BIBLE
BACKGROUNDS

BIBLE BACKGROUNDS

Explanatory Notes on the Bible

MERLE D. STREGE

Warner Press
Anderson, Indiana

Coordinator of Communications and Publishing
Church of God Ministries, Inc.
PO Box 2420
Anderson, IN 46018-2420
800-848-2464 • www.chog.org

To purchase additional copies of this book, to inquire about distribution and for all other sales-related matters, please contact:

Warner Press, Inc.
PO Box 2499,
Anderson, IN 46018-9988
877-346-3974 • www.warnerpress.org

Cover design by Mary Jaracz and Carolyn Kuchar
Layout design by Joseph D. Allison and Mary Jaracz
Content editing by Arthur M. Kelly
Copy editing by Stephen R. Lewis
Indexes by Stephen R. Lewis

ISBN-13: 978-1-59317-144-5
ISBN-10: 1-59317-144-7

Library of Congress Cataloging-in-Publication Data

Strege, Merle D.
Bible backgrounds : explanatory notes on scripture / by Merle D. Strege.
p. cm.
Includes bibliographical references.
ISBN-13: 978-1-59317-144-5 (hardcover)
ISBN-10: 1-59317-144-7 (hardcover)
1. Bible—Commentaries. I. Title.
BS491.3.S77 2006
220.6'1–dc22 2006027064

Printed in Canada.
07 08 09 10 /TC/ 10 9 8 7 6 5 4 3 2

Dedicated to

George H. Ramsey, Sr.

and to the memory of

Gustav Jeeninga, Frederick v. Shoot,

and E. Marie Strong

BIBLE BACKGROUNDS

Old Testament

The Pentateuch

Historical Books

Wisdom Books

The Prophets

New Testament

The Gospel Story

Paul's Letters

General Letters

Foreword

The Bible. It really is amazing. A book of books, spanning a huge period of time, a wide variety of cultures, written in challenging languages, available to us only in translations, argued about, researched, fought over, divided over, and died for. Yet it is still the primary source of knowledge about God and God's hope for an ever increasing number of peoples spread around the globe, in a vast and growing number of languages.

The Bible is the book for Jews, Christians, and Muslims. It covers thousands of years of history and development, yet we cannot go to a specific time, place, or event and say, "Here is where and when the Bible came into existence." It began as oral traditions—campfire tales—of immense and defining importance passed on by parent to child, generation to generation.

> Hear, O Israel: The LORD is our God, the LORD alone. You shall love the LORD your God with all your heart, and with all your soul, and with all your might. Keep these words that I am commanding you today in your heart. Recite them to your children and talk about them when you are at home and why you rise. Bind them as a sign on your hand, fix them as an emblem on your forehead, and write them on the doorposts of your house and on your gates. (Deut 6:4–9 NRSV)

From century to century through oral tradition, the message of God and the stories of the people of God were passed on by word of mouth. Eventually, it all came to be written down separately as letters, histories, accounts, genealogies, and records and finally collected into one volume—the one we call the Holy Bible.

As meandering in its development as the Bible seems, it speaks from a consistent and integrating perspective. This is the record of God's involvement with his creation. This book speaks with a unified voice and affirms these central truths: God is. God created all. God desires a relationship of deepening intimacy with a creation that more often chooses its own autonomous ways. God will go to nearly any end to woo his obstinate creation back into relationship with him and, through him, with others and the entire created order.

Larger and more personal than life, the Bible continues to help all persons come to grips with life's most important truths and challenges. Even if one is not a believer, there are no major life issues left out. There is no clearer picture of both the glory and depravity of human beings. There is no greater storehouse of simple, practical wisdom—how to live in such a challenging world. There is no greater guide to and through the mysteries of living. There are those, believers and nonbelievers, who say that there is no way to live well in this world without the knowledge and understanding that come through interaction with this book. As Dr. Strege says in the foreword, "The Bible may not be the sole foundation of American culture, but data from various sources strongly suggest that an attempt to understand [that culture] apart from the Bible would be...incomplete."

No book exists that is more important to the life of the church than the Bible. Its empowering witness to the Lord of the church, to the redeemer of humanity, to life wisdom, to our understanding of God, the Son, and the Holy Spirit, and to the body of Christ cannot be overstated. We are struggling enough to be the church *with* the Bible; without it, the church might very well slip into oblivion. How else do we know what God intends? How else do we know the Great Commandment and the Great Commission—the twin heartbeats of the church in the world? How else do I understand what it means to be called by God? How else do we understand what it means to be a fully devoted follower of Jesus?

In thinking about the purpose of the church, could one get more fundamental than these words from Paul: "...for building up the body of Christ, until all of us come to the unity of the faith and of the knowledge of the Son of God, to maturity, to the measure of the full stature of Christ" (Eph 4:12–13 NRSV). How could one achieve that without studying the Bible? There is no way for us to be formed into the likeness of Christ outside of a community of believers formed through knowing Christ. There is no way for such formation to occur without studying his life, opening ourselves to his words, and inviting him, the resurrected Lord, into our lives so that "the Advocate, the Holy Spirit, whom the Father will send in my name, [can] teach you everything, and remind you of all that I have said to you" (John 14:26 NRSV). It is not an overstatement to say that this central discipleship work of the church can be accomplished primarily through thoughtful, prayerful, and consistent Bible study.

In the life of the church, there are many essential tasks. There is no task, however, more central to the fulfillment of its commission than the study of the Bible.

This book, *Bible Backgrounds: Explanatory Notes on the Bible*, is designed to help both Bible student and Bible teacher navigate the sometimes smooth and other times turbulent waters of the Bible. In fact, *Bible Backgrounds* is written for the whole church so that we may better know the God about whom the book was written, through whose inspirational agency it came to be, and that we may better know what it means to be called God's people.

For many years, Dr. Strege has provided guidance, direction, insight, context, and information to help teachers and learners better understand Scripture. *Bible Backgrounds: Explanatory Notes on the Bible* contains that work and makes it accessible for wider use. *Bible Backgrounds* exists to help the church assist the Holy Spirit in the holy work of forming Christ in God's people. Foremost in all of his work, Dr. Strege is a child of the church, and *Bible Backgrounds* is informed by his study of, as well as his commitment to and love of, Scripture, the church, and its Lord. He and we offer this strong and thoughtful commentary to the discipling church.

Arthur M. Kelly
Anderson, Indiana

Preface

Upon picking up this book, those familiar with my previous work may ask, "What qualifies a historian of Christianity, and an Americanist at that, to write a book on the Bible?" It is a fair question. As I attempt an answer, I will also offer some reflections and observations that I hope will explain the character of the book's contents.

First, it is true that my academic specialization is American religious history. That said, it must be acknowledged that few books can match the Bible's influence on American life. According to a 1991 study, 45 percent of Americans surveyed said they had read the Bible during the previous week, and 71 percent agreed to some extent with the statement, "The Bible is the written word of God and is totally accurate in all that it teaches."[1] Several Gallup polls in 2004 indicated little if any appreciable change in these attitudes. Not only do Americans continue to regard the Bible highly; but it has profoundly shaped elements of their culture. The authors of *Habits of the Heart*, a perceptive study of cultural attitudes, reflected on the importance of two prominent American moral languages, systems of thought and criteria by which we decide how to live. One of these languages is individualism and its sense of independence. "Commitment" names the second language, and stresses the obligation or responsibility we owe to the group. In America, the biblical idea of covenant is a very important source of the language of responsibility.[2] The Bible may not be the sole foundation of American culture, but data from various sources strongly suggest that an attempt to understand it apart from the Bible would be difficult as well as incomplete. Although it is not my primary field of study, a working knowledge of the Bible has thus been important to my work as a scholar-teacher of American religious history.

Second, I have taught at institutions where professors do not occupy chairs as much as benches. This means that I have not infrequently been assigned, and often have volunteered to teach, the introductory Bible course at Anderson University. To support this assignment, I have maintained a serious reading interest in biblical scholarship. For several years, I have also taught a course on the history of the Christian interpretation of the Bible. While I am by no means the peer of my colleagues in biblical studies, I am not entirely uninformed about critical issues in the field and am conversant with methods by which Christians have read and interpreted the Bible across the centuries.

Third, I have studied and taught Scripture in the church for virtually my entire adult life. The primary arena of this work has been the Sunday school and has provided me an experience that reinforces my conviction that the Bible is, first of all, the church's book. While a seminarian, I began teaching adult Bible study classes and have followed that vocation in Church of God

1. Barna, *What Americans Believe*, 288, 294.

2. Bellah et al., *Habits of the Heart*, 27–51.

congregations in Vancouver, Washington; Walnut Creek, California; and two congregations in Anderson, Indiana—Park Place and North Anderson. On more occasions than I can recall, practicality and an eagerness to learn have led students in these classes to entertain and even occasionally generate ideas more common in the academy than the church. I still recall my trepidation at introducing the synoptic problem at First Church of God in Vancouver when Wally Cone interrupted the lesson with the bluntness only a retired logger could muster to declare, "Of course the Gospels are different; they were written by different people!" My experiences with scores, perhaps hundreds of Sunday school learners who share Wally's common sense suggest to me, at least, that the distance between the church and the academy may not be as wide as many believe. As of this writing, I am blessed to lead weekly sessions of the Bible study-class at North Anderson Church of God. The participants' love for the Bible, knowledge of its contents, and openness to new ideas and different points of view are an inspiration, and I continue to learn by participating in this extraordinary group. One member described us as a group reflection on the biblical text, one wherein we pray that our corporate meditation strengthens our practice of faithful discipleship. This, it seems to me, should always be the aim of biblical study in the church.

From the day I first responded to the call to vocations in the church and her academic institutions, the crucial importance of serious Bible study has been impressed upon me. The Great Commission declares that disciples are made through baptism and instruction. Disciples are made as they are taught everything that Jesus commanded. The church makes disciples primarily through teaching, and this means first and foremost the Bible—both the Old and New Testaments. We teach to the end that disciples will not only believe but also do the Word; Scripture is to be performed. We in the Church of God (Anderson) come by this appreciation for the practice of Scripture honestly, as do all latter-day descendants of the Pietist movement of Christianity. Our spiritual and theological ancestors certainly thought that the Bible is to be believed. Even more to the point, however, they believed that the Bible was to be lived, put into practice, in a word—*performed*.

What strengthens the church's performance of Scripture? Perhaps we should begin by identifying two assumptions that undermine that practice: (1) Performance of Scripture is not strengthened by the belief that the teacher's task is somehow to make the Bible more relevant. This notion assumes that on its own the Bible is irrelevant or, at least, not very interesting. But what is not relevant about life/death, war/peace, sin/wholeness, good/evil, sickness/health, sex/love, and God? The Bible addresses each of these and every significant dimension of human experience. Moreover, attempts to "make the Bible relevant" miss the point. In a real sense, the Bible is uninterested in being made relevant to us. Rather, it is we who are to be made relevant to Scripture as our lives are formed into a people capable of living faithfully with the God who is the Bible's primary subject. (2) This great aim of Scripture points to another mistake in the way we often read and teach the Bible: we think it is primarily about each of us as individuals. The American culture of individualism subtlety influences us to read the Bible as if "I," my interests, and even my curiosities are its principle concern. This tendency is illustrated in the cartoon on the office door of one of my colleagues. A Sunday school teacher replies to a question asked by one of the class members: "No, I do not know the calorie content of manna." The Bible is not interested in some of the questions we may bring to the text. It is surely about humans, but its basic concern is their relationship to the God who is the focal point of Scripture, the one revealed in its pages. Moreover, this God calls individuals to be a people, not ends in themselves. This claim is born out by the observation that in the original Hebrew and Greek, the vast majority of pronouns in both testaments are plural rather than singular. More often than not, Scripture collectively addresses the people Israel and the new people of God, the church.

The distinction between Scripture's address to individual or group leads to a crucial element of biblical interpretation. The church's performance of Scripture is strengthened by teaching that encourages us to see our lives in relation to the biblical text, but this perspective is enriched through *group* Bible study. Each of us reads the text to some degree in the light of our own experience, and that means none of us reads it in the same light. Each student sheds a different light, however slight the degree, on another's reading of the text. It was the early Church of God writer D. Otis Teasley who offered a vision of good interpretative practice when he described it as a three-cornered conversation among individual readers, the church, and the text of Scripture.[3]

Group study references several different associations. In my experience, the relationship among these groups resembles a set of concentric circles. The innermost and primary group is the immediate circle in which we regularly discuss the meaning and implications of the biblical text. This circle is surrounded both literally and also through time by its larger church group, sustained by its distinctive doctrinal and interpretive traditions—in conventional religious terminology, a *denomination*. It is important to acknowledge the particularity of one's interpretive practice. I am skeptical of claims to objectivity, as if the claimant can see from a timeless perspective unconditioned by history and location. Exceedingly rare is the person who does not interpret from some particular theological or, perhaps, intellectual point of view. It is often one's church affiliation that principally defines this perspective, and it is a mark of humility to acknowledge its limitations. However, these fellowships also belong to the Christian church, the whole body of Christ across time that has interpreted the text for the instruction and practice of faithful believers. This whole-church view means that an appreciation for the interpretive work of Augustine, Luther, Wesley, and many others informs the pages that follow. An even wider circle recognizes that before the church existed, there was the group called Israel, into which Gentiles have been grafted by Christ; insofar as possible, Christians must appreciate the fact that what they call the Old Testament is also read and interpreted by Jews as the Hebrew Bible.

3. Teasley, *Bible and How to Interpret It*, 107–114.

Taken together, these concentric circles comprise a vast household of faith, and none should be excluded from the task of faithful biblical interpretation.

Another group also contributes to the church's study of the Bible: the scholarly community, whose critical analysis can be appropriated by the church to encourage its faithful performance. Christian scholarship during the Reformation introduced a new historical awareness into the study of the Bible. John Colet, Erasmus, Johannes Reuchlin, Wolfgang Musculus, and John Calvin, among others, gave lectures and wrote commentaries that read the text literally but not literalistically, in the process breaking with the medieval tradition of allegorical interpretation. Reformation-era scholarship opened the door to the historical-critical analysis that became increasingly popular in the wake of the European Enlightenment. To be sure, this scholarship, informed as it was by new philosophical, historical, and scientific assumptions, questioned aspects of the biblical text in ways that many Christians found uncomfortable. Nevertheless, such analysis can benefit faithful interpretation of the Bible in the church. Nicholas Lash offers an insightful analogy that explains how this is so.[4] William Shakespeare, observes Lash, wrote his plays to be performed. It also is the case that a considerable body of critical scholarship has arisen in analysis of his work, even though Shakespeare's aim was not to give critical scholars meaningful employment; he wrote plays to be performed. Nevertheless, wise Shakespearean actors and actresses will read this critical literature in the effort to strengthen their performances. Similarly, the Bible was written to form the people of God and enable them to live faithfully with the God of Scripture; Scripture directs the performance of believers' lives. Ever since Otto Linn introduced the critical study of the Bible at Anderson College in the 1930s and at Warner Pacific College in the '40s, Bible teachers in the Church of God have shared Lash's belief that faithful performance of the Bible can be improved and not infrequently is informed only by critical scholarship. This book shares that conviction as it attempts to gather some of this scholarship with all of the aforementioned groups and bring them to bear on specific biblical texts. Admittedly, the product is a rather eclectic (some may think idiosyncratic) blend that addresses texts sometimes critically, or doctrinally, or devotionally, or historically, or in some combination.

A further word of explanation is due those who expect to find here a commentary on the entire Bible. These notes originally were prepared as supplementary material for users of the adult teacher's Sunday school curriculum published by Church of God Ministries. The Bible texts for that curriculum conform to the Uniform Lesson Outlines developed by the Committee on the Uniform Series. In a five-year cycle, series lessons cover the entire Bible but partially rather than examining every verse. Texts from virtually every book of the Bible are studied while no single book is considered in its entirety. The contents of this book, revised and edited from the original notes, comment on the texts selected for the CUS lesson outlines. Informed by the academic study of the Old and New Testaments, the goal of this book is not to provide technical information

4. Lash, *Theology on the Way to Emmaus*, 37–47.

but to help the church understand and ultimately practice Scripture more meaningfully in order that it may live more faithfully with its Lord.

These remarks cannot conclude without expressions of appreciation to the many people who have contributed to producing this book. More than a decade has passed since Richard Willowby asked me to take the assignment of Bible Background writer for the Sunday school curriculum of the Church of God. Obviously, without that invitation this book would not have seen the light of day. My particular friend Arthur Kelly suggested that more than a thousand pages of accumulated manuscript could and should be turned into a book, and he has patiently edited the revisions with skill and care. Joe Allison, coordinator of Communications and Publishing at Church of God Ministries enthusiastically supported the project and lent it his considerable publishing experience. Space will not permit me to name the many students and co-teachers who have participated in church Bible studies or college courses and whose questions and comments have stimulated new ideas and perspectives on the ancient text of Scripture. Their enthusiasm for the Bible and honest inquiry spur me on, and for this they also deserve the deepest thanks. My wife Fran, who insists that I conclude any session by tying things together and whose example of faithful Bible study and discipleship daily instructs me, our grown children, and now our grandchildren, contributes daily to my life and thus to my work.

One final word of appreciation is reserved in explanation of the dedication of this book. When I arrived on the campus of Anderson College in September 1965, Gustav Jeeninga, George Ramsey, Fred Shoot, and Marie Strong comprised the Anderson College Bible faculty. Their courses in Old Testament and New Testament, required of all undergraduates, introduced students to a Bible virtually unknown to us all. Their advanced exegetical courses and studies in Greek challenged students specializing in biblical studies by applying critical scholarship to the text of Scripture. Each was a memorable teacher. To his calling as a teacher, George Ramsey brought intellectual brilliance and an irrepressible enthusiasm for the classroom and the Bible—especially the *Revised Standard Version*. Fred Shoot possessed an uncanny ability to know how many verses of John's gospel each Greek student had translated and the puckish sense of humor to call upon a student to recite the verse immediately beyond the limit of his or her preparation. Marie Strong's Introduction to the History and Literature of the New Testament course followed a syllabus that well near exhausted the critical literature and was so large that the department insisted she charge her students a dime to defray printing costs. I shall never forget the day when honest Gus Jeeninga abruptly adjourned a class session because he had not been able to work out some intractable material to his satisfaction; he promised to have the issues worked out by the next session, and the whole class knew they had better be ready. The scholarly tracks of all four will be found across the following pages, and they deserve great credit for whatever is of value here. I also recall enough of their criticisms of my undergraduate papers to realize that none would agree with everything I have written. Whatever this book's shortcomings, the responsibility is mine alone.

Other professors have taught me much: George Kufeldt at Anderson University's School of Theology and, in another context, the late Milo Chapman of Warner Pacific College, to name but two. I also continue to learn from my accomplished colleagues in the Department of Religious Studies at Anderson. However, it was the four individuals to whom this book is dedicated who first awakened me and countless others to the disciplined study of the Bible. Dozens of their students now teach in colleges and seminaries. Hundreds more regularly preach from the Bible they taught us to read with a clearer, wider eye. The dedication of this volume means to acknowledge a deep and abiding personal appreciation as well as the church's debt to four of its outstanding teachers.

Merle D. Strege
Pentecost 2006

OLD TESTAMENT

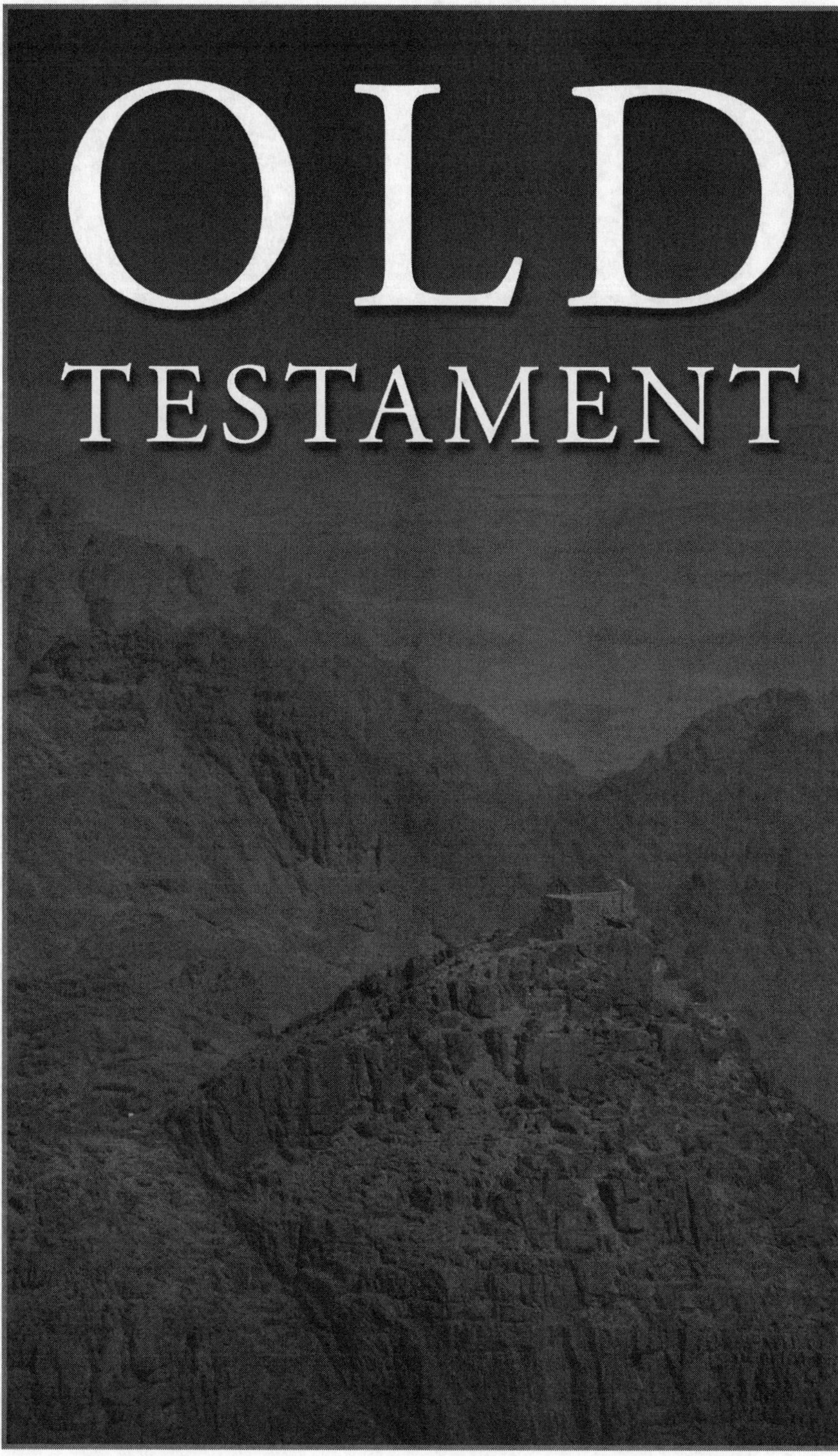

The law of the Lord is perfect and
revives the soul.
The Lord's instruction never fails,
and makes the simple wise.
The precepts of the Lord are right
and rejoice the heart;
The commandment of the Lord
shines clear
and gives light to the eyes.
The fear of the Lord is pure
and abides forever.
The decrees of the Lord are true and
righteous every one,
more to be desired than gold, pure
gold in plenty,
sweeter than syrup or honey from
the comb.

—Psalm 19:7–10 (NEB)

The commandment that I lay on you this day is not too difficult for you, it is not too remote. It is not in heaven that you should say, "Who will go up to heaven for us to fetch it and tell it to us, so that we can keep it?" Nor is it beyond the sea that you should say, "Who will cross the sea for us to fetch it and tell it to us, so that we can keep it?" It is a thing very near to you, upon your lips and in your heart ready to be kept.

—Deuteronomy 30:11–14 (NEB)

Genesis

In the Beginning
Genesis 1:1–2:4a

The Bible begins, quite literally, at the beginning. The name of its first book, *Genesis,* comes from a word that means "origins" or "beginnings." It derives from the Greek, which is the language of the Septuagint, the name of a collection of Greek translations of the Old Testament. The Hebrew name for this first book of the Bible is *bereshith,* which also means "beginning." It is the first word of the Old Testament in Hebrew. The book of Genesis deals with the beginning of the creation, to be sure, but this wonderful book is so much more. It contains narratives that tell the origins of many aspects of human life within Yahweh's[1] creation. The book also deals with issues, problems, and aspects of human experience. Not surprisingly, it has been the Old Testament book on which Christian writers have most frequently commented. It is also a favorite source of lecture and commentary by a wide range of writers and theologians all the way to the recent television program hosted by journalist Bill Moyers, *Genesis: A Conversation.*

Before the beginning of anything, there stands God. If we may speak so, the Bible is based on the idea that the most fundamental way to talk of God is by means of a story. Yahweh is the central character in biblical narrative, and the book of Genesis is no exception. This preference for narrative needs special attention. Old Testament scholar Walter Brueggemann says that biblical narrative is about concrete people and events, gives freedom to our imaginations, and expects passionate hearing. Story is crucial to Genesis because this book recounts the origins of Yahweh's calling the world into being and calling creation into relationship with him. This narrative is not without a point of view; the biblical narratives are not neutral about Yahweh's call. When we hear them, they call us to respond afresh and anew to the Lord God's call upon our lives.

The Israelites who wrote the Old Testament experienced Yahweh as Redeemer. Amid the competing religious and theological claims of other peoples of the ancient Middle East, Israel found it crucial to affirm that the God of creation and the Redeemer God of Israel were one and the same. Other ancient peoples told their own stories of the origins of the universe. (The technical term for such stories is *cosmogony.*) Many of those stories affirmed an idea of the created world that underwrote the notion that the natural world and its processes carry their own divinity. The Genesis narrative sharply disputes that claim. According to Genesis, the created order is not divine; it is rather the product of Yahweh's freedom and creativity. The material universe is indeed good; for it is the creation of the Lord God. But the affirmation of creation's goodness is a far cry from the claim that creation itself is divine.

1. *Yahweh* is the English equivalent for the name of God as formed by the four Hebrew letters YHWH.

Humans and their Purpose
Genesis 2:4–25

Just prior to resting from creation, God created humans and placed them in the garden called Eden. The creation of humanity raises two challenging questions: What exactly *is* the place of humans in creation? Does Yahweh keep them under a tight rein or give them freedom to use as their own possession? According to the Genesis narrative, humans are given authority over creation; however, it does not therefore become their possession. Humans rule over creation as a steward rules the household of his master. In the ancient world, stewards did not own their masters' property, but they were expected to care for it as if they did. By the same token, humans do not own the earth. God expects us to tend his creation carefully and responsibly. The idea that humans are stewards of the earth connects neatly to the notion of discipleship. Like stewards, disciples live under authority; they are expected to live according to the rule that such authority underwrites and are therefore accountable for their actions.

After completing the work of creation, declares the text, Yahweh rested. "But because humankind is in the image of God, the rest of God is [also] a promised rest for humankind...As it is kept by the faithful week by week, Sabbath is a disciplined reminder of how creation is intended...It exists for the well being of humankind (Mark 2:27) . . . Keeping Sabbath, that is, breaking with the world of frantic self-securing, is a way to know God and his commitment to his world. The rest of God is an invitation to form a new kind of human community."[2]

Before taking up the text itself, we will do well to remember that the biblical text is not interested in every question we may think to ask. A cartoon illustrates this reminder. The setting obviously is a Sunday school class where the teacher, in answer to a question, says "No, the Bible does not specify the caloric content of manna." The Bible does not and will not answer every curious question we may ask. At many points, it is legitimate and even the product of honest reading and biblical interpretation to say, "We don't know." Instead, faithful reading and interpretation asks, What is it that the Bible wants us to consider and understand from this text?

Reduced to its essentials, Genesis 2:4–25 brings us face-to-face with two fundamental issues. First, God calls humans to live in and tend a world that is God's creation and nobody else's. Second, the terms of human life in this world belong to God and nobody else. Many additional interpretations attach themselves to this text. But as terribly important as issues like the danger of sex, evil, death, and the fall are, this text does not offer answers to them. What our text does want us to consider and know is far more important than these. In the first place, human beings exist at the will of God—Yahweh called humans into being. They were placed in the garden that was also Yahweh's creation, and they were placed there in order to tend that garden. We must distinguish between work and toil. It is clear from 2:5 that Yahweh created the man "to work the ground"; from the beginning, work was part of God's intention for human beings. Work became toilsome only after Adam and Eve disobeyed God. Part of the curse laid on Adam was that his work would

2. Brueggemann, *Genesis*, 47.

become toilsome (3:17–19). Adam's divinely appointed work was that he would tend Yahweh's garden, that is, humans are the stewards of Yahweh's creation.

The second issue in this reading is that Yahweh sets the limits on human beings in Yahweh's creation. Adam and Eve were not free to set their own agenda or "actualize" themselves. The garden of Eden was not a democracy. Humans did not get to vote on the rules. In fact, "the man" did not even choose to live in the garden: "The Lord God took the man and put him in the Garden of Eden to work it and take care of it" (2:15). Life in the garden was governed by a divine grant of freedom with one restriction: the man was forbidden access to the tree of the knowledge of good and evil. Notice that the story does not explain the significance of the tree; the issue here is not the knowledge it might yield. What really matters is that Yahweh's command is at stake. It specifies the terms on which life before God is possible. Disobedience to God's command yields death.

Sin
Genesis 3:1–13

A. Bartlett Giamatti, late commissioner of baseball, traced the word *paradise* back to an ancient Persian term for the king's park. Small wonder that later Latin and Greek translators of the book of Genesis applied the term to the garden of Eden. Until sin entered the picture, the garden was a paradise, the place of perfection where Yahweh came to walk and enjoy. It was God's garden. Adam and Eve dwelt in paradise, not as its owners, but as stewards given the responsibility for its care. Even so, the garden was their home, and this terrible story often calls to mind, as John Milton titled his epic poem, a paradise lost. Genesis 3 tells a story of loss: lost innocence, lost friendship, lost paradise.

Is it possible that we have made too much of the serpent in the story? Yahweh, Adam and Eve, and Yahweh's commandment concerning the tree of the knowledge of good and evil occupy the center of the narrative. It becomes relatively simple and easy to wander off into discussions about the serpent. During the celebrated Scopes "Monkey Trial" in Dayton, Tennessee, in 1925, defense attorney Clarence Darrow asked William Jennings Bryan how he thought the snake got around before being condemned to crawl on its belly. Milton took the serpent to be Satan incarnate in another form. Our best advice is to follow the lead of the biblical text, which has nothing to say about the origin or meaning of the serpent. In 3:1, it suddenly appears. God and the first humans are already in place. They live in fellowship with one another, and there is a divine prohibition concerning the tree. "What counts is the prohibition, the authority of the one who speaks and the unqualified expectation of obedience."[3]

The serpent appears to ask a question about the command of God. Until this moment, the command had stood as command. To raise questions about this command suggested the possibility that things could be otherwise. Perhaps, for example, it was not a *command*; maybe it was a *suggestion*, an option for good living. The serpent's question not only undermined God's command as command, but it also transformed God from subject to object. Until this moment in

3. Ibid., 46.

the Genesis narrative, God is the actor, the subject who sets events into motion. The serpent's question demotes God and his command to objects for discussion. The question doesn't allow God to be God.

Although at first she defends God and the command, Eve eventually joins in this strange new discourse about God. Even though the serpent tricked her, using just enough of the right language to make his questions appear legitimate, Eve's entrance into the conversation set in motion the downward train of events. Such talk is destructive; it underwrites the possibility of an alternative to the way of the Lord. The cost of such conversations is the loss of God's friendship. Adam and Eve—and with them all of humanity—are thus deprived of their original righteousness.

Eve ate the forbidden fruit and Adam after her. The text then moves to a second loss. "They realized they were naked" (3:7). Before God came to the garden seeking Adam and Eve, before the terrible questions—"Where are you?" and "What have you done?"—the consequences of disobedience are already at work. Within the human heart, guilt is established even before the judge appears to pronounce sentence. Adam and Eve experienced new, strange emotions. Shame took the place of innocence, and fear replaced friendship. Having lost their original innocence, and friendship with Yahweh, Adam and Eve were about to lose paradise.

God Hears

Genesis 4

The story of sin's entrance into human experience expands in Genesis 4. Adam and Eve sinned against Yahweh. Now we learn of the origins of the sin of one human against another. This chapter tells the tragedy of the first murder. As awful and compelling as Cain's crime is, we nevertheless must not allow it to obscure other rich themes that fill this narrative. These include (1) freedom, (2) the problem of the brother, and (3) Yahweh as the One who hears.

1. *Freedom: "It's up to you."* A good rule of thumb in biblical interpretation is to resist the temptation to fill in the gaps in the story. Such gaps appear in Genesis 4. The text does not explain Yahweh's preference for Abel's offering over Cain's. Indeed, their names in Hebrew suggest just the opposite likelihood. Cain implies vitality and vigor, while Abel means "vapor" or "nothingness." This story foreshadows many in the Bible where Yahweh chooses the younger over the elder, a pattern made all the more striking when we recall that the ancient world commonly gave pride of place to the eldest male child. Yahweh's will often goes counter to the world's way of proceeding.

   Cain must deal with Yahweh's mysterious preference for Abel's sacrifice. In 4:6–7 Yahweh makes it clear that Cain is free to do right. The ball was in his court. "If you do right, will you not be accepted?" Life is not fair. Try as we might through public policy and government regulation, the playing field is not level. Nevertheless, says Yahweh, what you do with what you've received is up to you. That is the privilege and the responsibility of freedom.

2. *The problem of the brother.* Cain obviously misused his freedom by

murdering his brother. Freedom is a heavy burden under the best of conditions. The presence of others, the brother, makes freedom even more of a problem. "To live in freedom in the presence of the brother means that we must negotiate our lives as a never-ending series of choices in the presence of others whose lives touch ours—with God as the omnipresent observer."[4]

3. *Yahweh is the One who hears.* Yahweh sees and hears. No event, no thought, no deed escapes God's eye or ear. Many have thought that such a God repressed human freedom. The psalmist, on the other hand, took comfort in the idea that there was no place where God was not present. Genesis 4 offers another perspective on God's omnipresent ear. Abel utters not a word in this entire narrative, but Yahweh hears the voice of his blood crying from the ground. That Yahweh's ear hears the cries of hurt and alienation affirms that God hears the victim, the oppressed, and the hurting. Yahweh's ear gives them voice. They can be sure that Yahweh will hear, and when Yahweh hears, divine action is sure to follow.

Judgment and a New Beginning
Genesis 6:6–9:17

The story of the great flood is among the most familiar in Scripture. People who cannot recite a single Bible verse recognize Noah's name. In the hands of ancient Israel's storytellers and poets, this familiar narrative affirms some of the most fundamental theological convictions of Israelite faith. Yahweh's creation stubbornly and perversely resists his purposes. A deep problem thus has emerged in the relationship between Yahweh and the creation. "The creation has refused to be God's creation."[5]

The flood story also raises some challenges for teacher and student. Some Old Testament scholars contend that the first five books of the Bible are the compilation of interpreters and editors of the narratives and oral traditions handed down to them. In Genesis 7:2, for example, we read that God commanded Noah to choose "*seven* of every kind of clean animal" (my emphasis). The number seven may have been a nod to the Hebrew idea of completeness represented by that number. Three pairs of each animal plus one for the requisite sacrifice would bring the total to completion. But from Sunday school days, we have learned that pairs of animals entered the ark. Genesis 6:20 and 7:8 both speak of *pairs*—male and female. Scholars refer to this as a bringing together of two narratives or traditions.

What do these kinds of problems mean for biblical faith? The work of those who study the process by which the text of the Bible came to be helps us to see the living faith of Israel and the church. The biblical text is, in this sense, Israel's testimony of its walk with God. It is written that we, and all others who follow, also will walk in faith with God. Close study of the text's formation gives us opportunity to watch Israel's faith develop and grow. It is also important, however, that we step back and view the text as a whole, as it now presents itself to us in the canon of Scripture. Viewed from this broader perspective, such questions as whether Noah chose seven or two of

4. Ibid., 55.

5. Ibid., 74.

each animal recede into the background as the biblical text forces us to attend to the great and pressing theological themes that command our attention.

The theological issue confronting us in the story of the great flood is the crucial matter of life in the company of a holy and righteous God. From this narrative, we learn that Yahweh had high hopes for the creation. It was created good, every living creature drawing the breath of life that ultimately derives from God. However, it all went awry, and the world and its people became something much less than God desired. The story of the flood is a terrible indictment of human folly; it appears to be a story that can only lead to judgment and death. But death is not Yahweh's last word. Beyond death there is life. One family of questionable behavior is not much in the face of such calamity. In this tenderest of new shoots we find demonstrated Yahweh's powerful will for a new creation, including us.

Calling
Genesis 11:27–12:9

The exodus from Egypt was Israel's crucial experience of God's redemptive power and therefore the pivot of the Old Testament. From this crucial point, Israel's theological claims were cast. Amid the competing religious and theological claims of other peoples of the ancient Middle East, Israel found it crucial to affirm that the God of creation and the Redeemer God of Israel are one and the same, which Genesis does.

The collection of narratives about Abraham and his family opens up another of Israel's key theological assertions: Yahweh is the God of Israel's foreparents. From their new vantage point of freedom, Israel saw that the God who had freed them from Pharaoh had been active in human history and particularly the history of Israel's ancestors, and for a very long time.

In the call of Abram and Sarai (their names before God's call), Israel's patriarch and matriarch, Yahweh calls into being a new community, a clear alternative to the dominant culture surrounding them. Dealing with a new community brings issues of discipleship into sharp focus; we must ask: What kind of community? What are its defining characteristics and its chief virtues? The text is quick to answer through its description of the community's first ancestors.

One of the first things we learn about Abram and Sarai is that they were not likely candidates for the role of founders of a new community. Abram was already old. Even by Old Testament standards, a man seventy-five years of age was no spring chicken, hardly an age to begin wandering across miles of desert. His wife, Sarai, was barren. She had been unable to conceive so much as a single child, let alone be mother to a great nation. Yahweh's call cast these two people into roles for which their natural abilities were inadequate; however, another thing that we learn about Abram and Sarai is that they also displayed virtues that were absolutely indispensable for life in the new community Yahweh was calling into being through them: They trusted Yahweh. They placed their lives in Yahweh's hands. They were people of faith, and faith was the key to life in Yahweh's new, alternative community.

A Promise Fulfilled
Genesis 15–18

Land and an heir are the twin centerpieces of Yahweh's call and promise to

Abraham and Sarah (their new names after the call). This promise appeared to be outrageous. Both Abraham and Sarah had reached an age in which conception was no longer possible. All through the years when Sarah might have conceived a child, she was barren. In the cultural world of the Old Testament, childlessness was nearly always considered the fault of the woman, whoever she might be and whatever her situation; barrenness placed women in a precarious position. A wife was expected to produce children, that is, heirs to carry on the family name. A barren woman was subject to reproach and shame among other women and her husband's displeasure or even worse at home. Thus, barrenness signaled hopelessness.

The hopelessness of this childless marriage generates great tension throughout these chapters. Twice Abraham attempted to resolve the problem on his own. First, he proposed the idea that he adopt his trusted servant Eliezar of Damascus, a proposal that Yahweh promptly vetoed. Then Sarah suggested that Abraham conceive a child with her servant Hagar. (It should be noted that Sarah's proposal was an acceptable alternative to childlessness in Semitic culture.) Yahweh did not object on moral grounds; nevertheless, it was clear that the child born of this union, Ishmael, is not the child that Yahweh had promised.

Sarah and Abraham attempted to resolve the problem of her barrenness through all the measures at their disposal. The tension of this situation, however, could be resolved only through the word of the promising God. In fact, it was only Yahweh's promise that stood over against the hopelessness of Sarah's empty womb. Yahweh repeated this promise again and again—for fourteen years. After such a long wait, Sarah found the promise laughable. To conceive and bear a child at her advanced age would be like saying that the baby would be born in a geriatric ward and Medicare would pay the bills. Sarah indeed laughs, but this laugh is likely devoid of all humor. Her dry, sarcastic laugh is the sort we make when we realize that somebody has played a cruel joke on us. Meanwhile, Yahweh's promise endured.

Finally, the hopelessness and unrelieved tension of these two barren old people was resolved when "the Lord was gracious to Sarah as he had said, and the Lord did for Sarah what he had promised" (21:1). This, as Martin Luther said, is the word of the promising God. It is in God's character to promise, and any divine promise made is a promise kept. If barrenness is a metaphor for hopelessness, then Yahweh's promise stands equally for hope. The route out of hopelessness is to cling to the promise of God. Other names for this clinging are faith and trust. Indeed, *faith* and *trust* are at this point synonyms for the cornerstone virtue of the human's relationship to God.

Faith Tested

Genesis 22:1–19

The story of the sacrifice of Isaac demands our close attention, even as it encourages daring suggestions. The following is not the only possible reading of the story, but it attempts to take the story very seriously. The story is difficult for us to hear, in part, because of some of its claims about God. Perhaps we can read and interpret the story in a way to make the story about God and Abraham and their covenant relationship.

The narrative opens with Yahweh's shocking command that Abraham take his son Isaac to the land of Moriah and offer him as a burnt sacrifice. Why would God make such a terrible command? Child sacrifice was an abomination in Israelite society. That Isaac was Abraham's "only son…whom you love" only heightens our natural aversion to a God who would command the death of a child. It will not do to say that Yahweh wanted to test Abraham. The sentence "Some time later God tested Abraham" (22:1) does not explain Yahweh's motive; it describes the story that follows. If we want to understand Yahweh's motive for this test, we may find one at 22:12. There, God said, "Now I know that you fear God." After this dramatic narrative had run its course, Yahweh himself said, "Now I know," which seems to suggest strongly that God's motive in testing Abraham was that God wanted to know for sure about this particular man's faith.

Some will surely object to this line of thought, saying that since God is omniscient, God already knew the quality of Abraham's faith. That idea, however, is not without its problems. It still leaves us without an explanation for the test of Abraham. Worse, it leaves us with a picture of a God who is not above putting even his beloved covenant partner through an agonizing emotional ordeal. Then there is still the matter of the biblical text itself and its strong implication that Yahweh *wanted* to know. If the text presses us toward the idea that the motive for this test was that God wanted to know, should we shrink back from that implication? Surely we have here another example of biblical paradox. In this text, we have God wanting to know, while in many other biblical texts we find that God sees and knows all. That we take the Genesis 22 narrative at face value does not require us to set aside all those other texts. Instead, we must affirm the paradoxical and often mysterious way of God with the created order.

Yahweh is only the first subject of this narrative. There is also Abraham, who is the central figure. Does he have faith? Will he trust the command of the God who had promised him everything through the beloved Isaac? Few of us will ever face such a test, and for that we can be profoundly grateful; this test carried Abraham beyond the conventional domain of ethics and morality. The Danish philosopher-theologian Søren Kierkegaard rightly saw that Abraham's obedience carried him into a region where there were no rules for living. No Israelite moral code would justify the sacrifice of Isaac. There would have been no way to explain or justify that action to Sarah. In order to follow this command of God, Abraham had to act purely on faith, and here faith meant trust in the divine promise and command.

Abraham was faithful to the command of God. After the journey to Moriah, Yahweh knew that. On Abraham's side, there was faith. On Yahweh's side, there was promise. These were the terms of the covenant. The happy ending to this narrative is that the covenant between Yahweh and Abraham is reaffirmed and amplified.

Isaac's Sons: Deception and Blessing
Genesis 25:19–34; 27:1–40

Earlier we observed that the book of Genesis explains the origin of things through narrative. The book explains the origins of creation, the origins of the human creation, the origins of human sin, and the origins of the people Israel. The genealogies of Genesis trace the descendants of many peoples other than Israel. In that many Semitic peoples trace their ancestry to Abraham, the Genesis narratives also give accounts of their origins. The story of Hagar explains the origins of the Ishmaelites, related to the Israelites through Isaac's half-brother Ishmael. This passage contains a narrative that explains the sometimes stormy relationship between the Israelites and their neighbors the Edomites by remembering the tension between their ancestors Jacob/Israel and Esau during their early years.

The Genesis narratives are never simply about origins and not only about facts or events such as a newspaper reports. We always must remember that we are reading theological history. The Old Testament confronts us with the divine significance of these events. If we learn about origins along the way, so much the better; the central focus remains on Yahweh and his purposes for humanity through the calling of Israel.

When we reach the midpoint of Genesis, we begin the cycle of narratives that tell the story of Jacob, and in Jacob we face a serious problem. Jacob is a scoundrel, a grasper (the meaning of his name in Hebrew), and a deceiver. His is not the sort of character that parents would want their children to emulate. Compared with Abraham or even Isaac, Jacob is a poor representative of the family's third generation. The fact that Jacob is clearly not a moral example and that his motives are nearly always a mixture of faith and self-interest, however, is not without theological and moral insight. The text of Genesis understands that human motives are rarely completely pure and, more importantly, that Yahweh can and does work with and through such imperfect specimens as Jacob to achieve his purposes. Finally, it is not that Jacob is a worthy candidate to be used as the chosen vessel of God; rather, it is that God has chosen Jacob, imperfect though he may be.

These two familiar stories illustrate our point. It is difficult to take the side of a man who will give food to his starving brother only after negotiating a heavy price or who willingly tricks his blind and dying father out of one of the father's most sacred obligations to his firstborn. We know these things about Jacob, but we also know that Yahweh chose him over Esau. We do not know the reason for this choice, as we so often do not know God's motives. The divine will is inscrutable, not open to our examination or questioning. It simply is.

God chose Jacob over Esau. In so doing, Yahweh acted in a manner consistent with a pattern of divine choice that runs through all of Scripture. God frequently chooses the weak, the lowly, and the otherwise despised to fulfill his purposes. In doing so, Yahweh overturns the world's conventional way of ordering its own affairs. In the case of this narrative, the name of that conventional wisdom is "primogeniture," the right of the firstborn son to inherit all of his father's possessions. By such worldly wisdom, all of Isaac's possessions belonged to Esau, including the covenant of Yahweh. God, however, had other plans and so chose Jacob. The divine choice conferred blessing and, paradoxically, trouble. Blessing is the subject of this text, but soon trouble will unfold for Jacob, the man chosen by Yahweh.

Flight and Vision
Genesis 27:41–28:22

Yahweh's choice of Jacob began a life of both blessing and trouble for Jacob. Although he carried a special designation as the heir of the covenant promise, this designation did not insulate Jacob from a life of conflict. Through the long cycle of stories about him, it almost seems as if Jacob's special status and his conflicted life went hand in hand; he apparently could not have one without the other.

In this text, we find a story that frankly recognizes Jacob's conflicts. It begins in the aftermath of his deception of Isaac. Jacob has twice swindled Esau, who now harbors a murderous grudge against his brother. Only the fragile thread of Isaac's waning days stayed Esau's hand. Rebekah saw that it was only a matter of time before Esau, the warrior-hunter, would strike and that Jacob, the man of the tents, would forfeit his life. To prevent Jacob's death, Rebekah plotted to send him to her brother Laban in far-off Haran, the region Abraham had departed long years before and where he had found a wife for his son Isaac. There is a sense in which Haran remained home for the wandering family of Abraham, Sarah, and their descendants. Possession of the land of Palestine remained a promise. As long as it went unfulfilled, they were still sojourners in the land and could still cast an eye to distant Haran.

We must not lose sight of the fact that the man who journeyed to Haran was a fugitive. He and his mother had conspired to overthrow the law of primogeniture. Semitic societies prized the right of the firstborn, for it served as a means of controlling disputes between siblings. As such, it was a very important social institution for ordering and controlling possessions and therefore power. People believed in the law of primogeniture and its claims. By stating that Yahweh chose Jacob over Esau, the biblical text undermined the social order that rested on that law. So Jacob was not only a deceiver; he also acted in ways that challenged society's status quo. In part, this explains why it was such a scandal that the promise to Abraham and Isaac was also transmitted through this deceptive and disturbing fugitive.

While asleep on the desert floor at "a certain place" (28:11) as yet unnamed, Jacob the fugitive dreamed. In his dream, he saw angels descending and ascending a ladder above which stood the very person of Yahweh. God then repeated the ancient promise made to Jacob's forefathers; it now became Yahweh's promise to Jacob as well, and readers are left to contemplate the stark prospect that Yahweh's covenant blessing came to Jacob as the result of a carefully contrived deception. While that may be a problem for us, we do better to stay inside the story itself, to perceive that the narrative is simply that way—as life sometimes is itself. (Settlement of property and inheritance is seldom achieved without coveting and calculation. That is how it often is in families.) This powerful story speaks for itself. The narrative exemplifies what is generally true of the book of Genesis. This is not a spiritual treatise on morality. It is, rather, remembrance of how faith moves even in raw human experience. We must leave it at that.

Disappointment Overcome
Genesis 28:10–29:35; 30:1–24; 35:22–26

The first five books of the Hebrew Bible are called *torah*, a term frequently translated into English as "law." While it is true that some sections of the Torah contain prohibitions, rules, and regulations, large sections of these books are narratives rather than legislation. It is worth remembering that much of the Old Testament was written not by lawyers but by storytellers. In addition to "law," torah also may be translated as "instruction." Ancient Israelites often taught through stories. The Torah instructed Israel in the all-important matter of walking in the way of the Lord. The book of Genesis contains the stories of Israel's origins. Generations of Israelites told these stories to their children and grandchildren. Through this kind of instruction, each generation learned how the people Israel had come into being.

These texts gather several blocks of material around the theme of the origins of the twelve tribes of Israel. Long after the Exodus and long after their return to Canaan, Israelites told these stories for the same reason that Alex Haley wrote *Roots:* The narrative explained where they had come from, all the way back to the twelve brother-patriarchs. The father of these twelve sons was, of course, Jacob. His sons are called Israelites because he was renamed Israel after his all-night struggle with God at Peniel (see Gen 32). For our purposes, the great concern of these stories is to explain the origins of the Israelite tribes. These stories are like a parent answering the typical child's question, "Where did we come from?" In that sense, you can begin with 35:22–26, the list of the sons of Israel grouped according to their mothers.

The next question is obvious: Where did the mothers come from? Perhaps there is another: Why did Jacob marry more than one woman? The answer to that is simply that the law then permitted men to take more than one wife. Jacob fathered his twelve sons by four different women: Rachel and her servant girl Bilhah, and Leah and her servant girl Zilpah. This may shock twenty-first-century moral sensibilities, but this arrangement was quite proper and within the boundaries of Israelite marriage custom. There is no point in attempting to moralize Jacob's polygamy into the source of his later domestic unhappiness; to do so is a questionable interpretive practice because the text itself makes no such judgment.

That Jacob fathered children by four different women does not mean that he loved them all equally. In fact, Rachel is the great love of his life. Jacob's love for her is one major element of the stories. Jacob's uncle Laban deceives his nephew by substituting Leah behind Rachel's bridal veil. If one thinks back to the story of Jacob's deception of his father Isaac, we see something of an ironic twist here: Jacob the deceiver becomes Jacob the deceived. After discovering that he has married the wrong woman, Jacob insists on having Rachel too. Laban agrees, but requires Jacob to work another seven years to pay for his bride. The story does not yet end happily, for Rachel is barren.

Childlessness is a persistent problem in the Old Testament because the absence of heirs made the future insecure. This insecurity touched the entire community, but in an acute way, it threatened the childless wife. *Barren* is the word often employed to describe women who did not give their husbands what every Israelite thought was crucial—children, especially sons, to pass on the family name and through whom parents would be remembered.

Sarah was barren; Rachel was barren; Hannah was barren; even in the New Testament, Elizabeth, the mother of John the Baptizer, is barren. It is a hard word signifying something dry, lifeless, and infertile. Barren women are sad not only because they do not know the joy of motherhood but also because their friends and neighbors judge them to have failed their husbands by not bearing children, which the ancient world understood as a woman's chief purpose. God hears the cry of these women, however, and gives life where there had been only barrenness. Rachel, the beloved of Jacob, bears two sons, Joseph and Benjamin. Just as their father loved their mother more than his other wives, so Jacob also loved these two boys more than his other sons. This preferential love becomes important in later stories that explain Israel's origins as the people of God.

New Dependence on God
Genesis 32:3–33:17

Jacob's stay in Haran eventually ended, and he began thinking about his return to Palestine, the land of his youth, and the land to which he was entitled by Yahweh's covenant. Palestine was also the home of his estranged brother Esau, and any return on Jacob's part will be incomplete without a resolution of the conflict between them. Many years had passed since the two brothers last saw each other. Much had changed during those years. Jacob had acquired four wives and had become himself the patriarch of a large clan. In Semitic cultures, a man must be wealthy to afford so many wives, and Jacob had become a very wealthy livestock owner during the years that he served Laban. Characteristic of Jacob, deception and trickery tainted the negotiations for his marriages and his wages, and Laban proved to be a match for the trickster and tough bargainer. True to form, after deciding to return to Palestine, Jacob once again resorted to deception in order to move family, flocks, and herds out of Laban's sphere of influence.

Jacob's return to Palestine was not without obvious dangers. There remained the unresolved conflict with Esau, now very much an unknown quantity in Jacob's mind. Had his brother nursed the old grudge against him? Had Esau's anger cooled? Jacob could not be certain of his brother's attitude and therefore developed a plan, the kind of shrewd calculation at which Jacob excelled. Jacob was very skilled at formulating a plan to gain whatever it was that he wanted; he was not nearly as good at determining what he should want. In any case, plans were laid that Jacob hoped would turn aside Esau's anger unless he was either a barbarian or without interest in material gain. It is instructive to note, however, that for all his shrewd planning, Jacob also prayed—fervently. The very best of plans might not be adequate to protect him against Esau.

The content of Jacob's prayer is striking. He reminded Yahweh of the promise made at Bethel years ago. By restating the promise, Jacob declared his intentions to hold Yahweh to that promise. Surely this man lived up to his name—Grasper! His striving and grasping reached their peak in the struggle with God at the Jabbok. As this story opens, the identity of the one with whom Jacob wrestled remained undisclosed. Only at the end, after a nightlong struggle, do we learn that this was Yahweh.

The text begins to work something of a transformation in Jacob here. Until now we have seen only the shady aspects of his character. But at dawn on the Jabbok, we see a man who can wrestle Yahweh through the night to a draw. A person must have some redeeming characteristics in order to survive a face-to-face struggle with God. Jacob left the struggle chastened and with a new name. He had wrestled God face-to-face and lived to tell about it. From then on he was *Israel,* meaning "He struggles with God."

We should not permit this story to transform the reunion of Jacob and Esau into an anticlimax. It was crucial to the future of the family of Jacob/Israel that they return to the land promised to Abraham. With the polite refusal and forcing of rich gifts upon Esau, that return was accomplished. The land of promise and the people of promise were brought together once again.

Favored Son to Slave
Genesis 37:1–35

The conclusion of the book of Genesis narrates the life of Joseph, the man through whom the clan of Israelites moved to Egypt. The Joseph stories do not place the same extreme emphasis on radical trust in Yahweh as we find in Abraham. On the other hand, the scandal of the Jacob narratives is nowhere to be found in the Joseph material either. Instead, we find running through these narratives an emphasis on Yahweh's hidden call. Joseph's life is an amazing sequence of twists and surprises, contingencies at every turn. Nevertheless, through calamity and the extraordinary rise to power, at work in the narratives of Joseph are the hidden and inscrutable purposes of Yahweh. Disaster threatens Joseph and, we know, Israel's future at many turns, yet the will of God works through these events to bring his intentions to fruition.

The story of Joseph and "the coat of many colors" is familiar to many people from their childhood years in Sunday school. The phrase comes from the King James translation. The *New Revised Standard Version* translates it "a coat with long sleeves." By whichever phrase it is described, we get the picture of a special garment. This coat distinguished Joseph from his brothers. It made apparent to their eyes what they all felt in their hearts: their father loved him more than them. Joseph is the subject and the hero of these narratives, but this should not be allowed to obscure the fact that he contributed to the family tension that is so crucial to the story.

We need to be on guard concerning our understanding of family in this context. The sons of Jacob were themselves now mature men and heads of their own tribes. What we have here is a large and complex clan of related people, not a modern nuclear family. Relations among the sons are complicated; a first family was composed of the older sons and a second family was made up of Joseph and Benjamin, the two sons of Jacob's beloved wife Rachel. They were younger and somewhat sheltered, the apples of their father's eye. Their older brothers envied them for the love their father lavished upon the boys. This festering jealousy was worsened by two additional facts: Joseph was a tattletale, and Jacob had given Joseph an ornamental coat, a garment much nicer than anything owned by the older sons. There is no mistaking the brothers' resentment of Jacob's preference for Joseph. The text says that "they hated him" for it (37:4). Interestingly, the text also states that they "could not" speak kindly to Joseph. It is not that they would not but that their anger had so consumed them that they no longer possessed the ability to speak in a kind manner. It also seems to be the case that Joseph enjoyed the fact that Jacob preferred him. What else are we to make of his reports, first to his brothers and then to his father, of his two dreams? Even Jacob has to scold the boy for believing that the day would come when his own parents will bow down to him. Their father's preference for their little brother somewhat overstepped social custom and irritated the older ten. When Joseph more or less rubbed their noses in the fact, irritation gave way to hate, and hate gave way to a jealousy that tempted them to eliminate their problem.

The clan's relationships deteriorated even further after Joseph recounted his two dreams. Once again, we encounter Yahweh's undermining of conventional worldly wisdom. A son so far down in birth order could expect nothing, yet "this dreamer" told his transparent tales of a day when his whole family would bow before him. The dreams are crucial to the narrative. It is even more crucial that the dreams come from Yahweh. Although Joseph is the hero of these narratives, because their main theme is Yahweh's hidden but undeniable purposes, the central performer is Yahweh.

One day Joseph, dressed in his coat of special favor, carried a message from Jacob to the older sons. To their motive was now added the opportunity to kill him, as some of them were determined to do. Reuben and Judah, two of the oldest, intervened. Reuben thinks that he will be able to return Joseph to the safety of his father's side. Judah's intentions are less noble; rather than bring a blood-curse on their heads by killing him, the brothers should sell Joseph into slavery. When the Ishmaelite traders come along, Jacob's sons follow Judah's suggestion. All that remains is to tell their father.

Deception had become a way of life for Jacob/Israel. He deceived his father Isaac. He swindled his brother Esau. He deceived his uncle Laban. He considered deceiving Esau a second time on returning to Canaan from Haran. Eventually the tables are turned on Jacob. There is a certain element of humor in Laban's deception of Jacob in the Leah-Rachel marriage-go-round, but there is nothing funny about the appearance of his sons before Jacob, holding Joseph's bloodstained coat in their hands. Even worse, they do not actually say that wild animals killed Joseph. Instead, they allow their father to fill in the blank they created when they said, "We found this. Examine it to see whether it is your son's robe." Notice the distance they create between themselves and Joseph. They do not call him "our brother" but instead emphasize the relationship between Jacob and "his son" Joseph. Through his own interpretation of the partial facts, the deceiver is deceived.

By the time we reach the conclusion of this narrative, all of those involved believed that the dreamer (and therefore his troubling dream) was dead. The sons believed that they had eliminated the source of their trouble. By all appearances, Joseph the dreamer was gone. Verse 36, however, opens a little ray of hope by employing the word *meanwhile*. Since Yahweh originated the dream and since his ways are often hidden from human eyesight, the "meanwhile" of Genesis 37:36 hints that the dream and the dreamer are still alive.

The Rise of Joseph
Genesis 39:1–41:56

"The Rise of Joseph" would be a good title for the large block of material running from Genesis 39:1 through 41:56. How was it that a young Israelite man could be sold into slavery and yet rise to the highest appointed position in the Egyptian kingdom? Moreover, what stake had the people Israel in this young man's story?

In the course of answering such questions, we must first observe that the Bible touches every aspect of life, often looking at them in the most direct manner. We have an example of that in the early section of this block of material, which is driven by an explicit sexual theme. The Bible is not embarrassed by discussions concerning sex. (Remember, for example, the erotic poetry that is the bulk of the contents of the Song of Solomon). The attempt by Potiphar's wife to seduce Joseph is important to the story. His resistance to the seduction illustrates two personal characteristics that explain Joseph's eventual rise from slavery to governmental authority, namely his integrity and the affirmation that "the Lord was with" Joseph (39:21, 23). The Bible's account of the attempted seduction demonstrates the depth of Joseph's loyalty and trustworthiness. The offer of an illicit affair by a person so insistent and willing as Potiphar's wife creates a temptation that, sadly, many in Joseph's day and ever since have been unable to resist. The same virtues that Potiphar saw in Joseph and that justified the authority by which he had been set over his master's household now enable him to withstand temptation. Potiphar entrusted him with everything that he owned; little did the Egyptian realize that Joseph could also be trusted around his alluring wife.

Joseph's integrity, however, does not insulate him from the trouble caused by the lies people tell about him. To help him endure such moments, something more than honorable character is required. That leads us to the second quality that explains Joseph's rise to power. Potiphar believes his wife's tales about Joseph. She emphasizes his inferior social status by referring to him as "that Hebrew slave" (39:17). Joseph is an alien in Egypt; he is an Israelite and an outsider. Lies about aliens and strangers are almost always easy to believe. In his anger, Potiphar orders Joseph thrown into prison. Alone and a foreigner in Egypt, there is little hope that Joseph can ever escape this terrible situation—except that "the Lord was with him." Despite his splendid personal characteristics, Joseph's future appeared bleak. He was not, however, alone.

The Bible often uses the phrase "the Lord was with him [or her]" to explain the unusual powers, abilities, and successes of its great men and women. For example, King Saul succeeded as long as the Spirit of the Lord rested upon him. But in 1 Samuel 16:14 we read, "The Spirit of the Lord had departed from Saul." That absence inevitably led to Saul's downward spiral. Of course, the Lord was with David, and thus David was successful. The phrase signals divine favor and, ultimately, success. So it is with Joseph. Although imprisoned, Yahweh was with him, and this divine presence will improve Joseph's lot. The warden looks favorably upon him and assigns him important responsibilities. The Lord's presence also enables Joseph to interpret the mysterious dreams of his fellow prisoners, minor members of Pharaoh's court. That they are members of court is important because courtiers have access to Pharaoh, the one man in Egypt who has power to release Joseph. The fate of the two men unfolds as Joseph's interpretation predicted. One of the courtiers is executed; the other is restored to court. Alas, once free, he forgot the man who predicted his release and restoration.

Death surrounded Joseph in the dungeon. The privileged elite of the Egyptian ruling class wielded this power of death against their social inferiors. To have committed adultery or attempted rape against his master's wife would have brought a summary execution. Moreover, people could be thrown into prison on the whim of their social superiors. The minor court officials with whom Joseph was imprisoned could be executed for the simple reason that, knowingly or not, they angered somebody who held great power. When Joseph was eventually summoned before Pharaoh, he encountered the Egyptian who would determine whether Joseph would live or die. Yahweh, however, stood over against these imperial forces of death. On three separate occasions, Joseph found himself in dangerous, death-dealing situations. The first was with Potiphar's wife, the second with Pharaoh's servants in prison, and the third when he stood before Pharaoh himself. Three times, Joseph escaped death because Yahweh, the Lord of life and not death, was with Joseph and kept him alive, for God is about to do something in the land of Egypt.

God's intentions involve both Pharaoh and Joseph. God reveals these intentions to Pharaoh in two dreams. The meaning of these dreams is anything but clear to Pharaoh, who mentions them within the hearing of his cupbearer. The mention of mysterious dreams jogs the memory of the servant, who tells Pharaoh of one who can interpret the dreams for him. Pharaoh orders Joseph's release, and after he is made presentable, Joseph comes to the court.

Joseph first denies that he possesses interpretive powers. The statement is both pious and true. He repeats the statement he made to Pharaoh's servants in prison: God is the source of dreams and their interpretation. The Egyptian does not care about the ultimate source of the resolution of his problems; Pharaoh simply wants to know the bottom line. Unlike the court magicians, Joseph can provide answers. The dreams predict seven years of abundance followed by seven years of famine. Notice that the text is silent on the question of God's purpose. We are not told why God intends to act in this manner, only that he will. Since the Bible is silent on this matter, it is best that we follow its example.

Joseph interpreted Pharaoh's dreams and then offered a plan for dealing with their consequences. The combination of interpretation and plan suggest to Pharaoh that the best man for the job stands before him. He appoints Joseph as a kind of viceroy, with authority in all matters save those directly pertaining to the throne. Joseph's integrity and the presence of the Lord have raised him to a status that parallels the position he held as Potiphar's steward. He directs Egyptian preparations for the years of plenty and famine. From radical insecurity and dependence on the will and even whims of others, Joseph's rise is as dramatic as it is complete. Second only to Pharaoh, Joseph now wields an almost uncontestable power over the Egyptians and those who need their assistance.

Forgiveness and Reunion
Genesis 42–45

The Joseph of these chapters is a man at the height of his moral, spiritual, and physical powers. No longer the inexperienced, straitlaced youth whose dreams outraged his brothers and annoyed his father, neither was Joseph any longer the competent, trustworthy steward in Potiphar's household. Joseph has achieved power and position beyond the dreams and hopes of any Israelite.

This narrative yields some fruitful insights into the nature of human relationships and the power of forgiveness. If we examine some of the relationships between the key figures in this story and the moves they make to gain their desires, we discover a great deal. Each of the characters must come to terms with the others and with their past in order for all to be pleased. First, there is the aged figure of Jacob, still brooding the loss of his favorite son and distant from the others, save alone Benjamin. Second, we have the brothers, led by Reuben and Judah, who have not forgotten their sin against Joseph and their father. A terrible famine has rendered them desperate, passive, and dependent on others. Third, their brother Joseph, by contrast, is the agent who makes things happen. Events occur in the fashion he designs and for his purposes. Of course, Joseph also grasps the situation with a knowledge his brothers lack. While he knows their identity, his is a mystery to them. Such knowledge and position combine to give Joseph an unassailable power over his brothers and his father. Just as his dream foretold, they bow down to him. This is a moving and powerful story of testing. The brothers are tested and so is Jacob. Joseph tests his brothers to determine what kind of men they have become in the years of their separation. Jacob is tested, for he must trust his beloved Benjamin into the care of his other ten sons. In the end, their trust is rewarded and we learn that Joseph's enslavement, as well as the years of plenty and the famine, have meaning according to the larger purposes of God.

When they return from Egypt with their silver and grain, the Israelites tell their father of the harsh Egyptian and his demand that their youngest brother must return with them in order to secure the release of Simeon and allow them further trading opportunities in Egypt. At first Jacob will have none of this; Benjamin will not be permitted to leave his side. Reuben even offers his own sons as hostages (42:37). The clan does nothing while the famine only increases its hold on the land. It is clear that they must return to Egypt for more grain. Jacob, the old master wheeler-dealer, sends his sons back, loaded with gifts that he hopes will curry Egyptian favor.

Once again, the brothers find themselves in the presence of the strange and stern Egyptian governor. He inquires of their father and of Benjamin, who stands in their midst. Once again Joseph is moved to tears and must flee the room. When he returns, they all sit down to a feast, except they do not eat at the same tables. Genesis 43:32 shows us the strains that ethnic differences placed on any social gathering. The difference is more than ethnic. Aliens and strangers were typically considered ritually unclean by the host culture; to eat with the unclean was, as the text says, detestable. At dinner, Joseph slowly begins his disclosure. He orders that his brothers take their places according to seniority. They are amazed that the Egyptians could know the Israelites' birth order. The mystery and power of their host only increases in their eyes.

The brothers soon are on their way home, unaware that Joseph has contrived to have them arrested for theft. They are summoned back into his presence and accused of having stolen a silver cup. Confident that none of them is the criminal, they open their packs for inspection. To their great dismay, the cup is discovered in Benjamin's pack. Now comes the final test. When they learn that only Benjamin must remain in custody, the brothers refuse to abandon him as they once abandoned Joseph. Judah, who had sold Joseph to the Ishmaelite traders, now stands to take Benjamin's place. The men who once tricked their father into believing that Joseph was dead are unwilling to see Jacob grieve the loss of Rachel's other son. Judah's loyalty to brother and father move Joseph to reveal his true identity. For a moment, his brothers find themselves too terrified to speak. If this is truly Joseph, what revenge might he take on them for their actions against him?

Joseph sees through all the actions of his father and brothers to the larger purposes of God. All of this—his kidnapping and slavery, his rise to power—behind all these events, the unseen hand of God has been at work. "So then, it was not you who sent me here, but God" (45:8). God has been at work to preserve the clan of Jacob/Israel. Knowing that famine would threaten its future, God sent one of the clan—Joseph—ahead to prepare the way. If the people of Israel were not protected from the famine, then God's promise to Abraham—Joseph's great-grandfather—would be nullified, but that could not be since the word of the Lord never returns void. Joseph instructs his brothers to bring their father and all their households to Egypt. The favor he enjoys with Pharaoh they will also enjoy. So is the house of Israel saved by leaving Canaan to take up residence in Egypt.

As we move through this narrative, the disordered and confused tangle of relationships among all these figures is rewoven into a whole cloth. Restoration is not accomplished without tension and, in some cases, real struggles. At a distance, Joseph and Jacob struggle over the issue of whether or not Benjamin would make the journey to Egypt. The brothers struggle with their father concerning the proposed second journey, one they made only because the famine worsened. At the narrative's center is the struggle between Joseph and his brothers, right up to the wonderful moment when his true identity is revealed. Old wounds are finally healed in Joseph's theological explanation for all that had happened to this family. God has been at work to preserve their life.

One should not be too surprised if Romans 8:28 comes to mind as this story is read. That verse might be applied as Paul's theological summary to this story in particular and to the Genesis narrative as a whole. Had he known the verse, Joseph might have said, "Exactly!" It was Joseph's knowledge and his belief in that theological point that created the possibility that he would forgive his brothers. Without such theology, old, festering wounds would have crippled

Joseph's relationship with his brothers. If we truly believe that God works for good, then forgiveness is always a possibility.

A Dwelling, Not a Home
Genesis 46–49

These chapters close the long narrative of Joseph and the Israelites' move from Canaan to Egypt. By the end of the story, Joseph has been reunited with his father Jacob/Israel, and his entire clan has been resettled on some of the most fertile land that Egypt has to offer. This sounds like a happy ending. Nevertheless, a cloud hangs over the story. We know that Israel's good fortune is temporary; hard times will eventually fall on the people. The story foreshadows these hard times by Israel's request that he be buried in Canaan. Later, although he had lived his entire adult life and risen to great power in Egypt, Joseph will make a similar request. Like his father, he wishes to be buried back home. These requests remind us that, although the Israelites benefit from the wealth and fertility of Egypt, it is only a temporary dwelling. At best they are but sojourners, aliens, and strangers in the land of Egypt; it is not, nor can it ever be, home.

Joseph's reunion with his brothers means that they return to their father Jacob with the astounding news that Joseph is alive. Moreover, he has become a man of great authority in Egypt—"father to Pharaoh" (45:8). In fact, Pharaoh himself invites the whole family to move to Egypt. We know that a later Pharaoh will enslave Israel, and this knowledge adds a note of irony to this Pharaoh's invitation. Worries persist in Jacob's mind even after the clan has begun the long journey. In a dream vision, God reaffirms the ancient promise to Abraham, "I will make you into a great nation there" (46:3).

After a tribe-by-tribe summary of Jacob's descendants, the story gives us a tally in 46:27. Including Joseph and his sons, the number of Jacob's clan is seventy. Since the Hebrews believed that the number seven signified wholeness or completeness, that Jacob's descendants number seventy is a sign of exceptional fullness and blessing. Of course, provision must be made for this large clan. They are shepherds and herdsmen, and their large flocks will need good pasture and water. Joseph coaches his family in the speech they are to make before Pharaoh. Apparently, Joseph has a plan in mind that will settle his family on the best land in Egypt and keep them some distance from the direct authority of Pharaoh. Blood is thicker than water; Joseph wants the best for his family. Goshen was likely in the northeast part of the Nile delta and therefore some of the very best land for raising livestock. Pharaoh concurs in this arrangement, and the clan settles in Goshen.

Jacob/Israel lived for seventeen years in Egypt, long enough to be reunited with his beloved Joseph. Jacob lived to see Joseph's sons Manasseh and Ephraim and to bless them along with his other eleven sons. In the fullness of his years, the time of Jacob's death finally came. Before he died, he asked Joseph to swear formally by placing his hand under his father's thigh that he would take Jacob's body back to the family burial plot in Canaan. This Joseph promised, and when his father did indeed die, Joseph made good on his word. Egypt, after all, was not home, even though the house of Israel was to live there for a very long time.

Exodus

Preliminary Historical and Theological Considerations

Exodus 2:23–25; 5:1–2; 11:1–8; 12:29–32; 15:1–2, 19–21

Drive along the freeways near Athens, Greece, and you will find signs that indicate the next exit with the Greek word *exodus*. The word literally means "the way, or road, out." The second book of the *Torah,* which modern Bible scholars refer to as the Pentateuch, recounts the dramatic narrative of Israel's road out of Egypt. Centuries had passed since Israel and his clan sojourned as friends of Pharaoh, and Egypt had now become the "house of bondage." Their dramatic release is the pivotal event in Israelite history, and thus the exodus stands at the very center of the Old Testament. Yes, the book of Exodus follows Genesis, but in terms of its significance for Old Testament faith, the exodus is of the first importance. Through this singular event, Yahweh transformed a loose rabble of slaves into the people of God. The exodus made a nation, a people, of the descendants of Abraham, Isaac, and Jacob. In the spring of every year, Israel remembered the exodus through the celebration of Passover. It was *the* great religious holiday of the year; Passover commemorated the central event of Israel's faith and history.

Ironically, this absolutely formative event in Israel's life is shrouded in historical mystery. Egypt is rich in archaeological history, but it contains no direct references to the Hebrews or to any Hebrew names. Only the Old Testament refers to the exodus. There is no shred of evidence in ancient Egyptian artifacts that Israel ever dwelled in Egypt. On the other hand, several early Israelites bear Egyptian names—Moses, Hophni, Phineas, and Merari, for example. Furthermore, John Bright states, "There can really be little doubt that ancestors of Israel had been slaves in Egypt." For one thing, "it is not the sort of tradition any people would invent! Here is no heroic epic of migration, but the recollection of shameful servitude from which only the power of God brought deliverance."[6] Other ancient peoples recited tales of their former greatness; Israel tells a story of its own oppression— not the kind of story people tell to impress. It was not to celebrate their own heroic past but to sing the glory of the power of Yahweh, who delivered them, that Israel narrated this story.

The date of the exodus also has been a matter of scholarly attention. Most evidence points to a date sometime between 1300 and 1250 BC. Archaeological discoveries and our knowledge of the history of the petty kingdoms of Palestine all support a date earlier than the year 1200, but no earlier than 1300. Although we cannot be certain, it would appear that the Pharaoh at the time of the exodus was Rameses II.

The theological mileposts are that Israel groans and Yahweh hears; Yahweh's prophet, Moses, speaks for the Lord, but Pharaoh refuses to listen; the tenth plague—death of the firstborn—yields Israel's release; and Yahweh delivers newly freed Israel at the Red Sea. These mileposts are theologically important because aspects of God's character are disclosed. Yahweh is the central actor in the Exodus narrative; God is the hero of the story.

6. Bright, *History of Israel,* 110.

Moses, Aaron, and even Pharaoh, have important roles to play, but without Yahweh there would be no story to tell. This seems perfectly obvious, and yet important theological claims depend on our recognition that Yahweh is the one who initiated the action. Unlike the gods of the Egyptians (and the Canaanites), Yahweh was not an impersonal force of nature. Nature gods were believed to control the natural cycles so important to ancient agricultural peoples: birth, growth, decay, and the forces that contributed to them. Yahweh also made the rain to fall on the just and unjust alike, but Yahweh also acted in history to achieve the divine will and purpose.

The exodus testifies to Israel's experience and belief that Yahweh acts in human affairs. This strong theological claim says something very distinctive about the God of Israel, even as it distinguishes Yahweh from the gods of Israel's neighbors. Yahweh is a history-making God. Yahweh is revealed through certain historical events.

What is revealed of God in the story of the exodus? In the first place, Yahweh hears. God is not abstract but personal. Second, Yahweh hears Israel's groans. This groan-hear connection sets up a major Old Testament motif: Israel cries, Yahweh hears, Yahweh answers. Third, Yahweh hears the groans of oppressed Israelites. Slaves matter to Yahweh. Nowhere else in the ancient world did gods behave like this. Everywhere but in Israel, ancient gods sided with the powerful and wealthy. Yahweh is not a God who listens only to the rich and powerful, the best and brightest. Yahweh's ear is attuned to the cries of all, from the top to the very bottom of the social order.

The Call of Moses

Exodus 3:1–4:18

The book of Hosea calls Moses a prophet: "The LORD used a prophet to bring Israel up from Egypt, by a prophet he cared for him" (12:13). The book of Deuteronomy concludes, "Since then [Moses' day], no prophet has risen in Israel like Moses, whom the LORD knew face to face...For no one has ever shown the mighty power or performed the awesome deeds that Moses did in the sight of all Israel" (34:10–12). Moses towers over the men and women of the Old Testament, for in a very real sense he was the great founder of Israel's faith. To be sure, Moses did not invent this faith and its traditions. As a prophet, he was a spokesperson for Yahweh, the person who carried God's revealing word to the people. Of course, Moses was not the only prophet of Israel, but prior to the exodus, the Israelite tribes were a loose association of clans that shared a common ancestor in Abraham. After the exodus and during the wilderness sojourn, Israel became a people—the people of Yahweh. Moses was the key figure in that transformation.

Scholars use the term *theophany* to describe events such as we find in Exodus 3. *Theophany* means the appearance or manifestation of God to human beings. Such appearances happen at God's initiative; humans do not summon God. Theophanies occurred before Moses (see Gen 3:8; 15:12ff), but with Moses and in the theophanies that occurred during the wilderness wandering, Yahweh's appearances become more an abiding presence, e.g., the pillar of fire and the column of the cloud that marked the Lord God's constant presence among the people Israel.

The story opens with Moses tending sheep near Mount Horeb. Earlier we learned that Moses is a fugitive. He is also an Israelite, one of an oppressed people enslaved by Pharaoh. We also know that Moses has made a new home for himself among the nomadic peoples of Midian. He has married and is now in the service of his father-in-law Jethro. While tending his father-in-law's sheep, Moses sees a bush that burns without being consumed. Curious, he decides to make a closer inspection. From within the bush, a voice calls to Moses by name and warns him to approach no closer. As the text says, "God called to him from within the bush" (3:4), hence the warning; humans may not get too close to God, who is so holy that proximity to this God is dangerous to human life.

At this point, Moses steps into the story's background and Yahweh assumes central focus. We are about to learn who this God is. It is the God of Abraham, Isaac, and Jacob, who acts in a manner so unusual and atypical of gods. In the first place, Yahweh actually converses with Moses. Other gods might appear in dreams or visions, but Yahweh talks with Moses. That tells us something about Moses' status as the man who spoke face-to-face with God, even as it tells us that Yahweh is willing to talk with humans—even fugitive members of an enslaved race. God is willing to work with human beings, as becomes clear as the dialogue with Moses unfolds.

Yahweh's character is further disclosed by three verbs: "I have *seen*...I have *heard*...I am *concerned*..." (Ex 3:7). Yahweh notices and is moved by the Israelites' suffering. Who are the Israelites that their suffering should matter to God? Are they a great people? Are they proud warriors and conquerors? No, they are none of these. As a matter of fact, they are a little people, an unimportant people. In the eyes of the great Pharaoh, they are a people significant only for the number of bricks they can make in a day. Yahweh is the God who hears when people cry, not only the rich and powerful but also all people. Even oppressed slaves who believe that their cries fall only on deaf ears have voices to which the ear of Yahweh is attuned.

Now the story shifts its focus back to Moses. Because Yahweh is the kind of God who has seen, heard, and been moved, someone must go to Egypt. Someone must be Yahweh's chosen instrument of liberation. In the theophany on Mount Horeb, Yahweh calls Moses to lead Israel out of bondage. It was for Israel's sake that Moses was called. Moses' call was about Yahweh as much as it was about Moses. Yahweh is a God who hears slaves and who is "concerned about their suffering" (3:7). Somewhat characteristic of Old Testament call narratives, Moses initially proved to be a reluctant prophet. Other later prophets also wondered whether they were capable of the task to which they were summoned. Moses disputes whether he is really the one to do this great work of service to Yahweh. Will people believe him? He even lacks the public presence and the forceful speech necessary to command. Nevertheless, it is Moses whom Yahweh wants for the assignment, and so it is that Yahweh is willing to work with the reluctant prophet and his self-proclaimed limitations. If he is not a great public speaker, his brother Aaron can be drafted for the role of spokesperson. God has a ready answer to each of Moses' objections, and underneath each answer is the promise, "I will be with you."

Having been assured of Yahweh's presence, Moses does not immediately accept his calling but asks yet another question. He asked for the name of the god who was addressing him from the bush. "The God of Abraham, Isaac, and Jacob" is a description, not a name. Moses sought more than a phrase. We miss something of the impertinence of this question in our modern age of informality. In Hebrew thought, names are intimately connected with existence and the essence of personality. Names therefore inherently possess power. (Incidentally, this idea lies behind the Old Testament prohibition against taking the Lord's name in vain. One may not use Yahweh's name lightly, for the name itself is powerful.) In asking the name of the divine being addressing him, Moses' question called upon Yahweh to reveal himself. Yahweh did and told Moses that his name is (in Hebrew, *"YHWH"*) "I Am That I Am," or alternately, "I Will Cause to Be What I Will Cause to Be." In other words, God's name discloses God to be the source of all that is or ever will be.

Deliverance

Exodus 13:17–14:31

After Moses' appeals, after plagues that are nuisances, finally there comes into Egypt the terrible plague of death and with it the first Passover and ultimately Pharaoh's release of the Israelite slaves. These events conclude in Israel's miraculous deliverance from the Pharaoh's army at the Red Sea. There is some confusion over the name and location of this sea. Consult a map of the region, and immediately one sees the problem. If the Israelites marched to the Red Sea named on most maps, they would have marched farther and much faster than a well-trained army—unlikely for a group that included both the elderly and the very young. Then there is also the problem of translation. The Hebrew name for this sea is Yam Suph, which means "sea of reeds." Further confusing us, possibly, are the visual images of this event created by Cecil B. DeMille in his epic film *The Ten Commandments*. The faith that Yahweh delivered Israel from the Egyptians, however, does not need to believe that it was the Red Sea nor that events happened as DeMille pictured them. The story's importance rests on other, more important, theological points.

The first point to remember is that Israel's destiny rests in the hand of God. Israel lacked everything necessary for its defense. Although armed for battle (13:18), the Israelites could not be considered a significant military force. Only a matter of days earlier, they had been slaves, not soldiers. They were certainly no match for Pharaoh's charioteers. Moses may have been an extraordinary leader, but even the most extraordinary of leaders must sometimes depend on others. If Israel is to survive and arrive at its promised destination, it will not be by Moses' hand but through the power of God alone. The text tells of this power and the guidance it provided Israel: "By day the Lord went ahead of them in a pillar of cloud to guide them on their way and by night in a pillar of fire to give them light, so that they could travel by day or night" (13:21). The text also tells us that the pillars of cloud and fire were constant. The One who watches over Israel neither slumbers nor sleeps.

Yahweh watches over Israel, and Yahweh also will act in Israel's behalf. Camped by the sea, Israel is attacked by the Egyptians, suddenly repentant over having lost their cheap labor supply. Presumably, it was the pillars of cloud and fire that guided the Israelites to their camping place. Their escape routes cut off, the Israelites are quickly terrified by the sight of the Egyptian warriors. Certain that they are about to die, the Israelites demand to know why Moses has brought them to such a fate. They forget that it is Yahweh who has brought them to this dangerous, fear-filled place. It is Yahweh who once again will hear their cry for help. It is Yahweh who will save Israel. In all this, perhaps Israel will learn that in good times, as well as desperate times, its life depends on Yahweh and Yahweh's faithfulness.

God instructs Moses in the manner of Israel's rescue. He is to stretch his hands over the water that holds them in danger and blocks their route to safety. Moses follows orders, and a great east wind pushes back the waters of the sea. Through Moses, Yahweh opens a path to safety. Israel's path is also the road to Egypt's destruction. Pharaoh and his soldiers are easily discouraged. They pursue Israel along the path created by Yahweh. God's power, however, is power for life not death. Since Pharaoh means to destroy Israel, he will have to pay with his own life. Egypt's death means life to the Israelites, and so they sing: "The LORD is a warrior; the LORD is his name. Pharaoh's chariots and his army he has hurled into the sea...Who among the gods is like you, O LORD? Who is like you—majestic in holiness, awesome in glory, working wonders?" (15:3–4, 11).

Israel at Sinai
Exodus 19:1–20:21

Three months later, we find Israel camped at the base of Mount Sinai. They are now free as can be, or so it appears to them. They are no longer slaves of Pharaoh or afraid of him. In a much later context, African-American slaves interpreted this experience of freedom in the lines "Free at last, free at last. Thank God almighty, I'm free at last." Understandably, newly freed slaves might think that their new freedom meant that they were like the *scirocco*, the desert wind that blows wherever it will. Encamped in front of Mount Sinai, Israel is about to learn the dimensions of its freedom. Yahweh's gift of freedom does not license Israelites to do as they please.

Moses climbs the mountain and receives from Yahweh a message for the people. It reminds them of mighty deeds already done on their behalf. God is a God of purposeful action. In the case of Israel, that purpose is now disclosed. Yahweh has given Israel its freedom for the purpose of living as the covenant people of God. As long as they were slaves in Egypt, covenant faithfulness was impossible. Once free, life as the covenant people of Yahweh is a real possibility. Yahweh has freed Israel in order that they might be faithful to Yahweh. In the Bible, freedom and faithfulness to God go hand in hand. One is nourished and grows in the presence of the other.

Why does Yahweh desire Israel to live in covenant relationship? Before we answer that question, observe in 19:5 the presence of that little word *if*. Life with Yahweh is contingent on obedience: "Now *if* you obey me fully and keep my covenant..." (author's emphasis). And if Israel is faithful to the covenant, what then? Then "you will be for me a kingdom of priests and a holy nation" (19:6). Priests, of course, are mediators between God and the people. Yahweh desires that Israel will fulfill the role of mediator between him and all the peoples of the world. Through Israel, all are to be blessed. Yahweh seeks Israel for a covenant life together for the sake of the entire world.

The covenant proposed on Sinai is not the first such agreement between the Lord God and Israel. The Old Testament refers to several covenants, for the term [*berith* in Hebrew] characteristically describes Yahweh's relationship with human beings. Yahweh covenanted with Noah (Gen 9:8–17), Abraham (Gen 15), and David (2 Sam 7) as well as with Moses and Israel. The concept of *covenant* so pervades the Old Testament that some later Christian thinkers adopted it as the organizing principle of their theology. The most prominent of these were seventeenth-century English and American Puritans. The governor of Massachusetts Bay Colony, John Winthrop, described the basis of that colony as a covenant between the Puritans and God. In Winthrop's view, disobedience would bring divine judgment, but faithful living would lead to such an outpouring of God's blessings that other colonies would say, "The Lord make us like New England." One of the earliest documents of American political history, the *Mayflower Compact,* also testifies to the powerful historical influence of the biblical idea of covenant.

What are the terms of covenant love and faithfulness? Exodus 20:2–17 records these as the Ten Commandments. How does a person live as one of the people of God? Exodus answers, "Follow the commandments." The Ten Commandments, or Decalogue, often are divided into two categories, sometimes called tables. The first table contains the commandments that instruct us in our relationship to God, numbers one through four. The balance composes the second table. These instruct us in our relationships with other human beings. Together, the commandments serve as the foundation of the covenant between Yahweh and Israel. If the people will follow them, they will live and be a light to the nations. As the book of Exodus narrates, Yahweh gave Israel the Decalogue and other elements of Torah during the year in which the people were encamped before Sinai. It was a year of instruction in how the Israelites were to live in their new freedom. A faithful walk with the Lord, according to Torah, was the means by which Israel could fulfill her mediating role as the light to the nations.

Dr. George Kufeldt, retired professor of Old Testament at the School of Theology at Anderson University, frequently says of the Decalogue, "They are called the Ten Commandments, not the Ten Suggestions." This wry observation reinforces our tendency to interpret Torah as law more than instruction. While it is appropriate to think of commandments as law in some sense, it is also important to think of the Decalogue as instruction and ask, To whom and for whom do the commandments exist? Martin Luther interpreted the commandments to be addressed to each one of us, but he added that, in addressing the commandments to us, it is not for our own sake. Christians, said Luther, stand under the gospel; God saves us by grace through faith in Jesus Christ. Therefore we ought not obey the commandments in a misguided effort to earn God's favor.

God addresses the commandments *to* us but *for the sake of* our neighbor—understood here as anyone. God gives us the commandments to direct our attention toward our neighbors with their needs for respect, life, safety, and peace. Luther thought that Christians should joyfully obey the commandments, for they direct us toward the proper objects of our love and concern, such as our neighbor, and thus also help us get ourselves out of the center of our attention.

Luther's reading of the commandments fits nicely with the moment when Israel stood before Yahweh at Sinai. Three months earlier, God had miraculously delivered the Israelites from Egyptian bondage. Now they were free. Through the Sinai Covenant, however, Israel learned that they were not free to be whatever or whomever they desired. Rather, the covenant balanced Israel's newfound freedom with covenant loyalty—faithfulness—to Yahweh. At Sinai, Israel learned that freedom is not an end in itself. Life with Yahweh entails more than being free. According to the Bible, faithfulness completes freedom.

God Is Just and Merciful
Exodus 34:27–35

These verses conclude one of the most dramatic chapters of the Pentateuch. Once again Moses has been on the mountain. He has gone there to plead for Israel's life. The people had committed a great sin during his earlier absence. While Moses was on Sinai with Joshua, the people wearied of waiting for their return and asked Aaron to make a new god for them. Thus it was that he fashioned the people's gold and jewelry into a golden calf, the kind of god that the Israelites would have remembered from their days in Egypt. Moses and Joshua return to the camp just as the Israelites have broken into a riotous worship before their new god. Unwittingly, they have broken the first commandment God had given to Moses. It is hard to say who is angrier, Moses or God. The prophet smashes the stone tablets on which Yahweh had written the commandments, and Yahweh is determined to smash Israel. Moses, however, pleads with Yahweh for Israel's life. The future of this stiffnecked people hangs in the balance while Yahweh speaks "to Moses face to face, as a man speaks with his friend" (33:11).

Moses persuades Yahweh to give Israel another chance. The Lord commands him to carve another pair of tablets and once again writes the commandments for Israel's instruction. This second experience includes Yahweh's self-revelation to Moses. In response to his request, Yahweh passes by him, revealing as much of the divine presence as Moses' humanity can stand without being consumed. As he passes, Yahweh proclaims the essence of the divine character: "The LORD, the LORD, the compassionate and gracious God, slow to anger, abounding in love and faithfulness, maintaining love to thousands, and forgiving wickedness, rebellion and sin. Yet he does not leave the guilty unpunished; he punishes the children and their children for the sin of the fathers to the third and fourth generation" (34:6–7). Yahweh's passage before Moses transfigures him. He is not the same man who walked up Sinai to plead for his people's life.

After forty days and forty nights on Sinai, speaking to God as a man would speak to a friend, Moses returned to the Israelite camp. All this time Israel has been waiting, wondering about their fate. In his arms, Moses carries the two stone tablets, newly inscribed with the commandments. The people are saved; their covenant with Yahweh has been restored. Even before he arrives in the Israelite camp, however, Moses' appearance frightens the people. His face now possesses a radiance that is clearly apparent even at some distance. This radiance marks Moses as different from all other humans, and Israel is fearful of him. Even as humans may not gaze on God's glory, that glory now reflected in the face of Moses is too much for the Israelites to bear. Moses calls Aaron and the other leaders to come and speak with him. Once they are reassured, Moses can enter the camp and speak with the Israelites. But from this moment forward, there will be a barrier between Moses and Israel. In order to speak with his own people, Moses must veil his face; its radiance is too much for Israel. Only when speaking with Yahweh may Moses remove the veil.

Through the great mediator Moses, Yahweh remains with Israel. Even though they have sinned greatly, Yahweh forgives. Because Yahweh is gracious, slow to anger, and abounding in mercy, Israel will remain within covenant relationship. A new set of commandments replaces the first. Israel has the instruction, the *Torah*, which will enable it to walk humbly with Yahweh, if only they will obey.

Pilgrim People, Pilgrim God
Exodus 40:34–38

The Israelites broke camp at the foot of Mount Sinai. Fifteen months had passed since the exodus; the people had been camped before the mountain for a full year. At the beginning of that year, Yahweh had given the Decalogue to Moses, but the reception of the commandments was just the beginning of Israel's instruction in walking in the way of the Lord. It was a year of preparation for the journey toward the Promised Land. The year at Sinai brought awe-inspiring theophanies and crushing disappointments. Israel experienced God's presence and God's wrath during the Sinai encampment.

The book of Leviticus records much of the law, including the holiness code, given to Israel at Sinai. This law covers nearly every facet of Israelite life and society. The Leviticus code is so extensive that later Jewish rabbis told a story that was said to illuminate Israel's response to all of this detailed legislation. According to the story, on the first day of Israel's march away from Mount Sinai, the people marched a distance that normally would take two weeks; they wanted to get as far from the mountain as possible in case God had still more laws to prescribe.

The encounters, the giving of the law, the warnings, and the judgments—all of these prepared Israel for the journey toward Canaan. In Egyptian bondage, they had been no people, a nonentity among the peoples of the eastern Mediterranean. In the exodus and through the year at Sinai, Israel became the people of Yahweh. Little more than a year after the exodus, the people were free and now profoundly conscious of their relationship to Yahweh and of what Yahweh expected of them. They were about ready to begin their journey. One final step remained.

Throughout the Sinai encampment, Yahweh had resided on Sinai. Cloud and fire on the mountain signaled God's presence there. Ancient peoples, Israel included, generally thought of their gods in some sense bound to place. In this view, the rule of a people's god extended through the region they inhabited but no farther. This view prompted the exiled Israelites to ask, for example, "How can we sing the songs of the LORD while in a foreign land?" (Ps 137:4). Israel struggled to come to the theological vision of Yahweh as the ruler of all the earth. The Israelites at Sinai still wondered whether their God would remain present with them when they departed Sinai.

Numbers 9:15 says, "On the day the tabernacle, the Tent of Testimony, was set up, the cloud covered it." At the center of the tabernacle stood the Holy of Holies, the most holy place where Yahweh dwelled and where he spoke with Moses. The cloud signaled Yahweh's presence and Yahweh's command to march. Its presence also pledged to Israel that Yahweh would be with them all along the harsh desert miles. Not only had Yahweh prepared them for the journey, he also intended to accompany Israel. Pilgrim people were prepared and accompanied by a pilgrim God.

Leviticus

Sacred Space, Holy People

Leviticus 26:2–6, 11–13

The psalmist sang of the temple in Jerusalem, "How lovely is your dwelling place, O LORD Almighty" (Ps 84:1). The temple was a sacred place because it was the place of Yahweh's presence. They believed that God was present in the temple in a manner unlike anywhere else. The tabernacle preceded the temple as Israel's place of worship and the sacred dwelling place of God. In essence, the tabernacle was a portable temple; Israel carried it during the long journey from Egypt to Canaan. Once set up in the center of the Israelite camp, the tabernacle became Yahweh's dwelling place. Once dedicated, the tabernacle and its furnishings would be holy and the altar "most holy." It is clear from Yahweh's pronouncement that Israel would be a kingdom of priests and a holy nation with which God would dwell. What does *holiness* mean?

Church groups that emerged in the context of the nineteenth-century American holiness revival are inclined to interpret holiness in sharply moral or ethical terms. In such traditions as the Church of God movement or the Church of the Nazarene, holiness has been commonly understood as "heart purity," with the emphasis on purity. In this view, holiness is the absence of sin and its contaminating effects. To be sure, the Old Testament concept of holiness also requires purity—witness the prescribed ritual washings and anointings. But more than purity is attached to the Old Testament idea of holiness. Also important is the idea of separation. Objects and people set apart for the service of Yahweh are holy. To be profane (from a Latin word that means "outside the temple") is to use or employ the holy for unauthorized purposes or outside the bounds of the sacred. Once properly dedicated, the tabernacle became holy—separated to Yahweh.

No Israelite could profane the tabernacle without serious consequence. (Ancient Israel commonly believed that some places were sacred. The location of one of Israel's important shrines was the site of Jacob's dream-vision of angels descending and ascending the ladder. He named this sacred place Bethel, meaning the "house of God," because of this unusual manifestation of divine presence.) Modern people often do not fully appreciate this sense of sacred space. (I still recall, however, my mother's severe scolding after she discovered me using the kneeling bench at the front of our church's sanctuary [a term that derives from the Latin *sanctus*, "holy"] as a balance beam. She had a strong sense that it was a holy place. Even young children were to respect its sacredness.) Israel's sense of the tabernacle's sacredness was driven by similar feelings, but they were deeper and expressed much more strongly.

In the tabernacle's innermost area, the Most Holy Place, Yahweh resided among the people. There rested the ark of the covenant ["testimony" NIV], which held the most sacred objects of Israelite life—the two tablets of stone on which the Ten Commandments were written. The Most Holy Place was so sacred that only the high priest was permitted into it, and only once a year on Yom Kippur, the Day of Atonement. The ark was so sacred that no human hands were permitted to touch it. Members of the priestly class, the Levites, carried the ark on long poles that rested on their shoulders. Any person who touched the ark would die, just as any person who climbed onto Mount Sinai, Yahweh's dwelling place, would die. Yahweh's holiness is an all-consuming fire.

Israel devotedly crafted the tabernacle, Yahweh's portable dwelling place. Yahweh pledged to be their God and to walk before them in pillars of cloud and fire. Once completed, the tabernacle becomes the place where Yahweh fulfills another promise: "I will put my dwelling place among you, and I will not abhor you. I will walk among you and be your God, and you will be my people" (Lev 26:11–12). Happy are those people whose God is the Lord.

In a similar vein, Israel was the holy people of God. Like the tabernacle, Israel was not to be profaned. The people themselves, however, constituted a threat to their holiness. Through disobedience, Israel could profane itself. The people whom Yahweh chose to be his priests could abuse their freedom, soiling and profaning their holy character. Disobedience carried a terrible threat.

As disaster threatens the disobedient, so God stands ready to bless those who live in covenant faithfulness. Divine blessing comes to the obedient. Moreover, obedience to Torah yields blessings of stunning magnitude. Productive land, large and prosperous families, peace, and the abiding presence of Yahweh are promised to those who keep covenant with God. This overflowing generosity cannot but amaze modern people who are accustomed to an economics of scarcity. Obedience, trust, and abundance are fundamentally linked. This text from Leviticus daringly suggests, all empirical evidence to the contrary, that God abundantly rewards those who trust him. Leviticus 26 thus makes an astounding claim that flies in the face of the spirit of our modern age.

Numbers

A Holy God

Numbers 9:15–23

Yahweh's holy presence is no trifling matter. Once completed, the tabernacle becomes the place where Yahweh dwells and, therefore, where God and Israel meet. Because Yahweh dwells with Israel, they have a future and a guide. By the same token, because Yahweh dwells with Israel, certain areas of the camp become off-limits. Not even Moses may enter the Tent of Meeting; it was the place of the Lord's presence, and the glory of the Lord filled the tabernacle.

The term *holy* deserves some special attention. Often we take it to mean "morally pure" or "without sin." In Hebrew, the term has a larger meaning. Utensils used in tabernacle worship were declared holy. They had been set apart for divine service. Anything or anyone sanctified, "made holy," as such, was thus dedicated to God's use. But what did it mean to say that God was holy? Here the idea of sinlessness and separateness converge. God is wholly other and completely unlike humans not only morally but also in terms of God's own nature. The holiness of God is such that no human—not even Moses—may gaze at "the glory of the LORD" and live. To see God in the fullness of that glory is to be swallowed by its all-consuming holiness.

God's holiness is such a serious matter that many people have formed habits of reverence to honor it. Instead of writing the four consonants of the Hebrew alphabet that spell God's name (*YHWH*, which becomes "Yahweh" in English), the Old Testament writers substituted another less holy term, "the LORD." Wherever you see "the LORD" in the English-language Old Testament, you can be fairly certain that early Hebrew manuscripts had substituted that word for YHWH. When reading the Hebrew Bible aloud, pious Jews will pass over the phrase "the LORD" in silence because they believe even this substitute is too holy to be spoken by human voice. Very orthodox Jews will not write *YHWH* for fear that the paper on which God's name is written might fall on the floor and thus profane the name of the Lord.

The presence of this dangerously holy God in their midst generates respect among the Israelites. We should respect their respect for Yahweh's holiness. The Bible itself says that it is a fearful thing to fall into the hands of a righteous God (Heb 10:31). Besides, the presence of the Holy One in their midst conferred certain benefits on Israel. Yahweh's presence guided the people. The pillar of cloud and fire was a place of God's presence, a spiritual as well as geographical compass. Every Israelite could find his or her bearings by sighting the pillar. Look around, find the pillar, and people will discover not only God's presence but also where they are in relation to God. To be able to see oneself in relation to God is a gift and a grace.

In the company of Yahweh's guiding presence, Israel must develop a pilgrim attitude. Whenever the pillar moved, Israel broke camp and followed. When the pillar halted, Israel pitched camp. Sometimes the pillar did not move for weeks; sometimes it stopped only overnight. Living with Yahweh as guide required Israel to develop an attitude that regarded the journey itself as their home.

Faithlessness

Numbers 13:1–14:24

Regardless of Yahweh's presence in their midst, Israel grows restive and rebellious. Jealousy and fainthearted-ness festered until they broke open in rebellion. Moses' own brother and sister, Aaron and Miriam, became jealous of their brother's privileged position as both Israel's leader and Yahweh's spokesperson. The people were more willing to follow the cowardly advice of the majority of scouts who reconnoitered Canaan than they were prepared to trust Yahweh, as Caleb and Joshua encouraged. Together the sins of jealousy and faithlessness paint a sad picture of Israel as a people who had not grown according to Yahweh's intention.

What lines connect jealousy and faithlessness? These sins resemble one another in that they both manifest a kind of moral weakness. Jealousy rarely expresses itself in the full light of day. Rather it makes its home in the heart where it hides in a remote corner until asking, "Why do you think you're so good?" Miriam and Aaron were jealous of Moses and complained, disclosing their very small spirits. Believing themselves their brother's equals, they coveted his status and authority. Yahweh answered their complaints by drawing a distinction that elevated Moses above all other Israelite prophets. To the latter, Yahweh spoke in dreams and visions, but with Moses Yahweh conversed face-to-face. There is more: "He sees the form of the LORD" (Num 12:8). Yahweh's speech disclosed two facts: Moses' siblings were no match for their brother, and their jealousy had angered Yahweh.

Yahweh's anger also was kindled against Israel for their cowardly faithlessness. These people should have known better; they had witnessed with their very own eyes the Lord's mighty acts in Egypt and at the Red Sea. How could they have forgotten so quickly the Lord's miraculous deliverance? How could they turn their back on Yahweh, preferring instead the weak-kneed report of the majority? For one thing, the scouts had empirical evidence to reinforce their story. They had returned to the camp with a single cluster of grapes so large that two men had to carry it on a pole slung between them. Land that yielded giant grapes also must harbor giant warriors, and in fact, it did. Neither Joshua nor Caleb challenged the facts of the scouts' story; there *were* giants in the land. The dispute lay in what was to be done about them. Joshua and Caleb trusted Yahweh; the other spies and Israel did not. They were at that point where a faithless people and faithlessness breeds cowardice.

Taken together, the story of Miriam and Aaron and the story of the scouting expedition into Canaan leave us with the sinking feeling that something had gone very wrong with the project that began in the exodus. The people and some of their leaders were unraveling. Bickering and cowardice leave a bad taste in our mouths. So it was also with Yahweh, who was ready to cashier them all and make a fresh start with Moses. But Moses loved this people and begged Yahweh for their lives. At points the Old Testament pictures God in a curious, almost malleable light, and this is one of those moments. Moses got Yahweh to relent from his anger by pointing out that, were he to slaughter the Israelites, the Egyptians would hear of it and claim that Yahweh lacked the ability and the power to finish what he had begun in the exodus. This argument convinced Yahweh to take another course, and its consequences for Israel were nearly as disastrous as if the whole nation had been destroyed. Because of their rebellion, Yahweh required an entire Israelite generation to wander through the desert for its entire lifetime. Only faithful Caleb and Joshua were spared the consequences of Yahweh's anger. No one else of this generation lived to enter Canaan.

Deuteronomy

The Second Law
Deuteronomy 1:41–2:8

Second Kings 22 and 23 recount the reform of Israelite religious life led by King Josiah. A key element of this reform was the discovery of "the book of the law" in the temple treasury. Most scholars agree that this book was Deuteronomy. The discovery in 621 BC and the manner in which it was used to govern religious life in Judah are crucial steps in the process of canonization (the process by which books were officially established as holy books that belong in the Bible). It is clear that Josiah and the religious establishment of Jerusalem regarded "the book of the law" as authoritative. This was the first step in determining the writings that would have such status in Israelite life. First Deuteronomy and then the other four books of the Pentateuch became "Torah," the law in which the psalmist took delight. In this manner, probably no later than about 400 BC, Torah became the first of the three sections of the Hebrew Bible to be canonized.

Calling Deuteronomy "the book of the law" is something of a misnomer. It is not a law code but, more accurately, a series of three discourses. So Deuteronomy is better described as three sermons or one three-point sermon (4:44–11:25; 12–26; 28). Moses is the preacher, or prophet. These prophetic discourses take obedience as their theme.

In Deuteronomy obedience brings God's blessing; disobedience leads to judgment and defeat. This sentence sums up the theological idea known as the Deuteronomistic doctrine of reward. This doctrine works off a simple logic: If you do *x*, then *y* will follow; if you do not do *x*, then not *y* but *z* will come your way. The little word *if* thus carries enormous power. The doctrine stands at the very heart of Israel's belief that historical events do not simply happen, nor are they random. Events carry a heavy freight of theological and ethical significance. The freight is the revelation and expectations of Yahweh and what Yahweh expects of his people.

As Israel came to know God's character, they were expected to live consistent with that character. In a nutshell, Yahweh's people, Israel, were expected to walk in the way of the Lord. If they walked obediently in that way, then Yahweh would be with them and bless them. If they did not heed Yahweh's word, then trouble would dog Israel's steps all the way to Canaan.

Frequently, Deuteronomy traces episodes during Israel's journey through the wilderness in light of this doctrine. It is an all too familiar story: Israel rebels or disobeys and affliction follows; Israel obeys and Yahweh was with them, blessing their life. The cycle repeated again and again throughout Torah. Why didn't these people get the message and straighten up?

Perhaps we should ask whether we Christians of today are any more or less faithful than the Israelites of this narrative. We have a tendency to be critical of these people, as if, were we in their shoes, the wilderness crossing would have gone quickly and smoothly; as Lancelot says in the Lerner and Lowe musical *Camelot*, "Had I been made the partner of Eve, we'd be in Eden still." But isn't there something of this tendency to rebellion in all of us, even when we know that if we do not do *x* then z will follow?

The Deuteronomistic theology did not have a monopoly on ancient Israelite thought. There were those who interpreted the covenant with the Lord in absolute terms. Their view of Yahweh's faithfulness and promises led them to believe that Yahweh's covenant was everlasting. It could never end because Yahweh had spoken it. Over against this view of the covenant stood the Deuteronomistic doctrine of reward with its emphasis on the word *if.* That little word made Yahweh's covenant with Israel conditional. Israel had to meet the terms of the covenant if it was to remain in force. According to Deuteronomistic theology, the divine blessings of the covenant were conditional upon Israel's obedience to the word of the Lord. Moses' three sermons in Deuteronomy repeatedly refer to the events of the Exodus in terms of the Deuteronomistic theology. The consequences of those events underscore the importance of faithfulness to the Lord with whom Israel is bound in covenant.

What God Expects

Deuteronomy 5:1–21

It is not intended as a slight against attorneys to remind ourselves that storytellers and not lawyers wrote the Old Testament. We cannot be reminded too often that Torah is fundamentally a narrative. The Ten Commandments do not appear independently of that narrative, as if emblazoned on a plaque and hung on a wall. Rather, the commandments have a rich narrative context that will help us to see and understand what is going on. This narrative of God, Israel, and, in the New Testament, Jesus and the church is the most fundamental way to talk about God. Thus, we do not begin with the commandments and then move to the story as if the law is the only important part. Rather, we begin with the story in order to move to the Decalogue. It is the narrative that makes the law intelligible.

Deuteronomy means literally "the second law." We can take it in the sense of "the law repeated" or "the law stated again." Deuteronomy 5:1–21 illustrates this way of speaking. In Deuteronomy, the commandments are not given as if for the first time; rather, they are recited. Like their earlier occurrence in Exodus, the situation surrounding this recitation is pregnant with meaning. By the time we get to Deuteronomy, many years had transpired. Except for only a very few faithful old warriors, an entire generation had passed away. Now, the new generation was poised on the edge of Canaan, ready to enter into the land and take possession of it. Moses, the elder statesman of the old guard, rightfully worried about the possibilities of life under this new generation. How would they respond to the freedom that accompanied ownership of the land? Would they live by remembering the mighty deeds of Yahweh, or would they be tempted to some new and unforeseen way of living? In a word, would they remain faithful?

Repeated throughout Deuteronomy are two words—*hear* and *remember.* Time and again the phrase "Hear, O Israel" introduces important instruction. The phrase is very much on the order of saying, "Listen! Pay attention!" Once Moses had the people's attention, it became crucial that they remember. Israel would not live long in the new land if they forgot all that Yahweh had done for them, chastisement and rebuke as well as blessing. All of it had been instruction aimed at developing the virtue of faithfulness in Israel. Now, on the desert side of the Jordan, Moses offered one final restatement of the central teaching to walk in the way of the Lord, acknowledging Yahweh and all of Yahweh's ways.

A Politics of Memory
Deuteronomy 6:1–25

If one of the themes of Deuteronomy is "Listen," another surely is "Remember!" The book cares deeply for the present and future generations of Israelite children and their memory of Israel's past. Deuteronomy is also concerned to connect those memories to Israel's present religious life. The book dares to ask the question: What would life in Israel be like if nobody remembered Torah and its story of our forefathers and foremothers? Deuteronomy believes that life without Torah's moral and spiritual anchors would be terrible. To avoid this calamity, Deuteronomy sets out on a grand effort to reclaim Israel's future by educating its children in the great heritage of Torah. After the commandments have been read out, the reader is told that this declaration has been made for the sake of the coming generations. Israel's future is at stake; Deuteronomy wants to secure it by calling Israel to remember. If the children are not educated in their spiritual heritage, Israel's future will crumble into the dust. Deuteronomy aims to put in place a program of religious and moral education, at the center of which is the necessity of remembrance.

At the outset of this educational program, Israel is taught to recite one of the centerpiece passages of the Old Testament, the *shema* (she-mah). The term comes from the first Hebrew word of Deuteronomy 6:4, "*Hear*, O Israel." The verb is a command to listen. Once Deuteronomy has Israel's attention, it proclaims the commandment that Jesus quoted when asked which was the greatest commandment of the Torah. Then Deuteronomy urges parents to impress on their children the *shema* and the commandments. This is more than encouragement or friendly guidance. Israelite parents are under obligation to educate their children in these commandments nonstop: " when you sit at home and when you walk along the road," in other words, all day long (6:7).

Why is this relentless education so urgent? Deuteronomy looks to the possibility of a day when Israelite children will no longer understand the meaning of their religious practice. Then children will ask their parents, "What is the meaning of the stipulations, decrees, and laws the Lord our God commanded you?" (6:20). It would be the same as if our children asked us, "Why did the pastor dunk those people under water today at church? Why do people go to the front of the church and kneel to pray? Why were we served little cups of juice and tiny bits of bread?"

Deuteronomy instructs the parent to respond to the children's questions with a most interesting answer. The parent is not told to say, "Because the Bible says so," or "Because we've always done it that way." Parents are instructed, instead, to answer the questions by telling a highly condensed form of the great narrative of the exodus. This story is told in three economical verses. But why this narrative? Because it is the most important story in Israel's history. Before the exodus, they were nothing, a slave people without hope, a rabble. In the exodus,

Yahweh transforms Israel into a nation. They become a people, but not just any people; Israel becomes the people of God. With Yahweh, they have a future, and the name of that future is Canaan, the "land flowing with milk and honey." The parent tells the children this story because it gives meaning to Israelite religion and life. Had there been no exodus, the commandments would lose some of their meaning and relevance. Deuteronomy's hypothetical future child wants meaning-filled answers. One can answer such questions only by reciting the story of which he or she is part.

Deuteronomy 6:12 states this command in a negative form: "Be careful that you *do not forget* the LORD, who brought you out of Egypt" (emphasis added). Not forgetting or remembering was critical to Israel's "way of being together." In other words, its politics consisted fundamentally in acts of remembering. Not remembering the narrative of God's mighty works of redemption and formation put them perilously close to passing out of memory. Whenever Israel forgot them, she lost her way morally and politically; a disappearing people would result. The life and vitality of the people of God depended on their determination to remember.

Israel remembered through several different actions. First, in worship Israel sang songs that remembered the mighty acts of God. Examples of these memory songs are Psalms 105, 106, 135, and 136. The psalms were the hymnal of Israel, and these specific psalms could not but stimulate Israel's memory of all that Yahweh had done to redeem it. Second, Israel remembered through the great narratives of its past, told, retold, and later written as Scripture itself. The narratives of Yahweh and Israel form the largest portion of the first five books of the Old Testament, Torah, which we commonly call the "books of the law." Storytellers taught Israel the way of the Lord, with whom Israel was to walk, through stories of remembrance. Third, and of perhaps the greatest significance to Israel's memory, were the great religious celebrations of remembrance—the Feast of Tabernacles/Booths and, of course, the Passover Feast. Thus, Israelites celebrated and recalled the miraculous events that constituted them as a people. Each of these ways of remembering formed Israelites as the people of Yahweh. Formed as such, they could grasp who God was calling them to be and the mission to which that identity called them.

Yahweh also defined Israel's life through the commandments. The first and greatest commandment is recorded in Deuteronomy 6:4–5, the *Shema*. This brings us to the second powerful word of our study passage explicitly addressed to Israel: "Hear!" The force of this word can be illustrated by the familiar situation in which parents want their children's undivided attention. They say, "Listen!" or "Listen to me!" The statement following such an imperative cannot be taken casually. Since the command is to love God with all one's being, perhaps our obedience to that command ought to begin by paying attention with all of our being.

We ought not to skip over the fact that it is with our ears that the Old Testament expects us to attend with all of our being. No one may see God and live, so the eye cannot be the organ through which come attention and knowledge. Yahweh's primary, but certainly not his only, means of communication with Israel was the *word*. Prophets spoke the *word* of the Lord that came to them. The *word* is living and powerful, and it is the vessel by which Yahweh communicates with his people. Since that is so, it is imperative that the people of Yahweh listen.

Intrusive?

Deuteronomy 8:7–20

There once was a new pastor who, of course, wanted to get acquainted with all the members of the parish. One parishioner was a woman whose husband, a farmer, rarely attended worship. The pastor decided to pay a call on the farmer in the hope of getting on friendly terms that would help him become more regular in his attendance. The pastor drove out to the farm, which he observed to be wonderfully managed. When they met in the yard, the pastor opened the conversation by saying, "Farmer Brown, my, but you and the Lord have done a wonderful job with this farm. The orchard is neatly pruned. The fields are clean, and the livestock fat and well cared for." Farmer Brown replied, "Yes, but you should have seen it when the Lord had it himself."

Deuteronomy envisions a day when the Israelites will have come to an attitude not unlike Farmer Brown's. This text looks to a time when Israelites live in fine homes and enjoy all of the benefits of prosperity. On that day, the text asks, what or who will occupy the center of Israel's heart? And what circumstances will have developed that someone or something has taken Yahweh's place? It seems clear enough that this warns Israel against forgetfulness: "Be careful that you do not forget the Lord your God" (8:11). How was Israel to escape this forgetfulness and its terrible consequences?

Obviously to remember was the key to Israel's religious and political security. To remember meant to observe all of the Lord's commands, laws, and decrees. All of this divine legislation aimed at enabling Israel to live and walk with Yahweh. The goal of this walk was that Israel would be a holy people, pure and separated to the service of God and ready for the Lord's service. As such, walking in the way of the Lord encompassed the totality of Israel's life. As we have already said, Torah was much more than the Commandments, although they were at its heart. Torah covered virtually every facet of an Israelite's life from birth to death, governing details of that life ranging from diet to sex. Perhaps Judaism was made interesting because its law code told people what to do with their dishes and their genitals.

Much of this Torah legislation appears intrusive to modern people. This is due in part to the modern division of life into public and private spheres. Many of the aspects of life that Torah regulated, modern people regard as private. Thus matters pertaining to diet or the body are often regarded as "nobody's business but my own." Protestantism also has often regarded the law as somewhat intrusive and, even more so, opposed to God's grace. Thus we have frequently been taught to separate the law into two categories—moral and ceremonial. We then learn to consider the latter as a heavy and complicated burden of obligations. It is important to note, however, that the psalmist sang of the righteous person's delight in the law of the Lord (Ps 1). The law was Yahweh's gift to Israel and as such a sign of Yahweh's graciousness.

As we read the Old Testament passages that speak about all of this law, it appears complex to us because we do not live under it. Were we Israelites, however, that likely would not be the case. A simple analogy makes the point. Consider for a moment all the laws that you obey every day without ever consciously thinking of them. They don't come to mind because they are so much a part of your daily life. That you obey them imposes no great burden on you. It seems probable that much of Torah functioned in the same way for Israel. In countless regulations, small and large, Israel's observance of Torah kept alive the people's memory for Yahweh. Those acts of remembering were critical to Israel's moral life as the people of Yahweh. To fail to observe the commandments was to forget. To forget was to sever the link that bound Israel to the Lord.

Obedient Leadership

Deuteronomy 31:1–8; 34:5–9

The Israelites who neared the Promised Land of Canaan were the children and grandchildren of those delivered from Pharaoh in the exodus. That generation eventually died during forty years of wilderness wanderings, the judgment of Yahweh for their disobedient refusal to follow the advice of Caleb and Joshua. A new nation, purged and once again holy to the Lord, now marched toward the river Jordan.

Moses suffered the same fate as the other members of his generation. To be sure, he had not disputed the word from Caleb and Joshua. Great and obedient to God though he was, Moses was not permitted to enter Canaan. Numbers 20:1–13 tells the story of Moses' disobedience at Kadesh in the wilderness of Zin, where everyone suffered a parching thirst. In response to Moses' plea for Israel, Yahweh directed him to speak to a rock that water might flow forth. Moses struck the rock with his staff, as he had done on a previous occasion; water flowed anyway, but Yahweh was angry for Moses' disobedience and told him that he too would not enter Canaan.

It is interesting that Deuteronomy mentions none of this in explanation of why Moses was not allowed to cross the Jordan. Perhaps the story was so well-known that it did not bear repeating; twice, however, Deuteronomy offers another explanation for the fact that Moses could not enter Canaan. In 1:37 and again in 3:26 the text reads, "Because of you the Lord became ["was" in the latter] angry with me." We are left with the impression that Moses may have loved Israel too much, that he stood too strongly and too often to its defense. The context of these two passages strongly suggests that Yahweh became angry with Moses because of his unswerving loyalty to Israel, even on those occasions when Israel had proven disobedient and utterly faithless.

The man appointed by God to succeed Moses was Joshua, whose name means "Yahweh is salvation." This Hebrew name is transliterated by New Testament Greek as *IESUS*, which becomes in English, of course, Jesus; both names derive from the same Hebrew root. What kind of feelings would come over a person named to succeed such a man as Moses? Joshua is not to be blamed for worrying that he might not be up to the job. Even Moses had once similarly worried. As with Moses, so also Yahweh promised his presence. The Lord would go before and never forsake Israel. Additionally, Moses laid his hands on Joshua as a sign that he was to be filled with wisdom (34:9). Thus, Joshua could proceed in the confidence that Yahweh and the spirit of Moses' wisdom would guide him.

Joshua

God's Holy Presence
Joshua 3:7–17

Archaeological evidence points to a great political and military disturbance in Palestine during the years roughly from 1250 to 1200 BC. The evidence shows that the invaders broke the resistance of the inhabitants, although somewhat incompletely, and transferred their tribal center into Palestine. This evidence, most biblical historians agree, is connected to the conquest of the Promised Land by the Israelites.

But before Israel could mount a war of conquest, the people had to enter the land itself, accomplished at the river Jordan near a place called Shittim, locating Israel not far from fortified Jericho. The heart of the procession crossing the Jordan was the ark of the covenant. The ark was the holiest object in all Israel. In this gold-covered wooden chest the Israelites carried the stone tablets of the Ten Commandments. Moreover, the ark's lid, decorated with two cherubim, was called the mercy seat. Israel understood the ark to indicate the presence of Yahweh among the people and serve as his portable throne.

In ancient Israel, the idea of *holy* carried with it the concept of dread or "awe-fullness." One should not presume to draw too close to the holy God of Israel. Thus, for example, Israelites were expressly forbidden to walk upon Mount Sinai, the holy mountain of Yahweh. To do so without divine permission meant instant death. Moses, who stood in the presence of Yahweh, had to cover his face, so brightly did it shine with the reflected glory of the Lord. As the seat of God's presence, the ark also was a holy object, not to be handled with profane hands. Only the priestly tribe, the Levites, were authorized to carry the ark, a task that even they performed by hoisting the ark on long poles slid through golden rings fastened to its sides. To touch the ark, even in goodwill, was to die; it was holy.

On the day that Israel crossed the Jordan, the people were advised to keep their distance from the ark—about a thousand yards. They were to follow its lead from a respectful distance. When the Levites stepped into the river, the water stopped flowing. This was a sign of Yahweh's presence with the people. But Yahweh did not stop the Jordan for the sake of convenience. Rather, the sight of their holy ark on the shoulders of Levites standing on a dry river bed confirmed in Israel's mind that Yahweh was indeed with Joshua, even as he had been with Moses. A leadership transition had taken place, true, but the real leader of Israel remained on the throne and had pledged his eternal presence with Israel.

Remembering God's Mighty Acts
Joshua 3:7–4:24

Joshua is the first of several Old Testament books written from the perspective of the Deuteronomistic law. These books include Joshua, Judges, 1 and 2 Samuel, and 1 and 2 Kings. They demonstrate that the principles driven by the book of Deuteronomy have been proven true by events in Israel's political and religious history. This means that the great principle driving Israel's history is that God honors faithfulness to the covenant and punishes disobedience. Peace and prosperity are signs of Yahweh's favor and Israel's faithfulness. Social and political difficulties and disasters are the consequence of Israel's disobedience to the covenant. Through the books of the Deuteronomistic history, we thus read Israel's successes and failures as the history of its faithfulness and disobedience to God.

As we pick up the Deuteronomistic narrative in Joshua, Israel is about to cross the Jordan River. This historic event brings to conclusion the mightiest of Yahweh's actions in Israel's behalf—the exodus. When the last Israelite stepped onto Canaanite soil, the exodus was finished and a new mighty work was set to begin. If future Israelites were to live in trusting faithfulness to Yahweh, these mighty acts must be remembered. So Joshua ordered the people to construct a monument to the miraculous crossing of the Jordan, summarizing all the prior history. Twelve stones, one for each tribe, were plucked from the riverbed to create this monument to God's powerful action in and on behalf of Israel. The pile of stones stood against the day when future generations, perhaps ignorant of their heritage, would ask, "What do these stones mean?" That question provided a ready-made opportunity for the older generation to conduct a history lesson.

For Israel, history was far more than just one thing after another. The people of God lived as a people by remembering Yahweh's mighty deeds. Far more than manifestations of divine power, these deeds marked out Israel's life as Yahweh's people. To forget or otherwise neglect Yahweh's deeds was a recipe for moral and theological disaster. "More than a mere exercise in nostalgia, the act of remembering served the important functions of helping Israel to understand again who they were as a people and the kind of people Yahweh was calling them to be."[7] In Israel's history, the act of remembering was a moral and political act because it formed the people into a body of a particular character—the people of Yahweh. If Israel succeeded in living by its memory, the monument on the banks of the river Jordan could never be a mere pile of rocks. They were "a memorial to the people of Israel forever" (4:7), a reminder of Yahweh's mighty works.

Holy War

Joshua 6:1–5, 15–20

At the heart of today's study passage lies the concept of "holy war" or *herem* in Hebrew. The idea seems foreign to modern people, known to us today only in news media references to warlords and terrorists such as Osama bin Laden and terms like *jihad*. We may be somewhat perplexed to find that idea in the Bible. Nevertheless, the Old Testament certainly does use of the concept of holy war, and the conquest of Jericho is one of the most explicit examples of this practice anywhere in Scripture.

In Israel's practice of holy war, Yahweh was understood to be a warrior God. After the defeat of the Egyptians at the Red Sea, Miriam had sung, "The LORD is a warrior; the LORD is his name" (Ex 15:3). Not only was Yahweh a warrior, but he

8. Strege, *Tell Me the Tale*, 137. See also Strege and Willowby, *God's Redeeming Story*, chapters 2 and 3.

also possessed power to achieve victory. When the two ideas were combined, the people of Israel had the necessary ingredients to begin their ideology of holy war. It's important to understand that all of Israel's wars could not be brought under the designation *herem*. On certain occasions, Israelites went into battle in service to their king, in rebellion, or for other reasons. A conflict could be designated a holy war only if certain specific conditions have been met in (1) preparation, (2) personnel, (3) conduct, and (4) outcome.

1. *Preparation*. Almost by definition, a holy war had to be sanctioned by and include the active participation of Yahweh. The Lord directed and led the attack on Jericho. The elaborate instructions and repeated marches around Jericho were part of Israel's divinely directed preparation for battle.

2. *Personnel*. Israel's real battle leader was Yahweh. Joshua may have been Israel's military commander, but he took his marching orders from Yahweh. Yet even then, it was Yahweh's presence with Joshua that qualified him for his role as a leader.

3. *Conduct*. In a sense, the size of the Israelite army was not a matter of any real consequence. A major reason for the forty years of Israelite wilderness wandering had been their lack of confidence in Yahweh. When the people heard reports of giants and large armies, their courage left them. They still had to learn that Yahweh as leader determined the conduct of the battle. Another aspect of this conduct was the use of the ram's horn as a symbol of Yahweh's voice. As long as the people of Israel followed the Lord's instructions for the conduct of the war, they could be confident of victory, regardless of the size of their army.

4. *Outcome*. In some cases, the Lord gave Israel permission to sack the conquered city of its wealth (see Deut 20:10–20). In other cases, however, such as Jericho, everything within the city—all of its wealth, livestock, and people—were considered "devoted" to the Lord. This meant the destruction of all living beings and the confiscation of all movable wealth for the tabernacle treasury. The only exception was Rahab and her family in return for her assistance to the Israelite spies during their mission in the city. All else was devoted either to destruction or confiscation. To disobey this ban was to invite the most severe reprisals, as Achan and his family learned (see Josh 7).

Israel was confident that the God whose hand guided the course of history also acted through war to accomplish his purposes. This confidence was part of the Israelites' belief that Yahweh was the deliverer of Israel and the guarantor of victory in the war of conquest for the land of Canaan.

Renewing the Covenant
Joshua 24:1–25

After the destruction of Jericho and Ai, Israel engaged the residents of Canaan in a military contest for possession of the land. It was a war of conquest but not a war of extermination. This study passage describes the events through which some of these people became part of Israel.

Joshua 24 presents us with a scene in which Joshua was about to take leave of Israel. His service was nearly completed, and soon he would die. But leaders of Joshua's stature do not simply fade away. Just prior to the covenant renewal ceremony at Shechem, he had delivered his farewell address. Afterward he assembled all of Israel at Shechem for one final renewal of their covenant.

From the story itself, we can infer that conquered Canaanite peoples were present among the Israelite tribes who gathered at Shechem. We may conclude this from Joshua's references to the gods that he commanded the people to put away. Among the Israelites whose families once lived in Egypt, there were those who had kept Egyptian idols. It is altogether likely that Egyptian religion would have crept into Israel during the long centuries of slavery. The golden calf fashioned by Aaron probably was a representation of the Egyptian bull-god Apis, whose image the Israelite slaves would have seen frequently. One is hard-pressed to explain why Israelite slaves would keep and worship the idols of their former overlords, other than to lay such a practice at the feet of the stubborn and perverse human heart. That some Israelites possessed such idols seems clear enough from Joshua's command that they were to throw them away (24:14).

Joshua referred to three separate classes of idols. To be discarded were the "gods your forefathers worshiped beyond the River and in Egypt." The phrase the gods "beyond the River" refers to the Euphrates River, which, along with the Tigris, forms the Fertile Crescent. Centuries earlier, Abraham had left Paddan-Aram, near the northern corner of this region, to go to a land that Yahweh would show him, forsaking the gods of that region in the process. Those were the gods from "beyond the River" whose worship had extended into Canaan. Third were the gods of the Amorites, residents of the region who either were killed or assimilated into Israel.

Regardless of the origins of this idol worship, Joshua seems to have given all who would belong to Israel the same choice—those who would belong to the Israel of Yahweh must lay aside all rivals. In this we see the viewpoint that says that the status of an Israelite was religious as well as ethnic. In Joshua's mind, the cornerstone of Israelite identity was not a matter of race or ethnicity but the first three commandments of the Decalogue. Those who were willing to live in obedience to these and the other commandments were worthy to be called children of the house of Israel. This emphasis on obedience as a condition of belonging to the people of God is characteristic of the Deuteronomistic historians. It also seems to echo in Jesus' observation, however, that his brothers and sisters are to be found among those who do the will of his Father in heaven (Matt 12:50).

Judges

Cry and Answer
Judges 2

Two very important themes appear in the book of Judges. First we have the familiar theme of the Deuteronomistic history: Israel's disobedience brings Yahweh's displeasure and, therefore, trouble for the people; Israel's obedience brings blessing. Second, prominent in this book is the "cry-answer" theme. These two themes are interrelated. Israel disobeys, suffers divine judgment, and in their suffering the people cry out to God. Yahweh hears their cry and answers in the form of a "judge." The judge is Yahweh's agent through which Israel is redeemed and restored.

This cycle begins at Judges 2:2. Yahweh accused Israel, "Yet you have disobeyed me." Disobedience had its consequences. "Now therefore I tell you that I will not drive them out before you; they will be thorns in your sides" (2:3). Had Israel obeyed God, the conquest of Canaan would have gone differently. As it was, the people's disobedience cost them Yahweh's cooperation; the Canaanites would not simply melt away. They would be thorns in Israel's side.

The bad situation of 2:2–3 worsens in Judges 2:11–12. A lengthy period of time had passed, and the generation that earlier had suffered Yahweh's judgment was "gathered to their fathers." A new generation, more evil than their parents, replaced them. Three sins made the children worse than their parents: (1) They did not know Yahweh. (2) They did not remember the mighty acts of God. (3) They served the Baals (2:10–11). As Yahweh had promised, the gods of the Canaanites had ensnared Israel. Idol worship was so persistent in Israel that some explanation seems appropriate.

The Baals and the Ashtoreths were nature gods and goddesses. As such, they were believed to control the forces of nature that were important to people who derived their living from the land. Rain, sunshine, and the *fertility* of soil and livestock were matters of crucial importance to agricultural peoples whose lives depended on the land's productivity. Worship of the fertility gods and goddesses was believed to offer farmers and shepherds the chance to appease these forces and make them yield abundant crops and healthy and productive flocks and herds. Agricultural productivity mattered to Israelites as much as to any other people who earned a living from the soil. In the midst of Canaanite idol worshipers, the Israelites early and often were tempted to worship the gods and goddesses of their neighbors.

Idol worship, of course, disobeys the very first commandment. The people "provoked the LORD to anger" (2:12). God's anger meant bad consequences for Israel. The people suffered at the hands of their enemies. "The hand of the LORD was against them.... They were in great distress" (2:15). Enter the judges. The judge (*shophet*, in Hebrew) was more than the legal officer that the term brings to our minds. Judges also served as military leaders in the ongoing struggle against the still present Canaanite peoples. The judges delivered Israel from their calamities, but only if and when Israel heeded them. When the people followed the judges, life was good. When the people failed to listen, misery and turmoil followed; then the people cried out to Yahweh, who heard and answered.

What we have here is more than a general historical narrative. It is also a prescription for the proper life of the people of God. They are to live by God's mercy and grace. The commandments were mercifully and graciously given that Israel might live. They failed, and God chastised them so that they might cry and return to obedience and once again "keep the way of the LORD and walk in it as their forefathers did" (2:22). The Deuteronomistic historians and the cry-answer theme together constituted a model for Israelite life with Yahweh. If followed, the model promised life. If unheeded, it promised trouble.

History with a Purpose

Judges 4:2–9, 14–15, 22

The book of Judges narrates the period of Israel's history between the entry into Canaan and the beginning of the monarchy. But the stories of the judges are never simply historical narratives. They rest in a larger theological understanding of God and God's ways with Israel. As we read this material, we will need to keep some fundamental points in mind.

It is always important to keep in mind that Old Testament history is underwritten by a theological understanding. Historical events carry significant meaning for Israel's life because Israel believed that the Lord's hand governed the unfolding of history. God actively participated in the historical process, raising some people up and bringing others down. In Israel's view, the most dramatic example of this divine intervention and the making of history was the exodus.

Second, Israel believed that since God acted in time, what we term history is meaningful. History, in other words, was moving in a particular direction; it has a beginning and will someday end. We call this a linear view of history, and it distinguished Israel from the other peoples and religions of the ancient Middle East. These other religions thought of time as cyclical, simply following the round of the seasons of the year. Many of the gods were nature deities who were believed to control the seasons and the weather conditions that were of vital interest to agricultural peoples. Consequently, these people located their lives in the natural cycle that repeated itself annually. In such a view, the events of time have little ultimate or lasting importance because the major concerns of life will be the same year after year. The pull between these two very different conceptions of time and God's interaction with Israel created one of the major tension points in Israel's life during the period of the judges.

Little is known of Deborah other than she was the wife of Lappidoth. Rather than a judge, the text refers to her as a *prophetess*, a term that is slightly out of historical context in that prophets and prophetesses typically do not appear in Israelite history until after Samuel. Perhaps Deborah is called a prophetess because Israelite women did not lead men into battle, and that function was one of the roles of a *shophet*. Other than this however, the text clearly indicates that Deborah ruled Israel as a judge.

The story of Deborah raises some interesting questions about the role of women in ancient Israel. In the Semitic world of which Israel was a part, women did not hold any kind of leadership positions, yet in that man's world we find not one but two women playing key roles in this narrative. Clearly Barak, the Israelite general, respected Deborah and took his marching orders from her. The other woman in this story was Jael, who killed the Hazorite general Sisera (in a particularly grisly manner, it must be added). What does the text say to us about the gender of those whom God calls to service? At the very least, this text in Judges is not at all shy about reporting the leadership role of a woman. After all, it is Yahweh who calls servants to lead his people. The appropriate response is to follow those servants, whose credential is not gender but that their appointment is by God.

Mixed People, Mixed Religion
Judges 6–8

Three features of Israelite history form the backdrop for the story of Gideon. First an account must be made for the presence of such peoples as the Amalekites and Midianites in the land of Israel after the conquest under Joshua. Second, that these peoples lived in Israel leads to the long-term problem of religious syncretism (the combination of different religious system, beliefs, and practices) among the Israelites. Israel's religious syncretism of course broke faith with God and their promise to worship the Lord God alone. They always suffered as a consequence of having done such evil. In their suffering, Israel cried out to God, who heard their plea for help and answered through the call and sending of a new judge. This now familiar cry-answer structure is the third feature underlying the narrative of this text.

In the face of the story of Joshua and the conquest of Canaan, how are we to account for the presence of the Amalekites and Midianites, who posed such problems for Israel's peace and security in the Gideon narrative? If the Israelites had completely conquered the land when they entered, what were these people doing there? Many Bible scholars now think that Israel's conquest of Canaan was partial and unsystematic. They took what land they could and bypassed areas where the geographical terrain or armaments of their enemies proved too difficult to overcome. Thus, we have a picture of the conquest where the Israelites did establish the territory of their possessions as described in the book of Joshua. Within that territory there remained pockets of unconquered people whose resistance to the Israelite presence sometimes grew strong enough to threaten Israel's peace. During the era of the judges, the land was not defended by a standing army and was rather easily invaded, as in the case of the Midianites.

It must be said, however, that Old Testament situations and events rarely occurred independently of the presence and activity of God. There is a theological reason for Israel's fear and misery at the hands of Midian. The text identifies that reason in these simple terms: "Again the Israelites did evil in the eyes of the Lord" (6:1). God allowed the Midianites to oppress Israel in return for Israel's sin. What was so terrible a sin that it led to oppression that forced people to hide in caves like animals? The Israelites had broken the first and second of the Ten Commandments. It wasn't that they turned away from the Lord, but that they mixed the religions of the unconquered Canaanite peoples with the worship of the Lord. *Syncretism* is the term for this kind of mixing of religious traditions. In the Gideon narrative, God ordered Gideon to demolish an altar to Baal and to cut down an Asherah pole. Apparently the Israelites had added these cultic objects of Canaanite fertility religion to the religious practices associated with the worship of Yahweh. But Yahweh is a jealous God, and therefore syncretism is no better than apostasy. For this act of disloyalty, the Israelites suffered invasion and oppression.

Israel's suffering and pain repeatedly prompted the people to cry out to God for forgiveness and relief. Modern readers may wonder at Israel's amazing fickleness, forgetting immediately God's acts of mercy and deliverance. But remember that the stories of the judges cover centuries, ample time for succeeding generations to lose sight of the lessons learned by their parents and grandparents. It is even more important to see God's patient lovingkindness at work in the cry-answer structure that defined the covenant relationship between him and Israel. That Israel wandered is cause for repentance. That the Lord heard the cry and stood ready not only to forgive but also to come to Israel's aid is cause for amazement and worship. Such a God must be praised. In this relationship where Israel could cry out to the God whose ear missed no plea, the Israelites lived sometimes faithfully and sometimes not. However fickle Israel may have been on her side of the covenant, Yahweh's faithfulness to Israel abided. Such faithfulness is the love that will not let us go.

Adolescent Leader, Iron Foe
Judges 13–16

Of the men and women who led Israel during the period of the judges, none was less capable of governing himself, let alone the Israelite people, than Samson. The stories concerning him present the picture of an unruly man of immense strength and an appetite for trouble. That such a person could be a judge over Israel illustrates the persistent Old Testament point that success depends on the presence of the Lord. It would be very difficult to say that Samson was a role model, and we are left wondering why God would send his Spirit to rest upon such a wild and unpredictable man. But Samson was neither the first nor last biblical character whose personal life was less than exemplary and yet upon whom the Spirit of the Lord rested. In the Bible, success as a leader depends more on the presence of God's Spirit than upon personal virtue. This makes an important theological point about God's freedom. Nothing constrains God or God's choices. Throughout the Bible, God often surprises us in choosing those whom we would not—disreputable people, weak people, obscure people. In such choices, the point is repeatedly made that success depends not upon human ability but upon the presence of the Lord.

By Samson's day, Israel had acquired a new enemy—the Philistines. These were the people against whom Yahweh contended. These are those whose lives Samson made so miserable that they became obsessed with capturing and controlling him. The Philistines probably arrived in Canaan about the same time as the Israelites and settled on the coastal plain that extends inland from the Mediterranean Sea. That location placed them where they would immediately threaten the tribes of Dan and Judah. It is not insignificant that Samson was a member of the tribe of Dan. The Philistines were a well-organized, disciplined foe. They were a challenge Israel was not equipped to defend against. Furthermore, the Israelites had not yet learned the secret of forging iron, which meant that their softer bronze weapons were no match for Philistine armaments.

In the broad background of Israel's history, the Philistines first become a problem during the time of Samson. The scope of the Philistine problem grew throughout the lifetime of Samuel, culminating in their disastrous capture of the ark of the covenant. King Saul coped bravely but finally unsuccessfully with the Philistines. It was not until the reign of David that this threat to the peace and security of Israel was finally eliminated.

Ruth

A God for All Peoples
Ruth 1

The book of Ruth tells a story that was long recited in Israel's oral tradition before it was written and eventually became part of the canon of the Old Testament. It is a little surprising that this book was included in the Old Testament canon. The Torah, the first five books of the Old Testament, was the first division of the Old Testament to receive canonical status, followed by the division called the Prophets. The third and last division of the Hebrew Bible to be canonized is called Writings. It is here that the book of Ruth was located, in a sub-section called The Five Scrolls along with the Song of Solomon, Lamentations, Esther, and Ecclesiastes. In Hebrew tradition, one important criterion for a book's canonization was authorship. Books about or written by a prophet were highly regarded by a society that respected prophetic speech. The tradition held that Samuel was the author of the book of Ruth, and that belief may have been a determining factor in its acceptance into the canon. Impressively, the central figure in this story is a woman, and an alien woman at that. These important factors also bear on possible reasons behind Ruth's canonization.

The book likely was written after the exile and against a backdrop of rising Jewish nationalism and isolationism. Led by people such as Ezra, the postexilic Jewish community increasingly believed that their survival as a people depended on a policy of separation from all other people and their cultures. This attitude led to the requirement, for example, that Jews must marry only Jews. Ezra went so far as to require men to divorce their non-Jewish wives and marry within the community of Israel. This practice of Jewish separatism could easily become corrupted into an attitude that denied the Lord any interest in peoples and nations other than Israel. Separatism thus degenerated into the beliefs that the Lord cared exclusively for Israel and that God directed the events of history in consideration only of his covenant with Israel.

Some Jews challenged this attitude and the practices of exclusivism. Both Ruth and Jonah may have been written at least in part to protest the idea that God cared only and exclusively for Israel. These books counter Jewish exclusivism with stories that emphasize God's presence with and interest in Gentiles.

The story of Ruth begins outside Israel. During a time of famine around Bethlehem, an Israelite named Elimelech had moved his family to Moab, of all places. The Moabites were particularly detested in Israel because, among other things, they practiced child sacrifice to their god Molech. Israelite tradition reached back to earlier times to identify the Moabites as a despised people. According to that tradition, the annihilation of the population of Sodom and Gomorrah left Lot's daughters without marriage prospects. Instead of allowing God to provide a solution to the problem, the daughters seduced their father into incest. As a result, the elder daughter gave birth to Moab, the father of the nation called by his name. Thus, in the eyes of later Jewish exclusivists, it was bad enough that Elimelech chose to live beyond the borders of Israel. To live among the Moabites was even worse. Worst of all, however, Elimelech and Naomi's sons married Moabite women. Measured against the separatist policies of the postexilic community, Elimelech and his family looked like contaminated apostates.

Alongside the challenge to Jewish exclusivism, a second thread runs through the book of Ruth. That thread is women without husbands and the levirate law. In the world of the Old Testament, a woman was the property of some man. If she was not yet married, her father ruled her life. If married, that role fell to her husband. If widowed, her son or sons assumed responsibility for her. All of the men in Naomi's life were dead. That fact made her life not only sad but also precarious. Her decision to return to Bethlehem would not necessarily have improved her situation, nor would she have hoped that it would. Even though that was her home, in Bethlehem she would still be a childless widow and therefore without any means of protection or support. The lot of her Moabite daughters-in-law would be even worse in Judah, so she advised them to remain in their homeland. When she referred to the fact that she was beyond the possibility of bearing and raising new sons for Orpah and Ruth, Naomi was speaking against the backdrop of the levirate law. This social custom required a dead man's brother to take his widowed sister-in-law as wife and, if she was childless, father sons by her to continue the dead man's posterity. This custom once again illustrates the powerlessness of women in ancient Israel and their utter dependence on men. There is another actor in this story, however, one who cares for women, especially desperate women, and, as we shall see, also for those who were not born into the Israelite community.

David's Family Origins

Ruth 2–4

In these chapters, the two themes previously introduced are developed. The precarious and unprotected lives of the two women, Ruth and Naomi, come to be sheltered under the attention and care of Boaz, and the book's concluding verses sharply contest Jewish exclusivism.

Few other Old Testament books give us such detail concerning the ordinary affairs of Israelite common life. The residents of Bethlehem and the surrounding area were farmers and herdsmen, and the book of Ruth refers to them in their workaday routine. The book also makes passing references that indicate some of the problems and even threats that Ruth faced. The setting of Ruth 2 is the barley harvest, a season when everyone was busy with the crucial work of gathering the crop that would provide sustenance for the coming year. Even those who owned no land and had no crop to harvest were involved. Poor women were permitted to gather the leftover grain among the landowner's servants. This practice of gleaning was a socially and religiously underwritten custom that recognized the landowner's responsibility for the poor of his village.

In Ruth 2:9, we read that Boaz told Ruth he had warned his men not to touch her, a statement that alludes to her dangerous situation. She was a childless widow and not the responsibility of any man. Moreover, she was not an Israelite by birth. These two social facts combined to mean that, in the eyes of young Israelite men, the Law of Moses governing sexual relationships did not apply to her. It is almost paradoxical by today's standards, but in ancient Israel, a man who had a sexual relationship with a woman other than his wife was understood to have violated some other man's rights. If the woman was unmarried, her sexual partner had violated what amounted to the property rights of her father. If the woman was married, then it was her husband's rights that had been violated. Race and ethnicity also entered the picture, as Israelite women were to be respected by Israelite men; foreign women were not as fortunate. For these reasons, even as simple an act as gleaning put Ruth in a dangerous situation.

That Ruth and Naomi's life in Bethlehem was so precarious makes particularly impressive Naomi's stratagem to secure a new husband for her daughter-in-law. Some modern readers of this story may be troubled by its assumption that every woman needs a man, inferring from this that the Bible regards women as inferior to men. But that would be a mistaken inference. It is the case that Naomi had to work within the social conventions of her day, but she was anything but passive. Naomi is an intelligent and clever woman who knew the rules governing male-female relations and who used those rules in the interests of Ruth, whose kindness and devotion to her mother-in-law had impressed everyone in Bethlehem.

Surely such character deserved some reward, and that reward came through the working out of the levirate law. This law recognized the importance of descendants in a society organized according to male lineage. Thus, a deceased man's male relatives owed it to his name and descendants to marry the widow of the deceased and have children with her. It was this custom that Boaz recognized and followed in order to marry Ruth and bring the narrative to a happy ending. But not only did the house of Elimelech and Mahlon come to have a male descendant in little Obed, the baby born to Boaz and Ruth, and not only did Naomi come to enjoy the role of grandmother, but Obed also would live to father Jesse, who became the father of David, the great king.

The book of Ruth thus concludes with an ironic implied statement that rebuked Jewish exclusivists everywhere. The genealogy of David that includes Ruth says to its readers that even the greatest of Israel's kings had a Moabite great-grandmother. Few in Israel disputed that the Lord was with David. If that were so, then what did David's family tree have to say to the idea of ethnic purity that had arisen in postexilic Israel?

First and Second Samuel

Barrenness and Waiting

1 Samuel 1:20, 26–28; 2:1–8

The main portion of this passage is often called "Hannah's song" (2:1–8ff). But before we consider those verses, we must appreciate the reason behind her joyful song. Hannah celebrated what the Lord had done in her life. She had just given birth to a son. This was no ordinary birth, for the text tells us that Hannah had been barren. Not only was she barren, but also "the LORD had closed her womb" (1:5). Who was this woman that the Lord would take such an interest in her and her childbearing? The text does not answer that question; this is not a biography of Hannah. We do not read 1 Samuel to learn her life story or to moralize from it; rather, the information about her barrenness and its cause is the text's way of telling us that God was at work in Israel. Hannah's divinely appointed condition was an uneasy burden. To be a childless wife in Israel was a reproach. An Israelite woman's purpose was to be a wife and mother. Marriage was but the first step; husbands expected children, preferably sons. A barren wife was a failure. Small wonder that Hannah rejoiced when she discovered that she was pregnant and doubled her rejoicing on the day of Samuel's delivery.

In the Bible, the condition of barrenness nearly always suggests diminished hope. Barren land is fruitless; it yields no life. The barren desert lacks only moisture in order to be fruitful. Barrenness also suggests waiting. In her barren condition for many years, Hannah waited. Her hope for a child was a hope for her own fulfillment, and for this Hannah waited until hope began to fade into despair.

In 1 Samuel, Hannah was not the only one who waited. All Israel was waiting, because, like her, the nation was barren. In Hannah's day, late in the period of the judges, life in Israel was not good. The Philistines menaced from without while sloppy and unethical religion threatened within. Israel was waiting for a king, who ultimately turns out to be David. He would not be just any king but the Lord's anointed. David would sit on the throne that the Lord had prepared for him.

So Hannah sang. She sang of her deliverance from barrenness and of her restored hope. The Lord alone was Hannah's deliverer and hope. The Lord is a strange and marvelous God whose deeds are to be celebrated. Unlike the gods of Israel's neighbors, the Lord hears the cries of the poor and needy. Hannah was needy; Israel was needy. In the birth of Samuel, the Lord once again revealed himself as the source of Israel's hope and deliverance—the sovereign Lord who heard the cries of the earth's meek and broken. This was neither the first nor the last instance in which God would so reveal himself. There will come a day when another baby boy would be born in answer to Israel's barren hopelessness, and another woman would sing of the marvels that God had done.

We can make a connection between Israel's anticipation of David in the time of Samuel and Israel's wait for the Messiah in the time of Jesus. In both cases, there was great barrenness; in both cases, people waited for a deliverer. In both cases, barrenness gave way to life through an extraordinary birth; in both cases, the agent at work in the people's lives was the Lord God of Israel. Where the Lord is at work, life is sure to spring forth.

Social and Political Transition
1 Samuel 3; 7:3–14

In at least two ways, Samuel stands as a transitional figure in Israel's history. First, he bridges the era of the judges with the era of the prophets. The judges ruled Israel in simpler times when government was less complex. The office of judge combined many different functions—military commander, legal judge, and a religious leader through and by whom God's will was known and spoken. By Samuel's time, Israelite society had grown complex to the point that the several responsibilities of the judge had been separated. Social change, however, is rarely clean and swift; instead it often occurs in transitions. So it was with Samuel, who is sometimes called *judge* and sometimes *prophet*. That he would be a great prophet in Israel is foreshadowed by the comment made in the text just prior to the beginning of his story: "In those days the word of the LORD was rare; there were not many visions" (3:1). For and into such a time, Samuel was born.

Samuel presents us with a second transition in Israelite life—the shift from the cry-answer structure of the judges to the development of a monarchy. The Philistine threat continued to grow throughout Samuel's lifetime. This text concludes with the Israelite victory over the Philistines at Mizpah under Samuel's leadership. But the peace achieved at Mizpah was not permanent, and the Israelites had to live with the bitter fact that the Philistines had captured the ark of the covenant. To be sure, the Philistines had expelled the ark from their midst after God punished them for this outrage. Nevertheless, the people of the very God whose power it symbolized had treated the ark shabbily. That they had done so is an indication of their desperation. The powerful Philistine threat prompted the elders of Israel to rethink the cry-answer relationship to God. In time, they would ask that God appoint a king to rule over them like the kings of other nations.

Samuel was the man they asked to carry their request to God, a proposal he opposed. Samuel favored the old system of the judges. In this, he represented Israel's old guard, who were suspicious of kings and the things kings do with power. Thus, Samuel is a transitional figure between the earlier system of the judges and the new—in Israel—institution of monarchy.

Samuel lived through times of turbulent social and political change. Internal corruption and powerful external enemies threatened Israel's very existence as a people. Nevertheless, behind scenes of social change and the danger of battle, the inscrutable will and purpose of God were at work. God saw and God would guide. In some cases, God's will was known through the loud thunder and panic he created in the Philistine camp (7:10). In other instances, God made his will known through a quiet call in the night to a small boy dedicated to the Lord's service by a God-fearing mother. The changes confronting Israelite society and the external threat posed by the Philistines cannot be read simply as if that is all there is to the story. That there is a story in the first place is because of the perception that there is a God in Israel even when the Israelites refused to heed him. God would not be ignored or denied. Thus, God calls to Samuel out of the night to speak to Israel in a turbulent moment of crisis.

From Judges to Kings

1 Samuel 7:15–8:22

Samuel stood at a watershed in the history of Israelite politics. By *politics* we mean Israel's way of being together and the way it ordered its social, moral, legal, and economic life before Yahweh.

Samuel was the last of the judges. As such, he represented the old way of doing things. He also was the kingmaker, the one who anointed the chosen of the Lord. Clearly, he stood at a critical transition in Israelite life.

This text begins at a moment of uncertainty among the people of Israel. Samuel, their judge and leader, had grown old. The days of his leadership were dwindling. Foreseeing this, he had appointed his sons to succeed him. Unfortunately, these young men were not cut from the same cloth as their father, and their judgeships were marked by corruption. The elders of Israel worried about these deteriorating conditions, and understandably, it fell to the elders to express concern to Samuel. This was an extraordinary step, for in so doing the elders were saying that the old order was broken and in need of replacement. What was that old order?

During the era of the judges, Israelite government was a theocracy. The actual ruler, the monarch of Israel, was Yahweh. God governed Israel through the commandments, the Torah, and through the judges. In this order, the cry-answer relationship was crucial—Israel's cry and Yahweh's hearing and answering of that cry. In this manner, Yahweh cared for and led Israel internally and against their enemies. The aim of this divine rule was a people of justice and righteousness. That Samuel's sons "perverted justice" (8:3) stung with a particular bitterness, for the corruption of the judgeship attacked the very foundations of the theocracy.

That the elders came to Samuel seeking a change is especially important. As elders, they could be expected to stand for the old order; perhaps they even had a vested interest in that order. Their request for a departure from the theocracy signaled the depth of their discouragement as well as the corruption of Israelite life.

Samuel resisted the elders' request. Since he was so identified with the judgeship, Samuel understandably interpreted this request as a rejection of his leadership. Yahweh clarified this misunderstanding (8:7), but Samuel continued to resist. The idea of monarchy repulsed him, and his reasons are not hard to find. Kings may solidify society, but they exact a heavy price in return for order. Under Yahweh's theocracy, Israel lived at peace within its borders and beyond as long as the people lived in obedience to Torah. Then justice and righteousness provided the basis of a peaceful society. A king might also bring peace and social stability to Israel; however, kings rest their rule on a foundation other than Torah. Samuel described the foundation of monarchical rule in the list that runs from 1 Samuel 8:11 through verse 18. This is a description of an ancient, centralized royal bureaucracy. Such a monarchy would conduct a military draft, conscript laborers, seize Israelite girls for the royal harem, and impose a widespread system of taxation.

When the elders of Israel requested that he ask God to select a man for their king, Samuel had reasons other than personal pride for his reluctance toward anointing an Israelite king, and these reasons were based in the nature of monarchy itself. To the Israelites assembled at the shrine of God at Mizpah, Samuel explained that their request for a king was also a rejection of the Lord God as their ruler. There was more to Samuel's hostility: he feared that Israelite kings in the long run would behave no better than the kings of the surrounding peoples. Samuel foresaw all of this in the future of an Israelite monarchy, and yet the fundamental reason for his hostility lay in the implicit rejection of God.

Implicitly, Samuel seems to be asking, "Which do you want, Yahweh's order under Torah or a king's heavy-handed order?" Samuel ominously warned of a day when Israel would groan under its own king. The national memory could look back to the days of groaning under Pharaoh: far worse to groan under their own king. There was more, for Samuel warned Israel that Yahweh would not hear their groans. To reject Yahweh as ruler meant to reject the whole body of the old order, including the old cry-save structure. In the old days, when Israel cried, Yahweh answered. To ask for a king "like all the other nations" (8:20) was to give up the kind of divine hearing and answering that had marked Israel's walk with God in the past.

Monarchy under Saul

Samuel 9:1–10:27; 15:10–16:13

The first man anointed king over Israel was Saul, the son of Kish, of the tribe of Benjamin. The Benjamites occupied territory in the northern region of Canaan among tribes who referred to themselves as the House of Israel. The southern tribes, centered in the tribe of Judah, called themselves the House of Judah. This north-south division figures in the development of the early monarchy in Israel.

Saul is a tragic figure in the story of Israel's kings. He was courageous, sincere, and—in the beginning—faithful to God. Saul wanted to be a good king and do what was right for Israel. In the end, his sincere intentions proved his undoing.

Saul's reign began under the suspicion and grudging acceptance of Samuel. As we have already seen, the old prophet-judge bridged the old era of the judges and the new institution of monarchy. Samuel clearly preferred that Israel remain under the old arrangement of the judges and the loose confederation of Israelite tribes.

Although Israel had rejected the old system of God's rule, the Lord refused to be rejected. He granted the people's request and chose Saul to be their king. The text makes a point of describing Saul's height, that is, his stature. It isn't only that he was tall but that he possessed a commanding outward appearance. However, appearance isn't everything. God changed Saul's heart so Saul would be qualified for kingship not merely in appearance but also religiously. After this inward change, when "the Spirit of God came upon him in power" (10:10), Saul joined a band of prophets in what may have been an ecstatic religious dance.

In the ancient Middle East, kings had to have religious validation. The formal anointing of Saul acknowledged him as God's choice. That Saul "prophesied" in the Spirit of the Lord further legitimated that selection. All that remained was for Saul to lead the men of Israel into battle. This royal action he also fulfilled, now surrounded by "valiant men," the core of his fighting force, who had been persuaded by God that this impressive man could lead them.

Despite Saul's early promise, Samuel's fears about the institution of monarchy eventually came to fruition. Saul began to act like a king in his own right rather than one who reigned under the authority and with the blessing of God. First, Saul set up a monument to himself at Carmel after defeating the Amalekites (1 Sam 15:12). Second, although his army routed the Amalekites, Saul failed to carry out completely God's instructions concerning them and their property. It had been God's will that the Israelites fight a holy war against the Amalekites. Under the rules of such war, the Amalekites and all their property and goods were "devoted" to the Lord. That meant the Israelites were to take no plunder and kill every living being, whether animal or human. Saul modified those instructions, reserving the best livestock for a sacrifice to God and sparing the life of the Amalekite king, Agag. His desire to save some animals for a sacrifice seems reasonable, but why spare the life of his enemy? Perhaps Saul had begun to make a distinction between the lives of commoners and kings; the latter, even if foreign, deserved better treatment than the general population. Whatever the case, Samuel equated Saul's actions with idolatry—the worst of sins in Israelite religion. For his idolatrous disobedience, it was God's judgment that the kingdom of Israel would be ripped from Saul's hands.

Israelite kings never enjoyed the privilege of unilateral power. They may have worn crowns and sat on thrones, but God remained the real king in Israel. Kings might be able to act on their own for a season, but sooner or later God judged their actions, blessing the obedient and punishing the wicked. The spokespersons through whom God declared his intentions were the prophets. There was always a prophet around to keep the king in check. Saul had his Samuel, David had his Nathan, and Ahab had his Elijah. Prophets could be either kingmakers or king-breakers.

Having broken one king, Samuel made his way to Bethlehem to make a new one. This mission was filled with danger for the old prophet and for the people of Bethlehem as well. Who could know what Saul might do if Samuel's intentions were discovered? The trip, therefore, occurred under a ruse devised by none other than God. Samuel journeyed to Bethlehem apparently to make a sacrifice, although Bethlehem was not as important a shrine as Shiloh. Jerusalem at this time remained a Jebusite city and thus was out of the question as a religious site. Samuel had no religious reason to make a sacrifice at Bethlehem. His real purpose could only have been to anoint the man God had chosen to succeed Saul.

In the famous story of Samuel anointing David, notice the subtle manner in which the text elaborates and intensifies the narrative. The first son, Eliab, had the stature and countenance of a king, but that was insufficient. Is the text reminding us that Saul also had a commanding presence? Seven of Jesse's sons passed before Samuel while David, the eighth, tended sheep. In Hebrew thought, seven represented wholeness and completion; eight symbolized an insignificant addition. To be the eighth of anything did not convey distinction. While Samuel, Jesse, and the town elders waited for David's arrival, they all stood. Was this act of honor an anticipation of what was to come? Finally, even though Eliab's appearance was discounted because "the LORD looks at the heart" (16:7), the first information that the text gives us about David is that he was tanned and handsome. Eventually, this man would dazzle all of Israel.

The Death of Saul and the Rise of David

1 Samuel 31:1–2 Samuel 1:27

Saul's tortured life and reign ended on the battlefield at Mount Gilboa. The parallel account of these events in Chronicles makes the reasons for Saul's demise abundantly clear. First Chronicles 10:13–14 tells us the exact reasons for Saul's death: he was unfaithful to the Lord, he did not keep God's word, and he "even consulted a medium for guidance, and did not inquire of the LORD." That the Spirit of the Lord had departed Saul and left him to find his own resources is no excuse. Saul was still expected to live and act rightly. God's judgment can be harsh, reminding one of a seventeenth-century Puritan minister's reply to the objection that his sermons were too strict: "That, sir, is because I serve a strict God." Also note that the Chronicles account of Saul's bad end states that "the LORD put him to death" (10:14). First Samuel 31 tells the story of Saul's death in more detail, including Saul's final act of disobedience in his own suicide. Gravely wounded, he understandably did not want to be taken captive and tortured to death by the Philistines. Nevertheless, he was the Lord's anointed and therefore not to be harmed. Saul's armor-bearer respected this prohibition and refused Saul's request to kill him. Left utterly alone, Saul fell on his own sword and died.

No man stood to gain more from Saul's death than David. Ever since Samuel had anointed him years earlier at Bethlehem, David and Saul had stood in an ambiguous relationship to one another. Saul's reign began to decline, and David's star began to rise. But both of them were "the LORD's anointed," chosen by God to govern the people Israel. Israel's experience with monarchy was still quite new. The people hardly understood how to behave under the reign of one king, let alone two men with legitimate claims to the throne. To make matters worse, Saul gave no indication whatever that he was willing to abdicate in favor of David. Even after his personal disaster before Samuel at Gilgal, Saul intended to establish a dynasty. He deeply hoped that his son Jonathan would succeed him as Israel's king.

Jonathan, on the other hand, like most of Israel, loved David. Jonathan's sister, Michal, loved David and was married to him. Abigail loved David and also became his wife after her first husband died. Despite David's threat to Saul's throne and dynasty, in the midst of his paranoia and depression, Saul also loved David. It seems as though all of Israel loved David—and God was with him. Handsome, courageous, loyal, faithful, obedient, a poet-warrior, David was almost too good to be true. He was the kind of man who simply has to walk into a room to become the center of attention; all eyes fell upon him before he uttered a word. Had it been their right, the Israelites would have elected David their king. He was the Lord's anointed, the divinely appointed successor to Saul, and the best man for the job. The deaths of Saul and his sons eliminated the ambiguity in Israel's political situation, clearing the way for David to ascend to the throne. This was his moment.

It is a mark of David's greatness that he reckoned the hour of his success as the hour of his grief. He mourned the death of his bosom friend, Jonathan, and the death of the man Saul, who was his rival and who had repeatedly attempted to kill him. A cynic might say that David could afford to mourn Saul and Jonathan; plenty of time remained for monarchy. Perhaps, but there is no mistaking the sincerity and grief in David's moving lament for these men whom he loved.

The City of David
2 Samuel 2–5

The deaths of Saul and Jonathan did not give David an unobstructed path to the throne. The northern tribes called themselves the house of Israel in distinction from the southern house of Judah. These appear to have been more than symbolic names. Northerners were marked by a deep loyalty to Saul, and southerners were just as loyal to David. Judah quickly anointed David king over Judah after Saul's burial, but that act did nothing to heal the north-south division. Apparently, the house of Israel thought that Saul's successor should be a northerner. Abner, Saul's kinsman and military leader, put forward Ish-Bosheth, Saul's surviving son, as the legitimate heir to the throne of Israel. Bloody tribal warfare followed, marked by intrigue, murder, and blood revenge. This cycle of violence continued until Abner finally offered a peace initiative that proposed that David become king over Israel as well as Judah. In return for his statesmanship, Abner was murdered by David's captain Joab in revenge for Abner's killing of Joab's brother.

This picture of violence and political instability reveals David's rather precarious hold on the throne. His every action would be scrutinized for signs of favoritism toward either Israel or Judah. The choice of a site for his capital was especially important. Up until this moment, David conducted court as king of Judah in the southern city of Hebron. But this location would never serve as the location for the capital of a united monarchy. Northerners would resent a southern capital, and southerners would not tolerate a northern site. In this climate of suspicion, David demonstrated his shrewd political judgment by choosing a capital with which neither Israel or Judah could identify.

The citadel of Jerusalem, also called Jebus, had remained unconquered during the centuries following Israel's entrance into Canaan. It was one of those locations that had been bypassed and left in Jebusite control—and for good reason. Jerusalem—a much smaller version of the city than today—was located atop and around Mt. Zion. It was steep, craggy, and easily defended against invaders. That they had never conquered Jerusalem made it neutral territory as far as the houses of Israel and Judah were concerned. As such, it would make an ideal capital. The only problem was its strategic location. David, however, demonstrated a military prowess to accompany his political acumen and successfully attacked the Jebusite fortress. Neither southern nor northern, Jerusalem became in every sense of the phrase the city of David where he was absolute master, free of the jealousies and animosities of the houses of Israel and Judah.

Centered in Jerusalem, David's rule was to be modeled on the shepherd's care for his sheep. God intended David to become the shepherd-king over the people Israel. The image of the Davidic king as a good shepherd runs through the narratives of the kings of Israel and Judah, only to emerge again in the New Testament in Jesus himself. The first time we hear of David, he was tending his father's flocks. When God formally commissioned David's reign, it was in terms of the shepherd imagery. The prophet Nathan confronted David with his sin through the means of a story about sheep and shepherds. The ancient Semitic world pictured kings in such terms. They were fathers, benefactors, and protectors of their people. In the case of the kings of Israel, God stood ready to hold them to their high responsibilities.

God and Royal Power in Jerusalem
2 Samuel 7

Citizens of modern nations are accustomed to the legal separation of church and state government. Although the Bible and prayer are often elements of public ceremonies, such as the inauguration of the president of the United States, in the final analysis the American state papers—the Federal Constitution and the Declaration of Independence—do not use religious objects or symbols to legitimate government or nation. Our rhetoric often calls upon God for support, but according to the Constitution, the voice of the people is what finally matters most to elected officials. The relationship between religion and government in the ancient world differs markedly from this modern understanding. The reign of an ancient king, whether in Israel or any neighboring countries, needed the support of the priesthood and the public religious symbols of which they were custodians.

In 2 Samuel 6, the ark of the covenant suddenly becomes the focus of David's attention. For twenty and more years, nobody in Israel seems to have given much thought to this most sacred and powerful of Israelite religious symbols. The ark held the tablets of the Commandments. On top of the ark was the mercy seat, where abided the very presence of God. When carried into battle on God's authorization, the ark guaranteed Israel's victory over their enemies. As such, it connected Israel's present to the glorious days of the past when God abided among his covenanted people. Where the ark was, the Lord God was.

Remember that David had established his capital at the old Jebusite citadel of Jerusalem. While this neutral site held certain military and political advantages, it also had some disadvantages. Its principal shortcoming was that it lacked any religious significance in Israel's memory. Many important religious shrines dotted the countryside, places associated with a revelation of God or the memory of his acts. No such memories were associated with Jerusalem, and that absence created a potential weakness in David's rule. He could overcome that vulnerability, however, by moving the ark to his new capital, and so he did.

We need not interpret David's actions concerning the ark as those of a cynical politician looking for support for his regime. He combined political shrewdness and sincere faith in a remarkably pragmatic manner. David wanted and likely needed the ark in Jerusalem in order to maintain royal power, but when told that he was not the man to build a house for the ark, David humbly submitted to God's will. It turned out that the security of David's throne and his family dynasty rested on God himself and not on such a grand act of royal piety as the construction of a temple.

The concluding section, 2 Samuel 7, contains God's covenant with David. According to this pledge, freely given by Yahweh, God promised David that he and his descendants would sit securely on the throne in Jerusalem. Moreover, God promised his abiding love and presence to David and his successors. This covenant is the core of what is called the "royal" or "Jerusalem" theology. According to this view, God's covenant with David and his successors is unconditional. In this passage, God does not say, "If you obey, I will be with you." The promise is absolute; it contains no *if*. To be sure, God also promised that royal wrongdoing would be punished, but the punishment had limits; the kingdom would never be taken from David's family as it had from Saul's. God's covenant with David gave the royal theology a confidence and security that the Jerusalem theology did not originally enjoy. But this same theology carried the potential for overconfidence and even arrogance in kings who lacked David's love and trust in God.

"Thou Art the Man"
2 Samuel 11:1–12:25

In the first two sentences of 2 Samuel 11, we learn that something had gone wrong in David's rule over Israel. Springtime was the season for royal war making, and David was a great warrior. Saul had slain thousands, but David had slain ten thousands. Fearlessly, David had toppled the giant Goliath with a single well-aimed stone. Fighting men had volunteered for service under David because they recognized in him the kind of courage and valor that captures a warrior's vision and heart. But this spring—the implication is that this was the first time—David did not march off to war at the head of his army. Instead, he sent Joab in his place. To make sure that the reader does not miss the point, the text tells us, "But David remained in Jerusalem." For the first time, David had acted in a manner unworthy of him; he had not acted like a king.

Idleness, as the Puritans frequently reminded people, is the Devil's workshop. The idle king soon found trouble in the form of Bathsheba, wife of Uriah, a loyal soldier in David's army. Now at the height of his power, David could have anything he wanted, and he wanted this woman. There is no romance here, no words of love; there is only lust and its satisfaction. And the result is devastation and sorrow.

In the face of Bathsheba's devastating news, David acted with his customary swiftness and decisiveness. But these once admirable gifts are now employed in the service of a cover-up. Unfortunately for Uriah, he was open, honest, loyal, and completely trusting of David. The king used all of these exemplary qualities against him, ultimately murdering Uriah through a stratagem that left David just as guilty as if he had struck the mortal blow himself.

David's sin would not go quietly to the grave with Uriah. There was a God in Israel who would not look away from sin—even the sin of a powerful and enormously popular king. In Israel, royal power, even such power as David held, was limited by God's presence and will. Thus, Nathan the prophet spoke to David in the same relation that Samuel had spoken to Saul and that subsequent prophets would speak to the kings of Israel and Judah. Nathan came to David to disclose his sin and God's displeasure.

In the moment when his sin was revealed, when Nathan pointed his bony finger at the king and said, "Thou art the man," the greatness of David's soul is disclosed. He made no excuses. He did not feebly attempt to blame Bathsheba for bathing on her roof in plain view of the palace. He did not ask to see his psychotherapist. Simply, honestly, humbly, David confessed his sin.

God heard and forgave. Nevertheless, there were consequences to be suffered. The sin may have been private, but there would be public consequences to pay. Sadly, this sorry tale is a key episode in the subsequent history of David's family and all Israel.

First and Second Kings

Family Violence
1 Kings 2:1–4; 3:1–15

After his affair with Bathsheba, David's family slid into dysfunction, although it also may have been the case that this family was inherently unstable. Dysfunctional may not even be the right word. The structure of an ancient Near-Eastern monarch's family scarcely resembles the contemporary nuclear family. In the first place, David was a polygamist. Many Old Testament men had more than one wife. As a king, David was entitled to and kept a harem of many wives and concubines. The children born to these women were therefore half-brothers and half-sisters. In a patriarchal society such as ancient Israel, however, the blood relation was determined through the father. Thus, the text refers to all of them simply as David's children and as brothers and sisters, since he had sired them.

Of course, different mothers raised these children of a common father. In a culture where a woman's greatest achievement was to have children, the woman who bore David the son who would be his successor elevated her own status as well. It was an unstable arrangement from the beginning, ripe with jealousy, rivalry, and intrigue. Such a domestic climate inevitably produced problems. One of David's sons, Amnon, raped his half-sister Tamar, and her full brother Absalom killed Amnon to revenge her honor. Absalom later led a revolution against David that nearly toppled his throne. This was but the first of several attempted coups against David. We are left with a picture of a large extended family in disarray, headed by a man who could no longer quench the fires of jealousy and ambition.

In the midst of this turbulent family, Bathsheba also plotted to advance her son Solomon to David's attention and favor as successor to the throne. She achieved her purpose with the assistance of the prophet Nathan, the same man who once denounced David for his sin with her. All of this intrigue only intended to achieve that which David had promised, that Solomon would inherit the kingdom. This promise was in turn threatened when another of David's sons, Adonijah, seized his father's throne as his aged father neared death. Warned of this plot by Nathan, Bathsheba went to David and asked that his promise to Solomon be fulfilled.

"Uneasy lies the head that wears the crown." After David's death, Solomon did became Israel's king, but blood continued to flow. Solomon's henchman Benaiah killed Adonijah and Joab,

David's old captain and a man who had ruthlessly performed similar deeds in service to his master David. The transition in power was nearly complete. It only remained for Solomon to replace Abiathar with Zadok as high priest to make the administration his own and eliminate any threats to his new throne. Solomon may not have been the warrior his father was, but he proved to be just as ruthless and adept at politics and even shrewder than David at statecraft.

With domestic threats eliminated and foreign affairs stabilized through alliances, Solomon began a reign that also was marked by the Lord's favor. When God gave Solomon his choice of any desire that God might fulfill, Solomon asked for wisdom. His request so pleased Yahweh that he not only granted it but also showered blessings on Solomon. It is noteworthy that in the midst of God's promised blessings we find the word *if* (3:14). A new note had been sounded in the relationship between God and the kings of Israel. God's covenant with David's successors came to include a condition, fundamentally calling into question the old unconditional covenant between God and David.

The Temple and Solomon

1 Kings 5:1–8; 6:1–38; 8:4–9:5; 11

The kingdom of Israel reached its years of glory during the reign of Solomon. David's military prowess subdued the petty kingdoms, extended the borders, and established peace. Each of the three superpowers of the ancient Near East—Assyria, Egypt, and Babylon—was in a period of weakness and did not menace Israel. Foreign wealth flowed into Jerusalem while the Israelites also enjoyed domestic prosperity. In the midst of this golden age, Solomon determined to build a temple for God.

A subtle change distinguishes the motives behind David's and Solomon's desires to build a temple. David had been ashamed of the fact that he dwelt in a palace while the ark of the covenant rested in a tent. Solomon built the temple because God declared that it would be so. Solomon spared no expense in constructing the most glorious temple possible. Nevertheless, Solomon lived in a palace that was thirteen years in the making while the temple required only seven. Solomon was famed for his wisdom and the splendor of his court, but his heart did not match his father's passion for God.

Wise though Solomon was, he made mistakes. An especially critical mistake was an overconfidence that allowed him to think that elements of non-Israelite religions could rest alongside the worship of God. This tendency in Solomon first showed itself in his decision to hire a non-Israelite architect to build the temple. David had his faults, but he remained steadfastly loyal to God. In this, he was the "man after God's own heart," and in his loyalty to the Lord, David set the standard by which every subsequent Israelite king would be measured. His son Solomon inevitably was the first to be so judged and the first to be found wanting. As was so often the case in ancient Israel, the source of Solomon's sin was connected with the worship of Canaanite gods.

The problem with religious syncretism is that it blended elements of non-Israelite religion with the worship of God. The Canaanite religions focused attention and religious devotion on gods and goddesses that were believed to control the forces of nature crucial to agricultural peoples. When the Israelites, who were the children of slaves and had wandered the desert for a generation, settled in Canaan and began to learn the ways of farming, it was almost inevitable that they would follow the religious practices of their Canaanite neighbors. The Israelites seemed to assume that part of being a successful farmer in their new land must include worship of the gods and goddesses that their Canaanite farmer neighbors worshiped. Thus, elements of the fertility religions found their way into the worship of God.

Solomon's situation and problem, however, differs from the syncretism of the period of the judges. In the first place, by his day Israelites had lived on the land for several centuries and had established their own traditions. Through Samuel and David, this included a rigorous and strict adherence to Yahweh and Yahweh alone. Nevertheless, in his later years Solomon not only permitted the construction of shrines to foreign gods, but he also authorized that construction and worshiped these gods and goddesses in their newly constructed shrines. This is not syncretism but polytheism; either practice constituted a violation of the first and second commandments. Why would a man with Solomon's reputation for wisdom undertake such folly? The text's answer to that question is to blame his foreign wives. In this, we appear to have taken a step back from David's honest acceptance of responsibility for his own actions. David blamed none but himself for the sin with Bathsheba, but somebody else takes the fall for a sin that was Solomon's responsibility.

The description of Solomon's reign celebrates its glory and wealth. He ruled and kept a court in the manner of an oriental potentate. This high style included a large harem filled with hundreds of women. Solomon may have had a roving eye, but he married many of these women for the sake of political alliances. It was customary in the ancient world to seal a treaty between countries through a marriage of members of the royal families. The foreign princesses who married Solomon brought their gods and goddesses with them; it was neither required nor expected of these women that they convert to belief in Yahweh. By this route, pagan gods and goddesses found their way into Israel. Their patronesses in the royal harem asked Solomon for money and workers to build shrines to these pagan deities, and he consented.

Alongside God's unconditional promise to David that the kingdom would never be taken from him, there rested a parallel promise. Scholars refer to this promise as the cornerstone of the Deuteronomistic view of history. At its core, this promise centers in the word *if* and is the conditional side of Israel's life with God. *If* the people—and especially their king—will keep the commandments, then all will be well in Israel. But *if* the people—and especially their king—forsake God and his ways, then trouble and punishment will surely follow. Solomon neglected this *if*. It was a final mark of God's love for David that Solomon was permitted to die without witnessing the decline of his kingdom, but that decline would inevitably come because of his neglect of one little but all-powerful word.

The Divided Monarchy

1 Kings 12

Israelite kings were never free to act as other absolute monarchs. Monarchy in Israel was never absolute, but always checked by the power of Yahweh. Israelite kings were never free to govern according to their personal whim. Instead, they were to follow Yahweh's commandments—the Torah. From one perspective this qualification inherently destabilized the Israelite monarchy. Kings who disregarded or flouted Yahweh's Torah risked divine displeasure so great as to bring down their rule. Saul had disobeyed Yahweh, and the kingdom was taken from him. David forgot his obligation to shepherd his people, and terrible violence erupted among his own children. Solomon neglected the first commandment, which brought down the wrath of Yahweh on Rehoboam, who lost all but the tribe of Judah from the old kingdom of his grandfather David.

Monarchy in Israel also was unstable because of an apparent ongoing rivalry between the smaller tribes of the north (Israel) and the large southern tribe of Judah. Saul had been a member of a northern Israelite tribe. David came from the south and seems to have encountered some difficulty persuading the northerners to accept his kingship after Saul was deposed. Early on, David set up his royal court in the southern town of Hebron. Only when the elders of Israel went to him there and pledged their loyalty did David become king over all the people. Demonstrating his political shrewdness, David took a neutral site, the old Jebusite citadel of Jerusalem, for his royal city (see 2 Sam 5:1–7).

Such strong rulers as David and Solomon held the fragile royal coalition together. A lesser man, such as Rehoboam, could not hope to do so, even under better conditions than he inherited. So it was that the united monarchy collapsed under Rehoboam. Its instabilities were simply no match for the disintegrating forces of royal sin and tribal rivalry. The northern tribes rallied under Jeroboam, the son of Nebat, and threw off Rehoboam's yoke, leaving him to govern only Judah, the tattered remnant of the kingdom of David.

One additional word must be added to describe the man to whom the Israelites turned in their hour of need. Under Solomon, Jeroboam had been the leader of a group of forced laborers. That role gave him the opportunity to see the harsh treatment meted out to these unfortunate people. First Kings 11:29–39 gives an account of the prophet Ahijah's statement to Jeroboam that he would rule over the tribes of Israel after they were separated from the united monarchy. A divided kingdom and diminished power in Jerusalem was God's judgment on Solomon's descendants because he had permitted the worship of foreign gods in his kingdom.

The immediate cause of the monarchy's breakup was the insufferable arrogance of Rehoboam. He inherited a throne that was already showing signs of the heavy-handedness and corruption against which Samuel has once warned. Solomon's wisdom and the glory of Israel under his reign held in check the people's resentment of these increasingly harsh conditions. Almost immediately after Solomon's death, the people asked Rehoboam for relief from this system of royal domination. His foolish denial of their petition exposed the Israelite monarchy for what it had become: a despotic institution like that "of the nations" in almost every detail.

Once free of Jerusalem's authority, Jeroboam had to consolidate his rule as king over Israel. Jerusalem was the principal religious city for Israelites as well as Judahites. Ancient Israel, like all other nations, did not separate religion and the state. In fact, temple and monarchy tended to reinforce each other. The center of Israelite religious life was in Jerusalem, and Jeroboam foresaw that religious pilgrimages to the temple would take Israelites back to the city where Rehoboam ruled Judah from the royal palace. Jeroboam decided to redirect Israelite religious devotion away from Jerusalem toward shrines built in northern cities. Yahweh reigned in the temple in Jerusalem, but Jeroboam established the worship of idols at the historic shrines at Dan and Bethel, a name that ironically means "house of God" in Hebrew. Yahweh has been worshiped at these shrines in the days before Jerusalem's ascendancy. As Solomon had done before, and as so many kings would do after him, Jeroboam caused Israel to worship an idol in the place of Yahweh. The price of this sin was a tottering throne from which Jeroboam would eventually fall.

Ahab and Elijah

1 Kings 17–18

After Jeroboam became king over the northern tribes of Israel, he established his capital at the city of Samaria. He also reasoned, perhaps correctly but also to the demise of his dynasty, that the continued worship of God among his people might eventually incline them to reunification with Judah and Jerusalem, the site of God's temple. Jeroboam had already burned the political bridges connecting Israel and Judah. He burned the remaining bridge by abandoning the worship of the Lord in favor of idol worship as a way of distinguishing his kingdom from the southerners. This direct violation of the commandments earned Jeroboam the judgment of God, and the Israelite monarchy suffered through a period of instability and palace revolutions that ended only when Omri was able to bring a measure of union and peace to the situation. He was succeeded by his son, the infamous King Ahab.

Measured only in political and military terms, Ahab was an effective king. His reign was the second longest of the kings of Israel, and during it he stabilized the economy and the army. The kingdom of Israel was richer than that of Judah. It had better agricultural land, the basis for most ancient economies, and it also sat astride international trade routes, making Israel a natural commercial center. Ahab's ability enabled him to take advantage of these assets, and he built Israel into a strong and prosperous society. Ahab is not remembered for any of these achievements, however. Rather, people recall his name because he was a religious disaster and the enemy of the prophet Elijah.

Like his predecessors on the thrones of Israel and Judah, and after the fashion of oriental despots everywhere, Ahab kept a harem of wives. Many of these women had come to him to seal diplomatic treaties and military alliances. Non-Israelites, they brought with them the worship of the gods of their homelands. Solomon had permitted this worship through a policy of benign neglect. That was a shortcoming serious enough to warrant God's division of the monarchy. Ahab's sin exceeded Solomon's. Ahab not only permitted this worship, but he also engaged in it personally. Through his wife Jezebel, the worship of the Canaanite fertility gods Baal and Asherah was adopted as the religion of Israel and its kings. For this flouting of God's commandments Ahab would pay dearly.

The history of the Israelite monarchy differs markedly from the surrounding nations. The difference is that Israelite kings always had to answer to God, the true king over all Israel, and to the prophets, who were God's messengers to deliver his word of authorization and judgment. Although more than one prophet carried Yahweh's word to Ahab, his great opponent was Elijah.

Elijah was the first great representative of the prophetic tradition in Israel. Some might ask, Why not Samuel or Moses? Moses was a special case, the man who saw God face-to-face, and Samuel was a transitional figure between the old order of judges and the new institution of prophecy. The prophets were forthtellers, God's ambassadors sent to deliver his message. Often it was a message of divine displeasure and warning that required prophets to stand against kings. No prophet exemplified that stance more courageously or with greater determination than Elijah. Ahab's political and economic successes did not matter one whit in the face of his religious apostasy. The northern kingdom and Ahab might enjoy short-term prosperity, but his religious failure doomed his reign. God commissioned Elijah to deliver this message to Ahab face-to-face.

Israelite prophets and faithful believers in God found a determined opponent in Baalism. *Baal* is a Canaanite word that means "lord," master," or "husband" and signifies ownership. It is a generic term and could refer to any of several baals. Some had their own individual name: Dagon (Judges 16:23), Hadad, and Melqart of Tyre, likely the baal that Ahab's wife Jezebel worshiped. Baal was connected to fertility and was thought to be the god who controlled the winter rains. Israel's neighbors were agricultural peoples whose lives depended on a good annual harvest. It is no coincidence that the problem of drought and the need for rain are central to the great contest between Elijah and the prophets of Baal on Mount Carmel. Ancient Canaanite farmers answered those worries by worshiping Baal.

Among the Canaanite people, Baal had a female partner. Her name was Asherah (plural, Ashteroth), and she was the cruel goddess of sex and war. Since Baal and Asherah together controlled fertility, their sexual union was a crucial element in Canaanite religious practice. First Kings 16:33 says that Ahab made an Asherah pole. Today, anthropologists would describe this religious object as a phallic symbol. This public reference to sexual intercourse was mild compared to the lewd and lascivious worship of Baal and Asherah that included sexual acts uniting worshipers with official cult prostitutes. Israelites who slipped into Baalism violated not only Torah's commandments concerning sexual relations but also the commandment prohibiting the worship of any god but the Lord God.

Baalism seems to have waxed and waned among Israelites. It was a particular problem during the time of the judges, during the eighth-century BC, as well as during the reign of Ahab. In Judah, the kings Hezekiah and Josiah both suppressed Baal worship and were rewarded by God for their actions. No such champion appeared among the northern kings. In Israel, the prophet Elijah stood alone in the face of a king and queen determined to repress the worship of Yahweh and quite willing to be utterly ruthless in that pursuit. Jezebel ordered the murder of all the prophets of God that she could find. Elijah had escaped this bloody purge and now stood ready to contest the fundamental question of Israel's religious loyalty. Would they worship Baal or the true God?

The word *prophet* figures prominently in this narrative. Jezebel ordered the murder of all the prophets of the Lord. Obadiah preserved the lives of one hundred of those prophets. Four hundred prophets of Asherah and four hundred fifty prophets of Baal lived handsomely on royal subsidies provided by Jezebel. And, of course, there was Elijah. With all of these prophets of such different loyalties, what are we to make of the term *prophet*? What did it signify? It seems clear that during this period the role of the prophet was still under development. Such later prophets as Amos, Hosea, Isaiah, and Jeremiah were spokespersons for God, delivering oracles or sermons that were subsequently written and gathered into book form. Elijah also delivered God's word to Israel but left no book that carries his name. It is also obvious that *prophet* was something of a generic term in Elijah's day. It could be applied to the representative of any god, even one shown to be as impotent as Baal on the day that Elijah called fire down from heaven and Yahweh caused rain to fall on the parched land in a graphic demonstration of who was truly God in Israel.

Good News Is Bad News

1 Kings 22:1–40

This text is set against the backdrop of a period of intermittent war between the northern kingdom of Israel and the neighboring state of Aram. Aram is also known by the names of Aramea and Syria. This latter name is not to be confused with the vastly larger Assyrian Empire still farther northeast at the very top of the Fertile Crescent. Assyria was one of three great powers that contested with each other for control of the region, the other two being Babylonia and Egypt. Israel, Judah, Aram, and other small states on the western end of the Fertile Crescent fought with one another for territory during a brief period when all three great powers were in decline. Without the threat created by any one of the three, the smaller kingdoms were free to fight over such scraps of territory as Ramoth-Gilead, a town with a distinguished place in Israelite history but which had fallen into Aramaen hands. King Ahab coveted the return of the town and its surrounding territory. He determined to renew the conflict between his kingdom and Aram.

To ensure victory in the coming war, Ahab sought an alliance with Judah. He invited King Jehoshaphat to Samaria to negotiate arrangements. Jehoshaphat agreed to Ahab's proposal and pledged assistance, but he also added a proviso; he wanted the two kings to seek the advice and wisdom of God. In the ancient world of the Middle East, no responsible king would risk the enterprise of war without divine assistance. Even those who worshiped idols sought the support of their gods. In this sense, Jehoshaphat acted as would any king. Where Jehoshaphat differed from Ahab was in who it was that the former wanted to speak for God.

Ahab had surrounded himself with prophets, a standard practice in the world of the Bible. Kings needed people who could consult the gods and speak for them whenever royal decisions needed to be made, and so it had become customary to keep prophets on the payroll. We have previously encountered the large group of prophets who ate at Jezebel's table. Part of the royal bureaucracies of both Israel and Judah, these professional court prophets often played the role of religious advisers to the king. Of course, this system was deeply flawed in that any court prophet who wanted to keep his job had to give the king the advice he wanted to hear. It was not the kind of system that encouraged honest speech. So Jehoshaphat did not trust the word of Ahab's court prophets, not only for this fact but also for the far greater shortcoming that they were not prophets of Yahweh. In modern-day terms, Jehoshaphat wanted a second opinion. He asked Ahab to summon a "prophet of the LORD" who would speak the Lord God's word.

Ahab was caught between a rock and a hard place. He did not want to wage war without Judah as an ally, but he could secure that alliance only by agreeing to send for the one prophet who could speak the word Jehoshaphat had requested, Micaiah the son of Imlah. This man was a problem for Ahab because, unlike the court prophets, Micaiah told the truth—whether or not it would please the king. That Micaiah had nothing good to say to Ahab was, of course, because of Ahab's utter disregard for God and the commandments, a disregard most recently displayed in the wicked plot employed to gain the vineyard owned by Naboth (1 Kings 21).

However much they say otherwise, kings and rulers then and now are not inclined to surround themselves with truth tellers like Micaiah, particularly when they speak an unpopular word. Nevertheless, Ahab had to listen to Micaiah in order to secure Jehoshaphat's assistance. In what was surely one of the greatest of good news–bad news speeches ever, Micaiah told Ahab what he wanted to hear. His intended war against the Aramaens would succeed. On the other hand, to this positive word the prophet of the Lord added news that angered Ahab even as it must have struck fear in his heart. The allied armies would celebrate a victory that Ahab would not live to see.

The Work of Prophets
2 Kings 5:1–19

Whether in the northern kingdom of Israel or the southern kingdom of Judah, the rule of kings was always subject to the will and approval of Yahweh. In this kind of sociopolitical arrangement, the prophets therefore spoke with great authority. A king might ignore or even antagonize a prophet the way Ahab dealt with Elijah, but kings who disregarded or persecuted prophets risked the probability of divine displeasure. As noted earlier, prophets are divided into two groups: the writing prophets, whose books were eventually included in the canon of the Old Testament, and those who did not leave a written message. The earliest prophets, Nathan, Elijah, Elisha, and Micaiah ben Imlah, are members of this latter group and the forerunners of the prophetic movement that flourished in the eighth century BC when such men as Amos, Hosea, and Isaiah delivered messages that eventually became part of the law and the prophets.

We tend to think of prophets as seers, people who predict future events, and there is some element of prediction in many prophetic speeches. First Samuel 9:9 refers to this aspect of prophecy while it also makes a new distinction: "Formerly in Israel, if a man went to inquire of God, he would say, 'Come, let us go to the seer,' because the prophet of today used to be called a seer." A seer tells the future for people. That the "prophet of today" *used to* be called a seer suggests this predictive role. Since the prophet was no longer called a seer, we may conclude that some new role had been added. This new role was the prophet's function as Yahweh's messenger, the one who told forth the word of the Lord. Word and speech were characteristic forms of communication for prophets. True, some still had visions, but by and large the prophets of Israel and Judah began their messages—we may think of them as sharply set sermons—with the oft-repeated phrase, "The word of the LORD came to me."

We find another distinction between the writing and non-writing prophets. The writing prophets devoted their attention to large-scale issues—world politics, social justice, and national righteousness. To be sure, these issues mattered to the prophets because of the way little people were chewed up and destroyed by injustice and oppression. Their sermons attacking such injustices and sin define the writing prophets.

We are more likely to read and hear of the non-writing prophets engaged with *individual* hurting people. Several stories bring Elijah and Elisha into close contact with people with specific needs: a famished widow, a man victimized by royal greed and official corruption, a village with bad water, a widow with no oil, an old woman whose son had died, and Naaman the Syrian (Aramean) military officer who contracted leprosy.

Elijah and Elisha manifested Yahweh's power in Israel in ways that lay outside the channels of royal power. In this sense, they were more than prophets, either in the sense of seer or forthteller. They carried the title "man of God," a phrase we do not often find applied in the same way to the writing prophets. By his simple presence, the man of God served to remind people inside Israel and even beyond its borders that Yahweh was the true ruler and the real power in Israel and beyond. This reminder was a potential embarrassment to kings and military commanders who persisted in the belief that raw, coercive power kept them in control. Such men like to believe that they determine events. Thus, they are not likely to appreciate lessons taught by old men and servant girls, unless of course such lessons hold the key to life.

Endpoint

2 Kings 17:1–23

After 746 BC, the northern kingdom went into a steep decline at the moment when Assyrian expansion posed its gravest threat. Under Tiglath-Pileser III, Assyria first took the area of its eastern foe, Babylon. Once that task was completed, Tiglath was free to raid the smaller kingdoms to the west. In 743, he began a series of campaigns against Syria (Aram). At first, a coalition of the small kingdoms, led probably by King Uzziah of Judah, offered resistance. But Uzziah died in 742, and within four years the Assyrians were collecting tribute from most of the small kingdoms of the region—including Israel.

A strong nation with courageous and wise leadership would have been severely taxed by the situation facing

Israel, but the northern kingdom was anything but strong and her leadership a sham. Within the decade following the death of Jeroboam II in 746, Israel had five different kings. Three simply grabbed power without any grounds or legitimate claim. Jeroboam's son Zechariah was murdered after a reign of six months by Shallum, who was himself murdered after a reign of but one month. His murderer, Menahem, held the throne from 745 to 738, but only after a bloody civil war filled with terrible atrocities. Given the insecurity of his throne, Menahem may have willingly paid tribute to the Assyrians in the hope of their support. His son and successor, Pekahiah, was murdered by an army officer, Pekah, who seized the throne and eventually aligned himself with Rezin, king of Damascus, *against Judah* in the Syro-Ephraimitic war. At the moment when Assyria threatened from the north, Israel squandered its resources in a war against Judah. Clearly, political leadership in Israel existed in name only.

As bad as the condition of Israelite political leadership was, even worse was the decay of its society. Social crimes, paganism, debauchery, and sexual license in the name of religion completely undermined the national character.

By the time of Hoshea, the last king of Israel, anyone could see that nothing lay between Israel and the reality of occupation. In one final act of desperation, Hoshea sought the aid of the other great power of the region, Egypt. The tribute that he had been paying to keep the Assyrians at bay, he now offered to Egypt. But Israel was too far away from Egypt, whose army could not endure such a long over-extension. They accepted Israel's payments but gave nothing in return. God had turned his face from Israel, and Israel could find no earthly support. In 722, the Assyrian army conquered Israel. It is the Bible's firm conviction that none of this happened without God's knowledge and intention. This text contains a long and sad catalogue of the reasons Israel fell. Biblical faith sees in these events the hand of God working to bring about his purposes.

First and Second Chronicles

A Theological View on History
2 Chronicles 30:1–6, 8–12

As previously noted, the Deuteronomistic theology rested on the belief that the health of the covenant between the Lord God and the Israelites depended on obedience. This perspective underwrote what might be termed the conditional covenant, and is expressed, for example, in 2 Chronicles 7:14: "*If* my people... will...turn from their wicked ways, then will I hear from heaven" (italics added). The little word *if* establishes the condition: obedience. When Israel and, more specifically its kings, obeyed the Torah, then the nation would prosper. Disobedience, however, would bring judgment and ruin.

On the other hand, Deuteronomistic theology was contested by another understanding of Israel's covenant with the Lord. This opposing view was centered in Jerusalem and stated that the monarchy and its capital city could trust in the unshakable promise that God made to David: his house would always rule in Jerusalem.

One of the dominant events during the reign of Hezekiah occurred not in Jerusalem or Judah. That event was the fall of Samaria, the capital of Israel, in 722 BC along with the whole northern kingdom. The destruction of Israel had two effects on the people of Judah. In the first place, they felt the shock at the death and exile of their kin. Israel may have been a separate kingdom, but its people shared a common religious inheritance with Judah; the people of Israel were also the Lord's people and subject to the Lord's commandments. Second, worse than occupying Israel, the Assyrians obliterated it. The northern kingdom was simply wiped off the map. After the fall of Samaria, nothing stood between Judah and the ruthless Assyrians. Judah's kings had to confront the harsh political realities of life with a totalitarian and aggressive neighbor.

King Hezekiah is the key figure in this text. He must be studied against the checkered history of his family. On the one hand, his great-grandfather, the great Uzziah, who reigned for more than fifty years, was successful only so long as he was faithful to the Lord. Hezekiah's grandfather Jotham "did what was right in the eyes of the Lord" (2 Chron 27:2), but Hezekiah's father Ahaz did not live up to this standard. Ahaz ordered the creation of idols for Baal worship and encouraged worship at sites other than the temple in Jerusalem. Ahaz also practiced child sacrifice—an abomination among the Israelites. It is doubtful that he substituted pagan worship for the worship of the Lord. More likely, he combined elements of these religions, a common practice called syncretism. In any case, Hezekiah subsequently cleansed pagan shrines and idols from the kingdom of Judah. His sincere religious reforms clearly mark his obedience to the Lord, who rewarded the king's faithfulness by protecting him and his people against the Assyrian juggernaut. Just as the Deuteronomistic theology said, Hezekiah's faithful obedience brought blessing and peace to Judah.

As faithful readers of Scripture, we must be aware of the different literary styles and perspectives that appear in the biblical text. Chronicles is the work of a historian reflecting on the events of the two monarchies. The Chronicler looked back on these events and saw in them the basis for his theological point about obedience to the Lord God. The prophetic literature, however, is also the product of people who lived through some of the events about which the Chronicler wrote. The prophets' sermons are the primary literature of the period that Chronicles describes. The difference between these two kinds of literatures is similar to that of eyewitnesses' accounts and the historians who later describe the events in which the eyewitnesses participated. Other genres such as gospels, letters, and sermons also can be found in the Bible. We interpret better when we read the Bible not as a flat text but with some awareness of the specific style of literature and the variety of perspectives within the text.

Manasseh's Sins and Repentance
2 Chronicles. 33:1–13

If we compare the account of King Manasseh in 2 Chronicles with that in 2 Kings, we notice a distinct difference. The Kings narrative is quite silent on the subject of Manasseh's repentance. In fact, 2 Kings makes a considerable point of the depravity of Manasseh's reign. This king's sins make up a familiar list:

syncretism, astrology, consulting spiritual mediums, and child sacrifice—the shedding of innocent blood. Taken together, these sins constituted a terrible corruption of Israelite religion. Second Kings is uncompromising in its assessment of wicked King Manasseh; his rule was responsible for the destruction and exile about to befall the people of Jerusalem. Royal sin will lead to political disaster.

Second Chronicles is as uncompromising as Kings in its assessment of Manasseh's reign. The Chronicles account, however, includes material not found in Kings and reaches a very different conclusion about him.

How are we to account for this difference? For one thing, Manasseh's long life (to age sixty-seven) and his very long reign (fifty-five years) were normally sure indicators of the Lord's blessing. According to the Deuteronomistic theology, such benefits were never accidental; they were signs of God's favor. The problem was that Manasseh's reign, full of sin as it was, could hardly constitute a basis for divine blessing.

It is here that 2 Chronicles adds information that is absent from the parallel account in 2 Kings. Some commentators are skeptical that these events actually happened and worry that the Chronicler was so committed to the Deuteronomistic theology that he supposed that Manasseh must have done something good to have earned the blessings of prosperous reign and long life. These commentators conclude that the story of Manasseh's captivity and subsequent repentance are therefore inventions of the chronicler. However, others argue in favor of the historical accuracy of the Chronicles version of Manasseh's reign, pointing to contemporary accounts. In this case, then, Manasseh's biography perfectly fits the Chronicler's theological point of view. The king's long life and the prosperity of his reign are linked to his repentance.

We are still left with the problem that Manasseh seems to have undergone a rather light discipline, given the terrible nature of his sins. One would think that, especially when compared with the fates of other Judahite and Israelite kings, Manasseh might have suffered a worse punishment. His repentance seems to have mitigated those consequences—but only for a season. In the final analysis, the judgment of 2 Kings will hold. The sins of Manasseh had set the kingdom of Judah on a desperate downhill slide. As in the case of earlier rulers, Manasseh's reforms proved to be short-lived. His son Amon returned to the excesses and apostasy that marked the worst days of his father's reign. Who is to deny that the son had been introduced to these by Manasseh himself? In a real sense, then, Amon's sins would have been the sins of Manasseh—not personally, but in the sense that they were Manasseh's kind of sin. And the final verdict concerning these sins is that the whole nation would be punished.

Josiah's Reforms

2 Chronicles 34:1–33

Josiah succeeded to the throne of Jerusalem at the tender age of eight, too young to rule on his own account. It is likely that these first years of his rule were marred by the same kind of religious and social problems that afflicted Judah during the worst days of Manasseh and Amon. Nevertheless, the young man matured quickly and at sixteen began religious reform throughout the land.

The first stage of Josiah's reform witnessed the destruction of foreign gods and the elimination of religious syncretism. This project involved the cleansing and refurbishing of the temple in Jerusalem. Then, as now, repairs to buildings cost money, and in the process of removing funds from the temple treasury, members of the priesthood were surprised to discover a presumably long-neglected book of the law. Scholars agree that this law book was a copy of Deuteronomy, but they disagree as to whether it was freshly written in the seventh century BC or a long-lost product of the pen of Moses. Regardless of one's point of view, the discovery of the Book of Law was of momentous importance not only for Judah during the reign of Josiah, but for the subsequent history of the Old Testament.

Scholars generally agree that the Law or Torah—the first five books of the Old Testament—was the first biblical writings that Israel regarded as authoritative or canonical, as we say today. Deuteronomy, read aloud in the hearing of the people of Jerusalem, was clearly assigned the normative status that we assign to the books of the canonical Scriptures. *Canon* comes from a Greek word that means, by extension, "measuring stick." That which is canonical is the standard against which all else is measured. The law book discovered in the temple clearly possessed such a quality. When Hilkiah and Shaphan reported the contents of this book, Josiah immediately recognized that Judah was not living according to its standard. Measured against Deuteronomy, Judah's religious life was wanting. The newly discovered law book thus acquired canonical status—the first such acknowledgment we find in the Old Testament.

The text portrays that dismaying moment in Judah's religious life when king and people discover that neither preceding generations nor they had followed the Lord's commandments. The situation predicted in that book had come to pass. The children of Judah were so ignorant of their constitutive narratives that they could only ask their parents, "What is the meaning of the statutes and covenants that the Lord your God has commanded you?" In other words, "Why do we perform the religious acts that we do?" Having lost contact with their past, the people of Judah lost their sense of identity; that loss opened the door to religious syncretism and adopting the ways of the Assyrians— practices condemned by the prophet Zephaniah.

Josiah's reforms brought about religious renewal in Judah. As the text says of him, "He did what was right in the eyes of the Lord" (2 Chron 34:2). When Josiah died, all Judah mourned. For his faithfulness in restoring the true worship of the Lord God in Judah, Josiah was blessed not to witness the destruction of his kingdom. Nevertheless, that destruction remained in Judah's future.

In part, Josiah was responsible for this judgment. Although he moved aggressively to reform Judah's religion, good King Josiah did not devote similar attention to the social and economic ills that continued to afflict the poor people of the land. A century earlier, the prophet Micah had identified these. In the eyes of the prophets, it was never enough to reform religion alone. They inevitably linked true religion with the right and proper treatment of people. When he neglected social reforms, Josiah overlooked the biblical teaching that righteousness and justice are ultimately and thoroughly connected.

The Fall of Jerusalem
2 Chronicles 36:9–21

To the prophets fell the responsibility of declaring the word of the Lord to the people of Jerusalem and Judah. That word defined the meaning and significance of the events unfolding around them. It bears repeating that for the people of the Bible, historical events were never thought to be simply events. Rather, those events were freighted with significance. The meaning of history was to be found in the unfolding purposes of God, who demanded justice and righteousness of his covenant people.

It is left to 2 Chronicles, and the parallels in 2 Kings, to record the historical accounts of the fall of Jerusalem. It would be a mistake to think that either of these accounts was written from an objective or neutral perspective. Both Chronicles and Kings have a point of view about the reasons behind the collapse of the southern kingdom; in fact, it is a perspective that they hold in common. Neither regards Nebuchadnezzar as a free agent; he was the instrument of the Lord who intended to punish Judah for its terrible and persistent sin. Nebuchadnezzar might wage war, but behind the scenes God was working to accomplish his purposes.

Jerusalem and Judah did not collapse in one climactic battle. The rulers and people struggled through an agonizing decade and more before the final catastrophe. Following the Battle of Carchemish in 605, the balance of power in the region tipped in favor of the Babylonians. It became prudent for the surviving states—of which Judah remained one—to pay tribute to the Babylonian overlords. For these little kingdoms, the choice apparently was to either pay tribute or disappear. When the Babylonians temporarily failed to bring Egypt under subjection, King Jehoiakim rashly took this as a sign of Babylonian weakness and stopped paying tribute. The Babylonian army was still in the area, however, and turned on Jerusalem, where Jehoiakim finally met his end. His successor and son Jehoiachin (sometimes called Coniah) lasted only three months before capitulating in 598. Jehoiachin was marched to Babylon, along with several thousand people, mainly the aristocracy and the leading citizens of Jerusalem, including a temple priest by the name of Ezekiel, who later prophesied to the Exiles. This was the so-called First Deportation.

The Babylonians set up a puppet king in Jehoiachin's place, his uncle, who took the throne name Zedekiah. This period proved to be the most difficult in the career of the prophet Jeremiah. Since he, like the other prophets, saw the Babylonians as the instrument through which the Lord intended to discipline Judah, Jeremiah's prophecies counseled the remaining leadership to accept Babylonian rule. Four years into Zedekiah's reign, however, a revolt broke out in the Babylonian army, and the Egyptians under a new pharaoh attempted to break free of Babylon's yoke. The Egyptians encouraged the small states of Palestine—Judah included—to join an alliance aimed at securing their freedom. Heedless of Jeremiah's repeated warnings, Zedekiah allowed himself to drink deeply of the wine of nationalism as poured out in the words of the prophet Hananiah. The king learned too late which prophet authentically spoke the word of the Lord. Jerusalem was besieged and eventually capitulated. Zedekiah was taken prisoner. The last sight he witnessed before the Babylonians put out his eyes was the execution of his sons. In 587 BC, Zedekiah was led to Babylon in shackles, along with several thousand other exiles. As they marched down the road leading from the once proud City of David, their ears would have been filled with the sounds of the city walls being pulled down and their noses filled with the smoke of the fires that burned palaces and the temple of the Lord. Their defeat and humiliation was complete and terrible. The destruction of Jerusalem and the temple signaled the beginning of exile, and even more fundamentally for the faith of Israel, this cataclysm provoked a crisis of belief for many. Where was Yahweh in the midst of all of this?

Ezra

Cyrus, the Lord's Servant
Ezra 1

If the exodus is the most important event in the Old Testament, the exile and its aftermath stand second. Jewish religious institutions were altered dramatically by and after the exile, and new ones were created. The Torah was interpreted in ways that played a considerable role in reshaping Judaism all the way down to Jesus' day. Jewish theology had to take account of the sudden and unexpected turn that occurred in the exile . Only a handful of Israelites had believed that the Lord would use exile and captivity as means of disciplining his people. This stunning event forced theologians to reassess their understanding of God and his ways. In short, Jewish life and religious institutions needed to be reconstructed even as the temple and the city walls needed to be rebuilt. Ezra the scribe, Nehemiah the governor, and a group of postexilic prophets, including Haggai, Malachi, and others, were the key figures in this massive cultural, religious, and architectural rebuilding project.

The Persian emperor Cyrus I was a key figure in the exiles' return to Judah. This vigorous and aggressive military leader began his career as the king of a small vassal state within the orbit of Babylonian power. Cyrus was a Persian and a useful ally of the Babylonians in their defense against the Medes. Little did the Babylonians suspect that Cyrus was the real threat. Before they realized what a danger he actually was, Cyrus had waged military campaigns north and west of Babylon that made him the master of that region. By the time the Babylonians read the handwriting on the wall, it was too late to save their tottering empire. In 539, one of Cyrus's generals led his army into the city without a fight. A few weeks later, Cyrus entered Babylon as the master of the largest empire the world had yet seen, a territory stretching from what is today Afghanistan all the way to modern Turkey.

In the first year of his reign in Babylon, Cyrus decreed that the Jewish community and its religious institutions were to be restored in Jerusalem. Not only were the exiles permitted to take their personal belongings, but the Persians also released into their keeping the plunder that the Babylonians had stolen from the temple. These furnishings were given to Sheshbazzar, a descendant of the royal line of Judah who had been given a Babylonian name during the exile.

It is, of course, the affirmation of Scripture that such events as the return of the exiles are neither accidental nor happenstance. The book of Ezra is not content to explain the restoration as the product of Persian domestic and foreign policy. On the contrary, God is affirmed as the unseen presence that prompted Cyrus to action. That God was thought to move the heart of a Gentile named Cyrus was an important step toward the theology that affirms God as the universal sovereign of all people everywhere.

Worship amid Hostility
Ezra 3–4

The brilliant historian of Israel, John Bright, helps us gain a clearer perspective of the circumstances that confronted the first exiles who returned to Jerusalem. In the first place, there were not very many people—a population of perhaps twenty thousand. The size of the province of Judah had shrunk to not more than twenty-five miles from northern boundary to southern. "The newcomers faced years of hardship, privation, and insecurity…They were dogged by a succession of poor seasons and partial crop failures…which left many of them destitute, without adequate food and clothing. Their neighbors, especially the aristocracy of Samaria, who had regarded Judah as part of their territory and resented any limitation on their prerogatives there, were openly hostile."[8]

This background helps us appreciate the situation described in Ezra 3–4. The hardship and deprivation of the situation is not difficult to imagine. The exiles' very first act upon returning was to rebuild the altar on the site of the temple. Construction work on the temple had not yet begun; in fact, the foundation had not yet been laid. But the worship of God was the absolute center of Jewish life, and the exiles could not worship without an altar on which to conduct sacrifices. All worship, therefore, was out-of-doors, an everyday occurrence regardless of the weather conditions.

It is small wonder that the foundation of the new temple was laid amid shouts of joy and celebration. Once completed, the temple would symbolize a return to normalcy, even as it would remind people that the Lord God was once again enthroned in Jerusalem. Tears and the sound of weeping were mingled with shouts and celebrating. They may have been tears of joy. They may also been tears of anguish at the memory of what was irrevocably lost. There is an implication in 3:12 that the foundation of the second temple was laid out to dimensions smaller than the first temple. Perhaps some people wept when they noticed the difference. Still others may have been saddened by the realization that their community lacked the wealth and human resources to complete the construction project. Work indeed had begun, but some in the crowd might have wondered when, and how, they would ever finish.

The problem of resource shortages was compounded by the hostility of the Samaritan people just to the north of Jerusalem. The animosity started in what appeared to be a gesture of generosity. The Samaritans wanted to join in the work of rebuilding the temple, claiming that they had been worshiping the Lord through all the years since the Assyrians had conquered the region. These Samaritans were descended not from

9. Bright, *History of Israel*, 365.

the people of the northern kingdom of Israel but from the peoples the Assyrians had relocated on that land. As such, their worship of God would have been corrupted by an amalgamation of beliefs and practices imported from pagan religions. The Jewish leadership recognized this and, determined to restore the undefiled worship of the Lord, refused the Samaritan offer. The Samaritans reacted by hatching a scheme to halt work on the temple altogether.

In what was nothing other than a boldfaced lie, they sent a letter to the Persian King Xerxes that caricatured Jerusalem and its residents as a pesthole of rebellion, advising him that the city and its temple should be left in ruins. In the absence of any counter-testimony, Xerxes could not be blamed for believing this false message. In the Persian Empire, the king's word was absolute. When Xerxes said the temple construction must stop, it was halted until he might say otherwise. Therefore, the temple in Jerusalem languished in ruins for almost another two decades.

Resuming Construction
Ezra 5–6

Political upheaval troubled the Persian Empire, occasioned by the ascendancy of Darius I in the years 522–20 BC. During this time, the prophets Haggai and Zechariah read this political turbulence as signs of God's restoration of Israel through the work of one they anticipated to be the Messiah. As a result, Zechariah delivered a hopeful message that served to accelerate work on the temple. The work was grounded in both religious devotion and political expectations, but these colored the construction project with more than a hint of subversion in Persian eyes. Matters were made even worse by the fact that the people resumed construction in disregard, if not defiance, of the order of the previous king, Xerxes. The situation in Jerusalem was dangerous, especially after Tattenai learned that the Jews had restarted work on the temple. Tattenai was probably a Persian who held the political appointment of governor or satrap of the province of Trans-Euphrates. (The Persian Empire was divided into administrative units, each called a satrapy.) The satrapy Tattenai governed bore its name because of the perspective of the Persian kings, who viewed their empire from Susa, the capital city far to the east. From that vantage point, Palestine and the surrounding region lay far to the west, "beyond the Euphrates River," such as Trans-Euphrates. Older commentaries portray Tattenai as hostile to the Jews and the temple project. In light of what we now know of Persian policies, that portrayal seems unfair. The Persian policy toward subject peoples typically encouraged and even supported the worship of the local god or gods. The Persians believed that people who were free to worship their deities were less likely to rebel. When Tattenai inquired into the unauthorized construction going on in Jerusalem, he was simply doing his job. People were working on a project that his records indicated had been halted by King Xerxes. Tattenai would have been within his authority to punish those who had ignored the order. He also could have halted work while awaiting a reply to his letter to the new king, Darius. That Tattenai allowed the work to continue suggests a neutral attitude toward the Jews on his part. Such an attitude would have been in keeping with policy and with the posture of an administrative bureaucrat whose job is to carry out the policies of his superiors.

Tattenai reported the matter without prejudice to Darius, who ordered a search of the imperial archives to find the original decree of Cyrus authorizing the restoration of both people and temple. A clear paper trail in the archives verified the accuracy of the Jewish version of the story. Not only did Darius reaffirm Cyrus's degree, he augmented it with financial assistance from the imperial treasury. Darius added one final stroke to his order, insisting that all be carried out "with diligence." The word of an oriental potentate was to be obeyed without fail. To add the phrase "with diligence" lent a sense of urgency to his order. Bureaucrat that he was, Tattenai knew the significance of the added phrase, and the temple work went forward with renewed energy as well as new resources.

Commentator Mark Throntveit notes that the book of Ezra has a different tone than both Haggai and Zechariah. Ezra makes no mention of any messianic significance to the events of the day and the temple project. The book does not share the prophets' messianism, nor is mention made of their rebukes to Jerusalem's leaders and people.

Ezra and His Mission

Ezra 6:14–22; 9:1–10:14

The book of Ezra takes its name from the man who, although Jewish, nevertheless rose to a high position in the Persian court. A modern version of his title might read like this: Minister of State for Jewish Affairs. It is very difficult to date accurately the years of his ministry in Jerusalem. He was a contemporary of Nehemiah, governor there, and likely arrived in the city about 428 BC. The two men complemented each other; Nehemiah was the builder who brought order and stability to the physical structure of the city, and Ezra reformed its ethical life and religion. Ezra was known as a scribe, the term not carrying then the negative associations that it has in the Gospels. It was important to a scribe to write down an accurate account and to record the details that explained how events came to take place. The book of Ezra contains many such details.

In the world of the Bible, such great events as the reconstruction of the temple did not simply happen. Ezra took some pains to explain how this wonderful event had come to pass. As we have seen, the story of the temple's rebuilding begins in the reign of the Persian king Cyrus, who freed the exiles in Babylon, allowed them to return to Jerusalem, and decreed that the temple was to be rebuilt. Ezra 6:3–5 reports Cyrus's decree. As is often true of bureaucracies, Cyrus's decree seems to have been filed in the royal archives without anyone taking action on it. A later Persian king, Darius, recovered Cyrus's original decree and issued a decree of his own implementing the one issued by Cyrus.

Some who read this story may wonder why Scripture describes the rebuilding of the temple as the work of earthly kings and humble people rather than the work of God. The people of Ezra's day were not troubled by such questions, for they believed that such kings as Cyrus and Darius were instrumental causes. To be sure, their decrees may have been the immediate cause that sent events into motion, but what power had moved these kings to decree that the temple should be rebuilt in the first place? There the Israelites saw the hand of God at work. In such a view, that the temple was in fact rebuilt was ultimately the work of Yahweh, who worked even through the decrees of nonbelievers to accomplish his purposes. Ezra carried a personal commission from Artaxerxes, the new king of the Persians, which specifically covered religious matters in Palestine. Ezra's assignment was to normalize Jewish religious practices, a task for which he was well-qualified. According to Ezra 7:6, he came from Babylon and was "a teacher well versed in the Law of Moses, which the LORD, the God of Israel, had given." We will do well to ask why Ezra's assignment was necessary.

The warrior-kings of ancient empires often deliberately uprooted large segments of the populations of conquered nations. The Assyrians were masters of this practice and so were the Babylonians, although not to the same degree. Resettlement was used to reduce the possibility of revolt in the conquered nation. Once the land was nearly emptied of its original population and its leaders deported, the remaining society was likely to disintegrate. Customs, social mores, and religious sanctions would be forgotten. Rival peoples would eventually settle the land as squatters. Given enough time, some of these newcomers would intermarry with remainders of the original population, creating a mixed race. (The Samaritans of the New Testament came into being in this fashion.) Naturally, the religions of these mongrel peoples combined beliefs and practices from the various groups that had mingled their bloodlines in intermarriage. Such a process corrupted the religion of the original population. The result of this policy was a demoralized population that retained little or no memory of the past, its religious convictions, its customs, or the stories that sustained them. In this sense, to be demoralized is to be shorn of the elements that comprise a moral system.

Moral philosopher Alasdair MacIntyre has said that we can answer the question, What am I to do? only after first answering the question, Of what stories am I a part? The Jews of Ezra's day could not answer these questions because they no longer knew the Torah. As we have noted previously, *torah* is better translated as "teaching" or "instruction." Torah is Yahweh's instruction for Israel in the all-important matter of walking with the Lord. This is clearly more than a law code; it is the story of God, beginning at creation and continuing down to Israel's entry into Canaan. Ezra returned to Israel to find that his people had forgotten basic instruction in what it means to be the people of God and to walk with Yahweh. Without this instruction, they did not and could not know who they were or how they were to live. Through his role as the teacher of Torah to Jerusalem, Ezra helped the Jews recover their identity and, with that, their moral bearings.

One of the important consequences of Ezra's mission was the Israelites' sense that they were different from the peoples surrounding them. The religious practices of Israel's neighbors differed markedly from those spelled out in the Torah. Some of Israel's neighbors practiced child sacrifice, and many used forms of sacred prostitution; all worshiped idols. Ezra determined that Israel's only option, if they were to continue as a people, was to follow a policy of separation from all non-Jews. In his eyes, therefore, resolving the issue of racial/ethnic intermarriage quickly became critical to Israel's integrity as a separate and holy nation. This problem comes into sharp focus in Ezra 10.

Ezra's policy of forbidding intermarriage may seem harsh, especially in the eyes of modern people accustomed to the belief that they may marry anyone they choose. Ezra believed that Israel's future depended on the existence of people who were willing and able to live according to the Torah; only those with an undivided religious loyalty could walk in the way of the Lord. Since intermarriage threatened to divide Jewish religious loyalties, Ezra forbade it. In such policies as this, the religious and ethnic purity of Israel shared a common perspective and goal.

Nehemiah

Cupbearer to the King
Nehemiah 1–2

Two men dominated postexilic events in Jerusalem and its surrounding region—Ezra the scribe and Nehemiah, governor of the province of Judah within the Persian Empire. Nehemiah was an exiled Jew who had risen to prominence in the Persian court. He held the position of cupbearer to the king. The post was as dangerous as it was important. Assassination and palace intrigue were staples of Persian court life. King Artaxerxes I, whom Nehemiah served, had succeeded to the throne after his father's murder. Artaxerxes' grandfather was Darius I, who himself had gained the throne by engineering an uprising. The intrigue surrounding these despots required extraordinary measures to safeguard themselves and their families. The royal cupbearer tasted the king's wine before serving it and by this act determined whether the wine had been poisoned. Every day brought the cupbearer another risky drink.

The first seven chapters of Nehemiah are written as a memoir, a record of Nehemiah's activity in Jerusalem. This section reports his status as the king's cupbearer. But there is more to the story. One consequence of this custom was that cupbearers often enjoyed their king's confidence as trusted and loyal subjects. This would be likely, since the cupbearer risked his life daily in the king's service. Nehemiah seemed to enjoy such a relationship with Artaxerxes, who inquired one day why his cupbearer seemed so downcast. The source of Nehemiah's sadness was a report that Jerusalem's walls lay in ruins and that the city gates had been burned. That he was saddened by this report suggests that it was recent news—and this is something of a problem to our interpretation of the text. We might have thought that the walls had been destroyed during the Babylonian army's attack on the city. Nebuchadnezzar, however, had invaded Jerusalem more than fifty years prior to Nehemiah's sadness. Any destruction by the Babylonians could scarcely have been news to him. Nor would it explain why Nehemiah was afraid to mention the destruction to Artaxerxes. It seems more likely that Nehemiah had heard of a more recent destruction as the result of an attack that had occurred during Artaxerxes' reign. To bring such a matter to the king's attention would imply that he was a poor administrator, one who either didn't know or didn't care what was going on in a province of his own kingdom. Moreover, Artaxerxes had a reputation for sharp mood swings and a tendency to reverse his own decrees and policies; he might say one thing today and the opposite tomorrow. Quite naturally, then, Nehemiah would be apprehensive in reporting what he had heard about Jerusalem to a man who held absolute power of life and death over every subject in his kingdom, including his cupbearer.

Artaxerxes responded positively to Nehemiah's report and offered royal support for the proposed reconstruction of Jerusalem's walls, which meant that Nehemiah would have a military escort, royal letters of safe conduct, and authority to cut timber from the king's forest to be used for the city's gates. Although Artaxerxes gave his full backing to the project, Nehemiah did not believe that this support was merely happenstance. Thus he said, "And because the gracious hand of my God was upon me, the king granted my requests" (2:8). Once again we see that from the Bible's point of view events do not merely happen: Yahweh is in them and behind them. Since that is so, events disclose God and the divine purpose even as they define the difference between good and evil.

The larger context of the Nehemiah narrative helps us locate this moment in Western history. Artaxerxes reigned from 465 to 424 BC, and Nehemiah received his royal commission in 445. This means that his public career coincided with some of the great names of Greek history. Socrates was just beginning his career as a philosopher in Athens, the great city of Greece where such people as the playwrights Sophocles and Aeschylus were writing and where the great statesman Pericles oversaw the Athenian democracy. A Greek coalition had defeated huge Persian forces at the battles of Salamis and Plataea and established Greek authority around the rim of the Aegean Sea.

Judah's history in this same moment was not nearly so glorious. Political insecurity dominated Judah's affairs. After Zerubbabel, the territory was governed by Samaritan administrators. These administrators appear to have allowed their agents to lay a heavy tax burden on Judah as well as behave insolently toward its residents. Sanballat, Tobiah, and Geshem displayed an utter disregard for the traditions and well-being of the residents of Jerusalem. Their intolerable disdain reflected the poor state of Judah's life. Some towns were beginning to repopulate, but Jerusalem's population remained small. Ezra 4 recalls the false report sent to King Xerxes I some forty years earlier, a fabrication intended to get the Jews in trouble with the imperial government. In their hour of need, the Jews of Jerusalem turned to a kinsman who had access to power unmatched by anyone in Judah or Samaria.

Nehemiah went to Jerusalem armed with an imperial commission to rebuild the walls of the city. He also carried authority to requisition building materials from royal sources. Whether he also had been named governor of the new province of Judah is not clear, but he did come to hold that office. The fact that Judah slipped from their control could not have pleased the Samaritans.

The unfolding story will give us a picture of their attitude, but first it is important to understand the nature of Nehemiah's assignment. Nehemiah's name is most readily associated with the huge project of rebuilding the walls of Jerusalem. To be sure, his most pressing task was to provide a measure of security for the city, a political and military task, but he also deserves credit for working to restore Jewish political and religious institutions. Without those, the rebuilt walls would have encircled a hollow center.

Nehemiah under Trial

Nehemiah 6

Only after secretly inspecting the disrepair in the walls of Jerusalem did Nehemiah inform the people of his mission and set about organizing them for the work. It was for the protection and reinvigoration of Jerusalem itself that the walls were to be rebuilt, but recruits for the labor were levied from all across Judah. Since the city was not only the religious citadel of Judaism but also the political center of the province, all citizens had a stake in her revitalization and defense. Work proceeded rapidly, and in fifty-two days the walls had been rebuilt. Somewhat to the contrary, the Jewish historian Josephus reported that it took more than two years to complete the project. It may be fair to say that under Nehemiah the people closed in the walls and brought the work to a reasonable state of completion. However, the accomplishment to which Josephus referred must have included reinforcing the wall as well as finishing battlements and gate defenses.[9]

By any measure, Nehemiah and the workers accomplished a Herculean task in a very brief period. Skilled laborers were few, and the workers harassed by powerful enemies. Nehemiah may have had the full backing of Artaxerxes, but the king resided in an imperial capital hundreds of miles to the east. Much nearer, and for that reason more dangerous, were Sanballat, Tobiah, and Geshem. Sanballat and Tobiah in all likelihood worshiped Yahweh. They gave their children Jewish names, seem to have regarded themselves as Israelites, and were accepted as such by some of the leading families of Jerusalem.[10] It is also likely, however, that their worship of the Lord was corrupted by elements of Canaanite religion. On the other hand, Nehemiah's religion, formed and practiced in the decidedly minority community of exiled Jews in Babylon and Persia, was utterly free of any blending tendencies. He and the returned exiles were quite unreceptive—indeed, intolerant—of "Israelites" such as Sanballat and Tobiah. As far as Nehemiah was concerned, they were little more than pagans. Sanballat and Tobiah thus stood to lose on two scores. The new leaders of the community of Israel rejected them, and their political control of the region would be diminished by a revitalized Judah governed by Nehemiah. Accompanied by a third mischief-maker, Geshem the Arab, these men determined to disrupt Nehemiah's work.

They hatched three different schemes to intimidate him and the people of Jerusalem. The first scheme attacked the relationship between Nehemiah and Artaxerxes. Sanballat declared his intention to send a letter to the king that would accuse Nehemiah of treason. This letter was a reverse image of the one that Artaxerxes gave Nehemiah, authorizing his mission. Nehemiah was too secure in his relationship with the king to be cowed by threats of character assassination. He dared Sanballat to follow through with his threat. When their first scheme failed, the

10. Bright, *History of Israel*, 381.

11. Ibid., 382.

conspirators attempted to undermine the relationship between Nehemiah and God. Sanballat and Tobiah secured the services of one of their Jerusalem sympathizers, Shemaiah, to play the role of a prophet and lure Nehemiah into the temple, onto ground where a layperson had no right to be. The third scheme, an effort to separate Nehemiah from his popular support in Jerusalem, is not so clearly detailed as the first two. But it remains clear enough that the conspirators wanted to exploit the strained relationship between the Jerusalem nobility who had befriended them and Nehemiah. All three of the schemes aimed to discredit the governor, but all three failed. That they failed is a testimony to the resolute courage, loyalty, and faith of Nehemiah.

Balance for Moral Life

Nehemiah 8–9

The restored temple and walls of Jerusalem symbolized two important aspects of the life of the postexilic Jewish community in Judah. Once the walls were rebuilt, the people of Jerusalem enjoyed a measure of security. The newly completed temple gave the Jews a religious center. Some measure of pre-exilic life had thus been restored to Jerusalem.

At the same time, conditions had changed and never would be the same.

Israel, now sharply reduced in number, could not look to a nation-state for their identity and their unity as the people of God. God had promised Abraham a land. Israel had returned to the land, but it was no longer the country ruled by David and his successors. Ezra's great achievement was that he gave Israel a new center around which to build and understand themselves as God's people. As Ezra stood in the open square and read daily from daybreak to midday, the Law began to replace the land as the center of Jewish culture. Once they had heard and understood the Law, Jewish people could live as the people of God, regardless of their circumstances. Gathered about Torah, Israel could live out its divine calling without political autonomy. Ezra became known as the "Lawgiver" because he gave Israel the means to live faithfully, even though they were politically subject to the Persian kings.

Ezra and the Levites who assisted him in reading and interpreting the Law were beginning at square one. They were laying the foundations for the life and culture of the postexilic community just as surely as others had laid the foundations of the temple and Nehemiah had rebuilt the walls. For one thing, many of the people of Jerusalem had become so accustomed to speaking Aramaic, the language of their captors, that they had lost some level of ability to understand Hebrew, the language in which Torah was written. (The *New International Version* obscures this point by translating Nehemiah 8:8 in a way that suggests that the Levites explained the Law's meaning rather than interpreted its language.) It is likely that Ezra had brought a copy of Torah with him from Babylon. If the Jews in Jerusalem had no copy in their possession, then both the language and religious life had sunk to a low ebb. That the people wrung their hands and wept at the reading of the Law may be taken as a sign of their dismay at how badly things had gone wrong.

Without tradition, says Tevye, the milkman in the Broadway musical *Fiddler on the Roof*, life is precarious, as precarious indeed as a fiddler on the roof. As the tradition of Israel, Torah in postexilic Jewish life became the religious and cultural center of gravity for a community that believed that it was the remnant of the people of God. The Law—which we should understand as encompassing far more than a narrow set of religious functions—kept Israel on balance and enabled it to live in its strange, new postexilic world.

Roughly one hundred years passed before the missions of Ezra and Nehemiah restored the political and spiritual foundations of Jewish life. The narrative that recounts their accomplishments is a piece of salvation history. The whole of that history is the narrative of Yahweh's dealings with Israel—its calling, liberation, falling and restoration, destruction and renewal. Small wonder that the people of Israel were exhorted to teach it to their children and learned to recite it as a part of worship. In fact, Nehemiah 9:4–36 gives us a wonderful example of the recitation of Israel's salvation history as an act of worship. Before the assembled congregation the Levites—Israel's worship leaders—told again the story of Israel's life as the people of God. Through this narrative and no other, Israel must interpret its situation as a chastened people returned from exile. The people located themselves within this narrative and, once located, they could interpret their situation and understand it as an occasion for repentance and renewal.

By their separate but related actions, Nehemiah and Ezra stood at the very center of the renewal of Israel. Nehemiah had returned to Jerusalem to rebuild a city destroyed by the Babylonians and suffering through a long-term state of disrepair and discouragement. Ezra's mission was to rebuild Jerusalem's moral and spiritual inheritance. Whether carried into exile or left to suffer poverty and raids, the people of God were demoralized. The Jews needed more than to have their spirits lifted by some sort of religious cheerleader. Rather, decades of exile and victimization had badly eroded the moral and spiritual foundations of the nation. In the middle of the fifth century BC, those foundations required rebuilding just as much as the walls of Jerusalem.

More accustomed to reading the New Testament than the Old, Christians might wonder that a scribe played such a positive role in Israel's postexilic renewal. After all, some of Jesus' worst enemies can be found among the critics that the New Testament labels the "scribes and the Pharisees." Not all scribes were alike any more than all Pharisees opposed Jesus; one thinks of Nicodemus and Joseph of Arimathea. Ezra was a scribe devoted to the study of Torah, and Torah—instruction for walking in the way of Yahweh—was precisely what Israel needed. Without the great moral and spiritual moorings of their traditions, especially the great narrative of salvation history as recited by the Levites in worship, the Israelites could not locate themselves within Yahweh's larger purpose. Without this, Israel could not answer the question, What kind of people is Yahweh calling us to be? Day after day, Ezra stood surrounded by representatives of the tribes of Israel and read Torah into the living consciousness of the people. This act restored to them a lamp for their feet and a light for their path, making possible their renewal as the people of Yahweh.

Memory and Identity

Nehemiah 10:28–39

Ezra read out the Torah to the people of Jerusalem for the entire seventh month of the year. This month is the time prescribed to celebrate the Feast of Tabernacles or Feast of Booths. This religious festival commemorated the journey from Egypt to Canaan. Since the Israelites lived outdoors all during those years, the festival required people to work and sleep in temporary shelters in emulation of their ancestors. Apparently, the Jewish calendar had fallen into disuse by Ezra's day. Their descendants had forgotten about this celebration along with much of the rest of the Law. But they demonstrated a newfound resolve to keep the Law by immediately restoring the festival.

Not all the manners and customs of the Torah community were recovered as easily as the Feast of Tabernacles. One of the most difficult issues concerned racial intermarriage, and this problem pointed to a likely difference in religious attitude between the returning exiles and the resident Jews. Those exilic Jews were thrust into religious and cultural deprivation as severe as the economic straits to which they were condemned. The religious and political leadership had all been sent into exile. Many of the remainder left Jerusalem to settle in the elephantine colony of Jews in Egypt. It is likely that the prophet Jeremiah ended his days in this colony. The remaining people in and around Jerusalem lacked leaders and resources to practice their faith in the manner of their forefathers and foremothers. One indication that no leaders remained in Jerusalem is that, when the time came for restoration after exile, the new leaders—Ezra and Nehemiah—both came from elsewhere.

Without leaders and loosened from their moorings, the nonexiles drifted away from strict observance of the Law. However, while the Torah lost some of its importance at Jerusalem during the period of the exile, among the exiled Jews its significance greatly increased. In exile, the Jews kept the law faithfully because it was how they could maintain their identity as the people of God. Moreover, their very circumstances had the effect of isolating the bulk of the exiles into their own communities. Both circumstance and a policy of limited contact with the Babylonians—they were Gentiles, after all—combined to create a way of life among the exiled Jews that maintained a strict separation.

It is quite likely that intermarriage was a source of friction between the returning exiles and the residents of Jerusalem. It is tempting to reduce this problem to one where Ezra's objections to intermarriage were that he objected to Jews marrying outside the faith of Israel. But that is to read this situation in modern terms rather than those that existed in Ezra's day. Then, religion and ethnicity were not as easily divided as they are in modern societies. In Israel, religious practice reinforced ethnic identity and vice versa. Ezra's policy did not meet with instant approval, although in the end it was accepted.

These verses and the preceding chapters illustrate the importance of the Law for the covenant community of Israel. The renewal ceremony could not take place until the community had been ritually and practically cleansed according to the high standards of the returned exiles. Another crucial element in Israel's renewal was a lengthy recitation of the narrative of its life with the Lord, reaching all the way to Abraham. Before the people could renew their covenant relationship with God, Israel needed to know once again whose people they were. That identity rests on a foundation called memory. For a community that lives by remembering, the process of identity formation depends on the faithful narrative recitation of its past.

Esther

Beyond Israel's Borders

Esther 3:2–3, 5–6a; 4:7–16

The book of Esther is unique among all sixty-six books of the Bible because the name of God is not found in its pages. We can ask, therefore, why this book is included in the canonical Scriptures. Viewed from a modern perspective, the book seems quite secular—a story of Jewish heroism in the face of enemies willing to commit genocide against Israel. Perhaps we need to remember that, like the stories of Joseph in Egypt, of Moses, and of Daniel, the book of Esther narrates an episode where Israel is delivered from danger. That God is not mentioned in Esther does not mean that the Lord was not at work directing what modern eyes see as purely secular events. The Jews of the late Old Testament period could easily assume that if Israel was involved in the story, then so was the Lord—whether or not mentioned by name. On these terms, because Esther, like other Old Testament books, tells an extraordinary story of Israelite deliverance, it was judged to deserve a place in the canonical Scriptures.

Another aspect of this book worth mentioning is its complete lack of interest in the land of Israel. Commentator Jon Levenson contrasts this curious attitude to that of another Old Testament book that deals with Israel's connections to Persia: Nehemiah.[11] In that account, Jews living in the Persian Empire were downcast because they were far from Israel and Jerusalem lay in ruins. Mordecai and Esther seem to have been unconcerned about the status of the land of Israel; Persia was their home. They were full-fledged Jews of the Diaspora.

Levenson's observation suggests ideas about the book's origins and date of authorship. Esther was obviously written after the destruction of Jerusalem and the exile in 587 BC. The Persians, who decreed that the exiled Israelites could return home, in turn swallowed up the Babylonian Empire. Many Israelites did, but some preferred to remain in Persia. Remember that Israel had been in exile for fifty years, long enough for a generation to have grown well into maturity without ever having set foot in Jerusalem. For those Jews who had lived their entire lives in exile, the cities of the Babylonian and Persian empires were the only homes they had ever known. The text of the book does not refer to its author, but given the location of the events that it recounts, many scholars believe that it was written by a Jew living in Persia sometime during the fourth or third century before Christ.

If these theories about its date and location are accurate, then Esther is distinctive among the books of the Old Testament in another respect: It was written outside the borders of Israel. Some of the book's themes correspond to the theory that it was written in Persia. Postexilic Jews who did not return to their ancestral homeland faced the problem of life as

12. Levenson, *Esther*, 14.

a minority community. The tribal organization of the ancient Middle Eastern world ensured a precarious existence for any ethnic minority, especially one as stiff-necked as Israel. Moreover, the real trouble in the book of Esther begins when Mordecai refuses to bend his knee to the Persian official Haman. It is a scene reminiscent of the book of Daniel, where Jews are in trouble because they would bow down only to God. Esther does not explicitly state this religious scruple as the motive behind Mordecai's refusal, but it is a reasonable inference. It took courage for Mordecai to defy the arrogant bureaucrat Haman, just as it took great courage for Esther to enter the king's presence unbidden. In her world, men ordered women, especially when the man was an oriental despot. Esther's action was extraordinarily courageous, but then courage is always demanded of the people of God who are a minority in a dominant culture that knows not the Lord.

Comedy and Drama

Esther 8:3–8; 9:18–23

Like the description of some contemporary movies, the book of Esther could be labeled a dramatic comedy. For those familiar with the story, there appears to be very little humor in the Jews' desperate situation. A Persian official close to the king maneuvers affairs into a situation that threatens the lives of all Jewish residents under Persian rule. What comedy could there be in genocide? Yet the story begins with King Xerxes looking rather foolish. In the opening chapter, he appears to have had too much to drink when he ordered Queen Vashti to appear. Xerxes had thrown a sumptuous feast, and the men had been eating and drinking in the king's palace. The wealth, elegance, and furnishings of his house duly impressed Xerxes' guests.

In his drunken state, he foolishly summoned the most beautiful of all his possessions—Queen Vashti—that his guests would be even more envious of him. But the queen refused to answer this royal summons. Those of us who live in the Western democracies scarcely can imagine the insulting nature of Vashti's refusal. Vashti's refusal said, in effect, "Xerxes may be king of Persia, but he is not the master of his own house." A man who couldn't control his women was a laughingstock in that world. Although the story of Esther quickly shifts to Haman's deadly plotting, the book opens with a narrative joke about the man and the court who ruled the lives of the Jewish exiles in Persia. They must have told the opening sections of this story with a bit of a twinkle in their eyes because it made their Persian hosts appear inept and incapable of governing their own households.

Just over the horizon from the humorous opening of the book of Esther hung the ominous cloud of genocide. Haman turned his personal grudge against Esther's uncle, Mordecai, into a pretext for the slaughter of all Jews living within the Persian Empire. The narrative holds a dramatic reversal, however; for the tables were swiftly turned, and Haman found himself receiving all of the murderous treatment that he had planned for Mordecai. In these reversals, there is to be found a dark but clearly identifiable humor. The person who accomplished this reversal was the beautiful Queen Esther. Her identity as a daughter of Israel had been hidden from everybody in the royal household, and this is crucial to the plot, for no Jew save Esther could gain access to the king. Haman had played false with Xerxes: without referring to them by name, he told the king of a people whose stiff-necked customs warranted their destruction. Xerxes agrees to Haman's proposal without getting all the facts. Power without intelligence or understanding makes buffoons of those who wield it, no matter how deadly their buffoonery may prove to be. Only Esther could save the day by appealing to her husband for her life and the lives of her people.

Haman's overinflated ego and hatred of Mordecai and the Jews made him vulnerable. Twice in quick succession the tables were turned on him. These sudden reversals occurred just before Xerxes' summary judgment in favor of Esther's request. In the first, Haman unwittingly created the occasion whereby his enemy Mordecai was to be honored, and Haman had to oversee the awards. And the second, of course, was when Esther revealed her identity as a Jew and therefore was the target of Haman's purge. It was a cruel joke, to be sure. Haman, the crafty plotter against Israel, not only saw his murderous plans come to naught, but ultimately he also found himself the victim of his own evil designs. In the end, the joke was on Haman. Foiled by a beautiful woman, he forfeited property and life.

Job

A Challenge to Prosperity Theology
Job 1:1–3:3

Job is collected in the division of the Hebrew Bible called the *ketubim* or "writings," often referred to as Wisdom Literature. Old Testament scholar Walter Brueggemann says that the Wisdom writings offered Israel teachings in perspective for living. In other words, the older generation, in its life experiences with Yahweh in Yahweh's world, were teaching the younger generations a perspective tested over time. The elders' determination was to develop certain moral skills in the younger generation: (1) to appreciate that various aspects of life are interrelated and hang together (for example, what we do brings consequences and affects other people), (2) to acknowledge a mystery in the interrelatedness of life (we cannot control life or manage God), (3) to see our claims to knowledge as they really are and admit our limitations in knowledge (get rid of our idols), and (4) to arrive at the place where we trustfully submit and yield to God (life must be lived in faithful obedience to God). One side of the Wisdom Literature breathes the confident assurance that those who heed the way of wisdom will lead happier lives of blessedness. The other side is acutely aware of dissonance and contradiction in the world and its relationship with Yahweh. Sometimes the wicked prosper, and not all children trained in the way of the Lord follow that way when adults. The experience of contradiction makes this side of Wisdom Literature far less confident in set formulas for successful living. The book of Job stands in this latter tradition.

It was the common opinion of ancient Israelites, and, indeed, much of the cultural world surrounding them, that prosperity was a sign of divine favor. By the same token, calamities and suffering were believed to be punishment for sin. We find this idea prominent in the book of Deuteronomy, and for this reason, Old Testament scholars refer to the idea as the Deuteronomistic theology. In simplest terms, this theology states that God blesses the faithful and punishes the wicked; whether people are prospering or suffering, their condition is the divinely appointed consequence of their moral action and religious attitudes.

This theology has underwritten the assumptions of many Christians. For example, in the wake of a string of disasters that befell the Massachusetts Bay Colony in the 1670s, the Puritan ministers gathered to consider the reasons why God might have afflicted them. They concluded that, in their words, "God hath a controversy with New England." There was sin in the camp, and the colonists' problems were the direct result of that sin. If people would repent and mend their ways, then peace and prosperity would return to the colony. The book of Job considers such ideas as it critically examines the Deuteronomistic theology that underwrites them.

There is more than one perspective on life and blessedness to be found in the Wisdom Literature. Both Ecclesiastes and Job question the Deuteronomistic perspective, although in very different tones. Job is a masterful reflection on the problem of suffering and how it can be interpreted. We do not know the identity of its author, but clearly this was a theological thinker of unusual insight. The book's theological reflections on the problem of suffering take the form of a narrative about a man whose origins are obscure. His home, the land of Uz, is somewhat mysterious and not of recent knowledge. Job's story opens with a sense of "Once upon a time," not unlike the opening of Jesus' parable of the prodigal son. It is as if we are watching a universal drama unfold before our eyes. The problem of suffering is surely not unique to Job; in this he is every man and woman, boy and girl, but the book's theologian-writer took pains to make Job's situation specific and extreme.

Job was blameless and upright. In other words, according to the common theology, why should he suffer? But Job did suffer—and terribly. If *he* could fall prey to pain and calamity, then it can happen to anybody. In this way, the book's reflections on suffering are not only about Job's problems but also about those of anyone who suffers. There is a scholarly consensus that the book was written in the period of Israel's exile in Babylon. This consensus rests on the view that, in the midst of great tribulation, Israel reflected on the story of Job as a way of rethinking one of their standard theological assumptions. Israel's recent experience of suffering had brought revelation and new theological insight.

The problem of the suffering of righteous people is not the only question asked by Job. Another, perhaps deeper question is, Why do the righteous serve God? The question posed by Satan to God in chapter 1 is crucial to the theological discussions that make up nearly the entire book of Job. Having been asked by God about his faithful and obedient servant Job, Satan replied, "Does Job fear God for nothing?" This question puts the Deuteronomistic theology squarely at the heart of the discussions that will follow in the book. Satan believed that Job served God out of self-interest. If the Deuteronomistic theology is correct, then it is prudent to serve God; good things come to those who do. Did Job fear God because it was right to do so or because it earned him God's blessings? The Lord allowed evil to befall Job as a test of Job's motives. In so many words, God said to Satan, "Take away all the wealth, all the signs of my favor, and you will see that Job is serious about his faith; he serves me because it is right to do so and not for what he gets out of it."

(A word must be added here about the rather curious role played by Satan in the early chapters of Job. We have used *Satan* as a proper name for the Devil for so long that we scarcely think of the term in any other way. The name *Satan* actually is a transliteration of the Greek word *satanos*, which means "the adversary." In Job, the term does not necessarily refer to the Devil, for "adversary" clearly enjoys permission to enter the heavenly council where other angels also talk with Yahweh about the created world and human affairs. This council is the setting envisioned by the opening verses of Job. The adversary angel traveled about the earth observing all sorts of events and people. After his return to Yahweh's council, God asked this angel where he had been and thus began their conversation about Job.)

Many of us have heard or perhaps used the phrase *the patience of Job*. While meant as a term of respect, that phrase may lead us to misread the themes of this book. Hardly a patient man, Job insisted on asking questions—lots of them. This book is no pious meditation on patience in the face of adversity. Instead, we must read it as a deep theological consideration of fundamental questions concerning faith.

Job, of course, was completely unaware of the conversation that had taken place, and soon his suffering is well under way. Stripped of property and family, in chapter 2 he is physically afflicted. As the saying goes, when you have your health, you have everything. Shorn even of his health, Job now has nothing. Yet he refuses to complain. So far, he is the very model of steadfast faithfulness: "The LORD gives and the LORD takes away; blessed be the name of the LORD." As the text says, "In all this, Job did not sin in what he said" (2:10).

Comfort and a Demand
Job 2:11–23:12

Job's three friends—Eliphaz, Bildad, and Zophar—have come in for more than their fair share of criticism. Some of this harsh judgment is justified in that their persistent defense of conventional wisdom and piety led them to run roughshod over their suffering friend. Moreover, it does appear that their zeal for theological precision and insistence that Job agree with them blinded them to his need for compassion and consolation. Their friend was suffering terribly, and all they could do was argue theology—or so it seems. Before we dismiss them entirely, let's admit that these three friends possessed one or two admirable characteristics.

In the first place, the three men journeyed to Job's home for honorable motives. They came to comfort Job and sympathize with him. Since their last meeting, his appearance had changed dramatically. They found him in the posture of ritual mourning, sitting in dust and ashes, and spreading them on his head. Despite their shock and dismay, they did not run from his presence. Neither did they burst into noisy conversation to cover their awkward embarrassment. Instead they began to weep and wail. They tore their clothes and poured ashes and dust on their own heads, a sign that they had ritually joined their friend in his suffering. The three men sat quietly in this posture for a week until finally their friend spoke.

Job's first words shattered the silence *and* the conventional piety of his friends. He cursed the day of his birth, saying that it would have been better had he never been born. In Job's eyes, the birth of a child, any child, no longer brought joy. Life had become a bitter trial from which Job longed for release. It would have been better had he been stillborn. This attitude both surprised and challenged his friends and their theology. Each is a representative of that theological tradition. It had taught them that Job's condition must have some cause and that cause was sin in him. Within their theological frame of reference, this is the only possible cause. They concluded that the Lord had punished Job, and in their determined piety, they encouraged their friend to confess his sin. Their theology taught people that life was to be treasured as a gift from God. Anyone who cursed his or her birthday with the same breath insulted Yahweh, who gave life to all. In Deuteronomistic confidence, they promised that God would stay his wrath if only Job would repent.

This section contains a series of elaborate discussions between Job and his friends. Bildad made a speech in reply to Job's despair at his wretched condition and eloquently summarized conventional Israelite theological wisdom on this subject (8:1–6ff). He contended that God is just and that calamity such as Job suffered was only the just reward for sin. Sin always has its consequences, and where we see disaster, we may be sure that it is God's punishment. He did not moralize. Instead, he offered Job a way out of his situation (8:5–6). Bildad's analysis and solution were known to all pious Israelites: God blesses the righteous and punishes the wicked. Those who suffer need only repent and all will be well.

Job's point was that this conventional theology did not speak to his situation. The problem was that Job knew that he had not sinned and had nothing to confess. Job was not a dualist; he did not believe that God was the source of blessing and Satan the source of evil. Trouble as well as good comes from the hand of God (2:10). Job knew nothing of the agreement between the Lord and Satan; so as far as Job was concerned, God was the source of his misery. The problem was that Job could not figure out its cause or purpose. Early in his discussions with his friends, Job was as much a Deuteronomistic theologian as they; that is why his suffering was such a problem to him. He too believed that the righteous prospered and the wicked suffered. What troubled him was that he knew that he was not one of the wicked.

Bildad and his two associates came to Job sympathetically and with good motives. Unfortunately, their consolation rang hollow because they did not fit Job's experience. Job perceived that they were talking past one another, and the realization that he had not been heard drove him deeper into despair. There was only one with whom Job now wished to speak. Job dared to ask to argue his case before Yahweh, the judge of all the earth.

Faithful reading of this material must take care not to transpose the Pauline verse that all have sinned and fall short of God's glory back into the setting of Job. Much as we might be tempted to make it so, the issue in Job is not a discussion of original sin. The text itself refuses us that option when it tells us that Job was blameless and upright. We must keep to that point because it allows a new theological awareness to dawn in Job's consciousness.

It was his knowledge that he was without sin in this matter that enabled Job to question the Deuteronomistic theology of his friends, a theology that he once held but now began to leave behind. The knowledge that he had not sinned allowed Job to make what seems to be a terribly audacious proposal: Job wanted to put God on the witness stand in order to interrogate him. Job thought that he had a case against God. Just as God allowed the question of whether Job was serious about his obedience, so also Job had questions: Is God reliable? Why did God allow this to happen to me? These questions cross the mind of every innocent sufferer. Such questions drive the requests in 13:20–24; Job knew that he had not sinned and, therefore, he was willing to enter into debate with the Lord over the reasons for God's actions against him.

Composer George Frederick Handel has taught us to read Job 19:25 and following as a reference to Christ. Christians certainly want to interpret this passage as such, but is it? The literary shape of this passage is not prophecy, and it is asking too much of the Old Testament figure Job to think that he believed in the Christian Trinity. It is enough to say that Job believes that the Lord would ultimately vindicate him. The Lord knew the truth, and he would not allow Job to suffer in confusion forever. Job might earlier have had his suspicions about God and his trustworthiness, but in 19:20ff he returned to bedrock faith. The Lord is just. Despite appearances to the contrary, finally Job could rely on the justice of God. Scholars are divided over whether this text anticipates the doctrine of the resurrection. Some say no, but others conclude that 19:20ff is an Old Testament affirmation of the belief that Job would one day see his vindicator face-to-face.

Theological Revision

Job 27:2–5; 31:5–8, 13–15, 24–25, 28

The focus in these verses is on that moment in Job's life when he realizes he is utterly alone. His wife and friends had turned against him. His three friends are offended by his claims of moral uprightness, and their theological discussion had soured into denunciations of Job and his claim. As for his wife, much earlier in the story, she could offer only the cold counsel of despair when she advised her husband to curse God and die. Job had also waited for an answer from God, but so far the Lord had been silent. With support from neither family nor friends, bereft of human fellowship in his hour of need, listening vainly for the voice of God, Job stood alone. What would he say? What would he do? Where would he turn?

The biblical material takes the form of an oath. In his isolation, Job had nowhere to turn but to make the most solemn declarations of his integrity. The opening verses of chapter 27 declare Job's formal promise that he would never lie or speak any kind of falsehood. This is followed by his stubborn refusal to concede even the first point of Bildad's position in chapter 25. Job refused to yield his integrity.

Chapter 31 is an elaborate oath wherein Job opened every aspect of his life to public scrutiny and divine examination. Job declared his life to be an open book. Examine any and all of his public dealings—business affairs, relationships with his neighbors, charitable contributions to the poor, and so forth—and, said Job, you will find only righteous action. But Job's claim to righteousness was not limited to outward actions. He also invited people to examine his heart. Inquirers would find no unwholesome thought or attitude. He had not secretly lusted after a beautiful young girl or trusted in his great wealth; neither had he ever inwardly rejoiced at an adversary's misfortune or calculated his actions according to public opinion. In no aspect of his life had Job failed to live uprightly. To seal his declaration of righteousness, he repeatedly invited curses upon himself if anything he had said should be proven untrue.

Commentator Gerald Janzen points to developments in Job's character between the opening of the narrative and the oaths of chapter 31. Through his suffering, Job had changed. He could no longer rely on the Deuteronomistic theology, and he would no longer make foolish statements that denied God's gift of life. He had lived with God all through the years, and even in the face of divine silence, Job would in full integrity solemnly bind himself to God.

Out of the Whirlwind

Job 38:1–42:6

After a long series of debates between Job and his three friends, the Lord speaks, but not before a long discourse from a young man named Elihu who suddenly appeared without introduction in chapter 32. Elihu sided with the three friends, but the young man claimed a different authority for his speech. Until chapter 32, the discussion had been framed largely on the basis of human experience. Elihu, on the other hand, claimed divine inspiration for his discourse; he claimed to be a prophet. However, in Israel's experience there were false prophets as well as those who authentically spoke the word of the Lord. There is no transition from Elihu's "inspired" discourse to the beginning of the Lord's speech out of the whirlwind. It is as if Job was forced to choose between the two; he must decide which word was authentic and therefore the word that he would heed.

Out of the whirlwind, the Lord God spoke. The One who had been questioned now would question. All through the preceding debates and discourses, Job had consistently demanded his day in court. In those debates, he had been arguing against his friends; now Job turns to Yahweh. His righteousness was unfeigned and, in his eyes, unassailable. Job believed that this warranted a divine answer to the injustice of his suffering. In terms of the conventional theological wisdom on which the discussions had relied, Job deserved none of the misery that had befallen him. His demand that the Lord be called as witness was also a question about God's justice. In Job's view, if God blessed the righteous and punished the wicked, then, because Job was indeed righteous, his suffering called God's justice into question. Recall that the idea that the book of Job puts forward at least two major questions: (1) Why do the righteous suffer? and (2) Why are the righteous pious? At the beginning, Yahweh pointed to Job with pride, believing that Job worshiped God for no ulterior motive but purely for God's own sake. That confidence allowed Yahweh to permit the adversary to attack Job's family, property, and Job himself. Yahweh seemed confident that Job's piety was grounded on a foundation more certain than material prosperity. By chapter 38, however, Job's repeated demands that Yahweh give him his day in court seem to have convinced God that the adversary may have had a point; perhaps Job had served God because it was prudent to do so. At the very least, by chapter 38 Yahweh had grown weary of Job's complaints. It appears that questions remained, but suddenly it is Yahweh who is the questioner and Job who must answer.

Yahweh's lengthy discourse is a series of rhetorical questions that can be reduced to two fundamental issues. Essentially, the cumulative effect of all of these questions asked Job, Who are you? and Where were you? The second of these is answerable only with Job's words, "I was not." The rolling effect of the Lord's powerful questions is like successive peals of thunder, each one building on the previous until the ground shakes. "Where were you when I laid the earth's foundation?" "Who marked off its dimensions?" "Who laid its cornerstone—while the morning stars sang together?" And on they roll, question after unanswerable question until every aspect of the creation is covered, every aspect save one—humanity.

Job could not answer even one of these questions that asked, Where were you? But he could respond to the other basic question that the Lord God put to him. The Lord also asked, Who are you? In this massive set of unanswerable questions running through the whole catalogue of creation, human beings were not found as objects but as the subject that God addressed directly. Job was not an "it"; he was a "you" to whom the Lord would speak directly. On the other hand, we can ask whether Job was expected to answer these questions. Perhaps they were asked simply to put Job in his place. It was not that Yahweh was unsympathetic to Job's situation and to his plea for understanding; however, he had gone too far. A person can question God in anger. People can rage against God. But Job's rage had reached the stage of insolence and that was when Yahweh said, in essence, "That's enough. Where were you on the day I laid the foundations of the earth?"

The Lord's question, Who are you? is also an accusation. "Who [are you] that darkens my counsel with words without knowledge?" The speech from the whirlwind makes clear the utter transcendence of God. In the opening verses of the Lord's speech, Job was already put on notice. His little debating point about justice and unmerited suffering may have been significant in his own eyes, but its brilliance became darkness when measured against the Lord's transcendent splendor. Who are you? made its point; Job realized that he had been speaking of things that he really didn't know. Yet as a human being, he could be and had been addressed by God. Job's questions may have overreached themselves, but he alone of the Lord's creatures could answer this question. When the Lord inquires into the state of the soul, human beings alone in all the creation have the capacity to say, "I repent."

Yahweh questioned Job in this manner nearly all the way through chapters 38 to 41. Finally, in chapter 42, Job summons the courage to speak. The Job who speaks now is a very different man from the one we have heard throughout the book. Job had been transformed. Although they were not the answers Job originally sought, Yahweh had answered his questions. God had spoken in an extraordinary manner, transcending conventional wisdom. God's ways, so learned Job, are not our ways. Yahweh's answers to Job's questions reveal the majesty and glory of God, the Sovereign Creator of the universe. But the knowledge of God is also the knowledge of ourselves. Yahweh's revelation of himself to Job allowed Job to see himself as he really was. In the reflected light of God's glory, all that Job could do was repent. Job had heard of Yahweh in the past, but now he had seen God. In this knowledge that came by seeing lay a newfound respect: the fear of the Lord that is the beginning of wisdom.

Psalms

The Hymnal of Israel
Psalms 1; 19

It is not at all accidental that Psalms and Proverbs have been published frequently in pocket-sized editions of the

New Testament. The beloved evangelist Billy Graham reads from these two books every day because the Psalms direct our attention to God while the Proverbs point toward godly living in the world of human relationships. Of the Psalms, Martin Luther said, "There you look into the hearts of all the saints as…into heaven; and in that garden you see spring up lovely, bright, charming flowers…of all sorts of beautiful and joyous thoughts about God and his mercy."[12]

The Psalms have often been described as the hymnal of Israel. The superscriptions at the beginning of some of them indicate that they were used in worship, often for specific purposes. So, for example, Psalm 30 was used for the dedication of the temple, and Psalm 100 was to be sung in accompaniment to the giving of the thank offering. One hundred fifty psalms are collected in the book of Psalms, also called the Psalter, but other psalms appear in various Old Testament books. See, for example, Exodus 15:1–18, "The Song of Moses"; 1 Samuel 2:1–10, "Hannah's Prayer"; Isaiah 38:10–20, "Hezekiah's Song"; and Jonah 2:2–9, "A Thanksgiving Psalm."

The psalms of Israel are songs and poetry that express the full range of human emotion. Those who recited and sang these words expressed those feelings to Yahweh, their Creator and the one who set the course of their lives. One of the extraordinary aspects of the Psalms is the great freedom with which Israel spoke to God. As we read through the collection, it is clear that the writers of the psalms and those who sang them believed that they could speak to God about anything and in a wide range of emotions. Thus, some psalms express joy and delight in the presence of God while others rage and vent anger as they question God's purposes and action.

Psalm 1 has been described as a beatitude. Psalm 19 combines two themes so different as to suggest to some commentators that they are two psalms combined into one. The first six verses of Psalm 19 comprise a hymn that centers on God's revelation in nature. Beginning with verse 7, the topic switches to a meditation on the law. The law that the psalmist celebrated here was not so much a body of legal prescriptions as it was instruction in walking in the way of the Lord. And what person of faith would not take delight in that?

The Knowledge of God and the Knowledge of Humanity

Psalm 8

In reflecting on this psalm, one might find it helpful to find a place to view the sky at night. How vast is the expanse of space. Our own sun, the closest of those stars, is ninety-three million miles from the earth. Our solar system ends where the sun's gravitational pull loses its force—about fifty billion miles from our planet. Outside our solar system, the star closest to earth is *Proxima Centauri*, some twenty-five trillion miles away. Traveling at the speed of light (186,000 miles per second), it would take a human lifetime to make the round-trip from Earth to *Proxima Centauri* and back. Understandably, those who gaze into the heavens may feel insignificant against such immensity.

The psalmists were not astronomers and possessed no scientific knowledge of the stars, galaxies, and the vastness of

13. Quoted in Weiser, *Psalms*, 19.

space. Nevertheless, this vision inspired Psalm 8 and its praise for God the Creator, which is its first theme. But this poem is not simply a nature hymn; it is a psalm about the Creator God behind the vastness of space.

The second theme of Psalm 8 is a meditation on humanity. John Calvin (1509–64) taught Christians to appreciate the interrelatedness of the knowledge of God and human beings. The knowledge of God sheds light on the knowledge of human nature, and a true knowledge of human nature cannot be achieved apart from the revelation of God. Yet the gap between God and humanity is at least as great as the vast distances of space. The Old Testament expresses this difference between us and God as God's holiness. Measured against the holy, eternal God, a single human life looks pretty insignificant. Quite properly, the holiness and greatness of God evoke in us a sense of awe. When we take that awe as a starting point, we can appreciate what a miracle it is that God is mindful of us and cares for us.

Measured against God, human beings appear insignificant; measured against the balance of creation, those same human beings take on a more impressive stature. The painter and sculptor Michelangelo Buonarroti (1475–1564) lived during the high Italian Renaissance, a cultural and intellectual movement that sought to revive classical learning. Renaissance artists and scholars were particularly interested in the languages and achievements of human beings, and thus humanity became their subject, earning them the label "humanist." Their interests and motives, however, were a far cry from today's secular humanists. Many Renaissance humanists studied human arts and letters or portrayed humanity out of a deep Christian piety that drank from the well of such biblical passages as Psalm 8. Michelangelo sculpted his famous giant statue of David under such inspiration. He said he wanted to portray David as a man possessed of all the dignity and powers with which God had created human beings. It is said that when this statue was unveiled in Florence, people had already attached small slips of paper to it. On one of those slips was written the message, "How magnificent a creature is man!" Properly qualified, the psalmist would agree.

The One Who Watches Over Us

Psalms 23; 80; 121

There is no more beloved song or poem in the Bible than the Twenty-third Psalm. It speaks of God with such serene confidence and intimacy that we turn instinctively to its verses in times of grief. Small wonder that either in speech or print, Psalm 23 plays some part in many a Christian funeral.

Psalm 23 speaks of God as shepherd; so does Psalm 80. The image of the shepherd and his flock is admirably suited to describe the relationship between God and his people. Sheep are not among the brightest of God's creatures and utterly dependent on their shepherd to guide them to good pasturage and water. Without the protection of their shepherd, sheep are easy prey. It is easy to see how this metaphor could be applied to the relationship between God and Israel—especially if the poet had himself once cared for flocks of sheep.

There is, however, an interesting contrast between Psalm 80 and Psalm 23. The former speaks of God as the shepherd of Israel. That was conventional religious language in ancient Israel, expressing the relationship between God and Israel. Psalm 23 uses that same language, but it also applies the idea to the relationship between God and the individual: "The LORD is *my* shepherd" (emphasis added). It is almost as if David heard the verses of Psalm 80 and gave new focus to the divine-human relationship by personalizing it. The Lord God is the shepherd of *Israel*, but he is also *my* shepherd—personally and individually. Like Psalm 23, Psalm 121 also speaks of the believer's relationship with God in confident tones. This is not the crashing music of a symphony finale. This is not a hymn to be thundered; it is a lyrical poem to be sung gently: "He who watches over Israel will neither slumber nor sleep." Psalm 121 also contains some very familiar verses and, in the King James Version, a serious mistranslation. In that translation, Psalm 121:1 reads, "I will lift up mine eyes unto the hills, from whence cometh my help." More recent translations have rendered this "I lift up my eyes to the hills—from where will my help come?"

The reference to looking at the hills is neither accidental nor the product of a romantic vision of snowcapped peaks. Psalm 121 is one of a subgroup of psalms—120 to 134—that is sometimes called the "Book of Pilgrim Songs." Each of these psalms carries the superscription "a song of ascents." *Ascent*, of course, means "going up." So what does it mean that we have some songs that were sung while "going up"? The topography of Israel offers an explanation. On the west is the coastal plain, relatively flat land leading down to the Mediterranean Sea. On the east is the Jordan Valley. Between lies the central highlands—rugged, mountainous terrain. Jerusalem is located in these highlands on Mount Zion. Anyone traveling to the temple in Jerusalem quite literally had to go up. So we often find in Scripture the phrase *going up to Jerusalem*. The "Song of Ascents" is thus a psalm sung by people who were on pilgrimage, trekking up the rising terrain toward Jerusalem and the temple, lifting their eyes toward the house of the Lord.

Repentance
Psalms 32; 51

Repentance and forgiveness are the dominant themes of Psalms 32 and 51.

In the long tradition of Christianity, Psalm 51 is known as the "Psalm Miserere." It takes this title from the first word of the text in the Vulgate Bible, the Latin version prepared by the great Bible scholar of the ancient church, Jerome (c. 345–420). The *New International Version* translation of Psalm 51 includes a superscription saying that it was composed by David after his adulterous affair with Bathsheba. We should note that this idea is a commonly held tradition, but it is not part of the text in ancient manuscripts. Psalms 32 and 51 are two of the "Seven Penitential Psalms" (Ps 6, 32, 38, 51, 102, 130, and 143). From very early in the life of the church, these psalms played an important role in Christian worship. In the later Middle Ages, it was standard practice to recite these psalms at morning prayers during the season of Lent.

The early Christian theologian Augustine (354–430) interpreted Psalm 51:5 to warrant his idea that human beings were depraved in their very nature. To believe in the doctrine of human depravity is to say that human nature is a distortion of the original righteousness in which God created us. Morally misshapen creatures, in a depraved state, are, in Augustine's highly descriptive phrase, "turned in on ourselves." This means that we are all too prone to self-gratification and self-regard motivated by concern for the self rather than for God and others. Augustine's doctrine of human depravity is not the only interpretation of human sinfulness in the Christian tradition, but it certainly has influenced a wide range of Christian theologians and church teachers.

A striking feature of both Psalms 32 and 51 is their confident hope in God's forgiveness. Neither takes that forgiveness for granted, but both believe that a sinner's prayer of repentance will find God's open heart. David is described as the "man after God's own heart." Given his violent life, sometimes exacting a cruel revenge and certainly guilty of a terrible moral lapse in the matter of Bathsheba and Uriah, it is somewhat curious that David is described in such glowing terms. Obviously, it was not a consistently holy life that earned David this title. Thus David's psalms disclose God's readiness to forgive. David did not sin in order that grace may abound, but his psalms disclose a profound insight into the character of God who is "the LORD, a God merciful and gracious, slow to anger, and abounding in steadfast love and faithfulness, keeping steadfast love for the thousandth generation, forgiving iniquity" (Ex 34:6–7 NRSV). David trusted the Lord's capacity for forgiveness. It is the availability and power of God's forgiveness that breaks the power of the heart turned in on itself. If we will not trust in God's forgiveness and not break out of the circle of our own self-regard, we are condemned to lives of self-deception. The honest thing we can say about ourselves is "I have sinned." It is also a frightening statement to make without trust in God's forgiveness; however, when we fall back into the forgiving arms of God, that sentence leads to life as God always intended it to be.

Sacred Space
Psalms 42; 43

Form criticism is a method of Bible study that analyzes and compares blocks of material according to literary forms or types. This method has identified three major kinds of psalms when categorized according to form. There are (1) psalms that take the form of a hymn, (2) psalms that take the distinctive form of the lament, and (3) psalms of thanksgiving. Psalm 42, a hymn to God, is an expression of the psalmist's yearning for God and for familiar Jerusalem. This desire for a specific locale in which to worship may prompt a few questions from those who do not think of God as geographically located.

The world of the Bible typically identified some places and things as more holy—more sacred—than others. One thinks of the ark of the covenant or Mount Sinai; these are objects and places so filled with the presence of God that to touch them meant death. Shrines and altars were set up throughout Israel to mark off places where a special presence of God was tied to that locale. Thus, the Israelites gathered at Bethel (which in Hebrew means "the house of God"), a very important national shrine at the location where Jacob had his vision of the ladder to heaven. The temple built by Solomon replaced these local shrines over time and became the house of God. In its innermost recesses was the Most Holy Place, a location so sacred and filled with God's presence that the high priest of Israel entered only once every year. People who lived in the Bible world readily accepted the distinction between sacred and not sacred. The conventional term for not sacred is *profane*, which literally and originally meant "outside the temple." Speech did not need to be crude or vulgar to be profane in this sense; the term applied to any and all things that were not part of religious institutions and rituals.

This psalmist lived in a world that believed that some places were more sacred than others because God was somehow more present there than in other locales. It seems clear that he shared that belief. The challenge for us as faithful readers of this text is to consider this belief in light of the affirmation that God is everywhere, an affirmation we find not only in the New Testament but also in some passages in the Old Testament.

The Redeemer Is the Creator
Psalms 65; 104

Because the Old Testament begins with creation in Genesis, we tend toward the belief that ancient Israel's understanding of Yahweh began with the idea that God is the Creator. Theology must have a starting point, after all, and what could be more fundamental than the beginning where, as the text says, "God *created* the heavens and the earth." There is, after all, a rough and ready logic that says that creation must be the starting point of biblical faith; if God had not created the heavens and the earth, there wouldn't be anything. Our understanding of God must begin, we think, with the theological statement that God is the Creator, a logical enough response. But we must bear in mind that Israel's understanding of God developed historically rather than logically. God is revealed in history, and the path of history rarely follows the straight lines and right angles of logic.

In terms of its historical development, the faith of Israel begins with the exodus. This statement does not mean that Abraham, Isaac, Jacob, and the other patriarchs did not worship God before. It does mean that Israel's faith begins in the exodus event. This event is the pivot of the Old Testament in the same way that Jesus' resurrection is the pivot of the New Testament. In the Old Testament, everything revolves around the revelation that the God of Abraham, Isaac, and Jacob is the Redeemer of Israel. The exodus is the central event of Israel's life, revealing him to be that Redeemer. This event formed the faith that nurtured and sustained Israel through the years of wilderness wandering that followed the exodus.

When the Israelites entered Canaan, the faith of Israel was challenged in a way that prompted further development. The books of Joshua and Judges make it clear that the Israelites did not drive the indigenous peoples of Canaan out of the land. Although some peoples were conquered, many remained as neighbors. The Canaanites were farmers, and agriculture was their way of life. They were sensitive to the rhythm of nature and worshiped idols of nature gods believed to control that world. From the very beginning of Israel's life in Canaan, some Israelites were tempted to include the worship of these nature deities as part of the worship of the Lord God. Other Israelites resisted this temptation. They affirmed instead that the Redeemer of Israel was also the Creator of the world.

Psalm 65 is a wonderful example of this. The first section of the psalm celebrates the mighty acts of God that begin with Israel's redemption. The next section celebrates the Lord God who is the Creator and Sustainer of everything that is.

Augustine (354–430) solidified Christian belief in the doctrine of creation ex nihilo, meaning "out of nothing." He taught that before creation there was only God; nothing else existed. Augustine also taught that the general tendency of the universe ever since the fall was to lapse back into the nothingness from which God's word had called it. Only God's sustaining presence and will saves the creation from that collapse. So, said Augustine, God is Redeemer, Creator, and Sustainer.

The Lord of All People

Psalms 67; 96

When we study the Old Testament, it is always important to consider the changing social and cultural context during the centuries its books were written. During that time, the Israelites sometimes enjoyed peace and prosperity; sometimes they suffered famine, exile, and invasion. Under the reigns of David and Solomon, the nation enjoyed unmatched political power, wealth, and influence. At other moments, Israel knew only political devastation. The presence of idol worship, however, is a constant factor throughout Israelite life.

Sometimes within Israel, and certainly all around its borders, people worshiped deities other than the Lord God. The Moabites sacrificed to Molech, and the Egyptians to any of scores of deities. The Canaanite peoples worshiped Baal and Asherah. The presence of so many gods in close proximity inevitably provoked the question, Whose god is the greatest? Such a question brings to mind the famous spectacle on Mount Carmel. The comparison of one god against another is a long-term theme in Israel and lies behind the oft-repeated question, "Who [what god] is like the LORD [Yahweh]?" The obvious answer is "None."

The sixty-seventh and ninety-sixth psalms have something of the flavor of a comparison between Yahweh and deities of the surrounding peoples and cultures. There is more to these poems, however, than the assertion that the Lord God is bigger and stronger than any other God. What we find in these two entails the promise of a day when the Lord will be the God of all peoples because it is already true; the Lord God *is* the ruler over all creation.

Who was the intended audience for this strong assertion? It is likely that the psalmist aimed these poems at certain people within Israel. These psalms counter the belief that the Lord had covenanted with Israel and was the God of Israel—alone. In this interpretation, these psalms targeted an exclusivist attitude that asserted that the Lord's covenant with Abraham made Isaac's descendants the chosen people to the exclusion of all others. Alongside this self-centered interpretation, one finds another, broader and more inclusive view. Yes, the Lord God had chosen Israel for the purpose of being a light to the nations—but not so that Israel might congratulate itself on being God's elect. According to this perspective, God desires that all people, Israelite or not, worship and live in fellowship with him. Israel is not the end or goal of God's action but the means. This expansive view of God and his intentions for the world is the great burden of these psalms. It is, therefore, correct to say that they carry an evangelistic theme; each looks to the day when all peoples will live under God's righteous judgment and care.

Responsibilities of Authority
Psalms 72; 82; 113

All peoples of the ancient Near East were religious. There is no reference to any ancient nation that was atheist. Further, they were polytheistic, worshiping many gods. They also shared the practice of idolatry, and they held to the idea that there was a special relationship between the gods and the king. In some cases, the king was thought to be the earthly manifestation of one of the gods. Frequently, the king was referred to as a son of the gods. The point here is that throughout the ancient Near East, divinities and royalty were commonly associated with each other. The upper crust of society had a privileged access to these deities. The gods, in turn, favored the social elites. In other words, the gods were on the side of the wealthy and privileged.

Ancient Israel understood the relationship between the Lord God and humanity in marked contrast to her neighbors. The Lord God differed from the false gods of Israel's neighbors. Therefore, the psalmist asked, "Who is like you, O God?" There are many ways to measure the difference between the Lord and the gods of the Canaanites, Philistines, Egyptians, Babylonians, and Assyrians. One significant difference was that Yahweh's favor was not the special privilege of the king or the movers and shakers of Israelite society. It is distinctive to Israel's understanding that God is described as hearing the cries of the poor and the weak on the margins of their society and without power or influence. In the opening chapters of Exodus, we learn that God had heard the cries of his people—the enslaved Israelites. That God would hear *and answer* the cries of slaves distinguished him from all other gods worshiped by Israel's neighbors. This distinction is sometimes labeled "ethical monotheism."

The close relationship of justice with God gave the Israelites permission occasionally to rage daringly against God. Since God had acted in the past to free oppressed slaves, he could be relied upon when injustice appeared in later times. When justice was delayed, Israel felt free to confront God: Why do the wicked prosper? How long, O LORD, must we be made to suffer? When will you lift your hand in our defense?

The Lord was not a God only for the privileged and powerful. Moreover, God expected the privileged and powerful to share his concern for the marginalized. Thus, Psalm 82 describes God as presiding as judge over an assembly of the people. We can safely assume that the king and his associates are standing somewhere near the front of the room. It is to them that God hurls the question of verse 2—"How long will you judge unjustly and show partiality to the wicked?"—and the imperative of verses 3–4—"Give justice...maintain the right....Rescue the weak and needy... deliver them..." (NRSV). Since the Lord cares for the poor and the downtrodden, those who would be his people are obligated to share in that concern.

Poets and Songwriters
Psalm 73

Bible scholars and theologians increasingly encourage us to read the Bible as a narrative. It is the great story of God, Israel, Jesus, and the church. This story begins in Genesis (beginnings) and concludes with Revelation. As these scholars point out, large sections of the Bible are written in narrative form. The majority of material in the first five books of the Bible is narrative, as are Joshua, Judges, Ruth, 1 and 2 Samuel, 1 and 2 Kings, 1 and 2 Chronicles, Esther, Ezra, and Nehemiah. The Gospels and the Acts of the Apostles also are written in narrative form. The great task we face as the people of God is to locate our own individual stories within this larger framework of the story of God. Then we can begin to perceive who we are and what kind of people God is calling us to be.

Of course, large sections of the Bible are not narrative. One such nonnarrative book is Psalms. We would be foolish and wrongheaded were we to try to interpret this material as if it were a narrative. How, then, are we to proceed? Two related reading strategies can be used to connect the Psalms (and other nonnarrative biblical material) with the great biblical narrative of God, Israel, Jesus, and the church.

First of all, we ought to remember that the Psalms are a written product of the great story of God. They are themselves situated within that story; it is their context. For example, many psalms were written by David, a key figure in the story of Yahweh's dealings with Israel. The shepherd boy wrote the "Shepherd's Psalm" and later became the Shepherd King of Israel. When he perverted that role, the prophet Nathan confronted the king with a story about another corrupt shepherd. Through the telling of the story, David faced up to his sin and, according to tradition, wrote Psalm 51. All of this was because Israel had experienced Yahweh's reign as the firm yet loving hand of a shepherd. Take those two psalms out of the great narrative and they lose much of the rich web of meaning that helps us to interpret them.

The second reading strategy connects us to the great narrative as we locate our own lives within the story of God. Psalm 73 is a wonderful example of that strategy. The psalmist lived in Israel, a people who had tasted and seen that the Lord was good. In their long history they often had cried to the Lord, and Yahweh had heard their cry and redeemed them. Their experience within that narrative had formed them as a people who praised Yahweh as the champion of the oppressed and the God who punishes the sins of the wicked.

Now comes the problem, because the psalmist knew of wicked people who were prospering. Even worse, getting away scot-free with their ill-gotten wealth had made them arrogant. They despised the very name of God. This just didn't compute. The presence of such people within Israel contradicted the great story of God and tempted the psalmist to turn his back on righteous living (73:12–14).

Almost at the point that the psalmist had reached the end of his rope and could no longer live with this contradiction, he entered the temple for worship. Surrounded by all the temple furnishings and memorabilia of Yahweh's faithfulness to Israel, the psalmist came to his senses. He regained his perspective and orientation. Faith was rekindled. Trust in Yahweh and Yahweh's ways was reborn. The psalmist once again found the means of living in Yahweh's love and the hope-filled expectation of Yahweh's justice.

To reach such character as the people of God will require of us frequent and faithful work locating our lives within God's story.

A Story-Formed People
Psalm 78

This psalm underscores the point that we have been making: there is no more fundamental way to talk about God than story or narrative. The psalmist included us in the promise to "tell the next generation the praiseworthy deeds of the Lord" (v. 4). Deeds, of course, are acts. Acts can be recounted only through the use of action words—verbs. Verbs convey a sense of motion through time; a description that uses such verbs will likely have a beginning, middle, and ending. Where these three features are present, we have the makings of a narrative—a story. Many people believe that *story* means fiction or that stories are naive forms of entertainment best suited to children, but only a moment's reflection enables us to see the shortsightedness of these assumptions. Television and print journalists regularly provide us with news stories that tell viewers and readers "what really happened." And the narrative structure of nearly the entire contents of the first five books of the Bible and all of the Gospels of the New Testament should convince us that stories are not merely for children.

The people of God—whether Israel, the old people of God, or the church, the new people of God—are a story-formed community. We are a people who are formed morally and politically through telling the stories that make up our defining narrative. Psalm 78 reminds us of the importance of that task. Telling those stories sometimes leaves the people of God with riddles and mysteries that defy simple answers. The recognition of some of these historical riddles is the special burden of Psalm 78.

What are some of these riddles? The psalmist wondered, and wants us to wonder, why it is that some of those who have seen with their eyes what God has done have wandered away from divine fellowship. Psalm 78 should be read as a cautionary tale, a story to be remembered and pondered so that we and our children might benefit from remembering the mistakes of a previous generation that fell by the wayside.

The Living Faith of the Dead
Psalm 119

Psalm 119 is an extended meditation and celebration of torah in the life of the worshiper. The one who sings Psalm 119 delights in the instruction of the Lord. Its teaching is to be fully obeyed. The person who sings this song prays that Yahweh will not allow him to stray from the commandments. In verse 11, for example, the psalmist says, "I have hidden your word in my heart that I might not sin against you."

What does it mean to carry the word of God in the heart? About a generation ago, educators decided that memorization was a bad thing for children. As a result, rote memory work passed into the category of activities that should not be part of learning. This attitude infected many approaches to Christian education as well, with the result that many adolescents and young adults who have attended church and Sunday school all their lives nevertheless struggle with biblical literacy. The word of God clearly has not been hidden in their hearts.

The ancient Israelites believed that the heart was the center of a person's being. From the heart, as Jesus said, come forth the actions that identify a man's or woman's character. That the word of God was hidden in the heart signified the psalmist's moral and spiritual orientation. So long as a person follows Yahweh's torah, that person does not sin against the Lord. Torah is but a small part of Scripture, and memorization of large sections of Scripture may not guarantee an upright life. But ask yourself whether you would rather walk through life with the Lord's instruction or without it.

Torah provided Israel with traditions that gave stability and meaning to their lives. *Tradition* here need not mean something musty, old, and irrelevant. It need not signify the dead faith of the living; *tradition*al can mean the living faith of the dead. Torah comprises Israel's primary tradition. The Torah in which the psalmist delights includes the story of Yahweh's dealings with Israel, enabling the psalmist to understand who he is and what Yahweh expects of him. The psalmist sings of biblical tradition, a lamp for our feet and the light by which we can walk through life as the people of God.

Our life path may take us through green pastures and beside still waters. It may take us through the valley of the shadow of death. The apostle Paul, imprisoned in Rome and presumably under sentence of death, asked Timothy for several items. "The time has come for my departure," he wrote (2 Tim 4:6). At such a moment, what possessions are of such importance to Paul that he would ask Timothy to bring them to him?

Paul asks only for a cloak, for warmth against the damp cold of a Roman dungeon, and his scrolls and parchments. We do not know their contents for certain. The text does not provide enough information to warrant strong inferences. Might these scrolls have contained notes and sketches of theological ideas Paul wanted to work out in further detail? Perhaps. But if time was short, if only a month or two remained in Paul's life, is it unrealistic to think that he would want scrolls containing the Scriptures to read for comfort and light?

We must, of course, remember that any scriptures read by Paul would have been what Christians call the Old Testament. None of the Gospels existed, since his own letters were the earliest written elements of the New Testament. Reading from the Old Testament means that he would have been reading from the same books in which the psalmist delighted, the word that he celebrated as a "lamp to [his] feet and a light for [his] path."

Proverbs

Seek Wisdom

Proverbs 2:1–15

One theme of Israel's Wisdom Literature reflected on negative aspects of human experience. We may not like to think about them, but few of us live to old age without experiencing pain, suffering, and calamity. The books of Ecclesiastes and Job explore this darker side of human experience in the light of faith in Yahweh. But Wisdom Literature also has a positive side. The Proverbs express the confidence that life will go well if we will follow certain guidelines.

This delightful and insightful collection of observations and sayings provides the wisdom necessary to a confident life as the people of God. Long before the publication of *Life's Little Instruction Book*, the Proverbs were guiding people on the pathway of a life of happiness in the company of God.

Proverbs 2:1–15 explains the benefits of wisdom. The little word *if* assumes a prominent role in verses 1–4. The text tells us that *if* we accept the wisdom of the older generation—their words and commands—and *if* we seek understanding and search for wisdom with the same eagerness that we pursue wealth, then we will understand the fear of the Lord and find the knowledge of God. Such fear and knowledge are the beginning of wisdom; only a fool would despise them.

Verses 6–8 of chapter 2 turn our attention to the God who, if we will fear him, is the source of wisdom. Verses 7 and 8 particularly express that buoyant confidence that is one side of Wisdom Literature. To the upright, God gives victory. God is a "shield" to those who walk blamelessly. He "protects the way of his faithful ones." This sounds like Bildad, Eliphaz, and Zophar talking to Job. How can we reconcile the optimism of Proverbs with the drama of Job or the cynicism of Ecclesiastes?

The answer to this question takes two forms. In the first place, the people of the Bible thought differently than we. Westerners tend to think in terms of either-or, black or white, this way or that. We tend to think that if something is this way, then it cannot be another. The people of the Bible could and did choose between starkly contrasting alternatives ("Choose you this day whom you shall serve…"), but they also thought inclusively. At times they could think both-and as well as either-or. In the second place, the Bible itself guards against one-sided and overstated interpretations. If you press the optimism of Proverbs too far, the Bible will insist that you pay attention to the perspectives of Job and of the psalmist who cried out to know why the wicked prosper. The optimism of Proverbs and the darker view of Job, in other words, are both true; the canonical shape of Scripture will not allow us to take only one of them and freeze it as a hard and fast position.

An Education in Perspective
Proverbs 3–4

If, as Old Testament scholar Walter Brueggemann describes them, the books of the prophets gave ancient Israel an education in the passions, then the wisdom writers provided them with an education in perspective. In no Old Testament book is this perspective any clearer than in Proverbs. Generation after generation, Israelites sought to pass down a set of observations regarding the best way to live. In the same way that Christians hope that the character of their children will be formed by their spiritual instruction, ancient Israelites hoped that training in wisdom would form certain virtues in their sons (in the ancient world girls did not receive this kind of education).

The first of these virtues is an appreciation of life as interrelated in all ways, including moral, spiritual, and physical. Second, instruction in wisdom helped young Israelites acknowledge that underneath the relationships of the moral, spiritual, and physical worlds there abided a transcendent mystery.

One of the marks of a wise person is the humility born of an awareness that there are certain things beyond the knowledge and capacity of human beings. Third, the aim of the wisdom literature is to bring the next generation to the place where it trustfully submits to the Lord and his ways. The wisdom writers taught Israel to believe that there is a way of wisdom for the people of God and to come to a practical, living knowledge of that way. So it was that they repeated these words:

> Trust in the LORD with all your heart,
> and do not rely on your own insight.
> In all your ways acknowledge him,
> and he will make straight your paths.
> Do not be wise in your own eyes;
> fear the LORD, and turn away from evil.
> It will be a healing for your flesh and
> a refreshment for your body
> (Prov 3:5–8 NRSV).

Wisdom's Final Authority
Proverbs 3:1–8, 11–15

The book of Proverbs contains a good deal of practical advice that might be labeled "worldly wisdom." It is not hostile toward God but is like the advice a person might have read in *Poor Richard's Almanac*, such as "A penny saved is a penny earned." So, for example, we have such proverbs as "A soft answer turns away wrath." This sort of proverb is part of the conventional wisdom of the ancient Middle East. The Israelite people taught this wisdom to their younger generations. Very often the Proverbs present this kind of worldly wisdom in the form of an address from a parent or a sage whose advice instructs the listener, often addressed as "my son."

In Proverbs 3, "We might suppose that...again it is a parent or wisdom teacher who speaks, and that his instruction...or directives...are aimed at enabling the young man to find his way in the world and make a success of life. This impression is not contradicted by the motive clause in verse 2, 'for they give you increased length of days, and years of life with well-being.' We might suppose that [this] is an educational discipline in the strict sense...and that the source of authority is either the seniority of the parent or the sagacity of the wisdom teacher."[13]

As soon as we get to verse 3, however, it is clear that the wisdom taught in chapter 3 is quite unlike the conventional wisdom of the ancient Near East. The instruction of chapter 3 intends to guide the learner beyond simply getting on in life. Chapter 3 may use the standard Wisdom forms, but the content has been radically altered. The old, worldly wisdom, as William McKane has pointed out, is turned upside down. The reader of this book is subject more to God than to the authority of a parent or teacher.[14] The instruction, language, and thought patterns of Proverbs 3:3 clearly remind us of Deuteronomy 6:6–9. Proverbs' reference to Deuteronomy therefore strongly places its wisdom teaching in the great Israelite tradition of Torah, the instruction that God gave to Moses for Israel during their encampment at Sinai. The authority on which this wisdom rests is the authority of Moses, the covenant, and the God who gave it to Israel. Verse 5

---

14. McKane, *Proverbs*, 290.
15. Ibid.

continues the pattern of locating Proverbs' wisdom in the traditions of Israelite religion. In this case, Proverbs connects wisdom to worship. Verses 5 through 8 can be cross-referenced to the Psalms, the great hymnal of Israelite religion. Compare the following passages to Proverbs 3:5–8: Psalms 4:5; 5:8; 111:10; and 38:3. The wisdom of the Proverbs could be heard whenever and wherever certain of the Psalms were sung in worship.

Wisdom rooted in the fear and worship of Yahweh will yield long life. It confers riches and honor, but it's not finally a guide to wealth and success. Beyond the quest for worldly success loom the larger matters of the life lived in faithful discipleship to God. The Proverbs take conventional wisdom and locate it in this larger context. Without God, a successful life would not be complete at all. The wisdom that is rooted in Torah and in Israelite worship is "more precious than rubies; / nothing you desire can compare with her" (3:15).

Wisdom Begins in God's Character
Proverbs 3:27–35; 14:21

These passages provide a series of advisory sentences that are negatively framed. Each verse (3:27–31) begins with the phrase "Do not. . . ." These verses teach the specific attitudes of neighborliness and benevolence as well as a general attitude of goodwill toward all. The law of hospitality governed general relationships between desert peoples. Neighborliness and benevolence were values rooted deeply in a world where a harsh environment could easily become deadly. The law of hospitality was accepted by all and indeed was so universally practiced that it took precedence over hostile or unfriendly relationships. The law required even enemies to call a truce in the face of the unrelenting heat and dry climate. People were obligated to provide even their enemy with water and shelter against the desert. We may consider the proverbs of neighborliness to have developed with the law of hospitality in the background.

As noted earlier, there are strong parallels between this section of the Proverbs and the book of Deuteronomy. Given those parallels, it makes good sense to read these proverbs as specific applications of Torah and thus extended guidance for life as the people of God.

The series of verses that offer negative advice is joined together by a common concern for those vices and attitudes that threaten public order. Malice and spiteful intrigue will undermine public life, as will false accusation and envy. The public good is threatened even by the person who puts off until tomorrow the good that lies in his or her power to do today. In all these attitudes, there lies a threat against public order and a strong social fabric.

Verse 32, though, shifts the topic. Now we are taught the reason for the prohibitions of verses 27–31—the character of God. As the people of God, we are to take on his character. God detests a perverse man such as would engage in the kind of activities that have just been forbidden. Instead, God draws "the upright" into his very confidence. "Yahweh abhors the intriguer, but the candid and upright man who knows the virtue of openness and simplicity has the ear of Yahweh, is assured of unbroken guidance and will be more effective than [the devious man of intrigue]."[15]

16. Ibid., 301.

Once again, we find that wisdom, even the wisdom that conducts human affairs, begins in the character of God.

Proverbs 14:21, summarizes this teaching about good relationships between neighbors. Here we find guidance for the special relationship between neighbors where one owns many possessions and much wealth while the other is in need. If wisdom begins in the fear of the Lord, then it begins in the *Shema*: "Hear, O Israel, the LORD our God, the LORD is one. Love the LORD your God with all your heart and with all your soul and with all your strength" (Deut 6:4–5). To this law, Jesus added the second, which he said was like it: "Love your neighbor as yourself" (Lev 19:18). Wise dealings with our neighbors are rooted in Torah, which directs our attention toward Yahweh, who is to be feared and loved, and our neighbor, who is to be cared for with the same regard as we would wish for ourselves.

Parents and Children
Proverbs 6:16–35

One of the prominent words in the wisdom writings is *instruction.* Since the wisdom writers aimed at shaping the perspective of future generations, this instruction would be a key means to that end. Although the contrast should not be pressed too far, while pulpit and sermon are the home of the prophets and preaching, the classroom is the location of the sages who set down the wisdom sayings. Their writing may lack the urgent passion of the prophets, but that does not mean the message is also lacking in force. Excitement must not be mistaken for importance. A well-lived life is the product of common daily decisions as much as the result of watershed crises. The Wisdom Literature frequently and routinely focuses our attention on the moments and choices of daily life.

In the book of Proverbs, particularly in chapters 1–9, the voice of wisdom alternates between the instruction of God and of a parent. Behind this parental instruction there abides the eternal word of the Lord. But the person whose voice we hear is a father instructing his children, and typically his son. So, for example, in chapter 6 we find the repeated use of the phrase *my son*. This might be a teacher referring to one of his students, or a parent addressing his or her son before offering a series of proverbs that are the fruit of experience: "A little sleep, a little slumber, / a little folding of the hands to rest— / and poverty will come upon you like a bandit, / and scarcity like an armed man" (Prov 6:10–11). (Note that the proverb does not say that poverty is caused only by laziness. That would be to invert and distort its logic, which concludes that, whatever other conditions may lead to poverty, laziness surely will.) This is practical wisdom born of past experience; however, when we arrive at verses 16–19, we find this practical wisdom anchored to a very direct statement that lists attitudes and actions that God detests. In other words, the instruction of parents backs up the instruction of God.

The voice in this passage begins in God's instruction and then shifts to a parent's moral advice about sexual matters. Verses 24–26 may sound as if men are, more or less, the innocent victims of evil temptresses, but such thinking is balanced by the two proverbs of verses 27 and 28 that make it clear that in matters of sexual immorality "it takes two to tango." These two sayings capture the rich, down-to-earth quality of much of the Wisdom Literature—not at all unlike the farmer who says, "Well, you can't lie down with dogs and not expect to get fleas."

Internalizing Wisdom

Proverbs 15–17

Human speech is an extraordinary gift. Ancient Israelites believed that words possess a certain reality-making power, and nowhere is that belief more apparent than in human relationships. Words can raise us up or bring us down; they can nourish or devastate. Many of the proverbs found in these chapters concern themselves with the use and abuse of speech. The speech of wise men and women can easily be contrasted with the speech of fools. Not only does the speech of the wise dispel anger and restore calm, but sages also add to the general deposit of knowledge. It is part of wisdom to expand knowledge and insight. A wise person does not hoard knowledge but shares it so that others might benefit. Moreover, sages not only add to the general knowledge of the whole body, but they do so with style. They are eloquent and know how to turn a phrase. By way of contrast, "when fools speak, folly overflows like water bubbling up from a copious spring."[16]

The following true story illustrates as precisely as any the purpose that lies behind the collection and preservation of proverbs such as those found in chapters 15 through 17. When I was a boy, my cousins and I looked forward to our annual October pheasant hunt. We all lived in or near Minneapolis and St. Paul, but my father, grandfather, and uncle arranged these annual hunts with one of our relatives who farmed on the rolling prairie of southwestern Minnesota. My cousins and I were not yet old enough to carry shotguns, but since none of the men in the group owned a birddog, we were brought along as substitutes. One lovely autumn afternoon, my father and I wandered through a cottonwood grove onto the lane of the farm adjoining Cousin Wesley's. The owner and a friend were standing in the yard and immediately saw us as we emerged from the grove. Nearly all of the farms in that region were posted, meaning they could not be hunted without permission. The farmer leaped to the conclusion that we were hunting his land, jumped in his pickup, and tore down the lane.

When he reached us, the farmer and his friend angrily confronted my father. In that tense moment, he grabbed for Dad's shotgun. My father immediately let go and said, very quietly, "If you'll calm dawn, I can explain how we got here." He proceeded to identify us as relatives of the neighboring farmer and that we had gotten off his farm accidentally. We hadn't meant to be hunting anywhere without permission. The tension defused by this explanation, the farmer returned Dad's shotgun, and we went on our way.

I was shocked and more than a little embarrassed by my father's utter lack of manhood. He had let that angry farmer take his shotgun without a hint of defiance. Dad read my mind and broke the silence by asking me to think about the confrontation. Three men, a boy, and a loaded shotgun made the elements of a potentially lethal wrestling match. Then Dad said, quoting the King James English he had memorized as a boy,

17. Ibid., 478.

"The Bible says, 'A soft answer turneth away wrath.' And it does." More than forty years have passed since he taught me that lesson, but it shines today as brightly as the sun of that October afternoon.

We err if we think that the book of Proverbs offers little other than the substance of memory drills. These sayings are for our moral formation as the people of God. Learning that a soft answer turns away wrath entails internalizing that message in order to answer softly when confronted by anger. This proverb and all the other wisdom sentences of this book are meant to be memorized, then internalized, so that we can become wise.

Timeless Truths

Proverbs 19:17; 22:1–4, 8–9, 16, 22–23; 23:10–11

These texts are taken from a section of the book of Proverbs that is made up of single-sentence statements. Not unsurprisingly, Bible scholars refer to this section—Proverbs 10:1 to 22:16—as sentence literature. A single proverb can be studied as an isolated saying or grouped together around a particular theme without doing violence to the text itself. The manner in which individual proverbs have been grouped together in these readings is an example of this latter approach. We can legitimately ask Proverbs, "What does the Bible have to say about poverty and responsibility for the poor?" and gather up an answer composed of several proverbs taken from many different chapters. Unlike other books of the Bible, the context of the specific passage is not all that crucial for appropriating the instruction of the Proverbs.

Commentator William McKane sees a paradoxical quality in the sentence literature of the Proverbs. On the one hand, a proverb is ancient and concrete, very explicit in its images. On the other hand, a proverb is also immortal and open to future readers. The paradox is that the proverb acquires immortality because of its particularity. "Better a dry crust with peace and quiet / than a house full of feasting, with strife" (17:1) is a saying that is both concrete and timeless. One need not have been born in ancient Israel or speak Hebrew to appreciate the moral lesson it conveys. One can imagine a group of elders seated by the town gate entertaining one another with recitations of these single-sentence aphorisms. Many a gray head would nod in agreement as the saying brought to mind lived experience. Not incidentally, on the fringes of the group stood the younger men and perhaps an unusually bright and perceptive young man who listened and learned in this manner from his elders. Such sayings invite us to listen and similarly be instructed.

It would be easy to over-romanticize this setting. We would then fall into the mistake of thinking that the era of the Old Testament, and Proverbs in particular, was some kind of golden age when every boy and young man took to his heart the moral instruction of his elders. We know from the biblical narrative itself that such was not the case. Samuel's sons wandered into corruption and perverted justice. Many of David's sons proved to be disappointments. One of them even attempted a palace revolt. That there are children who ignored their parents' instruction then does not nullify the moral import of the Wisdom Literature now. Indeed, there is a kind of rough and ready poignancy to the

Proverbs. This instruction is important; those who follow it will be wise and live well and their lives honored, while those who ignore wisdom earn for themselves the label *Fool*.

These texts also gather together proverbs that have God's regard for the poor as their subject. Wealth and poverty are both subjects that come under the scrutiny of the Proverbs. It is clear that the book of Proverbs has nothing against wealth, but today's lesson also makes it abundantly clear that God cares for poor people, whose powerlessness is not to be taken advantage of by those who hold social and economic power. Those who do so, or who otherwise injure the poor, invite the wrath of God.

Available to All

Proverbs 28:4–10, 13

Wisdom is different from expertise. Experts possess knowledge that the rest of us do not. We call plumbers to fix plumbing problems because they know something we do not; that knowledge is their expertise. Wisdom, however, is not the personal or secret property of the wise. Wisdom is accessible to all.

Wisdom is generally available to all those who, as Jesus would later say, "have ears to hear." Since this wisdom is generally available, it really belongs to the entire community of Israel. In fact, that general availability has something to do with the way many of the wisdom sayings of the Proverbs came into being. Imagine an evening at the edge of the village or city, at the gate where the elders, the wise men, of the town would gather to talk and reflect about life. This was their place and their responsibility. While they sat, one of them might say, "Better a poor man whose walk is blameless..." and the rest of the elders gathered in the circle would reflect on this opening phrase. What had their walk with Yahweh taught them about poverty? To what might it be compared? Are there things worse than poverty lived by those whose lives are blameless? The village elders turned such questions over in their minds. Perhaps one would break the silence with a phrase that he thought might appropriately finish the sentence. Perhaps someone contributed a word or two. Slowly, bit by bit, the remainder of the sentence took shape: "Better a poor man whose walk is blameless...than...a rich man...whose ways...are...perverse." Perhaps a head or two would nod in agreement. The village council or elders generated many of the proverbs of practical wisdom in a fashion something like this. Many of the proverbs are the distillation of lifetimes of the community's lived experience as the people of God.

Chapter 28 reinterprets the vocabulary of wisdom. There is a marked contrast in this chapter between the wise person who is righteous and the fool who is wicked. The way of wisdom will be the way of a blameless life, the way of one who keeps Torah, who does not turn a deaf ear to the law, who has discernment, and who confesses and renounces sin. The way of the fool stands in direct contrast, and the one who follows this way will not be kept safe.

Wisdom and piety thus go hand in hand in the Proverbs. The man or woman who fears God and follows his instruction will be kept safe and successful, although Proverbs takes care to define success in terms other than material prosperity. On the other hand, the person who defies Yahweh and confronts him without proper respect and fear will only meet disaster.

Ecclesiastes

The Hidden Purposes of God
Ecclesiastes 1:1–4:14, passim

It is a vast understatement to say that the Bible is an extraordinary book, and among the qualities that make it so is the Bible's balance—the way in which it refuses to allow careful readers to emphasize one point to the exclusion of another. As we have already seen, the book of Job questions the theology that affirms blessings as a sign of God's favor and suffering as divine punishment. It is not that Job is right and the Deuteronomistic theologians wrong. The Bible affirms that both are right but that neither should be pressed too far. One of the greatest theological testimonies in the Old Testament is the goodness and trustworthiness of the Lord. But, as Old Testament theologian Walter Brueggemann notes, the Old Testament also contains a countertestimony, a minority point of view. Ecclesiastes, described by one commentator as the strangest book of the Bible[17], is part of the countertestimony tradition of the Old Testament.

The message of Ecclesiastes seems so alien to the balance of Scripture that we sometimes think it odd that this book was included in the biblical canon. When was the last time you heard a sermon based on Ecclesiastes? Nevertheless, Christians are people of the whole Bible. The book of Ecclesiastes is part of the canon of Scripture, and we may not act as if it is not. It is part of the Wisdom Literature of the Bible, and like the book of Job, it reflects on some of the negative aspects of life.

18. William P. Brown, *Ecclesiastes*, 1.

Brueggemann says that the wisdom writings offered Israel a perspective for living, the older generation teaching the younger a perspective tested out in their own lives. The elders are determined to develop certain moral skills in the younger generation. They want this generation to appreciate that the various aspects of life are interrelated and hang together (for example, what we do brings consequences and affects other people). They want youth to acknowledge a mystery in the interrelatedness of life (we cannot control life or manage God) and to see our claims to knowledge as they really are and admit our limitations in knowledge (get rid of our idols). And they want youth to arrive at the place where we trustfully submit and yield to God (life must be lived in faithful obedience to God).[18]

Within the body of Wisdom Literature, Ecclesiastes still stands out for the difference in its message and spirit. The book of Proverbs confidently guides its readers, offering wise observations on almost every aspect of human experience and activity. On the contrary, in many passages Ecclesiastes is not as confident as Proverbs and breathes a spirit of world-weariness. It is almost as if Qoholeth, the author of Ecclesiastes, whose name in Hebrew means "the Teacher," had seen enough. "Vanity of Vanities," said Qoholeth, which is the Hebrew way of saying "utterly meaningless." "Everything is meaningless" (1:2). If we were to stop there, all we would have is the counsel of despair. This odd message leads some Old Testament scholars to suggest that the book may have been written during a time of dramatic cultural change and economic

19. Brueggemann, *Theology of the Old Testament*, 680–81.

hardship, for Qoholeth repeatedly asked what was to be gained for all the toil and hardship of daily living. All of the activities of life that the Proverbs celebrate, Qoholeth pronounced meaningless. But that is not quite the whole story.

Nearly all of us can name people whose prayers for healing were not answered in the way they wished. One of life's most terrible facts is that people do experience awful calamities when the order and constancy of the universe seem to come unglued. Everything falls to pieces and life becomes meaningless and absurd. Ecclesiastes voices the complaint of those for whom life has become raw and meaningless; through this book their pain and hopelessness are articulated.

The message of Ecclesiastes is, however, not utterly hopeless. Underneath what seems meaningless, the processes of God are at work. (By the way, many baby boomers will instantly recognize verses in this text, even if they are completely unfamiliar with Ecclesiastes. In the mid-'60s the Byrds popularized a portion of these chapters with their song, "Turn, Turn, Turn.") In the pairings that make up the verses of this poem, no aspect of human experience is excluded; the deplorable is included along with that which we welcome—killing as well as healing, discarding as well as keeping, uprooting as well as planting. What is to be learned from such mystery? Underneath the storms and uncertainties of life, "I know that everything that God does will endure forever" (3:14).

The Gift of Today
Ecclesiastes 11:7–12:8

Commentator William Brown thinks it likely that the Ecclesiastes was written during a broad period of cultural uncertainty and drift. Widespread social and economic changes prompted people throughout the Middle East—from Egypt to Persia—to question the wisdom they had inherited from their forefathers. Readers may wonder why they should bother to study such a book if it has such a gloomy attitude toward human existence. The answer is not too difficult; we study this book for the same reason Thomas Mallory climbed Mount Everest: "It is there." Ecclesiastes is one of the canonical books of the Bible, and the whole Bible is intended for our instruction and growth as the people of God. We are not free to pick and choose the books or passages we like, for desire often directs our preferences rather than guides our needs, and sometimes we lack the wisdom to know the difference.

Ecclesiastes is included in the canon of Scripture because of its inspired wisdom. But what kind of wisdom is it that views life as vanity? What a far cry this is from the book of Job, where suffering is real and raw and yet Job's faith could say, "I know that my Redeemer lives." By contrast, Qoholeth seems to have given up on life and adopted a spirit of world-weariness. Two points are worth remembering here. First, the Bible is not a flat text; it is the product of many pens working at many places across many centuries. To make this historical observation in no way invalidates the doctrine of biblical inspiration, but it does acknowledge that human beings were involved in the writing of the books of the Bible. Human beings are part of culture, and human beings and cultures both change—growing and maturing, and declining. The Bible reveals God to us, but it also discloses the growth and development of Israel's understanding of God. All one need do is read through the Psalms carefully, for example, to see this understanding rooted in the full range of its walk with the Lord. All the human emotions are packed into its verses—joy (even ecstasy) peace, worry, fear, rage, despair, contentment. Ecclesiastes offers us a piece of wisdom set at a particular stage of that walk.

Christian discipleship calls us to reflect on life and the practice of faith in all the seasons of human experience. To follow Jesus is more than enthusiastic worship and good times with the community of believers. Ethics, our way of living as the people of God, is another vital aspect of our spiritual and moral growth. The Wisdom Literature of the Bible is particularly focused on ethics. It is here that Ecclesiastes offers us wisdom that will reorient our perspective as the people of God. In these verses, wisdom links two human experiences in what appears on the surface to be an unlikely combination.

Perhaps only Qoholeth could put joy together with death. Christians face death in the joy of the resurrection, but Qoholeth was not a Christian. So how could he talk about joy when he was also aware that death surrounds life with a limit that cannot be escaped? Ecclesiastes reminds us that not one of us will get out of this alive. We will all die. The Christian hope sustains us for the future that lies beyond the grave, but Qoholeth's reminder also helps us to focus on today, on this life and all the relationships and gifts with which God has filled it. In these, we are to take delight. In these, we are to take all the joy that is possible.

Song of Songs

Erotic Love

Song of Songs 2:8–13; 7:10–12; 8:6–7

The book of Ecclesiastes says that there is a time for everything, and in the Old Testament, "everything" includes love. When we think of love in the Bible, the idea that comes most readily to mind is *agape*, the self-giving love of which Jesus is the perfect expression. The Bible speaks of other kinds of love as well, however, and the Song of Songs celebrates the love of erotic desire.

Some translations of the Bible title this collection of love poems the "Song of Solomon," while other translations call it the "Song of Songs." The latter title is taken from the first two words of the book and is a particular Hebrew grammatical construction familiar to Bible students. In other Old Testament passages, we find such phrases as "holy of holies" and "vanity of vanities." This pattern of a word stated in the singular followed by the same word in the plural is the way the Hebrew language expresses the superlative. It is like saying "the most holy place on earth," or in the case of the title of the book we will study today, it is like saying this is the best song of all.

Solomon traditionally has been considered the author of this book. Some scholars question the traditional view of authorship. Solomon is mentioned by name in 1:1, but the grammatical construction is ambiguous. Either Solomon wrote it or else the book describes him as the lover who is the subject of the poems. In either case, Solomon's name is closely connected with this collection of love poems.

To be perfectly frank, the Song of Songs can legitimately be called a collection of erotic poetry. But let's be clear: the word *erotic* does not mean dirty, however much it has been used in that way in modern times. *Erotic* comes from the word *eros* and names the specific kind of love that longs for another and desires intimate union—soul as well as body. There is no more powerful expression of eros than the romantic love of a woman and a man. As beings created by God, eros is part of the human experience. Erotic love is part of God's good creation. As such, it is an aspect of the human experience to be wondered at and celebrated. Under the influence of dualistic patterns of thought, Christians insisted for centuries on reading the Song of Songs as an allegory of Christ's love for the church. To do so is to deny the first meaning of these poems. They celebrate the natural, God-given delight in one another that women and men express sexually.

The verses under consideration are taken from three different poems in the collection. The first of these (2:8–13) sings of the desire that grows between two lovers to be together. The setting of this poem is springtime, when "a young man's fancy lightly turns to thoughts of love," Tennyson wrote. Later poems in the collection make explicit reference to body parts, but here the relationship between lover and beloved begins first in the intimacy of presence to one another. Sex comes later; here it is enough that the lover and beloved desire to be in one another's presence. In that intimate communion, they take delight in each other's company. This theme continues in the second passage (7:10–12). The third passage (8:6–7) marvels at the power of romantic love. The attraction and physical desire of two people for each other is "as strong as death" (8:6), which is to say, stronger than any other human experience in earthly life.

Isaiah

The Song of the Vineyard
Isaiah 5

Isaiah received his dramatic call to speak the word of the Lord in the final year of the reign of King Uzziah (also known as Azariah) of Judah, about 742 BC. We must say "about" because the calendars in the ancient world lacked the accuracy of modern methods. Therefore, Isaiah began preaching a little later than Amos and Hosea, but nearly the same time as Micah in Judah. These four prophets, along with the Judahite prophets Zephaniah, Nahum, and Habakkuk, are classified as pre-exilic, that is, they prophesied in the years before the invading armies of Assyria carried Israel into exile and the Babylonians did the same to Judah. That Isaiah's call came to him in the temple at Jerusalem has led some to speculate that he had been a professional court prophet. He is somewhat unusual among the biblical prophets for his familiarity with the temple and his belief that the city and monarchy eventually would figure in the restoration of Israel. We can say with some confidence that Isaiah was a citizen of Jerusalem, likely a member of its upper class, during the tumultuous second half of the eighth-century BC. From his position in Jerusalem society, Isaiah shared many of the same conclusions as Micah concerning the evils in Judah and the divine judgment to be poured out there.

As Isaiah began preaching, the real question for him was the future of Judah. Although roughly twenty years down the road, the destruction of the northern kingdom was a foregone conclusion. Israel and its capital Samaria were doomed. Isaiah's prophecies concerning Israel spelled out her doom. Both Amos and Hosea had preached to try to save Israel. They had called upon the Israelites to return to the Lord while his face might still be found. But their warning and pleading fell upon deaf ears. Neither prophetic preaching nor diplomatic and military reversals could dent the arrogance of the Israelites. With proud hearts they boasted, "The bricks have fallen down, but we will rebuild with dressed stone; the fig trees have been felled, but we will replace them with cedars" (Isa 9:10). Since Israel would not heed the call of Amos and Hosea to return, it fell to Isaiah to announce her doom. Since she would not be purified, she would be destroyed. Ephraim as a people would be wiped away. Isaiah's preaching really had no role to play in Israel's future since her fate was sealed.

Most of his ministry was aimed at Judah, but on a few occasions he addressed Israel also, primarily concerning her final destruction. None of those messages performed this unhappy task with greater clarity or eloquence than the sermon in Isaiah 5.

Old Testament scholars call this the "Song of the Vineyard." Set as a poem, this discourse is among the most elegant and powerful in all the prophetic literature. Isaiah set his announcement of Israel's doom in the metaphor of a vineyard and its owner. God is the owner; Israel and Judah the vineyard. Although

God lovingly and tenderly cared for this vineyard and provided for its every need, "it yielded only bad fruit" (5:2). What is a landowner to do with such a plot of ground? Better to cut one's losses; so Isaiah concluded about God's mind toward Israel. Isaiah 5:26–30 describes the Assyrian army, the instrument of God's wrath, waiting to march across Israel. But what of Judah? They too were part of the Lord's weedy vineyard. Must Judah suffer the same fate as her northern sister? Would the spectacle of Israel's destruction prove sufficient as a warning that Judah must mend her ways or suffer a similar fate?

Injustice and Its Deserts
Isaiah 6

Judah did not experience the material prosperity of Israel. Although the people of Judah also dabbled in Baalism, they did not as a whole descend as far into the depths of religious syncretism and idolatry. Not that the Lord would tolerate even minor offenses in this area. The Lord is a jealous God, and even the slightest nod toward a false deity merited his wrath. Flirting with idolatry was bad enough, but to a breach of the commandments Judah added the sins of injustice and exploitation. As Isaiah said, he lived among a people of unclean lips; falsehoods, deceit, clever manipulation, bribery, extortion, and idolatrous worship passed across those lips.

Isaiah said that such sins deserved punishment. Israelites would be punished and also Judahites. One feature of his prophetic call in chapter 6 is the statement that Judah should not be allowed to hear God's word of warning, lest the people repent and be spared the punishment they deserve (v. 10). Isaiah declared that ruin and devastation would visit his people and their land. This message applied equally. Remember, Isaiah delivered this message in 742, about twenty years before the fall of the northern kingdom. He could see the Assyrian army marching into Israel and then threatening Judah. These terrible developments would not occur apart from God's permission and design. According to Isaiah's message, Assyria was the instrument of God's judgment.

As noted, Isaiah shared the message of divine judgment with Amos, Hosea, and Micah. But like Hosea, Isaiah did not restrict his message only to "gloom and doom." He also held out some small measure of hope. Even as Hosea had looked toward a day when Israel would come home, Isaiah also prophesied a hopeful future in the Davidic monarchy. The theme of hope appears already in the word that God spoke to Isaiah in the temple. In language that parallels the famous messianic prophecy of chapter 11, Isaiah 6:13 speaks of the stumps that would be left after the invaders had gone. But, said Isaiah, a "holy seed will be the stump in the land."

The Sign that God Is with Us
Isaiah 7

The monarchy in the northern kingdom had declined to a point where its department of foreign affairs neglected Assyria in favor of waging war against its smaller neighbors. This policy extended so far as entering into an alliance with the Arameans for the purpose of making war against Judah. Note the irony. Israel preferred to war against the people of God by making alliances with neighbors who were not. Bible historians refer to this as the "Syro-Ephraimitic" alliance that led to war. "Syro" stands for Syria, another name for Aram, and Ephraim was an alternate name for Israel.

Ahaz, king in Jerusalem, feared the Syro-Ephraimitic alliance and with good reason. Judah lacked fertile land for agriculture and also was situated off the major trade routes. This combination made for a weak economy. Weak economies do not make for strong armies. Judah would have had her hands full fighting the Israelites alone. Israel's bargain with the Aramaens gave them an insurmountable advantage over Judah. Ahaz knew that if war came, his army would be routed. He needed an ally, and he found it in, of all people, the Assyrians. It was a scene that has been played repeatedly in world history. Little powers fighting among themselves seek aid of superpowers. The world of the Middle East in 742 BC closely resembled alignments during the Cold War, except that the superpowers were not the Soviet Union and the United States but Assyria and Egypt.

Isaiah came to Ahaz with a word from the Lord. (Incidentally, it is this apparently easy access to the king that leads some Old Testament scholars to conclude that Isaiah was a member of the Jerusalem upper class.) His message sounds like the words of a foreign policy adviser, except that its ultimate source was God and not the mind of the prophet alone. Isaiah's first message to the king sounded a note of confidence (7:7–9). That Ahaz did not take this intended confidence was not a sign of his humility or piety. He was among those Judahite kings who had strayed from God, descending to the level of child sacrifice. So we ought not to place much stock in the false piety of his stated intention not to ask for a sign from God (7:12).

Isaiah's second message to Ahaz contains verses that Christians read annually during Advent. We read them as a prediction of the Messiah—Jesus of Nazareth. That they are so is the firm conviction of our faith. As faithful readers of the Scriptures, however, we must also read these verses in their immediate context—the Syro-Ephraimitic alliance and the coming war Ahaz quite properly dreaded. Isaiah told Ahaz that a child was to be born, a sign that God was with Judah. In the context of his own time, the point of Isaiah's prophecy was not the child but events that would occur during the child's early years. Women in Judah gave their infants a mixture of curds and honey to wean them off mother's milk. When Isaiah says that the land of the two kings dreaded by Ahaz would be laid waste before the child ate curds and honey, he was saying—in the immediate context—that in only a short time the Syro-Ephraimitic alliance would collapse. In any case, that alliance was not the real threat, as Isaiah said. Ahaz ought to have worried about the real power in the region—the very people with whom he had struck a bargain. In aligning himself with the Assyrians, Ahaz had gotten into bed with the enemy.

Some will wonder whether such a reading is appropriate for Christians. Does our faith require us to read Isaiah 7 exclusively as a prediction of Messiah Jesus? If we also read this passage according to its historical context, will our faith be undermined? I want to answer no to both questions. Faithful reading of the text allows the scripture to mean all that it can. Isaiah 7 was a message to a rightly troubled king in the middle of the eighth century BC. It is also a message to all those who would believe on the name of Jesus for salvation.

The Prince of Peace

Isaiah 9:1–7

Responsible interpretation is one of the crucial tasks that confront every teacher of the Bible. Those who teach anywhere in the church's educational ministry know and feel the importance of this responsibility. We desire to teach the Scriptures faithfully and in a manner that encourages the growth and development of followers of Jesus. Faithful teaching includes the obligation to be faithful to the text itself so that we teach all that the text can mean. This text calls us to this latter kind of faithfulness.

There is a rabbinic saying that Scripture means all that it can mean. This suggests the possibility of more than one meaning for a text. Like several writings of the prophets, chapter 9 can be interpreted in ways that follow more than one line of thought. This is particularly true of Isaiah, Micah, and Jeremiah. Matthew, Luke, and Acts read and employed some of the sayings of the prophets as predictive references to Jesus of Nazareth as the Messiah. These Gospels have trained centuries of Christians, us included, to read Isaiah 9:1–7 almost exclusively as a prediction of the coming of Jesus. These verses are some of the most memorable and lyrical passages in the entire Bible. They are especially recalled during the Christmas season and re-echoed for us in Handel's great oratorio *Messiah*. We read them as pointing to a hope that comes to fruition in Jesus as the child who would be called "Wonderful Counselor, Mighty God" (9:6). This became part of the messianic hope of the people of Israel, which they thought would be fulfilled in a king who would deliver them from their enemies. Some saw this fulfilled as early as Hezekiah. Christians, of course, find this to be a proclamation of the coming of Jesus Christ as Savior.

It is appropriate for Christians to interpret this text as a prediction of the Messiah, but we also must understand that the historical context warranted another legitimate interpretation. Isaiah 10 refers to a people who have walked in darkness and later in the chapter to the people of Ephraim and Samaria—alternate references to the northern kingdom of Israel. At the time Isaiah delivered this sermon, Israel was slipping into the death agony of its struggle with Assyria. It had gone so far as to ally herself with the Arameans in a military coalition against Judah. In Isaiah 7, we read that, at the Lord's whistle, flies and hornets will swarm from Assyria and Egypt to sting Israel—a metaphorical reference to the arrow and spear tips of the invaders.

Against all of this background, Isaiah announced the coming of the Immanuel-child, one who according to the calculations of Isaiah 7:14ff was soon to be born. This child would restore order, justice, and righteousness to a society that was disintegrating. According to this line of interpretation, Isaiah was prophesying the coming of a political ruler who would give Israel those desires for which people of every time and place have yearned: a just and righteous society where people may live in peace and without fear, a society made so by good and wise leaders. This is the interpretation that we might call the message to the original hearers.

The original message was valid for its time and place. But if, as the rabbis said, Scripture means all that it can mean, then Isaiah 9:2–7 also may be interpreted as we Christians do in the Advent season. These phrases, in their very majesty, sound, and rhythm, predict the glory of a Messiah who offers human beings the hope that is the alternative to all human governments and systems of order. We sing of a God who rules by stooping to our condition and promises a kingdom not of war and violence but of peace.

The Peaceable Kingdom
Isaiah 11:1–9

Isaiah proclaims a messianic hope for peace in chapter 11. In some detail, this poem describes what the Messiah will be like. He will come from the family of Jesse and hence be a part of David's line. The Spirit or breath of the Lord will be upon him. Qualities of wisdom, understanding, counsel, and power will be there. He will know and respect the Lord God.

The authority of the Messiah will not simply lie on the surface but will be based on a deep righteousness. He will be concerned about the needy and the poor. Righteousness and faithfulness will be his hallmarks. Even the harmony that was lost in Eden will be restored. This *shalom*, this wholeness and peacefulness, will be ushered in by one coming as a "little child."

One of the rich words of the Old Testament is *shalom*, generally translated as "peace" but involving a harmonious whole in the lives of nations and individuals. It involves completeness of life in good health, righteousness, and justice, all under the blessing of God. *Shalom* is close to *holiness* and adds up to salvation for humankind.

The artist Edward Hicks rendered several paintings under the title *The Peaceable Kingdom*. Each of them eloquently and simply portrays the spirit of this text. Oxen calmly chew their cud alongside lions that remain majestic but without ferocity. A child rests its arms on the shoulder of a lioness while a sheep lies at rest next to a wolf. Beasts of prey and their natural sources of food peacefully and unnaturally coexist. Although their title is not precisely biblical, it calls to mind the vision of a universe at peace given to us in Isaiah 11:1–9.

Many Christians have read this text as a prophecy of God's millennial rule through the Messiah. In this view, the fully instituted kingdom of the Lord will bear marks conforming to Hicks's vision of a world of creatures completely at rest and at peace with one another. Isaiah may have had such a view in mind, but it is important to remember that he also was concerned about the events of international politics in his own day. The Assyrians had destroyed Israel, and no buffer stood between them and Judah any longer. Fear of Assyria's next move dominated the foreign policy decisions of Judah's kings. But Assyria never mounted a successful campaign against the southern kingdom and eventually was subjugated by the Babylonians. In view of the prophets' frequent references to Assyria as a lion, perhaps we can also read Isaiah's vision as a prophecy of the day when the great predator Assyria would be made subject like all the nations that had been its prey. The Babylonians would make the Assyrian lion lie down with the lamb of Israel.

The first verses of Isaiah 11 deal with the character and government of the messianic king. We read them every Advent as prophecies that were fulfilled in Jesus of Nazareth. They also are expressions of Isaiah's disappointment with the kings of Judah in his own time. As with the other prophets of the eighth century BC, we know very few of the details of Isaiah's life. But one clear difference between him and his contemporary Micah, for example, is Isaiah's easy reference to the temple and royal government. It is clear enough that Isaiah found Judah's monarchy to be a sad departure from the days of the great David and that the prophet looked to a day when the people of God would be ruled by a king who possessed character traits not present in the rulers of his day. The name of this ruler would be Immanuel, and he would be the sign of Yahweh's presence.

The world still looks for governors and statesmen whose administrations are guided by wisdom, knowledge, and the fear of the Lord. We all wish to live in societies founded upon justice, righteousness, and faithfulness. It is a desire at least as old as Isaiah. Christians differ as to their views of the character of the messianic kingdom. Some see that kingdom through the eyes of Edward Hicks and look to a day when all the creatures of the earth—humans and otherwise—will live in a supernatural peace. Other Christians see the messianic kingdom as an inner life of a peace-filled spirit in each individual human being who lives under Christ's rule and reign. Yet all Christians affirm as a chief article of their faith that the Messiah has indeed come and that his name is Jesus.

Comfort and Renewal

Isaiah 40:1–11

Many scholars conclude that two authors composed Isaiah. They see the first thirty-nine chapters as written by the historical Isaiah, out of an orientation eight centuries before Christ and prior to the destruction of Jerusalem and the Babylonian exile. They see chapters 40–66 as written by one or more prophets with a sixth-century orientation near the close of the exile at a time when the return to Jerusalem and its rebuilding are imminent.

Conservative scholars themselves are split on this matter. Whether or not the book has one author or many, there is broad agreement that we have here a book of both rich diversity and meaningful unity. It proclaims to our spirits personally and to the church across the centuries that it is the inspired word of God.

The words of Isaiah 40 recall the melody of the tenor air from Handel's *Messiah* with its gentle tones of comfort and tenderness. But who is the text addressing in these verses, and what is the life situation of the original readers of the text? The theme of Isaiah 40 is comfort and renewal. This message was aimed at the exiles who had endured fifty years of captivity in a foreign land where everything from language to customs, even the diet, was alien. Little, if anything, about their Babylonian surroundings reminded them of home. There was no temple and therefore no proper worship. Even the geography was unfamiliar—the flat basin of the Tigris-Euphrates valley versus the hills of Judah. Of course, the presence of soldiers daily reinforced the people's awareness of captivity. Despair seasoned the bread of exile. Psalm 137 provides some sense of their bitter hopelessness.

Isaiah 40 announces comfort and hope to people who desperately needed to hear such a word. They had lost everything—homes, families, familiar institutions of government and religion, and even their belief that the Lord was still with them. Against such hopelessness, Isaiah 40 proclaims a word that refuses to credit the counsel of despair and the temptation to abandon faith in God. Underwriting this message is the confidence that the Lord remains faithful to his covenanted people. The God of Abraham, Isaac, and Jacob is, in Martin Luther's phrase, the "promising God." His covenanted promise is sure, and the people of God can rely on that, even in the most desperate of life's moments. The metaphors and images of this chapter reinforce the idea of the Lord's constancy and faithfulness. The new hopeful action of the sovereign God on behalf of the exiles is described in language reminiscent of the exodus. Once again Israel will cross a desert to freedom through the power of God. Isaiah 40 delivers a message that says that because God had covenanted with Israel he would not abandon them to exile. Their misery was at an end. Soon the Lord would restore his people and take them home.

Who were the messengers and agents of God's comfort? Who was to speak tenderly this word Israel so desperately needed to hear? Surely such a prophet as Isaiah was one such messenger, but it is also likely that the text has in mind the same heavenly beings surrounding the Lord's throne in Isaiah's famous temple vision in chapter 6. The Lord's majestic court is populated with beings whose purpose is to execute his will, and his intention in chapter 40 is that Israel is comforted and hope is restored.

All of this has reference to the original readers, but we are entitled to ask also about ourselves, who are clearly not Israel in exile. What does this text have to say to us? We can interpret Isaiah 40 in at least two directions. The first is to read the text as did G. F. Handel when he wrote his magnificent oratorio. In this case, we will interpret it in light of the salvation history that culminates in the life, death, and resurrection of Jesus. The "comfort" of the text is a foretaste of the comfort offered to all who believe on the name of Christ. But we may also, second, extend the text's pastoral meaning. We can interpret it as a word of comfort to those suffering souls whose hope and faith in God are threatened by calamity. It is especially such persons who need to hear the word of scripture that promises that the comforting, hope-filled "word of our God stands forever" (40:8).

The Servant of the Lord
Isaiah 42:1–9

This text is the first of four "servant songs" found in Isaiah. The songs are some of the most intensely studied passages of the Old Testament. At question is who the servant really is. Scholars have proposed many possibilities: (1) The servant was a personification of the people of Israel as a community. They would have been called, sent forth to serve, suffered, and won final victory together. (2) The servant might have been the writing prophet himself. The first three servant songs have sometimes been looked at that way. God could be calling the prophet, sending him forth, going with him through suffering to victory. (3) The servant was or would be a specific but unnamed historical figure other than the writer. (4) Centuries later, the Gospel writers identified Jesus as the suffering servant. Here certainly was the ideal, humble leader sent from God, one whose death enabled the forgiveness of his people's sins. Jesus also identified himself with the characteristics of the servant described in these songs.

And so it is that the figure of the suffering servant comes through sharply to Christians, who see Jesus in that role, making possible the forgiveness of their sins and challenging them to live and serve in the spirit of the true faith. While the nation of Israel may have been an early attempt at living up to the servant role, it is in Jesus that we Christians find a complete fulfillment.

Isaiah 42 introduces the formal title of the "servant," one also found in chapters 49, 50, 52, and 53. This title is variously applied throughout this section of the book of Isaiah. In chapter 41, the people of Israel are collectively called the Lord's servant. In chapter 45, the text refers to Cyrus, King of the Medo-Persian Empire, as the "anointed" of the Lord and thus presumably also a servant who does God's bidding. Since the term can be applied to any number of individuals or collectively to a group of people, it is not always easy to determine the identity of this "servant." Isaiah 42 specifically connects the servant with justice. This justice is not an insular or private justice; the servant will bring justice to all the nations. The prophets of ancient Israel taught the idea that justice denied in one locale is justice denied everywhere. According to this idea, one unjust act is like the proverbial rotten apple that spoils the entire barrel.

Garrison Keillor of *A Prairie Home Companion* tells the story of a friend who wrote him a long letter in which the friend confessed to being tempted to have an illicit affair with an associate at work. The man and his coworker were to attend a conference in a city some distance from their hometown. There they would find the anonymity that they believed would permit their sexual liaison. Before departing for this trip, the man decided not to go through with the plan, and the reasons for his decision give insight into the prophets' understanding of justice. The man chose to honor his marriage vows for the sake of his family and his community out of a dawning awareness that evil and injustice are never restricted to their immediate locale. Rather, they have an insidious way of spreading to the eventual contamination of community and society. Understood thus, the unjust act of an individual is never his or hers alone, and there is no such thing as limited injustice. Justice denied in one place is justice denied everywhere.

The book of Isaiah underwrites this idea of justice. It would not do for Israel to petition the Lord for a leader to secure justice for Israel while all other nations suffered. The servant of the Lord would bring justice to all the nations for three reasons: (1) The Lord is the sovereign God whose rule extends over all peoples and who therefore has an interest in the well-being of people and nations everywhere; (2) if there is justice only in Israel and injustice elsewhere, then Israel's justice will be precarious and only temporary; and (3) such a state mocks Israel's divinely appointed role as a light to the Gentiles.

There is no arguing with Isaiah's strong identification of the servant as the one who brings God's justice to Israel and the nations. This is not to be confused with righteousness, which the servant also mediates. As has often been said, righteousness refers to the relationship between God and the human creation. Justice, on the other hand, concerns human affairs and is underwritten by

God's determination that these affairs will be fair and equitable. There is, in other words, a "this-worldly" dimension to the work of the servant whose coming Isaiah predicted. He comes for the sake of justice as well as righteousness among Israel and all the nations.

Israel's Redeemer and the Lord of All

Isaiah 44:21–45:8

This text is among the prophecies addressed to the exiles just at the moment of their release from captivity and return to Judah and Jerusalem. In this context, it is worth reminding ourselves that prophecy has as much or more to do with *forth*telling than it does with *fore*telling. Many of the prophecies of the Old Testament are to be understood as sermons; they had a definite point to make to the audience of that day. Isaiah 44 and 45 is an example of that very kind of prophetic statement.

The subject matter of the book of Isaiah changes sharply between chapters 39 and 40. The situation of the first 39 chapters is that the kingdom of Judah lived under the threat of Babylonian invasion. The prophet's message in chapters 1–39 threatens the imminent judgment of God. The chapters from 40 on are addressed to people for whom the Babylonian invasion and exile were accomplished facts. After chapter 40, the message comforts and offers hope in the promise that exile will end and the Israelites will return home.

Isaiah 44 declares that Israel's punishment for the sins of the past is over. It reveals some of the most important qualities of the God who stood ready to restore Israel. God would not forget his people, although there must have been days in exile when they felt as if God had forgotten. God had swept away Israel's sin; it was like the morning mist that is burned off by the warmth of the midmorning sun. Isaiah 44:22 declares God to be the Redeemer. God is the maker of heaven and earth, the one who exposes the empty words of false prophets and fulfills the words of his true messengers. God is the one who said to Israel, "Return home." This God declared that Jerusalem, which the Babylonians destroyed, would stand whole and proud again; the ruined homes of little Judean towns would once again hear the sound of laughter and life.

Isaiah 44 and 45 also say something about how the exiles' return would take place. Isaiah 44:28 and 45:1 make positive reference to a man named Cyrus. This Cyrus was the king of the Persians who invaded Babylon. The prophet's positive reference to him is striking. Cyrus was the "shepherd," the "anointed," whose right hand God took into his very own. Isaiah 45 makes clear God's intention to clear Cyrus's path to conquest.

The idea that God would use a heathen king as his chosen instrument is not unique to Isaiah. Other Old Testament books affirm God's sovereign power over the nations. Nevertheless, the internationalism of Isaiah is stunning in its scope. These prophecies reveal something very important about God. The God of Israel is the God of all the nations. Whether or not those nations acknowledge him (45:4), God is sovereign and may do with them as he will. If they listened to the message of Isaiah, the people of Israel could not think of Yahweh as a provincial little God interested only in the fate of the Jews. Even as he is Lord of all creation

(44:24), God is Lord of the nations. God is God over the entire world and desires the redemption of all peoples.

A Light to the Nations

Isaiah 49:1–6

The Old Testament is sometimes perceived to focus entirely and inwardly on the chosen people. The second servant song provides a very different outlook. The servant's mission certainly includes the people of Israel themselves, but it goes far beyond that. The people of Israel were chosen but not only for their own benefit. They are also the elect who are to take the good news of redemption out across the world.

The broader purpose of this song appears in its opening lines. An intimate dialogue between God and the servant is opened up to include "you distant nations." Even while it is the servant's mission to "restore the tribes of Jacob," the servant is to be "light for the Gentiles." God's message of salvation is to be taken to the ends of the earth.

Here the question of who the servant is raises its head again. If the servant is the community of Israel, then this call speaks of the whole nation as an evangelist. If the servant is the writing prophet, then his role goes beyond the major task of encouraging the people of Israel in a very troubled time to understanding that he has a message of God for the whole world. If the servant is the prophesied Messiah, as the gospel writers proclaim, then it is clear that Christ and his followers have a message of salvation for the whole world. Throughout all of these interpretations, we end up with a strong communication from God that his redemption is meant to be carried to all peoples. As followers of God's servant, Jesus Christ, we share in that mission.

A new mood characterizes Isaiah 40 and the following chapters. Once again Israel had hope, and hope made the future a possibility. The despair of exile gave way to the hope of going home and the new thing the Lord God would perform among the nations and in Israel. These chapters carry the message that the Lord is sovereign over all gods and peoples. Bel, Nebo, and the other gods of the Babylonians were no match for the God of Abraham, Isaac, and Jacob. Isaiah affirms Cyrus, the Persian king who decreed the end of Israel's exile, as the Lord God's servant. The Lord governs the affairs and movements of all the nations. This sovereignty gives all of human history a hope-filled future.

While it may have been a relatively new idea in Israel that the Lord governed the affairs of all the nations, Israelites were quite comfortable with the notion that the Lord directed their own history. Behind this idea lay the prior notion of God's election of Israel. The Israelites celebrated their election, even as they disagreed about its meaning and purpose. Some Israelites interpreted their election as a sign of God's special favor; they were therefore special and somehow superior to all other peoples. Other voices in Israel challenged this view, saying that the nation had been chosen not as a sign of favor but because the Lord had conferred on Israel a special mission. Thus, in Exodus 19:6, the Lord told Israel that they were to be "a kingdom of priests and a holy nation." The same note of servanthood sounds in Isaiah 49. The prophecy declares that Israel is to be the vehicle to carry the Lord God's salvation to all peoples everywhere. This text was surely a comforting word for the exiles: even after their shame and deportation, the Lord had a grand future in store for his people. They were not a rabble coming home to weeds and thorns where buildings and walls once proudly stood. They were the servant people of the sovereign God, who had chosen them to be a light to the nations.

The God Who Remembered

Isaiah 50:4–11

An enduring, faithful relationship flows between God and God's people. Despite exile and defeat and despite the disobedience of the people of Israel and the punishments sent upon them, God has not forgotten them. In the midst of troubled times, the servant suffers. The relationship between God and God's disobedient people has been strained but not completely broken. In the midst of it, God and his servant are able to communicate. The all-powerful, transcendent God is able to come close and open the ear of God's follower. God is able to stand close down through history despite all the disruptions. The servant knows that God will be faithful and that God cares in the midst of the suffering. So he has set his "face like flint." He will endure. He will be steadfast.

Again the question of who the servant is has influenced our interpretations of this song. But whether the servant is the people of Israel, the prophet himself, some other historical individual, or the expected Messiah, the lesson of the song is the same: God is faithful. Those who follow and serve must endure across time in order to fulfill the mission God has given them.

Ultimately, Jesus Christ is that servant, and we as the servant church find our strength in the God who stands by us. We are called to listen to God, speak for God, and serve faithfully in God's name steadily across the years. Our faces are to be set like flint.

Remembering God

Isaiah 51:1–6

The immediate historical focus of this passage is on Jews in the midst of their captivity during the exile in Babylonia. Part 1 of Isaiah had been warning the Jews about the dangers of such captivity as they drifted from God and as the power of their nation declined in the face of growing Assyrian and Babylonian power. At first, representatives of the northern kingdom of Israel were taken captive, and then as the sixth century dawned, Jews were taken to Babylonia during the reign of Nebuchadnezzar. While a few prospered, most sorrowed and suffered.

When Cyrus, the king of Persia, came to power, he followed a policy of returning captives to their homelands. His edict of 538 BC set in motion the end of the exile and the rebuilding of the temple at Jerusalem, completed about 515 BC. All of these things are about to happen within the historical focus we find in Isaiah 51.

So chapter 51 proclaims that blessings are in store for the chosen people, now captives in Babylon. They are to gather strength from their memories of what God has done for them in the past, particularly through father Abraham and mother Sarah. Isaiah holds out the hope that the desolate ruins of Zion, destroyed long before, can be made into a new garden of Eden. In 51:4–6, the promises of God's justice and salvation are lifted up. People and nations will come and go, but the redeeming God remains the same.

The Suffering Servant

Isaiah 53:1–6, 10–11

Isaiah 53 summarizes, in eight verses, the longer fourth servant song of Isaiah 52:13–53:12. Here the idea of a leader who suffers, who is humble, who is not attractive physically, but who is ready to lay down his life for the sins of his people comes to a rich climax. Some of the most stately and beautiful passages that Christians have voiced in describing their Savior are to be found here.

"He had no beauty or majesty to attract us to him." His followers would not come to him because of the usual attributes of a princely ruler.

"He was despised and rejected by men." This leader would not come on a wave of popular approval based on charm and political savvy. In fact, he was to be distinctly unpopular.

"A man of sorrows, and familiar with suffering." He would know pain deeply and intimately, day after day. He could link with all of suffering humanity.

"We all, like sheep, have gone astray... and the LORD has laid on him the iniquity of us all." Sin is a central factor in the life of the world; this servant will take it all upon himself as he suffers and dies so that sin may be defeated.

Here are laid down by an ancient Jewish prophet the words and phrases that would become the hallmark of a Messiah, born as a baby in a stable, champion of an unpopular cause, and victim of a persecution. By Christ's sufferings, we are healed and achieve a final victory.

A Feast for All

Isaiah 55

Isaiah 55 contains some of the most familiar and memorable verses in all of the Old Testament. Many of these verses possess a lyrical quality that has enabled songwriters to set them to music. Several modern spiritual songs and choruses are based in these words. A strong note of celebration runs through this chapter, so perhaps it should be no surprise that its verses have been set to song.

Feasting was typically an element of any ancient Israelite celebration, and that is certainly also the case here. In Isaiah 55, the Old Testament anticipates the New Testament in the proclamation of this stunning news: anyone, and everyone, is invited to the Lord's final banquet, and there is no charge. Rich and poor alike are invited. The names of the homeless are on the guest list right alongside the names of those who live in mansions and who own summer homes on oceanfront property. Political and military leaders are invited, and so are the little people whose lives are thrown into confusion by conquerors and invading armies. No money is necessary; everything is free for the taking.

This text casts a vision of a day when all the nations will gather at the table of the Lord God in the great feast. No longer will the world be divided into the categories of Israel and "all others," the Gentiles. In the great feast, Israel will extend God's invitation to people not known, and at the feasting tables, Israel will exchange introductions with others who do not know Israel.

The shadow side of this picture is that some refuse the Lord's invitation. Either they insist on paying or determining the menu or the guest list. Thus they "spend money on what is not bread, and [their] labor on what does not satisfy" (55:2). In so doing they have missed the point of the feast. The host is the sovereign Lord of the universe. There is no possibility of attending the dinner on one's own terms. Either you accept the Lord's invitation on its own terms or you do not attend. Of course, the name for the terms of God's invitation is "grace."

Most people who live in the democracies of the West find it difficult to put themselves into this particular situation in the world of the Bible. The common people of that world knew what it meant to be excluded on the basis of social class. The nearest parallel in modern society would be exclusion on the basis of race. Quite to the contrary of any social, ethnic, or economic distinction, the good news of Isaiah 55 heralded a new day when whosoever will may come.

This magnificent prophetic poem invites Israel to return to the bosom of covenant fellowship with Yahweh its God. If we read this song in light of previous texts in Isaiah, we see that the moment has arrived when Yahweh will invite Israel to return. But the exiles must return to Yahweh before they can return home. Isaiah 55 eloquently invites the exiles to come home to Yahweh. This poem invites the people to be reconciled with their God.

To drive home the effect of God's invitation, the prophet used a series of references to Israel's past. In verses 1–3, he drew on the people's memories of desert journeys where food and water were scarce. Israel remembered several such deserts. There was the wandering in the wilderness after the exodus. Most recently for the exiles, there would have been the memory of the terrible desert crossing in Nebuchadnezzar's chains. As prisoners of war, they would have been treated roughly and given very short rations of food and water. Now, through the prophet, God invited the exiles to a fellowship where water flowed freely and where food was in inexhaustible supply. Most amazing of all, it was free for the taking; there was no charge.

Perhaps we are given here an insight toward interpreting God's declaration that God's ways are not ours. In human terms, the price of goods is determined by the law of supply and demand. In God's terms, anyone can eat and drink, whether or not they have money to buy. The prophet also called the exiles' memory back to the covenant. This was by no means a new idea to the exiles. Indeed, when the first prophecies against Jerusalem were uttered, many Israelites would not believe that the city would be destroyed. They refused to believe because of their interpretation of the covenant with David. Isaiah 55:3 refers to this covenant. Before the fall of Jerusalem and the exile, many Israelites believed that Jerusalem would never fall captive. They believed this on the basis of God's promise to David that his "house" or dynasty and Jerusalem would last forever (2 Sam 7:8–16). Here Isaiah referred again to this covenant; it was still in force. There was more; because of this covenant, other people who as of yet did not know Yahweh or his ways would also come to the Lord. The people of the exile were thus mediators; their covenant promise would be the means of the salvation of the Gentiles.

Isaiah 55 is a poem of great comfort and consolation. If Israel would but return to the Lord, they could go home and be made new. It is tempting to read this chapter solely as a word of comfort addressed to us or any other person who is suffering and in need of consolation. It is such a word to be sure, but we also might pause to consider what such a text says indirectly about the God who freely offers such comfort and consolation. There are those who believe that the Old Testament is only about law and that grace is reserved to the New Testament. It is hard to see how Isaiah 55 is not about grace. These verses reveal God as gracious—water and food are available without cost; God unconditionally promises that his covenant with David will last forever. These verses also reveal God to be far above feeble human reasoning. This is why Israel could return home. God would not hold the people's sin against them. If they would but seek his face, if they would call on this God whose ways are mysterious but who is near, then they could go home singing and clapping their hands for joy.

Worship and Justice
Isaiah 58

Isaiah 58 contains two key words. One is *fasting;* the other is *justice.* Fasting is a spiritual exercise in which persons forsake something generally regarded as good for the sake of a higher good. In this sense, fasting is an act of worship, and so we have a connection established between the instruction of Isaiah 58 and the practices of worship. The other key word in Isaiah 58 is *justice.* It is justice, *mishpat* in Hebrew, that is the criterion for determining true and authentic worship.

Isaiah 58 speaks in a voice that harmonizes with the other great pre-exilic and exilic prophets—Amos, Hosea, Micah, and Jeremiah. Each and all of them insisted that unjust social relationships affected a person's relationship with God: there can be no righteousness apart from justice. The problem is not that people were irreligious. It is not that people were indifferent in their religious commitments. It is not that they were hostile. That kind of attitude would easily fall under prophetic condemnation.

Quite to the contrary, Isaiah 58 addresses a people who loved to worship. These persons were precise and correct in their worship and absolutely correct about its forms and practices. They had memorized the proper forms and the psalms to be sung and were happy that others saw them enjoying their religion and piety. And yet, "in their very exercise of religion they miss the essential point, God's order of compassionate justice."[19] The prophet sharply attacked this mistake and judged such worship to be utterly unacceptable to the Lord God. By way of contrast, Isaiah 58:6–7 presents us with a majestic picture of the kind of worship endorsed and desired by God.

Isaiah 58 underscores a model of worship with corporate and social dimensions that are absolutely necessary if we are to call ourselves true worshipers of the one true God. "It is a rigorously moral understanding that places the one who would be true to God on the side of the same ones whom God reached out to help and empower, those suffering injustice at the hands of authorities, those imprisoned for acts of conscience, those denied their fair share of the land's produce, those denied housing and proper clothing, those turned away even by their own relatives."[20]

This text challenges readers at the point where they may be accustomed to thinking that worship is largely an individual matter. Like other prophetic texts, Isaiah 58 insists that while we may sing enthusiastically, pray fervently, and

19. Hanson, *Isaiah 40–66*, 204.
20. Ibid., 205–6.

generally enjoy ourselves in church, without and apart from our commitment to God's compassionate justice, our worship may be a waste of time.

Rebuild, Restore, Renew

Isaiah 60–61

Isaiah 60 and 61 are located in the section of Isaiah that speaks immediately to the situation of the exiles upon their return to Jerusalem. What were their circumstances, and what did they find at the end of their long journey back home? We might envision the return of the exiles as something more like a trickle than a flood. Small bands of exiles rather than a single, mass migration made their way home. When these weary travelers reached their destination, they found a devastated city. It was worse than they remembered because of decades of neglect and inattention. Weeds and thistles had taken root in the seams of the pavement and in places that once had been the interiors of buildings. Imagine the feelings at the sight of bushes having grown up and obscuring the location of the altar of the temple or a badger making its den in the corner of a building that once had been somebody's home. People weary and fatigued by the long journey from Babylon could only be dispirited by such sights and the realization that nothing was as it once had been.

Isaiah 60 and 61 expound on the theme announced at the conclusion of chapter 59: "'The Redeemer will come to Zion, to those in Jacob who repent of their sins,' declares the LORD" (59:20). In its original situation, the promise of the Redeemer's return is Yahweh's pledge to return to his temple on Mount Zion and accomplish the renewal of his people after exile. Jerusalem and the temple would be rebuilt and thrive once again. Comfort and consolation would be meted out abundantly to all in need.

Centuries after the restoration of the exiles and Jerusalem, Jesus opened the scroll of Isaiah in the synagogue at Nazareth. To those assembled, he read Isaiah 61:1–2 and declared that these verses had been fulfilled in their hearing, giving a new and vastly broader significance to the promise of divine comfort and renewal. Thus, a strong gospel link connects to this text. Jesus' life and teachings add up to good news about salvation. He expressed the purpose for his salvation mission when he returned to his synagogue in Nazareth and, according to Luke 4:18–19, read from Isaiah 61:1–2. Here Jesus was citing "glad tidings" or good news as proclaimed by the prophet. It was just as timely for Jesus' hearers in Nazareth as it was for Jews returning discouraged from the exile and finding desolation and ruin.

There are important common elements in the good news repeated in Isaiah and Luke. The Lord has anointed a bearer of the good news. It is good news especially for the sorrowing, the prisoners, the poor, the disadvantaged. We get further insight into the nature of this gospel linking both eras by the three *r*'s mentioned in 61:3–4. Those who receive the good news will be called on to rebuild, restore, and renew the ruined, devastated world and lives of people around them. All of this is to happen in an atmosphere of beauty, gladness, praise, and righteousness. There is always good news at the heart of God's redemption of his people, whether it is in Old Testament, New Testament, or current times.

A New Heaven and a New Earth
Isaiah 65:17–25

Once again we have before us a vision of the peaceable kingdom promised by God in Isaiah 65:17-25. Is this vision nothing more than "pie in the sky in the sweet by and by"? Was Isaiah offering discouraged people a narcotic vision of some other time and place in order to dull their pain and disappointment? Or was the prophet giving people a vision that says that the present is not what God wills and that the people's efforts to rebuild their city and society can be measured only against this vision of God's eternal intentions for creation?

Recall that the word *servant* in Isaiah 42 can be read to mean the people Israel. The whole people Israel is thus interpreted as a kingdom of priests whose task it is to be the light to the nations. But even the servant of the Lord can become tired and discouraged—especially when events do not live up to expectations. When the fulfillment of our hope is deferred into an obscure future, discouragement quickly takes root. Discouraged people are easily tempted to dream because their dreams and visions salve disappointment and numb the pain of unrealized hopes.

The exiles who returned to Jerusalem found a set of conditions that did not easily bend to the people's vision of a rebuilt city and society. Problems quickly arose. There wasn't enough money for a construction project of such magnitude as rebuilding Jerusalem. Even if money had been sufficient, there were not enough workers. In the first decades after their return, the exiles made very little progress in rebuilding their beloved Jerusalem. Discouragement and perhaps even unbelief crept into their hearts. Their suffering hindered their seeing how justice and peace might be restored. They could either separate God's promise from their physical life and assign it to the spiritual realm, or they could hold firm to that promise, working toward and waiting expectantly for its fulfillment.

The vision of the new heavens and the new earth pictured in Isaiah 65 is not a spiritual drug to be read whenever we are discouraged with the status quo, whenever it seems to us that the powers that pretend to rule this world are just too entrenched and too strong to be overcome. This text is not to be read whenever we want a foretaste of the way things will be in another time and place. On the contrary, this text is a call to arms. Isaiah 65:17–25 presents the people of God with a picture of the kind of world God has always intended the creation to be.

Jeremiah

Hardness of Heart
Jeremiah 6–7

Jeremiah is famously described as the Weeping Prophet. Except perhaps for Hosea, no Old Testament figure discloses more completely the heart of the Lord wounded by the faithlessness of his people. Jeremiah belonged to the priestly clan of Anatoth from the tribal region of Benjamin. This family background connected Jeremiah to the tribes of the northern kingdom of Israel and may help to explain his interest in those tribes.

Chapters 2 through 6 of the book of Jeremiah contain a considerable body of sayings directed against the temptation of the Canaanite fertility cults that had proved to be so persistent a problem in Israel. In this section, Jeremiah employed Hosea's metaphors of adultery and prostitution to describe Israel's religious faithfulness. This parallel suggests that in the first years of his prophetic work, Jeremiah assimilated the themes of the great prophets of the preceding one hundred and fifty years. These themes join the theological issue for which Jeremiah called the people to repentance (6:26), but verses 27–30 indicate that the people were already "hardened" and would not do so.

No Old Testament prophet understood better than Jeremiah that God had run out of patience with Judah. In fact, many scholars think that Jeremiah marks the theological high point of the Old Testament because he so clearly identifies with Yahweh's determination that Judah must forsake its evil ways and return to right religion. That determination is evident in Jeremiah 7, the so-called "Temple Sermon."

This chapter is set down as the "word that came to Jeremiah from the LORD." Yahweh gave Jeremiah both the sermon's content and also the instructions about the manner in which it was to be delivered. Jeremiah was ordered to deliver a message that offers little comfort to people arriving for worship just outside the temple. They have come to worship in security and comfort, confident that they are Yahweh's people and that Yahweh loves them and will protect them. What they hear is, "Reform your ways" (7:3). Imagine a scene where a man or woman, not an authorized minister, stood outside your church and loudly proclaimed as you walked by that you needed to reform your ways.

As with much of Jeremiah's preaching, this sermon turns on the word *if.* Jeremiah delivered a message that emphasized the possibility that Yahweh might turn away from them if they did not follow the way of the Lord marked out in the Torah. Many of his listeners believed in a very different theology that insisted that the covenant between Yahweh and Israel was everlasting. They believed that God would not turn away from Jerusalem and the line of kings that ran back to David. They believed that Yahweh's promise to David (cf. 2 Sam 8–16) included security and prosperity for Jerusalem. These people had no *ifs* in their theology. These were the people who said, "This is the temple of the LORD, the temple of the LORD, the temple of the LORD" (7:4), as if no sin could separate them from Yahweh.

Against this theology of comfort and security, Jeremiah directed his message. Not only could Judah and Jerusalem sin and sever their relationship with Yahweh, but the prophet declared that they already had and that they must return to God. Throughout his sermon, he insists that God will forgive, but only "*if* you really change your ways." (7:5), "*if* you do not oppress...and *if* you do not follow other gods" (7:6). In Jeremiah's mouth, the great covenant between Yahweh and Israel is not absolute but conditional. God will not wink at sin. God will not look the other way simply because of the covenant. Since God will not overlook injustice and oppression, those who fail to act justly and who oppress others must expect disaster.

Jeremiah invokes a painful memory to remind his listeners of the disaster that is possible when people persist in their sin. He mentions the name of Shiloh (7:12), recalling Israel's defeat by the Philistines several centuries earlier. Israel's loss at Shiloh was more than a military defeat. Shiloh was the site of the tabernacle and therefore the most important religious shrine in Israel. There Eli's two unjust and corrupt sons, Hophni and Phineas, persuaded the Israelites to remove the ark of the covenant from the tabernacle and carry it into battle in order to defeat the Philistines. Their desperate measure backfired, and their enemies captured the ark itself. The ark held the mercy seat, the place where Yahweh abided in Israel's midst. So when the ark left Israel, in an important respect, so did God. Jeremiah's reference to Shiloh is thus a frightening reminder that those who persist in sin run the risk of God's departure—the real disaster.

False Hopes and Judgment
Jeremiah 19; 21:1–10

The word of the Lord came to the prophet Jeremiah during the worst days of the kingdom of Judah. Jeremiah preached during the terrible years of social, religious, and political decay. The northern kingdom of Israel was but a memory, swallowed up more than a century earlier by the Assyrians. In Judah, idolatry had become commonplace, and the people of God had sunk to the practice of child sacrifice, an abomination in the sight of God. A series of weak kings succeeded to the throne of David, men who were incapable of stabilizing Judah internally. Neither were they any match for the external threat posed by the great and powerful Babylonian, King Nebuchadnezzar. This text is a message delivered at the moment when that threat had grown so great as to frighten nearly everyone in Jerusalem.

A small circle of royal counselors in Jerusalem stubbornly clung to a point of view that scholars today call the "royal" or "Jerusalem" theology.[21] This theology interpreted Yahweh's promise to David in 2 Samuel 7:8–16 to mean that Yahweh would never forsake the monarchy or the city of Jerusalem in which it resided. Yahweh had made a covenant with David. Since Yahweh's word was absolute, Jerusalem and the king could rely on Yahweh's protection. In Jeremiah 21:2, these people gave voice to their expectation: "Perhaps the LORD will perform wonders for us as in times past so that he [Nebuchadnezzar] will withdraw from us."

Jeremiah did not share this point of view; in fact, he thought in very different terms. He shared with the Deuteronomistic theology the perspective that history unfolds as the judgment of Yahweh. Everything hinged on the little word *if*. If the people lived faithfully according to the Torah, then God rewarded Israelite faithfulness with peace and prosperity. On the other hand, Israelite faithlessness, understood in terms very much like marital infidelity, brought disaster. It was Jeremiah's sad duty to tell the people of Jerusalem that the *if* clause of their covenant with Yahweh had come due. No more chances; it was too late for that.

We should not be surprised that Jeremiah's preaching did not attract many followers. After all, who wants to believe that the only remedy is one that will kill some of us? The severity of Jeremiah's message was enough to drive off most people. That the Jerusalem theology was available as an attractive alternative

22. On the subject of the royal theology and the covenant, see Strege and Willowby, *God's Redeeming Story,* 34–41, 63–69.

only added to Jerusalem's tendency to discount Jeremiah's preaching. If we are honest with ourselves, we will probably admit that most of us would rather take honey than vinegar. The people of Jerusalem were no different, and they could point to a scriptural text and a time-honored interpretation as anchors for their point of view. Of course, hopes pinned to the Jerusalem theology proved to be fruitless, and regardless of their convictions, they were trampled under the feet of the Babylonian soldiers who marched into the city.

The invasion and destruction of Jerusalem were not Yahweh's final word of judgment. The little word *if* still remained. Exile would bring repentance and with it the possibility of restoration and renewal. Jeremiah 19 and 21:1–10, read in isolation from the rest of this book, make Jeremiah appear one-sidedly harsh. He was, however, also the prophet who consoled Jerusalem with a promise that on the other side of destruction and exile a new heart would replace their flinty old one. Yahweh would write a new covenant, not on tablets of stone but on the heart.

Sins Theological and Ethical
Jeremiah 22

Jeremiah's prophecies against Judah identified two different kinds of sins. One of these was the sin of religious syncretism.[22] Like the kings of Israel, some of the kings of Judah had either permitted or introduced the worship of foreign gods. It does not appear to have been the case that they entirely eliminated the worship of the Lord in favor of these gods. Rather, the kings added the worship of these gods to the temple or permitted this worship in the surrounding countryside, combining elements with the worship of the Lord. Some scholars believe that religious syncretism was a problem in Israel from the days of Joshua and that its practice rose and fell depending on the royal determination to root it out. With the exception of only a few kings, during the period of the divided monarchy, syncretism had become a widespread and persistent problem. Syncretism violated the command to have no other gods before Yahweh, so we might think of it as a theological sin.

The other great sin against which Jeremiah prophesied was injustice. Jeremiah was the great prophet of the exile, and the bulk of his sermons and oracles focus on the imminent threat of Babylonian invasion and what Judah must do in the face of this threat. Destruction and exile raised huge theological questions concerning God's covenant with Israel. The most pressing of those questions asked whether the Lord cared any longer for his covenant people. If God did not protect Judah against invasion, could he be trusted? A major task of Jeremiah's prophecy was to answer such questions by reinterpreting the covenant. We will explore this idea further, but we should not allow the profundity of Jeremiah's message to overshadow his attention to the sins in Judah's behavior that were the root cause of its destruction. As much as syncretism, injustice was part of that cause, and injustice is an ethical sin— a sin and not merely a moral lapse.

This chapter ties together a series of prophetic oracles against the two kings who succeeded the great reformer Josiah.

23. To be sure, he never used this term of more recent derivation. We employ the word *syncretism* today to describe the blending of widely different religious traditions.

First, Jeremiah criticized Josiah's son, Shallum, and, second, the grandson—the despised Jehoiakim. This judgment focused on the injustice of their respective reigns. Recall that from the time of David, the king was to be the shepherd of his people. Under this compelling metaphor, the king was understood to be the one who secured Israel against harm. His responsibility was to defend the nation against external threat and protect those without social and economic power from those who might be tempted by status and wealth to exploit the powerless. Alas, the kings of Israel and Judah did not always fulfill the shepherd's role; in all too many cases they were among the predators. The prophets consistently attacked this problem and named it as a sin and an affront to the justice of the Lord. Some of the most memorable verses of the Old Testament come from the lips of such prophets as Amos: "Let justice roll on like a river, righteousness like a never-failing stream!" (Amos 5:24); and Micah: "What does the LORD require of you? To act justly and to love mercy and to walk humbly with your God" (Mic 6:8). Like his famous predecessors, Jeremiah also prophesied against injustice, one of the sins that led to the nation's downfall.

Hope through the Fire
Jeremiah 25–26

One can imagine that by the year 600 BC, fear and panic raced through Jerusalem as Judah's political situation became increasingly desperate. Two of the three superpowers of the Middle East—Assyria and Egypt—had collapsed in the face of Babylonian aggression. Until Assyria fell, a faction of leaders in Jerusalem favored a strategy of seeking Assyrian protection from Babylon. That possibility disappeared when Assyria fell. Similarly, when the Babylonians defeated the Egyptians at the Battle of Carchemish in 605, Judah lost its only other potential ally of any significance. That the kings of Judah even considered these alliances with foreign powers and their gods is a measure of their diplomatic desperation. Any such alliance would make Judah a vassal state and require the people to pay heavy tribute for military protection.

Jeremiah's open declaration that the Babylonians were about to destroy Judah was a message scarcely calculated to calm the anxieties of Jerusalem dwellers. Ancient people did not receive bad news any better than we do today. In times of national crisis, political leaders are inclined to insist on universal loyalty among citizens. From the point of view of the Jerusalem establishment, the crisis demanded solidarity; this was no time to weaken the nation's resolve with talk of destruction at the hands of invaders. To the king and his advisers, Jeremiah's prophecies sounded like defeatism. Moreover, another faction of the Jerusalem leadership pointed to the Lord's promise to David that his descendants would always rule in Jerusalem and that, by implication, the city would never be captured or destroyed. Those who held to this promise believed that since the Lord's solemn word could never be voided, the monarchy and its capital city need not fear invasion. Thus, when Jeremiah forecast the city's destruction, this faction was ready to charge him with treason. From their point of view, Jeremiah's prophesying contradicted the word of the Lord.

Jeremiah might have been executed on the spot were it not for the voice of reason that came from the elders of Jerusalem. They were the people who remembered that an earlier prophet, Micah, had prophesied against Jerusalem but did not suffer execution as a result. Jeremiah also called into question the corrupt behavior of the Jerusalem establishment and the theology that legitimated it.

Jeremiah's sermon to Jehoiakim announced the arrival of trouble, but not without a small glimmer of hope. It might still not be too late to repent, but even if the worst were to befall Jerusalem, there would be a divinely imposed limit to its punishment.

Comfort and Grace

Jeremiah 30–31

These chapters come from the section of Jeremiah often described as the "Book of Comfort." The historical situation is that Jerusalem and Judah had not yet been captured by the Babylonians, but the ax was about to fall. In this terror-filled situation, Jeremiah spoke a word of hope-filled consolation. The Lord's final word would not be the destruction of Judah. On the other side of calamity, the people Israel would find hope and renewal.

The entire Bible must be read and interpreted with high regard, but these chapters deserve an added measure of respect. There is nothing in the experience of white North Americans—not even the terrorist attacks of September 11, 2001—that can serve as an analogy to help us appreciate Judah's plight. The United States and Canada have enjoyed a long period of peace at home, free from invasion and occupation. Europeans and Asians who lived through World War II are much better prepared to relate to the threat of destruction and exile that loomed over Jerusalem. The Holocaust remains as the almost perfect parallel to the situation that Judah faced at the moment Jeremiah delivered the messages of the Book of Comfort. Because such horror has scarcely touched many of us, out of respect for the suffering and dead, we must take great care that we do not read this text casually or come to quick and easy interpretations.

Imagine a situation you wanted to escape or overcome, but all possible avenues are closed. The people of Jerusalem faced precisely that situation on the eve of the Babylonian invasion. Judah was diplomatically isolated. Her pitiful little military force was no match for the Babylonian army. When war finally came, everyone in Jerusalem knew it would be a slaughter. But military defeat was only prologue to the pillaging, looting, and rape that would follow. Such were the practices of warfare in the ancient world, and when those horrors had subsided, the survivors would be herded off to Babylon and exile. The weakest would not survive the journey, and those who reached their new foreign home could only wonder what their fate would be as aliens in a strange land.

Jeremiah's word of comfort to the terror-filled community that awaited the destruction combined several themes. First, he told the people that Jerusalem's destruction was a consequence of their own sin. There is very small comfort in that, except to recognize that the calamity of exile was the Lord's means of disciplining his people. This leads to a second theme, namely that those whom the Lord disciplined had not been abandoned. There were voices in Jerusalem who wailed that the Lord had cut them loose and that all hope was gone. Jeremiah refused to give credence to despair. Third, Jeremiah looked beyond the exile and saw a hope-filled future; the Lord's people would be restored.

For a long time, Christians have read Jeremiah's hope-filled promise of a new covenant as a promise of the new relation that would come through the Messiah. This reading is made all the easier if one thinks of the old and new covenants as the Old and New Testaments. Old Testament scholar Walter Brueggemann objects to this reading because it ignores the text and doesn't take into account the return of the Israelite community after the exile. Brueggemann goes on to maintain that the "old" and "new" covenants of Jeremiah 31 refer to the Israelite community before and after the exile that began in 587.[23]

It is very difficult for Christians to read Jeremiah 31:31ff as anything but the promise of the new covenant in Christ. Perhaps this is a place where it is best to remember that the Bible means all that it can mean. To recognize this point allows us to read such texts as this and hear the voice of God addressed to future ages as well as to a people who stood in terror at the sight of their world collapsing around them. If grace is an attribute of God, and that gracious God is eternal, then it is not too much to believe that grace also marked the Lord's relationship with Israel. That grace, signaled in the Book of Comfort, offered hope to people in Jerusalem in 587, even as it offers hope today.

24. Brueggemann, *Commentary on Jeremiah*, 292.

Lamentations

Despair and Hope

Lamentations 1:12–16; 3:22–24, 31–33

The destruction of Jerusalem, and particularly the temple, wrote the finishing lines to a profound theological crisis among the people of Judah. These people could not grasp the destruction of the temple in light of the belief in God's special election and protection of God's people, Israel. How do you explain the terrible suffering of God's chosen people in light of God's sovereignty?

Prophets such as Jeremiah and Ezekiel offered sermons and oracles that helped those who remained in devastated Jerusalem make sense out of what had happened. Similarly, the poems collected in the book of Lamentations articulated both the pain of Judah's suffering and the hope that the Lord might relent and restore it.

The poems were composed very shortly after the destruction of Jerusalem in 587 BC. The author still remembered vividly all the terrors and horrors of that event, and there was very little of the hope that was rekindled later by prophets such as Ezekiel. The poems of Lamentations evoke the raw emotion of despair.

The structure of Lamentations orders this rawness by imposing a strict construction on its message. It is composed of five poems, the first four of which are acrostics (the first line of the poem begins with the first letter of the Hebrew alphabet, *aleph*, the second, *beth*, and so on through the entire alphabet). It was a way of expressing the completeness of Israel's desolation and despair.

The poet needed the entire alphabet to depict the last full measure of suffering. In chapters 1 and 2, the first line of each stanza begins with a successive letter of the alphabet. Chapter four is the same, except that each stanza is only two lines long rather than three. Chapter three is the most elaborate of the acrostics; in this poem, the stanzas are three lines long and each line of the stanza begins with the same letter, the pattern being repeated through the entire alphabet. Chapter 5 is not acrostic, yet still conforms to the Hebrew alphabet in that its number of lines is the same as the number of Hebrew letters.

Traditionally, Jeremiah was thought to have written this book, but there is little internal evidence for that view. In fact, there are reasons to believe otherwise. The book gives evidence of the broken trust of the nations on whom Judah had relied for assistance, but Jeremiah was outspoken in his hostility to such alliances. And Lamentations remembers the high hopes set on Zedekiah; this does not square with Jeremiah's blunt prediction that the king would be given over to the Babylonians. For such reasons, it seems better to leave the authorship of Lamentations uncertain.

Ezekiel

No Excuses, Please
Ezekiel 18

The prophets of Israel may be divided into several useful, distinctive categories. There are a small number of *non-writing* prophets, such as Samuel, Nathan, Elijah, Elisha, and Micaiah ben Imlach. They take their classification because no book of their sermons and oracles is part of the Old Testament. The *writing* prophets are divided into *major* (Isaiah, Jeremiah, and Ezekiel) and *minor* (all those prophets whose books are gathered into the book of the Hebrew Bible called the "Book of the Twelve"). The writing prophets also are categorized according to the period of their activity in relation to the exile (587 BC): pre-exilic, exilic, and postexilic. Ezekiel is a writing prophet whose messages were delivered before and during the exile.

"No stranger figure can be found in all the goodly fellowship of the prophets than Ezekiel. His was a stern personality, and not very winsome, in which one senses contradictions. A harsh demeanor conceals passionate and, one suspects, profoundly repressed emotion. His teaching has now the dryness of a priestly torah, now a soaring, if undisciplined, eloquence.... Ezekiel was scarcely what we would call a normal man. Yet he stood like a watchman over his people (ch. 3:17–21), announcing Yahweh's righteous judgment with the authentic voice of Israel's normative faith."[24]

Ezekiel is often called the "prophet of individual responsibility," a title earned for him by sayings like those found in Ezekiel 18. While his argument does clearly advance the idea that individuals are responsible for their own actions, we must take care that we do not make Ezekiel into a modern-day individualist.

Very near the time of the fall of Jerusalem, voices could be heard quoting the old proverb, "The fathers eat sour grapes and the children's teeth are set on edge." The proverb was widely understood to mean that the Lord held succeeding generations accountable for the sins of their parents.

25. Bright, *History of Israel*, 336–37.

Exodus 34:7 supports this meaning, but the proverb was being quoted with the implication that the Lord's ways were not right or fair (cf. Ezek 18:25). The prophet's message in chapter 18 was aimed at this murmuring. Presumably, people in Jerusalem were complaining that the disaster about to befall them was judgment for the sins of previous generations and that punishment was misguided. They might have asked, "Why should we have to suffer for our parents' wrongdoing?"

Ezekiel answered this question with an elaborate argument. He works through three succeeding generations and makes the point that anyone who sins will suffer the personal consequences. The current generation of Jerusalem dwellers had itself earned the Lord's wrath. This text should be read not as an anticipation of modern theories of individualism, but as an argument that allowed nobody in Jerusalem any excuses; the misery about to descend upon the city was the fruit of their own misdeeds.

Life Where Once Death Reigned
Ezekiel 36–37

Few modern criminal justice systems employ the sentence of exile. To modern people, exile does not seem to be a serious form of punishment. Certainly, it would be inconvenient to be exiled to another country, perhaps highly so, but we would not be inclined to think, like the Israelites, that exile is a living death.

People of the ancient world, Jews and non-Jews alike, believed that few punishments were worse. This belief was rooted in ideas about the relationship between individuals and society. These ideas are nearly the opposite of modern thought. Ancient people thought of the individual as an extension of the larger group. Thus, people gained their identity and reason for being through this relationship. If that relationship was severed, a people lost their identity and became nonentities. Although a hand severed from the body still possesses a hand's shape, it may no longer be a hand because it cannot perform the functions of a hand. In the world of the Bible, this way of thinking applied to people. Exile radically separated people from the larger body and sent them far from home; they lost their ability to function properly. They were condemned to a living death. For these reasons, ancient peoples thought that exile was a terrible punishment indeed.

The prophet Ezekiel lived during the same terrible times as Jeremiah. The great difference between them is that Jeremiah was not among the people sent into exile. Bible scholars think that Ezekiel likely arrived in Babylon with the first group of deportees in 598 BC. His prophetic ministry lasted from 593 until about 571.

Until the final collapse of Jerusalem in 587, Ezekiel delivered stern warnings to the city (see Ezek 1–24). In exile, Ezekiel's message began to change as Yahweh's word of consolation and hope came to him. Israel would not be made to eat the bitter bread of exile forever. Out of the dust and ashes of defeat, out of the shame, despair, and living death of exile, hope might still live. The famous vision of the valley of dry bones is just such a message.

Ezekiel 36 and 37 are sermons delivered to the Israelite community in exile. Jerusalem had been laid waste. The king, aristocracy, and religious leaders of Judah—including Ezekiel himself—had been deported and marched into the precarious existence of exile. This community in exile found it easy to believe that they had no future. When people believe that they lack a future, hope becomes impossible and despair triumphs. Judah in exile could only sit by the rivers of Babylon and mutely rage against its captors, impotently wishing that somebody would smash the heads of Babylonian toddlers on the rocks [cf. Ps 137].

In the aftermath of Jerusalem's fall and in the first years of exile, the raw wounds of humiliation and defeat remained open. Only after they began to heal could prophets such as Ezekiel bring up the subject of return and renewal. Both subjects come up for consideration in chapters 36 and 37. The latter contains the memorable vision of the valley of dry bones. The Lord commanded Ezekiel to "prophesy" (preach) to the bones, having first asked, "Can these bones live [again]?" By implication, the question extended to Judah and Israel. Could Israel, dead in exile, live again? Could life be restored to the dead streets of Jerusalem? God only knew. What great faith it took on the part of the prophet to preach to the dead bones of the whole house of Israel. If one did not know whether the bones may live, who but people of faith and obedience would preach to them?

"This remarkable narrative (Ezek 37) perfectly epitomizes the function of prophecy at a crucial moment of history. The [exile] community, which has lost its will to survive, is vivified by the spirit activated by the word of God addressed to the community…Everything depends on God. Bones cannot stand by their own power…The people of God could not live *as God's people* through their own power. Everything depended on God. The answer to Yahweh's question, '*Can* these bones live?' depended on Yahweh's intention. In Ezekiel 37:25–27, that intention was disclosed. The word of the Lord, which came to the prophet Ezekiel, was that Israel would live again. In the explanation of the vision (vv. 11–14)—again, a feature typical of the book—that future is identified as settlement in the land [of Israel]."[25]

Much the same spirit animates the sermon in Ezekiel 36, although not in the same dramatic setting as chapter 37. Ezekiel promised Israel that the Lord would restore them to their homeland. But this promise was set in a context and declared to be for a purpose larger than God's concern for Israel itself. Chapter 36 completes a warning that Ezekiel gave to Edom, Israel's neighbor, remembered for taunting the exiles as they marched into captivity. Edom "went too far," and the Lord would bring it down.

In part, this message answered the question about God's sovereignty, a question that any thinking person would have been compelled to ask: If this could happen to us, is the Lord really sovereign? Ezekiel answered that question by taking over the priestly explanation for the fall of Jerusalem. The exile was the result of the pollution of the land by idolatry and arbitrary violence. This answer was crucial, for it reasserted God's omnipotence and sovereignty over the nations: exile was the result of the Lord's judgment, not his impotence.

Ezekiel asserted that God's reasons for returning the exiles to Jerusalem had to do with the Lord's regard for himself and his name among the nations.

26. Blenkinsopp, *History of Prophecy in Israel*, 204.

Daniel

The King's Table and the King's Man
Daniel 1:3–16

The book of Daniel takes its name not from the author but from the subject of several of the narratives collected here. Israel lived in a threatening situation at the time of the book's composition. People in exile live under constant threat, as they never know when and if their captors will turn on them. Scholars suggest two possible dates for the time Daniel was written, both of which were times when Israel lived under terrible threat. Some conclude that it is the product of an exile, perhaps even by that name, who wrote in Babylon between 587 and 538 BC. Other scholars say that Daniel was written much later, probably during the Maccabean revolution about 168 BC. In their view an anonymous writer composed the book, partly from stories about the exile Daniel as well as in the apocalyptic style that became increasingly popular after the year 200. A fact in support of this second view is that the literary style of apocalyptic did not otherwise appear until after that date. It remained popular for three centuries, down to the time of the New Testament book of Revelation. Another argument in favor of this later dating is that apocalyptic writers generally preferred to remain anonymous, naming their books after one of the great worthies of the Old Testament.

If Daniel were written during the Babylonian exile, it was addressed first of all to people who actually lived in the situation. If, on the other hand, the book was written during the second century, it would have been first read by Israelites whose land was occupied by the armies of the Seleucid overlord Antiochus Epiphanes, one of the successors to the great empire of Alexander the Great. It was Antiochus who desecrated the temple in Jerusalem, forcing the Jews to sacrifice a pig on its altar. Whether in exile or living as an occupied people, the book of Daniel is addressed to people who live in a captive situation where life is fundamentally insecure.

The story recorded in chapter 1 will be familiar to most Bible readers. On the surface it is a simple narrative about temptation and the honorable and faithful resistance put forth by Daniel and his friends. If, however, we read this story in light of Israel's powerless situation, this familiar narrative might appear to us in a new light.

Daniel and his friends were among the exiles transported from Judah to Babylon by Nebuchadnezzar. Life in exile was uncertain, bitter, precarious, and hopeless. As Psalm 137:4 says, "How could we sing the Lord's song in a foreign land?" (NRSV). Nebuchadnezzar nevertheless provided a few of these exiles an escape from their hard life. He invited them to move from the outskirts of his great and glorious city into the very center of power—to live in his palace, sit at his table, and eat his food.

We should be suspicious of kings who act so generously toward their captives. Why would Nebuchadnezzar do such a thing? The text says that the best and brightest of the Israelite young men received Nebuchadnezzar's invitation. Did he want to recognize their talent and ability? Was there a shortage of intelligent, handsome Babylonians? Or was this a strategy to pacify exiles who would not be happy until they were allowed to return home?

How might a king prevent the revolt of captive people living within the borders of his nation? One way would be to treat very generously some of the natural leaders among those captives and invite them into the palace to become the king's friends. As the king's beneficiaries, these bright young men would later find it easy to tell their fellow Israelites that they really had nothing to fear from the Babylonians, who, after all, really were nice people. Thus, Nebuchadnezzar plotted a strategy that would lead them to forget the true situation of exile for them and their people.

The centerpiece of this strategy was food. Nebuchadnezzar wanted the men to assimilate by eating the rich food of the royal Babylonian diet. The men declined, asking instead for water and vegetables. They decline because those who eat the king's food become the king's possessions. Rich, delicate cuisine is not the real temptation here; it lies deeper. To sit with the king was to be included among the powerful. If they would but eat the king's food, even more power would come their way. But these young men refused and insisted on eating vegetables and drinking water, the same food eaten by their fellow Israelites in the camps and shantytowns on the outskirts of the city. The young men insisted on remembering their connections to the people of God. They will belong to God and the people Israel, not Nebuchadnezzar.

Be Certain of Who You Serve

Daniel 2

The book of Daniel differs markedly from other prophetic books. In fact, much of Daniel is written in a style very different from prophetic speaking and writing. This style, called apocalyptic, developed after the last of the Old Testament prophets had stopped speaking. Not all of the book of Daniel is written in the apocalyptic style. Chapters one through six are a collection of narratives concerning Daniel and other Jewish exiles in Babylon. Here we read familiar stories of the lion's den, the fiery furnace, the handwriting on the wall, and the exiles' refusal to eat the rich food on King Nebuchadnezzar's table. These stories seem straightforward enough and reasonably simple to interpret. But Daniel 7–12 presents a very different picture. Here we read descriptions of strange beasts and obscure numerical combinations. The text is anything but straightforward, and we are left wondering about the meaning that seems to be hidden underneath several layers of symbolism.

Biblical apocalyptic writing (the New Testament book of Revelation is the other great example) has often been described as a tract for hard times. The beasts, numbers, and strange visions are all a secret code language by means of which oppressed Jews encouraged one another and strengthened their hope and faith in God's final act of deliverance.

However, commentator W. Sibley Towner believes that Daniel also has a message for the people of God living in relatively good times. "This book glows with a deep conviction that God will not fail to achieve his redemptive purpose in the world. It glows with the trust that tyranny and oppression in all their forms are not the wave of the future but that the outcome of the human experience is finally the vindication of faithful obedience, goodness, and truth. God wins in the end, and all who seek to keep the faith with God are winners as well! That is a faith which can sustain the saints in good times and bad. It is a faith that the contemporary secular world longs to affirm, but mostly cannot.... It is a faith which can lead us away from [do-nothingism] and apathy and can energize us for the task of working for the good and safety of the creatures of the earth in the company of other persons of good will."[26]

Daniel 2 is found in the narrative section of the book. Here we see Daniel attached to the court of the king of Babylon, mighty Nebuchadnezzar. Daniel and his friends were among the best and brightest who were marched from Jerusalem to Babylon. Moreover, they were the cream of that crop, because they were selected to be admitted into the circle of Babylonian sages, magicians, and astrologers who served Nebuchadnezzar. The world into which they had been invited was both pampered and dangerous. This king was an absolute monarch, an oriental potentate whose word was law and whose every whim was to be taken seriously and indulged. Nebuchadnezzar held the power of life and death in his hands, and in Daniel 2, we discover just how dangerous was the world in which Daniel lived. For little or no reason the king had decreed that, on pain of a horrible death, his sages must tell him both the content and meaning of a recent dream. This demand was too much for Nebuchadnezzar's professional sages, and the task was left to Daniel. Through the power of God, a point that Daniel made at great length, he fulfilled the king's demands. The lives of *all*—Jewish exiles and Babylonian sages alike—were spared.

27. Towner, *Daniel*, 4.

Life for an exile was precarious. Life was also precarious for the restored Jews of the post-exilic community. Even today life remains precarious; most of us cannot insulate our lives against decisions made by other people with more power and authority. Daniel served at the court of a man whose will and word could be benign one moment and malignant the next. Daniel not only survived but prospered in that precarious world because he faithfully served God, who was even more faithful to Daniel.

Arrogant Power
Daniel 3:14, 16–25

The story is told that once when President Lyndon Johnson was returning to the White House from Andrews Air Force Base, he departed Air Force One and started walking toward the nearest helicopter. Unknowingly, Johnson walked toward the wrong one. A young airman noticed the President's error, ran up to him, and said, "Mr. President, that's not your helicopter!" Unimpressed, Johnson brushed the young man aside and replied, "Son, they're all my helicopters." This story illustrates the arrogance of power. It is such arrogance—coupled with God's response to it—that lays at the heart of this text.

The story begins with an act of arrogance. Nebuchadnezzar ordered the erection of a statue bearing his likeness. This statue was so big that it sat outside, and it was golden. What people order the construction of lavish monuments to themselves? Nebuchadnezzar, however, was not finished. Once the statue was set up on the plain of Dura, he commanded that on signal all the people in his kingdom were to drop whatever they were doing and worship his likeness. This is arrogance upon arrogance.

Neither God nor those of God's people who are faithful would allow such presumption to go unchallenged. It was reported to Nebuchadnezzar that three young Israelites had refused to obey the royal decree. These were young men of stature, some of the very men to whom the king had once acted kindly but they would not bow before his image. Their disobedience unsettled the royal power. How would it look to the rest of the people of Babylon? Neither Nebuchadnezzar nor any other king could afford such disobedience among his people. The young men must be destroyed. An example had to be made of them to reinforce the royal power their defiance had undermined. When word got out that these disobedient young men had been incinerated, the rest of the population would quickly fall into line.

Nebuchadnezzar's plan was flawed. Although the furnace where they were to be thrown was superheated, the young men escaped harm. Their hair was not singed; their clothes had no hint of smoke in them. Even worse for the king, a godlike figure was reported to have been seen in the furnace with the young men. Nebuchadnezzar did a quick about-face. He decided that the God in whose name the young men defied his order was really worthy of praise, and he ordered that Babylonians were not to utter any word against the God of the Israelites.

Psalm 24 poses the question that runs through the entire New Testament: Who is the King of glory? The answer comes ringing back: The Lord, he is the King of glory! The Bible steadfastly refuses any and all human effort to take the place of God as the true king of glory. The struggle between earthly kings and the heavenly king runs all the way from Israel's request that Samuel anoint them a king to the Jerusalem mob's shout that it had "no king but Caesar." God simply will not put up with rival claims to his authority. It doesn't matter whether the king is from Israel or Judah, Assyria, Babylon, or Rome; those who set themselves up as gods will be confronted by the true God. The confrontation in this text reveals God as the king who is faithful to his people. Sometimes, as in the case of the story of the fiery furnace, that confrontation occurs through the witness of the faithful people of God. Their faithfulness receives an extraordinary reward. By decree of a freshly rebuked Nebuchadnezzar, the God who preserved the young men in the depths of the furnace was known in Babylon as the God of Shadrach, Meshach, and Abednego.

Handwriting on the Wall

Daniel 5:1–7, 25–28

This text moves forward in time from the reign of Nebuchadnezzar to the last ruler of the Babylonian Empire, Belshazzar. Although the text refers to him as the king, in actuality he served only as vice-regent when his father was absent from the city. One other technicality must be cleared up. The story calls Nebuchadnezzar the "father" of Belshazzar. We should understand that term to mean "ancestor." The Bible often employs this usage, as in the statement, "a wandering Aramean was my father" (Deut 26:5 RSV), which was to be repeated by members of every generation even though "father" refers specifically to Jacob.

Belshazzar has thrown a party for a thousand nobles of the kingdom.

While we may know little of Belshazzar's character, what matters in this story is that he had been drinking heavily and was not in his right mind. Under the influence of alcohol, Belshazzar issued a very foolish command. He ordered the chalices and goblets, the fine gold and silver vessels, that the Babylonians had stolen from the Jerusalem temple to be brought before him. They had taken sacred objects as the booty of war when they conquered Jerusalem generations earlier. Whatever the cause of an unsound mind, emotional or chemical, acting under such limitations can get you in a lot of trouble.

So long as the temple vessels remained in the royal treasure chamber, no harm befell the Babylonians. But the day came when Belshazzar ordered them brought before him. Drunk with power as well as wine, he ordered the goblets and pitchers filled for his guests. The party-goers drank from vessels devoted to use for the worship of the God of Abraham, Isaac, and Jacob. Worse, they poured out libations, customary drink offerings, to the Babylonian idols. The use of these sacred objects in this manner profaned them. They were holy, that is, to be used only in the service of God, but Belshazzar used them outside the temple and its purpose for them. Not only did he profane them, he committed sacrilege; he used them for the worship of gods other than the one true God of Israel.

Just as Yahweh did not suffer the arrogance of Nebuchadnezzar, God would not permit Belshazzar's profanity and sacrilege to go unpunished. In the midst of the partying, a hand suddenly appeared and wrote four mysterious words on the palace wall: *mene, mene, tekel*, and *parsin*. No one could decipher their meaning, but someone recalled an old wise man, one who remembered God's ways of dealing with the world: Daniel. The old sage was summoned, and he translated the words into a message that struck terror into Belshazzar's heart: "You have been weighed in the balances and found wanting" (v. 27 RSV). Daniel reminded Belshazzar of Nebuchadnezzar's fate for similar acts of arrogance. The king's sacrilege had been observed and it would be punished. A new world power, the Medes and Persians, would rip from his hand the power he had misused. Sin does not go unpunished. The moral order of God's creation and human society within it will be reaffirmed.

Biblical people believe that the universe operates within a moral system that cannot be violated without penalty. People might be able to ignore that order for a while, perhaps even a very long time, but sooner or later those violations come to light and there will be penalties to be paid. God and God's moral order will not be mocked forever; the wheels of God's justice might grind slowly, but they never stop. God's justice and righteousness will outlast and eventually bring to account every violation of them. This is an element of the character of God. The story of the handwriting on Belshazzar's wall reveals this to be so.

The Prayer of an Exile

Daniel 9:3–6, 18–23

The context of Daniel 9 differs from the book's earlier chapters in one way and is similar in another. The new thing about Israel's situation was that the Persians were now in power. The Egyptians and remnants of the Assyrians had been defeated by the Babylonians at the Battle of Carchemish in 612 BC. The Babylonian kingdom fell in turn to the Persian Empire under Cyrus in 539 BC. These empires were the superpowers of the Middle Eastern world during the years from 800 to 330 BC. They swallowed small kingdoms like Aramea (Syria), Israel, and Judah, or forced them to serve as puppet states. The Babylonians had destroyed Jerusalem in 587 BC. Several deportations carried a sizable segment of the population into exile. The first chapters of the book of Daniel are set in the time of Babylonian domination.

By chapter 9, however, the Persians had seized Babylonia and thus the Jewish exiles now served new masters. Under the Babylonian kings, the exiles knew that they had few prospects for returning home. But now that the Persians were in power, the future looked more promising. On the other hand, their situation had not changed in that they were still exiles. They were still captive, held against their will in a strange land. That captivity was no different for the fact that Persians now held power. The raw, daily reality of the exile is the context of Daniel's confession and prayer in chapter 9.

On one level the exile could be interpreted as nothing more than an unfortunate consequence in which the little nation of Judah got in the way of the Babylonian superpower. To understand the story in this manner would be to read the Israelite situation from the standpoint of the international politics. To the Israelites, however, events were never simply events; they were expressions of God's will. According to this theological view of history and its events, the people of Jerusalem were carried off into exile for reasons larger than the political and military ambitions of Nebuchadnezzar. In Israel's theological view, their exile was a direct consequence of their sin; they had disobeyed the Lord and exile was the divine judgment against them. Events are never simply the result of human action; rather, there is behind human intention and action the purpose of God working out his good and perfect will.

This theological perspective was an underlying assumption of Daniel's prayer. The prayer, therefore, in 9:4 quickly moved to confession. Israel was in exile because they "have been wicked and have rebelled...have turned away from your commands and laws...have not listened to your servants the prophets" (vv. 5–6). For these reasons, and for others that the prayer lists, "the Lord did not hesitate to bring the disaster" (v. 14).

The great prophet Jeremiah also followed this Deuteronomistic interpretation of historical events. Second Chronicles 7:14 is a clear example of this biblical way of thinking: "If my people ... will humble themselves and pray and seek my face and turn from their wicked ways, then will I hear...and will forgive their sin and will heal their land." Daniel's prayer followed the same pattern. He knew that the people had sinned; that was the theological explanation for the fact of exile. The only way out was to seek the Lord's face, to humbly confess sin, and to ask for restoration. Daniel knew that the exiles' return depended utterly on the mercy of God; they had done nothing to merit their restoration. So he prayed that God would lead them home for mercy's sake and for the sake of the ruined temple in Jerusalem that, so long as it and Jerusalem lay in ruins, made the people of God a shame and a laughingstock in the eyes of the world. This, implied Daniel, was no way for the people of God to live; neither was it the way that the God of Abraham, Isaac, and Jacob should be known among the nations.

Vindication in a New World
Daniel 12

Apocalyptic comes from a word that means "revelation." Something has been hidden and through this writing is about to be disclosed. Daniel and Revelation are the two books of the Bible to employ this style of writing, but there were many other apocalyptic writings that were not admitted into the canon of Scripture. Wide differences can be found among these writings, but they generally shared the conviction that history as they had known it was coming to a close and that events of their day contained signs of the cosmic struggle between God and Satan. Furthermore, apocalyptic writings shared the belief that the historical events of their day carried signs of this struggle. These books wanted to describe the impending crisis of history, God's final judgment, the vindication of God's faithful people, and their blessedness in a new age about to dawn.[27]

Theologically speaking, apocalyptic writings take a very dim view of the present world. They see the world as led astray by fallen angels and polluted by sin; "it is an evil world, a world in rebellion against God, a secular world, very nearly a demonic world. Yet it was not doubted that God was in control and would soon come to judge the world, consigning Satan and his angels and those who have obeyed him to eternal punishment, and saving his own. Eschatology[28] here appears in a new dimension. What is awaited is no longer a turning point in history, however dramatic—but a new world (age) beyond history."[29]

Israel's prophets had anticipated the coming "Day of the Lord." To be sure, they saw it as a day of judgment. But the prophets also saw God's redemption of his people occurring through that judgment. In their view, the Day of the Lord was not the end of history but a dramatic change in its course. Apocalyptic writing appropriated the concept of the Day of the Lord from the prophets but invested it with a new meaning, even further enlarging its significance in the process. In apocalyptic writing, the Day of the Lord means that history is not turning but ending. This difference in meaning has sometimes led scholars to say that apocalyptic writings represent a pessimistic view of the world over against the more hopeful view taken by the prophets. The prophets thought that the world was evil, but not so bad that the Lord would not redeem it.

Characteristics of apocalyptic writing underlie Daniel 12. However, in addition to these themes, we find in this passage the most unambiguous of Old Testament texts concerning the resurrection of the dead. "Multitudes who sleep in the dust of the earth will awake (v. 2)." The concept of the resurrection of the just and the unjust was a late development of Old Testament understanding. In fact, in Jesus' day there were still many Jews, primarily the Sadducees, who rejected the idea altogether. But it cannot be denied that this glorious, hope-filled description is part of the vision of biblical faith here in this text.

27. Bright, *A History of Israel*, 3rd ed., 455–56.

28. Eschatology refers to beliefs about the end of time.

29. Ibid., 456.

Hosea

Marriage to a Prostitute

Hosea 1–2

A faithful reading of Hosea pays great rewards to its readers, even as it makes demands. This book looks unflinchingly at the decaying relationship between Israel and God and describes it in symbols and language rarely spoken in polite company. Hosea also contains some of the most moving passages in the Old Testament and, indeed, in the entire Bible.

Hosea was a younger contemporary of Amos. He delivered his message to the northern kingdom of Israel sometime during the years 786 and 746 BC. We do not know much about Hosea's life, but the little we do know exceeds by far our knowledge of most of the other Old Testament prophets. We learn this information in the first three chapters of his book, where we find the details of his unhappy marriage to a woman named Gomer. This marriage consisted of five stages: (1) Hosea and Gomer entered into a marriage covenant. (2) Gomer broke their covenant by committing adultery as a prostitute. (3) Hosea was about to punish Gomer, which was his right under the law. (4) Although free to cast her away, Hosea could not let his wife go. (5) At the last, Gomer would return.[30] During their marriage, Gomer gave birth to three children. There is no certainty that Hosea was the father of any of them. There is no certainty that they even had the same father.

In his unhappy marriage, Hosea saw a metaphor for Israel's relationship with God. This metaphor was the heart of the word that he delivered. In Hosea's view, Israel was a faithless spouse who had violated her covenant with God by playing the harlot and whoring after the false gods and goddesses of the Canaanites. Mention has been made of the sexual practices that were part of Baal and Asherah. Although difficult to imagine, it may have been the case that the people of Israel had reached a point in their religious confusion where they mistook these fertility rites for the authentic worship of God. Hosea 2 paints a picture of a confused people who attributed the productivity of their land to Baal and who continued some of the celebrations that were part of Israel's religious life under the Lord.

Hosea's metaphor for Israel's faithlessness reached all the way to the naming of Gomer's three children. Whether or not he was their biological father, Hosea asserted the Israelite husband's right to name the children born to his wife. The first of these children he named Jezreel, for the broad fertile valley that also served as a major trade route. It was the site of a bloody purge carried out by Jehu, commander of the Israelite army. Both King Joram II and his mother, the infamous Jezebel, were killed in this revolt. (Unfortunately, the Judean King Azariah was also a victim of this purge, although unintended.) Jehu's rebellion and the savage way he conducted it isolated Israel from her neighbors and left her without allies when the Assyrian armies marched down from the north later in the eighth century. Ancient military commanders preferred to engage opposing armies in flat open areas where they could make the most effective use of their chariots. When the Assyrian army defeated the Israelites, the battle occurred in the Valley of Jezreel.

31. Gentz, *Dictionary of Bible and Religion*, s.v. "Hosea."

Hosea named Gomer's other two children symbolically, to warn Israel of its precarious situation. In Hebrew, *Lo-Ruhamah* (1:6) means "not pitied," signifying that when the Assyrians eventually arrived to plunder Israel and carry the people off into exile, God would observe these events without pity for his former spouse. *Lo-Ammi* (1:8) means "not my people." Long before, God had chosen Israel, saying, "I will be your God and you will be my people." Hosea's symbolic naming of the third child threatened Israel with nonbeing.

How Can I Abandon You?
Hosea 11

The books of Hosea and Jeremiah stand above the rest of the Old Testament in their intimate portrayal of the heart of God. Hosea 11 describes God's love for Israel in the tender terms. It also reveals God's heart pulled in two directions. Like Hosea with Gomer, the Lord was determined to punish Israel for her harlotry. But Hosea loved Gomer, and God loved Israel. How could he let her go?

The Assyrian Empire that menaced Israel from the northeast was a brutal and repressive totalitarian state. Its armies followed no rules of war, but ruthlessly savaged the countryside and people they invaded. As a means of insuring against later rebellion in occupied regions, the Assyrians routinely deported large numbers of the population from one nation, replacing them with people deported from another occupied territory. This mixing of peoples debased their religions and cultures and left them impotent and utterly subjugated. That was the fate awaiting Israel scarcely more than two decades after Hosea and his message. The Assyrians would destroy Israel "without pity," the name of one of Gomer's children.

God knew the fate that awaited Israel, and his heart was deeply moved. At the risk of trivializing this love, like a modern-day parent God could say, "My child, this will hurt me more than it will hurt you." Hosea 11 expands on God's relationship with Israel by adding the metaphor of parent-child to the previous idea of husband-wife. God spoke with words that reveal the pain of unacknowledged love. He had done so much and had given so much to Israel. But who did Israel thank for all of these blessings? Not the Lord, their true source, but Baal.

In the gentlest of images, God said that he taught Ephraim—another name for Israel—to walk. All we need to do is close our eyes and remember the gentle encouragement parents give to toddlers on the verge of taking their first steps. We stoop to their level and reach out our arms, coaxing, encouraging, and ready to catch the youngsters. So it was in the first days of God's life with Israel. He led them with "cords of human kindness"; we can imagine an ancient device woven to support a toddler not much different from a modern baby walker. It must be said that these are maternal images. Israelite fathers wanted their wives to bear children, preferably sons. But men were not extensively involved in rearing children; that was "women's work." It is instructive of our conception of God that he described his relationship with Israel in such motherly terms.

God raised Israel and gave his child love and blessing. Yet God also acknowledged that his people would reject that love. He knew that soon the Assyrians would rape and plunder the land. And so God, the judge of the universe, asked, "How can I give you up, Ephraim? How can I hand you over, Israel?" (11:8). Could God really treat Israel no better than Admah and Zeboiim, two cities on the plain destroyed along with Sodom and Gomorrah? In a sentence that raises some perplexing theological questions, God declared, "My heart is changed within me; all my compassion is aroused." God, the Holy One, must do what is right, even as Abraham had asked God on the eve of the destruction of Sodom, "Will not the Judge of all the earth do right?" (Gen 18:25). Thus, God declared that a remnant would be spared and saved from the coming Assyrian onslaught. God would not wink at Israel's sin, but neither would God utterly destroy. It was Hosea's vision that some of God's children would learn through their suffering, and the Lord would bring them home.

Joel

Iniquity Punished, Boundless Mercy
Joel 1–2

Joel was a common name among Israelites because of its theological affirmation. In Hebrew, Joel means "Yahweh is God." We know nothing about this man other than his father's name. Unlike many of the other prophets who dated their sermons and oracles according to the reign of the kings of Israel and Judah, Joel didn't bother to date his work at all. Commentator James Limburg reckons the date of Joel's prophecy according to several internal references to events of the day and concludes that Joel may have delivered it around the year 400 BC. However, this date is not certain.[31]

31. Limburg, *Hosea–Micah*, 58.

As we have said repeatedly, in the Bible and especially among the prophets, events are never simply historical events; they are freighted with theological significance. If we reflect on the work of the majority of the prophets, we find that they interpreted the great political events of their day in terms of Israel's faith and its covenant with the Lord. They saw God's hand in the fortunes and reversals of the northern and southern kingdoms and their people. Joel also saw God's hand at work in history, but in his case the crisis confronting Israel was not political but agricultural. A great swarm of locusts, commonly grasshoppers, had invaded the countryside, and they menaced the life of Israel as surely as any army that marched across its soil.

Ultimately, the land, and consequently farming, is the foundation of any society. None of us would last very long without the crops and livestock produced by the men and women who live in the country. This is a common-sense fact of life that may have been obscured for the majority of the nations we call developed, whose people live in cities and suburbs and shop for food in supermarkets. Food products are there in such abundance and come from such a variety of sources that the thought of a food shortage rarely occurs to us. Such was not the case in Joel's day, nor is it so in all too many places in our world, even today. Agricultural crises mean widespread famine in a nation where the vast majority of people raise their own food. The plague of locusts that spread across Judah in Joel's day threatened to consume the crops that were the very lifeblood of the people. This was more than a few bugs jumping around the edges of a wheat field on a hot August afternoon. "At the sight of them, nations are in anguish; every face turns pale" (2:6).

The plague of locusts was not the end of Joel's story. Even more memorable was the deliverance from this plague worked by the hand of the Lord. Thus, the prophet began his sermon with the command that the people were to tell this tale of affliction and release to their children, and their children, down through the generations. They had witnessed yet another of God's mighty acts, and its story must be told and retold. This story begins with the plague of locusts and ends in God's deliverance. In between, we find Joel's prophetic insight into its meaning. Sin was the occasion that brought the plague on Israel, and Israel's repentance would lead to the Lord's forgiveness and deliverance.

Christians tend to remember Joel 2:28–29, especially in connection with the book of Acts. But the centerpiece of this passage is found in 2:13. There Joel applied the broad fundamental categories of the faith of Israel to the concrete and specific situation confronting him and the people. He quoted Exodus 34:6, the text where the Lord God revealed as much of himself to Moses as Moses could bear. Connected to verse 7, this is one of the great foundational texts of the faith of Israel. All the adjectives and the paradoxes of biblical faith are there. God punishes, but God is compassionate. God will not wink at sin, but God forgives. Joel lived in the center of that faith, and his work as a prophet was to encourage Israel to live there as well. In the final analysis, his sermon shows us one way in which the great theological affirmations of biblical faith were applied to the highly specific and concrete situations of life. Consistently, the prophets applied such affirmations in ways that encouraged or restored Israel's hope in God.

Amos

A Hard Message in Good Times
Amos 1–2

In the eighth-century BC, the international situation surrounding such small kingdoms as Israel and Judah underwent dramatic and ominous change. The Assyrian Empire awakened from a period of dormancy and began flexing its military muscles. Always aggressive and ready to demand tribute, a newly revitalized Assyria spelled serious problems for its little neighbors. In 800 BC, those problems were barely visible on the horizon, but they were there nevertheless.

The men who first saw them were the great prophets of this century: Amos, Hosea, Micah, and Isaiah. These men saw more than Assyrian militarism in the events about to unfold. The prophets also saw the judgment of God. The events of history carried a crucial theological and moral message. Nobody saw that message with greater clarity or declared it more courageously and forcefully than the prophets.

Amos was chronologically the first of the eighth-century prophets. He was a shepherd in Tekoa, a village in the southern kingdom of Judah. To this simple, honest man, the word of the Lord suddenly came. It was a word of warning and judgment against several of the little kingdoms of the region, including Judah and Israel. In a few decades, Assyria swept all of them away save Judah. But the large majority of Amos's message was directed to the northern kingdom of Israel.

Underlying Amos's message is the Deuteronomistic doctrine of history.

Amos looked at Israel's religious and social life and found injustice, immorality, and idolatry; in short, the people of the northern kingdom had utterly failed in their covenant obligations to Yahweh. The wealthy class ground down the poor, selling them into forced labor and using their economic power to gain an unfair advantage. Justice became the private property of the rich, and justice available only to some is not justice. During the rites of the Canaanite fertility religions that had replaced the worship of God, fathers and sons visited the same temple prostitutes. Amos saw all of this and knew that God's wrath surely would break out on Israel.

The eighth-century prophets delivered an unpopular message to people who believed that they could ignore it. Amos was a foreigner in Israel, a man whose home was in another country. Israelites displeased with his message could tell him to go home and mind his own business. To further complicate Amos's task, Israel was enjoying economic prosperity. When times are bad, people will listen more attentively to the word of the Lord than in more prosperous times. Amos's listeners saw their prosperity as a sign of God's favor and anticipated even greater times in the coming "day of the Lord." Amos's word to this badly mistaken people was that their prosperity was hollow and their society morally bankrupt. The day of the Lord was indeed about to dawn, but it held only disaster for Israel.

Straight Talk about Social Justice

Amos 4–5

It is a common misconception of the Israelite prophets that they were primarily concerned with predicting future events. To be sure, prediction did figure in many prophetic sermons. First and foremost, however, prophets addressed the state of affairs current in their own time. They spoke of the future because that was where the consequences of Israel's folly would bear fruit. A common way of describing the classical prophets of the eighth century BC is to say that they were "forth-tellers" as much if not more than they were foretellers. The prophets were powerful preachers who bluntly identified Israel's and Judah's sins. They fearlessly named them, and their sermons exposed the errors in popular religious beliefs. Prophecy in Israel was rooted in strong preaching that did not blanch at the public proclamation of the sins that would lead to future disaster if the people and their leaders failed to repent.

Men such as Amos and Micah noticed the little people who were ground down by injustice in their society. Others might shrug their shoulders and say that in any society there will be some who cannot compete; they might look the other way or simply ignore injustices. Amos was not such a man. To him, as well as to other prophets, it mattered that corrupt bureaucrats overtaxed widows. It mattered that only the wealthy got the verdicts they wanted in court. It mattered that shrewd and dishonest merchants rigged their scales to increase their profit margins. Such injustices had become systemic in Israel. In the face of systemic injustice, we are tempted to say, "Well, of course it's wrong, but what can anybody do about it? Life's not fair." In the summer of 1999, American farmers could not buy a loaf of bread in a grocery store with the money they were paid for a bushel of wheat. Amos would have been their champion.

Amos's sermons identified God as the defender and avenger of injustice's victims. According to Amos, unless Israel returned to God and God's commandments, disaster would fall upon the nation. God would not stand idly by while his people refused to do justice and love mercy. The eighth-century prophets and much of the Old Testament tightly join together God's expectation that justice and righteousness will characterize the corporate and individual life of his people.

Righteousness describes the proper vertical relation among humans and God. *Justice* is the quality that is to determine the horizontal relationship between human beings. Amos linked the two requirements so that absence of one diminished the other as well. There can be no righteousness without justice, and there can be no justice without righteousness. The word of the Lord that came to Amos declared that God couldn't care less about Israel's worship as long as those worshipers ignored the injustices and the hurt in their society.

Popular among people of the northern kingdom was the belief that the "day of the Lord" would dawn soon. As they saw it, this day would restore Israel to the glory of David and Solomon. They expected God to pour out peace, prosperity, and security upon Israel. Amos stood this image on its head. The day of the Lord was coming, to be sure. But it would be a day of darkness and not light. The day of the Lord would bring judgment and not glory. The day of the Lord would bring military disaster and exile. Amos's interpretation of this phrase, "the day of the Lord," could not have run any more counter to the popular religious beliefs of his day. But the fearless prophet was not seeking popularity. He sought only to deliver the word of the Lord—the word of justice and righteousness—that had come to him.

The Courage to Speak for God
Amos 6–7

Amos was among the earliest of the writing prophets. The book that bears his name and is composed of his prophetic judgments (called oracles) parallels the narrative of 2 Kings 14:21–29. As already noted, Amos was a shepherd—a layperson, in other words—from Tekoa, a village in the southern kingdom of Judea. Although a Judahite, Amos prophesied in Samaria during the years from 760 to 750 BC.

As if his prophetic work as an outlander in Israel was not difficult enough, Amos also delivered his sermons at a moment of unequaled prosperity and security. If it is the case that hard times and disaster softened Israel's heart and prepared it for Yahweh's word, then prosperity closed their ears to that message. Amos began preaching when Jeroboam II had successfully extended Israel's borders. Expanded borders meant increased wealth flowing into Samaria. Money flowed freely, and the upper social classes benefited from these political and economic conditions. Amos 6:4–6 details some of the sumptuous lifestyle of the Israelite upper class. They were wealthy enough to afford ivory inlaid furniture and dine on aged prime beef and mutton. They bought wine to drink "by the bowlful" and pampered their bodies with expensive creams and moisturizers. The common theology of that day interpreted prosperity as a sign of Yahweh's favor. Amos would find it very difficult to persuade wealthy and complacent Israel that God was displeased with them.

Second Kings 14:26–27 refers to the suffering of everyone in Israel and that Yahweh used King Jeroboam II to eliminate external threats to Israelite security. However, Jeroboam II also is said to have continued the idolatrous practices of Jeroboam son of Nebat. Furthermore, Jeroboam II also either created or allowed domestic injustice to flourish. Some Israelites were wealthy, but not all were. The wealthy exploited the poor: "They sell the righteous for silver, / and the needy for a pair of sandals" (Amos 2:6). The powerful in Israelite society also corrupted the legal system so that justice was denied to the oppressed (2:7). While some Israelites reclined on expensive furniture and indulged themselves, other Israelites cried out in their misery and oppression.

Israelite religion included the idea of the "day of the Lord," (*yom Yahweh* in Hebrew). Hearkening back to the old theocratic ideal of "cry-answer," the day of the Lord was to be a time of release and recovery, a day when Yahweh heard the cry of the oppressed. In Amos's day, wealthy Israelites had corrupted this idea, however, interpreting it to their own advantage and denying the poor any hope of future restoration. "Israelites of this era looked forward eagerly to the 'Day of the Lord.' They believed that this 'day' [or era] would inaugurate an age of peace and freedom from the aggression of their enemies. Israelites thus anticipated the Day of the Lord as a time of lightheartedness, security, and celebration. They were already prosperous; the arrival of the Day of the Lord would add military security to their already abundant material life."[32] It was also the case that such security would permit the wealthy to continue their exploitation of the poor. Through their reinterpretation of the day of the Lord, the wealthy robbed the poor of perhaps their last possession: hope.

Amos sharply criticized the new interpretation of the day of the Lord. As he proclaimed the word of the Lord, it became clear to the residents of the Israelite capital of Samaria that the day of the Lord would bring darkness rather than light. Judgment, not celebration, would be the order of that day. Idolatry and injustice would bring down the northern kingdom in the day of the Lord.

Obadiah

The very short book of Obadiah is unlike much of the prophetic literature in a few key ways. It begins with an announcement that what follows is the vision of Obadiah. Although the idea of a vision is not unique to this book, it is far more common to find the prophets saying, "The word of the Lord that came to ______." The ear, not the eye, was the more typical organ of revelation among the Old Testament prophets. Second, and more important, Obadiah is a prophetic oracle of divine judgment delivered primarily against Israel's neighbor, Edom. The Israelites are only marginally addressed in the entire book, and not directly by name. That is highly unusual. Third, Obadiah, the shortest book in the Old Testament, is also an example of intertextuality. The book begins by restating a passage from another of the prophetic books. What we have in Obadiah is one prophet building a sermon on a text from an earlier prophet's work. Other examples of intertextuality exist

32. Strege and Willowby, *God's Redeeming Story*, 97–98.

among the prophetic books, but they are rare. When all three of Obadiah's rarities are combined, the result is a very distinctive book.

The name *Obadiah* means "servant of the Lord." The text says absolutely nothing else about this man. His message is terse and direct, and there is little time for introductions. In fact, "time is short" might serve as a theme for the entire book.

The first five verses of the book closely parallel Jeremiah 49:9, 14–16. The parallel is so close that scholars conclude that Obadiah had access to Jeremiah's prophecy. If that is the case, then we can speculate that Obadiah's vision was the product of his meditation on Jeremiah's message. Obadiah's sermon against Edom is what he saw because of his reflection on an earlier prophet's word. On that basis, Edom is the central subject of Obadiah's sermon.

Edom and its people have a long history in the Old Testament. The territory of Edom was located south of the Dead Sea. Its northern neighbor was Moab; to the south and east was desert. Edom shared its western border with Israel, specifically the tribe of Judah. Harsh and barren terrain, Edom was distinctive for the reddish rock formations of the region. (In fact, *Edom* in Hebrew means "red region.") Jacob's twin Esau was the patriarchal ancestor of the Edomites. Just as the relationship between the two brothers was often contentious, so also the relationship between Israel and Edom was filled with strife. In the days of King Saul, Edom was numbered among Israel's enemies. David defeated the Edomites and made them a people subject to Israel. They revolted during the reign of King Jehoram of Judah about 850 BC.

Among Israel's painful memories of the exile, one that stood out was the behavior of the Edomites at the time of Jerusalem's destruction. In Israel's eyes, this behavior was all the more blameworthy because the Edomites were kinsmen. Instead of sharing their relatives' grief, the Edomites behaved as if they were Israel's enemies. Obadiah says that they gloated and rejoiced in Jerusalem's downfall and joined in looting the city. According to verse 14, the Edomites also handed over refugees to the Babylonians. The Israelites never forgot nor forgave this traitorous behavior. Several Old Testament books refer to the Edomites and call down the Lord's wrath upon them, including Psalm 137:7; Isaiah 34; Jeremiah 49:7–22; Lamentations 4:21–22; Ezekiel 25:12–14; 35:5–6; and Malachi 1:2–4. These passages all either state or echo the sentiment that Edom will pay for its sins.

We might be tempted to read the book of Obadiah as a call for Yahweh to avenge Israel against its neighbor, but that is to interpret this book as motivated by pettiness. Instead, we might interpret this book as having looked into the Lord and his ways and found eternal moral principles. First, God's concern for the weak and defenseless must extend to all people. Edom played the role of bystander in Jerusalem's hour of need, and it is for the refusal to come to a neighbor's aid that Edom would suffer. Second, there is a moral order in God's universe that balances out the consequences of sin with the sin itself. A terrible inversion of the Golden Rule, this order says, "As you have done to others, so it shall be done to you."

Jonah

Yahweh Is Lord of All

Jonah 1–2

Jonah is another of the shorter prophetic books that, like Amos, Micah, Hosea, Obadiah, and Nahum, were collected together in the Hebrew Bible in a single volume known as the Book of the Twelve. Jonah is unique among the Old Testament books of the prophets. Although some prophetic books contain narrative sections, Jonah is entirely a narrative. The subject of this narrative was a man named Jonah, the son of Amittai, a prophet in the northern kingdom of Israel during the reign of Jeroboam II (786–746 BC). This was the period of Assyrian political ascendancy and expansion. The city to which he was called, Nineveh, was the capital of the Assyrian Empire. In other words, Jonah's story is told against a backdrop of threatened Assyrian power.

It is important to distinguish the date of the narrative's setting (the dramatic date) from the date when it likely was written (the date of publication). The story was part of Israel's oral tradition long before it ever was written down. Passed down from one generation to the next, the story of Jonah was likely written during the postexilic era, when many Jews believed that the Lord's covenant eliminated the possibility that the Lord cared at all for non-Jews. This is the idea of ethnic exclusivism, also challenged by the book of Ruth.

The corollary of this exclusivity was that God treated all other nations with an attitude of benign neglect. But a more virulent form of exclusivism espoused an active hatred of non-Jews, especially if they were threats to security. Beyond question, the greatest and most fearsome threat was the Assyrian Empire, and it did not take much at all to incite Israelite hearts to a cold and bloodthirsty fury against the Assyrians. Nahum 3 is a chilling expression of that hatred. This point of view stated that God had nothing positive to say or do to the Assyrians.

The story of Jonah had been told for many generations, but it was written in a moment of intense Jewish exclusivism. Many Old Testament scholars have concluded that the book was written as a criticism of the form of Jewish exclusivism that spawned hatred of the non-Jews. Certainly, the reluctant prophet Jonah was a man who appears to have shared this venomous hatred. Jonah was not trying to escape his calling; he was objecting to the people to whom the Lord was sending him. Jonah did not want the Ninevites even to hear a word of warning and mercy from God; he definitely did not want to be the mouthpiece to give them that word.

The Assyrians were not worthy of the Lord's mercy and salvation and ought to have been excluded from it. However, the Old Testament also insists that the Lord will have mercy on whomever he will. In any case, divine mercy and grace are always gifts that no person—neither those inside the covenant community nor those outside—can ever merit or deserve in any way.

The Reluctant Prophet

Jonah 3–4

The narrative continues. Jonah has just been vomited onto dry ground by the great fish that had been his unwanted host for three days. We can only imagine how this experience would have shaken the man who would be the Lord's prophet. The second time the Lord called Jonah to be his prophet to Nineveh, there were no further attempts to flee. Jonah obeyed—but still with considerable reluctance.

The city to which Jonah was directed was large and notorious. One translation of the Hebrew says that Nineveh was a "city great to God." The phrase describes size, not moral or spiritual character. Nineveh is elsewhere in Jonah described as an "exceedingly great" city, so large that a person would need three days to walk from one side to another. By the standards of the ancient Near East, Nineveh was huge, and its size was matched by its reputation for cruelty. Nineveh was the capital of the Assyrian Empire, a militaristic society that practiced state terrorism. The prophet Nahum called it "vile" (Nah 1:14), "the bloody city, all full of lies and booty" (3:1 RSV), and compared it to a den of lions (2:10–12) and a prostitute (3:4–7). He said that when Nineveh and its empire collapsed, people everywhere would rejoice.

In the eyes of the original readers, the idea that God had called Jonah to preach in Nineveh was nearly unthinkable. It would be roughly comparable to a situation in which a Jewish person would be called to preach to Nazis immediately on the heels of the Holocaust. Small wonder that Jonah proved to be less than enthusiastic in his preaching. His message consisted of only a warning: "Forty more days and Nineveh will be overturned" (3:4). There is no hint of divine mercy and forgiveness; there is no suggestion that repentance of heart and life was an option open to the Ninevites. Jonah preached a message of judgment without hope because Jonah was a preacher who did not care for his congregation. The word "overthrown" (RSV) in Jonah's one-sentence sermon is the same word used to describe God's devastation of Sodom and Gomorrah. Jonah would gladly have danced on the ruins and ashes of Nineveh.

Despite Jonah's dull preaching, Nineveh repented. From the lowest to the highest, mourning and repentance was the order of the day. The Lord God noted their change of heart, and as the text says, "He had compassion and did not bring upon them the destruction he had threatened" (3:10). Jonah may not have cared about the Ninevites, but God did. Despite all the bloodshed, all the evil, and the great wickedness of the city, the Lord cared about these people.

The central message of Jonah is that God does not have only one chosen people; all others are also objects of his love and attention. There is no wickedness that cannot be repented, because God's mercy holds open the door to forgiveness and restoration. In the face of this insight into God's character, Jonah could only grumble.

But there is a kernel of truth in Jonah's complaint. In 4:2, Jonah quoted from Exodus 34:6–8, a text that has been described as Israel's core testimony to the character and faithfulness of God. Jonah must have been astonished to find himself quoting these words in reference to the Lord's care and regard for the people of Nineveh as well as the people of Israel. Astonishment will be equally great in the hearts of all who mistakenly believe that God's love and care extend no further than the boundaries of the covenanted people of God.

Micah

Who Was Micah and When Did He Prophesy?

Micah 3; 6:1–8

Amos and Hosea prophesied in and to the northern kingdom, Israel. In 722 BC, the Assyrian army under Shalmaneser V marched into the streets of Samaria, Israel's capital city, and the northern kingdom disappeared. Prior to the destruction of Israel, the kings of Judah believed that they were protected by the small states that lay between them and Assyria. By the end of 722, that buffer zone no longer existed. It then became Judah's turn to worry about Assyrian expansionism and what that might mean for them.

Micah was the first eighth-century prophet to speak in and to the kingdom of Judah. He delivered this message during the years from 742 to 687 BC, which made him a younger contemporary of Hosea. Micah's prophetic career also overlapped the years of the great Isaiah. It is quite rare to find one prophet mentioning another, but Jeremiah 26:18 refers to Micah as a prophet of the time of King Hezekiah and cites Micah 3:12. As with most of the prophets, we know very little of Micah's personal history. He lived in the small town of Moresheth in the hill country southwest of Jerusalem. We do not know his occupation, but he clearly identified with the small farmers and villagers of that region. Some scholars have thus thought that Micah was himself a farmer. Others have seen in some passages of his book evidence of a man of high standing in his community, someone with the self-confidence to look the religious and civil leaders of Jerusalem in the eye. Whether the former or the latter, Micah's prophecy stated God's case against Jerusalem in uncompromising terms.

What was the word of the Lord through Micah? Micah identified economic and political exploitation and corruption as religious shortcomings. As the capital and by far the largest city in Judah, Jerusalem controlled the surrounding region economically and legally, as well as politically. The moneyed class lived in Jerusalem and from their comfortable homes controlled the rural economy. It was a situation reminiscent of the plight of modern-day farmers who are forced to accept low prices for their livestock and grain while others reap a profit. In the bluntest of terms, Micah accused the Jerusalem establishment of consuming the little people of the countryside. Even worse in Micah's eyes was that the religious and judicial leadership joined in this exploitation. Money was at the heart of the problem. Judges would give the "right" verdict for a bribe. Priests would not teach without a fee. Court prophets told fortunes only when paid. All of this, said Micah, was an offense to God.

Micah 6 states God's case against Judah, and the Jerusalem establishment in particular, in the language of a legal brief. God spoke as a prosecutor bringing an indictment against an accused criminal. The Lord had a controversy with his people. People in Jerusalem refused to hear this indictment on the grounds of their belief that God would never allow harm to come to the city. Jerusalem was the site of God's temple, after all; it was the center of Israelite religion. Residents of the city took comfort in these facts and falsely concluded that because of them God would never permit any harm to come to the city. Micah's indictment of the Jerusalem establishment directly challenged this line of thought. He dared to state the unthinkable: Jerusalem would be destroyed. Why? Because the religious and political leadership of the nation refused "to act justly and to love mercy and to walk humbly" (6:8) with the Lord.

Habakkuk

Living by Faithfulness
Habakkuk 3:2–6, 17–19

The prophecies in the book of Habakkuk concern the same events about which Jeremiah prophesied. This material can be dated from roughly 627 to 598 BC. Like many of the prophets, little is known of Habakkuk. He is one of a very few that the text names a *nabi*, (a prophet). That he is so named leads some scholars to the view that Habakkuk may have been an official or cult prophet. The word *cult* here should not send up warning flags. It is used here to describe established forms and institutions of religion. Cult prophets were attached to the temple in Jerusalem; they earned their living by prophecy.

Cult or temple prophets struggled with the temptation to make sure that their prophetic oracles did not threaten or offend. After all, the ancient kings, patrons of religious institutions who requested predictions from the temple prophets, were inclined to kill the messenger who delivered bad news. One thinks of Jehoshaphat's request to Ahab that they get a word from the prophet before waging war and Ahab's reluctance to call for the prophet Micaiah ben Imlach, who always prophesied ill of Ahab. Habakkuk did not yield to the temptation to add sugar to the strong medicine he declared to official Jerusalem. All of the signs pointed to Judah's destruction at the hands of the Babylonians, and Habakkuk minced no words in declaring so. To his warning of disaster, however, he added a word of instruction about living through a time when the Lord's voice was not likely to be heard.

"Habakkuk...typifies the faithful person who has to live in the world as it is and has grown weary with the world's ways of wickedness."[33]

In Romans 1:17, Paul wrote that "the righteous will live by faith." This idea was not original with him but is a quotation of Habakkuk 2:4. Luther interpreted Paul to mean that as long as a man or woman has faith, no sin can separate that person from God. In the context of the prophet's words, however, Habakkuk 2:4 reads differently. Much as in the final prayer that ends his book, the prophet said that faithfulness to God is the means by which the believer can live through any circumstance. Even when all external indicators suggest that faithfulness to God is a waste of time—when the vines bear no fruit, when the fields are barren, when rubble fills the once vibrant streets of the city—in such circumstances, righteous people will still trust the Lord with all their hearts, souls, minds, and strength. Such trust is a good working definition of faithfulness.

33. Elizabeth Achtemeier, *Nahum–Malachi*, 35–36.

Zephaniah

"Day of Wrath"
Zephaniah 1:12; 3:1–5, 11–13

As the second half of the seventh century BC drew to a close, the most astute and spiritually gifted of Jerusalem's preachers gazed eastward from the city walls. Beyond the horizon, the political sky darkened under the threat of a new superpower. At this moment, Judah remained under the Assyrian thumb as a vassal state expected to pay heavy tribute to its overlords, but the Assyrian Empire was sliding into decline. Before the century's end, the fall of Nineveh in 612, coupled with the rout of the Egyptian army at the Battle of Carchemish in 605, signaled the end of Assyria. The victors in this battle were the Babylonians, a reinvigorated, expansionist empire that coveted the little kingdoms of the western end of the Fertile Crescent even as it had swallowed Assyria whole. Not since Isaiah and Micah (700) had a prophet preached in Jerusalem; but during the reign of Josiah, prophecy reasserted itself in Judah in the preaching of Zephaniah. He saw danger beyond the eastern desert.

Josiah reigned from 640 to 609 BC. Although his reign is justly remembered for religious reform and the discovery of the "Book of the Law," Josiah's years were marked by the ominous buildup of Babylonian power. Josiah and his people did not suffer during his reign, but the handwriting was on the wall. Zephaniah was the first to announce its message.

Nothing is known of Zephaniah, except that his family is identified back four generations. We are simply left to ponder the significance of this naming, unique among the Old Testament prophets. What we can say about Zephaniah is that his message was radical and universal. According to his prophetic sermons, all of the nation-states of the western Fertile Crescent—the mighty as well as the petty—were soon to feel the full weight of God's judgment.

Zephaniah aimed his message particularly at the powerful, growing reality of syncretism at the court. There is no disputing the fact that Zephaniah's preaching showed the Lord's anger with Judah. Neither was there any means of softening this anger. Here we read descriptions of the fully disclosed wrath of God. It is not surprising, then, that when later poets wanted to describe this wrath they returned to the words of Zephaniah. Perhaps no musical rendition better captures this awesome wrath, even terror, than that of Verdi's moving and powerful *Requiem*.

Haggai

First Things First
Haggai 1:2–14; 2:1–5

The prophet Haggai was one of the earliest postexilic prophets. According to Haggai 1:1, the word of the Lord came to this prophet "in the second year of King Darius." This king ruled Persia from 522 to 486 BC. It had been roughly twenty years since Cyrus had liberated the exiles and allowed them to return home. Persia was still the dominant political power. It was customary to date events according to the reign of the monarch. Because of this, we can date Haggai's prophecy to the year 520. If his prophetic career was limited to the three prophecies that make up this book, it was a short career. We are told that three messages came to him, the first in the "sixth month," the second in the "seventh month," and the third in the "ninth month." Approximately three months span the length of Haggai's prophetic career.

Haggai's prophecy opens with a sharp rebuke directed toward Zerubbabel, a descendant of David and by Persian appointment governor of the province of Judah, and toward Joshua, the high priest. Haggai rebuked them for being inattentive to the temple rebuilding project, but Haggai had another complaint to file against the two leaders. Apparently Zerubbabel and Joshua had rather quickly gotten to work building houses for themselves while they neglected the reconstruction of the house of the Lord. This is the force of Haggai's rhetorical question in 1:4. Haggai's question highlights the moral and religious distance between Zerubbabel and David. Recall the splendor of David's palace and his embarrassment before God. Without the prompting of others, he had concluded that it was improper for him to live in a "house of cedar" while Yahweh's home was only a tent. We have only Zerubbabel's silence, so neither good nor bad motives or attitudes may be attributed to him, but it is nevertheless ironic that this descendant of David needed Haggai to get him moving on the construction project.

Haggai also saw the wretched lives of the residents of Judah, their poor harvests and impoverished economy. In his view, Judah's poor state of existence was directly related to the fact that the temple stood unfinished on Mt. Zion. His prophetic oracles essentially are sermons delivered as divinely authorized theological comment on the religious, political, and economic affairs of Jerusalem and its people. Nevertheless, Zerubbabel and Joshua answered Haggai with, at best, a lukewarm attitude. In effect, they said, "You know, the timing is just not right; we're not ready to start building yet." There seems to have been a preoccupation with personal economic matters. The inference is that the people had other items they either wanted or needed to take care of first. To Haggai, this attitude was one of indifference to what was proper and right; Yahweh must have a temple of presence, and matters in Israel would not be right until he did. Things would not be well in Israel until the Lord's house was rebuilt.

Haggai believed that the reconstruction of the temple was crucial to Israel's future. Until then, Yahweh's new thing in Israel would be delayed. Haggai looked forward to a "time when all the nations were to worship Yahweh and bring him their treasures, and, surprisingly enough, he believed that this time was already imminent (2:6–9). It was for this time, when [Israelite religion] would throw off its national limitations and become a universal religion [for all people, Jew and Gentile alike]—the time of the Messiah—that the temple had to be built."[34]

Haggai does not refer to the edict of Xerxes, which demanded that work halt on the temple. This absence is likely explained because the first of Haggai's sermons was delivered before the start of the work on the temple. But he was not the sort of man to be troubled by whether this project would displease the Persian king. In Haggai's view, the Lord God merited infinitely more attention and regard than any earthly potentate,

34. Von Rad, *Old Testament Theology*, 283.

even the king of so mighty an empire as the Persian. The Lord was without a house, and that was the central problem. No wonder that the fields of Judah produced such sparse crops and the vineyards' yields were so small. This lack of bounty was the work of the Lord. The turning point would come when the Jewish people demonstrated their love for the Lord by laying the cornerstone of the new temple.

There is reason to believe that, as was so often the case with Israel's prophets, Haggai's sermons coincided with political unrest in the larger world of the great dominant powers. A new claimant to the Persian throne, Darius, was not the clear successor. He was from a lesser line of the royal family but made his way to the top through a combination of intrigue, violence, and effective propaganda. His throne remained shaky until he was able to consolidate his power. Haggai's prophetic sermons, with their clear messianic hopes, fit neatly into the first two years of Darius's reign, from 522 to 520 BC.

Haggai's sermons and oracles represent something of a shift in the direction of Old Testament prophecy. The temple and the proper performance of religious obligations were matters of great importance to him. Haggai's stress on these issues strongly suggests that he was an official prophet of the religious establishment—perhaps an insider. Many of the pre-exilic and exilic prophets were outsiders, that is, men who came from walks of life far beyond the circle of court and temple life. Isaiah and Ezekiel were the two outstanding exceptions to this generalization. Like those two giants, Haggai's great devotion to the Lord's cause demonstrates that not all establishment insiders were corrupt or false in their worship of Israel's God.

Zechariah

Rebuilding Postexilic Society
Zechariah 4

The prophet Zechariah lived in Jerusalem during the years of Haggai. If he is the same Zechariah mentioned in Nehemiah 12:16, then we know that he was a member of a family of priests. His name means "Yahweh has remembered." "It is a conservative name, evoking a sense of continuity with earlier Israelite tradition. Such a name suggests that Yahweh remembers what he did for and with Israel at an earlier period. And it presumes that he will act again in a similar manner."[35] Both prophets said that they received the "word of the Lord" in the second year of Darius, King of Persia. Haggai and Zechariah delivered this word to the people in the form of prophetic messages. Unlike Haggai, however, Zechariah appears to have received his messages through the medium of visions. The language he used to describe his visions bears a striking resemblance to some of the symbolic language of Daniel in the Old Testament and the Revelation in the New.

We must interpret Zechariah's prophecy in the context of Israel's situation in Jerusalem after the return from exile. In some important respects, the people were faced with the task of rebuilding their society as well as the walls of their houses and city. A generation of leadership had been lost in the exile. It would have been the responsibility of this generation to transmit the inherited traditions and values of Israelite life and religion to the next generation. Without

35. Petersen, *Haggai and Zechariah 1–8*, 110.

the lost generation of exiles, there were few people to answer basic religious and social questions.

Zechariah's visions and prophetic messages focus on such matters. "These visions were, in a sense, the way Zechariah did his theology. In them, he is explaining why and how Yahweh will undo the results of iniquity; how Yahweh will be present in Jerusalem.... Zechariah reports that Yahweh will no longer be localized in his temple. Instead, Yahweh will be a wall of fire around the city. And as for the city itself, Jerusalem will be a different urban entity from what it had been earlier. It will exist without walls.... [In this case] Zechariah...was being hardheadedly realistic. The city walls of Jerusalem were not rebuilt for another century."[36]

Zechariah's prophecies directly addressed what had to have been a critical issue for many of Jerusalem's citizens: Without walls, how would the city be protected? He also addressed other similar questions. The ceremonial structures of Israelite religion imposed standards of purity and holiness, but with the temple lying in ruins, the old customary practices by which first the temple priesthood, and ultimately the people, were ritually cleansed could not be performed. What was to be done? Zechariah's visions provide a solution. The high priest "Joshua was to be cleansed in the ritual setting of the divine council, though not by [God] himself. Once this agent of communal purification had himself been cleansed the polity of the new community could begin to function."[37]

Where Haggai focused on rebuilding the temple, and related other issues to that central task, Zechariah's visions took in a broader perspective. For him, the issue was rebuilding Israelite religion and society. The challenge before the people, in Zechariah's view, was to implement plans and procedures for a new religious and social order. Repeatedly, the visions of the first four chapters refer to a measuring line or a plumb line, a standard tool of builders, who must constantly measure their construction against the irresistible force of gravity. This provides a striking image of the way Yahweh's servants will measure the reconstruction of Israelite religion and society by referring to the divine will.

Looking for the Messiah
Zechariah 8

Christians have not been the only ones reading certain passages of the books of the prophets as foretelling the Messiah. Many Jewish readers have interpreted them in the same light. The difference between us is in naming the identity of the promised Messiah. Christians affirm that Jesus is that Messiah; those Jews who are not secularized still await the Promised One of Israel. This wait on the part of Jewish readers is not new to modern times, nor even to medieval Judaism. The wait for the Messiah dates back to the time of the exile.

The Jews who returned from Babylon faced a dismal present and a daunting task. Their prospects were bleak, and in hardly any sense would a reconstructed Jerusalem and Judaism resemble what they remembered of the past. Nearly all of the institutions and order of pre-exilic life had been demolished. They would not be recreated after exile. The verses from Malachi were uttered in the slender gap between promise and unrealized

36. Ibid., 115.
37. Ibid.

fulfillment. Zechariah's prophetic oracle is messianic in its hope and its description of a completely restored Jerusalem and Judah. Given the hard life and miserable living conditions of the returned exiles, it may be understandable that a prophet should stand forth to paint a picture of a bright and wonderful future.

Zechariah delivered this message at a moment when international politics permitted such hopes, about the year 520 BC. King Darius's hold on the Persian throne was insecure enough to encourage a belief among some Jews that the moment of political liberation and national renewal was just around the corner. It seems clear enough that Zechariah, and his contemporary Haggai, interpreted the upheaval in the empire as an event preliminary to God's mighty interruption of history. It is also likely that their preaching created some of the enthusiasm that resulted in the rebuilding of the temple.

Zechariah continued to preach after Darius stabilized his political situation. That stabilization did not dissuade Zechariah from his belief that the Lord would soon overthrow the Persian overlords through the work of the Messiah. These were bold and inflammatory words. They were also, for that moment, mistaken. Zechariah pinned his hope for a restored Jewish community on Zerubbabel. Surely he was the Lord's anointed. Of course, Zerubbabel proved to be a huge disappointment for anyone who, like Zechariah, believed him to be the Messiah. What does this disappointment signify for Zechariah's prophecy? We can affirm the truth of his vision through its application to another time and place. There is another lesson to be learned from Zechariah's misplaced hope. It behooves all of us to remember that only God knows the time and place of his intervention. When we start forecasting the time and means of God's actions, we stand a good chance of being embarrassed as well as just plain wrong.

Malachi

God's Messenger
Malachi 3–4

The book of Malachi is actually an anonymous collection of prophetic sayings that date from the period after the temple was rebuilt but before the arrival of Nehemiah and Ezra. In Hebrew, Malachi means "my messenger," and the use of this phrase seems to be taken from the phrase in Malachi 3:1. Nothing is known about the person who first uttered these sayings. Scholars generally agree that Malachi lived after Haggai and Zechariah. Those two prophets had spoken with the intention of stirring up the recently returned exiles to their responsibility for rebuilding the temple. In Malachi, the existence of the temple is an assumed fact (see 1:10; 3:1, 10). Furthermore, and this is part of Malachi's major complaint, even with and in the temple's presence, the people and their religious leaders had fallen into spiritual decline. Corrupt religious practices had to be corrected.

Despite the jubilation that erupted when the second temple was dedicated, shortly afterward it became clear that community morale was low. Life was still hard, and it was manifestly certain that the good old days of pre-exilic life were not about to return anytime soon. The returned exiles became disappointed with their lot, and that led to "disillusionment and this, in turn, to religious and moral laxity."[38]

The situation confronting faithful people of God was almost as dangerous as the exile itself. If the community's integrity could not be restored, it stood to lose its distinctive character as the people of the Lord God. When that happened, the complete dissolution of the people Israel would surely follow. The past could not be recreated, and new forms and institutions were clearly needed. It was the mission of Nehemiah and Ezra to be the agents of social, religious, and cultural renewal. But as the sermons of Malachi were being delivered, the arrival of Ezra and Nehemiah was still somewhere in the future. Malachi's sermons, therefore, must be seen as anticipating their later work. It was given to this prophet to do the very important first work of reestablishing some of the most elementary concepts of Old Testament religion, starting with the idea of faithfulness. In this, he targeted what might be termed a set of religious malpractices.

The first malpractice concerns temple worship. The problem is that priests and people have conspired to permit the use of imperfect animals in the rituals of the temple. The law required sacrificial animals to be perfect and without blemish. Yahweh would be dishonored by any sacrifice that was less than perfect. Of course, then as now, the best animals fetched a greater price at market and served as better breeding stock. To offer such prize animals as temple sacrifices cost a farmer or shepherd dearly. It would have been difficult for these people to see their best livestock literally go up in smoke. Suppose one were to substitute an animal with only a small blemish, perhaps only a little tiny wart on the inside of a hind leg? Didn't Yahweh want the people of God to live in economic health and prosperity? From God's perspective, imperfect sacrifices rob God of the honor and worship that are the proper gifts of the people of God. That the sacrifices are not subject to inspection or enforcement is irrelevant. Any obedience worthy of the name begins in the honor that prompts us to do our duty even when nobody else is watching.

Malachi's second malpractice complaint was directed against the temple priesthood. Here we find a foretaste of the controversy that arose between Jesus and the priestly class a few centuries later. From Malachi's perspective, the priests had betrayed their calling. They were to have preserved knowledge and guided the people in their walk with Yahweh. Instead, as Malachi said to them, "You have turned from the way and by your teaching have caused many to stumble; you have violated the covenant with Levi" (2:8). Sadly, Malachi's complaint echoed those made by so many prophets before the exile. Yahweh called Israel and blessed it. Nevertheless, the people had broken faith with their God and the covenant that would have brought them life.

God once again had a controversy with his people. As in days past, the prophet stood to threaten judgment. God's hope for this people was constant: if only they would hear and return, they might avoid judgment. God's hope remained constant and so did the promise. Those who heard and returned would be restored to covenant fellowship. "'They will be mine,' says the LORD Almighty, 'in

38. Bright, *History of Israel*, 3rd ed., 378.

the day when I make up my treasured possession. I will spare them, just as in compassion a man spares his son who serves him'" (3:17).

Malachi does not mince words, nor does the book blur the distinction between righteousness and wickedness. It is the case that some of the wicked had prospered, but that was no reason to conclude that faithful service to God was without benefit. Malachi confidently rested on a fundamental belief in the moral coherence of the universe created by God. It may be true that wickedness can bring a measure of profit, but such instances are but temporary interruptions of the rhythmic beat of a moral life. These interruptions notwithstanding, faithfulness to God must rest in the assurance that God will not always wink at unrighteousness. There will come a day—the famed "day of the Lord"—when those who flouted the Lord's just and righteous ways will receive their due, as will those who kept faith through the trials and difficulties of life.

Speaking through his messenger the prophet, the Lord once again directed Israel's attention toward a future day of judgment. By Malachi's lifetime, the prophets had been issuing this warning for centuries. People who thought that the Babylonian conquest and exile had been the promised day of the Lord must have been dismayed to learn that it still lay in the future. In that day, another Elijah would speak for God (4:5).

Centuries after Malachi, the people of Judea remembered his words and asked if John the Baptizer was the promised Elijah.

NEW
TESTAMENT

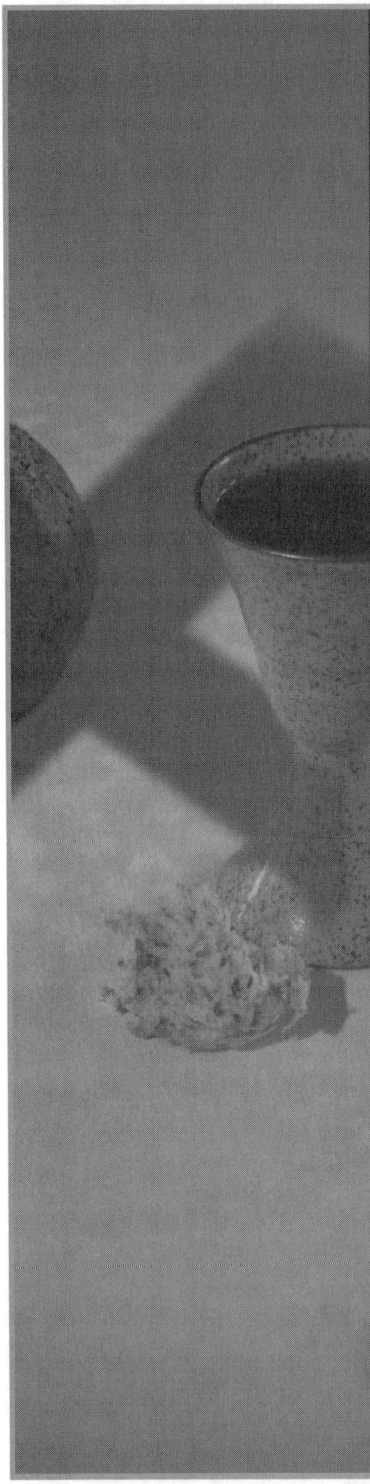

In the beginning was the Word, and the Word was with God, and the Word was God. He was in the beginning with God. All things came into being through him, and without him not one thing came into being. What has come into being in him was life, and the life was the light of all people. The light shines in the darkness, and the darkness did not overcome it. …And the Word became flesh and lived among us, and we have seen his glory…

—John 1:1–5, 14a (NRSV)

For Christ is the end of the law so that there may be righteousness for everyone who believes. Moses writes concerning the righteousness that comes from the law, that "the person who does these things will live by them." But the righteousness that comes from faith says, "Do not say in your heart, 'Who will ascend into heaven?'" (that is, to bring Christ down), "or 'Who will descend into the abyss?'" (that is, to bring Christ up from the dead). But what does it say? "The word is near you, on your lips and in your heart." (that is, the word of faith that we proclaim); because if you confess with your lips that Jesus is Lord and believe in your heart that God raised him from the dead, you will be saved.

—Romans 10:4–9 (NRSV)

Matthew

Family and Authority
Matthew 1:1:6, 18–25

Each of the four Gospels tells the story of Jesus; yet each narrates that story in its own way and, in a number of instances, with content unique to that Gospel. Mark keeps the cross in sharp focus while John portrays Jesus as the Savior of the world. Only Luke 15 contains the beloved parable of the prodigal son, and only Matthew contains the Great Commission, where the act of making disciples involves teaching as well as baptizing. In the context of the gospel of Matthew, the gospel work of making disciples refers to Jesus' great teaching, the Sermon on the Mount. If we understand this point, then we can see that the great burden of Matthew's gospel is ethics, addressing the question of how then followers of Jesus will live.

Imagine that you are a Christian believer of the first century with access only to Matthew's gospel. You have never heard of the gospel of Luke or any of the birth narratives contained in Luke. How differently would you remember the birth of Jesus? What points of Matthew's infancy narratives would you emphasize and try to remember?

The genealogy of Jesus takes up more than half of the first chapter. Genealogies are some of the least read verses of the Bible, but perhaps we are not reading them with sufficient attention. Matthew must have had some purpose in including this information beyond satisfying readers' curiosity about family trees. What might we learn from this condensed family history? In Matthew's gospel, the function of the Christmas story is to establish the authority of Jesus, the great rabbi of uncommon presence who teaches all to follow his ethical instruction. It is a kind of Christian Torah. Matthew establishes this authority by answering the unstated and crucial question, Who is Jesus? Later in this same gospel, Jesus himself puts this question to his disciples, "Who do the people say that I am?" The opening verses of Matthew's gospel lay the foundation for an answer.

Matthew traces Jesus' ancestry through Joseph's side of the family. Given that the text states explicitly that Joseph was not the child's natural father, how can Matthew trace the child's lineage through Joseph? Jewish adoption practices allowed an adopted son his father's inheritance and name just as much as if he were a natural child. Matthew's genealogy is, therefore, no mere rationalization. In Jewish tradition, Jesus was the adopted son of Joseph and had every right to claim David as his ancestor.

Second, Jesus' genealogy links him to Abraham. This connection describes Jesus as both a true son of Israel and in the line of descent from its great shepherd king, David. These genealogical links to Israel's former greatness had to be established if Jesus' teachings were to have credibility among Jewish readers. Matthew also locates the well-known circumstances of Jesus' birth squarely within the stream of the Jewish prophetic tradition. None of these things simply happen. As Matthew states, "All this took place to fulfill what the Lord had said through the prophet" (1:22). Such statements are an important element in Matthew's way of doing theology. Here we come to see Jesus and his mission in the context of Yahweh's long relationship with Israel. That long history comes to sharp theological focus in Matthew's use of Isaiah 7:14: "They will call him Immanuel—which means, 'God with us'" (1:23).

A third element worth noting is the presence of four women. The list is decidedly male, so it is remarkable to find the names of any women. But these four are unusual. They are Tamar, whose son Perez was fathered unknowingly by Tamar's father-in-law, Judah; Rahab, the harlot of Jericho who sheltered the Israelite spies before the city's destruction; Ruth, who was not even Israelite but a Moabitess; and the "mother of Solomon," who is unnamed, but we know her as Bathsheba, who committed adultery with David. The mention of these names would raise a few Jewish eyebrows as well as recall memories of faithfulness. Why include them? That these four women are included in Jesus' genealogy strongly links him with all of humanity—Gentile as well as Jew, sinner as well as those righteous under the law. The Messiah was born to all and for all.

Matthew's text makes no mention of Caesar, a census, shepherds, or angels singing in the heavens. Instead we read a narrative open to the point of view of Joseph. Tracing Jesus' genealogy through Joseph is only one example of this gospel's awareness of Jewish customs and traditions. A second illustration is that the Hebrew Bible—what Christians call the Old Testament—is quoted extensively. All of this constitutes strong evidence of the Jewishness of this gospel above the others. Many New Testament scholars believe that Matthew was written after Mark and Luke, in part to show the ongoing connection between Jesus and the "Law and the Prophets."

Matthew's gospel places a heavy emphasis on doing as opposed to simply receiving or having faith. Faith and ethics are not treated as separate themes in this gospel. Its emphasis on doing shows up already in the account of Joseph. Luke tells the story of the nativity with Mary in the forefront, in contrast to Matthew's way that makes Joseph the main human actor. This is a bit strange to our way of thinking since Joseph is neither the biological father nor the person who will carry and deliver the child. Nevertheless, Joseph is the central actor in the Matthean nativity story. Much is made of the virtues of justice and righteousness displayed in Joseph's character. There may be even more here than a hasty reading discloses. Since Joseph was both just and righteous according to the law, his religious obligation was to divorce Mary upon learning that she was pregnant. It was not anger that prompted Joseph to divorce Mary but the piety born of deep religious convictions. To all external appearance, Mary was guilty of fornication. Jewish culture and society regarded this as more than a moral failing; for a woman to have sexual intercourse before marriage was a crime punishable by death. Joseph's religious obligation before the law was to annul their marriage contract. However, we most resemble God, as Shakespeare said, when mercy seasons justice. Joseph was a merciful man.

The Law and righteousness may have required divorce and Mary's death, but Joseph resolved to act mercifully. There would be a divorce, but it would be handled privately to spare Mary public humiliation.

The second angelic message that Joseph received warned him to flee. The insane and murderous Herod was plotting to secure his throne. Once again, Joseph acted and the child's life was preserved. The parallel between the flight to Egypt and God's preservation of Moses should be noted.

There is more to Jesus' authority than family connections. He is the son of humanity and Israel, *and* the Son of God. The story of Jesus' miraculous conception and the visitations surrounding it establish that he is the Son of God. The birth of Jesus is seen neither as chance nor coincidence; it is the result of God's prior action. Through the extraordinary births of Israel's past, God had prepared a way of blessing and renewal for the people. As with Samuel and John the Baptizer, the Lord was once again at work in Israel, and this birth will be for the redemption of Israel and the sake of the entire world.

Christians read this account through the lens of their confession of faith that Jesus is "very man of very man" and "very God of very God."[1] More than a claim about his nature, Matthew's birth story directs us toward Jesus' unique purpose. God's preparations for this birth mark Jesus as a child of special destiny. His authority as a teacher flows from this beginning. Matthew's gospel tells us that Jesus was born to this authority to be Redeemer.

1. These phrases are taken from the Chalcedon Creed, the formalized declaration issued by the Council of Chalcedon in AD 451.

Visitors from the Gentiles
Matthew 2:1–12

Matthew's account of Jesus' birth gives us a no-frills narrative of the birth of Jesus—until we get to chapter 2. The story of the magi's visit is unique to Matthew.

Mystery surrounds the magi. Neither their names nor their home country is reported, only that they were "from the east." East could mean anywhere—Persia, Babylon, Arabia, or the vast expanse of the Fertile Crescent that stretched away to the north and east of Palestine. "From the east" may be a phrase intended to signify not a geographical location but a status; the magi are Gentiles. The magi are portrayed as the first of the many non-Jews who recognized Jesus as the Messiah and God's Christ for the entire world. *Magi* is the plural of *magus*, the term from which we get our word *magician*. Whether magicians or astrologers, they were members of a far-flung and populous group and would have been strangers in a family gathering surrounding Jesus.

An evil presence hovered over their visit. This had nothing to do with them or their profession and everything to do with Herod, king of Judea. In a word, Herod was insane. A client of the occupying Roman overlords, he ruled ruthlessly with an arrogant self-confidence born of the knowledge that Rome would back him as long as he did its bidding.

The Romans left the internal affairs of his kingdom to Herod, and he used that imperial neglect to his advantage. He deprived the Sanhedrin, the ruling council, of all political powers, limiting its authority to religion. During his reign, Herod bribed Roman officials to keep him in power; drowned his own son; suspected his second wife (he had five wives altogether) of adultery with an uncle and ordered the man executed; and murdered or otherwise ordered the deaths of scores of people who threatened his hold on the throne. Mentally deranged at the end of his life, Herod settled disputes within his own family by killing members of rival factions.

The magi's visit to Herod's palace placed them within the grasp of a man who had virtually no respect for the traditions of Judaism and who would stop at nothing to secure his power. His malign appearance in Matthew's gospel serves as a stark contrast to the reign of Israel's true king born in Bethlehem.

Forerunner

Matthew 3:1–8, 11–17; 11:2–29; 14:1–12

These texts focus on the identity and preaching of John the Baptist and the baptism of Jesus. While Matthew's gospel says nothing about the relationship between Jesus and John, Luke's gospel reports that they were cousins. A glance beyond texts of the Gospel narratives raises some interesting observations about John. In the first place, he was of sufficient importance to be mentioned in Josephus's great history of the Jewish people. There John is praised for his piety and prophetic leadership; readers are told that Herod executed him for fear that John's preaching might lead to political uproar.

Second, John was the leader of a renewal movement. He had disciples who persisted as a group until after the resurrection and the missionary expansion of Christianity. Some scholars raise the possibility that Jesus initially may have been one of John's disciples. That may explain Jesus' appearance at the Jordan and his request to be baptized. If that were the case, Jesus rapidly increased as John decreased, a change of directions to which John humbly submitted.

Third, John attracted sufficient attention from Herod Antipas to warrant prison. Herod's motives may have been political *and* personal. The text tells us that John had criticized the marriage of Herod to his sister-in-law Herodias, a violation of the Torah. From his jail, John sent some of his disciples to Jesus with the all-important question: "Are you he was who is to come, or should we expect someone else?" Given John's declaration at Jesus' baptism, this seems a strange question. It is the one, however, faced by every person who has seriously considered Jesus. John asks this question not only for his people, Israel, but also for us: Who is this Jesus?

Jesus replies to the crowd of onlookers and John's disciples by telling them to report to John what they had heard and seen. In verse 5, Jesus then enumerated some healing miracles and the fact that good news was being preached to the poor. Nevertheless, the mood of expectancy surrounding John helped create a climate of uncertainty around him and Jesus. Was this strange man who preached repentance the Anointed One of God? If not him, was there another? It was John who took himself out of the running, declaring that he was but the forerunner of the long-expected Messiah.

Although obvious to us, we must always remember that distance and other factors inhibited communication in the ancient world. Rumors and gossip only worsened the problem of separating fact from fiction. Jesus' self-revelatory claim simultaneously reveals John's identity. It is commonly asserted that the centuries on either side of Jesus' birth were characterized by intense apocalyptic expectation. It was a moment ripe with the expectation that God was about to act in dramatic and world-changing fashion. This mood among first-century Jews made it an era when people stood on tiptoe, so to speak, in anticipation of the coming of God's Anointed One. In this mood, popular Judaism looked forward to the return of the spirit of Elijah. The texts of Matthew, Mark, and Luke all bear the marks of this anticipation, as the name of Elijah often appears in connection with Jesus.

Malachi 4:5 predicted that the great and fearsome prophet of old would return and prepare Israel for the coming of the Lord. One finds this idea of the returning Elijah running throughout the Gospels right up to Jesus' crucifixion. In Matthew 11, Jesus responded to this apocalyptic sense of urgency: John was in fact the returning Elijah. Of course, that answer also reflected back on Jesus; if John carried the mantle of Elijah, Jesus must be the Anointed One.

In addition to John's unusual clothes and diet, he was distinguished from other popular preachers by the fact that he baptized people. The English phrase *John the Baptist* translates a Greek phrase that is more accurately rendered, "John, the one who baptizes." To baptize means to dip or to immerse. Long before John, the practice already had been understood as symbolic of divine cleansing. (Compare, for example, Elisha's instructions to Naaman the Syrian commander in 2 Kings 5.) Ritual washings were familiar in Judaism, but John connected the practice to his message of repentance. John initially found it unnecessary for Jesus to be baptized, telling Jesus that he instead should baptize him. In this way, John subordinated himself to Jesus, for Jesus said that his submission to baptism was not an act of repentance. Instead it was symbolic of obedience and righteousness. This act of submission on Jesus' part brought forth God's announcement of Jesus as his Son and, further, a declaration of divine pleasure in Jesus' act of submission.

Temptation and Obedience
Matthew 4:1–17

It is the special burden of Matthew's gospel to demonstrate that Jesus is the Messiah who fulfills Old Testament promises. Matthew repeatedly quotes Old Testament passages to document this claim. Matthew 4:15–16 is one example of many.

Neither this nor any of the New Testament gospels should be read as biography, at least not in the strict sense of the term. They are not reports such as we might read in a daily newspaper. The Gospels do not merely inform or spread news; they also encourage belief in Jesus as God's promised Messiah. The Gospels do not offer an objective, value-free account of the life of Jesus. Neither do they provide all of the details of his life nor a description of his physical appearance. Instead, they tell the story of Jesus in such a way as to invite readers to respond and to make a decision. The details they provide are only those sufficient to that end. All four of the Gospels are guided by this evangelical purpose.

This text clearly demonstrates Matthew's intention that readers make a decision about Jesus. Taken together, the stories of Jesus' wilderness experience show his capacity to withstand temptation as well as his authority over Satan, who had no power over him. As a later text says, "[He] was in all points tempted like as we are, yet without sin" (Hebrews 4:15 KJV). The same Spirit that, only a few verses earlier, descended on Jesus in confirmation of his obedience now drove him into the wilderness to be tempted. This was a divine testing. Just as God once tested Abraham's obedience, God also tested Jesus. That God tests people in the Bible cannot be denied. That Jesus later taught his disciples to pray for deliverance from times of testing also cannot be denied. This testing is terrible, for it opened Jesus to the wiles of the tempter at points where Jesus was most vulnerable.

The first temptation was to satisfy hunger. Jesus had been alone in the wilderness fasting for forty days. Surely God would not begrudge a hungry person a little bread transformed out of stone. Jesus' answer prioritized the needs of the soul over those of the body. Bread will sustain the latter, but only the word of God nourishes the soul. The second temptation tested Jesus' piety. Jesus would soon preach a message of trust in the heavenly Father. Surely God would not refuse an extravagant demonstration of love and trust. To recklessly test God's faithfulness is no mark of piety.

The third of the temptations was the most insidious and clever. Satan promised Jesus all the kingdoms of the world—unlimited power. Think of all the good that could be accomplished, all of the hurt that could be healed, and all of the misery undone. True, one would have to get his hands dirty mixing with the world, but surely the good accomplished would far outweigh that. This diabolical offer attempted to get Jesus to break the first commandment by appealing to his character as the one who brings healing and wholeness. By quoting Deuteronomy 6:13, Jesus turned his back on worldly power and the one who offered it.

Hebrews speaks of Jesus as having "learned obedience" (5:8), and we should not be afraid of interpreting his wilderness experience as one of those times of testing. This is to be taken with deadly earnest. Three times, Jesus repels temptation with a quotation from the Old Testament. The Devil then departs. He has been defeated through Jesus' obedience to the word of Scripture. The narrative closes with an act of divine approval. Angels now come and minister to him. Divine blessing follows obedience.

Disciples

Matthew 4:18–22; 9:9–12; 10:1–4

We are inclined to picture Jesus' disciples as a tight-knit group of twelve, each called to follow Jesus within a narrow timeframe. These texts, however, will not support such a view and open up some other considerations about the Twelve and others of Jesus' followers.

Although often used interchangeably, the words *disciple* and *apostle* have very different meanings. Jesus first called the Twelve to be his disciples. A *disciple* is one who accepts a discipline of a master. *Apostle* comes from the Greek word meaning to send a message; an *apostle* is a messenger. The disciples eventually became apostles, but only after their instruction and only after Jesus commissioned them.

For a full study of these verses, compare the parallel passages in Mark and Luke. Compare Matthew 4:18–22 with Mark 1:16–20 and the larger account in Luke 5:1–11. Many scholars think that an inner circle of Jesus' followers existed, consisting of Peter, James, and John. At the very least, they were the disciples who accompanied Jesus both to the Mount of Transfiguration and the garden of Gethsemane. Andrew also may have been part of the inner circle, for when some Greeks asked Philip to show them to Jesus, Philip first sought out Andrew (John 12:20ff). In any case, the call of James, John, Peter, and Andrew is told with a particular fullness that concludes with Jesus' announcement that these former fishermen will thenceforward follow a very different course.

The account of Matthew's call comes in Matthew 9:9–12 (the parallels are Mark 2:13–17 and Luke 5:27–32). Luke calls this tax-collector-turned-disciple Levi, leading some to conclude that this man's name was Matthew Levi. Whatever his name, in the Matthew narrative, his call occurred after the Sermon on the Mount. If Matthew Levi was in the crowd that day, presumably he was not one of the Twelve; his call came later.

Last, there is the significance of the group's title, "the Twelve." Matthew lists them and notes that Jesus gave them such authority that it altered their relationship with him. Formerly they had been disciples; here Jesus gives them authority and then calls them apostles. (Compare Matthew 10:1–4; Mark 3:13–19; and Luke 6:12–16.) Clearer in the Markan account than in Matthew is the picture of a large following out of which Jesus called the Twelve. Within the Twelve, there was likely the inner circle. Scholars have long attached significance to the number twelve, interpreting this as a symbolic connection to the twelve tribes of Israel. The tribes were but a memory in Jesus' day, but the number twelve naturally connected the disciples, Israel's memories of lost glory, and hope for restoration and the Messiah.

The Sermon on the Mount
Matthew 5–7

Blessedness (Matt 5:1–12)

We may think of the Sermon on the Mount as a kind of Christian Torah—that is, instruction in walking in the way of Jesus. Matthew concludes with the Great Commission, where the crucified and resurrected Lord directed his followers to make disciples by baptizing them and teaching them everything that they had been commanded. Presumably this "everything" must include the Sermon on the Mount at its very heart. What we have then in the sermon is the core of Jesus' teaching concerning the formation and ethical life of his followers. To be a Christian is to be a disciple of the Lord Jesus; the Sermon on the Mount is the discipline according to which his followers are to live. Jesus' sermon is congruent with the divinely appointed responsibilities and roles incarnate in his very person—teacher, ruler, and judge at the end of time.

The Sermon on the Mount gives us an elaborate account of Jesus' instruction and the way of life he offers his followers. The famous Beatitudes open that account. The Greek word used here indicates the idea of blessedness. Some English translations use *happy*, although another Greek word is typically used to convey that sense. From the human point of view, happiness means a comfortable lifestyle free from sickness, money worries, and family problems. Christians tend to share this perspective except when challenged to view life from a spiritual vantage point. Reflective study of the Beatitudes will provide this challenge. How can tears be better than laughter? How can righteousness compete with the glitter of the world? How can suffering become more attractive than carefree living? Is everything about the Christian life a paradox?

Surely this is a rather odd list of conditions for blessedness. Who would think that the poor are blessed, or the lowly, or the mournful, or the persecuted? In the world of the New Testament, such people often were thought to be under a curse, or their calamities believed to be divine punishments in consequence of some sin. Jesus' benediction upon the suffering reversed this bit of religious wisdom. The Beatitudes open with a word of comfort for those who had been excluded from God's love and care.

Jesus also pronounces God's benediction on the merciful, the righteous, the pure in heart, and the peacemakers. That the door to God's favor is opened to the suffering does not mean that it is closed to those who have walked in the way of the Lord. Jesus makes it clear, however, that blessedness comes to those who have so lived "because of me." Jesus is the new standard of righteousness and the new criterion for life and blessing.

Law or Instruction (Matt 5:17–20, 38–48)

In Matthew, there is no tension between the Law of Moses and the gospel of the kingdom come in Jesus. Early in the Sermon on the Mount, Jesus states his solidarity with the "Law and the Prophets." This phrase refers to the two canonical divisions of the Hebrew Bible. Jesus declared that not the slightest stroke—a reference to the *yoth*, the smallest letter in the Hebrew alphabet—would disappear from the Law of Moses until "everything has been fulfilled."

Martin Luther distinguished the law and gospel to a greater degree than perhaps any other figure in the history of Christianity. Luther's antagonism toward the law originated in his inability to reach a sense of the forgiveness through the penitential practices of medieval Christianity. The years he spent in an Augustinian monastery only deepened Luther's sense of his own sinfulness and a dread of standing in the presence of the divine and righteous Judge. Luther saw Old Testament law in the same terms and placed the gospel over against it, regarding the law as a burden intended to drive us to despair and thus into the arms of the gospel.

Some contemporary Bible scholars now think that Luther may have misread the law as it was understood in Jesus' day. The law appears to modern readers as alien and preoccupied with small details, but to the people of first-century Judaism, the law was no great burden. Consider an analogy between the Law of Moses in Israel and the complex web of laws that govern life in most nations. Think of the many laws obeyed daily in any culture without conscious thought about them—traffic laws and municipal laws, to name two.

Most people do not get into their cars with a copy of their state traffic laws under their arms; they know the laws relevant to that situation and, for the most part, follow them. Something similar is likely to have existed in first-century Judaism. Torah could hardly have been alien to the people of that culture but instead provided the atmosphere of tradition that surrounded them. Not all cultures share the antitradition attitude so prominent in America. In Jesus' day there were surely many who, like Tevye the milkman in *Fiddler on the Roof,* believed that without the traditions of the Mosaic Law, life would be insecure indeed.

To those who feared him as a legal anarchist or those who desired complete freedom from the law, Jesus announced his intention to preserve the law rather than destroy it. This word may have disappointed some, even as it comforted others. But as he considered various points of the law, he added his own interpretation. Characteristically he said, "But I tell you..." The phrase implicitly claims the speaker's authority to interpret the law as Jesus did. Thus, he read the law in intensified applications. It isn't enough simply to avoid murder or adultery; Jesus read the law to encompass our hearts. On the question of divorce, Jesus appears to have been in conflict with the law, for Deuteronomy 24 expressly permits what Jesus refused to allow. Later, in Matthew 19, Jesus explained his teaching in greater detail. Taken together, the passages indicate a harmony between Moses and Jesus on this matter. Jesus basically agreed with the law but extended its reach. In Matthew's gospel, the law, then, is not the enemy of Jesus and his followers; rather, it is instruction for walking in the way of the Lord.

Prayer (Matt 6:1–21, 25–34)

The middle chapter of the Sermon on the Mount might be subtitled "Putting Our Earthly Life in Heavenly Perspective." The Law of Moses and its interpretation recede to the background while matters of piety and attitudes toward material possessions step into the spotlight.

The foil against which Jesus set his instruction on piety and prayer was that class of people he called "the hypocrites." Who were these people? Instantly, the word *Pharisees* comes to mind because we are familiar with their sharp dispute with Jesus. Interestingly, the text does not identify the hypocrites any further than by the term *hypocrite.* We do not know for certain they were Pharisees, although most likely some were. On the other hand, some Pharisees probably were quite sincere in their practice and not prone to public piety in search of praise. It was not a class of people or a religious party that Jesus had in view; he took aim at a particular attitude. Hypocrisy is not a vice restricted to scribes and Pharisees.

In his sayings on piety and prayer, Jesus spoke about public and private life in a manner that deserves some attention. Usually, we read these sayings against the backdrop of modern distinctions between these two spheres of life. Particularly in the United States, people are trained to think of religion as restricted to the private sphere of life. In America, no one can tell you what to believe, but the price of this freedom has been the reduction of religion's voice in the public square when policy is debated. Americans are free to believe or not believe just about anything they want as long as they keep those beliefs to themselves.

In ancient Jewish life and culture, religion knew no such restriction. Neither was life divided so neatly into public and private spheres. Families were not nuclear and isolated but extended and interrelated. Houses were small, so more of life occurred in public. Religion was not reduced to acts of worship but extended into the conduct of people's daily lives—the foods they ate or avoided, the dishes they used, and even governed occasions when sexual intercourse was not permissible. Jesus' instructions on piety and prayer reflect a cultural world where public religious acts were common and where the temptation to hypocrisy was equally common.

In a world where religion was a public matter, Jesus was concerned with the location and attitude of his disciples' prayers and with their contents. In our world, one notable exception to the public/private distinction is prayer in public venues. We are increasingly accustomed to the sight and sound of public prayer. People routinely ask a blessing on meals in a restaurant. Students gather about a high school flagpole for an early morning prayer service. Professional football players kneel and bow their heads in the end zone before tens of thousands of screaming fans. Of course, not everyone shares this enthusiasm for public prayer. Once, after watching a batter make the sign of the cross just before entering the batter's box, ex-Yankee catcher and folk philosopher Yogi Berra remarked, "Why don't we just let God sit this one out?"

Given the widespread incidence of public prayer in the late twentieth century, how are we to read Jesus' teaching that his followers should pray in secret? In part, we seem to have a question of motive and in another part a question of distinguishing Jesus' followers from the conspicuously public religious works of hypocrites. In the first case, Jesus told his disciples that public piety does have a reward; the reward is whatever people think of those who practice it. Of those who wish to make a spectacle of their praying or good works, Jesus said, in effect, "Whatever people think of them, that is their reward." God, on the other hand, will bless far more those who pray and do their good deeds in secret. Perhaps it was because that time and place was so characterized by outward religious expressions that Jesus taught his disciples another way in order to separate themselves and their religious practices from the publicly pious.

In this same passage, Jesus taught his disciples the familiar words of the Lord's Prayer, sometimes called the "Disciples' Prayer." (Notice that Matthew's version of this prayer, as also is the case with the version in Luke 11:2–4, omits the closing doxology, "For thine is the kingdom and the power and the glory forever." This sentence appears to have been added in later versions of this prayer that appeared as early as the end of the first century in a church manual called *Teaching of the Twelve Apostles*. For centuries, Western Christians did not conclude the Lord's Prayer with this doxology. It first appeared in an English version of the Lord's Prayer in the 1637 edition of the Scottish Book of Common Prayer and from there has made its way into customary usage among Protestants.)

A second block in Matthew 6 contains sayings about money. Ah, money! As a wise preacher once said, "It is much easier to get the saints to separate themselves from sin than to persuade them to separate themselves from their money." Consider the fact that Jesus spoke about money far more frequently than he did about matters of sexuality. And yet, if one listened only to contemporary American evangelicals, one would get the distinct impression that the latter had dominated his teaching. When it comes to money, none of us—neither the rich nor the poor—is immune to the temptation that "one dollar more" will solve our problems. According to the Deuteronomistic doctrine of reward and also much of the Proverbs, wealth is a blessing. Maybe. Jesus seems to regard it as something of a problem as well.

Relationships among Disciples (Matt 7:1–5, 12–20)

Matthew 7 is the third and final chapter of the Sermon on the Mount and the section that deals primarily with relationships. Here Jesus taught primarily about the quality of attitudes toward and interaction among his followers. We often read the sermon as if it was addressed generally to all people. That is certainly the case, in the sense that we desire that all would become Christians and thus the sermon applies to all. But in another sense, the sermon is addressed specifically to those who are Jesus' disciples. We see some of this specificity in chapter 7.

The opening verses of Matthew 7 can be read as Jesus' instruction to his followers concerning relationships within the group of disciples. This fellowship is classless, and a hierarchy has no place. No person within the fellowship may assume the role or the authority of a judge, and the relationships among followers are to be governed by kindness and generosity. The thrust of Matthew 7:2 comes very close to the spirit of the Golden Rule, in effect saying, "Insofar as you judge at all, judge others in the same manner and with the same spirit that you would want to be judged."

Jesus' famous saying about not looking for specks of sawdust in our neighbor's eye is also to be taken as instruction on relationships among his followers. Incidentally, this saying also illustrates a turn of speech found in Semitic cultures—"oriental hyperbole." Often used as a teaching device, this figure grossly overstates a point to lodge it in the hearer's memory. Jesus' saying about the "log" or "beam" or "plank," depending on the translation, is also memorable for its humor. It is an image to provoke laughter. To be sure, Jesus' mission had a very serious purpose, and we should never lose sight of that. On the other hand, neither should we allow even the shadow of Jesus' cross to obscure the delight and humor that sometimes punctuated his teaching.

The saying concerning false prophets and teachers also needs to be read initially in its first-century context. From Acts and other sources, we know that miracle workers, wandering preachers or prophets, and false messiahs were all part of first-century Judaism. It was important—indeed crucial to the future of the church—that Jesus' followers be warned against the possibility of such imposters. One commentator concludes that the saying about good and bad fruit was intended to be applied as an index of good and bad leadership.

Today, followers of Jesus read the Sermon on the Mount not only in its first-century context but also as instruction to us on the character and conduct of our discipleship. These teachings are to govern our relationships within the church as much today as they did among Jesus' first followers. Their guidance leads us in the path of faithful living as members of Christ's church.

Power to Fill a Half-Empty Glass
Matthew 8:23–27; 14:14–21

Matthew tells these miracle stories as eruptions of the power of the rule and reign of God. Jesus displays power not only over nature and the natural elements of life, but such also takes aim at the frailty and weakness of the faith of his disciples.

Perhaps you have seen the *Hagar the Horrible* comic strip in which Hagar is asked whether his glass is half-empty or half-full. The Viking slurps down the remaining contents of the glass and then says, "I hate philosophical questions." Hagar's disinterest aside, most of us know some people for whom the glass is always half-empty. Folks of this mind-set always seem to find the one or two minor glitches in a program that was otherwise a resounding success. Whether we label them pessimists or realists, these people are the target of these two miracle stories as they exponentially increase the stakes of faith.

"We will drown." The first story deals with authentic, palpable fear. We are no longer discussing attitudes but raw emotions. Jesus and his disciples were in a small boat on a storm-tossed sea; death by drowning was impending. The evidence indicated that their boat would go down. This was no idle fear; some of the disciples were, after all, fishermen and quite familiar with storms at sea. They awoke the Lord, sleeping below deck, and begged him to do something to save them. To their amazement, he did, but only after first rebuking them for their lack of faith. The disciples' amazement is curious. After all, they had asked Jesus to act. Apparently they believed that he could rescue them from their peril. Were they surprised only by the manner in which Jesus acted? Where was the littleness of their faith? Was it that they found it difficult to believe that God would preserve their lives on the storm-tossed sea? Or was it perhaps that they made their request of Jesus only partially trusting that he possessed the power to rescue them? Perhaps the scope of the disciples' faith was always too limited.

"They will go hungry" (and, by the way, so will we). The miracle of the loaves and the fishes underscores the disciples' limited grasp of the possible ways the rule and reign of God can redeem hopeless situations. In this case, they had presented Jesus with the problem: more than five thousand hungry people. Jesus gave the problem right back to the disciples: "You give them something to eat." Here the disciples' glass was not even half-empty. Jesus relented and told them to bring the people to him who could answer the problem.

The Greek New Testament uses two different words for the miracles Jesus performed. John typically uses the word *semeion*, which means "sign." The miracles are signs that point to Jesus and the claim that he is the Logos, the Word, of God. The three Synoptic Gospels use the word *dunamis*. This word is related to English words such as *dynamo, dynamic,* and *dynamite.* It has to do with power, especially eruptions of power. In the context of Matthew, Mark, and Luke, *dunamis* is an eruption of the power of the rule and reign of God. Jesus' miracles are the first rays of the dawning light of the Kingdom. Faith is the key that enables the disciples to grasp them for what they are. The miracle of miracles is that only a tiny bit of this faith is sufficient. That we need faith only the size of a mustard seed is a good thing for those of us who tend to see our lives as glasses half-empty, who fear that we are about to drown in a sea of problems, and who have a hard time seeing all the possibilities God has in store for us. If these two miracles demonstrate that the power of God's rule can alter the rules of nature to conform to his purpose, then perhaps these stories also point to the possibility that God's love and power can overcome our too little faith.

Power over Death
Matthew 9:18–31, 35–36

Matthew 9:18-38 contains four miracle stories. In these stories Jesus (1) raises a young girl from the dead, (2) heals a woman through the mere touch of his outer clothing, (3) restores sight to two blind men, and (4) restores speech to another man by exorcising a demon. Taken together, the stories display Jesus' power over sickness, death, and the demonic world.

Here we have a narrative within a narrative. The account of the woman with the issue of blood interrupts the larger account of the synagogue leader's desperate effort to get Jesus to come to his house for the sake of his dying daughter. Think how impatient the synagogue ruler must have been, waiting for Jesus to talk with the sick woman who simply reached out to touch Jesus' cloak. Every minute spent in conversation on the street brought his daughter that much closer to death. By the time they reached the man's house, the musicians and ritual mourners had already arrived—the "noisy crowd" mentioned in 9:23. To this group Jesus announced that the girl was not dead but asleep.

Because death was a frequent and familiar visitor in the ancient world, friends and family members could surely determine if the young girl had died. It is perhaps this knowledge that provoked their laughter at the ridiculous claim that she was merely sleeping. Others in the crowd might have rejected Jesus' claim on religious grounds. Not all first-century Jews believed in life after death. Pharisees did, but they were a small minority compared with other religious factions and the general population. So, some in the crowd laughed at Jesus' statement because their own beliefs did not include the possibility of resurrection. Whatever the source or motivation of this laughter, Jesus' startling act became the talk of the region. Nothing, not even Jesus' express warning, could prevent the ever-widening circle of stories about the health-giving power that flowed from his fingertips. Thus, the raising of Jairus's daughter became still another manifestation of God's rule and reign come in the person of Jesus of Nazareth.

Politics of Separation or Forgiveness
Matthew 12:22–32, 38–40

All four Gospels agree that a variety of people challenged Jesus and created conflicts with him. On a few occasions, Jesus himself seems to have prompted the tension with a well-aimed question. Sometimes those who fell into conflict with Jesus were called simply "the Jews." At other points, they were referred to as "scribes." But the most familiar term the Gospels use to describe Jesus' opponents is "the Pharisees." Who were these people, and why did they take such sharp exception to Jesus' message and ministry?

The Pharisee movement is first mentioned during the rule of John Hyrcanus, who became ruler of the Jews in the years after the Maccabean revolt (about 134 BC). The Pharisees may have begun among a group known as the *hasidim*, "the devout or pious ones." One of their major characteristics was a very strict attitude toward and interpretation of the Law of Moses, or Torah; the Pharisees tried to live according to those teachings as closely as possible.

The word *Pharisee* comes from the Hebrew word *perushim* and means "the separated ones," a definition that provides us with a clue about some of their commitments. Pharisees practiced a policy of deliberate separation from the dominant Roman culture. Pharisees were deeply concerned to preserve both Judaism and the Jewish people, and the best way to accomplish that goal was through an interpretation of the Torah that resulted in strict separation from everything considered ritually unclean. If a religious barrier could be built to divide Judaism from the ritually unclean Gentile-Roman world, thought the Pharisees, then Israel could be saved.

In a certain sense, the Pharisees were some of the most devout people in the larger Jewish world. They were zealous in their worship and highly detailed in their obedience to the Torah. They also believed in the resurrection of the dead, the existence of spirits and angels, and the reality of rewards and punishment after death. Some of these beliefs they of course shared with Jesus.

Often people who are zealously committed to a cause refuse to admit alternate viewpoints and become rigid and inflexible in their own commitments. This seems to have been true of the Pharisees, and thus we begin to understand something of the nature of their sharp opposition to Jesus, who preached a message that announced the forgiveness of God as available to all. One can scarcely imagine a message more offensive to the Pharisees.

There may be yet another aspect to the Pharisees' intense opposition to Jesus. Unlike the wealthy and aristocratic Sadducees, the Pharisees came from a social background much closer to that of Jesus. Recall that the occupation of Saul of Tarsus was tent-making, a trade similar to carpentry. Jesus' disputes with the Pharisees were sharp perhaps because they shared some common beliefs and were from the same social class. In that sense, their conflicts, more like family quarrels, were more intense than disputes with strangers or people of more remote beliefs and social classes.

Preaching in Parables

Matthew 13:1–13, 34–35

Among preachers, there is the truism that their listeners can and do remember illustrations with greater clarity than the teaching points of a sermon. Even as there is no more fundamental way to speak of God than narrative, it also may be that we human beings are formed to respond best to stories. Jesus made extensive use of stories as a teaching device, and the parable was his favorite form. Stories and parables are open-ended, often capable of multiple interpretations. It may be, therefore, that some listeners entirely miss the point. Wouldn't a simple, straightforward statement of the main points be more economical and less risky of confusion? In modern terminology, why not simply cut to the chase?

Jesus' disciples may not have shared the modern world's impatience, but they did question his habit of teaching through parables. The English word *parable* comes from the Greek *parabole,* which means "to lay alongside." In other words, a parable is a comparison. But what is being compared to what? Two scholars contributed greatly to our ideas about Jesus' parables—C. H. Dodd (*The Parables of the Kingdom,* 1935) and Joachim Jeremias (*The Parables of Jesus,* first published in German in 1947). Although the two differed significantly, they also shared the view that Jesus employed parables as more than sermonic illustrations; in them, the kingdom was proclaimed as being here and now and available to those who heard. Since the work of Dodd and Jeremias, New Testament scholars have generally taken the view that Jesus' parables need not be interpreted rigidly as having exclusive meaning; they employ the language of metaphor and do not impart information in a straightforward manner. After all, to speak metaphorically is to speak of one thing in terms of another. This does not mean to suggest that Jesus used parables to confuse or obscure his meaning; rather, it is consistent with the fact that some of his hearers came to understanding and others did not. Jesus himself said, "Those with ears to hear let them hear."

Jesus did not invent the parable form, nor was he the first to use it. The rabbis used it to teach points of the law. Jesus used it to illuminate his teachings on the kingdom of God. Jesus taught his followers that this kingdom was already among them; it is not out of place to say, with the early church theologian Origen, that Jesus *was* the kingdom of God in person. In Jesus' parables, the kingdom's immediacy has three important aspects or consequences for his listeners: (1) if the kingdom is present, then judgment threatens those who will not hear or live according to its precepts; (2) especially for those who have been oppressed but also for all who follow Jesus, the kingdom brings joy; and (3) many of the parables provide necessary and specific instructions for life under God's reign.

Some grasped Jesus' point, and some did not. The disciples' question about teaching in parables was prompted by the parable that reinforces this fact. The parable of the sower is not an analysis of farming techniques. Farmers in the ancient Mediterranean did not employ modern methods. The plow that most of us think of when we hear the word had not been invented. Jesus' parable assumes familiarity with broadcast seeding, a method that usually got some seed into soil prepared with a rudimentary implement but also scattered some seed onto ground too thin to support a crop. Anyone who has ever planted a garden knows that some of God's creatures will snatch up seed not intended for them. Nevertheless, some seed germinates and matures into a good crop.

Isn't this a description of the various understandings of Jesus' teaching about the kingdom of God? Then and now, news of the kingdom is spread. Then and now, some of this news falls on deaf ears and never takes root. Then and now, the news takes root and flourishes, but only for a season. Then and now, the news is snatched away before germinating. Then and now, the news is heard, takes root, and matures into full discipleship. Some people refuse to hear—despite our sincere efforts—but there are also those who will respond with scarcely any work on our part.

We are often tempted to moralize from Jesus' parables, but remember that Jesus is describing the kingdom of heaven. The reign of God, like the rain that nourishes the earth, falls on the unjust as well as the just. God's reigning activity can be found in places where little apparent good comes of its presence and where men and women will ignore its signs. But God's reigning work will take root in other hearts, soft and made responsive by any of countless life situations. Jesus is not describing the way the things of the kingdom *should* be, nor is he offering a description about the way the kingdom *will* be in the future. Nor is he describing a method of Christian evangelism; rather, he describes the ruling activity of God at work in the world.

No More Outsiders
Matthew 15:21–31

The story of the encounter between Jesus and the Syro-Phoenician woman must be considered against the backdrop of prejudice that defined ethnic relationships in the ancient Mediterranean world. Ancient peoples typically believed that their own ethnic group, its social and religious customs, was superior to others. For example, ancient Greeks thought of their own culture as "Greek" and all others as "barbarian." Alexander the Great, himself a Macedonian but having been educated in Greek ways and knowledge, considered it his mission to spread the achievements of Greek civilization to the people in lands subjugated by his armies. Sometimes this spread was accomplished brutally and with the worst kind of cultural bigotry. The soldiers of a ruler of one of Alexander's successor states forced residents of Jerusalem to adopt aspects of Greek religion. This forced sacrilege led to the Maccabean revolt of the second century before Christ.

The Jewish people were not immune to ethnocentrism—the belief that my people, my religion, and my ways are superior to all others. The Jews, of course, divided the world between themselves and all others—namely Gentiles. At least from the time of Ezra, the Jewish people had practiced a way of life that drew a clear line between themselves and all other people. We see the effects of that cultural practice in the New Testament church where Paul labored to bring Jew and Gentile together in the unity of Christ. Perhaps a greater surprise to us is that this attitude also appears in some of the stories of Jesus in the Gospels.

In this narrative, Jesus and his disciples had traveled north to the region of Tyre and Sidon. These were Canaanite or Phoenician towns on the Mediterranean coast north of Galilee. The narrative does not explain Jesus' intention, but Jesus' appearance in what was clearly non-Jewish territory once again marks him as following an agenda very different from the Pharisees. (Early in Matthew's gospel the magi appear, and from that point forward people from far beyond Israel's borders are welcomed into the Kingdom that Jesus proclaimed.) Whatever Jesus' reason for the trip into Phoenician territory, the first section of his conversation with this mother desperate to save her child was marked by the tension that governed Jewish-Gentile relationships.

Three times she begs for Jesus' help. At the first two times, Jesus rebuffed her with harsh-sounding comments that presuppose Israel's primacy. What is going on here? Where is the gentle

Shepherd? Perhaps Jesus' initial rebuffs were intended to test her faith. She was, after all, a Canaanite and may have approached Jesus out a set of superstition and a belief in magic. In this scenario, Jesus can be seen as testing—and ultimately rewarding—her faith. Once it had been seen that her request was grounded in authentic faith, Jesus granted the great desire of her heart.

We ought also to consider the fact that this story follows a sharp discussion between Jesus and the Pharisees (15:1–20) on the often-debated question of clean versus unclean. Jews considered Gentiles to be unclean, but the faith of the Canaanite woman stood in sharp contrast to Jewish separatism. The narrative shows that Gentiles, as well as the house of Israel, may enter into fellowship with Jesus. After the close of the New Testament era, Christianity became overwhelmingly Gentile. We should not allow this vast numerical superiority, however, to obscure the great truth that we non-Jews are the latecomers, who through Christ have been admitted to the people of God.

Who Is This?

Matthew 16:13–23

The book of Hebrews opens with the words, "In these last days he [God] has spoken to us by his Son" (1:2). The Son did not carry words; the Son *is* the Word. In his published lectures on Christ, the German martyr-theologian Dietrich Bonhoeffer said, "The only real question which now remains is: 'Who are you? Speak for yourself!'…It is also the question of faith: 'Who are you? Are you God himself?'"[2] The early church struggled profoundly with questions concerning the person and work of Christ. Texts such as Hebrews 1:3, "The Son is the radiance of God's glory and the exact representation of his being," when considered against the background of basic religious and theological assumptions, raised crucial questions about the nature of Christ and his ministry. Some early Christians were devoted to the idea that God is one; therefore, they read Hebrews 1:3 to say that *radiance* means "similar to" but not "the same as" and *representation* means one who stands in the place of another. At the same time, other Christians insisted that the Logos and the Father were "of the same essence."

In AD 381 at the Council of Constantinople, Christians confessed the doctrine of the Trinity, that God is "one essence in three persons." Centuries later, such theologians as Bonhoeffer wondered whether the council had asked an inappropriate question. It appeared to him that the question uppermost on their minds was, What are you? The question that mattered most to Bonhoeffer in addressing Christ was not What? but Who?

Matthew 16:13–23 turns on the question, Who? Jesus first asked his disciples, "Who do *people* say the Son of Man is?" (emphasis added). The disciples dutifully reported what they had heard. Popular religious belief expected the return of the spirit of bold and faithful Elijah. Many believed that "the Elijah's" return would begin the consolation and renewal of Israel. In this mood of heightened expectancy, some identified Jesus with "the Elijah" or another of the great prophets of Israel's past.

Having heard popular sentiment about him, Jesus then turned his questions on

2. Bonhoeffer, *Christ the Center*, 30.

the disciples themselves: "But what about you?...Who do you say that I am?" The question does not call for analysis; it is not a request for information. Neither does it call for another secondhand report. The question cuts to the heart of the matter. When we ask, "What are you?" Jesus becomes an object for analysis, a thing to be examined and analyzed. Matthew 16 brackets out questions about Jesus that begin with *what;* they are not permitted here. Instead, we are forced to come to terms with Jesus as the subject, the One who initiates. As subject rather than object, Jesus now stands in relation to the questioner. So the question, "Who are you?" forces us to consider Jesus in relation to us. Carried to its logical conclusion, the question forces each person to consider Jesus in relation to himself or herself. Our answer makes all the difference.

The World Upside Down
Matthew 18:1–4; 20:17–28

The apostle Paul obviously had specific audiences in mind as he wrote his letters. To the Galatian Christians, for example, he wrote, "You foolish Galatians! Who has bewitched you?" (3:1). To the Philippians, he wrote with a love and confidence that he rarely bestowed on the Corinthians. New Testament scholars now think that the Gospel writers also had specific audiences in mind as they wrote. Luke's gospel opens, for example, with his salutation to a man named Theophilus. In a similar vein, scholars set forth the idea of a Matthean community to which the gospel according to Matthew was addressed. Matthew addresses many issues that would have been of special concern to Jewish Christians, questions about their discipleship in light of Torah and the status of the law in general. In Matthew, Jesus teaches more in the manner of a rabbi, for example the Sermon on the Mount. At the beginning of the discourse, Jesus *sits* to teach, assuming the formal teaching position of a Jewish rabbi.

Let's assume that a first-century Matthean community did in fact exist. How might that group of Jewish Christians read this text and how would that reading influence ours? These two passages both emphasize a reversal of roles. Normal values are turned upside down. Those who are thought to be of least importance would be acclaimed the greatest; those who generally were regarded as the greatest would find themselves standing at the end of the line.

People of the Matthean community might have been tempted to think of themselves as the greatest. In a church that was attracting more and more Gentiles, they might have believed that they deserved pride of place. After all, Jesus was a Jewish boy, one of their own. Shouldn't the ethnic heritage they shared with him count for something in a church founded on Jesus' crucifixion and resurrection? Just as James and John's mother was prompted to ask for privileged positions for her sons—Who gets reserved seating? Who doesn't have to stand in line?—the Jewish Christians of the Matthean community might have assumed a superiority.

Anyone reading the sayings of Jesus—then or now—under the assumption of some sort of privileged position in the church is in for a rude awakening. Jesus reverses the standard calculation of importance. Under the rule and reign of Yahweh, children have an importance that Jewish society could scarcely imagine. Culturally, children were the possession, indeed the property, of their parents. In the Kingdom, however, people can neither expect nor claim such privilege. They must accept a status similar to children and be willing to live trustfully by the will and grace of God.

In Matthew 20:17–28, Jesus had just finished the parable of the laborers in the vineyard, concluding the story with the same upside-down reading as in 18:1–4. He said it more bluntly in 20:16: "So the last will be first, and the first will be last." His point seems to have been utterly lost on James and John's mother, as she immediately asked for "first" for her boys. Sitting next to Jesus could be dangerous, as he pointed out to those close to him; it would mean sharing the fellowship of his suffering. To their credit, James and John answered that they were ready to share that cup with their Lord. Jesus repeated the theme of these texts in his concluding saying that greatness lies in serving. Those in the community called church, whether Matthean or modern-day, are called to this upside-down greatness, not privileged positions.

Receiving and Extending Forgiveness

Matthew 18:15–18, 21–28, 32–33

Jesus' sayings on forgiveness in Matthew 18 follow his teaching about the value of "the least." Matthew 18:6–35 frequently makes use of themes common in Jesus' teaching: shepherds, servants, and children. Each of these groups held low status in Jewish society. Respectable members of upper-class Jewish society despised shepherds. Shepherds spent long periods away from home and therefore could not protect their women—an important norm of Semitic culture—and thus appeared irresponsible and dishonorable. Shepherds sometimes grazed their sheep on other people's lands; therefore, the entire class was generally considered to be thieves. The lot of children in the ancient world was similarly difficult. They were the weakest and most vulnerable part of Jewish society.

Jesus' teachings transform these people of low social status into people of moral worth and example. As much as anyone else, they too had the potential to forgive that was critical for life under the rule of God. Jesus told his listeners that they must become like children. He held up as a moral example the shepherd who leaves ninety-nine sheep to find one that is lost. By speaking of the lower classes so positively, Jesus already began raising their social status.

The context of a particular passage is always critical to our interpretation. In the case of the parable of the unmerciful servant, the context is a discussion about the importance with which Jesus treats forgiveness. In other words, we are dealing with a block of material that might be read as instructions to Jesus' followers about their relationships with each other. The larger context is Jesus' instruction to his followers about the importance of their regard for and attention to one another. In our time, these teachings should challenge our tendency to think of discipleship in exclusively individualistic terms. Following Jesus will bring into focus our relationships with other people.

We start with the disciples' curiosity. But are they curious about the Kingdom or about their own destiny in that

Kingdom? Jesus answers their question with a series of parables that deals with human relationships: selfishness, regard for those whose innocence makes them vulnerable, the restoration of broken friendships, and forgiveness. We might read the parables of Matthew 18 as social parables because they explore the relational dimensions of discipleship. There is, after all, life in the Christian community that is a consequence of following Jesus.

Peter asks Jesus about forgiveness: should one forgive as often as seven times? The rabbis taught that one should forgive three times, but not on the fourth occasion. Peter's increase of forgiveness to seven times appears to be a considerable moral advance. Any pride that Peter might have felt in this superiority would have been immediately deflated by Jesus' reply that forgiveness should be extended not merely seven times but "seventy *times* seven" (v. 22 NKJV, emphasis added). Forgiveness, it appears, must flow like a river in a flash flood.

Jesus' parable tells the story of two debtors. The first debtor owed a king 10,000 talents, and the second debtor owed the first 100 denarii. Since a denarius (singular for *denarii*) was roughly equal to a day's wage for the majority of persons in the crowd, an annual income amounted to somewhere between 350 and 400 denarii. One talent, however, was equivalent to 6,000 denarii. The first debtor owed the king *10,000* talents. For the crowds listening to Jesus, 10,000 talents was more money than they could imagine. To repay his debt, the servant would have to work every day of the week (except the Sabbath, of course) earning *twice* the daily rate for more than 19,000 years. This model assumed no interest for the loan. Clearly the servant could not repay the debt. The servant did not need to repay this impossible sum because the king forgave it. Having been stupendously released of a mind-boggling debt, the servant immediately refused to forgive the second debtor of a far smaller amount. Compared to 10,000 talents, what was a measly 100 denarii? Word of this got back to the king, who became justifiably angry with his unforgiving servant.

This parable draws on the covenant undergirding Jewish faith and society. That covenant pointed in two directions—vertically toward Yahweh, who insisted on Israel's righteousness, and horizontally toward the people of God, whom Yahweh insisted deal justly with one another. In this two-dimensional parable, Jesus' teaching about the Kingdom was based on the covenant's judgment that there can be no righteousness without justice and no justice without righteousness.

In the economy of God's reign, forgiveness is offered in proportion to its practice. To practice forgiveness is also to receive forgiveness. As God has forgiven those who become followers of Jesus, so are they in like manner to forgive. In the face of the conclusion of the parable of the unmerciful servant, we might very well ask whether the Christian community can exist, or whether Jesus' disciples can grow in that discipleship, in the absence of the practice of forgiveness.

At the End of the Day
Matthew 20:1–16

Matthew 19:16–30 sets the context for Jesus' parable of the workers in the vineyard, especially Jesus' saying that "many who are first will be last, and many who are last will be first" (19:30). This material includes the familiar story of the "rich young ruler," as he is called in the King James Version. Wealth is the central issue of the story. The young man had obeyed the whole of the law, but when Jesus told him that the one needful thing to inherit eternal life was to sell all that he owned, give to the poor, and follow Jesus, "the young man...went away sad, because he had great wealth."

Here we are told of a group of day-laborers who receive the same wage, but some of these people have worked for an entire day in the hot sun. Others worked only half as long, and still others barely arrived in the vineyard before quitting time. Nevertheless, all are paid exactly the same amount. What a strange idea in our day of equal pay for equal work! Indeed, this parable contradicts the conventional wisdom. It is difficult to imagine any setting, from kids mowing the backyard to factory workers to teachers, where we would accept the conditions imposed by the owner of the vineyard.

Remember, however, this is a parable about the Kingdom. It is a description of the rules that govern life under the reign of God, not the conventional wisdom of our world. Under the reign of God, even those who didn't get called when the notices first went out still have the opportunity for full payment.

That Jesus taught and preached largely among the "people of the land," poor persons who could barely eke out a living, likely meant that when they either watched this story unfold or later heard about it, they would have nodded their heads in agreement. "Isn't that just like the rich? They just can't let go of their money." They even may have chuckled at Jesus' hyperbole about camels and needle eyes. But the disciples, apparently not getting the point, earnestly asked, in effect, "Well, if this wealthy and righteous man cannot enter heaven, who can?" (Remember, wealth in those days was typically thought to be a sign of God's favor.) Peter, nervously making Jesus' point again in a self-interested way, reminded him that the disciples (who were by no means wealthy or middle-class to begin with) left everything to follow him. Jesus then reassured Peter that he and his fellow disciples would have a seat in eternity. Those followers who had left houses and family would receive "a hundred times as much" and would "inherit eternal life." Not only would they be included, but showers of heavenly blessings also would rain down upon them.

This familiar story amazed Jesus' followers. Perhaps they still were not completely convinced. Jesus taught that God's forgiveness was freely available and that God stood ready to accept anyone and everyone. The disciples and most of the people in the crowds were accustomed to being last. At or near the very bottom of the social ladder, they lacked the wealth and social power that underlay the life of privilege and religious respectability of such people as the rich young ruler. These "people of the land" more or less assumed that the wealthy and privileged would have first access to heaven, just as they enjoyed first access to the goods of Jewish society and religion. When Jesus came teaching that God's reign covered everyone according to forgiveness that was open to all, it was a message almost too good to be true for the common people of the villages of the Galilean countryside.

From time to time, they had to pinch themselves to make sure this wasn't a dream. Could it really be true that they—the last of their society—were the first under God's reign?

In such a context and to such amazed listeners, Jesus told this wonderful parable. Many people will come under the rule of God. The surprise and joy of God's rule is that not only do the first of Jewish society have access to the Kingdom, so do the last. Even more wondrous, under the rule of God, "the last will be first, and the first will be last." Most wonderful of all is that we who are not of the house of Israel also can be saved.

Triumphal Entry
Matthew 21:1–13

These verses portray two famous scenes from the Gospels: Jesus' triumphant entry into Jerusalem and the cleansing of the temple. Matthew does not specify the day that Jesus entered Jerusalem; neither do Mark or Luke. It is John who reports that the entry occurred five days before the Passover. It is from this latter source that the church's memorializing of the triumphal entry known as Palm Sunday comes.

Matthew's account of Jesus' life and ministry gives us a picture of Jesus as a wandering preacher, teacher, and miracle worker who traveled through the little towns and villages of Galilee. There he remained until near the very end of his ministry, when he set his face toward Jerusalem (Luke 9:51). Until that decision, Jesus was reasonably out of harm's way. Galilee lay a good distance from Jerusalem and the Sanhedrin. Pontius Pilate also ruled from Jerusalem; Roman authority did not weigh quite so heavily in Galilee as in Judea and the capital. Jesus' decision to go to Jerusalem, therefore, gave his enemies easier access to him. Although precariously close to those who meant to kill him, Jesus moved freely about the city of Jerusalem, teaching and preaching just as he had in Galilee. The one exception to this general description is the event known as the cleansing of the temple.

New Testament scholars debate the significance of the incident in the temple. Some argue that Jesus' attack on the moneychangers was focused on them alone. Others contend that, in driving out animals and moneychangers, Jesus intentionally challenged the whole temple system. Changing the Roman *denarius* into temple coin was a standard practice. The temple moneychangers were not the only moneychangers, but their location in the court of the Gentiles was the most convenient. Secular currency was unacceptable and had to be converted into temple currency in order to purchase animals for sacrifice.

There is some reason to think that people from the surrounding countryside went along with the arrangement for convenience sake, even if that might mean losing a little in the exchange. Consider the problem of transporting a live animal over many miles to be sacrificed in Jerusalem. The law required that any sacrifice be completely unblemished; any kind of injury along the rough journey would make the animal unacceptable. It is reasonable, therefore, to think that many people were willing to pay higher prices or a fee for changing money as part of the overall cost of making a sacrifice in the Jerusalem temple. If that was the understanding and practice of many temple worshipers, then we must read the temple cleansing as an attack on the whole system rather than a select group. If we view these incidents from this perspective, we likely will revise upward our estimate of the size of the crowd calling for Jesus' death later that week.

Living Expectantly
Matthew 24:45–25:13

The parable of the ten virgins concludes a section of the gospel according to Matthew often called the Little Apocalypse. Apocalyptic thought developed in Israel when the prophetic movement declined after the Israelites returned from Babylonian exile in the late fifth and then the fourth centuries before Christ. Although often warning that God's judgment was about to fall on Israel, the classical prophets held out hope that God would restore Israel and that the people of God, even if only a remnant, would be redeemed.

Apocalyptic writing also held out hope, but of a different kind. In biblical apocalyptic, hope anticipates the end of the age when the Lord will ring down the curtain before the creation of a new heaven and a new earth. Such hope results from the judgment that the world is too far gone to be redeemed. God's only alternative is to destroy and begin anew.

Apocalyptic thought flourished among the Jewish people during the centuries just before and after Jesus' birth. The disciples' request about the end of the age fits neatly into this expectancy. Jesus responded with a description that has haunted some people ever since, especially those who have tried to discern the signs of the end. The religion channel of any cable TV system testifies to the continuing presence—and futility—of this interest.

Near the conclusion of the Little Apocalypse, Jesus told his followers that "not even the angels in heaven, nor the Son, but only the Father" knows the timing of the last days (24:36). Since the timing of the end is unknown, it is best to be continuously prepared for its arrival. That is the message of this text.

One of the eagerly anticipated events of my boyhood was our annual October hunting trip. It was one of those male bonding experiences that people love to analyze today. All I knew then was that my father and grandfather, my uncles and cousins, and I would spend a day walking the cornfields and fencerows of western Minnesota in search of the Chinese ring-necked pheasant. One cool, brilliant afternoon a pheasant rooster jumped into the sky off to the left of the line of men and boys walking the field. My father, a crack shot, whirled but did not shoot because there were people in the line of fire between him and the bird. The shot belonged to the hunter on the end of the line, but we heard no shotgun report and watched as the bird flew safely out of range. During lunch, my father asked the hunter why he hadn't fired. The man replied, "Well, I wasn't expecting him over there." Late that night as we pulled into our driveway, my dad asked in a voice half to himself and half to me, "Why would a person go pheasant hunting and not expect birds?"

That, of course, is the point of the parable of the ten virgins. Why prepare for a wedding if you are not willing to take care of all the details? You won't get a second chance. Be ready, today.

An Unprofitable Servant

Matthew 25:14–30

In the gospel of Luke, Jesus uses the phrase "kingdom of God," a phrase that rarely appears in Matthew. There we typically find the phrase "kingdom of heaven." There is essentially no difference between the two. The apparent distinction can be attributed to the differing backgrounds and audiences of the two writers. Luke was a Greek convert to Christianity; the use of the term *God* invoked no special pious difficulties for him. Matthew, writing out of the beliefs of a Jewish Christian, could take no such liberties and so had to invent a substitute for *God*, a name Jews and Jewish Christians believed too holy to speak or write. He simply writes "heaven," the domain of God. So the two phrases mean essentially the same.

However expressed, this phrase has to do with the impossibility of humans gaining mastery over the kingdom. We tend to interpret *kingdom* as a place, as in the "kingdom of England," but a better translation of both Greek phrases, *basileia tou theou* (kingdom of God) and *basileia tou ouranou* (kingdom of heaven) is the "ruling activity" or the "reign" of God. Such an interpretation underscores the force of God's action. *Kingdom* is more verb than noun; it is what God is *doing*. Furthermore, Jesus' parables of the kingdom have a puzzling quality about them because they are not easily reduced to a single, easily grasped point. The parables' puzzling quality resembles Jesus' teaching about the kingdom of God: after all is said and done, the kingdom belongs to God and not to us. Indeed, our claims to have unlocked the mysterious "lo, it is here, now it is there" quality of God's rule are among the best indicators that the kingdom remains far from us. One cannot grasp God's rule; one may only live within or under its authority.

If the parable of the laborers in the vineyard illustrates the category of joy among Jesus' parables, then the story of the talents emphasizes the category of judgment. Imagine yourself in the crowd as Jesus tells this story. As hearers, we are invited to pass judgment on the overly cautious servant who refuses to invest his master's money. It's one thing to hoard our own belongings; it's quite another to allow that which another has entrusted to us to lie fallow. The cautious servant is unprofitable and a drain on the economy of his master's household. Unproductive servants are liable to dismissal. "If we read this parable such that the master is God, then who is the unprofitable servant? Who would Jesus' hearers have understood the servant to be? He is the type of pious Jew who comes in for so much criticism in the Gospels. The parable was intended to lead such persons to see their conduct in its true light. They are not giving God his own; they are defrauding him".[3]

Sheep and Goats

Matthew 25:31–46

As we consider the parable of the sheep and the goats, we should consider where it is placed in Matthew. This is a parable about judgment, and it may be more than coincidental that, as the last of Jesus' parables, it appears just before his arrest and trial. Judgment is in the air. Jesus was about to be judged falsely,

3. Dodd, *Parables of the Kingdom*, 119.

but at the last judgment all will be summoned before the righteous judgment bar of the Lord.

We might inquire into the identity of the sheep and the goats. If a parable is a comparison, then to whom was Jesus referring by these terms? Notice that the parable begins with the statement that "all the nations" will be gathered before the Lord. Is this phrase simply another way of saying "everybody," or should we take it in the sense that nations are people groups? Western and especially American individualism presupposes us to read it as a summons to each individual person. The ancient world thought of individuals as extensions of their people group—the nation—and it is certainly within the realm of possibility that the phrase "all the nations" means exactly what it says. In other words, the image is of groups rather than individuals who answer God's summons.

For centuries, biblical writers referred to Israelites and their leaders under the metaphor of sheep and shepherds. As far back as David, and perhaps especially with him, Israel had understood itself to be the sheep of God's pasture. David the shepherd boy was called to be the shepherd king of this people. Jesus spoke of himself as a shepherd and described part of his mission as the rescue of the lost sheep of Israel. The metaphor of Israel as a flock of sheep was firmly rooted in Jewish speech. By the same token, if Israel was a flock of sheep, Jews understood Gentiles to be goats, much less desirable animals.

As is so often the case in Jesus' teaching, this parable turns conventional understanding on its head. When the parable began, Jesus' listeners thought they understood the direction it would take. After all, they knew the meaning of *sheep* and *goats*. It becomes apparent, however, that they did not know Jesus' meaning. Some criterion other than ethnic identity now determined who was at the left and right hands of the Lord. The new criterion dealt with ethics and the attitude one takes toward Jesus.

Especially in Matthew's gospel, Jesus' teaching pays great attention to ethics. In one place, he even said that not everybody who calls him "Lord" will enter into eternal life; eternal life is reserved for those who do the will of God. This seems to give Christian ethics priority over a proper confession of faith, and it fits well with the thrust of the parable of the sheep and the goats. Here statements count not nearly as much as deeds. Furthermore, "doing" is not simply a matter of avoiding sin; rather, "doing" means positive acts of Christian charity, works of mercy, and generosity.

Christians sometimes seek to know the identity of "the least of these." After all, if we are to do works of charity, shouldn't they be properly directed? But part of the parable's force is that neither the sheep nor the goats knew that they were serving the Lord when they served the "least of these." So perhaps, like the neighbor in the parable of the good Samaritan, the "least of these" is anybody in need of Christian charity.

Betrayal

Matthew 26:3–15, 20–25

In his epic masterpiece *The Divine Comedy*, the great Florentine poet Dante described hell as an inverted cone that became narrower the deeper one descended into its bowels. In Dante's vision, Satan was forever imprisoned, bound fast at the waist in a frozen lake. Captive with him were the souls of three arch-traitors: Cassius and Brutus, the treacherous friends of Julius Caesar who murdered him on the Ides of March, 44 BC; and Judas Iscariot, the man who betrayed Jesus.

We are accustomed to the idea that sin is sin; no sin is worse or better than another. Every sin is an infinite offense against God. Dante, on the other hand, obviously thought that some sins were worse than others. The deeper into hell one travels, the worse sins and their punishments become. It may seem strange to us, but Dante thought that sins of fraud were more serious than sins of violence, that is, counterfeiting is worse than murder. How outlandish from our perspective, but this inversion reflects Dante's thought about the bonds of trust that make a society possible in the first place. If we cannot trust anybody, human society becomes impossible. Chaos would replace order, and human beings would degenerate into subhuman creatures. The very worst violation of trust, in Dante's view, was an act of personal betrayal. The most despicable act of betrayal in the history of Dante's Italian heritage was the murder of Julius Caesar, and the worst in Dante's Christian heritage was Judas's act of giving up his Lord to a Jewish leadership.

Matthew's account of Jesus' betrayal carries an air of foreboding. Jesus and the Twelve are in Jerusalem. He knew that he would soon be crucified and told them so. The text tells us that the leaders of the Jerusalem establishment were intent on Jesus' death. Then one night a woman poured expensive perfume on his head, and he told his indignant friends that it was a sign of the anointing that would soon be performed on his corpse. Death hung heavy in the air, but as yet Matthew does not tell us when or how these terrible events will unfold.

Later in the week, at the Passover meal, Jesus stunned his disciples with the announcement that among them reclined his betrayer. This was unthinkable, and yet each of them in turn asked whether he was the traitor. It seems a curious question. Did these men have so little understanding of themselves that they could not say with any confidence that they would not betray Jesus? Early Christian commentators interpret Jesus' announcement and the fact that Jesus did not immediately name his betrayer as an eleventh-hour opportunity for Judas to repent. Jesus had washed the feet of all twelve and was not willing that any would perish. John Chrysostom says that the Lord "was willing to allow the others to be alarmed, just for the sake of redeeming this one."[4]

Perhaps the disciples' question reveals more self-awareness and insight than first meets the eye. Maybe it was good that they were aware of a weakness that could turn any one of them into a traitor. It is no vice to confess one's weakness. Chrysostom says that Jesus finally disclosed the traitor's identity to allay the fears of the other eleven. At least they could take comfort in the knowledge that it was Judas and not one of them. However, one in the group pledged that he would never betray Jesus. Before the rooster crowed that rash pledge-maker had denied his Lord three times.

Agony
Matthew 26:26–30

The hours in Gethsemane were the last moments that Jesus would share

4. Simonetti, *Matthew 14–28*, 246.

with any of his disciples before his crucifixion. He intended that they spend this time together in communion with God. Although their spirits were willing, the disciples' bodies were weak, and they fell asleep while Jesus prayed. Even before his arrest, Jesus already was alone.

The Master and his disciples had departed the upper room for a garden. They had eaten the Passover. His betrayal was imminent; Judas had already been dismissed and was searching for the temple guards. Perhaps Jesus and his disciples left the room rather than see the place of Passover fellowship defiled by an act of perfidy. In any case, they walked to Gethsemane not in flight but in search of a place of prayer. To this holy spot, Jesus invited Peter, James, and John, leaving behind the others as he had done only weeks earlier at the Mount of Transfiguration. The three members of the inner circle had been privileged to behold the Son of God in his glory standing with Elijah and Moses. Now they beheld the Son sorrowful unto death. This was also glory, the glory of the undying love of God for human beings, a glory that accepted alienation and death before it would see us go unredeemed.

The text says that Jesus became overwhelmed in the face of what lay ahead. What is the focal point of this sorrow? Early church teachers agreed that Jesus was not mourning for himself; rather, he sorrowed over the disciples who would soon flee and deny their association with him. Only a matter of minutes earlier, he had revealed Peter's impending timidity and utter lack of loyalty. True friends find no joy in confronting their friends with their shortcomings; such moments become occasions of mutual grief. Then there was Judas. Surely the sorrowing love of the Good Shepherd extended even to the man who at that very moment was leading armed guards to the garden. Jesus had said of this man, "It would be better for him if he had not been born." Finally, Jesus sorrowed over Jerusalem and its people, who had so often in her history turned against the prophets. All of these sorrows were held in the cup from which Jesus drank in the garden. The name of that cup is *agape*, and as the American preacher and theologian Horace Bushnell once wrote, "There is a Gethsemane in all love."

In great agony of spirit, Jesus asked if the cup of sorrow and alienation might be lifted from his lips. "If it is possible" is not a phrase that questions, as if Jesus is asking whether God has the power to remove the cup; rather, said early Christian theologian and exegete Origen, the question must be referred to God's justice. Even God is limited by the sphere of his own justice. Because God is just, he may not act unjustly; whether the cup might be taken from Jesus is not a question of God's power but whether in so doing God's justice would be violated. Jesus was asking whether there was a way consistent with divine justice for him to escape the cup of sorrows. There was no way out because God's justice cannot finally overcome God's love. Indeed, God's justice requires God's love.

It is the church's confession that Jesus was truly God and truly human. In the view of John Chrysostom, asking this question demonstrated Jesus' true humanity. Christians need not be shy about saying so. This question reveals a moment of deep human pathos; but in the next sentence, Jesus disclosed the strength born of his complete identification with the Father: "Yet not as I will, but as you will." (26:39).

"In order to make clear that he is truly God and truly human, words alone would not suffice. Deeds were needed. So he joined deeds with words in order that even those who had been highly contentious may believe that he both became man and died. Admittedly, some still do not believe that this was so. But many more would have been unable to have believed if his face had not been seen at Gethsemane."[5]

Crucifixion

Matthew 27:38–54

In our day, capital punishment has come under close scrutiny. Many in American society question whether the death penalty is evenhandedly applied. They note that some convicted criminals are more likely than others to receive a death sentence and to be executed. Other Americans have advocated changes in the methods, such as death by lethal injection.

The Romans also executed people in many different ways, but not out of a desire to avoid cruel or unusual punishment. The victim's social status typically determined the method. Quicker, less torturous forms were employed for people of the upper social classes, while the lower classes and slaves were executed by methods that most would describe as hideous. Crucifixion was the worst, a form of execution reserved for criminals from the lowest social classes. To suffer crucifixion not only was to die; it was to be slowly tortured to death in the most shameful of circumstances. Rome used crucifixion to send a message.

Matthew's account of Jesus' death is spare in detail. There is no doubt that Jesus suffered excruciating pain. Whether Matthew intends that we meditate on this physical suffering is another question and a legitimate one. For Matthew, it seems, alienation is more important than physical wounds. One notes in particular the taunts and jeers that members of the crowd hurled at him as he was dying between the two robbers. Utterly alone, Jesus cried out the prayer of abandonment—"My God, my God, why have you forsaken me?" It is a prayer for the great paradox of that moment: the Son suffers the abandonment of the Father and the Father suffers the death of the Son. Who but the Son of God could offer a prayer to the God who had abandoned him? In so praying, Jesus quoted Psalm 22:1 in Aramaic, which some in the crowd confused with a call to Elijah. In the minds of some watchers, the apocalyptic darkness that unnaturally settled over the entire countryside could have raised the possibility of Elijah's return. In the end, however, Romans—not even Jesus' own people—pronounced the final verdict on Jesus: "Surely he was the Son of God!"

Recall that Jesus was crucified during Passover, the highest Jewish festival. Joseph of Arimathea's actions of claiming and removing Jesus' body from the cross required extraordinary courage and commitment. According to Torah, the law that Jesus came to fulfill, to touch a corpse was to become ritually unclean. Joseph's act prohibited him from participating in Passover.

5. Ibid., 255.

To become identified with Jesus in such a public way could only mark him as one under official suspicion. In this way, the Christian virtue of love transforms ordinary courage into an extraordinary witness to faith and the power of the good news of forgiveness that Jesus taught and that his death purchased.

Resurrection
Matthew 28:1–20

Matthew's account of Jesus' resurrection includes details not found in the other gospel narratives. Only Matthew mentions an earthquake, the descent of an angel, and the stupefying effect of these events on the Roman guards. In fact, only Matthew refers to these guards at all. In Matthew's narrative, Mary Magdalene and the "other Mary" arrived at the tomb, felt the earthquake, and witnessed the sudden appearance of an angel who rolled away the stone to reveal an empty tomb. One might expect these women to be alarmed; hence the first words that the angel speaks are, "Do not be afraid." Fear had reduced the guards to a dead faint. As soldiers of an empire that stood opposed to the resurrected Lord, these soldiers had reason to be afraid. But the angel told Jesus' followers that they had nothing to fear. More than thirty years earlier at Jesus' birth, angels had spoken the same message to those who were fearful. At the beginning and the conclusion of Jesus' life on earth, the message remains constant: there is no need to be afraid.

The angel knew that the women had come to the tomb to complete Jesus' burial. The angel adds the phrase, "who was crucified." Why was it important to add that descriptive phrase? The women did not need to be reminded of the manner of Jesus' death. It was the faith of the early church that insisted on remembering that Jesus was "the crucified and resurrected Lord." The cross, an emblem of shame and a social stigma, had become the occasion of thanksgiving. This remembrance marked Christians as a distinct group among ancient Mediterranean religions. Few adherents of Greco-Roman or mystery religions worshiped a crucified God. And if they did, few would be willing to admit it publicly. It was a rare citizen of that world who would have voluntarily identified with a crucified God, yet Christians made that precise identification. When Roman persecution began in the second half of the first century, these Christians quickly found themselves living as the church under its own cross.

The fifth-century Latin bishop of Ravenna, Peter Chrysologus, commented on the stone of the empty tomb in a manner particularly befitting the church's Easter worship: "An angel descended and rolled back the stone. He did not roll back the stone to provide a way of escape for the Lord but to show the world that the Lord had already risen. He rolled back the stone to help his fellow servants believe, not to help the Lord rise from the dead. He rolled back the stone for the sake of faith, because it had been rolled over the tomb for the sake of unbelief. He rolled back the stone so that he who took death captive might hold the title of Life. Pray, brothers, that the angel would descend now and roll away all the hardness of our hearts and open up our closed senses and declare to our minds that Christ is risen, for just as the heart in which Christ lives and reigns is heaven, so also the heart in which Christ remains dead and buried is a grave. May it be believed that just as he died, so was he transformed. Christ the man suffered, died, and was buried; as God he lives, reigns, is and will be forever."[6]

In Galilee, the resurrected Jesus commissioned the eleven. His words have fueled the missionary endeavor of the Christian church ever since and are known as the Great Commission. Three verbs describe the activity of Jesus' followers: (1) make disciples, (2) baptize, and (3) teach. The first verb, *matheteusate*, is written in the imperative mode; it is a command. The latter two words, *baptizontes* and *didaskontes*, are both participles. Grammatically, we have a sentence where the latter two participles shape the meaning of the command. In other words, disciples are made through the actions of baptism and teaching. Jesus also specifies what the disciples are to teach—"to obey everything I have commanded you" (28:20). In Matthew's gospel, a good place to start such teaching would be with the Sermon on the Mount. It also should be clear that the kind of moral transformation required in this sermon occurs over a long period of growth and maturation in the presence of the Spirit. In other words, "making disciples" is the work not of an instant but a lifetime. Coming to faith in the triune God who saves through Christ Jesus inaugurates a life of transformation. Baptism confirms believers as they set out on that pilgrimage. Learning in the context of the church is the arena by which such lives are advanced.

6. Ibid., 306.

Mark

Announcing and Making Good News

Mark 1

Of the three Synoptic Gospels, Mark is generally agreed to be the oldest, and according to many New Testament scholars, the one that provides the basic outline and content for Luke and Matthew. In all likelihood, Mark was written not long after AD 60. There is a very ancient tradition that Mark wrote his gospel on the basis of the preaching and recollected stories of the apostle Peter. The early church historian Eusebius (*c.* 260 to *c.* 340) reports this tradition dating back to the second century.

Commentator Robert H. Gundry states that the gospel according to Mark was written with a particular theological purpose.[7] To appreciate this purpose, we must remember the utter shamefulness of death by crucifixion. In Greco-Roman society, the cross was more than a terrible instrument employed to ensure a slow and painful death. It was an execution reserved for the most heinous criminals from the lowest social station. Execution by cross was intended to stigmatize the victim, and it was successful. Ancient people avoided walking through even the shadow of a cross. As early Christian missionaries and evangelists spread throughout the Roman world, one very likely barrier to the credibility of their message was the news that the Savior had been crucified. Those of us who have transformed the cross into an article of jewelry can scarcely appreciate what an impediment it was

7. Gundry, *Mark*, 1026.

to successful Christian witness. Gundry argues that part of Mark's purpose was to overcome the scandalous news of a crucified Savior, to write a defense of the life and message of Jesus.

Action characterizes Mark's gospel. We will not find here the long discourses of Matthew or John. Neither do we read narratives concerning Jesus' birth or childhood. Mark describes only the adult years of Jesus' life and ministry. Since there was little likelihood that the Romans would crucify Jesus for anything that he might have done as a boy, it is Jesus' adult actions and teachings that had to be narrated for their innocence of any wrongdoing. Because it is Jesus' deeds that hold Mark's attention, he characteristically uses the Greek phrase *kai euthus*, which is translated "and immediately," "right away," or "straight away."

The gospel according to Matthew begins with Jesus' genealogy; Luke with Jesus' birth, and John with Jesus' identity. Each focuses on Jesus. The gospel according to Mark, on the other hand, opens with an announcement about the message of Jesus. Verse 1 announces the beginning of the good news (gospel). Then two well-known and respected historic voices are quoted: Isaiah and Malachi (verse 2 from Mal 3:1 and verse 3 from Isa 40:3).

Today's scholars debate the identity of Malachi, but the proclamations ascribed to him were part of the prophetic canon of Mark's day. The book of Malachi was written to and for a people living in a time of chaos. Besieged with great threats, their belief in God's promises wavered. Malachi reaffirmed the law and its promise and told them that there would be a herald who would come to alert the people to the time of God's fulfillment of the law.

Mark quotes Isaiah to add further detail concerning the herald. A voice crying in the wilderness would declare that his calling was to pave the way for one greater than he. Mark's readers would have understood this reference readily because it was the custom of that day for emissaries of an official to precede him in order to repair the roads for his chariot and to alert the people to his coming.

Mark begins the story about Jesus by explaining that the beginning of the account does not start with Jesus' birth or with his ministry, but with the messages conveyed by the prophets generations earlier. Mark then describes John, who came "baptizing in the desert region" (1:4) and proclaiming, "After me will come one more powerful than I" (1:7).

Several distinct actions are entailed in this block of material. They are (1) Jesus' baptism at the Jordan, (2) the call of the first disciples, (3) Jesus' exorcism of an evil spirit, and (4) teaching and healing in Capernaum. One might ask whether there is even another action—the temptation in the wilderness—but Mark's account of that is so sparse that it seems better understood here as an extension of the baptism narrative. Some commentators and interpreters have contended that the gospel of Mark is primarily a theology of suffering; everything in Mark revolves around or extends from Jesus' cross.

But there is also a great deal of glory in this gospel. We find two instances of that here in the opening passages. Heaven opened and God's Spirit descended upon Jesus after he rose out of the water. What can be more glorious than God's declaration of pleasure at our actions? God said to Jesus, "With you I am well pleased."

Not just pleased—*well* pleased. Second, the demons were shown to be subject to Jesus' authority. History is full of powerful people who maim and kill. Here we read of one who used his power to heal and redeem. That is heavenly glory come down to earth.

In Jesus' day, it was customary to ask male members of the synagogue to read and then speak about a passage of the Bible. Men who were recognized as visiting rabbis were especially extended this courtesy. It would have been common for an animated discussion and debate to follow after the presiding rabbi interpreted a particular passage of scripture. The whole premise of scriptural study and enlightenment rested on the power of one's interpretive ability, and rabbis vied for the honor of forwarding an interpretation that held up under the scrutiny of their peers.

This is the setting of Jesus' teaching in the Capernaum synagogue. Instead of igniting the expected debate, however, Jesus' interpretation and instruction inspired uncontested amazement. The other rabbis offered nothing to refute it, and the congregants were struck by a conviction that what Jesus said was true.

After what has turned out to be a sermon instead of debate, an outburst from an evil spirit, acknowledging Jesus as the "Holy One" (1:24), took place. It is not too much to imagine that this possessed man had attended the synagogue and had heard rabbis speak before, but it was in Jesus' presence that the evil spirit must bear witness. Since Jesus did not want his identity established by the enemy, he first silenced and then evicted the evil spirit. Word of this spread, and people came from all over with their sick and possessed. Then came a leper, a man ravaged by a highly contagious disease. Jesus touched and healed this man, risking possible infection and certain ritual impurity. Then Jesus instructed the man to comply with Mosaic Law by submitting to inspection by a priest and making the necessary offering to God. Whether the man obeyed on these points we do not know, but he did not remain obediently silent. Interest in Jesus grew to such a degree that he could no longer go unrecognized into any cities of the region.

The Spirit of the Law of Moses
Mark 2:1–3:6

Mark 2:1–3:6 contains stories that share a common theme of conflict. Very early in Mark's gospel, a tension develops between Jesus and the religious establishment—the Pharisees and teachers of the law. This tension concerns the interpretation and keeping of the law: When is it permissible to heal? Can the commandment to rest on the Sabbath never be broken—even to do a good deed? God commands us to be a holy people and to shun the very appearance of evil, so should we ever be seen partying in the company of known sinners? This tension also concerned the larger and more ominous question of whether Jesus was guilty of blasphemy, a crime liable to capital punishment.

Alongside this deadly prospect, there was also some rather petty carping. Jesus' critics drew comparisons between John's disciples and the Pharisees, who both practiced fasting as an act of religious devotion, versus Jesus' disciples, who were said not to have fasted. Once passions had been sparked, any issue, from the greatest to the utterly trivial, had the potential for becoming a flashpoint.

Ever since Martin Luther, Protestants have lived with a certain tension of their own. This particular tension lies in the domain of theology and ethics. Luther's famous emphasis that justification is by faith alone has variously been interpreted to mean that salvation depends on faith and nothing else; in other words, no acts or series of acts can purchase a man or woman's salvation. Luther himself took the position that the only thing that separates a believer from God is unbelief; in other words, the believer who stops trusting in God ceases to "have faith." While nearly all Protestants agree that we are justified through faith in Christ, many, including most of the Wesleyan-Arminian persuasion, still appreciate the necessity of works. After all, doesn't James clearly state that without works faith is dead?

As soon as we open the subject of good works, we are on ground that was very familiar to Jesus and the Pharisees. Let's grant the latter a point. Religious practices are important to the development of mature disciples. Engaging in the disciplines of prayer and fasting are practices that strengthen and deepen spirituality.

Today Protestant writers produce a growing body of literature that emphasizes the importance—even the necessity—of practicing the elements of the Christian faith. But does this mean that the Pharisees were correct in their increasingly ominous and interminable dispute with Jesus? What was the issue that so sharply divided them from him?

Mark 2:1–3:5 describes events that show Jesus acting in violation of accepted religious norms and conventions. First, Jesus made an audacious claim to being able to forgive sin (2:5). Second, Jesus associated with a tax collector, his tax collector associates, and sinners (2:14–15). Tax collectors, particularly Jewish collectors, were reviled traitors since they were agents of the Roman occupation. Third, Jesus' disciples did not observe the fasts (2:18). Fourth, Jesus' disciples worked (picked grain) on the Sabbath (2:23). Fifth, Jesus himself worked (healed) on the Sabbath (3:3–5).

Through these events, Mark not only elaborated on Jesus' authority; he also demonstrated the distinction Jesus made between the Law and the people-made rules and regulations attached to it. For instance, the Law said, "Remember the Sabbath"; the rules said, "Don't pick an ear of corn on the Sabbath." Read in this light, the tension between Jesus and the interpreters of the Law should not be read in such a way as to dismiss the Law out of hand. Jesus is portrayed as having kept the spirit of the Law. The Law thus is valid and also liberating over against the deadening hand of the rules that claimed to be the correct interpretation of the Law.

The centerpiece of these conflict stories is Jesus' habit of associating with unclean and unsavory people—tax collectors and sinners. Tax collectors came to their positions through bribery and then extorted their own fellow Jews to recoup the bribes paid to the Roman overlords. Traitors as well as extortionists, tax collectors were twice hated. "Sinners" was a category that could include just about anyone with whom nice, respectable people did not associate. In case anyone wanted to quibble, Jesus provided plenty of ammunition. He was seen in the company of women, none of whom was his wife, violating a strictly observed Semitic taboo. Jesus didn't stop there; he was even known to have spoken to prostitutes. The Law of Moses, especially as the Pharisees interpreted it, forbade such disrespect for proper relationships. Jesus did not advocate disregard for the Law; however, he countered critics with the observation that the sick need a physician more than the healthy. People and their need take preference over self-righteous observance of the Law that misses its spirit.

Sabbath Healing

Mark 3:1–6

Jesus' running controversy with the Pharisees and others surrounds this famous account of healing on the Sabbath. We often attribute only sinister motives to the Pharisees; in the Gospels, we see them only in opposition to Jesus. But there is more than this to the Pharisees. Jesus also received positive hearings from Nicodemus, Joseph of Arimathea, and Gamaliel, all of whom were Pharisees.

Our word *pharisee* comes from a Hebrew word that means purity through separation. The Pharisees sought to preserve Israel through separation from the Gentiles. The means of that separation was the Law of Moses, which included a growing body of oral interpretation. To live faithful to the Mosaic Law would, in the Pharisees' eyes, clearly mark Israel as the people of God. Of course, consenting to and supporting a point of law becomes a problem when the law is applied to concrete life situations. This is precisely the issue at hand in Mark 3:1–6.

The Law of Moses commands us to "remember the Sabbath and keep it holy." The Pharisees strictly interpreted that commandment—no work of any kind on the Sabbath. Puritans and other Protestants applied this commandment to the Christian day of weekly celebration, Sunday, and legislated a whole set of laws that required most businesses and government offices to close on Sunday. Persons over the age of fifty can remember when even simple purchases became difficult on Sunday. Those practices were not entirely misguided. To keep one day in seven for the remembrance of the Lord and for our rest remains as it always has been, part of the divine intention for our lives.

Jesus' quarrel with the Pharisees did not concern the Sabbath commandment itself, but their interpretation of it. His question in Mark 3:4 is a little like the trick question sometimes asked of men, "Have you stopped beating your wife?" It forces respondents to make a choice between alternatives, neither of which is especially pleasant. Jesus' question was a trap; either answer would force a concession from the Pharisees. Yes, the Sabbath is to be remembered and kept holy, but there are also exceptions. As Jesus said on another occasion, "The Sabbath was made for people, not people for the Sabbath."

Power over Deadly Forces

Mark 4:35–5:13

In one way or another, the miracle stories found in Mark 4:35–5:13 are connected by the idea of death. In the first story, Jesus' word calmed a storm that threatened death to the disciples. In the story of the Gerasene demoniac, Jesus healed a man whom the demons had forced to dwell in a graveyard. In the final story, Jesus demonstrated his power over death by bringing back to life a young girl whose demise was so certain that mourners had already gathered and started their sad work.

Death connects the three stories, but their message is that Jesus has power over the threat of death as well as death itself. Jesus' authority is the basis of this power. Miracles in the Synoptic Gospels are *dunameis*, plural of *dunamis*. The Synoptic Gospels agree that miracles are eruptions of divine power—the power of the rule and reign of God. Jesus had but to speak a word and the power of God's rule erupted, transforming a desperate situation into one of peace and joy. Such power rests on authority. Thus the disciples, their fears quelled as readily as the storm, asked one another, "Who is this? Even the wind and the waves obey him!"

The miracle stories in Mark 4:35–5:13 follow a geographical pattern that suggests a circular trip out of Galilee and back. Jesus and his disciples started on the western shore of the Sea of Galilee and encountered the storm during their sail across the sea. Once across, they disembarked in the region of the Decapolis, the "Ten Cities"—Gentile country. The Gerasene demoniac was not a Jew (and thus an explanation for a large herd of pigs in the vicinity). Jesus' power and mercy are not restricted to the house of Israel, but these Gentiles seemed not to know what to make of this man whose authority and power produced such extraordinary events, so they asked him to leave. Pharisees and teachers of the Law wanted to kill Jesus, and the Gentiles were bewildered by him. In response to their invitation to leave, Jesus returned to the other side of Galilee, where Jairus begged him to heal his daughter. Some know not what to make of Jesus and thus dismiss him. Others are desperate for his presence and touch.

Commenting on the healing of the demoniac, the early medieval churchman Gregory the Great took note of the fact that Jesus directed the restored man to witness to the miracle that had been performed on his behalf. Putting these words into the mouth of the demoniac, Gregory wrote, "A legion of demons has been, as I believed, cast out of me. I would prefer merely to forget all of this that I have known and simply to rest at the feet of the Savior. But lo it is said to me, so strongly as to compel me against my will, 'Go home to your friends, and tell them how much the Lord has done for you, and how he has had mercy on you.'[8] Many times we, like the disciples, would like to tarry in the Lord's presence, find a place to rest, and bask in the warmth of his gracious love and kindness. And yet there remains work to be done, even as there was for the one who had been so brutally abused by the demons.

"Only" Have Faith
Mark 5:21–43

It is a commonplace that faith is at the very center of the Christian's relationship with God. The medieval theologian Thomas Aquinas referred to faith, hope, and love as theological virtues because they all pertain to God. Faith was the virtue on which, said Thomas, hope and love rest because faith must precede them. Many stories in Mark consider aspects of this crucial Christian virtue from the perspective of the interaction between Jesus and several different people who are either said to

8. Oden and Hall, *Mark*, 71.

have faith or whom Jesus encouraged to exercise their faith.

So far in Mark we have learned that Jesus can be directly connected to the messianic prophecies and that he contended with the powers of evil and nature and was served by angels. We also learn that he taught with authority, healed all manner of disease including leprosy, cast out demons, forgave sin, attracted loyal followers, and drew the attention of the entire region. The gospel of Mark relays all of these things in a rapid-fire, nonstop sequence. The only respite readers are allowed is Jesus' explanation of the parable of the seed. Then this short pause is followed by a dramatic story about the man with the legion of demons. We come now to 5:21 in which Jesus was met by yet another great multitude.

Breaking through all this momentum and anticipation stepped one man, Jairus, a synagogue official—not a peasant, not somebody weak or infirm, but a man of position, power, and, most likely, wealth. In all humility, however, Jairus fell at Jesus' feet in the posture of debasement. Need will do such things to us. Jairus was willing to lay aside dignity and social claims for the sake of this appeal. When we hear his request, we realize he was a man moved by fear of loss. While it is true that his dramatic appeal indicated his great love for his daughter, it was the desperate fear of losing her that brought him to Jesus' feet.

This story is particularly interesting for the way it unfolds. Jairus, one of the presiding officials of the local synagogue and therefore of some stature in his community, had hurried to Jesus on a desperate errand. His daughter had fallen ill and was on the verge of death. Upon finding Jesus, Jairus did not scruple over protocol. Important official or not, he became a person begging for favor or help. There was not a moment to be lost, so Jesus rose and accompanied Jairus. The journey and the narrative were interrupted by another person seeking Jesus' help.

We could read Mark 5:24b–34 as another healing narrative. In fact, it is nearly as long as the story of Jairus's daughter, excepting the fact that this second narrative occurs inside the first. The "inside narrative" tells of the woman who had been bleeding for twelve years. Like Jairus, she too was desperate and had determined to risk everything on one bold venture. Her powerful faith had led her to believe her healing did not depend on touching Jesus' person or on him touching her. "If I can but touch the hem of his garment." Her faith in Jesus opened the door through which his healing virtue flowed, and she was made whole. Jesus took notice and wanted to learn the identity of the one who had touched him.

What of Jairus, his daughter, and their need at this precise moment? The last thing Jairus could have wanted was for Jesus to interrupt their hasty journey in favor of one anonymous person in the pressing crowd. Not a moment was to be lost, and yet here was Jesus stopping in that mob to ask, "Who touched me?" Even worse, from Jairus's point of view, was that the woman was discovered. Now Jesus wanted to talk with her. She had become the singular object of his attention and he seemed to have completely forgotten the desperately ill little girl. Just as Jesus told the woman that her faith had made her whole, some messengers arrived with word that the little girl had died. In his grief-stricken dismay, Jairus can be forgiven for thinking, *If only he hadn't stopped, my daughter would be alive and well.* But Jesus continued on toward the house and said to his bewildered petitioner, "Don't be afraid; just believe."

In this passage, two people believed, which is to say they had faith. But they believed in different circumstances, and their faith made different demands of them. The woman believed in Jesus, having exhausted every other alternative. He was her last hope; nevertheless her faith was strong enough that she reached only for his cloak. At the moment when Jesus said "Just believe" to Jairus, all hope seemed to have been lost. Jairus had to believe in the face of hopelessness. And yet Jesus said "just"—"only" in the King James Version—as if faith were effortless, as if it were no greater than a mustard seed.

Hometown Skeptics

Mark 6:1–13

The first half of Mark 6 deals with rejection and the shadow of death. Jesus had just raised Jairus's daughter, once again demonstrating his power over death for all to see. This extraordinary explosion of divine power was followed, however, by rejection back home in Nazareth. To make matters far worse, on the heels of Jesus' repudiation in his own hometown came word that his cousin John the Baptizer had been executed, another victim of state murder at the hands of the man Jesus called "that fox"—Herod Antipas.

John's death carried ominous implications for Jesus. If the state could execute a prophet on the whim of a teenage girl, then Jesus' own life wasn't secure. That his own neighbors rejected him so easily served to underscore the growing danger.

Fresh on the heels of his victory over death, Jesus went home to Nazareth. When the Sabbath arrived, Jesus went to the synagogue and began to teach. Mark does not report the content of Jesus' instruction. Is this an omission, or does it make the point that it was Jesus' authority to which his neighbors objected? The grammatical construction of the Greek here is significant. Mark employs a verb form that suggests the townspeople of Nazareth were astonished even as Jesus taught. This implies that Jesus' neighbors had already made up their minds about him and had prejudged him and his message. Thus they asked, in essence, "Don't we already know this man and his origins? Don't we know his occupation? Don't we already know his family?" The prejudice of the townspeople obscured the truth and left them quite blind. To identify Jesus as a carpenter missed the comparison at the beginning of Mark's gospel: Jesus is greater than John the Baptizer, and the people of Nazareth should have recognized that fact. Similarly, Jesus' true identity was the Son of God, but all that his neighbors could see was that he was the son of Mary.

In response to the prejudiced reaction of the people of Nazareth, Jesus quoted an aphorism, a short pithy saying that captures the essence of the situation (6:4). We should avoid the conclusion that the source of the prejudice against Jesus was his occupation. Whether in Palestine or in the Diaspora, Jewish people did not look down on manual labor. The apostle Paul took pride in the fact that he supported himself with the work of his hands, and tent making was not high on the list of respected forms of labor. No, the source of the prejudice among the good citizens of Nazareth, as with peoples of other times and places, was ignorance and a stubborn insistence that they could not be mistaken.

The text says that Jesus performed only a handful of minor miracles in Nazareth and attributes this absence of the miraculous to the town's lack of belief. The text says that Jesus himself was amazed at their lack of faith. Let's take special care here as we interpret this text. It would be easy to conclude that the power of God is unavailable to those who lack faith, leading us to think that if our faith is weak or nonexistent, God's power will be frustrated. Two points are worth remembering. The first is theological. We need to exercise caution lest we make human faith greater than God's power. Second, we must avoid the logical error of concluding that because Jesus performed no miracles in Nazareth because of weak faith, he acts in that way in every case. That our prayers are not answered in the manner we seek is not a sure indicator of weak or absent faith. Many a believer has been unnecessarily troubled by that mistake in logic.

Tradition and Iconoclasm
Mark 7:1–23

Whenever someone gets busy doing good in fresh new ways, critics gather. In Mark 7, religious leaders complained about the way Jesus' disciples did not follow custom and ate with "defiled" hands. Mark's account here is not about breaking the basic law of God but about codes tied to human tradition and custom. This text reflects a respect for God's law and distinguishes it from the cluster of secondary regulations and traditions that grew up around it.

At certain points of Jewish religion, Jesus showed himself to be a genuine iconoclast. The Gospel accounts generally portray him as sincerely respecting the Mosaic Law, but by the first century Jewish religion had added a considerable body of interpretation to the Law. A major element of that body of interpretation was the so-called *halakah*, the "oral tradition." As legal precedents shape the interpretation of law in United States courts, so the *halakah* combined with the Mosaic Law to govern religious practice among the Jewish people. The Pharisees were the primary arbiters of this practice, and they employed it to separate themselves not only from Gentiles but also from the people of the land, those who occupied the lower rungs of the Jewish social ladder. In Mark 7, Jesus sharply criticizes not the law but, as he called them, "the traditions of men" that interpreted the law and governed Jewish religious life.

The Pharisees regarded the law and the oral traditions as cut from the same cloth. In their eyes Jesus' criticism of the oral tradition was tantamount to attacking the law itself. From this perspective, Jesus was a dangerous iconoclast, a man whose teaching could not be permitted to continue because of its potential to upset or destroy the religious status quo. On the issue of ceremonial washing, Jesus uttered some of his sharpest words of criticism yet in Mark's gospel. Again, the conflict may have begun in Jesus' preference for the needs of the people over legal precision. Some Pharisees saw the disciples eating bread. Perhaps this bread was leftover from the miracle of the loaves and fishes. It may have been the first opportunity the disciples had to eat anything in quite a while. There may not have been fresh water available in which to wash. We cannot say for sure, of course; but the Pharisees caught the disciples in violation of religious practice, and Jesus immediately came to their defense. (Mark's lengthy explanation of Jewish ritual washing in this passage reinforces the general belief that he wrote his gospel for a Gentile audience. Jewish readers would not need an explanation of this practice, while Gentiles would be mystified by a less than complete account.)

Ritual washing, as directed by Pharisaic interpretation and practice, was but a symptom and not the disease eating away at Judaism, and Jesus quickly moved the discussion from symptoms to the heart of the problem. He drew a sharp distinction between the commandments of God and the traditions of human beings. The commandments were to be followed, of course, but the traditions were empty. Even worse, in some cases, the traditions supported religious practices that contradicted the commandments. Here Jesus raised a specific point concerning one such tradition. As a means of increasing piety, a tradition developed that said that whatever goods were declared "devoted to God" had the highest religious priority. Apparently, some Jews devoted a portion of their means to God that otherwise would have been used for the support of their parents. An act that had the appearance of piety masked disobedience to the commandment to honor father and mother. Jesus used this as an example of the bankruptcy of a religion concerned with externals rather than the condition of the heart.

As usual, Jesus turned the tables on the Pharisees. What appears to be beautiful religion is actually ugly morality. In declaring all things clean, Jesus did not declare the law null and void. The great ancient commentator and theologian Origen makes the following point: "According to Mark, the Savior 'declared all food clean,' so we are not defiled when we eat those things declared to be unclean by those who still desire to be in bondage to the letter of the law. But we are then defiled when our lips, which ought to be bound with good judgment as we search for correct balance and weight, speak recklessly and discuss matters we ought not."[9]

In our own time, we participate in the Christian community and are stabilized by our own religious traditions. Important as those practices are, in the spirit of Jesus' teachings in Mark 7, such traditions are no substitute for our personal commitment to the Lord. The most serious sin appears to be an inner disregard of the law, even more serious than deliberate acts of outer disobedience or the breaking of customs.

A Witty Gentile Mother
Mark 7:24–37

The gospel according to Mark makes geographical references frequently enough that it would be a good practice to read it with a set of Bible maps. They would show, for example, that Jesus and the disciples were on a tour that took them into Gentile territory to the north of Galilee. That Jesus spent significant time among Gentiles is important with respect to the Jews, who needed to see that Jesus came for all human beings. But if indeed

9. Ibid., 99.

Mark's gospel was written primarily for Gentiles, then those readers also would find encouragement in the numerous instances when Jesus traveled and ministered outside Galilee and Judea.

The first story centers on a curious conversation between a Gentile woman and Jesus in which her determined, bold faith won the day. Jesus and his disciples were resting. According to the text, he had hoped to remain incognito, but his fame was making that impossible. Upon hearing of Jesus' presence in town, a woman boldly begged for his healing touch on her possessed daughter. Jesus refused the woman's request with a harsh proverb. The extended meaning of the proverb is captured by Robert Gundry: "Emphasis falls on…'first' in Jesus' reply, 'Let the children [i.e., my Jewish disciples] be satisfied first [i.e., be fully taught].' 'First' implies that the woman's daughter may receive the salvific benefits of God's kingdom at a later date. But the next clause, 'for it is not good…to take the bread of the children [i.e., the time and effort needed to teach my disciples] and cast it to the little dogs [i.e., to Gentile children like the woman's daughter],' makes the delay so indefinite that in effect Jesus is denying the woman's request."[10] The harshness of this reply seems out of character with the standard portrait of Jesus as friendly, gentle, and receptive. After all, Jesus had once told his disciples to make sure that children were free to come to him and not to be forbidden. How could that same Jesus now call a needy young girl a "little dog"?

Faced with this apparent contradiction, modern readers speculate about his motives in talking this way to the Syro-Phoenician woman. Some conjecture that perhaps Jesus was half joking, testing the woman's faith, or setting the limits of his ministry according to the time available to him on earth. Perhaps we would do well to follow Mark, who resists the temptation to determine his motives. Sometimes it is permissible to read the Bible and be left with an unanswered question.

The text is more interested in the woman's bold response to Jesus than in his motives. She was not put off by his refusal but retorted with a witty reply of her own. That she was so nimble-witted at a moment when her mind was surely on her daughter was certainly admirable. The woman had the presence of mind to reply that even dogs were permitted to lick up the crumbs that the children knocked off the table. Like the importunate widow, the Syro-Phoenician woman refused to take no for an answer. With certain admiration, Jesus told the woman that her witty reply, grounded in a bold faith, had won the day.

The second story in this text is straightforward and easier to follow. Once again Jesus was in Gentile territory, this time the region of the Decapolis east of the Sea of Galilee. Once again, the one who needed help—a deaf and dumb man—was a non-Jew. Once again we find the tension between Jesus' desire that the news of such miracles not be broadcast and its inevitable rapid spread. The story concludes with the disciples' wonder at all that Jesus had done and done so well. We are left with the implication that this man is truly the Son of God. What was implied was about to become explicit in the words of Peter the Jewish disciple and by a Gentile centurion at Calvary.

10. Gundry, *Mark*, 373.

Fides Quae, Fides Qua
Mark 8:27–9:8

Medieval Christian theologians used a pair of very similar Latin phrases to express two sides of faith: *fides quae* and *fides qua*—"the faith that believes" and "the faith that is believed." Noncreedal traditions such as the Church of God tend to be formed more by the faith that believes. We might term this *experiential* faith, trusting in God with all of one's heart, soul, mind, and strength. In this sense, faith is, to borrow a phrase from Protestant theologian Paul Tillich, living with reference to God as "ultimate concern."

On the other hand, the faith that is believed refers to the *content* of faith, typically summarized in a statement of beliefs such as the Apostles' Creed or the Westminster Confession of Faith. Christians who subscribe to such statements are said to have "confessed" the faith, meaning that they have witnessed to their belief in its truth.

The first of the two narratives recorded in Mark 8:27–9:8 centers on Peter's answer to Jesus' identity question, "Who do you say that I am?" He actually began this series with a broader question, "Who do people say I am?" As is so often the case, Peter was the disciple at center stage. He provided the definitive answer, "You are the Christ." We should note here that Mark, like the other synoptic writers, provided a translation for Gentile readers. Peter would have spoken in Aramaic, the everyday language of first-century Palestine, and would have spoken a word here much nearer the Hebrew *Messiah*. But few Gentiles spoke or read Hebrew or had knowledge of the Jewish context that would enable him or her to correctly understand the word *messiah*. So Mark provided the Greek equivalent—"the Anointed One." This simple sentence uttered by Peter has come to be called his confession of faith. It is an example of the faith that is believed, the content of Christian faith. Christians are people who believe, with Peter, that Jesus is the Christ, the Messiah of God. That is not the only thing Christians believe, but it is the starting point.

To grasp the surprise of this passage, it is important to understand the conventional expectations regarding the Messiah held by Jesus' contemporaries. The Israelites resented to the marrow of their bones the Romans and their occupation. The very real misery of Jewish subjugation had fostered a belief that the Messiah, if he came in their day, would overturn the Roman rule and establish Israel as the preeminent kingdom of the day. Those who looked to such a restoration thought of the kingdom of God as physical and political. Such a kingdom would, of course, have spiritual implications in that the restoration of the Davidic kingdom was expected to draw the entire world to recognize God as the only One High Almighty and the Israelites as his chosen people. Nevertheless, a physical messianic reign was uppermost in the minds of many.

Mark delivers an account of Jesus that demonstrates Jesus' unique authority and power and recounts his challenges to those conventional expectations. In a way, this aligned Jesus with expectations of a political messiah—at least without directly saying so, but highlighting implications of this political expectation. However, Mark's account also creates a backdrop for the great surprise of chapter 8. Suddenly (there is that characteristic Markan immediacy), Jesus is moving in a direction directly opposed to conventional expectation. He—not the Romans—would be killed. His kingship called for denial, crosses, dispossession, and death—not recognition, crowning, possessions, and life. To the disciples, it was as if the wind had been knocked out of them and they were left gasping for air. How could this be?

The second story recounts the transfiguration of Jesus. Nearly a week had passed since Peter's confession of faith at Caesarea Philippi, and Jesus had taken Peter, James, and John to the top of a mountain. There the disciples were startled by a dramatic change in Jesus, his clothing, and by the appearance of Moses and Elijah. The Jewish people revered Moses as the great lawgiver; they looked for the coming of Elijah just before the arrival of the day of the Lord (Malachi 4:5–6). Moses and Elijah talked with Jesus, thus setting the stage for God's command that the disciples were to listen to him. Jesus thus stands with the personalities that embody the Law (Moses) and the prophets (Elijah), which is to say the revelation of Yahweh in Scripture. The disciples similarly experienced the fullness of divine revelation—Jesus, the Christ and Savior. This experience was "the faith that believes"; there is no content but an experience so stunning that Peter wished they could build enclosures for each of the three and listen to them converse up there on the mountain.

It would not do for Jesus and the disciples to remain on the mountaintop. Their experience was extraordinary but had to end. There was crucial work that remained to be done. We might also want to ask whether their experience on the Mount of Transfiguration was connected to Peter's confession a week earlier. Such a question suggests that in the all-important matter of faith we err if we try to separate the faith that believes from the faith that is believed. In the final analysis, can we have one without the other?

"Help My Unbelief"

Mark 9:14–37

The scene at the beginning of the narrative in Mark 9:14 is a direct continuation of the story of the transfiguration. Jesus, Peter, James, and John descend the mountain and return to the nine waiting disciples. Before the reunion, however, the nine had become embroiled in a dispute with a large crowd. In the center stood a man and his demon-possessed son. The nine disciples disputed about this boy with some teachers of the law. The disciples had attempted to exorcise the demon that tormented the son and had failed.

As Jesus and the three disciples approached, people in the crowd noticed them and ran to see Jesus. The text says that they were "overwhelmed with wonder," a phrase that Mark uses in this grammatical form only on two other occasions. This form connotes extreme agitation or emotional distress. What could have provoked such a reaction in the crowd? One reasonable answer is that the radiant whiteness of Jesus' clothing remained after the transfiguration. At no point does Mark indicate that this brilliance had faded. Commentator Robert Gundry wonders whether Mark wants his readers to assume that the transfiguration continued all the way to Golgotha. This would be one way to heighten Jesus' innocence over against the injustice of his sentence. In that way, the shame of the cross—a very prominent concern of Mark's gospel—would also be combated.[11]

Mark describes the boy's seizures and convulsions with unusual detail. The demon had extraordinary dominion over its young victim. Although Jesus had promised his disciples the power to perform exorcisms, they had failed. Alongside the disciples' failure was the unbelief of some in the crowd. The teachers of the law did not believe; neither did many others, one in particular—namely the father. The spread of unbelief was broad enough to provoke Jesus to ask in exasperation, "How long shall I put up with you?" But he relented and commanded the boy to be brought to him.

The centerpiece of this narrative is the ensuing exchange between Jesus and the boy's father. After answering Jesus' question concerning his son's condition, the father blunders into an embarrassing plea: "If you can do anything, take pity on us and help us" (9:22). The request reeks with doubt. Who in his right mind would attach such a condition to a request made of Jesus? Perhaps we should exercise a little compassion and understanding toward this unfortunate man. For years, he had watched seizures cast his child about, threatening his life with fire and water. Finally the chance came to see a man with the reputation for helping people like his boy, but Jesus was absent, and his disciples couldn't produce the desired relief. The man's hopes had been dashed. Unbelief had crept into his heart, so he attached that little word *if* to his request. We can read this condition in either of two emphases: "*If* you can do anything..." or "If *you* can do anything...." The latter reading takes some of the sting out of the man's *if*. It would be as if the man was saying, "I've tried the others and they couldn't help. Can you?"

Plenty of offense remains even if we take the softer reading. Jesus seized on that little word, *if*. He rebuked the unbelieving father with a statement that said the desire of the man's heart was within his grasp if only he could summon up enough faith. Now the man shouted back his reply, "I do believe; help me overcome my unbelief!" Only moments earlier, all hope had been dashed, but the appearance of Jesus had revived belief and transformed despair into hope. Yet there remained some residue of unbelief. It was for the elimination of those last doubts that he cried. Many of us live in a similar tension. We believe, but circumstances of life often beat us down, and in that dark, damp soil the spores of unbelief find all kinds of places to take root. Ultimately, it is a cry of belief that asks the Lord to help us with our unbelief.

The Rich Young Ruler
Mark 10:17–27

The word *gospel* "can signify a literary genre, a particular theological message, or a canonical writing normative in the life of the church. The gospel of Mark is all three: a collection of traditions about Jesus presented in story form, a narrative constituting good news about God and his Kingdom, and a writing that occupies a place of fundamental importance in the Scriptures of the church."[12] As a Gospel writer, Mark's purpose is to

11. Ibid., 487–88.

12. Williamson, *Mark*, 1.

bear witness to Jesus as the Christ, the one who proclaims God's rule and reign and who is the incarnate rule of God. At many points that rule came into conflict with the powers that pretend to rule this world, and at other moments the rule of God personally manifest in Jesus confronted people who were not hostile but pulled toward lesser loves. Thus we have the famous story of a wealthy young man who wanted to follow Jesus but who also loved the things of this earth.

The story of the man traditionally known as the "rich young ruler" is poignant and biting. It is a story about wealth, and there is no escape from this fact for readers in the highly developed Western world. We often measure our own standard of living against others who are wealthier than we, just as frequently neglecting to make the comparison the other way. By any reasonable worldwide standard, middle-class North Americans turn out to be wealthy, and we will simply have to read this story in that awareness.

At the beginning of this narrative, the text tells us that Jesus had "started on his way" (10:17) but does not explicitly state his destination. If we consider the wider context, we might say that Jesus was on his way to the cross. Already, on two different occasions, Jesus had predicted his impending passion. The shadow of the cross fell across Jesus' path, even though he and his disciples were still in Galilee. When the text tells us that Jesus met the rich young ruler on his way, we should consider the cross as part of that way. The cross relativizes this encounter. Given Jesus' destiny in Jerusalem, the young man's wealth cannot but lose some of its importance.

The young man addressed Jesus as "good teacher," a salutation that seems to us respectful. Early Christian commentators on this passage nevertheless roundly condemn the young man. Ephrem the Syrian found in this salutation an arrogance born of the knowledge that the man had kept the law and that he "called Jesus 'good,' as if he were offering him a favor, just as some favor others with honorary titles. [The Lord] fled from that by which people favored him, so that he might show that he had received this goodness from the Father...[and that] the Son is good in just the way that the Father is good."[13]

Perhaps Jesus rebuffed the young man's salutation as a way of testing his sincerity. If so, the young man seems to have passed this initial test, for he answered in a manner that elicited Jesus' loving response. But the next test was more difficult, and this time the young man failed. In response to Jesus' word to sell all his possessions, the young man departed with a heavy heart. "He did not follow. He just wanted a good teacher, but he questioned who the teacher was, and scorned the identity of the One who was teaching. 'He went away sad,' bound up in his desires. 'He went away sad,' carrying a great burden of possessiveness upon his shoulders."[14]

Clearly this story is a hard teaching. Christians have attempted to lessen some of its bite by interpreting Jesus' saying about the camel and the needle's eye with reference to an unusually small gate in the Jerusalem city wall. There is no evidence to indicate that this gate existed before the ninth century—many centuries after Jesus' earthly ministry. Better to take comfort in Jesus' declaration that with God all things are

13. Oden and Hall, *Mark,* 139.

14. Ibid., 143–44.

possible and see the problem of wealth under the canopy of God's grace.

Privileged Positions
Mark 10:32–52

The gospel according to Mark is especially concerned to respond to the shame of the cross and to emphasize the fact that Christians worship a crucified Savior. Of course, Jesus' crucifixion is not the end of the story. In the resurrection of Jesus, God reversed the verdict of the Jewish religious leaders, Pilate, and the crowd that had clamored for his death. The two stories told in Mark 10:32–52 emphasize God's way of reversing conventional expectations.

The first of these stories is the familiar narrative that finds James and John coming to Jesus with a self-serving request. The little band had reached Jerusalem, and they are about to enter the city. Jesus had just spoken of his impending suffering, death, and resurrection. This seems a strange moment to ask, as did these two brothers, for special consideration. Perhaps they thought they might not get another chance. Perhaps they completely misunderstood Jesus and were anticipating the establishment of a worldly kingdom. For whatever reason, James and John seized the moment to ask for high-level cabinet positions.

"You don't know what you are asking." After some words on the suffering they would indeed share with him, Jesus helped James and John to see what they had actually requested. In the process, he also mollified their understandably irritated colleagues. Here we see Jesus once again reversing the assumptions of the dominant culture—"the world." Under the rule and reign of God, greatness is defined by serving. If you want to be great, James and John, you will need to serve others. This is not the way of the Gentiles, which is to say, the way of the world.

A few years ago on a late summer day, a worldwide television audience watched the funerals of two women. In England, Princess Diana was buried amid pomp and circumstance while half a world away the body of Mother Teresa of Calcutta was also laid to rest. Diana was a world-famous celebrity who lived all too much of her adult life in front of cameras and paparazzi. In the world of the rich and famous, she was great. Mother Teresa spent her life among some of the most impoverished people anywhere on the globe. All she did was bring comfort, care, and the love of Jesus to the most desperate of them in their final days. Teresa was so great according to the standards of the Kingdom that she won the world's acclaim but then gave it away. In the Kingdom, greatness is measured by service.

The second story also contains a reversal. At Jericho, only a few miles from Jerusalem and the triumphal entry of Palm Sunday, Jesus and his disciples were walking along the road in the midst of a large crowd. Bartimaeus, a blind beggar, sat unnoticed. He was begging because that was the only option open to a blind man without a family. His was a miserable, impoverished life on the very edge of starvation. Out of this deprivation, he called out to Jesus, using the descriptive name "Son of David." This was a phrase of great distinction and honor. In applying it to Jesus, Bartimaeus was in effect calling him the king of Israel. Above the din, Jesus heard the beggar's voice and asked him to approach. Jesus wrote Bartimaeus a blank check, "What do you want me to do for you?"

The beggar asked for sight, and his request was granted. We usually say that seeing is believing, but in this case believing was seeing. Greatness is service. Believing is seeing. A week after Bartimaeus received his sight, death gave way to life. Of such is the kingdom of God.

Palm Sunday
Mark 11:1–18

The narrative of Palm Sunday begins with Mark's notice that Jesus and his disciples had reached Jerusalem. It was in Jerusalem that Jesus' life and ministry would reach their fulfillment. Approaching the city from the east, the little band would have traveled near or through the small suburban villages of Bethphage and Bethany on the slopes of the Mount of Olives across the Kidron Valley from Jerusalem. Somewhere in the vicinity of one of these villages, Jesus sent ahead of him two of his disciples with instructions to fetch a colt. The colt was an ass foal that had never been yoked or ridden and worth a good deal of money. Even though the disciples were asked what they were doing when they untied the colt, no one offered any objections.

Coming into the city riding a colt would have conveyed an interesting message. Kings and important dignitaries rode into cities. They did not walk. Jesus' entry on the colt was an entry of one with position and authority; however, it was also humble. The fact that Jesus chose a colt and not a chariot communicated an attitude of humility. While valuable, a colt was not a conveyance used by the very wealthy.

It should be noted that while humble, the Jerusalem entry was accompanied by great generosity. The colt's owners generously shared it. The people greeting Jesus were extravagant in their adoration. Many of them were poor but still threw down their only cloaks to honor his passing. They climbed the trees and cut large palm leaves. The huge crowd sang an antiphonal: one chorus shouting "Hosanna," the other answering with "Blessed is he."

All was accomplished just as Jesus had said. This predication and its fulfillment are more than a preamble to the triumphal entry and more than a transition. This brief story depicts Jesus as the master of the situation, even though events were about to unfold that would question that fact. The teacher who was about to be celebrated and cheered would be crucified and dead before the week was out. But Jesus knows this and is the true master of events, illustrated by the accuracy of this prediction as well as the fact that he rode peacefully into Jerusalem on the back of an unbroken colt.

The text tells us indirectly that Jesus and his disciples stayed in Bethany rather than in the city of Jerusalem itself. This was Passover week; the city would have been teeming with religious pilgrims come to participate in this the holiest week of the Jewish calendar. Mary, Martha, and Lazarus lived in Bethany. The text does not specify, but we might conjecture that he stayed with these loyal friends. In any case, early in Passover week Jesus and his disciples walked back into Jerusalem and entered the temple. He had visited that site the day before, after his triumphal entry, and taken in the scene. The text "but it was already late" suggests that

Jesus had formed a plan of action even before his first visit. Just exactly what Jesus had in mind became clear on the following day.

It is here that we find the strange incident of the barren fig tree. On his way into the city, Jesus, hungry, saw a fig tree in full leaf but bearing no fruit. Despite the fact that it was not the season for ripe figs, Jesus cursed the tree and it withered within twenty-four hours. Why would Jesus curse a tree for not bearing fruit out of season? The answer may lie in the possibility that Jesus did not expect to find fruit on the tree but buds, which were edible. The tree should have been in bud at that time of the year, and when none were to be found, Jesus cursed the tree for its barrenness. Even in the best possible light, the curse of the barren fig tree portrays a different side of Jesus. This is not the gentle teacher who taught forgiveness and love. The Jesus who cursed the fig tree is the man about to enter the very citadel of Jewish religion and life and throw it into disarray. Perhaps he had a right to be edgy. An attack on the temple moneychangers and merchants was sure to bring repercussions.

Much has been said to portray the moneychangers and merchants as a group of swindlers bilking innocent religious pilgrims who had traveled to Jerusalem to fulfill their spiritual obligations. This reading draws a distinction between the moneychangers and the temple proper, but we may ask whether such a separation is appropriate. After all, the temple needed the moneychangers and merchants in order to function. The priesthood and religious leaders of Jerusalem had to regard this attack as an attack on the temple itself. From their perspective, anybody who acted as Jesus had was a dangerous enemy of the system and needed to be eliminated.

Empty Chairs at the Table

Mark 14:1–25

In many Christian churches, the service of the Lord's Supper is called "Holy Eucharist," from the Greek *eucharisteo*, "to give thanks." This reading is taken from Mark 14:22 where Jesus is reported to have given thanks for the meal shared in the upper room. Other traditions refer to this service as Holy Communion. Roman Catholics often refer to it as the Mass, a term that derives from the Latin *messe*, "meal." In remembering the Lord's death, we are to unite around this table. How sad and ironic that this service has often divided Christians.

In 1529, four Protestant reformers and their associates gathered at the castle of the landgrave Philip of Hesse. Philip had invited them to a meeting, known as the Marburg Colloquy, for the purpose of achieving some degree of unity among the growing number of European Protestants. Its chief participants, on one side, were Martin Luther and his close friend and fellow professor at the University of Wittenberg, Philip Melanchthon. On the other side were, from Zurich, Huldreich Zwingli and his associate John Oecolampadius. Literally in between them geographically and theologically stood the mediating reformer Martin Bucer of Strasburg. Luther and Zwingli agreed on several major points. The major issue on which they could make no headway was their varying interpretations of Mark 14:22–25.

Although he distinguished his views from the Catholic theology of the

Eucharist, Luther held to the idea that Christ was in some sense actually present, mingled in the elements of Communion. His is but one of several different expressions of the doctrine of the "real presence." For Luther, when Jesus said, "This is my body," he was referring to the bread that he and the disciples were about to eat. Zwingli had been strongly influenced by Erasmus of Rotterdam, the Dutch Christian humanist , who was a man of simple piety and peaceable ethics. Following this lead, Zwingli sought to simplify Christian faith and worship wherever possible. He believed that the service of the Lord's Supper was symbolic, that Christ was not actually present in the elements of the meal. For Zwingli the saying "This is my body" had to be understood as a reference to Jesus' flesh and nothing else.

The Marburg Colloquy broke up without reaching agreement. In fact, their sharp debate drove Luther and Zwingli even further apart. A few years later, Zwingli died in battle, and when Luther heard the news he is reported to have said, "Hell has gained a noble spirit; fare thee well, thou scorpion." Unfortunately, this kind of suspicion and mistrust continued to govern the attitudes of European Christians on the issue of the Lord's Supper. In 1542, little more than a decade after the Marburg Colloquy, Emperor Charles V called all the contending factions together for a meeting at Regensburg (also called Ratisbon) in an attempt to reach consensus on Christian teaching. Representatives from the Lutheran, Reformed, and Catholic traditions attended, as did the ever-present Martin Bucer. The Regensburg Colloquy actually reached agreement on the doctrine of justification, stating that believers are justified by faith and that good works do not earn but declare justification. For a brief moment, all European Christians were united on a major point of Christian doctrine. Then the conferees turned their attention to the next item on the agenda, the Lord's Supper. On this issue the meeting ground to a halt. Nobody present would concede even a minor point, and the Colloquy at Regensburg broke up after the participants repudiated even the matters on which they had previously agreed.

The table of the Lord is no place for division. The Lord's Supper is the meal that should heal and unite. It is the memorial meal of a peaceable community gathered to remember the one whose death makes salvation possible and by which the church itself is constituted. The Lord's Supper is at the heart of a way of being the church that begins in such sacred acts of remembrance.

The Great Reversal

Mark 14:55–64; 15:1–2, 12–15

In Jesus' trial before the Sanhedrin, the three main groups of his accusers joined forces against him. The chief priests, elders, and the teachers of the law assembled to create a Jewish court. The hearing they conducted, however, was little more than a show. Jesus would not be presumed innocent, and the judges and so-called jury were anything but impartial. Jesus' accusers had made up their minds some time earlier, and before the trial began his fate was already sealed. Witnesses would in fact be called to give false testimony. Jesus' enemies had assembled this mockery of justice not to inquire into his teaching but for the purpose of formally rejecting both him and his claims. There was no question of conviction. Jesus' accusers had prepared a scenario that guaranteed he would be found guilty according to the Law of Moses.

Two different but related charges were brought against Jesus. The first was that he was heard to say he would destroy the temple and in three days rebuild it better than it had been. This charge has a basis in Jesus' action in cleansing the temple of the moneychangers earlier in the week. Some might contend that this was no attack on the temple but merely the elimination of corrupt practices that had attached themselves to the temple's periphery. However, to attack the moneychangers and temple merchants was to attack the temple itself because they provided a service that enabled the sacrificial system to work smoothly. In this connection, modern-day Christian readers should try to appreciate the seriousness of this charge against Jesus. A sizeable segment of the Jewish population regarded the temple as the dwelling place of Yahweh. Proper worship and temple piety were, in the view of these people, necessary to the well-being of the people Israel. To speak against the temple threatened that well-being and was a very serious matter. To profane the house of the Lord in this manner could therefore be construed as an act of blasphemy.

The second charge against Jesus was blasphemy, pure and simple. In response to the high priest's question whether he was indeed the Messiah, Jesus answered affirmatively and that "you will see the Son of Man sitting at the right hand of the Mighty One and coming on clouds of heaven." If the Jerusalem religious leadership was looking for an excuse to condemn Jesus, he handed it to them on a silver platter. According to the law, he was guilty indeed—if the charge was true. On the other hand, if Jesus' words and deeds did mean the end of the temple and sacrificial systems, he would indeed have destroyed the temple and the priestly caste, replacing them with himself as the new High Priest. If indeed he was who he claimed to be—the Messiah of God—a charge of blasphemy could not hold water.

The trumped up charges against Jesus turn out to be true not only according to the law but also in fact. But because they are true in fact, he is not liable to judgment under the law. Unwittingly, his enemies used the truth to bring about his unjust death. The law found Jesus guilty. Under its provision, he was indeed guilty of blasphemy. But—and this is the great "however"—God raised Jesus from the dead, which makes this a matter of the truth of Jesus' claims and puts all who believe in him under grace and not the law.

Crucified and Resurrected

Mark 15:33–39; 16:1–8

"Darkness came over the whole land." It is difficult to plunge deeply enough into the meaning of Mark 15:33, so layered is it with thick symbolism. Yet it is a verse with which we spend very little time. In fact, most of us want to spend as little time reflecting on the crucifixion as possible. Good Friday services cannot avoid the temptation to refer more to the resurrection than spend time meditating on the crucifixion. Yet without entering as fully as possible into the crucifixion, our appreciation of the resurrection wanes pale and shallow.

Darkness fell. The climate of the East is hot and dry. The sun shines most of the time, and it is bright. The landscape is of white limestone, and contrasts between light and shadow are sharp. In the middle of the high sun afternoon, darkness fell. It did not come on like the dusk; it came as if with a switch—and it swallowed the whole land. Imagine it.

Jesus cried out "God! Why have you forsaken me?" The triumphant Messiah of Thursday was confessing abandonment on Friday. Followers heard this from his own mouth. Mockers, misunderstanding his words, rallied and looked for the dramatic appearance of Elijah. What prospects for confusion.

Jesus shrieked and died. Imagine the despair of some, the evil exultation of others. Feel the breath go out of your own lungs. It's over. Nothing can be done now. Hope dissolves. You sob. You hear the Roman centurion whisper, "Truly, this man was the Son of God." Was. *Was*. Your face is in the dirt, muddied by your tears. *Was!*

The veil of the Holy of Holies tore clean through from top to bottom. According to the Talmud, the veil was sixty feet long, thirty feet wide, with a depth the width of a hand's palm. It was so heavy, according to the Talmud, that it took three hundred priests to lift it. Imagine your bone-jarring shock as you realize that the holiest place on earth was no longer hidden and restricted from view, no longer inaccessible.

Imagine yourself standing outside the tomb looking at a man in a white robe. You blink your eyes. He is still there. Your mouth is suddenly dry and you start to shiver. He says, "Don't be amazed. Jesus, whom you seek, is risen. He is not here. Go and tell." You run, tripping over weak knees and trembling muscles. Nothing is as it should be. You can't speak. Your tongue won't move because your mind can't think. You know nothing but raw fear—fear birthed by the knowledge that nothing you've known is as it should be, nor will it ever be as it was.

Jesus' resurrection signifies the death of death. So the fifth-century theologian and bishop Augustine wrote, "He died, but he vanquished death; in himself he put an end to what we feared; he took it upon himself and he vanquished it, as a mighty hunter he captured and slew the lion. Where is death? Seek it in Christ, for it exists no longer; but it did exist and now it is dead. O life, O death of death! Be of good heart; it will die in us, also. What has taken place in our head will take place in his members; death will die in us also. But when? At the end of the world, at the resurrection of the dead in which we believe and concerning which we do not doubt."[15]

The fourth century bishop-theologian Gregory Nazianzen marveled at the way a comparatively few drops of blood renew the whole world. "Many indeed are the wondrous happenings of that time: God hanging from a cross, the sun made dark and again flaming out, for it was fitting that creation should mourn with its creator. The temple veil rent, blood and water flowing from his side.... The happenings at the sepulcher and after the sepulcher; who can fittingly recount them? Yet no one of them can be compared to the miracle of my salvation."[16]

Finally, Peter Chrysologus meditated on the stone that sealed Jesus tomb: "Is it from the door of the sepulcher, or of your own hearts? From the tomb, or from your own eyes? You whose heart is shut, whose eyes are closed, are unable to discover the glory of the open grave. Pour then your oil, if you wish to see

15. Ibid, 244–45.
16. Ibid., 235.

that glory, not on the body of the Lord but on the eyes of your own hearts. By the light of faith you will then see that which through the deficiency of faith now lies hidden in darkness."[17]

Luke

Matters of Form and Content

Luke 1:1–4; 1 Corinthians 15:1–4; 1 John 1:1–4

Although we refer to them almost universally as "books," the writings that make up the New Testament actually take a variety of literary forms or genres. Recognizing these different forms is important to biblical interpretation; a particular text can be read more profitably if we understand its form. Luke is one of the three Gospels called the Synoptics because of their common perspective on the life and ministry of Jesus. Corinthians, on the other hand, is one of several letters written by the apostle Paul. The letters of John, along with the gospel according to John, bear such a distinctive quality that scholars refer to them as the Johannine Literature. These texts were written at different moments in the early history of the church; they serve varying purposes but share a common narrative. Paul's Corinthian letters are commonly dated between AD 51 and 54. Many scholars believe Luke was written between AD 65 and 70. The Johannine writings appeared near the very end of the first century. Three different people, writing in different moments, inspired by the same Spirit, testify to a shared gospel tradition.

17. Ibid., 241–42.

Before any of these were written, the early church *spoke* the good news (scholars refer to this as the "oral tradition"). Scholars speculate on the existence of writings, perhaps early collections of the sayings of Jesus, that may have appeared before Mark's gospel but during the era of the oral tradition. The texts from Luke, Corinthians, and 1 John each refer to that first spoken gospel. What were its contents?

In the ancient Greek manuscripts, the sources of the English Bible, Mark's gospel carried no title. It simply said, "The beginning of the gospel about Jesus Christ, the Son of God." This beginning already suggests some of the content of the oral tradition: Jesus Christ, Son of God, Savior. The first letters of each word in this phrase form the famous acrostic *ICHTHUS*, which is also the Greek word for *fish*. Early in the history of the Jesus movement, the sign of the fish symbolized the spoken gospel. Paul's account of the gospel that he received (1 Cor 15:1–5ff) expanded on this message but did not materially alter it. He specified Jesus' crucifixion, death, and resurrection as God's action through which human beings are saved. Jesus the Savior, the "One-Who-Saves," was the indispensable figure in all three writings. This is no new idea tacked on to Paul's message after he left Corinth. We can safely assume that "this gospel [by which] you are saved" (15:2), that is, the oral gospel that Paul preached when he was in Corinth and to which he referred in this letter, included the life and teachings of Jesus, the crucified and risen Savior.

Luke's gospel opens, "Many have undertaken to draw up an account of the things that have been fulfilled among us" (1:1). New Testament scholars devoted decades of study to these ancient documents and their background. From this study, as well as recent archaeological discoveries, we have learned that a great many gospels concerning Jesus began to circulate. These offered highly unusual or novel interpretations of his life and ministry. The book of Luke may have been written, in part, to set the record straight in the face of some of these fanciful accounts. For the sake of the young church, it became increasingly important to write words about the Word. As 1 John testifies, this Word—this *Logos*—was with God from the very beginning and incarnate in Jesus of Nazareth. John had seen and heard this Word and lived in the joy of fellowship with the Word. John wrote that others, including us, might know the joy and life born in fellowship with the Word, the *Logos* of God.

The Forerunner
Luke 1:5–80

As with the Old Testament, we must remember that the primary subject of the narrative of the New Testament always remains God. The Gospels and Acts are not simply biographies; they are narratives concerning the action of God in Christ and the Holy Spirit in the life of the church. The persons who figure in these narratives are not the primary subjects. Their presence helps to round out the story, but they are not the agents who make things happen; God, Christ, and the Holy Spirit—the Trinitarian God—is the who makes things happen.

More explicitly than any of the other Gospels, Luke explains the method by which he composed his gospel. In the opening preamble, Luke explained to a person named Theophilus (meaning "friend of God") that many different accounts of Jesus' life and ministry already had been written. These narratives had been compared—presumably quoted—in the preparation of Luke's gospel. Theophilus also is told one of the purposes of this gospel: "So that you may know the certainty of the things that you have been taught" (1:4). This motive helps us understand that this is a *gospel* and not a biography. A biography attempts to tell the complete story of a person's life. A biography does not, necessarily, ask the reader to come to a set of convictions about that person. Luke's gospel, on the other hand, leaves out many aspects of Jesus' life because they do not contribute to his main purpose: *that those who read this narrative will come to belief in Jesus as the Messiah of God and, believing, have eternal life in his name.*

Along with Mark and Matthew, Luke is one of the Synoptic Gospels, but the gospel of Luke also contains material that is not found in the other gospels. The parables of Luke 15 are unique to this gospel. So also is the nativity section. Special to Luke, then, are some of our most treasured stories about Jesus and some of the most beloved of his parables. Small wonder that this gospel is the favorite of many Christians.

The figures of Zechariah and Elizabeth are focal points of Luke 1:5–80. They are important to the story of Jesus as the parents of John the Baptizer. Moreover, Elizabeth was the first person to speak a word in witness to the extraordinary action of God in the incarnation. When her cousin Mary, pregnant with Jesus, visited Elizabeth, Elizabeth testified to the stature of this child on the basis that "the baby in my womb leaped for joy" (1:44). One of the main features of Elizabeth and Zechariah was their age; they were too old to have a child. Moreover, even when Elizabeth was of an age to bear children, she was barren. Many commentators appropriately focus on the miraculous birth to these aged people, but another important aspect is the fact that as aged people they represent what we might call "the old."

"God is at work from within...the institutions, rituals, and practices of Judaism. The couple is of Aaron's line, Zechariah is a priest, they are blamelessly pious in all of God's commands and ordinances, and the word of God comes in the temple. For Luke, God works in and through the normal avenues of life in the believing community. Luke...lays out a fundamental conviction: continuity with Israel's institutions, rituals, and faith puts one in a position to be used for God's purpose. The old (in this case, an old couple) will usher in the new."[18]

From the time of his encounter with the archangel Gabriel, Zechariah had been speechless. It was a Jewish father's right to name his children, and names were customarily passed down through family generations. Gabriel had instructed Zechariah to disregard custom and name the boy John. In Luke's gospel, John is the forerunner for Jesus in two important senses. First of all, John's birth prepared the way for Jesus' birth. His parents were elderly and childless. The plight of barrenness and the way God answered that plight through the extraordinary births of special children is a long-term theme of the Bible. It reaches all the way back to Abraham and Sarah. Thus, we learn that Elizabeth's child was extraordinary. She was kin to Mary, and her extraordinary child stood in relation to the even more extraordinary child to be born to Mary. Second, of course, John's message of repentance prepared the way for Jesus' gospel of God's forgiveness and acceptance of outcasts and sinners.

As soon as Zechariah had named his son, the aged priest's tongue was loosed, and the first occasion of its use was to praise Yahweh and offer thanksgiving. The elderly couple had walked obediently before God; God had answered their prayers, and now Zechariah would sing the Lord's praises.

The elderly priest's song is called the "Benedictus" from the first word of the text in its Latin translation and can be divided into two sections. Verses 68–75 begin with thanksgiving to God for his mighty act, but Zechariah thanks God not for John's birth but for the impending nativity of Israel's Redeemer. Yahweh had "raised up a horn of salvation." The phrase symbolically refers to God's power, and the language here is reminiscent of several psalms that praise Yahweh for his deliverance of Israel. In this first section, Zechariah thanks and praises God for the promise that the birth of Jesus would keep. Yahweh had remembered his covenant with Abraham and, by virtue of that remembrance and divine mercy, Israel would be redeemed. The people would be freed to serve God without fear in holiness and righteousness all of their days.

The second section of the "Benedictus" turns our attention to the newborn John. Since John is the forerunner of Jesus, Zechariah's description of his son's work cannot be divorced from Jesus and his mission. John's conception and birth were miraculous, but that did not make him the Messiah. John was the prophet of the Most High God

18. Craddock, *Luke*; 26.

and his role was to prepare the way for Israel's Redeemer. Without Jesus, John's existence had little purpose. As with Hannah and Samuel of old so also through Elizabeth and John, the Lord was at work in Israel, and the result of this work would be salvation and blessing for people who lived in the shadow of sin and death.

Mary
Luke 1:26–56

Many Protestants are uncertain about Mary, the mother of our Lord. They are quite certain that the Catholic veneration of Mary accords her a status too high for any mortal. Generally speaking, Protestants respect—even honor—Mary and see in her a model of Christian humility and obedience, but they refuse to venerate her, a refusal that fundamentally separates them from Catholics.

In the earliest centuries of the church, Mary's place in the Christian tradition took a considerable step forward. In the city of Alexandria, Egypt, Christians began referring to her by the use of the word *theotokos*, in Greek "the God-bearer," using this word partly to make a claim about the divine nature of Jesus. To name Mary the *theotokos* was a way of saying that her son was but God himself. The use of the term makes a certain kind of Christian sense. If Jesus is God, then the woman who gave birth to him is the God-bearer or, as the phrase came to employed, the mother of God.

During the third and fourth centuries, as the church worked out the doctrines of the Trinity and incarnation, church worship played an important role in resolving those debates. Alexandrian Christians refused to give up the use of *theotokos* in worship, and it remained in the church's vocabulary of worship. It was almost inevitable that Mary's stature in the eyes of ancient and medieval Christians would grow.

Most Protestants, however, interpret this text as the narrative of a young woman extraordinarily open to God's action in her life. Occasionally, we make too much of Mary's age and make her a model of precocious spirituality. She was no doubt in her mid-teens when she became pregnant, but we must remember that people grew up more quickly in that time and place. The idea of a lengthy adolescence between childhood and adult life is a fairly recent and largely Western development. Mary became pregnant at an age when most women in her society married and began having babies. It is not her age that distinguishes Mary; it is her obedience, courage, and faith.

A word concerning the social world of this narrative is also in order. Luke 1:27 refers to the formal relationship between Mary and Joseph. The New International Version reads that they were "pledged to be married." Other translations read "betrothed." In either case, something more than a modern-day engagement is occurring. Galilean marriage custom included two "weddings." The first was a kind of public declaration of marriage—a betrothal ceremony. After this ceremony, the couple was considered to be married except that they did not yet live together and therefore did not engage in sexual intercourse. Cohabitation came only after the second ceremony, a wedding nearer to our understanding of the term. It seems likely that Mary and Joseph were in the period between the betrothal ceremony and their actual wedding at the time of Gabriel's visit.

Protestants take Mary as one of the first and most important New Testament examples of trusting submission to the will and purposes of God. If we look carefully at the text, however, we find that her first reaction to Gabriel's salutation is not trust. It is not too much to say that Mary's role as the mother of the Lord begins in astonishment. We should not find this terribly surprising if we start with the fact that it was an angel who brought word to Mary of her favor with God.

More often than not, in the world of first-century Judaism the appearance of angels was startling, for they were somewhat fearsome creatures. In the cases of both Zechariah and the shepherds of Bethlehem, before anything else, the angels assured them that they need not be afraid. Gabriel, one of the seven archangels of later Judaism, delivered a salutation to Mary that troubled her—and this before he got to the heart of his announcement. Only in the angelology of the popular North American Christianity in the late twentieth and early twenty-first centuries have angels become kindly guardians who are instantly received as spiritual friends. We should take care not to project back onto the text modern-day notions about angels but allow the text to speak for itself.

Throughout Luke 1 and 2, "Mary is portrayed as favored of God (v. 30), thoughtful (v. 19; 2:51), obedient (v. 38), believing (v. 45), worshipful (v. 46), and devoted to Jewish law and piety (2:22–51). Luke names her in the company of believers when the church began (Acts 1:14)...However, we must be careful to notice that none of her qualities is offered as the reason God chose her; that reason lies tucked away in the purposes of God."[19]

The main element of the text here is the song that Mary sang in response to Elizabeth's salutation. This song is called the "Magnificat" from its title in the Latin Vulgate edition of the Bible. The Vulgate translation was virtually the only version of the Bible read by Western Christians for approximately eight hundred years. Throughout that period, only a very small percentage of medieval Europeans were literate. Nearly all of their knowledge of Christian life and doctrine came to them through visual presentations of the gospel and elements of the Christian tradition and the Scriptures they had been taught to memorize. One such piece was the Magnificat, which has been sung during the evening hour of prayer called vespers ever since the sixth century. Today's Anglican service called Evensong also includes Mary's poem.

The poem is noteworthy for its disclosure of Mary's character. First, her praise to God had little to do with God's choice of her; she did not sing about herself but about what God had done. This is a mark of humility. Second, as commentator Fred Craddock notes, Mary was so certain that God would do what had been promised that she sang of this as if it was already an accomplished fact. This observation depends on a reading of the Greek verb forms. Fred Craddock notes that we "should also consider the [use of the past tense to express future action] as a way of expressing the confidence and the certainty as though they already were."[20] Mary was not afraid to place the events

19. Ibid., 27–28.

20. Ibid., 30.

of her life within the larger purposes of God. What God would do through her, Mary found to be consistent with what God had done in the past.

Last, Mary put into sharp relief the character of God's past action: the lowly are raised and the exalted are brought low. The gospel according to Luke champions the cause of the lowly and the oppressed. Where Matthew's gospel often applies a spiritual interpretation to Jesus' teachings, Luke sees their earthly significance and application. Luke records Jesus' statement in Nazareth inaugurating his ministry. According to that statement Jesus took his mission to be to "preach good news to the poor...to proclaim freedom for the prisoners, and recovery of sight for the blind, [and] to release the oppressed" (4:18). Luke's version of the Beatitudes also carries a list of corresponding "woes" that specifically targets the rich (6:20–26). While Jesus was not concerned with only the earthly aspects of life, faithfulness to the biblical text leads to the conclusion that Jesus' preaching of the nearness of God's rule and reign included both spiritual and physical aspects of human life. Luke's gospel makes this dual aspect of Jesus' message very plain.

Nowhere is Luke's concern for the oppressed and downtrodden more evident than in the prominence of women in his gospel. Women were scarcely more than property in the social world of the Bible. They had few rights, and the right to speak in public was not one of them. In Luke, however, women possess a voice that expresses their dignity as children of God. Elizabeth and Mary were but the first of many women who speak and act meaningfully in Luke's gospel. Neither of these women was a passive receiver. Both spoke and acted as moral agents who understood and obediently agreed to God's action concerning them and Israel. Each in her own way publicly articulated the significance for Israel and the world of the divine action upon their lives.

The Nativity
Luke 2:1–20

From our vantage point after nearly two thousand years of Christian history, it is hard to believe that early witnesses to Jesus' life could have been mistaken about any element relating to it. However, that is precisely the case with Luke's dating of the birth of Jesus. On such matters, we will do well to remember a few important points. First of all, the ancient world possessed no accurate timepieces or calendars. The best that anyone could do was a sundial. That the solar year lasts for an extra fourth of a day means that over a span of centuries calendars grow massively inaccurate without some form of correction, such as the insertion of a leap day every four years. Ancient calendars possessed no such device. Second, no CNN stood by to record and report news events. Such writers as Luke worked from very fragmentary sources; some inaccuracy would be only natural. Third, the purpose of Luke's gospel is that people will come to faith in Jesus as the Savior, the Christ of God. In light of that evangelical purpose, it is not so important that we cannot reconcile the reign of Herod the Great with the date of a census when Quirinius was governor in Syria.

The *names* of Luke 2 carry far more significance than the *dates*. In the space of four verses, Luke referred to Augustus, Quirinius, and David. Luke's first-century Gentile readers would recognize the first name immediately, the second probably, and perhaps the third. All three people had name recognition among Luke's Jewish readers. Such names convey a sense of worldwide scope. The Emperor Augustus constructed the famed Pax Romana, the Roman peace that spread stability and security over a vast region from England to Arabia. Quirinius was the regional representative of that imperial power. The name of David hearkened back to the days of Israel's glory. Through the mention of such names, Luke set the infancy narrative on a world stage. "Luke and his audience know that the ripples sent forth by the immersion of Jesus in the Jordan will eventually begin to change the course of the Tiber."[21] The birth of Jesus was an event of cosmic significance.

Ancient historians customarily dated events according to the reigns of rulers. Thus, we find Luke dating events in the lives of John and Elizabeth, and Joseph and Mary by reference to the great and mighty of their world: Julius Caesar's nephew and successor, Augustus; and Quirinius, governor of Syria. Luke did more than refer to the great and near great for chronological reference points. Commentator Fred Craddock thinks that Luke wrote with a "basic conviction that emperors, governments, and laws serve the purpose of God, often without knowing it. In this, Luke agrees with Isaiah 45:1. Caesar Augustus is more than a date for the story; he is the instrument of God's will. There does not have to be a miracle or an unusual event for God to be at work. God works miracles in Luke, to be sure, but God works without them, too."[22] It is worth remembering that Luke wrote as a historian *and* a theologian. Today's scholars typically find that an odd combination. The working assumptions and axioms of modern scholarship separate the two fields of inquiry. Thus, most scholars hold to the view that historians write on the basis of objective or at least verifiable evidence and analogy while theologians have no such reliable bases for their conclusions. Such assumptions did not intrude on Luke's work as a writer. Instead, he saw history as the unfolding of God's will. Luke wrote as a careful historian but also in the full conviction that God's wider purpose lay behind specific historical events.

Already the great reversal of which Mary sang in the Magnificat was slowly but surely underway. The great and the mighty, the movers and shakers of the ancient world, were not the powers that they imagined themselves to be. Caesar Augustus may have decided that it would be a good thing to take a census of his empire's population, but his decision served the will and purpose of God. In a sense, Caesar was taken down a notch, from the primary cause of everything to a secondary cause whose actions ultimately brought about what God purposed. In the story of Jesus' birth, Caesar and his governor were not the central actors. Humble Galilean peasants assumed the role of main character. Caesar was no longer a cause, but merely an explanation.

By way of contrast to Caesar Augustus, Mary was a simple village girl, a young woman whose only birthright was to hard work and watch other more privileged people go to the front of the

21. Raymond E. Brown, *Birth of the Messiah,* 414.

22. Craddock, *Luke,* 34.

line. Like her son, she had been born into a society stratified by social classes. The barriers between these classes prevented social mobility. By far, poor people made up the largest class, a class much larger than the others. Enormous social distance and differences in wealth insulated the wealthiest from the poorest classes of the Roman Empire. The nativity story in Luke forestalls and eliminates any potential barriers that would deny poor and powerless people access to the Savior. Jesus could not have been born in circumstances any more rude or bare of decoration, conditions not far removed from those with which poor people were quite familiar.

Part of Luke's theological conviction is that God's action can be and is accomplished everywhere, among the meek and lowly as well as the great and powerful. Luke shares this conviction with the Old Testament, which also teaches that the great and powerful of the earth can be unwitting instruments of God's will. On occasion, God breaks into history in miraculous ways, but God also works in the everyday decisions of men and women. To do so may not be exciting or entertaining, but God is not interested in putting on a show.

Luke 2:1–20 includes the observation that Mary "pondered" all of these things. What things? There is the testimony of the shepherds. There is also the name that she and Joseph had given the child at the instruction of Gabriel. *Jesus* is a Greek transliteration of the Hebrew *Yeshuach*, which can also be rendered as *Joshua*. The name means "Yahweh is salvation." Joshua of old had been mightily used of God. Would her son also be such a man? To what kind of deliverance or salvation would her son lead Israel? Mary could not have known the answers to such questions and others that must have filled her mind. In the face of so many unknowns, her immediate steps were to follow the way of obedience.

That Jesus' birth was announced first of all to shepherds continues the great reversal. This birth was not a media event. The angels made no announcements in the palaces and great cities of the Roman Empire. Instead shepherds were the first to hear the news. In Jesus' day, shepherds were anything but gentle, noble, or kind; they were often considered dishonest and beyond the law. It is also the case, however, that these shepherds watched flocks outside Bethlehem, the home of Israel's great shepherd king. There is some possibility that they may have been special shepherds who watched flocks of sheep destined for temple sacrifice in Jerusalem. Whether or not this was the case, shepherds were the ones who heard the news of the Savior's birth before any other. Those accustomed to being considered as the last and the least of society were suddenly early participants in the great reversal worked in the reign of God that broke into history in a stable not far from where they watched their flocks.

To be sure, as verses 1–4 tell us, Jesus' birth would have an effect on the political empires of the world, but the day also would come when heaven itself will be shaken by his death on the cross. Therefore, at the time of the Savior's birth, "the heavens declare the glory of God" (Ps 19:1). The implications of this angelic singing meant that the shepherds need not fear and that there would be peace. The masses that lived under Roman rule knew about peace, but the Pax Romana exacted a terribly high price in terms of bloodshed and outright fear. The Romans enforced their peace at sword point. In the Roman world, fear made peace possible. In the Savior's reign, there also would be peace, but of a completely different character. The Savior's peace came because angels sang to all of humanity, "Fear not!"

Epiphany
Luke 2:21–40

Luke's infancy narrative closes with a scene at the temple in Jerusalem. No mention is made of the visit of the magi, nor of Herod's order to kill all male children under the age of two. Luke gives us a picture of a peaceful return to Nazareth with a brief pause in Jerusalem in order to fulfill the legal requirements concerning ritual purification after childbirth.

The idea of ritual uncleanness strikes many modern people as odd and the taboos and regulations associated with it as complex and inconvenient. In many ancient cultures, however, and today's traditional cultures, the idea of clean/unclean was and remains widely accepted. Ancient Israel took very seriously God's statement, "You shall be holy; for I the LORD your God am holy" (Lev 19:2 RSV). To be holy meant to be separate unto God. Ritual cleanness was one way of indicating that separation. The people who lived within this system of ceremonial cleanness and uncleanness did not view it as intrusive or burdensome. It was one of many elements that constituted the way things were.

Leviticus 12 governs the condition of uncleanness associated with childbirth. For males and females alike, an emission of blood or other body fluids created a state of ritual uncleanness. Completing the prescribed ritual cleansed and restored the person to full participation in the community of Israel. Joseph and Mary followed these Levitical regulations, bringing Jesus to the temple "on the eighth day" to be circumcised and to offer a sacrifice of two doves in keeping with the prescribed rules. In this, they were obedient and observant Jews.

Mary and Joseph's Torah obedience is joined to the faithfulness of Simeon and Anna. These two aged, faithful servants of God watched as the couple and the infant Jesus fulfilled the law's requirements. The text honors the old man and woman for their faithful hope in the coming Messiah. Simeon offered a moving prayer of thanks to God for allowing his servant to see the day of Israel's glory and the Gentiles' revelation. Anna further testified to the role the child Jesus would play in God's plan of redemption. At only eight days, Jesus was already being revealed to the world.

The liturgical churches celebrate a religious feast day called Epiphany. This celebration occurs on January 6 or on the Sunday between January 2 and 8. At this celebration, the Orthodox churches commemorate the baptism of Jesus, while the Western churches commemorate the visit of the magi. Prior to both were the events involving Anna and Simeon at the temple in Jerusalem. These two testimonies manifested the identity of Jesus to those who were standing nearby. In the newborn infant, hope and faith found completion. Here too Jesus was disclosed or manifested. He was no common child; his life would change Israel and the entire world.

The Boyhood Incident in the Temple
Luke 2:40–52

As previously noted, the term *biography* is somewhat misapplied to the canonical Gospels. None of them tells Jesus' complete life story; two do not mention either his birth or childhood. In none of the four do we read anything like a modern biography that tries to explain in some detail the formative influences that shape a person's development. While some nineteenth-century Protestant theologians in Germany attempted to reconstruct the details of Jesus' life, their efforts miss the point: the Gospels are *gospels*. They were written so people would have sufficient information about Jesus to come to saving faith in him and to grow as his disciples. The Gospels were written so we might believe in Jesus and have eternal life through his name. There were ancient accounts of Jesus' life that more closely resemble biography. None of these was admitted to the New Testament canon. Of the canonical Gospels, only Luke tells us anything about Jesus' boyhood, and that is the story of the incident in the temple. This one episode is all we are told of the years between Jesus' infancy and the beginning of his public ministry.

Why would Luke tease us with one charming narrative when there is so much more we want to know? Perhaps this one story is sufficient to the purpose of Luke's gospel. If we think in such terms, we should not read this passage as insight into the dynamics of Jesus' family or his relationships with Mary and Joseph. This story is much more than an almost forgotten detail of Jesus' boyhood. Instead, we might read it as a bridge between the infancy narratives and the opening of Jesus' ministry.

The narrative describes Jesus as a boy whose parents raised him faithfully in the traditions of Israel. Faithful and observant Jews, Joseph and Mary made the trek to Jerusalem annually for the great religious festival of Passover. Not all Jews did so, and this text along with others helps us to see that Jesus was reared as a true son of Israel. At every milestone of their son's life, Mary and Joseph faithfully discharged their responsibilities as Jewish parents. He had been circumcised on the eighth day according to Torah. Also according to Torah his parents had presented Jesus in the temple and made the requisite sacrifice of two doves as prescribed for a firstborn son.

Age twelve was a significant moment for Jesus to be back in the temple, for it is the age of *bar mitzvah*, the time when a Jewish child becomes a son or daughter of the covenant (for girls the term is *bat mitzvah*). In the Judaism of Jesus' day, when a boy reached the age of twelve, he became a son of the covenant and thus a man. It is no accident that the one story from Jesus' boyhood included in Luke's account concerns this highly significant age. In Jewish eyes, Jesus had become a man, and as a man he owned each of the prior events and actions made in his behalf. Even before his birth, signs and miracles attended his life. At the proper moment, his parents had presented him in the temple. It was time for Jesus to honor—by his own decision—all the indicators and expressions of faith that had been made for him. As a man he would have to own for himself his divinely appointed destiny, and so he did. When his distraught parents found him talking theology with the rabbis and learned sages of Israel, he asked them if they realized that he needed to be about his father's work. Although Mary and Joseph had raised Jesus in the faith of Israel, they were still mystified by this question. It would not be the last time a saying of Jesus left his hearers puzzled. Now that he had owned the mission appointed him by God, tension would rise between Jesus and those who heard, but did not quite understand, his words.

Going Public
Luke 4:14–30

Luke's gospel includes a narrative that emphasizes the issue between the followers of Jesus and those who denied his lordship. This narrative also strengthens and gives certainty to the Christian teaching about Messiah Jesus. Luke 4:14–30 opens just as Jesus enters Nazareth, the village that was his home, in the northern district of Palestine called Galilee. He had just returned from the southern district of Judea where he was baptized by his cousin John. Afterward, Jesus spent forty days alone in the desert, where he was tempted by Satan. Overcoming the three separate temptations, Jesus returned to Nazareth, "in the power of the Spirit," as Luke 4:14 says. The fresh manifestation of the Spirit's power not only signifies Jesus' victory over temptation but also his faithfulness to God, on whom it depended. On the homeward journey through Galilee, Jesus stopped to teach and heal, but his real destination was his hometown. Jesus had experienced victory twice, at his baptism and again in the desert. In the full joy of this double victory, he now inaugurates his ministry.

On the Sabbath, in Nazareth, Jesus attended the town's synagogue. The synagogue was still a fairly recent development in Jewish religion and life. Many New Testament scholars think that the synagogue developed among the Babylonian exiles. Their connection with Jerusalem and the temple severed by miles and miles of searing desert, the exiles quite naturally formed the synagogue as a divinely approved alternative. By the first century AD, the synagogue had developed fully as a religious institution and served three important functions. It was a (1) house of prayer, (2) place for study, and (3) place of assembly. The synagogue did not replace the temple; it was not simply a smaller, local temple. No sacrifices were performed in or near synagogues; that remained restricted to the Jerusalem temple. But synagogues played a very important role as places where the traditions of Judaism were taught and any male member of the synagogue had the right of speech in its assembly. On the occasion described in Luke 4, Jesus exercised that right.

When he entered the synagogue at Nazareth, Jesus already was becoming famous as a teacher. Exercising his privilege as a male of the village, he stood to read. The text does not say whether he requested the Isaiah scroll or that it was simply handed to him unbidden. Nevertheless, he finds Isaiah 61:1–2 and reads it. This passage would have had an unmistakable meaning in the ears of the men sitting in the synagogue. The Isaiah passage looked forward to the coming of the Messiah, the one who would bring with him the acceptable year of the Lord. Jesus handed the scroll back to the attendant, and now all eyes were fixed on Jesus. The silence was deafening. What will he say? Without fanfare Jesus simply said, "Today this scripture is fulfilled in your hearing."

The late John Howard Yoder, Mennonite theologian, offers an interesting and instructive reading of Jesus' speech in Luke 4:18ff. Yoder links Jesus' reading of Isaiah 61 to the idea of the year of jubilee.[23] The phrase "year of the Lord's favor" (NIV) provides the connection between the jubilee as prescribed in the book of Leviticus, the description of God's action in Isaiah, and also in Jesus' use of that text in Nazareth. The jubilee year occurred ever fiftieth year and was a year during which sweeping social and economic changes were to occur in order to restore Israelite society to the balance and equality of the days of Joshua. Yoder contends that Isaiah 61 promises a social and economic renewal in terms of the jubilee legislation and that it would be a mistake to ignore this dimension either in Isaiah or in Jesus' reading of Isaiah 61 at Nazareth.

That Jesus read the Isaiah passage does not in itself account for the hostility directed toward him. The synagogue members may well have anticipated the coming of the "year of the Lord's favor." Only after Jesus took the further step of claiming that the scripture had been fulfilled that very day were the hearts of his fellow townspeople stirred against him. To make such a claim was tantamount to a claim to be the "Servant of the Lord" predicted by Isaiah—indeed the Messiah, the agent through which the Lord God of Israel would bring about this dramatic transformation. The people of Nazareth thought they knew Jesus well enough to make a judgment about his claim. Perhaps their familiarity with him and his family bred a little contempt. Jesus recognized this attitude in them when he commented on the honor that prophets often receive everywhere but in their own hometown. Not willing to compel their belief, Jesus let people think of him what they would in a familiar but haunting phrase, "Those who have ears to hear...."

Jesus' claim challenged the villagers' conventional theological wisdom. He is aware of this and quotes to them a proverb that places him alongside Elijah and Elisha, two prophets who rarely got a fair hearing from Israelites earlier in Israel's history. Jesus' claim is disturbing for another reason. He referred to episodes from the two prophets lives when they ministered to the widow of Zarephath and Naaman the Syrian—Gentiles. This was to declare that these prophets received a more favorable hearing from non-Israelites, even though it was to Israel that Yahweh had sent them. In making this comparison with past treatment of the prophets, Jesus is telling his fellow villagers that things are always the same in Israel. Yahweh's people reject Yahweh's prophets. That explains why the people of his own home town refuse to accept his reading of Isaiah—and their fury with him and his words.

Taking Up One's Cross
Luke 9:57–62; 14:25–33

In his famous little book *The Cost of Discipleship*, Dietrich Bonhoeffer, the pastor-theologian martyred by the Nazis in 1945, wrote these words: "When Christ calls a man, he bids him

23. Yoder, *Politics of Jesus*, 28–33.

come and die."[24] Bonhoeffer described a popular conception of God's grace that asked little or no human response in return as "cheap grace." He wanted his readers to understand and appreciate the high cost of God's grace—not only in terms of the divine sacrifice of God's Son, but also in the radical obedience that Bonhoeffer understood to be the proper human response to that costly grace.

The shadow of a cross falls across Luke 9:57–62 and 14:25–33. This cross was the one that Jesus carried to Golgotha. It is also the cross that Jesus asks each of his disciples to carry—from that day to this. The church that read these words shortly after Luke wrote them saw the cross's shadow with a clarity that those closest to the event, that is, Jesus' disciples, could not yet fully understand.

Jesus' call to take up the cross is situated in the narrative between Peter's confession of faith and the transfiguration. Both were high moments in the disciples' faith pilgrimage. In fact, Peter, James, and John were so caught up in the experience on the Mount of Transfiguration that they wished to remain there. As glorious as these moments were, Jesus needed to tell his followers the whole story. The life of discipleship was and is more than simply a matter of belief—having one's doctrinal ducks in a row—and moments of high worship. The life of discipleship also extended beyond trusting Jesus—important and necessary though that was. The principles of action and commitment must be added.

Scholars have dubbed this large section of Luke as the Travel Narrative. It begins with 9:51: "As the time approached for him to be taken up into heaven, Jesus resolutely set out for Jerusalem." Until this moment, life with Jesus may have been physically taxing but not dangerous. In Galilee, Jesus and his followers enjoyed a broad freedom made possible by the distance between them and the authorities in Jerusalem. Danger increased, however, as the distance between Jesus and Jerusalem closed. Jesus would soon make the ultimate sacrifice, and he asked his followers for a matching commitment.

Jesus' response to the man who requested a little extra time to care for his aged father jangles our ears. Can the Jesus who was so concerned for children be so callous toward the elderly? The tension of this saying was increased in the context of a common interpretation of that day that said that caring for one's aged parents was part of the commandment to honor parents. To say "Let the dead bury their own dead" (9:60) appeared to be counsel against obedience to one of the commandments. The harshness of Jesus' words might be softened slightly by applying the passage from Luke 14; perhaps this is only another way—pointed to be sure!—of telling his would-be followers that they should count the cost. Following Jesus would not be easy; it could end up costing people their lives and the lives of their loved ones.

These hard sayings of Jesus so impressed some of the radical reformers who were among the forerunners of the Mennonites and Hutterites that they spoke of a "bitter Christ" to balance what they saw as Martin Luther's excessive emphasis on the "sweet Christ." Those radical reformers saw very clearly

24. Bonhoeffer, *Cost of Discipleship*, 99.

the shadow of the cross falling across their path of discipleship. They concluded, therefore, that the church is a community that lives under the cross. "When Christ calls a man, he bids him come and die."

Sending the Seventy-Two

Luke 10:1–9

Typically, when we think of Jesus, we think also of the Twelve. This group picture dominates our imaginations so that we sometimes are a bit confused by such texts as Luke 10. Here Jesus commissions *seventy-two* of his followers for the work of spreading the news of the kingdom of God. Sending out so many followers suggests a description of the Jesus movement that might look something like the following. Surrounding Jesus are the twelve disciples; among them there appears to be an inner circle—Peter, James, and John. Surrounding the Twelve is a larger group of followers, some of whom are merely curious, others who tag along for a while, and still others who seriously follow Jesus but not as part of the Twelve. Thus, we have the comparatively large group that Jesus sent out into the Palestinian countryside ahead of him.

The sending of the seventy-two occurred as Jesus made his way from Galilee to Judea and eventually Jerusalem. This journey, taking in a large section of the gospel according to Luke (9:51–19:44), continues the Travel Narrative, that unfolds after Jesus "resolutely set out for Jerusalem" (9:51). It is not difficult to envision a shadow hanging over this journey. Jesus was on his way to Jerusalem, the city with a reputation for killing God's messengers. Some of the parables he told along the way emphasized the point that time was short, others hinted darkly of the future, and some spoke specifically of death. The situation called for rapid and widespread evangelistic activity. Every town along the route to Jerusalem had to be alerted to Jesus' imminent arrival. Soon the Master would arrive.

What advice did Jesus give these who announced his presence? In essence, travel light and be wary. Announce that God's shalom rests on households as you visit them. Remain as long as the welcome mat is out, but do not make yourself a burden. A first-century manual of church life, *The Teaching of the Twelve Apostles*, gave nearly the same advice to missionaries spreading out across the Roman Empire.

The seventy-two were to announce, "The kingdom of God is near." Upon their return, they joyfully reported that even the devils had submitted to the power of God manifested in word and deed. The seventy-two announced Jesus' presence—the rule and reign of God incarnate—and they exorcised demons, a ray of the spiritual dawn that announced the near presence and soon arrival of the Lord.

The seventy-two sent out by Jesus could be called missionaries. They were commissioned to announce the arrival of God's ruling activity in Jesus. This witness is the fundamental nature of missionary work. The church also witnesses to the arrival of God's rule. The church is not the Kingdom but the witness to God's presence and ruling activity in the world. If the church is such a witness, then all who are members of Christ's body are called to be missionaries.

Who Is My Neighbor?
Luke 10:25–37

We begin with a question. Some rabbis—Jesus included—were engaged in a favorite pastime. They were discussing Torah, instruction in walking in the way of the Lord. One member of the group asked Jesus about the requirements for eternal life. The question was intended to examine Jesus and, perhaps, draw him out into the open. To the question, the expert rabbi replied with another question of his own. It is unnecessary to attribute this question to hostility because Jesus was following standard rabbinic teaching and discussion methods as was the expert in Torah. We should expect any serious member of this discussion to ask, Who is my neighbor?

So begins one of Jesus' most famous parables. Americans who cannot name half the Ten Commandments know the phrase *Good Samaritan* and can use it in a manner consistent with the parable that bears its name. This parable also gives its name to a recreational vehicle owners' club. We seem to know a Good Samaritan when we see one, but the parable does not mean to describe Samaritans. By means of this story, Jesus answered a question that asked for the identity of the neighbor so that the Torah could be followed faithfully.

The hero of this story was a Samaritan, a member of a despised race. Galilean Jews traveling to Jerusalem often took a longer journey around Samaria rather than the much shorter route through it. They did not want to get Samaritan dust on their sandals. It is commonplace to note the proud religious pedigrees of the priest and Levite who passed by the victim on the far side of the road. Occasionally, one hears reports of experiments that use a staged scene to determine whether people today will stop to assist a stranger who needs help. You can be sure that when a minister or a seminary student does not stop to render assistance, that failure is broadcast with relish. We seem to find it humorous or ironic when clergy behave more like Jesus' opponents than their Master. There is nothing in this parable, however, to suggest that clergy are to be held to a standard of compassion higher than anyone else. No double standard divides Jesus' followers.

The nineteenth-century Danish thinker Søren Kierkegaard offered an insight about the identity of the neighbor. He also distinguished between neighbor love and friendship. Kierkegaard noted that romantic love and friendship are preferential; that is, we choose our friends or we fall in love with those people we desire as friends or loved ones. Friendship and romantic love are based in preference for the company of one person over another. On the other hand, neighbor love—the kind that Jesus taught—said Kierkegaard, is not at all about preference. In Kierkegaard's view, anyone we might chance to meet is our neighbor. The love Jesus spoke of does not concern itself with preference. This love (*agape* in Greek) is concerned with the well-being of the other— whoever that other might be. So, says Kierkegaard, if you want to know who your neighbor is, you need look no farther than the face of the first person you encounter. This is your neighbor and, therefore, a potential recipient of your care and concern. This radical openness to the other seems neither practical nor always safe in the world we occupy. But that does not excuse us from reflecting on Kierkegaard's observation that *agape* is not about preference. The parable of the good Samaritan seems to support him on that point. After all, the Samaritan does not appear to have determined the identity or ethnic heritage of the victim. All he did was go out of his way to help somebody in immediate need. It seems then that Jesus' answer to the question opened the definition of neighbor to include just about anybody.

Active and Contemplative

Luke 10:38–42; John 11:20–32

Narratives that tell of encounters between Jesus and the two sisters, Mary and Martha, appear in Luke and John; neither Matthew nor Mark mentions Jesus' friendship with these women. Jesus was a friend to the entire family, the two sisters, and their brother Lazarus, but Lazarus figures only in one story and that after he had died. It is Jesus' friendship with Mary and Martha that takes center stage. The fact that he enjoyed such a relationship with two women raises an important point about him.

Jesus kept an extraordinarily open and engaging attitude toward women. In the Semitic world in which he resided, women were considered property. Men educated boys and young men, preparing them for active, public lives. Girls were prepared for marriage and a life of domesticity. Until their wedding, they were the property of their father; once married they were the property of their husbands. Women's lives revolved around family and hearth, and men expected them to stay there. This social arrangement effectively limited a woman's social contact to one man—her husband or her father. Contact with other men in public earned a woman a dangerous reputation. Against this prevailing social attitude, Jesus kept company with women and enjoyed friendships with some. Mary and Martha are among the best known.

We should not allow modernity's more relaxed relations between the sexes to obscure the scandal that Jesus' enemies would have been quick to point out when he entered the house of these two women. Lazarus is not part of Luke's narrative and presumably was not home. What reason could a Jewish man have for entering the home of two women? Jewish culture possessed few, if any, wholesome answers to that question. Even worse, the text tells us that one of them, Mary, "sat at the Lord's feet." This phrase indicates that Mary took the role of a disciple in flat contradiction of the policy of more conventional rabbis who refused to permit women disciples.

John's portrayal of Mary and Martha is quite consistent with Luke's. Both evangelists show Martha to be the bustling, active personality and Mary the more subdued and reflective. Martha is always busy doing; Mary prefers thought and reflection. The two, along with Lazarus, had some connections with the Pharisees. When Jesus arrived at their home after Lazarus's death, he asked Martha whether she believed that her brother would rise from the grave. Her answer strongly suggests that Martha believed in the general resurrection at the end of the age. This belief was standard Pharisaic teaching in Jesus' day. We should not allow the hostility that characterized Jesus' relationship with most Pharisees to blot out the very friendly relations he enjoyed with others. Nothing in the Gospels suggests any hostility between Jesus and Nicodemus, for example. Further, it must be remembered that it was the Pharisee Joseph of Arimathea who arranged for the burial of Jesus' body at a moment when nearly all of Jesus' friends and disciples had deserted him.

In Luke, the story of Mary and Martha appears immediately following Jesus' teaching about neighborliness through the parable of the good Samaritan. If we were to engage in a bit of canonical criticism, we might compare these two stories and find that they both concern "being" and "doing." The Torah scholar had all of his theological ducks in a row but appears to have had difficulty when it came to action. Martha, on the other hand, was all action with little or no reflection. The implication of Jesus' teaching for the scholar is that constant analysis must give way to helpful action and that any needy person will qualify as the recipient of that action. For the bustling doer, on the other hand, the one needful thing is to take time for reflection. Jesus aimed at something higher than a commitment to one or the other. Perhaps what we need is the wisdom to know when it is time for each.

Kingdom Priorities
Luke 12:13–21

A multimillionaire once was asked how much money is enough. He answered, "One dollar more." The theme of the first half of Luke 12 deals with wealth and the all too human tendency to measure worth in terms of material possessions. Jesus raised this issue with uncomfortable frequency. He probed the human heart's attitude toward wealth more often than he dealt with issues concerning sexual ethics. It is both interesting and a bit ironic that contemporary evangelical Christians who pride themselves on faithful reading of the Bible reverse that emphasis.

The ominous knowledge that Jesus and his disciples are journeying toward Jerusalem helps us interpret Jesus' parables in this section of Luke's gospel. The threat of arrest, trial, and death lends particular significance to Jesus' sayings. Having set his face toward Jerusalem, he travels in the direction of that threat, so we should expect him to teach with a new air of gravity about matters of ultimate concern. His teachings along the way help us to critique our own values and commitments in the light of eternity.

The heart of Jesus' parable about building bigger barns can be found in his saying, "A man's life does not consist in the abundance of his possessions" (12:15). The parable follows and illustrates this saying. The wealthy farmer died on the very night he had laid plans for his future ease. He had measured his life, including his future, by his great wealth. In his judgment, God called the man a fool. The force of the question, "Then who will get what you have prepared for yourself?" (12:20) suggests that God thinks that amassing great wealth carries with it a corresponding neglect of God. On the other hand, Jesus' saying, "This is how it will be with anyone who stores up things for himself but is not rich toward God" (12:21), seems more open to the possibility that a person could be rich in things but also rich toward God. What clues can we pick up that will enable us to find a consistency between the two?

It is possible that the text doesn't allow these two perspectives to be harmonized. Think, for example, about Jesus' saying that a camel would sooner pass through the eye of a needle than a rich man enter the kingdom of God. That seems pretty cut and dried, but the disciples still asked, "Who then can be saved?" To this question, Jesus replied that all things are possible with God (Luke 18:18–29). Perhaps Jesus wanted to prevent his listeners from making hard-and-fast rules about wealth and salvation. In the process, he placed the burden of interpretation squarely on their shoulders.

Following the parable of the wealthy farmer comes Jesus' famous discourse about the lilies of the field and the birds of the air. The centerpiece idea is that "life is more than food, and the body more than clothes" (12:23). Recall that Jesus said these things on the journey that would be his last. The treasure waiting in heaven relativizes material blessings as well as all the cares and worries of life. That great treasure is the only enduring measure of value.

The Great Banquet
Luke 14:15–24

Luke, who almost universally is believed to have been the author of both Luke and Acts, was a Gentile, an outsider to the Jewish community of Palestine. His gospel bears the marks of a person who had experienced firsthand the sting of exclusion. Thus, we find a particular sensitivity to those whose social stations similarly excluded them from the mainstream of religious life. The parable of the great feast is but one illustration of this Lukan attitude.

The parable of the great feast or banquet in Luke 14:15–24 set the stage for the three parables about lost things in Luke 15. Interestingly, the parable of the prodigal son also refers to a banquet or feast. In fact, running through the entire Travel Narrative is the motif of being invited to come to some kind of celebration. Throughout this section, Jesus and his followers are frequently "not received." The parable of the great banquet and the three parables of the lost reverse roles. Jesus, the traveling guest, becomes Jesus the host who invites everyone, sinners included, to the great feast of the kingdom of God. Jesus now receives. "Though this ministry of Jesus is not new, what now becomes lucid in light of the journeying-guest motif is that Jesus journeys to Jerusalem, inviting folk in the present as Lord of the household of the Kingdom to his banquet. And it is the Pharisee-lawyers (scribes) who are the arch-antagonists to this journeying."[25]

This parable is a comment on the Jewish religious leaders' rejection of Jesus. In it, Jesus makes use of "the symbol of the heavenly banquet [which] was a traditional one for the bliss of the good time coming, when the kingdom of God should be revealed."[26] As is often the case, Jesus turns the tables on respectable religious leaders who presume to understand the nature and appearance of God's rule. The parable strongly suggests that the "righteous" will—or have—rejected the invitation to the banquet while tax collectors and sinners accept. That these "unrighteous" are invited at all is but a further glimpse of God's graciousness. The parable may

25. Moessner, *Lord of the Banquet*, 158.
26. Dodd, *Parables of the Kingdom*, 93.

be read further as Jesus' playful but serious retort to the Pharisees' and legalists' complaints about his teaching: the kingdom of God is like the banquet Jesus describes.[27]

The Loving Father
Luke 15:1–2, 11–24

Luke 15 is about things that are lost: a sheep, a coin, and a child. It contains perhaps the most beloved of all Jesus' parables, the one most people know as the parable of the prodigal son. New Testament scholar Joachim Jeremias thought that such a title misplaced the story's emphasis and preferred to call it the "parable of the loving Father."[28] By either title, our hearts are moved as soon as we hear the familiar words, "There was a man who had two sons."

In ancient Palestine, the law governing property distribution between a father and his heirs was clear and precise. The father could pass on property through a will, or second, he could give land to his sons while still living. In the first case, the son held possession of the land as well as the right to dispose of it as he saw fit. In the second case, the son only possessed the property; he could not dispose of it as long as his father remained alive. In the parable, the younger son wanted to turn his inheritance of land into cold, hard cash. He asked for something to which he was not entitled. There is also the sheer impudence of the boy's request. It is as if he had said to his father, "I do not want to wait until you die. I want my inheritance right now." The son's request trampled on the fifth commandment as well as on legal custom. Jesus' listeners would have been shocked at such hardness of heart. Family members and neighbors could only despise a son who made such a request.

Luke 15 opens by referring to the grumbling of Pharisees and scribes about Jesus' habit of associating with sinners. The "lost" parables must be read first as his answer to their carping. God takes no greater joy than in the sinner who comes to his or her senses and asks forgiveness.

In the traditional cultures of Kenya and Tanzania, people often object to the fact that the people in this story are unnamed. They will ask, "What is the man's name? What was his family? What was his village?" In those cultures, people's names and family connections serve to identify them and locate them in the social world. That a person's name is unknown therefore leaves matters open-ended and empty. Perhaps that is as it should be. Nameless characters allow us to write our own names into the story. At some point in our lives, we have all played the prodigal and the Father waited for us. At other points, we may have played the older brother. Our discipleship calls us to a love like that of the Father, a love that waits, a love that rejoices when one who was lost is found.

The Demands of the Hour
Luke 16:1–13

Many Bible readers will be familiar with the verse: "You cannot serve both God and money." Far fewer will be familiar with the parable that precedes it. At first reading, it is a curious story in which Jesus seems to be praising the unscrupulous conniving of an

27. Ibid., 95.
28. Jeremias, *Parables of Jesus*, 128.

embezzler. The parable cuts in two directions, and careful interpretation must take notice of both applications.

Jesus' summary comment about serving God or money identifies one teaching point in this parable. Jesus frequently referred to money. Most of the people who heard him speak and teach were "people of the land" who owned very little and eked out their daily existence. Mostly, they were just plain poor; their circumstances forced them into relentless worry about their daily needs, which they believed money would relieve. The tendency to believe that more cash will solve all of our problems is but a reminder that money can present a moral issue for the impoverished as well as the wealthy.

The manager in this story was responsible for the orderly government of his master's household. The Greek word for this responsible position is *oikonomos*, from which we get our word *economics*. The *oikonomos* looked after his master's interests and saw to it that the many enterprises of the estate ran smoothly and harmoniously. That was the ideal, but the manager in Jesus' story failed to measure up to the task. He had in fact embezzled from his master, who in the face of rumors about his servant suddenly asked for a reckoning. Heavy financial obligations were involved, the amounts totaling more than eight or nine years' wages. In order to escape detection, the steward conspired with his master's debtors to reduce the amount they owed, in some cases cleverly suggesting that they make out their new bills in their own handwriting so that all appeared normal. Money had ensnared the *oikonomos* and driven him into a spiral of deceit that utterly betrayed his honor and trustworthiness. Money had tempted him into becoming a self-contradiction.

Why would Jesus praise such behavior? In this case, we are concerned not so much with money as with what Jeremias calls the "challenge of the hour."[29] Here Jesus is saying, in essence, "It may be too late. Repent and change your heart by whatever means you can." The people who reported the incident to Jesus had every right to be upset with the dishonest *oikonomos*. But in praising him, Jesus wanted his listeners to see that they too were in imminent danger, but a danger far more serious than that facing the servant. "This man was [prudent] ... i.e. he recognized the critical nature of the situation. He did not let things take their course, he acted, unscrupulously no doubt...but boldly, resolutely, and prudently, with the purpose of making a new life for himself."[30] It isn't that Jesus praised the servant's actions; it is as if Jesus were saying, "For you, too, the challenge of the hour demands prudence; everything is at stake!"[31]

Persistence
Luke 18:1–14

Luke 18:1–14 focuses on prayer and the attitudes of those who pray. These verses tell of three different individuals who prayed. It will be useful to compare and contrast the attitudes of these three people.

First, we have the importunate widow. We are sure to encounter problems if we press the meaning of this story further than the widow and her attitude, but it is very easy to do so. If this is a parable

29. Ibid., 180.
30. Ibid., 182.
31. Ibid.

about prayer, and the widow is cast in the role of one who prayed, shouldn't we take God to be represented by the judge who is in a position to grant this woman's petition? This conclusion stretches the meaning of the parable too far and in ways is uncomplimentary toward God. Jesus said that God knows and gives better than parents who would not give a stone to a child who had asked for bread. In this parable, we are therefore better off focusing solely on the woman.

Jesus had special compassion for widows. Theirs was an especially precarious place in ancient Jewish society. It was a man's world, and women were highly dependent on men for their well-being. A widow was forced to depend on her son for food and shelter. There is no son in this parable, however, from which we can infer that she had no man to take care of even her most basic needs. She was extremely vulnerable in that society, and vulnerability made her desperate. The people who listened to Jesus would have instantly recognized the widow's dilemma, and they would have known women who shared her plight. Those same listeners may also have known such local village officials as the judge—petty men with an inflated self-image. But the widow's desperation had given her a shamelessness that ended in triumph. She must have justice; since there was none but the judge to grant it, she pursued her request beyond propriety.

Second, there is the Pharisee, who also prayed shamelessly. His shamelessness is placed in stark contrast to the widow. The woman's request was grounded in desperation, the Pharisee's in self-righteousness. Standing in the temple, a very public place, he prayed to be heard—by God, by his fellow worshipers, and by himself. The people who listened to Jesus tell this story also were acquainted with Pharisees, men who prayed aloud while standing on the street corner.

Shame also figures in the attitude of the tax collector. Of course, to mention the phrase *tax collector* in ancient Galilee was to incite resentment toward this despised minor class of the Roman bureaucracy. In the minds of Jesus' listeners, "justified tax collector" was an oxymoron. Nevertheless, Jesus told them that this man went to his house justified. Why? The tax collector prayed in such shame that he could not lift his eyes to the heavens. Aware of the immense moral distance between God and himself, the only possible prayer left to the tax collector was a confession of his sinfulness and a petition for divine mercy.

From these stories, we see that some forms of shamelessness are appropriate to prayer while others are not. Deep humility and even shame are appropriate to prayer for, in the ancient language of the *Book of Common Prayer*, "We have done the things we ought not to have done, and left undone the very things we ought to have done."

Grace for "Known Sinners"

Luke 18:15–19:10

Jesus' announcement that he and his little band were bound for Jerusalem might very well have sent a shudder through his disciples. Mostly small-town folk and country people, they rarely visited the large capital city. Galilee was a backwater province with a reputation for rough-mannered people whose dialect and behavior easily distinguished them and their ways from the sophisticated and polished environment of Jerusalem. Then too, there were the Romans. The governor, or procurator, Pontius Pilate ruled from Jerusalem at the Fortress Antonia. Surrounding him were the inevitable collection of bureaucrats and other persons seeking to curry Roman favor. Also garrisoned at Jerusalem were soldiers who enforced the famed Pax Romana. The Roman occupation weighed heavier in Jerusalem than in Galilee. While Jesus and his disciples certainly would have encountered Romans back home and during their travels, the number and significance of those contacts was likely to increase the closer the group came to Jerusalem.

Most segments of Jewish society took offense at one aspect of Jesus' teaching: his message that God's rule and reign welcomed any and all people. His attitude toward money and political power threatened the socially privileged, moneyed interests in Jerusalem. Such teaching was comparatively safe in distant Galilee. In and around Jerusalem, though, this message was bound to fall on the ears of people with the means and ability to do something about a man they considered a troublemaker. Nevertheless, Jesus neither altered his message nor changed his habits of association.

After setting his face toward Jerusalem, Jesus traveled to the ancient city of Jericho. It was in that ancient city that the famous exchange between Jesus and Zacchaeus occurred. Stopping to speak with a tax collector, and then continuing to go to his house to eat with him, could only incite the Pharisees watching Jesus to drastic measures. Nearly all Jews, rich and poor, city dwellers and rural folk, young and old, despised men such as Zacchaeus. Few Jews would have thought that God's rule and reign could ever include tax collectors.

To begin, there was the man's name. Although we cannot state so with absolute certainty, it seems possible that Zacchaeus may have changed his name to give it a more Greek or Roman appearance and sound. *Zacchaeus* is an unusual Hebrew spelling. More likely, this man's name was actually Zaccai, which he had lengthened and Hellenized by adding a Greek suffix. In the eyes of many, such an act constituted an unpatriotic betrayal of one's own people and culture. Added to Zacchaeus's questionable politics was his distasteful occupation. The office of tax collector was a particularly juicy plum in the Roman Empire. As long as rates were not so extreme as to promote rebellion, Roman government was unconcerned about the receipts gathered by their collectors. All that mattered to the Romans was that they got their share. Tax collectors were thus free to collect whatever they wished, sending Rome its tax revenues while pocketing the balance. Men such as Zacchaeus often charged excessive rates in order to recoup the money they had originally used to bribe the Romans for the job. The system was corrupt, and as is often the case, ordinary people ended up paying its costs.

Nearly anybody in the Jericho crowd could quickly come up with two or three reasons to hate Zacchaeus. Once hatred had taken root, those same people would easily have concluded that God, like them, had no use for the little weasel. Quite contrary to prevailing sentiment, however, Jesus announced that salvation had come to Zacchaeus's house. To offer God's grace to tax collectors such as Zacchaeus—not far from Jerusalem—could only increase the Pharisees' opposition to Jesus.

The Last Supper
Luke 22:7–23

During the Middle Ages, Christians were heavily oriented toward visual aspects of the faith. In a world where few people could read or write, it was certain that even fewer could read Latin, the language of worship and the Bible. It is to be expected, therefore, that aspects of Christian practice that did not directly depend on the written word took on added importance. For this reason, icons and relics of all kinds assumed significant roles in the public and private devotional lives.

Over the centuries, no part of Christian worship came to be venerated or regarded with more respect than the service of Holy Communion. The annual Jewish celebration of Passover provides the backdrop for the meal shared by Jesus and the disciples, which is symbolically reenacted by Christians when they gather for Communion. According to Fred Craddock, the Passover thus governs Luke's account of the upper room meal. The language of verses 19–20 later "came to be interpreted in sacrificial terms as atonement for sin. However... the Passover lamb was not a sin offering. The lamb sacrificed for sin was another ritual; the Passover lamb was the seal of the covenant, and the Passover meal commemorated that covenant offered to the faith community by a God who sets free. Jesus' blood seals a new covenant offered to the faith community by a God who sets free."[32]

Christians have often asked, "What happens here?" when coming to the Lord's Table, and their many different answers have served the unfortunate effect of dividing us. Perhaps we should ask a different question. Perhaps we should take a page from the Passover liturgy that guides every observance of this formative moment in Judaism—including the one in the upper room. Instead of asking what happens, perhaps we should ask: Why have we come here? Why do we come to this table? Why do we wish to eat this bread and drink this cup?

We come to this table to remember. "Our corporate act of remembrance forms our character after the image of Christ. In eating bread and drinking from this cup we remember and thus identify with the crucified Lord to the purpose that our lives might proclaim his sacrificial death until he returns."[33]

On This Rock?
Luke 22:31–34, 54–62; John 21:1–22

Peter has long been the favorite of many a follower of Jesus, perhaps because he is so representative of human nature. The Gospels portray Peter as impetuous and enthusiastic. He is so bold as to declare his allegiance to the Messiah and willingly follow Jesus even unto death, but when the moment came to act on that allegiance, Peter could muster only denial. After the resurrection, Peter seems to have forgotten his failure, for he was so eager to talk to Jesus that he could not wait for the boat to reach shore; he jumped into the water and swam. And when Jesus inquired pointedly into Peter's love, his feelings

32. Craddock, *Luke,* 256.

33. Strege, "Ecclesiology and the Lord's Supper," 127.

were hurt. None other of the disciples blew as hot and cold as Peter.

Peter, of course, was not this man's given name. He was Simon bar Jonah—Simon, son of John. Jesus nicknamed him *Peter* at Caesarea Philippi after his famous declaration that Jesus was "the Christ, the Son of the living God" (Matt 16:16–18). Protestants and Catholics alike have made much of this incident. Catholics interpret this passage to mean that Peter is the "rock" (*petros*, in Greek) on which the church is built. Protestants attempt to score an interpretive point from the different gender of *petra*, the form used to refer to the rock on which the church was built. In their view, Jesus was making a play on words. Proponents of both arguments must be reminded that Jesus spoke Aramaic, not Greek, and the Aramaic *Kepha* takes only that form. *Kepha*, incidentally, is the word that is translated "Cephas" in some older versions of the Bible.

One way to think about these two texts is to contrast them in time and place. Jesus predicted Peter's betrayal at a very dangerous moment in their life together. Jesus and the disciples were in Jerusalem. Galilee and its safe distance from the capital was a memory. Their days were light and happy in Galilee where big crowds followed them and some of Jesus' fame overflowed onto his disciples. In Jerusalem, by contrast, those who were believed to be Jesus' associates found themselves in a precarious situation. Speaking Aramaic with a Galilean accent was enough to raise suspicion. Peter and the other disciples recognized their danger. They were under no illusions that things in Jerusalem would be as simple as they had been in Galilee. Peter had talked of prison and death. The other disciples vowed their willingness to take up the sword in Jesus' defense. Never mind that their relative safety behind closed doors might embolden them in a manner that would evaporate in the hot glare of the day. Peter and the other disciples appreciated the danger of this moment.

All is different in John 21:1–22. In some ways, things were back to normal. Peter, Andrew, James, and John had returned home and resumed work in the family business. Back in Galilee, they were safe, and they had returned to the comfortable routine of the days before Jesus had called them from their nets. As they spotted a figure on the shore, grilling fish and warming the flat bread of the Middle East over a fire, familiar feelings stirred. A stunning catch of fish confirmed that it was the Lord. In the rush to get ashore, Peter remembered to take his clothes along. Was this only modesty? Did Peter think that clothing his naked body would also cover his traitorous behavior back in Jerusalem? Or had he blotted out what was too painful to be remembered?

Jesus would not allow Peter to forget without being forgiven. Three times—once for each denial—the Lord asked his disciple whether he loved him. What a searing moment! On a sunny beach with a picnic all prepared, just like the old days, Peter was forced to remember. But forgiveness and healing came.

Who Killed Jesus?
Luke 23:13–49

Who was responsible for Jesus' death? Mel Gibson's recent movie, *The Passion of the Christ*, potently refocused attention on this question. The person who ordered Jesus' death was Pontius Pilate, governor of the Roman province of

Judea. The Romans gave a broad grant of power and authority to the social elite in conquered territories, but that authority stopped short of the right to authorize and execute capital punishment. That grim responsibility Rome kept for herself. If Jesus was to die at the hands of the state, a Roman official would have to sign the death warrant. By the date of Jesus' trial, however, Pilate was in a delicate position.

Earlier in his administration, Pilate had acted rashly, attempting to introduce Roman battle flags and military standards into the city of Jerusalem and to dedicate some golden shields in his Jerusalem residence. Both actions violated agreements between the imperial government and the Jews, inflaming the passions of these people whose rebellious nature made them poor subjects in the first place. The threat of riots forced Pilate to back down. Later he tried to seize funds from the temple treasury to pay for a civil engineering project, which also led to open resistance and bloodshed. Pilate's difficulties in governing the Jews were certain to be noticed back in Rome. The imperial policy was to govern its provinces with a kind of benign neglect, collecting taxes and preserving the peace. Since the far-flung Roman army could not simultaneously muster enough soldiers to meet rebellions in several quarters of the Empire, it was important for Roman governors to rule in such a way as not to incite local populations.

The consequences of previous errors have a way of presenting themselves later in less demanding situations. After interrogating Jesus in what was more a hearing than a full-scale trial, Pilate concluded that Jesus had committed no crime and certainly did not deserve to be executed. The baggage of Pilate's previous blunders now came back to burden him. His career could not afford another bad report to his superiors in Rome. Faced with the threat of still another riot and possibly worse, the Roman governor acquiesced to the demands of the Jews. None of this excuses him.

We might also say that the Jews were responsible for Jesus' death. In the centuries following Jesus' crucifixion, Christians labeled all Jewish people as "Christ-killers" and used that excuse to commit unspeakable atrocities against them. We will never know the horrific number of men, women, and children who have been tortured and killed—in most cases by people who claimed the name of Christ—for no reason other than they were Jewish. Without stooping to such bigotry, however, we can say that the Jews in the governing council and those howling for Jesus' crucifixion were responsible for his death. In the former case, we have people who were determined to get rid of Jesus. In the latter, we see a screaming mob whose passions, for whatever motive, had been ignited beyond the point of reason. As Pilate discovered, there was no arguing with the crowd. They demanded Jesus' death, and he gave them what they wanted. Human beings are capable of acts in groups that they would seldom commit as individuals. One would like to think that the day after Jesus' crucifixion the people who made up the mob had come to their senses and were filled with regret. That does not reduce their responsibility for their actions.

Historically speaking, the Roman governor and the Jewish people both must be held accountable for Jesus' death. Much of modern American

Protestantism has sentimentalized Jesus, making him altogether nice, someone who went about doing good and encouraging people to love one another. We ought to ask ourselves whether the Romans or the Jews would execute a person for being nice. Surely they recognized in Jesus someone who threatened to turn the world upside down. Theologically speaking, since Jesus died for the sake of the world's sin, the whole world—past, present, future—is responsible for his death, which did transform the world.

The Road to Emmaus

Luke 24:13–49

We have reached a point in Luke's narrative at which many historians have balked ever since the early days of the nineteenth century. The rules of modern history make it very difficult for such scholars to accept Jesus' resurrection from the dead as a historical fact. Historians demand evidence and analogies in human experience. In the case of Jesus' resurrection, we have the testimony of Scripture and the witnesses it reports. This testimony can be evaluated and either accepted or rejected. Historians ask that this testimony be corroborated by analogy. In other words, historians want the event to which the witnesses testify to have parallels in human experience. But what do we do when the witnesses testify to an event unparalleled in human history? Jesus' resurrection is unique, a one-of-a-kind event. Human experience holds no analogies. This line of thought has led some theologians to the conclusion that the only response to the resurrection is faith—belief and trust that God raised Jesus from the dead, on the basis of the testimony of witnesses coupled with one's personal encounter with the risen Lord.

Two of Jesus' followers, one a man named Cleopas, had an encounter with the risen Lord as they walked to their home in Emmaus on the first day of the week following Jesus' crucifixion. The identity of the other person is unknown to us, although Christian art has often portrayed the second traveler as male. Despite the Gospels' accounts of several women among Jesus' followers, it has been typical to think of them first as men. In the case of the Emmaus travelers, however, a recent argument raises the strong possibility that the second person was Cleopas's wife. We infer this because the travelers invited Jesus to stay with them in their home. First-century Jewish culture expected males to marry and raise a family. These expectations were so strong that it would have been highly unlikely to find two Jewish male adults sharing a house. Hence we conclude, despite many beautiful paintings to the contrary, that Jesus' hosts in Emmaus were husband and wife.

Regardless the gender of these two people, as a result of their experience with the risen Lord, "their eyes were opened and they recognized him" (24:31). They rushed back to Jerusalem to tell the others, only to hear the disciples' report. Jesus had appeared to "the women who had come with Jesus from Galilee" (23:55), namely Mary Magdalene, Joanna, and Mary the mother of James, as well as unnamed others (24:10), and also to Simon Peter. Into the midst of this stunned little group, the Lord himself appeared. These first witnesses to Jesus' resurrection were forever changed by their experience. This change was moral in the crucial sense that their characters were transformed. Courage replaced fear. Trust and confidence replaced timidity and unbelief. Their encounter with the risen Lord changed fearful little people into men and women capable of resolute action and courageous witness. As Paul would later write, these disciples were new creatures in Christ.

On the basis of their example, we are entitled to ask, What are the moral consequences of the resurrection? This question does not discount the importance of Jesus' crucifixion and resurrection in terms of the sinner's justification and hope of eternal life, but we also must ask about transformation. The people who exited the room after their encounter with the resurrected Jesus were decidedly different from those who had walked down Golgotha three days earlier. God raised Jesus from the dead, and that worked a moral transformation in Jesus' first followers. What does it work in us?

How might the early church have told this story? It is, of course, a narrative that depended on the central event of Christianity, the resurrection of Jesus from the dead, and was told as a testimony to that event. Certainly it would also have reminded the early church of Jesus' promise that he would never leave or forsake them. It was also a narrative that reminded Jesus' followers that he was present in forms and ways that they might not recognize. In the final analysis, the early church told this story in a manner and for reasons similar to those that prompt us to tell it. The birth of Jesus ushered into the world a presence that would never leave or forsake us.

John

The Word Became Flesh
John 1:1–18; 20:30–31

John 20:30–31 explains this gospel's controlling purpose, and it is not history. Like the Synoptics, the gospel of John contains many of the most important events of Jesus' life and ministry. But historical writing typically does not attempt to persuade readers to religious belief. Yet this is precisely the purpose behind this gospel: "But these [miraculous signs] are written that you may believe that Jesus is the Christ, the Son of God, and that by believing you may have life in his name."

The phrase "Jesus is the Christ" underscores the obvious but important point that *Christ* is not Jesus' last name. *Christ* is the English translation of *christos,* which is the Greek equivalent of the Hebrew term *messiah.* Both of these terms mean "the Anointed One." To name Jesus the Messiah makes this claim about him: he is Israel's Anointed One, chosen to redeem the nation. The Greek New Testament's translation of *messiah* as *christos* enlarges the sphere of redemption to include the Gentile world. *Christos* becomes a title of cosmic proportions, and the first eighteen verses of John (New Testament scholars refer to these as the gospel's prologue) speak to this universal significance.

Only at the conclusion of the prologue do we find the phrase "Jesus Christ" (1:17, a literal translation from the Greek meaning "Jesus the Christ"). Until this point, John's gospel has employed the term *Word* to refer to the Son of God prior to the incarnation. *Logos* is the Greek term that the English

Bible translates "Word." The idea of *logos* is not a newly minted word or idea; it had circulated in Greco-Roman thought world for centuries. Philosophers and some religious thinkers thought of *logos* as impersonal "reason," that is, they thought of reason in the abstract, without any qualities of personality. These thinkers held that all rational beings possessed *logos* to some extent.

John took over this term and, in his prologue, linked it to *christos*. Then, at 1:14, he announced, "The Word became flesh and made his dwelling among us." This announcement raised critical theological issues with which early Christianity struggled. They touch the very center of the Christian confession that Jesus is the Christ—the belief that John 20:31 declares to be critical to belief in Jesus. In the first place, to say that the Word became flesh implies a time when the Word was without flesh. Thus, we draw a theological distinction between the eternal Son of God, the Word who was God (1:1), and Jesus of Nazareth. The *Logos* preexists the creation and everything in it (1:2–3), including the historical figure of Jesus. The *Logos* entered history uniquely, in a "one and only" way (1:14), as it became incarnate (flesh) in Jesus of Nazareth.

Incarnate in Jesus, the *Logos* brings grace and truth to humanity. Indeed, the incarnate One is full of grace and truth, which stand in superior relation to the Law of Moses. The incarnate *Logos* also reveals God. We have already been told that the *Logos* is God and shares in God's creative power. Only the "one and only" *Logos* (the Greek word *monogenes* means "the only one of its kind"), who is God, can reveal God to those who have never seen God. Incarnate in Jesus of Nazareth, the *Logos* reveals God to humanity. The incarnate One is the Christ, through whom comes grace, truth, and the revelation of God. The Revealer and the Redeemer are thus one and the same, incarnate in Jesus.

The Witness of John the Baptizer
John 1:19–34

Careful biblical interpretation must pay attention to what we can know of the historical, social, and literary contexts surrounding the individual books of the Bible. Admittedly, some degree of speculation comes into play, since the scholars who study these contexts work very much like detectives, piecing together enough clues to form a measured judgment. Current scholarship offers the hypothesis that the gospel of John originated in a Johannine community of Christians who had broken sharply with the Jews of the synagogue. This community was under attack from the Jews; according to the scholarly hypothesis, the sharpness of this attack influenced the shape of John's gospel.

In the gospel of John, people often known only by the label "the Jews" constantly question Jesus. It is as if he and his followers were somehow on trial—if not formally in court then certainly in public opinion. Unlike in the Synoptics, John the Baptizer appears in John's gospel only long enough to bear witness to Jesus as the Christ. John is but the first of a series of witnesses who appear, each testifying on behalf of Jesus like witnesses in a trial. "[S]ome see in John's Gospel a protracted judicial process...in which favorable witnesses like John [the Baptizer] and later a series of things and persons like Jesus' 'works' (5:36), the Father (5:37), and the Scriptures (5:39) are pitted against accusatory witnesses."[34]

John 1:19–34 is the first witness to Jesus in John's gospel. Back in 1:6, we learn that "there came a man who was sent from God; his name was John." According to John's gospel, John the Baptizer's ministry of preaching and baptizing had no primary purpose of its own. Instead, its purpose was to testify concerning the light of the Logos entering the world in the person of Jesus. John 1:19–34 covers the content of John's witness, with added comment from the following day in verses 35–42.

John's testimony begins, perhaps a little oddly, by denying that he was the Christ. John makes this denial to the priests and Levites sent by "the Jews of Jerusalem" to interrogate him. Part of the puzzle concerning this gospel's reference to "the Jews" is that the term could be applied to nearly anyone living in Jerusalem; it was a very Jewish city. To use such a phrase is like saying "some Danes from Copenhagen" or "some Irish from Dublin" unless, of course, John wishes to augment the ethnic sense of "Jew." In fact, John did precisely that, for in this gospel "Jew" signifies those who opposed and were hostile to Jesus and his community of followers. We should understand that those in Jerusalem who sent priests and Levites to question John the Baptizer were not motivated by curiosity. Rather, they are antagonists throughout the entire narrative.

John the Baptizer denied that he was the Christ, the Elijah, or even a prophet. His denials took this form because many people in first-century Palestine fervently anticipated the restoration of Israel, an event that was connected to the appearance of the Messiah or the spirit of Elijah. It was an age when people stood perpetually on tiptoe waiting for these events to unfold. John's witness included more than these denials. He went on to identify himself as the forerunner of the One whose sandals he was unworthy to untie.

The day after the priests and Levites asked their questions, Jesus stepped out of the crowd to be proclaimed by John as "the Lamb of God who takes away the sin of the world!" (1:29). To this announcement was added testimony citing evidence to support John's final witness, stated in very formal language: "I have seen and I testify that this is the Son of God" (1:34). Those who accused Jesus and his followers heard in these words the first defense of his innocence.

The Miracle at Cana
John 2:1–11

Jesus, his mother, and the disciples had been invited to a wedding in Cana, a Galilean town not far from Nazareth. The text gives us no clue as to the identity of the bridal couple. If this were a biography, the writer would naturally want to supply this detail, but for John's purposes the names are irrelevant to the story. The narrative does not even refer to Mary by name; she is called "Jesus' mother," and Jesus himself addresses her as "Dear woman." (The New International Version softens the apparent stiffness in this form of address by inserting the word *Dear,* which does not appear in the Greek text. It reads simply "Woman"). Jesus is the only one named in this narrative. He is the central figure in the story.

34. Sloyan, *John,* 12

At least three different points of consideration can be found in this narrative. First, there is the matter of who may direct or compel Jesus' attention. Second, the quality of the wine that miraculously appeared in the water jars and the reputation it imputed to the host deserves comment. Last, John refers to this event as a "sign," and we must consider the direction or meaning toward which that sign pointed.

Jesus' mother had noticed that the wine was in very short supply, and her pointed reference to this potential social blunder implies her belief that Jesus could take care of the problem. It seemed a rather petty matter. Is the power of the Son of God available to keep our parties from going bad? At first Jesus rebuffed her both by form of address as well as the reminder that his hour had not yet come. The timing of that hour was at God's disposal and no other. God and God alone directed the course of Jesus' life.

Second, although it raises concerns for Christians whose ethics prohibit the consumption of alcoholic beverages, apparently Jesus transformed water into wine of a very high quality. The master of ceremonies for this wedding feast apparently knew his wines and commented on the irregularity of reserving the best wine until the end of the banquet. The custom was to bring out the cheap stuff when too much food and drink had dulled palates. Only an extremely generous host would reserve the best wine until the last. Jesus' extravagant gesture attached a similar label to the bridegroom who had benefited from Jesus' action.

Last, John called this miracle a "sign." The Synoptics typically refer to Jesus' miracles as *dunamis,* eruptions of divine power, but John stated that this miracle was a sign pointing to the glory of the One who performed it. Those who lived in the presence of the incarnate One had, as John 1:14 says, "seen his glory." They saw it first in the sign of water turned to wine.

Jesus and Nicodemus
John 3:1–17

This text continues the witness motif that John employs. The circumstances are slightly altered, but words and phrases such as *verdict* and *stands condemned* appear by the conclusion of the passage. There is often some form of judgment going on in John's gospel, and this text extends that sense.

The Pharisee Nicodemus differed markedly from "the Jews" who accused Jesus. In this respect, he appears here as a defense witness. Were we reading the text as first-century Jews, Nicodemus's attitude toward Jesus would surprise us. After all, he was a Pharisee and a member of the Sanhedrin, the ruling council of Jerusalem. In consort with the high priest of the temple, the Sanhedrin governed Jerusalem.[35] To be sure, the Roman governor or prefect firmly controlled the province; however, since they wanted to avoid riots and other troublesome disturbances, the Romans preferred to leave local and municipal government in the hands of local rulers. If local rulers proved unequal to the task, Roman overlords were ready and able to enforce the "Roman peace." As a member of the Sanhedrin, Nicodemus was a member of the privileged elite of

35. For an enlightening description of the political situation in Judea and Jerusalem, see Sanders, *Historical Figure of Jesus,* 15–32. Sanders's painstaking historical scholarship offers an alternative view of the nature of political arrangements in Roman colonies.

Jerusalem, the sort of people among whom would be found Jesus' accusers. Such a person visiting Jesus, honoring him with the title *Rabbi*, is a surprise.

Nicodemus's visit is also a surprise because he was a Pharisee. Marcus Borg contends that one key source of the dispute between Jesus and the Pharisees lay in their radically different understandings of the nature of God's rule. The Pharisees taught that God's rule demanded a "politics of holiness." This phrase contains the idea that Israel's survival depended on the strict practice of the holiness code. The Pharisees believed that such practice would result in Israel's separation from contamination by the surrounding Roman world. Strict observance of the rules and regulations of Torah, which the Pharisees insisted upon, would separate Israel from the world and thus save the people of God. On the other hand, says Borg, Jesus taught a "politics of compassion." Not legal obedience but the practice of compassion in imitation of God's forgiveness becomes the proper expression of life under God's rule. In his view, the people of God live by forgiveness rather than legal obedience. Borg contends that these very different ideas of the nature of God's rule created much of the dispute between Jesus and the Pharisees.[36]

That a Pharisee and a member of the Sanhedrin would visit Jesus at all is surprising, so we should not wonder that Nicodemus called at night. That he paid Jesus the compliment of visiting for the purpose of an honest conversation stands as yet another witness to Jesus' authenticity as the Christ. However, their conversation is filled with contrasts: (1) Nicodemus visited Jesus, the Light, in the darkness of night. Should we read Jesus' words in 3:21 as a rebuke? Was Jesus chiding Nicodemus for coming under cover of the very darkness that "men loved"? (2) Jesus told Nicodemus, a full-grown man, that he must be, literally, "born from above" (NRSV). The birth of which Jesus spoke has nothing to do with human generation; it is "of water and the Spirit," but "birth from above" was not a term that Nicodemus recognized from the religious vocabulary of Judaism. Therefore this "teacher of Israel" did not understand, which surprised Jesus. The give-and-take of conversational debate would not win the day. What would?

In 3:12 and following, Jesus' speech took a new direction. Confession (in the sense of witness) replaced conversation. Jesus bore testimony to himself, and on the basis of this testimony, Nicodemus would have to make his decision; that is, offer his verdict, as to the question of whether Jesus was the Christ. We have no clue as to Nicodemus's answer, but his courageous presence at the cross when Jesus' body needed to be buried proclaims his final verdict.

The Woman at the Well
John 4:7-25, 28–34, 39–42

Consider the possibility that a person who knew everything about you visited your town. This person could remind you of everything you ever did or said. Obviously, this person could share that knowledge with your friends—and your enemies. How would you feel about such a presence in your hometown? After talking with Jesus, an unnamed woman at the well of Sychar ran to her neighbors with news of "a man who told me everything I ever did."

36. Borg, *Jesus—A New Vision*, 86–90; 129–42.

Sychar was a town in Samaria, and that piece of geographical information is important. Jews (as we are told in 4:9) "do not associate with Samaritans." The chasm separating these peoples was deep enough that Jews, thirsty though they might be, would not drink from the same well as Samaritans. From the Jewish point of view, the Samaritans were a mongrel people, the result of intermarriage among ethnic groups that carried back all the way to the era of deportation and immigration forced upon the northern kingdom of Israel by the Assyrian empire in the eighth century BC. Through marriage reform, Ezra had legislated ethnic purity among the exiles and people of Jerusalem (see Ezra 9–10). This policy became the basis for later Jewish claims to an ethnic purity that they believed elevated them socially above the Samaritans. Jews and Samaritans also followed different religious practices, and this was a major point of division. While both worshiped Yahweh, the Samaritans worshiped in a temple on Mount Gerizim that they had permitted Alexander the Great to build for them. To the Jews of Jesus' day, only the rebuilt temple on Mount Zion in Jerusalem constituted the house of Yahweh. Divided by social custom and religious practice, Jews had no reason to overcome their prejudice against the Samaritans.

Jesus' simple request for a drink of water from Jacob's well transgressed a social and religious barrier constructed over centuries. That he, a man and a stranger in town, made this request of a woman broke yet another taboo. Ordinarily, men and women did not associate in settings ungoverned by strictly observed social mores. To flout those mores even in innocence raised suspicions about the woman's sexual ethics. The woman took no offense at Jesus' violation of this important social barrier. Perhaps she had grown accustomed to male insults and liberties.

The first part of the conversation centered on water. As is so often the case in the Gospels, Jesus employs common elements to open spiritual significance. His request for a drink led to a discussion of his status: Was he greater than Jacob? Clearly the answer was yes, but more was at stake than a simple claim to unmatched greatness. If the Samaritan woman only knew the gift of God that Jesus offered, she would have the answer both to her question and to the riddle of her life. Jesus was greater because he offered "living" water, a phrase that commonly signified the running water of a stream rather than stagnant well water. Jesus invested the term with new significance; his water is the gift of eternal life.

The woman did not understand. In response to his direction that she find her husband, the woman replied that she had none, opening new discussion topics—her marital history and the nature of worship. This conversation, in turn, led to the woman's proclamation of the Messiah as well as Jesus' declaration, "I who speak to you am he" (4:26). The woman described the expected Messiah as one who will explain everything. Jesus has done so, even down to the private details of her life. In her heart was born the possibility of belief, so she ran to town to tell her friends.

By the time that John's gospel was written, a sizable body of Christians had grown up among the Samaritans. John 4:39 locates the origin of the church in Samaria in the testimony of the woman at the well.

The Sign of Bread
John 6:1–68

The miracle of the loaves and fishes is one of a very few of Jesus' miracles to appear in all four Gospels. In John's gospel, the miracle serves the very specific function of pointing to a truth about Jesus. John did not tell this story simply to encourage belief in Jesus as a wonder-worker.

The Synoptic Gospels treat Jesus' miracles in the same manner and see them in a light different from John. In fact, the Synoptic Gospels refer to this miraculous event with a word that John's gospel does not use. The Synoptic Gospels use the word *dunamis* in reference to Jesus' miracles. The word means a manifestation, perhaps even an explosion, of power. John's gospel often refers to Jesus' miracles differently. For John, foremost, this miracle points to Jesus and the teaching that he is the "bread of God" (6:33) come down from heaven to give life to the world.

Although it sometimes uses *dunamis*, John also and more typically uses *semeion.* Translated into English this word means "sign." John viewed Jesus' miracles as indicators or pointers meant to shed light on a truth about Jesus. Whereas *dunamis* points to the Kingdom, *semeion* points to Jesus.

It surely is the case that the same event can point in both directions, but if we are to interpret the Bible in all its richness, we want to be aware that John saw aspects of Jesus' miracles in a way that differed from the Synoptics. Common to John's gospel is a form of composition where we read a comparatively brief account of a "sign," such as the feeding of the five thousand (fourteen verses in John 6), followed by an extended commentary on the truth about Jesus toward which the sign points (44 verses, John 6:25–69). At Sychar, Jesus had told the woman at the well that he was living water; those who drank from him would never thirst. That idea of satisfaction is repeated in the miracle of the loaves and fishes; those who ate the living bread would never hunger. Drawing upon the Old Testament tradition of manna, the miraculous "bread" that nourished and sustained Israel through the wilderness, Jesus forthrightly announced to his audience, "I am the bread of life" (6:48).

Jesus said, "If anyone eats of this bread, he will live forever. This bread is my flesh, which I will give for the life of the world" (6:51). From this text, it is not difficult to see how only a century or two later Christians came to understand the Lord's Supper as a sacrament where Christ was present in the elements of bread and the cup. Certainly it was the case that pagan Roman critics knew such texts as John 6:52–61, for among the rumors against Christians was the assertion that their worship included cannibalism. A literal interpretation of Jesus' saying so offended his audience that "many of his disciples turned back and no longer followed him" (6:66). Nevertheless, the Twelve remained, for, as Peter said, "Lord, to whom shall we go? You have the words of eternal life" (6:68).

The Truth That Sets People Free
John 8:12–59

John 8 contains some of the sharpest verbal sparring between Jesus and the Jews in this gospel. It is not too much to say that Jesus gave these people something of a tongue-lashing. How else may we interpret such sentences and phrases as "You do not know me or my Father" (8:19); "If you do not believe that I am the one I claim to be, you will indeed die in your sins" (8:24); or "You belong to your father, the devil" (8:44)? The tension between Jesus and his accusers grows throughout John 8. Jesus points out their desire to kill him, and their determination was frustrated only because the appointed time of Jesus' death had not yet arrived. Then, too, Jesus' cleverness also secured him against the Jews who wanted to stone him there and then (8:59).

In this chapter, Jesus reserves some of his sharpest rebukes and charges for a group that John names "the Jews who had believed him" (8:31). Note that the King James Version reads "those Jews which believed on him." The New International Version also uses this verse to begin a paragraph while the King James Version does not. These differences point up the decisions that committees sometimes face when translating the original languages into English. Based on the Greek text, either translation is appropriate. What are we to make of this curious difference?

In John, "the Jews" typically signals people who opposed Jesus' work and who publicly harassed and accused him. The New International Version translators apparently decided that the sharp rebukes that follow verse 31 would not have been intended for those disciples who continued to follow Jesus. That conclusion certainly seems warranted. From the context, therefore, the New International Version translators decided that Jesus must have been addressing some who once believed that he was who he claimed to be and who, subsequently, had abandoned their belief. In the New International Version reconstruction of the scene, Jesus exchanged sharp words with a group of former followers who had turned hostile. Indeed, these former disciples appear to have nurtured hostility into murderous intent.

A second explanation for the heightened tension between Jesus and his accusers can be found in Jesus' naming of God as a witness in his behalf. The section beginning at 8:12 continues the theme of accusation and witness that has been described earlier. The Pharisees certainly could not be faulted for insisting that Jesus produce a witness other than himself to answer the charges against him. They appealed to a rabbinic tradition that required a second witness. Few modern courts would acquit the accused solely on the basis of that person's word, but the Pharisees initially were confused by the news that Jesus' Father would testify on his behalf. As Jesus elaborated on his relationship with the Father, he also laid claim to the Father's role and authority as judge. While Jesus' accusers judged him unfairly, God also judged and had "much to say" (8:26), and all of it was reliable since it came from an unimpeachable witness. The possibility of this judgment would not deter Jesus' accusers, as he himself knew. Thus he referred to the day "when you have lifted up the Son of Man" (8:28). The phrase, of course, points toward Jesus' crucifixion, but to lift up also means to exalt, and we are certainly permitted to interpret Jesus' crucifixion as the exaltation through which the entire world might be saved.

Accusations, testimony, witnesses, and judgment—John 8 gives us the impression that people were deciding between

Jesus and his accusers to find the truth. "Even as he spoke, many put their faith in him" (8:30). There they found the truth that would set them free.

The Resurrection and the Life
John 11:1–6, 11–15, 38–44

Beset by personal calamity and deep in his own physical misery, Job asked the question, "If a man dies, will he live again?" (Job 14:14). It may be that we should read this as an ironic and hopeless question. The Old Testament gives very little indication that the people of that time period hoped in the possibility of life after death. For them, death was the end, ushering the deceased into sheol, the house of the dead. It is also possible, however, to read Job's question as an anticipation of the changed beliefs of the New Testament era. Not all Jews agreed in belief in the resurrection. The Sadducee party rejected any belief in life after death. On the other hand, long before the beginning of Jesus' ministry, the Pharisees were teaching the view that all the dead would be raised in a general resurrection at the end of time. In this text Martha, sister of the dead Lazarus, seems to express such a belief and thereby raises questions about its origins. Had Jesus taught concerning the resurrection on some previous occasion? Were Lazarus and his sisters among the handful of Pharisees sympathetic to Jesus? Although such questions cannot be answered finally, they help us consider the context in which Jesus conducted his work.

The shadow of death hangs across nearly this entire story. Lazarus had died. Perhaps worse for Jesus and the Twelve, Mary and Martha's home was in Bethany, a suburb of Jerusalem. A trip to Judea would put the Galileans' lives in serious jeopardy. In fact, Thomas gloomily suggested that the disciples join Jesus on the sad journey so they could all die together. The finality of death, the grief and loss that it brings, overwhelms people in this story. Even Jesus was "deeply moved in spirit and troubled" (11:33). Like everyone in the group of mourners at Lazarus's tomb, Jesus also wept.

We have here the most dramatic of the miraculous signs that, in John, point to a great truth about Jesus. After he fed the five thousand, he said to his disciples, "I am the bread of life." In the same manner but in a much more emotionally charged setting, Jesus replied to Martha's belief in the general resurrection by saying, "I am the resurrection and the life." Shortly thereafter, Lazarus walked out of his grave.

We Christians mourn the loss of our friends and family members. Death remains bitter gall and the mystery that brackets earthly life. But we do not ask whether the dead will live again. To be sure, we grieve, but, as Paul said, not as those without hope. Our Savior has told us, and in his own resurrection shown us, that he is indeed the resurrection and the life.

The Purpose for Jesus' Death
John 12:23–28, 30–37, 42–43

Up to this point in John's narrative, Jesus has been prevented from harm from those bent on his destruction. The gospel offers the simplest of explanations for Jesus' preservation: his "hour" had not yet come. In other words, Jesus' death would not occur without the Father's permission. John 12:23 announces the arrival of that moment: "The hour has come for the Son of Man to be glorified" (12:23). Here Jesus speaks of his death, and like his first listeners we must ask how death on a Roman cross could glorify the incarnate Logos of God.

John's gospel repeatedly uses the phrase "lifted up," twice in fact in this text. One of those verses explicitly refers to the manner in which Jesus would be put to death. This is not news in the gospel of John. In 3:14, Jesus makes an analogy between his cross and the story of Moses and the bronze serpent in Numbers 21:4–9. Afflicted by poisonous serpents, the rebellious Israelites sought out Moses to give them relief. He did so by casting a serpent of bronze and hanging it on a pole with instructions that any person bitten by a snake need only look at the bronze serpent for healing. Similarly, says Jesus, all those who looked toward the Son of Man who is lifted up also would find the cleansing and healing gift of eternal life. For John, that Jesus would be lifted up signifies much more than a shame-filled death by crucifixion. True, resurrection followed crucifixion, and on Easter Jesus would be fully glorified, but in a very important sense Jesus' glorification began in his being lifted up—at crucifixion. For it would be Jesus' crucifixion, his being "lifted up from the earth," that would "draw all men" to himself (12:32).

The cross as Jesus' glorification speaks specifically to the theological and moral theme that people cannot keep their lives by holding on to them. Jesus refused to hoard his own life. In fact, he had come to die; that was his reason for being. Seed, stored in burlap sacks, remains seed and its potential unrealized. The purpose of a seed is to die, to be buried, and to germinate into a plant that will yield many seeds.

These sayings of Jesus, written near the close of the first century, must have appeared prophetic to John. Jesus—who by the year 150 Justin the Martyr called the *logos spermatikos*, the full embodiment of the "seed of reason"—had fallen to the earth. Through his death, countless new stalks of Christian wheat had germinated and were themselves bearing fruit. Jesus had been lifted up from the earth, and men and women of many different ethnic and racial groups were being drawn into his body, the church.

Over the centuries, Christians have offered several different interpretations of the significance of the cross. The letter to the Hebrews teaches that Jesus' death on the cross is the perfect sacrifice paid for sin. Within a century, Christians interpreted the cross as the instrument by which Jesus defeated sin and death and ransomed humans from the power of darkness. Around the year 1100, Anselm of Canterbury put forward the idea that Jesus' death satisfied sin's infinite offense against God's goodness and honor. Each of these interpretations catches an important aspect of the significance of the cross. Another view, developed by Peter Abelard, stressed the compelling power of Jesus' sacrificial death. Abelard thought that Jesus' death was so unselfish, such a pure act of self-giving, that humans could not help but be attracted to him by the power of his moral example. By itself, Abelard's interpretation is incomplete. Nevertheless, it gives us insight into Jesus' saying that his death would have the power to draw all to him. Thus we sing, "In the cross of Christ I glory."

Servanthood
John 13:1–17

Nearly all Christians observe baptism and the Lord's Supper. Some call these special services ordinances while others refer to them as sacraments. This latter term comes from the Latin *sacramentum,* a word that originally signified the oath or pledge taken by a soldier. In time, the word came to mean a "promise." The great theologian Augustine said that a sacrament is a "visible sign of an invisible reality." In Augustine's view, one shared by countless Christians, that reality was God's grace; a sacrament thus came to be understood as a divine pledge or promise of God's grace. On the other hand, *ordinance* comes from the same root as *ordained* and carries with it the sense of having been commanded. An ordinance is an act that has been ordained or decreed. In the accounts recorded in the Gospels, Jesus commanded his followers to baptize, to eat and drink the Lord's Supper, and to wash one another's feet. Hence, many Christians refer to these acts as ordinances.

Comparatively few Christians observe the ordinance of footwashing. Many have interpreted Jesus' saying, "You also should wash one another's feet" (13:14), to mean that Christians ought to serve one another. According to this view, Jesus' act of washing the disciples' feet was intended as an example. John's narrative of this moving gesture is all the more striking because of the absence of any reference to the Lord's Supper. Our attention is thus focused on this menial act of service.

Some of this focus may be explained by the gospel's strong claim that Jesus *is* the Passover. He is the Passover Lamb who takes away the sin of the world. It is no coincidence that Jesus died on the Day of Preparation, as sheep were slaughtered at the temple to make ready for the blood offering the next day. In John's account, Jesus' body lay in the tomb while Jerusalem ate the Passover. John's teaching that Jesus is the Passover takes attention away from the Lord's Supper as it elevates the significance of footwashing.

Footwashing was and remains a menial act of humility. Humility, however, is not the point. Jesus did not wash the disciples' feet to make either them or himself more humble. Jesus' followers are to serve one another. One may contend that humility is indispensable to a servant attitude, but the text points in a different direction. To Peter's objection at the prospect of the Lord serving him, Jesus answered, "Unless I wash you, you have no part with me" (13:8).

> Submission to a cleansing at Jesus' hands...is the proper disposition for partaking in the sacrificial drama to follow. Being bathed by Jesus means being symbolically taken into the event of the cross. It is likewise a model of service for the disciples.... But one must be washed by Jesus to have a part in him."[37]

Humility is not, therefore, the necessary condition to be met in order to serve one another. Rather, the condition of servanthood is that we must be washed by Jesus. We must stand with him at the cross. We must enter into the fellowship of his suffering. As modern-day disciples, we must submit to his authority as our Teacher as well as our Savior and place our lives at his

37. Sloyan, *John,* 169.

disposition. Even more than humility, submission is the key to servanthood within the fellowship of the church. Such submission and service, Jesus promised, will be blessed.

People of Love

John 13:34–35 (Mark 12:28–34; Luke 6:27–31)

John 13:34–35, Mark 12:28–34, and Luke 6:27–31 each speak to the Christian virtue of love. The Markan passage defines love in relation to the Torah. In the Lukan passage, Jesus radicalized the idea of love. In John's gospel, Jesus made love the central characteristic of the Christian community, the church. Taken together, these passages prompt us to think of Christians as a people with a heritage of love, a radical practice of love, and who are defined by love.

At the outset, we must distinguish between love as a feeling and love as a command. Western culture has had much to say about the former. The feeling of love—being in love—is the virtual foundation of the recording industry and Hollywood movie studios. We do not control or command these feelings; thus we say that we fall in love.

In a very different sense, John 13:34–35 and Mark 12:28–34 describe love as the subject of God's command. In Mark, a "teacher of the law," a rabbi, asked Jesus for an opinion about the greatest of the commandments in Torah. As one would expect of any reverent Jew, Jesus answered by quoting the *Shema* (Deut 6:4). The Jew who followed this text could be said also to have kept the first commandment of Torah. To this text Jesus added Leviticus 19:18, "Love your neighbor as yourself." Neither commandment is optional for the people of God. As George Kufeldt, my Old Testament professor, said of the Decalogue, "We do not call them the Ten 'Suggestions.'" They are stated in the imperative form, "You *shall* love." In citing these commandments, Jesus told his listeners that love was more than warm feelings or a kind disposition. It demands something more of us than simply being nice.

The dimensions of Jesus' radical extension of the love commandment become clear in Luke 6:27–31. He instructs us to love our enemies. The text does not even hint that enemies will become friends or that those who hate, curse, or mistreat Christians will suddenly repent of their actions. In other words, we can expect that those who do not like Jesus' followers will persist in their attitude. The enemy remains an enemy, yet from Jesus' point of view that doesn't matter: "Love your enemies." An enemy is a person with whom we do not associate. We *like* our friends and prefer their company. I fish with some of my friends and play golf with others; I would not invite an enemy to join with me in either. I cannot be commanded to like or prefer those who are my enemies; I am not required to enjoy their hatred, cursing, or mistreatment of me, but I am *commanded* by my Lord to love them. In case I have questions about the way to express this love, Jesus also provides me with a standard by which to measure loving action. We call this standard the Golden Rule.

The text from John's gospel places Jesus' commandment to love at the very center of the Christian community. In Luke, Jesus commanded his disciples to love their enemies. In John, he commanded them to love one another. In the face of some very ugly church fights and schisms, we might ask which is more difficult, to love one's enemy or church people? In that we choose neither enemy nor fellow church member, the two resemble each other. We are no more privileged to select who may enter the church through Christ than we can choose our blood relatives. We are stuck with our relatives, whether by blood or grace. The church is no country club. As Jesus said in John's gospel, his followers are defined by love, not by preference.

Love is the line running through these three texts. But love, especially love of our enemies, is not natural to us. We must be commanded to love those whom we would otherwise reject. Since we are commanded to act in this unnatural manner, we must be trained. The church—the community of love where people who are strangers nevertheless love one another under the Lord's command—is just such a training ground. Learning to love the saints and strangers of the church trains us to turn the other cheek—even to our enemies.

The Promise of the Spirit
John 14:15–18, 25–27; 16:7–15

The setting for John 14:15–18, 25–27 and 16:7–15 is Jesus' farewell to his disciples. This is sometimes called the "great discourse" uttered by Jesus just prior to his arrest and trial. As such, it is Jesus' last teaching opportunity before his death, a time for saying only the most important things that must be said. Understandably, the disciples were deeply troubled in their spirits. What sort of future lay in store? What was to become of them once their Lord had left? The pastoral tone of these words is unmistakable as Jesus comforted the disciples with word that the Holy Spirit would come to replace him.

The King James Version translates the Greek word *parakletos* (transliterated, *paraclete*) as "Comforter" while the New International Version reads "Counselor." Literally, *paraclete* means "one who stands alongside." The word calls to mind the idea of an advocate, rendered accurately by the term *counselor.* But where does the King James Version get *Comforter*? Apparently the translators were influenced by the Latin term *comfitare,* which the Vulgate edition employs to translate *paraclete. Comfitare* can mean "comforter," but it can also mean "strong fortress." The latter term carries the idea of a defender or, once again, an advocate. The point here, however, is that by using the term *Comforter* the translators did not have in mind a downy-soft blanket. The Spirit promised by Jesus is an advocate, a strong defender, who stands alongside and in the place of Jesus, the resurrected and ascended Lord.

The Spirit is more than a replacement, for the Spirit is sent by the Father in the name of the Son. The Spirit is also a teacher and guide; the Spirit would call back to the disciples' minds everything that Jesus had taught them. The Spirit is in the Father and in the Son. The Son is in the Spirit and in the Father. The Father is in the Spirit and in the Son. The divine *perichoresis*[38] of this Trinity of divine persons is clearly implied in this passage.

Jesus told the disciples that the Spirit would convict, judge, and guide. These might seem a rather strange trio to join

38. The Greek word *perichoresis* means "interplay," but with connotations of complete harmony, as in dance partners who are in perfect sync with one another.

together, but the idea that links these three roles is Jesus' saying that the Spirit is the "Spirit of truth" (14:17). The presence of truth convicts the world and passes judgment on it. Falsehood and deceit stand exposed by truth's revealing light. It is not that truth must actively pursue all manner of sin and unrighteousness; rather, it is that they are revealed for what they are in the light of truth's presence. The coming of the Spirit of truth makes such disclosure possible.

Since the Spirit knows the truth and is the source of truth, it follows that the Spirit will be a reliable guide for those who seek the truth. The Spirit's role as guide suggests the image of a pilgrimage. The truth is something we pursue more than possess. Complete knowledge of the truth lies somewhere in the future. In such a view, knowledge is not static nor the Spirit an agent of indoctrination. Instead, we journey toward the truth in the company of the only sure and reliable guide, the Spirit. Therefore, we are not forced to walk alone, without truth, until we reach journey's end. The Spirit will speak and teach us through the way that lies ahead. In the company of the Spirit of truth, we already live a truthful existence.

Jesus, the True Vine
John 15:1–17

John 15:1–17 employs the culture of the vineyard to speak of the desired relationship between disciples and Jesus. The Bible often uses images drawn from everyday life as metaphors, and the vineyard is employed in both the Old and New Testaments. The great prophets Jeremiah, Ezekiel, and especially Isaiah (e.g., Isa 5:1–7) spoke of Israel metaphorically as a vine or vineyard. Jesus' hearers could easily draw on this familiar agricultural sight to apply his teaching to their own situation. That Jesus' disciples are grafted into him means everything. In fact, it is not at all too much to say that those who are disconnected, severed from the true vine, are no Christians at all.

Jesus' lesson about the true vine and the gardener expresses the ancient world's idea about the relationship of individuals to larger groups. We find the same kind of idea in Paul's teaching about the church as the body of Christ. It is important to consider this idea carefully because it differs so fundamentally from modern ideas about individuals and the group. Ever since the eighteenth century, much of Western political thought has stressed the idea of the individual as individual. In this view, individuals join together with each other to form a society. A society is the product of many individuals binding themselves (entering into a "social contract") in a group. Social contract political thought considers the individual as the basic unit and societies as the end product of an action taken by many individuals.

Modern or Enlightenment political thought reversed the relationship between individual and group as it had been understood in the ancient world. In Jesus' day, the society or community was understood to be the basic unit and individuals were extensions of it. In this view, connection to the larger society was critical to the selfhood of men and women. We might make a comparison between this idea of a political body and the physical body of a human being. In one sense a hand is a hand as long as it can perform the functions of a hand—throwing a baseball, holding a fork, wielding a golf club. When severed from the body, a hand can no longer perform those functions. This loss of function can be taken to mean a loss of identity; a hand that can no longer perform as a hand is really no longer a hand. Applied to the social and political assumptions of the ancient world, this relationship means that individuals have identity only so long as they abide in a larger society or political body.

Jesus said to his followers, "Remain in me, and I will remain in you. No branch can bear fruit by itself; it must remain in the vine. Neither can you bear fruit unless you remain in me" (15:4). Those who abide in Christ obey his commands and bear fruit. They live within the sphere of his love, meaning that they both receive and express Christ's love. Those who follow Jesus are to love in imitation of his example.

The theologians Augustine and Thomas Aquinas both distinguished between two kinds of love—*benevolentia* (love that desires the good of the person loved) and *concupiscentia* (love that desires to gain something from the person loved). The first is modeled on God's love; the second selfishly turns the beloved into a possession. Jesus tells his followers that they are to love unselfishly, indeed benevolently, with goodwill toward those whom they love. In this way, Jesus loves his followers; in this way, his followers are to love one another.

Love of the kind that Jesus commanded changes the terms of the relationship between him and his followers. Until this moment they had been servants; from now on Jesus would call them friends. Jesus is the master who also is friend. Traditional Christian doctrine teaches that Jesus holds three offices: prophet, priest, and king. We must consider the possibility that here in John 15, Jesus added a fourth royal office—friend. The one who was called the "friend of sinners" takes us into a relationship of love that enables us to be called the "friends of God."

Church and World

John 17:1–6, 9–11, 15–24

Jesus' High-Priestly Prayer, as John 17 is often called, sharply sets his disciples against "the world." The world is a dangerous place, full of hatred for Jesus' disciples. Although they live in the world, Jesus' followers have no part in it. The Johannine writings all share this attitude that radically separates Christ and culture, the community of Jesus' followers and the world. Theologian H. Richard Niebuhr aptly sums up this radical separation:

> That world appears as a realm under the power of evil; it is the region of darkness, into which the citizens of the kingdom of light must not enter; it is characterized by the prevalence in it of lies, hatred, and murder; it is the heir of Cain. It is a secular society, dominated by the "lust of the flesh, the lust of the eyes and the pride of life," or, in Prof. Dodd's translation of these phrases, it is "pagan society, with its sensuality, superficiality and pretentiousness, its materialism and egoism." It is a culture that is concerned with temporal and passing values, whereas Christ has words of eternal life; it is a dying as well as a murderous order, for "the world passes away and the lust of it." It is dying, however, not only because it is concerned with temporal goods and

> contains the inner contradictions of hatred and lie, but also because Christ has come to destroy the works of the devil and because faith in him is the victory which overcomes the world. Hence the loyalty of the believer is directed entirely toward the new order, the new society and its Lord.[39]

In John 17, Jesus prayed for his followers in a way that clearly set them apart from the world. He prayed for their protection from the world even as he thanked God that the disciples, save one, had been preserved during the days of Jesus' ministry. Some Christians have worried that this Christ-against-culture attitude sets up the possibility of a church that insulates and isolates itself from the world. These people ask the questions: But didn't Jesus come to save the world and not condemn it? If Christians withdraw from the world, how can the world be saved?

The answer to these questions lies in John 17:20 and following verses. In these verses, Jesus' prayer connects the sanctification and unity of "those who will believe…through their message." As Jesus' followers are made one through the power of the sanctifying Spirit of truth and love, the world will come to believe that God sent Jesus (17:20–21). If Jesus' followers live in unity and holiness (that is, if the church will live as the body of Christ), then such a lifestyle creates the possibility that the world will recognize that it is the world and not the church. Such awareness is the necessary first step toward the world's salvation. It is through faithful discipleship that the church who is truly determined to follow Jesus loves the world. Loyalty to Christ is not a strategy of withdrawal to remain aloof from the world. Rather, loyalty to Christ enables the world's salvation.

Pilate

John 18:31–38; 19:12–16a

Pontius Pilate was the Roman procurator, or governor, of the province of Judea from AD 26 to 36. The accounts that come to us from extra-biblical sources portray him as a heavy-handed bully. On several different occasions, Pilate's use of his uncontested power disclosed his brutal, overreaching attitude. Philo of Alexandria reported that Pilate's administration was so disrespectful of Jewish religious beliefs that once the emperor himself ordered Pilate to desist. Philo went on to describe Pilate as guilty of insult, rape, murder, and inhumanity. He rather routinely incited the Jewish people to protest.

Pilate once marched the Roman legions into Jerusalem bearing their military standards with the image of the emperor. The Torah expressly forbade all images, and the actions of Pilate's soldiers offended the religious convictions of the inhabitants of Jerusalem. On another occasion, he intended to take money from the temple treasury to construct an aqueduct to increase Jerusalem's water supply. When crowds gathered in protest, he ordered Roman troops to bludgeon the crowd into silence and dispersal. Eventually, Pilate was recalled to Rome as a result of even worse treatment of Samaritan leaders.[40]

39. Niebuhr, *Christ and Culture*, 48.

40. *Interpreter's Dictionary of the Bible*, s.v. "Pilate."

The picture of a harsh and brutal Pilate that comes from such ancient writers as Philo and Josephus does not entirely square with the Pilate portrayed in the Gospels. The Pilate we see in the Gospels seems rather passive and reluctant to take action. This reluctance seems out of place in a man who once ordered Roman troops to surround a crowd of protesting Jews and keep them under guard for five days. In John's gospel, Pilate seems to have wanted to avoid trouble and ended up an unwilling tool of Jerusalem's religious elite. How do we account for this apparent difference in the sources' portrait of this man?

According to John, the real villains are people he referred to characteristically as "the Jews." Of course, these were not all Jews but a group of Jewish leaders. It wasn't until the climactic week of Jesus' life that the Romans entered the picture, and this because "the Jews" wanted Jesus executed. There is some difference of scholarly opinion here. According to the text, the Jews sought Roman involvement in Jesus' case because they said that only Romans could issue a death warrant. Jews were permitted, however, to use capital punishment in such traditional forms of execution as stoning. In Judea, only the Romans executed condemned criminals by means of crucifixion, and apparently that is the fate the Jews desired Jesus to suffer. To accomplish their purpose, they would have to gain Pilate's approval.

After questioning Jesus, Pilate protested to the crowd that he could not determine that Jesus had committed any crime, certainly not a capital offense. During this interrogation, Pilate asked the famous question, "What is truth?" It is tempting to read this as the ironic or sarcastic question of a world-weary bureaucrat, but we also see here the stark contrast between Jesus—the Truth—and a false and deceitful world that refused to acknowledge him. In either case, Pilate was reluctant to condemn this man in whom he could find no fault. Nevertheless, he gave in to the demand of the crowd. Pilate was in a difficult position. His previous administrative blunders may have raised questions about his ability to enforce the Roman peace in this part of the world. Perhaps he worried that his superiors in Rome were watching his every move. The Jerusalem leadership played him as if that was the case. In the end, they forced Pilate to choose between his political reputation and the life of an innocent man.

Jesus Crucified and Resurrected
John 19:16–30; 20:1, 11–18

In Book III of *Paradise Lost*, John Milton offers his interpretation of the moment when God the Father and God the Son entered into a covenant for the sake of lost humanity. Puritan theology was framed on the biblical theme of covenant, and good Puritan that he was, Milton saw a covenant that joined the Father and the Son within the very Trinity itself in the work of human redemption. As Milton depicted the moment when God foresaw the sin of Adam and Eve, he asked of all the citizens of heaven for one who would stand forth to offer satisfaction for this infinite sin against the infinite God; divine justice demanded recompense.

> Say, Heavenly Powers, where shall we find such love?
> Which of ye will be mortal, to redeem
> Man's mortal crime, and just the unjust to save?

Dwells in all Heaven charity so
  dear?
He asked, but all the Heavenly
  choir stood mute,
And silence was in Heaven...[41]

The voice of the Son of God crashes through the hush, promising to stand in the place of fallen humanity. The eternal Word through whom worlds were made will enter human history and subject himself to death.

Jesus' cross stands at the center of human history. His crucifixion and resurrection join to create the fulcrum on which the entire New Testament balances. These verses get to the very heart of the matter between God and humans. These are matters of such bedrock importance that one lacks adequate words to stress their significance. A few reminders, however, are in order.

(1) Although today the cross is a common object of decoration, in the first century it was commonly regarded as hideous. Romans used the cross to execute people whom they wanted to torture slowly to death. Death by crucifixion also marked a person socially. Like many other cultures then and for centuries after, Romans used several different forms of execution. Criminals of higher social standing were executed quickly, with comparatively low levels of pain. The execution of traitors, rebels, and slaves was an altogether different matter. They were crucified to send a message to anyone who might be thinking about revolution and as a mark of social stigma. Thus, it would never have occurred to Jesus' disciples to hang little crosses on chains around their necks any more than people today would wear necklaces sporting a miniature electric chair.

(2) Jesus was crucified between two thieves. This detail is not what held John's attention; it was the simple matter of a sign, a sign that had to do with Jesus' royal title. During Jesus' trial before Pilate, the Roman governor had asked whether Jesus was indeed king of the Jews. To a Roman diplomat, the whole scene must have seemed preposterous. How could the man standing before him be a king of any people, even a subject race such as the Jews? Hence Pilate's question to Jesus, "Are you the king of the Jews?" (18:33) can be read as heavily laden with sarcasm. By the same token, the sign that he ordered placed on Jesus' cross, "Jesus of Nazareth, the King of the Jews," (19:19) was not intended to honor either Jesus or his Jewish accusers. (In Western art, many depictions of the crucifixion show a sign above Jesus' cross on which are found the initials, INRI. These initials stand for the Latin version of the inscription Pilate ordered: *Iesus Nazarenus Rex Iudaeorum*). Pilate's sarcasm also was directed at the Jewish people he governed; that their king died such a degrading death degraded them as well.

Jesus' accusers understood the insult, and what is more, they did not want this man for their king. During the trial, Pilate had asked them whether Jesus was their king, and the chief priests had shouted back, "We have no king but Caesar" (19:15). They made their choice, and thus they wanted nothing to do with the man who hung on the cross underneath Pilate's sign. This man was not their king, so they went to Pilate and demanded that the sign be removed. But

41. Milton, *Paradise Lost*, 98.

Pilate would have nothing more to do with them or their dirty business this day. The Jews wanted nothing to do with Jesus. Pilate wanted nothing more to do with either Jesus or the Jews. "What I have written, I have written" (19:22). The Jews were dismissed, having been told, in effect, "Deal with it."

Only John's gospel includes the detail about Jesus' seamless robe, and unlike the Synoptic Gospels, John says that the sponge soaked in vinegar was raised to Jesus' lips on a stalk of hyssop. The Synoptics use the word *reed*. These two usages in John may be oblique references to the temple priesthood and the Passover. The high priest wore a seamless linen tunic. Was John hinting here at Jesus' role as the great High Priest? Similarly, hyssop was used as part of the Passover meal, which gives us grounds to ask whether John wanted his readers to remember Jesus once again as the "Lamb that takes away the sin of the world." While these details are peculiar to John's gospel, on another point he agrees with the Synoptics. All four Gospels have Psalm 22 in mind, and John pointedly cited it as the Old Testament scripture bearing on Jesus' suffering and alienation from God. Jesus had come to his own people, but they did not know him. In the end, they denied him. The Roman governor viewed him as an object of sarcastic scorn. Alienated from humanity and from God, Jesus breathed his last, saying, "It is finished." His work was complete, not "in the sense of over and done with but brought to consummation."[42] His work was complete.

(3) The theme of "Jesus falsely accused" runs all through John's gospel. Repeatedly, witnesses have appeared who testify on behalf of Jesus. The crucifixion and resurrection bring this theme to its dramatic conclusion and make an extremely important theological point. The Jews demanded that Pilate execute Jesus because he had broken the commandment forbidding blasphemy: "We have a law, and according to that law he must die, because he claimed to be the Son of God" (19:7). Torah was the law and Yahweh gave Torah to Israel. By this law a blasphemer must be put to death. From the standpoint of the Law Jesus stood justly accused *unless* he was who he claimed to be. The crucifixion was, in this sense, the Law's accusation and judgment against Jesus. But the crucifixion was not the final verdict. After Good Friday came Easter. In raising Jesus from the dead, God made a judgment in favor of Jesus. The tables were turned. Since Jesus was indeed who he claimed to be, he could not be guilty of blasphemy. Thus he was falsely accused under the Law but, raised by the power of God, vindicated in his claim to be the Son of God.

Easter Faith
John 20:1–29

In John's account of the first Easter, the resurrected Lord appeared in the garden only to Mary Magdalene. Earlier, Simon Peter and "the beloved disciple" (presumably John) had run to the garden upon her witness that Jesus' tomb was empty. John's account connects the empty tomb with only these three of Jesus' followers. Mary remained behind after Peter and John returned to the city. Then and there she encountered the risen Lord—but not before mistaking him for the gardener. Not until that evening did Jesus appear to the disciples.

42. Sloyan, *John*, 211.

A word that comes to mind from John in considering the Easter narrative is *ignorance.* We need not take this in a mean sense; we are not calling names here. It is simply that one is impressed by what Mary and the disciples seemed not to know. Much remained of which they were still ignorant. They neither knew nor did they immediately recognize what had transpired. Mary witnessed to this ignorance when she told Peter and, we believe, John, "They have taken the Lord out of the tomb" (John 20:2). Presumably "they" refers to somebody with sinister motives. Interestingly, Jesus' resurrection from the dead as an explanation of the body's absence seems not to have been a possibility for Mary. She seems to have thought that grave robbers had been up to some mischief or a well-intentioned gardener had perhaps rearranged things.

Peter and John also examined the tomb. Of John, verse 8 says, "He saw and believed." But this statement is followed immediately by, "They still did not understand" (v. 9). We believe before we understand. We may also believe in order to understand. Understanding and belief come to Mary a little later when the resurrected Lord called her by name. Then her eyes were opened and she saw both physically and also in the sense of insight. It is in this combined seeing that she returned to the disciples with the astounding sentence, "I have seen the Lord!" (20:18).

By the time of the writing of John's gospel, various interpretations of Jesus' life and death were already circulating. Some of these conformed to the Gospels while others did not. One such view historians now call Docetism. Docetists were dualists who thought that spirit/soul was good and matter/body was evil. In fact, matter—including human flesh—they considered so evil that Docetists contended that the eternal Word of God would never allow himself to be contaminated by contact with human flesh. Thus, they interpreted Jesus' life to mean that the Logos/Word of God only *appeared* to take on humanity. In actuality, the incarnation was an illusion. So said the Docetists.

John 20 and 21 take considerable pains to describe the resurrected Lord in material as well as spiritual terms. On two separate occasions, Jesus suddenly appeared in the midst of a gathering of disciples. The text takes care to inform us on both occasions that the doors were locked. Clearly, walls and locked doors pose no barrier to the resurrected Lord; however, to leave the account as such would have invited Docetists to press their claims that the divine Logos/Word only appeared to take on human flesh. Bodies do not suddenly materialize out of thin air.

By the same token, one cannot physically touch a spirit. One week after Jesus' first appearance to the disciples, he appeared again. Before the room was locked, but this time Thomas, who had been absent from the first meeting, was now present. He had been skeptical of their story and insisted that unless he could touch Christ's very wounds he would not believe. Once again, Jesus appeared and now granted Thomas his desire. For those early Christians worried about Docetism's threat to the faith, the story of Thomas served to illustrate powerfully the fact that, even after his resurrection, Jesus possessed a physical body that could be touched. Chapter 21 makes the same point even more graphically. Apparitions and ghosts do not eat. Here we are told that Jesus had prepared a breakfast of bread and fish for the disciples. The implication is that all ate—Jesus and the disciples, once again in narrative fashion disputing the Docetist interpretation of Jesus. In the context of the late first century, these narratives were read as saying, "The risen Lord is not a disembodied ghost! He is no apparition! God has raised him from the dead—body and soul."

In John's gospel, Jesus pronounces two beatitudes. The first comes in 13:17 after Jesus washed the disciples' feet. Those who do such things, he says, will be blessed. The other beatitude appears in 20:29. In contrast to Thomas, who had to see in order to believe (but whose stubborn persistence had served to make a point about the risen Lord's body), Jesus pronounced a particular blessing on all those who have not seen and yet believe.

Acts

The "Gospel of the Holy Spirit"
Acts 1:3–14

It is now a commonplace of New Testament scholarship to refer to Acts as the second volume of the work that began with the gospel according to Luke; together they are called "Luke-Acts." A comparison of the prologues to the two books, Luke 1:1–4 and Acts 1:1–2, will demonstrate this connection. Luke-Acts is a two-volume literary unit that tells the narrative of Jesus and the church empowered by the Holy Spirit. Of course, the life, death, and resurrection of Jesus form the center of this narrative. His ascension thus closes the gospel according to Luke as it also opens Acts. In Acts, the ascension serves as the final sign of Jesus' lordship.

Theologically speaking, Acts is the book of the Holy Spirit. *Apostles* may appear in the title in some versions, but the Holy Spirit commands the action from Pentecost forward. Peter and then Paul take prominent positions in the narrative, but the most important figure is the Holy Spirit. Acts 1:8 lays out a map or strategy for the expansion of the gospel. Directed by the Spirit, Jesus' closest followers witnessed to the death and resurrection of Jesus, first in Jerusalem, then in the surrounding province of Judea and into neighboring Samaria until at last the church expanded "to the ends of the earth."

The Holy Spirit is the soul of the church and thus the divine source of its life and motion. In Acts, the warm, enlivening breath of the Spirit blows through upper rooms, carries apostles from one district to another, gives others visions, and generally moves the church to action. The Spirit sets new members in the body of Christ; the Spirit gifts them and, through gifting, calls them into the Lord's service. In Acts, that service above all else means witnessing to the new life born of Christ's death and resurrection.

In the wake of persecution, the very earliest Christians identified themselves to one another by making the outline of a fish. A cross would have been too obvious; besides, ancient peoples were so offended by the very idea of crucifixion that they would not even walk through the shadow of a cross. The Greek word for fish is *ichthus*, which Christians used as an acrostic. Each letter of *ichthus* was the first letter of the phrase "Jesus Christ, God's Son, Savior." That phrase represented the very core of the good news. Undergirding that phrase were the testimonies of the persons who went out to the tomb on Easter only to find it empty.

In Acts we read of the promise of the Spirit. Although Jesus' resurrection thrilled his followers beyond words, those same followers wondered about the future. Acts 1:3–14 does not give us many clues about the subject of Jesus' talks with the disciples during the forty days following the resurrection, other than a general reference to the kingdom of God. Surely some if not all the disciples began to wonder what events were to occur next. It is in this context that the resurrected Lord promised that the Holy Spirit would soon fall upon his disciples. Of course, any promise requires the one to whom it is made to wait. A promise means that something will happen in the future; until that moment arrives, the one who received the promise must wait.

Sometimes we wait patiently and sometimes not. There is a note of that latter mood in the disciples' question concerning whether the moment had arrived when Jesus would restore Israel's glory. To that question, Jesus replied with a lesson about the limits of human knowledge. It is a lesson worth remembering whenever we fall prey to the temptation to unlock the secrets of the future, especially when trying to discern God's purposes in advance.

So the disciples returned to Jerusalem and awaited the promised Spirit. During their wait, they did what they could. They restored the number of disciples to its original twelve by selecting Matthias. And "they all joined constantly in prayer, along with the women and Mary the mother of Jesus, and with his brothers" (1:14). What better way to await God's promise?

Undoing Babel
Acts 2:1–4, 37–47

Acts is not only the book of the Spirit; it is also the book of the church. In Acts, we find the formative narratives of the church's early days. No event is of greater importance in those days than that described in Acts 2:1–4, 37–47. Paul teaches that the church is the body of Christ; the Holy Spirit is the soul of that body, the animating force that leads and guides it. Acts 2 relates the arrival of the Spirit promised by Jesus and the consequences for the tiny new church.

Theologian Stanley Hauerwas reads this narrative as the restoration of Babel. Recall the Genesis story of King Nimrod, who had arrogantly attempted to build a tower that would reach all the way to heaven. This monument to the king angered God, who turned it into a monument to human folly. To frustrate the tower's completion, God gave its builders different languages, making communication impossible. The world's many cultures and languages were thus born out of confusion. One of the sad outcomes is the frequency with which confusion has descended into strife and warfare.

Acts 2 narrates the undoing of this confusion. One consequence of the Spirit's activity was that everyone in the crowd on Pentecost could understand Peter and the disciples as they spoke: "Each of us hears them in his own native language" (2:8). Babel had led to disunity, but the arrival of the Spirit at Pentecost established the church as God's one body, a people of unity.

Unity in the place of disunity is one consequence of the Holy Spirit's presence. Jesus' followers, newly emboldened, is another, and Peter is the great example of this. On the basis of his behavior during Jesus' trial, few would have predicted that Peter would become such a bold and articulate preacher.

Peter's sermon was not calculated to entertain or please his listeners. He didn't attempt to ease them into the church by making them comfortable. There was no effort here to minimize their situation or help them picture God as nice. Instead, he reminded them that they, "with the help of wicked men, put [Jesus] to death by nailing him to the cross" (2:23). This was strong medicine that got even stronger when Peter made it clear that God's resurrection of Jesus stood directly opposed to this death and to those who were responsible for it. Hearing this, the crowd asked what they might do to be saved, and upon Peter's reply, three thousand souls were added to the church.

One additional consequence of the Spirit's work at Pentecost was that the Jerusalem believers took a different attitude toward their possessions. Many honest Christians tend to think of their possessions as their own. The church at Jerusalem offers a contrasting image. The church, first united through the power of the Spirit, was also one in table fellowship and in the property they held in common. Across the centuries, there have been Christians, such as the early Mennonites and contemporary Hutterites, who have been attracted to this ideal and followed it as one element of the full embodiment of Christian community.

Healing at the Beautiful Gate
Acts 3:1–10; 4:1–4, 13

The long narrative of Peter, John, and the man who was healed at the Beautiful Gate of the temple, found in Acts 3:1–10; 4:1–4, 13, witnesses to the Spirit's power to heal physical as well as spiritual maladies. The narrative also shows John and the still freshly transformed Peter in direct confrontation with the ruling religious authorities of Jerusalem. The Spirit also had worked powerfully in these disciples to enable them to speak articulately and confidently to a group whose power ordinarily would have intimidated most people of the disciples' social status. But this was no ordinary situation, and these were no longer ordinary men, for the Holy Spirit had come and was at work in the church.

Acts 2 concludes with a picture of the church that is withdrawn and hiding behind closed doors. It is a church that is safe and warm, where everyone knows everyone. But the gospel is to be shared and, in order to share, the church must reach beyond itself. The Spirit prompts the church to this action, and the church's action is formed around the gospel.

Peter and John attended prayers in the temple and were drawn to the lame man because the gospel was not meant to be hidden behind the closed doors of the church. When Peter and John saw the lame man, they gave him their most prized possession. They had no money, but the two disciples did have the power of the gospel, and they had just been praying in the temple. In the presence of this man who had not taken a step in his entire life, the disciples' prayer life and the gospel converged in the power of the Spirit.

We sometimes focus on the signs and wonders worked by the Holy Spirit in Acts. It is important to remember, however, that the Spirit acts in consort with and for the sake of the gospel. Peter's speech, addressed to the crowd that gathered to watch the lame man leap and dance, clearly makes the point. For the second time in Acts, Peter delivered a speech that was centered in and eloquently related the gospel of Jesus.

Peter began his speech by deflecting any praise away from himself and John toward God. The disciples' spirituality did not heal the lame man; neither did they possess any secret power to heal. Peter wanted his listeners to understand that magic was not the source of this miracle. At some points, people can confuse magic and religion. Magic is the claim to know and possess the ability to conjure and manipulate the forces of nature and even the gods. Religion never makes such a claim, but attributes the healing power to God. Peter made this distinction when he said, in effect, "Don't look at us. We didn't make this happen. It was the God of Abraham, Isaac, and Jacob who made the man able to walk" (see Acts 3:12–13).

The theological claims of Peter and John landed them in the middle of a controversy. In our world where church and state are constitutionally separated, the debate between the disciples and the Jewish ruling council may seem curiously outdated. In ancient Jerusalem, there was no separation of religion and politics or church and state. Religion could never be restricted to the private and personal recesses of one's own heart. On the contrary, religious convictions almost automatically carried very public consequences. Peter's speech and his theological claims struck at the very center of Jewish life, religion, and thought. The ruling council could not dismiss his words as the private ramblings of a religious fanatic. Therefore, they questioned him, and he answered in what must be described as a full-blown theological debate. The big surprise was that these rough-hewn, back-country fishermen handled themselves so well against the learned officials of the council. As in the case of the lame man, the disciples' success before the council was not to their credit, but to the Holy Spirit's.

Barnabas

Acts 4:32–37; 9:26–27; 11:19–30; 15:36–40

These four small units of scripture combine to give us what remains, admittedly, a sketchy portrait of Barnabas, a key figure in the early years of the church. Each unit displays some aspect of his character. Perhaps the place to begin is with the name by which we know him. Think of various nicknames given to people because of some defining characteristic: Slim, Swede, Curly. Barnabas is not a family name but a nickname meaning son of encouragement, and the text goes out of its way to tell readers that the disciples gave this name to the man formally called Joseph of Cyprus. Barnabas's presence was itself an encouragement to the life of the young church in Acts, even as he also actively encouraged others. He played an unusually positive role on developments in early Christianity.

We first meet Barnabas in the middle of a description about the early church and wealth. He was a Levite, a member of the priestly tribe, from the island of Cyprus. This is another way of saying that he was a Diaspora Jew, part of the dispersion that sent Jews all across the Roman Empire and beyond. Living in a society that was largely Gentile, Barnabas likely learned *koine,* the form of the Greek language that made international communication possible in the Roman Empire. A working knowledge of Greek would come in handy for any missionary. Acts 4 and 5 report the communal nature of the Jerusalem church. Propertied members of the church apparently were expected to sell their land and turn the proceeds over to the church treasury. Barnabas's willing participation stands over against the devious scheme of Ananias and Sapphira. Even if Luke intended no comparison, the contrast leaves Barnabas as a shining example of willing and faithful discipleship.

The next we see Barnabas, he is still in Jerusalem where he appears to have risen to a position of some prominence among the church leadership. Saul of Tarsus, newly converted and just returned from Damascus, tried to make contact with the church in Jerusalem. Understandably, Christians there suspected a plot. Saul had yet to live down his reputation as the ravager of the church. His sudden desire to join the fellowship would not have been the first time that an agent provocateur had attempted to gain admission to a secret group only to betray it later. But just as he had risked his personal wealth for the sake of the church, now Barnabas stood forth to risk his life—and perhaps the lives of the church leadership as well. Barnabas was the one to take Saul at his word, bring him to the Apostles, and speak as his advocate.

Saul's conversion and Christian witness turned out to be authentic. Since Barnabas had vouched for him, perhaps the Jerusalem church elders recognized in Barnabas the gift of spiritual discernment. The text describes him as a good man, filled with the Spirit and faith. When word came from Antioch that Gentiles were converting to the young Christian movement, the elders naturally sent Barnabas there on a fact-finding mission. He not only gave his blessing to this development, but Barnabas also took steps to ensure its extension by traveling to Tarsus in search of the man he believed was the right assistant for the work of teaching in Antioch—Saul, soon to be known as Paul. At this early stage, the relationship between the two men is caught in the phrase "Barnabas and Saul."

Acts 11:19–30 reports the famous Jerusalem Council. Again Barnabas was present, only this time it was as a member of the team "Paul and Barnabas." They had only recently completed a highly successful missionary tour of the province of Asia Minor. Many Gentiles converted to the new faith and, along with the Gentile Christians at Antioch, their presence in a church whose majority was Jewish Christian was bound to raise the question of whether the Torah applied equally to Gentiles as to Jews. At Jerusalem, Barnabas sided with Paul on this issue; the Law was to apply to Gentiles only in a very restricted sense. However, a reading of Galatians 2:13 suggests that Barnabas had lingering questions about this issue. This eventual difference with Paul may have had more to do than is apparent with the subsequent separation of this evangelistic team (Acts 15:36 and what follows).

Facing Persecution
Acts 5:12–42

It seems clear enough that Luke thought that the good news alleviates physical misery as well as release from the guilt and power of sin. The outbreak of this revolutionary healing gospel, powered by the Holy Spirit, turned Jerusalem topsy-turvy. Beginning with the lame man at the temple, the disciples healed many people suffering from physical maladies, confirming, as Acts narrates it, not just the gospel of Jesus; it is part and parcel of the good news. So in Acts 5 we read of miraculous healings that continue unabated. The disciples quickly earned a reputation for the ability to heal. This reputation grew to the point where people laid their suffering friends and relatives in the street where Peter's shadow might fall upon them as he walked by.

Jerusalem was astir with the actions and the message of the disciples. The rumors about Jesus' resurrection stubbornly persisted, coupled with the city's growing interest in his followers. This was anything but "business as usual" for the Jewish religious and political bureaucracy. In the face of the disciples' confidence and Spirit-filled power, the Jerusalem elite appear to have been a rather inept crew. They ordered the arrest of the disciples—also now called apostles, that is, "messengers"—expecting the usual strategy of threats and intimidation to work their desired effect. But the disciples were no longer men to be bullied. Filled with the Spirit, they stood up to the religious authorities in Jerusalem, even at the risk of imprisonment. God's power reached into their dungeon, undoing the order to jail the apostles before the ink was dry on the warrant that put them there. There was little the Jerusalem elite could do to quell the movement now spreading through the city they once thought they controlled.

In the face of the growing Jesus movement, the religious leaders were reduced to an impotent gag order on the disciples. But silence was the last thing on the mind of the suddenly articulate Peter, who soon found himself hauled in to face the Sanhedrin. Here the authorities and bureaucrats made a curious charge. They were upset and apparently worried that Peter was set upon assigning them the responsibility for Jesus' crucifixion. One wants to ask why they feared the truth that Peter once again forthrightly proclaimed.

His bold speech and the disciples' unwillingness to keep silent backed the Sanhedrin into a corner. A cornered adversary is especially dangerous. Their moral and religious bankruptcy now exposed, some in the council were determined to eliminate the troublemakers. At this point, the respected rabbi Gamaliel stood to oppose the majority's plan to escalate the violence. His wisdom, coupled with the presence of Nicodemus and Joseph of Arimathea, should remind us that not all intellectuals and members of the Jerusalem establishment opposed Jesus and his followers. Gamaliel reminded the Sanhedrin that other men had led revolts and created uprisings only to quickly fade from view. Time would tell. The Jesus movement would suffer the same fate unless it was truly sent from God. And if it was, the Sanhedrin was powerless to oppose it. Gamaliel's advice carried the day. The Sanhedrin stopped short of asking the Romans to execute the apostles but not short of a good beating. The storm clouds of persecution were thickening. The official number of lashes in a flogging was thirty-nine, enough to kill many people.

In the Face of Persecution
Acts 5:17–42; Hebrews 10:19–39

The New Testament does not gloss over the harsh realties of Christian life. Hebrews includes words like *suffering*, *insult*, and *confiscation*. The people to whom Hebrews was originally addressed had endured each of these and more. They stood in need of encouragement and instruction about how to go on in their discipleship under such threats. Acts 5:17–42 illustrates both the fact of persecution in the early church and the encouragement and strength that the young Jesus movement received from God's hand.

The Hebrews text encourages readers in practical matters of discipleship, but these practical matters of Christian living are grounded in theological concepts. The life of faith is rooted in the new covenant between God and humans. This unique covenant offers Christians privileges that they are to claim. Central to that uniqueness is Jesus Christ, the great high priest of the church. Hebrews reads the new covenant in terms of God's covenant with Israel. Thus, we find many references to features of Jewish religious life and worship. Taken together, they illustrate the potential of religious symbols to carry more than one meaning. Indeed, that multiplicity of meanings was precisely the source of friction between first-century Jews and Christians. Each group believed that it and it alone correctly interpreted the story and symbols of God's covenant with Abraham.

Medieval Christians commonly placed three theological virtues alongside the four cardinal virtues of justice, courage, temperance, and practical wisdom. The theological virtues are faith, hope, and love. Hebrews, unsurprisingly, refers to all three. Hebrews reminded readers of privileges under the covenant in Christ, but it also exhorts them to live out their responsibilities. God's love for us in Christ the high priest and resident in the Christian community, coupled with the faith and hope that also are privileges of the new covenant, combine to strengthen us for a life as the people who walk with the promising God.

If Hebrews presents a theological framework, Acts 5:17–42 provides an example of how that theology is lived out in the face of persecution. This story comes from the very earliest days of the Christian movement when Jesus' followers directly confronted the Jewish religious establishment. The issue between them went to the very heart of Judaism: Was Jesus the Messiah? The Jewish establishment answered in the negative; Jesus' followers answered yes. It was also the case that Jesus' followers were completely without social or political power and at the mercy of the Jewish leaders. Their political power, however, was no match for the power of God. Shortly after they order the arrest and imprisonment of some of the apostles, "an angel of the Lord opened the doors of the jail and brought them out" (Acts 5:19).

Ethnic Dissension
Acts 6:1–8; 7:55–8:1

Acts 6:1–8 and 7:55–8:1 frame the story of Stephen, the first Christian martyr. The narrative begins with a problem that was recurring in the life of the first-century church. Dissension arose in Jerusalem among Christians of different ethnic backgrounds. A large majority of Christians in Jerusalem were of Jewish origin. Moreover, they thought of themselves and the new faith as thoroughly Jewish. These Jewish Christians continued to attend prayers in the temple, and they also debated other Jews about Jesus' place in Judaism. These Jewish Christians testified that Jesus was the "Righteous One," as Stephen called him (7:52)—the Messiah of Israel. In these earliest days of Christianity, Jewish believers thus saw themselves as a movement within Judaism that brought its fulfillment.

First-century Judaism was not monolithic, and neither was the early Jesus movement. Jews were divided into several different religious and political factions (the Pharisees, Sadducees, Zealots, and Essenes). They were also somewhat divided culturally ever since the destruction of Samaria in 722 BC and their dispersion throughout the Mediterranean world. By the first century, Jews were scattered from Babylonia to Rome. The Jews who lived outside Galilee and Judea lived in a Gentile world and necessarily learned Greek, the Gentile language that served as the international medium of communication in that era. That the New Testament was originally written in Greek illustrates the broad reach of this culture and language. Periodically, these Greek-speaking Jews returned to Jerusalem either for extended visits or permanently relocating there. Some of these people became believers in Jesus and are the Grecian Jews referred to in Acts 6:1. The problem that erupted in the Jerusalem church had to do with the feeling of Greek-speaking Jewish Christians that they were second-class members of the church. This budding cultural conflict hints of the deeper Jewish-Gentile friction that later agitated nearly all of the Pauline churches.

The Jerusalem church had grown to a point where the Twelve could not effectively address all matters pertaining to its life. Some sort of division of labor was necessary. "In saying 'It is not right that we should give up preaching the word of God to serve tables' (6:2), the apostles are not disparaging such work; they are taking decisive action so that this necessary social (and liturgical?) administration might be assured—even though their words imply that the task of preaching is a primary apostolic duty."[43] We should not think that the only responsibility of seven deacons was ensuring the fair distribution of food to the widows and poor. One of the seven was Stephen, who possessed powerful gifts of preaching and healing. It was Stephen's preaching and other activities that attracted the attention of the Sanhedrin and eventually so angered them that they turned into a mob bent on killing him.

Associated with Stephen's killers was Saul of Tarsus, a Pharisaic Jew of the dispersion. Fluent in Greek as well as Hebrew, trained in the liberal rabbinic tradition of Hillel under Gamaliel, Saul lacked his teacher's wise tolerance. Zealous for the law and the traditions of his forefathers, he believed that the only way to deal with the Jesus movement was to suppress it, ruthlessly if need be.

The Church Suffers and Spreads
Acts 8:1–40; 13:1–3

Acts 8 begins with Saul's consent to the death of the Stephen. Our word *martyr* transliterates the Greek *marturos*,

43. Willimon, *Acts*, 59.

"witness." Stephen was stoned to death because his fearless sermon—"witness"—enraged the Sanhedrin. What could Stephen have said to provoke his listeners to such an extreme?

Stephen delivered a sermon in which he referred to Israel's frequent disobedience and its long, stormy relationship with God. Stephen began with Yahweh's call to Abraham and quickly moved forward in time to the long centuries of Israelite slavery in Egypt. He dwelt long and carefully with Israel's stiff-necked, rebellious attitude under the great leader Moses. This narrative was retold to make a point: "You stiff-necked people with uncircumcised hearts and ears! You are just like your fathers: You always resist the Holy Spirit!" (7:51). Stephen finished off the point by telling the Sanhedrin that in consenting to the death of Jesus, the Righteous One, they had "betrayed and murdered him" (7:52). That was more than enough to anger Jerusalem's religious elite, but Stephen testified that, just then, he had seen the heavens opening up and Jesus standing at the right hand of God. This vision was more than his listeners could bear. They rushed Stephen out of the city and stoned him to death. It was hot work, so they removed their outer robes and laid them at the feet of a young Pharisee named Saul of Tarsus, who watched the bloody scene with approval.

Saul was a determined enemy of the young Jesus movement. He regarded it as the worst sort of folly, a heretical offshoot of the true faith of Israel. As such, it was to be suppressed and eliminated. It is worth remembering that virtually nobody in the ancient world believed in freedom of religious expression; that is a much more recent idea. After Christianity became the official religion of the Roman Empire in 381, Christians even persecuted pagans. Later, during the Protestant Reformation, with John Calvin's approval, Reformed Christians at Geneva burned at the stake people who did not share their convictions. Still later, Puritans hanged four Quakers on Boston Common for the crime of being Quakers. We should not be too surprised at Saul's rush to eliminate Christians. It is only another chapter in a long and lamentable story.

Following the martyrdom of Stephen, violent persecution broke upon the church in Jerusalem. We do not know for certain that he was the leader of this campaign, but Saul of Tarsus "breath[ed] out murderous threats against the Lord's disciples" (Acts 9:1) and was bent on the church's destruction. Fearing for their lives, Christians living in Jerusalem fled the city. In this flight lies the second phase of the spread of the gospel.

Before his ascension, Jesus had told his followers that they would be his witnesses in Jerusalem, Judea, and Samaria, and to the uttermost parts of the earth (Acts 1:8). The gospel radiated out from its epicenter at Jerusalem. Bible students see in Acts 1:8 an outline for the entire book and often call it the "plan of Acts." The narrative begins in Jerusalem and ends in Rome. In between lies the story of the spread of the gospel, starting with the encounter between Philip and the Ethiopian. As previously, in Acts this spread was the work of the Holy Spirit, who uses persecution as a means of evangelism.

Philip appears to have been among those who fled Jerusalem in the face of Saul's persecution. He traveled first to Samaria, where he encountered a man named Simon. Miraculous healings and other signs accompanied apostolic preaching, and these extraordinary manifestations of spiritual power attracted Simon's attention. This was no accident, as he was by profession a sorcerer. Bible sorcerers and magicians occupied the gray world between religion and the malign forces of evil. People did not think of them as witches or warlocks but rather as manipulators of the spirit world. Sorcerers and magicians were believed to have knowledge of that world. Some of them—the magi of Matthew 2 (*magi* is a form of the word from which we get *magician*)—even used this knowledge to find their way to Jesus. Simon the sorcerer was a member of this general class. But Simon was inordinately attracted to the power by which Philip healed, apparently more interested in power than in the other aspects of the gospel. Finally Simon offered to pay Peter and John, who had subsequently traveled to Samaria, so he could receive the Holy Spirit. The apostles of course rebuked Simon, but his request gave his name to the practice of buying and selling leadership positions in the church that has ever since been called "simony."

Under God's direction, Philip departed Samaria for the region west of Jerusalem on the Gaza road. There he encountered an Ethiopian eunuch, a high official from the court of the *Kandake,* the queen of that people. The Middle Eastern world had long employed the practice of castrating young males for later employment in service where trustworthiness was especially critical. That this particular Ethiopian was reading the book of Isaiah is therefore doubly ironic. As a Gentile, his race disqualified him from Judaism. As a eunuch, according to the law in Leviticus, he was barred from ever entering the temple. We must not overlook these two facts. The Spirit directed Philip to a man who had no hope of salvation according to Judaism but who had every hope of salvation according to the gospel of Jesus. The story of Philip and the Ethiopian clearly and strongly implies that the gospel is for everyone. If the gospel is for everyone, then the church that is the community of that gospel is also for everyone.

Acts is, of course, the story of the scattering of the gospel seed unto the uttermost parts of the world. We see how that seed first left the mother church at Jerusalem and spread to Samaria. Later on, no person did more to scatter this seed than Saul himself. By the time we get to Acts 13:1–3, Saul is no longer the man who ravaged the Jerusalem church in 8:1–4. A few verses farther on (13:9), Saul is symbolically renamed Paul. Saul's conversion is so complete that he cannot even go by the same name. The one-time persecutor has been set apart for the work of scattering gospel seed.

Easter and the Damascus Road

Acts 9:1–31; Luke 24:1–12

Luke 24:1–12 and Acts 9:1–31 focus on Easter. The Luke passage is the familiar account of the women's visit to the empty tomb and the angels' announcement of Jesus' resurrection. Acts narrates the dramatic conversion of Saul of Tarsus on the Damascus road. At least two different approaches can be employed to link the two.

One way to consider these two texts is to examine them for the common element of surprise and sudden transformation. In both texts, God's power radically alters the expectations people bring to their situations. On the first

Easter, the women walked to the tomb in grief, their hopes and belief shattered by the crucifixion of Jesus. They had watched death's awful finality settle over his body, and on Sunday they approached his grave with no expectation other than to make final preparations for a proper burial. They had to revise their expectations immediately upon arriving at Jesus' tomb. They expected to find guards; none was present. They expected to find the tomb sealed; it was open. They expected to find Jesus' body; it was gone. The women went to the tomb expecting death; instead they were surprised by life. Easter is God's great reversal, the transformation that offers humans the ultimate hope.

Like Easter, and because of Easter, Saul's conversion is marked by reversed expectations. Saul departed Jerusalem determined to wreak havoc on the Christians in Damascus. This important Gentile city had a very large Jewish population, large enough to support several synagogues. The Jews there knew of Saul and the harm he had brought on the church in Jerusalem. Saul expected to persecute Jesus' followers in Damascus; instead he joined them. Ananias expected to go into hiding; instead he sought out Saul. Saul's former Jewish associates expected to welcome him to Damascus; instead they plotted his murder. The great reversal of Jesus' resurrection reversed the direction of Saul's life and the lives of people around him.

A second connection between Luke 24:1–12 and Acts 9:1–31 can be developed by considering the reality that the story of and witness to the resurrection formed the central message of the early church. On the heels of Saul's conversion, the gospel dramatically spread both ethnically and geographically. We will do well to remind ourselves of the core content of that gospel. Many New Testament scholars conclude that 1 Corinthians 15:3–7 is a concise summary of the gospel proclaimed across the Mediterranean world. Paul said that this gospel was the one he received. Does that mean that this message was part of his instruction under the disciples at Damascus? We cannot answer that with certainty, but it certainly seems logical to infer that it was. This gospel proclaimed that Jesus was crucified "for our sins...that he was buried, that he was raised on the third day"—all of this "according to the Scriptures"—"and that he appeared to Peter, and then to the Twelve." Jesus is the crucified and risen Lord. The same Jesus whose resurrection is celebrated on Easter is the Lord who appeared to Saul on the Damascus road and whom the converted persecutor Paul proclaimed from Jerusalem to Rome.

The Unity of the Church
Acts 10

Ever since the tower of Babel led to the division of human beings according to language, cultural and ethnic differences have played a large role in human relations. In some cases, ethnic awareness is benign and harmless. For instance, Americans still keep different customs at Christmas, often on the basis of the homeland of their immigrant ancestors. But in as many cases, ethnic difference is employed to demean, suppress, and, in the worst cases, destroy. We all have heard jokes that portray members of some ethnic groups as ignorant and degraded. Demeaning humor is finally not funny. In the extreme, the killing for human beings' "ethnic cleansing" takes ethnic difference to the level of the demonic.

Jews and Judaism followed the ancient world's pattern of ethnocentrism. By the era of the New Testament, Jews maintained a strict separation between themselves and non-Jews, who were, of course, called Gentiles; however, Jewish ethnocentrism added its own theological rationale to the standard attitudes of ethnic superiority. Jews pointed to God's covenants with Abraham and Moses as signs that God had chosen them and that they were therefore special. That belief contained an element of truth. God had chosen Israel, but as the means through which all peoples might be saved, not so that Israel could consider itself superior to those peoples.

Jewish ethnocentrism and separation intensified after the exiles returned from captivity in Babylon. Among Ezra's reforms was an insistence that the Jewish people be ethnically pure. Thus, he required all Jewish men to divorce their wives if they were of any other race. Later the Pharisees built what some scholars call a "politics of separation" on the tradition of Jewish ethnocentrism. The Pharisees believed that Israel would survive and return to its former glory only if its people maintained a strict wall of separation between themselves and the non-Jewish world. This policy influenced the lives and attitudes of Jews who were not part of the pharisaic party as such. It is also important to remember that powerful religious customs and practices reinforced the politics of separatism. The idea of clean and unclean that underwrote the laws of kosher not only governed everyday diet but could easily be extended to include separation from those peoples who ate unclean foods.

Acts 10 points to one of the great issues in the early church: Can the Gentiles be saved? Since Jesus' life and ministry occurred largely within and among the Jewish people and culture, the first Christians naturally enough were Jewish and assumed that Jesus was the Messiah of Israel. That he was also the Lord of the Gentiles was an idea that took the church awhile to accept. Against this background of ethnocentrism stands the story of Simon Peter's encounter with a Gentile believer, a Roman soldier who was "a righteous and God-fearing man" (Acts 10:22). Through this encounter, Peter came to the awareness that God "accepts men from every nation who fear him and do what is right" (10:35). This revelation played a vital role in the early church's realization that the gospel was not the private property of the Jews. If that was true, then the church would need to embrace the whole world and not limit its work to Israel alone. This amounted to a double conversion. God-fearer though he was, Cornelius needed to be converted to the Way. Peter, although already a disciple of the Lord Jesus, needed to be converted to the realization that the gospel is for everyone—the Jew and also the Gentile.

As is so often true of Scripture, God is the real subject of this narrative. God's angelic messenger spoke to Cornelius at Caesarea. God sent Peter a message through a vision. Before the story ended, the Holy Spirit was poured out on the Gentiles. God was the agent who brought about and was also the meaning of these events. The Acts narrative is the story of the unfolding mission of God: that the whole world may know the good news of salvation in Christ.

Gentiles at Antioch
Acts 11; 13:1–3

The irrepressible Spirit of God continued to spread the good news until it spilled over the cultural barrier of the Jewish people and religion. We have witnessed the Spirit's work in the lives of Peter and Cornelius. That story paves the way for the account of the church at Antioch and its dramatic expansion of the scope of gospel work. After hearing Peter's testimony, the Jerusalem church elders declared, "So then, God has granted even the Gentiles repentance unto life" (11:18). At Antioch that declaration bore fruit in the lives of Gentile believers.

The gospel spreads through all sorts of means. The Holy Spirit will not be blocked forever. The Spirit will find a way. In Acts 11:19, as in Acts 8:4ff, the good news was spread even through the effects of persecution. Stephen's death (Acts 7) unleashed a storm of persecution against the believers in Jerusalem. Antioch, a city some two hundred miles north of Jerusalem, became home to some who fled the city. Although intended to destroy the church, the persecutors' efforts succeeded only in expanding it. The Spirit has a mission for the church, and the Spirit blows where the Spirit wills.

Jesus and his disciples were all Galileans, and yet, from Jesus' passion and resurrection forward, Galilee plays a smaller and smaller part in the story of the expanding church. Perhaps Galilee was simply too small and too far off the paths of commerce and communication to be any kind of center for the Christian movement. In that sense, cosmopolitan Jerusalem, with its far-flung contacts to the wider world, offered a more attractive location for the church's leadership. Location may have been a critical factor, but we ought also to consider the influence played by certain attitudes, especially provincialism.

There were those Jewish Christians whose world was described by the borders of Galilee and Judea. For them, Jesus and his teachings represented the fulfillment of Judaism. They believed Jesus to be the Messiah of Israel, the Anointed of God who fulfilled the law and prophets. These people believed that the Jewish Messiah was for the Jewish people—period. Evangelism beyond the cultural borders of Judaism did not occur to them, and if it did, they rather quickly dismissed the idea as a fool's errand.

Other Jewish Christians thought differently. The New Testament sometimes refers to these people as "Hellenists," from the Greek word meaning "Greek." It is not necessarily that Hellenists were Greeks, but that they were sympathetic to the Greek-speaking world, that is to say, the entire Roman Empire. They could speak *koine*, the everyday Greek language in which the New Testament was originally written. Although themselves Jewish, the Hellenists' possession of this crucial linguistic skill enabled them to move about confidently in the Gentile world. Saul of Tarsus is perhaps the greatest and best example of the Hellenists.

Saul may have been the greatest of the Hellenists, but he was certainly not the first. Today's Bible lesson refers to "men from Cyprus and Cyrene" who traveled to Antioch and took the momentous step of including Greeks—which can signify any non-Jewish, Greek-speaking person—in the audience of potential gospel listeners. Today we are so accustomed to the idea that the gospel is for anyone and everyone that it can be difficult for us to appreciate the significance of this attitude and its consequences. It decisively answered the question, Who is the gospel for? And yet, the decisive step at Antioch required confirmation by the leadership in Jerusalem.

The momentous step of bringing the Gentiles within the gospel's reach had to be judged by the teaching of Jesus. The elders in Jerusalem were responsible for interpreting that teaching. After concluding that the gospel was for Jew and Gentile alike, the elders also insisted that new converts be diligently instructed in the new faith. As William Willimon comments, "Christianity…is a religion to be discussed, learned, debated, and taught. It was 'in Antioch that the disciples were for the first time called Christians' (v 26). Here is a faith so strange, so against the grain of our natural inclinations, that only by careful instruction and long-term nurture can it be apprehended in the lives of those who would believe."[44]

The church's evangelistic efforts took a dramatic turn at Antioch. Until this moment, Gentile conversions happened rather piecemeal. If a Roman centurion or an Ethiopian court official took an interest in Jesus and wanted to be saved, well, that was fine. The difference at Antioch was that here Gentiles were made the focus of Christian witness. The Ethiopian eunuch more or less overheard the gospel, but the Christian witnesses at Antioch spoke directly to the Gentiles. Quite intentionally, the eternal life of the gospel was made available to non-Jews by those who believed that nice people did not eat with Gentiles.

The text declares that "the Lord's hand" (11:21) was with the evangelistic efforts of the church at Antioch. These conversions were central to the Acts narrative, even as conversion is central to the life of the church. Moreover, in Acts conversions are testimonies to the power of God. Conversion is not the end of the story but the beginning.

Conversion inaugurates a new way of life, a new form of existence where we increasingly learn to envision the new possibilities that God has in store for the church. Those new Christians who opened the door to the Gentiles at Antioch had themselves been converted and as such opened, however tentatively, to a new way of seeing the people of God. That new fellowship—the people of God—embraced both Jew and Gentile as believers.

New Out of Old
Acts 13

The Antioch church was an extraordinary church. According to the Acts narrative, this body of believers lived on the edge of the new thing that God was doing in their midst. They first embraced that divine newness in the evangelism of the Gentiles. Second, they globalized their evangelistic efforts by commissioning Barnabas and Saul (Paul) for this work in obedience to the command of God. The Christians at Antioch were willing to innovate— and willing to risk—in order to advance the gospel.

The leadership at Antioch also made this church distinctive. Of those listed in Acts 13:1, three deserve special mention. Barnabas was the most senior on the list. A native of Cyprus, he was a Jew of the Diaspora, meaning a Jew who lived primarily in the Greek-speaking

44. Ibid., 106.

culture of the Greco-Roman world. This world extended even to the Scriptures that Barnabas read, a Greek translation of the Hebrew Bible (what Christians call the Old Testament) called the Septuagint. That would have been the Bible with which Barnabas likely was most familiar. As Barnabas, so Saul was a Diaspora Jew. His hometown of Tarsus was located on the southwestern shore of Asia Minor (modern-day Turkey). The third person deserving special mention is a man named Manaen—about whom we know nothing other than what the text tells us. Clearly, Acts wants us to notice this man, for from the text we learn that he "had been brought up with Herod the tetrarch." Manaen had been raised in privileged surroundings that tended to produce people like Herod, political lackeys who wished to curry favor with Rome. Nevertheless, Manaen had been converted. Along with Saul, his conversion represented a dramatic departure from his former life.

The second half of Acts 13, in particular, contains several quotations from the Old Testament. These serve to remind us that in the New Testament church the Old Testament was not at all old. It was the church's only text and therefore simply "the scriptures." Old Testament books cited in Acts 13 include Psalms, Isaiah, and Habakkuk. Today scholars refer to this practice of the text citing an earlier text as intertextuality. Old Testament scholar Walter Brueggemann sees something very important at work in the life of the biblical community that allows it to read and then cite scripture in this way.

> [Intertexuality] is not simply a literary device…to observe in the midst of a text. It is also one of the principal strategies taken up by this [scriptural] community, whereby the community is able to remain itself in the midst of many temptations and pressures. This texted community lives through time by its intentional, long-established utterance. We who would belatedly enter into that discourse must marvel at the glad saturation in the text undertaken by its members, and must see to our own attentiveness to that same saturation.[45]

The church is formed by the great narrative of God, Israel, Jesus, and the church recorded in the Scripture. Like the church in Acts, the church of today must be a "texted community" saturated in the Scripture not only in terms of knowledge but in the formation of our character as the people of God. It is through such situations that the church may become a people capable of living faithfully to the God revealed in Scripture.

A Missionary Church
Acts 13:14–52

We stand at the far end of the Christian tradition from the days when that tradition was first formed. Thus, we often have a little trouble imagining that what has now been Scripture and the teaching of the church for nearly two thousand years once itself was new and in the process of formation. And yet, that is exactly the situation as narrated by Acts where we read of new, and in many cases, surprising developments in the early church. A fresh and fuller reading of these biblical texts requires us to try to set aside our knowledge and familiarity with

45. Brueggemann, *Theology of the Old Testament,* 80.

the Christian faith and read these stories as first-time eyewitnesses to the events they recount.

Acts 13:14–15 and 42–52 deals with the first intentional missionary journey in the history of the church. The simple, matter-of-fact tone of Luke's narrative understates the significance of the Antioch church's momentous decision. In today's media-saturated society, the first enterprise of virtually anything—including many church activities—seeks full press coverage and splashy announcements. Quite the opposite seems to have been the case at Antioch, and part of the power of the Acts account is its simple, straightforward narrative of decisions and events that decisively changed the course of history.

The Gentile-oriented church at Antioch commissioned two of its leaders, Paul and Barnabas, to spread the gospel still farther beyond the land of its origin. Their journey took them to places where increased contact with Gentiles was inevitable. Not that the missionaries either forgot or ignored their own people. Paul's standard missionary practice was to find the local synagogue and there preach the gospel first to the Jews. Acts 13:16–41 contains the message that Paul proclaimed at the synagogue in Antioch of Pisidia. Presumably this was the basic sermon that he delivered wherever he encountered a body of Jewish people. Pauline practice was to preach first to the Jews but also then to the Gentiles. Himself a Jew of the dispersion, a Roman citizen, and therefore much more at home in the Gentile world than the Palestinian Jewish Christians, Paul's personal history and background made him exceptionally well-suited to the task of Gentile evangelism.

It would be wonderful to report that everyone who heard Paul and Barnabas also received the gospel. That would be untrue and perhaps also unrealistic. Jesus himself had said that the Kingdom is like a farmer broadcasting seed; some fall on good soil, some on thin soil, and some on hard and stony ground. Among Paul's listeners there were some stony hearts. While it is important to remember that some Jews did become believers, Luke also pointed out Jewish opposition to the gospel and explained its sources. At Pisidian Antioch, Jewish opposition was grounded in mere pettiness. At Iconium, some Jews simply refused to believe. It is also the case that some Gentiles either misunderstood or opposed the gospel. Gentiles at Lystra mistook Barnabas and Paul for the Greek gods Zeus and Hermes. Gentile merchants at Ephesus got angry with Paul and his associate Gaius Aristarchus because the gospel message cut into profits from sales at the pagan temple of Artemis. Opposition could come from any quarter. The recurring pattern in Acts, however, is that Jewish opposition to the gospel, coupled with Gentile receptivity, explains the rapid growth of the good news among the non-Jewish peoples.

Debate Over Entrance Requirements
Acts 15:1–2, 6–15, 19–20

Several years ago in a cover story on the changes in American Catholic church life since the Second Vatican council, *Time* magazine quoted an elderly Catholic lady in Iowa as saying, "Well, I hope I die soon so I can die a Catholic!" The woman had lived through sweeping changes in practice that had markedly affected her own religious life, and she was not happy with the result. Many people hold very tightly to the traditions of their religion. Because religion deals with the most basic level of our being, believers become unsettled when their traditions are questioned or altered. This unsettledness is due to more than mere discomfort in the face of change. Like Tevye the milkman in *Fiddler on the Roof*, many people believe that in the absence or alteration of religious tradition life becomes morally and theologically precarious.

The success of the Gentile mission raised questions about the religious traditions kept by Jewish Christians. Recall that the church in Jerusalem and Judea was composed of a large majority of Jewish Christians. Recall further that these Jewish Christians did not think of the Jesus movement as the development of a new religion. They understood Jesus and his teachings as the fulfillment of the law and the prophets. Therefore, Jewish Christians saw no conflict between the ritual and traditions of Judaism and the teachings of Jesus. In fact, they expected converts to the Jesus movement to learn and keep the traditions of Judaism. Outsiders to these traditions—namely the Gentile converts to Christianity—wondered whether their new faith required them to keep the Law of Moses.

A faction within the Judean church, Jewish Christians who perhaps were once or still remained Pharisees, insisted on uniformity among all believers. According to their view, since Jesus was the fulfillment of Judaism and not one jot or tittle of the law was to pass away, it was necessary that all male Gentile converts undergo circumcision. This was among the most important of Jewish traditions. Circumcision was the sign of God's covenant with Abraham and required of all males as a condition of admission to the covenant people of God. It was unthinkable that Jewish parents would not circumcise their sons. In the eyes of many Jewish Christians, it was equally unthinkable that converts to the way of Messiah Jesus should not undergo circumcision. Raising the issue of Gentile Christian circumcision as an open question would unsettle Jewish Christians who thought that this tradition was simply a given, a fact of life as the people of God. How could so central and important a tradition suddenly be optional?

The Jerusalem conference of the early church convened to consider questions related precisely to matters of religious tradition and obligation. What elements of the Law of Moses were binding on all Christians, Jew and Gentile alike? Were Gentiles to be circumcised? Could they consume meat that was cut from animals offered in sacrifice in pagan temples? James, elder of the mother church in Jerusalem, advised Gentile Christians that while they were excused from the expectation of circumcision and much of the Mosaic Law, nevertheless some elements of that law remained binding for them as well as their Jewish brothers and sisters.

Timothy

Acts 16:1–5; Philippians 2:19–24; 1 Timothy 1:1–3; 2 Timothy 1:3–5

In the New Testament church, perhaps no person more than Timothy combined in his person the ancient division that separated Jew from Gentile. Timothy was Paul's beloved son in the gospel. Paul said so to other Christians, even as he told this directly to

Timothy himself. The child of a marriage between a Jewish women and a Gentile man, Timothy stood to symbolize the church's overcoming of ancient suspicions and prejudices.

There remain in the modern world many places where people are divided by race or religion. To recall some of these is perhaps to begin to appreciate the ancient world's separation according to caste and ethnicity. Thus, Jews separated themselves from the *goyim*, the Gentiles, through a system of rules and regulations called *kashrut*, "kosher." Gentiles, which is to say all those who were not Jews, were thought to be unclean. They ate animals that the Torah said were unclean—pork chops, lobster, and shrimp, to name a few. From our perspective, such sanctions appear to govern only elements of everyday life that have nothing to do with religious faith. But first-century Judaism was a religion that believed that God's law covered every aspect of life—from religious ceremonies in the temple to the manner in which a Jewish wife cleaned and stored her dishes. Judaism was the religion of the covenant people of the Lord God and as such could not be restricted to only the spiritual realm. Rather, religion, according to the Torah, was about the physical and material aspects of life as well. Circumcision was the most important symbol of the special covenant of Jews with God.

Jews lived in the world of the Gentiles but not of that world. Some of those Jews became followers of Jesus, but that conversion did not mean that they stopped being Jewish and following all of the customs of *kashrut* according to the manner in which they had been taught. So it was that the conversion of Gentiles could not help but raise very large questions for the fledgling Christian community. Since these Jewish Christians looked at Jesus as the promised Messiah, they quite naturally looked at him as the fulfillment of the Torah, even as predicted by the prophets. For these Christians, the Torah remained very much in force. From their point of view, since that was the case, any Gentile who became a Christian was expected to keep the commandments. As children of the covenant with Abraham through their conversion to Christianity, these Gentiles needed to undergo circumcision, or so contended the Jewish Christians.

Paul and Timothy met on the former's second missionary tour of Asia Minor. The young man's spiritual legacy was impressive, as were the signs of his own faith. Paul saw great potential in him and determined to take him on the journey, and Timothy appeared to have gifts that would prove of great benefit to the church. This was always Paul's litmus test: Will this person, will this action, add to the life of the church? Will it strengthen the body of Christ? Prior to leaving Lystra, however, there was a technicality that had to be addressed. Since Timothy's father was a Gentile, and because fathers controlled the lives of their children in the ancient world, Timothy never had been circumcised. Now, the Jerusalem Council had declared that Gentiles need not submit to this procedure. Nevertheless, the same Paul who had argued that very point in Jerusalem now required Timothy to be circumcised before joining him and Silas. Paul the rabbi even performed the procedure himself.

Timothy's willingness to undergo circumcision is perhaps an indication that the decision at Jerusalem had not yet persuaded Jewish Christians. Paul feared their reaction if word spread that an uncircumcised half-Jew was engaged in gospel work. It is surely a sign of submission and an expression of the young man's willingness to be of service to Christ and the church. Timothy was willing to place his life in service—not on his terms, but on those of the church.

The Open Door to Europe
Acts 16:6–15, 27–33

The Antiochene church's decision to send Paul and Barnabas as missionaries changed the course of history. As much as Jews, Gentiles subsequently became the focus of evangelism. The missionary expansion of the church soon reached even more historic proportions. Thus far, Luke's narrative in Acts has recounted the exploits of the apostles among people on the western edge of the Asian continent. Christianity grew first in Asian soil. These verses tell the story of the gospel's step onto the European continent, where it eventually became the overwhelmingly dominant religion. One can hardly overestimate Christianity's influence on Europeans and their culture from ancient times throughout the Middle Ages and beyond—all of this because Paul and his companions answered the call.

The events described in Acts 16:6–15 and 27–33 occurred on what we now refer to as Paul's second missionary tour. The trip began out of his concern to visit the churches that he and Barnabas had established when they first traveled to the island of Cyprus and the towns of the Roman province of Asia. Before their departure, the partners on the original journey had a falling-out over a third member of the group. Barnabas wanted John Mark to accompany them again, but Paul disagreed because he had quit the first tour. This split carries more than a little sadness. Years earlier, it was Barnabas who, upon inspection of the rapid increase in the number of Gentile converts at Antioch, had remembered Paul and had gone searching for him at Tarsus. Sooner than others, Barnabas had recognized Paul's potential as a leader of the young church, and eventually the two men shared many labors in its cause. Nevertheless, when the time came to leave Antioch, Barnabas took John Mark to Cyprus and Paul selected a new partner, Silas, for the trip back to the churches of the province of Asia.

To Paul's group soon was added the man who became his beloved associate, Timothy, a well-respected follower of Jesus who lived in the town of Lystra. Some scholars conclude that Luke also was a member of this group. At Acts 16:11 the narrative switches from a third person account to first person; Luke started using the pronoun *we* as if he was a traveling companion. We cannot say with certainty when Luke might have joined the little missionary band. Did he depart Antioch alongside Paul and Silas, or did he join them somewhere along the way? In any case, it was a group larger than the original duo that came to Troas.

Troas was a standard port-of-call on the northwest coast of the Roman province of Asia. Its location meant that it naturally faced west toward Europe. It was a natural meeting place for merchants and sailors from east and west. There is little mystery in Paul's vision of a European—a man from the province of Macedonia, north of Greece, across the Hellespont. Many Europeans walked the wharves and streets of Troas. Paul and the other members of the apostolic band could scarcely have missed them.

It is both interesting and instructive that Paul's vision did not remain private. It may have been him alone who saw the Macedonian man asking for help, but the result was the group's common understanding that the message of the vision included all of them. Acts 16:10 balances private vision with corporate decision. Paul alone had seen and heard the Macedonian cry, but the entire group—"we"—prepared immediately to leave for Macedonia because all—"we"—had concluded that God had called "us"—the entire group—to preach the gospel.

The Gospel Knows No Boundaries
Acts 17:22–34

Athens was the greatest intellectual city of the ancient Mediterranean world. During the age of classical Greek civilization, this comparatively small city-state produced three of the finest philosophical minds of the Western world: Socrates (469–399 BC), his pupil Plato (429–347 BC), and Aristotle (384–322 BC). Plato founded a school, the Academy. Aristotle, who studied with Plato there, later founded his own school called the Lyceum. These outstanding thinkers laid a foundation for philosophy at Athens that made it the home of speculative thinking for centuries afterward. The two schools of thought mentioned in Acts 17, the Epicureans and Stoics, continued Athens' tradition of philosophy more than three centuries after Aristotle's death.

Epicureans and Stoics both practiced philosophy with the intent of freeing the soul from the cares and problems of this world. In other words, they employed sophisticated intellectual tools in the pursuit of a life of happiness. In doing so, they rejected the crude polytheistic religion of the Greco-Roman world. The gods of that religion were little more than larger-than-life projections of human characteristics with no great moral advantage over men and women. Therefore Greco-Roman mythology was filled with stories in which some gods behaved almost like spoiled children who got whatever they wanted merely because they were stronger than anyone else. Such tales disgusted philosophers like the Epicureans and Stoics, who preferred to think in abstract principles rather than anthropomorphic myths. They would have ignored the statues crowding Mars Hill (Areopagus) as mere props for the superstitious. That hill served more as the gathering place for those who wanted to engage in philosophy than a place of worship.

This meeting begins with Paul reasoning (17:17) with members of the local synagogue about Jesus as the Messiah, a customary Pauline strategy. Some philosophers overheard him and wondered what "this babbler" (17:18) meant by such talk. To the Epicureans and Stoics, Paul's *theological* language, such as his positive references to God and God in Christ, would seem to have been a step backwards into unnecessary god-talk. To hear him out, they nevertheless invited him to address the philosophy discussion group on the Areopagus.

Paul's address is an interesting example of the effort to state the gospel in language that draws on the vocabulary and ideas of the listeners more than those of the speaker. The name for this strategy is apologetics, which means to make a learned defense of the faith. Notice that in his speech Paul rather uncharacteristically did not refer to the Scriptures of Israel. Instead he attempted to present the good news of God's action in Christ in the vocabulary of his philosophical audience. Paul's speech was an effort to meet his listeners more than halfway.

We would have to say that Paul's speech got a mixed reception. Some listeners sneered at the idea of the resurrection. Their disbelief may have been rooted in the Greek idea that the soul is immortal but not the body. In their view, the resurrection of a body was unnecessary. The number of people converted to belief in Jesus as a result of this speech was quite small, leading some scholars to conclude that the strategy of Paul's speech either backfired or was flawed from the start.

One final historical footnote: the one named male convert on the Areopagus was Dionysius. Centuries later a Syrian Christian signed the name Dionysius the Areopagite to a collection of writings that stimulated the growth of Christian devotional writing and mysticism in the medieval Orthodox and Catholic churches.

Two Trusted Co-laborers

Acts 18:1–4; Romans 16:3–4; 1 Corinthians 16:19; 2 Timothy 4:19

Acts refers to a pair of gospel workers named Aquila and Priscilla, leading with the husband's name. In his first Corinthian letter, Paul followed that same pattern, but in Romans and 2 Timothy he reversed the order of their names. Is there some significance to this change? Had Priscilla assumed a leadership role in the churches where she and her husband served? Or can we consider the possibility that this name order is random, that Paul did not mean to suggest anything by it? Such questions ought to be considered when reflecting on the composition and writing of the New Testament. Is there the possibility that some of the words, particularly lists of names in the letters, are written with no large significance other than simply to say hello? Or is every word, prepositions included, freighted with significance and meaning in just exactly the order they appear in the text?

Aquila and Priscilla were Jewish refugees from Rome. They had been expelled during the reign of Emperor Claudius and had fled to Corinth where they met Paul. These two Jewish people were among the few members of the Corinthian synagogue to give Paul a fair hearing, let alone convert to Christianity. Convert they did, however, and they opened their home to Paul, where he not only stayed but also worked at the trade of tent making that he shared with Aquila. In the ancient world, small tradesmen such as Aquila performed their work at home. It is not likely that Paul carried tools with him, so if he was to support himself financially, he would need to find someone like Aquila who owned tools, a shop, and a willingness to take on new help. Priscilla and Aquila turned out to be unusually supportive. Paul later described them as his faithful co-workers. They traveled with him and eventually returned to Rome prior to Paul's arrival as a prisoner, for he sent greetings to them at the conclusion of his letter to the church there.

How did early Christianity regard these two dedicated gospel workers?

Ambrosiaster comments on Romans 16:3–4, saying, "These were Jews who, after they believed, became co-workers with the apostle because they had believed correctly and were thus able to persuade others to accept the right faith. Apollos, for example, although he was learned in the Scriptures, was nevertheless taught the way of the Lord more correctly by them. This is why Paul calls them his fellow workers in *Christ Jesus.*"[46] The second- and third-century theologian and exegete Origen said that the fact that Paul and the churches gave thanks for Priscilla and Aquila "shows that [they] were hospitable to Gentiles as well as to Jews. Hospitality is highly esteemed both by God and by man."[47] And the great fourth-century preacher St. John Chrysostom expanded on this point, saying, "Here Paul hints at their hospitality and financial assistance, holding them in admiration because they had both poured forth their blood and had made their whole property available to everybody. Notice how noble were the women Paul named. They were in no way hindered by their sex from following the path of virtue, and this is only to be expected. *For in Christ there is neither male nor female.*"[48]

One additional commentator, Pelagius, suggested that all Christian churches down to his own time in the fifth century should give thanks for Priscilla and Aquila; for in risking their lives to save Paul's, they preserved the teaching of the man whose works have done so much to shape a Christian understanding of what he called the gospel of Jesus Christ.[49]

46. Bray, *Romans*, 370.
47. Ibid.
48. Ibid., 370–71.
49. Ibid., 371.

Saying Good-bye
Acts 20:18–32

In Acts 20, Paul is on the return leg of a missionary tour that had taken him from Troas to Philippi, Thessalonica, Athens, Corinth—where he remained an especially long time—and Ephesus, leaving new churches everywhere in his wake. We find him about to set sail for Jerusalem. Even though he had a sense of foreboding about this journey, Paul was determined to go, compelled as he was by the Holy Spirit.

Paul's speech to the Ephesian elders was marked by repeated references to humility. He was not engaging in some sort of self-contradictory boasting about being humble. By the time of this address, Paul had acquired opponents within the church as well as without. People who were supposedly his brothers and sisters in Christ had questioned his apostolic credentials, falsely accused him, and spread malicious rumors about his work and character. It is understandable that Paul would want his associates at Ephesus to have a clear and accurate account of his attitudes and practices if, as Paul himself believed, he would never have another opportunity to talk with them.

The Christian virtue of humility stood in countercultural opposition to the values and ideals of Roman society. Romans were militaristic conquerors. By the New Testament era, their armies had occupied a territory that stretched from Persia in the east, across North Africa and Europe, to England in the northwest. Romans asserted that their soldiers enforced a Pax Romana, a "Roman peace" across the *oikumene* (from which we get "ecumenical"), the "inhabited earth." As is often the case with conquerors, the Romans overestimated the sweep of their power. Power, might, honor, and glory were coveted in the Roman world of conquest and achievement, such that the sentence, "I am a Roman citizen" was uttered proudly and often not without a certain arrogance.

Against the Roman virtues that glorified personal achievement, Christianity put forward a very different understanding of the ideal person. Paul had encouraged the Philippian Christians, "Your attitude should be the same as that of Christ Jesus" (Phil 2:5). Paul taught his churches that Jesus is the model of human existence as God had always intended it to be. Paul practiced what he preached. He asserted no privilege that might demand special favor or attention in the church. He sought financial contributions for the relief of famine-stricken Christians in Jerusalem but took nothing for his own pocket, supporting himself and his associates by the work of his own hands. As taught and exemplified by Paul, Christianity could not but appear to run counter to the ideals and values of the dominant culture of Rome. Countercultural religion implies a criticism of those values. Eventually, the Romans recognized that criticism and began taking steps to eliminate it. Opposition grew into waves of imperial persecution that recurred for 250 years.

On the eve of his departure for Jerusalem, Paul may have glimpsed the terrible future that threatened his beloved church. He certainly had a sense of foreboding about his personal future. Nonetheless, he also believed that he himself and the church were secure in the hands of God, who would neither forsake nor leave them alone in an increasingly hostile world.

The Life of Paul

Acts 26:12–23, 27–29

One of our most important sources for biographical information about Paul comes from Acts 26:12–23, 27–29, which occurs near the conclusion of Acts. The text itself is his last recorded defense of Christian faith and his discipleship. In the classic tradition of apologetics (from the Latin *apologia*, meaning "to defend"), Paul recounted to King Agrippa the narrative of his conversion to Christianity and consequent life as a disciple and apostle of the one Paul customarily called "the Lord." Paul's narrative included some biographical details that will be expanded here.

We know from the New Testament that Paul grew up in Tarsus, a city in southern Asia Minor. Presumably he was born there, although the text does not state that specifically. Growing up a Jew in an important regional center of the Roman Empire meant that Paul—or Saul, his given name—was raised as one of a large number of Diaspora Jews, even as his first missionary partner Barnabas. Jews who resided in Judea or Galilee lived within a dominant culture that was Jewish. Diaspora Jews lived within a small, close-knit Jewish community surrounded by the dominant Greco-Roman—Gentile—culture. Survival in that culture dictated that Jews learn to negotiate their way in the Gentile world. One crucial aspect of that negotiation was to acquire the language of that culture. Thus, Paul early on learned to speak and write the common Greek of that day—*koine*, the language of the New Testament. It should not be terribly surprising to us that when the early church sought candidates for missionary work, the first two they selected were

Diaspora Jews who had converted to Christianity—Barnabas and Saul.

From Paul's defense, we also learn that he was a Pharisee. This is not new information at this point in the Acts narrative, but presumably it was news to Agrippa. Our word *Pharisee* transliterates a Hebrew word meaning "the separated ones." A Pharisee is one who is separate—but from what? The Pharisees were those who lived separately from all that was ritually unclean. Such a mind-set would be even more indelibly stamped on a small community of Jews living far from Jerusalem and surrounded by Gentile culture. So it is that Paul described the Pharisees as the strictest sect of Judaism and himself as a Pharisee of the Pharisees (Acts 23:6; Phil 3:5).

Paul had studied with the famed rabbi Gamaliel. Presumably this was the same man who cautioned the Jerusalem leadership against a policy of persecution against the young church, saying that if it was of God, they wouldn't be able to kill it in any case. If this was the same Gamaliel, then clearly Paul at least on this occasion did not heed his teacher's advice. Early on, Paul embarked on a policy of violence directed against the church. The earliest mention we have of him in this connection puts him at the scene of Stephen's stoning, and that raises intriguing questions about Paul's whereabouts during the last week of Jesus' life. Might he have been in Jerusalem? The text reports nothing at all about this possibility, and since any answers to that question would be conjectures from silence, it is best not to push down that road. In any case, the road that mattered most in Paul's life was the one that led to Damascus.

Romans

Apostles and Geniuses

Romans 1:1–13, 16–17

Although it is not exactly accurate to apply the label "systematic theology" to Paul's letter to the Romans, it does express a comprehensive understanding of God's salvation in Jesus Christ: *through faith in Christ God's righteousness is available to all people.* Paul repeatedly calls this the *euangelion,* the "good message" or gospel. Unlike his other letters, this one was sent to a church (probably a group of house churches) that was not the product of Paul's missionary labor. Also unlike his other letters, pressing church problems do not seem to have been the apparent occasion of Romans. The gospel had arrived in Rome well in advance of Paul. He laid out his theology of salvation as a means of introducing himself to the Roman Christians before he arrived among them. We cannot date Romans with any greater precision than that it likely was written sometime between AD 55 and 64. In the wake of his arrest and hearings in Judea, Paul had begun his journey to Rome, under guard, to appeal his case before the emperor. We can surmise that Romans was written somewhere along the route, perhaps in either northern or southern Greece.

Paul opened Romans with the conventional form of letter writing in the ancient Mediterranean world—a signature and salutation at the very beginning. But he also adapted this form to suit his own purposes. He expanded the salutation to include, in verses 1 through 5, a capsule version of the gospel and the contents of the letter's main body. At the outset, Paul also identified himself: a "servant of Christ Jesus, called to be an apostle and set apart for the gospel of God."

In his path-breaking commentary on Romans, the famed Swiss-German theologian Karl Barth (1886–1968) made a considerable point that Paul was an apostle and not a genius. Barth sharply distinguished between the revelation that comes from God and the knowledge born of human ability. That Paul identified himself as an apostle signifies that he is a messenger who carries the message of another: the gospel Paul preached and the subject of this letter was not the product of his own mind, however intelligent he may have been. The gospel is grounded in the unique self-revelation of God in Jesus Christ. This revelation comes from above rather than from human insight.

Ancient Christian commentators on Romans were especially interested in the other word that Paul used to identify himself—"servant" or, more pointedly, "slave." Origen (c. 185–c. 254) thought that Paul's use of this word expressed his humility; "for he serves Christ not in the spirit of slavery but in the spirit of adoption, for Christ's service is more noble than any freedom."[50] Other ancient commentators saw no distinction between Paul and any other follower of Jesus. Everyone is called to the service of Christ. The calling to Christ's service and apostleship was not for Paul alone. As Theodore of Mopsuestia

50. Bray, *Romans*, 3.

(c. 350–428) observed, "All things are servants of Christ, and he is Lord of all. Therefore Paul calls himself a servant first of all, thereby encouraging the rest to do likewise."[51]

Bad News, Good News
Romans 3:1–4, 19–31

To borrow a line from a form of humor, these verses contain both bad news and good news. The good news is that God has made available to human beings a righteousness that is not connected to the Law of Moses but "comes through faith in Jesus Christ to all who believe" (3:22). Before we get to that good news, however, we must deal with the stark reality of the bad.

First, we need to remind ourselves of a commonplace of careful Bible study. The earliest biblical manuscripts lack notation—chapter and verse divisions and numbers. In fact, the early Greek manuscripts of the New Testament were written without punctuation, and in many manuscripts, every line of text is written only in large case letters. Recalling this basic information about the text will prevent us from making overmuch of current chapter and verse divisions as if they were important breaks in Paul's argument. They are not, and nowhere is that any truer than in Romans.

The first twenty verses or so of Romans 3 summarizes a lengthy argument that Paul has been making through most of the first two chapters of the letter. In the words of Paul Achtemeier, that argument runs something like this:

> We have learned that we cannot look to our collective past for any kind of comfort or salvific aid. Whatever our ancestry, whether Jewish or gentile, it has distinguished itself principally by its resolute sinfulness and rebellion against God. Our past has left us the inheritance of being unacceptable to God through our separation from him. The root of our problem is the human propensity to put non-gods in the place of God. Such idolatry clearly means the rejection of the Creator for a deity more pliable to our wishes. Basically, idolatry means not trusting God to be the kind of God we can live with. God's reaction to that lack of trust in him has been to allow us to "get away with" our desire to have something other than him for god. Paul has called that abandonment of us by God "God's wrath."[52]

Clearly, human beings face a problem; theologians term it the "human predicament." Some have couched this predicament largely in terms of human ignorance. Others have held that human beings have sufficient moral reserves to climb out of this predicament if sufficiently aided from beyond themselves. For Paul, the problem went deeper into human nature than a clouded or inadequately informed intellect. The solution to our problem lies on the other side of the divide between sinful, idolatrous creatures and a righteous God. The solution can come only from God through Jesus Christ.

Abraham's Righteousness
Romans 4:2–3, 13–25

Near the end of Romans 3, Paul asks whether God is God exclusively of the

51. Ibid., 4.

52. Paul Achtemeier, *Romans*, 66.

Jews. He followed with a rhetorical question affirming the Lord as the God of the Gentiles as well. Paul's discussion of faith and the law in chapter 4 is anchored to this strong affirmation that the God of Abraham, Isaac, and Jacob is the God of all peoples.

The question occupying Paul's attention here is this, On what basis was Abraham justified before God—law or faith? There is little dispute that Paul addressed this question, but we also must consider the larger issue that framed it. The problem of ethnic difference, specifically the matter of Jews and Gentiles, vexed nearly every first-century congregation with which Paul was acquainted. For Jewish Christians, the confession that Jesus was the Messiah naturally entailed the belief that he fulfilled the Law of Moses and thus was the hope of Judaism. That in turn made them heirs of all the promises of the Bible concerning the people of God. But the law had been given only to the Jews through Moses. What about those people—the Gentiles—to whom the law had not been given? Since they had no connection to Moses or the law, on what basis could they inherit God's promised salvation?

Some Jewish Christians contended that the righteousness of God could be made available to the Gentiles, but only if they placed themselves under the law. These were the people who insisted to the Galatians, for example, that Gentiles undergo circumcision as the entry point of a new relationship with God and thus membership in the church. Paul argued that this demand was flawed in two respects. In the first place, it was mistaken in the priority it gave to Israel, thus his insistence that God is the God of all peoples. Second, Jewish Christians were mistaken in their understanding of the basis of the possibility of right standing—righteousness—before God. For them it was the law; for Paul that basis was faith.

In chapter 4, Paul made a large point of the fact that, even prior to undergoing circumcision, Abraham, whom the Jewish Christians considered their forefather, trusted God—which is to say that he had faith in God. Paul understood Abraham's obedience to the requirement of circumcision not as a meritorious act that effected righteousness but one that declared "the righteousness that he had by faith while he was still uncircumcised" (4:11). For Paul, this is the clearest possible evidence that Abraham's righteousness rested not on any act of obedience on his part but solely on his faith in God. Since human beings must trust God's grace for righteousness, there can be no grounds for boasting; we ought not boast of what we have not done.

To augment his point, Paul read the promise that Abraham would be the father of many nations as dependent on faith rather than law. The Lord God promised that Abraham would father many nations, not one. If righteousness comes by the law, then Abraham would be the father only of the Jews. But faith is the basis of righteousness, so all who trust God for salvation through Christ are descendents of Abraham—the man of faith. That Abraham is the ancestor of all the faithful thereby is the means by which God's promise is fulfilled: Abraham is the father of all peoples anywhere—Jew or Gentile—who through Christ trust in God for righteousness.

A Gracious Peace
Romans 5:1–11, 18–21

Commentator Paul Achtemeier writes that Romans 5:1–11 is closely connected to 4:23–25 and elaborates on three themes that are introduced in the earlier passage: (1) righteousness, (2) Christ's death for sins, and (3) Christ's resurrection for righteousness. Achtemeier also identifies specific structural elements of this discussion that indicate Paul was following specific forms governing the presentation of a formal argument.

Paul's instruction here follows this line: We have been set right with God through the death and resurrection of Jesus. Grammarians call this an indicative sentence because it declares the way things are. From this statement, two additional conclusions may be drawn. It follows that if we have been set right with God, we also have peace with God; from this it follows that we can face our future with confidence, even when that future contains adversity.

The element that makes Christian confidence possible is God's grace. St. John Chrysostom (c. 347–407)—a Greek nickname that means "the golden mouth" given to him because of his great skill as a preacher—said of this grace,

> If God brought us near to himself when we were far off, how much more will he keep us now that we are near!... What grace is it to which we now have access? It is being counted worthy of the knowledge of God, being forced to abandon error, coming to a knowledge of the truth, obtaining all the blessings which come through baptism. For the reason he brought us near in the first place was that we might receive these gifts. For we were not reconciled merely in order to receive forgiveness of sins; we were meant to receive countless additional benefits as well.[53]

Chrysostom wrote these words at a moment in the church's life when many believers still keenly remembered the suffering endured by Christian martyrs under Roman persecution. God's grace is so powerful that, even in the face of such adversity and the world's attempts to undermine faith, faith and confidence in God will grow. Adversity only serves to strengthen our confidence (see 5:3–5). Christian martyrs laid down their lives in devotion to God, whose act of redemption through Christ surely is worthy of such sacrifice. But how much more extraordinary is it that Christ died in devotion to human beings, strangers far away from God? This is the "one act of righteousness" (5:18) that makes possible justification and life for all.

Objective and Subjective Relations
Romans 6:3–8

In the company of other witnesses, Paul also could say that he had seen the risen Lord. This revelation came on the Damascus road, and little of Paul's life remained the same after that extraordinary meeting. In fact, Paul spent the remainder of his life living out the consequences of his encounter with the crucified and risen Lord. Those consequences can be neatly divided into objective and subjective categories.

---

53. Bray, *Romans*, 128.

Objectively speaking, the consequence of Paul's conversion was a change in his relationship with God. Now he was *justified*, meaning that he had been made righteous through the sacrificial work of Christ on the cross. To be made righteous is to be set in proper relation, just as when we order a word processor program to justify a document's margin. But faith in Christ and his resurrection also signified a change in Paul himself. Not only was he justified, he also became a new creature in Christ. Paul gave baptism a singular importance here as he described it as the means by which we identify with Christ's death and resurrection. This is the subjective consequence of Christ's resurrection. Those who believe in him are raised in baptism to a new life. In one sense, new life is to live in the hope of the resurrection. In another sense, and Romans 6:1ff requires this consideration, another consequence of Christ's resurrection is a new moral life. Identification with Christ introduces us to a new way of living—a new lifestyle expressive of the new creature in Christ who we are privileged to become.

Nature's Lost Good

Romans 8:18–27, 31–34, 38–39

"Nature also mourns for a lost good." The sentence comes from the pen of the German-American theologian Paul Tillich (1886–1965), actually from a sermon of that title. Tillich drew on verses from Romans 8 to expound the gravity of sin and the glory of God's grace for the created order.

The enormity of human sin set the universe off center. As Paul said, the natural world, like God's human creation, is subject to frustration. In other words, the created world cannot achieve or be all that God intended at Creation's first light. It cannot achieve the ends for which it was created. Sin is the agent of this frustration. It would be silly to say that creation sinned, and so Paul declared. The source of this frustration lies not with creation but in "the will of the one who subjected it" (8:20). By whom did sin enter the world but through the first human beings and their disobedience? Therein lays the source of creation's problem.

One may interpret Paul in either of two equally legitimate directions. On one hand, he can be read as offering instruction concerning the origins of evil and its consequences for the created order. On the other hand, we can interpret this passage in terms of the modern-day suffering imposed on the natural world by human selfishness and waste. The sight of one Styrofoam cup on a lakeshore or an aluminum can in a streambed is sufficient to remind us of the ravages that human beings wreak on our natural environment—that is, God's created order.

God's natural creation is not alone in its suffering. Human beings also suffer, and some aspects of this misery arise in the dissonance that human sin originated between us and our natural environment. Anyone who has tried to raise a garden or clear a living space out of the forest can testify to the ways we and nature sometimes seem to be working at cross purposes. If you live where there are raccoons, you had better be sure to plant enough sweet corn to ensure that you will harvest their leftovers. Or consider the world of microbes and the fact that hospitals—places dedicated to the preservation and recovery of human life and health—are also home to some of the most stubborn, antibiotic-resistant strains of bacteria. Germs that once were susceptible to antibiotic drugs mutate into resistant forms.

In certain respects, we inhabit a benevolent and friendly environment, but in others the natural world is a hostile home. Ironically, and sadly, human actions have helped to make it so. Whether for humans or for the created order that they inhabit, this existence is not the final word. Ultimately, wrote Paul, all creation will be renewed in a glorious final restoration of all things according to God's original design.

Self-Righteous Idolatry

Romans 10:1–17

A perceptive teacher once observed that the history of Christianity could be written as the human refusal to accept the gift of God's salvation. In Paul's eyes, that history began with Israel's refusal to trust in Christ. As he described this problem in Romans 10, the issue centered less on Christ than on the law. From Paul's perspective, his fellow Jews preferred to trust in a righteousness earned by obedience to the law over the righteousness that comes by grace through faith. We must acknowledge that insistence on a performance-based righteousness is not peculiar to Israel; it is a characteristic that resides deep in the human heart.

Paul was deeply troubled by two questions concerning the Jewish people: Why does Israel still not believe, and will Israel ever be saved? The gift of the gospel to the Gentiles almost simultaneously marked a great reversal. Those who pursued righteousness—the Israelites, especially those like Paul who were zealous for the law—had not attained it. But those who had not pursued righteousness—the Gentiles—had obtained the righteousness that comes by faith. The people who had been given the law and who worked hardest at becoming righteous remained in pursuit of it while those who were without both law and an interest in righteousness had found it. Rather, it had found them. This seemed manifestly unfair.

Perhaps the unfairness is only apparent and not actual. The righteousness that comes by faith in God is essentially a matter of trust. We trust in God's grace to save us, to justify us, to put us into right standing with God. The Law of Moses aimed at establishing the same kind of trust. The psalmist sang of his delight in the law of the Lord and the light that it shone on his walk with the Lord God. But the human heart, colored as it is with the tendency to self-regard, transforms the law from a thing of grace into a mechanism for trusting in our own efforts. Instead of relying on God, we believe that we can achieve righteousness through obedience to the law. Perversely, we would rather trust in our own efforts. The person who says, "Trust in God, but keep your powder dry," appears to trust dry gunpowder about as much as God.

There is more than a whiff of idolatry about a person who pursues righteousness through self-effort. Such people trust in their own capacities and personal resources more than God's grace. In this context, misplaced trust is another name for idolatry, but we should not assume that those who misplace their trust do so arrogantly. Many persons mistakenly believe that they will be saved if they are good enough and live in desperate fear that they are not. Whether in arrogance or fear, to trust creature rather than Creator remains idolatry.

The gift of salvation through faith seems so simple as to be almost too good to be true. No wonder so many people down through the ages have found it difficult to believe. Someone brings the message, and now we know in whom to believe. Believing, we call upon his name to save us—not through anything we have done but because he wants to save and will do so graciously through the merits of Christ. In Paul's description of the dynamics of Christian evangelism, one is struck by the fact that it comes through hearing. And hearing involves words that pass unseen through the air from the speaker to the listener—by faith and not by sight.

Indicative and Imperative

Romans 12:1–3, 9–21

Thus far in Romans we have considered the grace of God primarily in relation to the problem of a sinful and rebellious humanity. We have seen how God's grace overcomes sinfulness and offers the possibility of a new relationship between God and the man or woman who believes in Christ. Romans 12 shifts our consideration of grace. Here Paul begins to discuss the transformation worked by God's grace on our relationships, beyond our relationship with God. He first discusses relations among the body of believers, moves to the community outside the body, and concludes, in Romans 13, with the governing authorities.

God's grace pardons all who believe. God's grace also empowers believers to live transformed lives. In previous sections of Romans, Paul taught the pardoning grace of God. This grace makes possible the new situation in which righteousness is available through faith. As Paul wrote, this is the way things now stand between human beings and God, which is to say that in this passage Paul wrote indicatively. In Romans 12, he shifts from the indicative to the imperative mood, drawing the moral consequences of our new situation. In effect, Paul declares, "Since you live in the new righteousness that is by faith in Christ, live like it." The Greek verbs of Romans 12 are written in the imperative mode. They are not suggestions for Christian living but expectations or even commands stated in clear and direct language; the lifestyle and relationships they structure are not options for higher spiritual living but basic Christian discipleship.

Grace must structure relationships within the body of Christ. Early Christian expositors of the Scriptures saw how the vitality of the church depended upon healthy relationships among all of its members. Those early teachers further saw that Christians accomplish more when working together in harmony than when acting independently of one another. Origen (c. 185 to c. 254) thus wrote:

> One person gives all his energy to the wisdom of God and the teaching of the Word; he is the eye of the whole body. Another...looks after the needs of the brethren and of the poor; he is the hand of the holy body. Another is an attentive listener

to the Word of God; he is the ear of the body. Another is busy admonishing the slack, comforting the suffering and aiding those in need; he is without any doubt called the foot of the body of the church. Each of these has his special task, but none can function properly without the others.[54]

Government

Romans 13:1–14

The great Christian theologian Augustine of Hippo (354–430) movingly describes his conversion in Book VIII of his masterpiece, *Confessions*. He was one of a small group of bright and earnest young men who contemplated becoming Christians. For none was this decision lightly made, but it appears to have weighed more heavily on Augustine. His reluctance had much to do with his deep attraction—perhaps addiction—to sex. So strong was this attraction's control over him that Augustine knew that, for him, conversion to Christianity would require a celibate life. Under great conviction and in agony of soul, Augustine struggled between his powerful sensual desires and the call of God upon his life. One evening, while reflecting on his plight as he paced through the inner garden of his house, Augustine heard a voice say, "Take and read. Take and read." He returned to a copy of the Bible he had left lying on a table and his eye fell on Romans 13:13–14 ("Let us behave decently, as in the daytime, not in orgies and drunkenness, not in sexual immorality and debauchery, not in dissension and jealousy. Rather, clothe yourselves with the Lord Jesus Christ, and do not think about how to gratify the desires of the sinful nature"). Augustine promised to follow this exhortation, confessed his sin, and was baptized a Christian. He went on to become the most influential voice in Western Christianity for the next thousand years.

Augustine's encounter with the letter to the Romans happened several decades after Emperor Constantine had converted to Christianity. His conversion brought peace to a church that had lived through nearly 250 years of periodic waves of persecution. The government of imperial Rome waged war on Christians in ten major periods of persecution. Christians knew that the government was not their friend; they must have puzzled over the words of Paul in Romans 13. Paul, of course, had written those words before the beginning of Roman persecution. Scholars estimate that he wrote Romans about AD 57. Tradition says he was martyred under Emperor Nero, about the year 65. By the time of his death, in other words, the government that Paul believed posed no threat to those who do good was persecuting Christians. By the end of the century, the church had suffered through many trials. As John of Patmos wrote the Revelation, he gave vent to the idea that the imperial government was a monster bent on devouring the church.

Paul had written that "rulers hold no terror for those who do right" (13:3). While true, it was also the case that governments assume the right to define right and wrong. Christians were able to live at peace with the empire while they were a movement so small as to escape government view. When Christians became more numerous, they could not

54. Ibid., 310.

help but be noticed, particularly when they refused to sacrifice to the Roman gods and especially the emperor. Although often requiring little more than burning a pinch of incense, Christians abhorred idolatry, even if it was the religion of the dominant culture. The dominant culture enjoys the power to define right and wrong, and in pagan Rome a refusal to sacrifice to the gods constituted both atheism and an attack on the sociopolitical system. Those were the so-called crimes for which Christians were persecuted.

We must remember that the government of Rome was often brutal, behaved ruthlessly toward even the slightest opposition, and possessed a large and well-trained army to enforce its will. It would have been quite pointless for Christians to rebel against the powerful empire. To be sure, as Paul wrote Romans, the empire had not yet begun persecuting Christians. Nevertheless, he could easily have foreseen the inevitable results of armed rebellion and therefore advised Christians to live at peace with everybody. Eventually, the Christian church triumphed over the pagan empire without ever fighting a military battle. In that respect, we must take care to notice that Paul bracketed his advice about Christians and government between sayings about the importance of love (12:9 and 13:10), which he called in another letter "the most excellent way" (1 Cor 12:31).

Servants of One Another

Romans 14:1–13

Paul's instruction to Christians in Romans 14 appears as something of a paradox, if not a flat-out contradiction. He begins with a ringing endorsement of Christian freedom. What troubles the conscience of one believer may not bother another in the slightest. Each, declared Paul, ought to mind his or her own business. The issue that prompted this discussion was the old matter of eating meat, a problem for Christians because in the ancient Roman world nearly all meat available for purchase had come from the carcasses of animals sacrificed in idol worship. Paul clearly stated the solution: "The man who eats everything [including sacrifice meat] must not look down on him who does not, and the man who does not eat everything must not condemn the man who does" (14:3).

If the discussion ended here, we would have no contradiction, apparent or otherwise. Before this chapter concludes, however, Paul seems to have taken the opposite point of view. In verse 15 he writes, "If your brother is distressed because of what you eat, you are no longer acting in love. Do not by your eating destroy your brother for whom Christ died." Are we to acknowledge the tender consciences of our fellow believers and live accordingly, or are we free to follow the dictates of our own conscience? The freedom that Paul granted each believer in 14:3, he appears to have taken away in 14:15.

The apparent contradiction in Romans 14 can be resolved with some help from Martin Luther (1483–1546). The famed Ninety-Five Theses were three years old when Luther published three remarkable essays, all in the year 1520. Together they are called the "Reformation Treatises." The last of them, published late that year, is titled "On the Freedom of the Christian." Luther framed this essay on two seemingly contradictory statements that parallel

Paul's instruction in Romans 14. Luther put the matter like this: The Christian is a perfectly free lord of all, subject to no one. And the Christian is a perfectly bound servant of all, subject to all. The manner in which Luther resolved this apparent paradox holds the key to understanding Romans 14.

A Christian is a perfectly free lord of all, subject to no one. Following Paul closely on this point, Luther staunchly affirmed the freedom of the Christian. For Luther, faith frees us from the condemnation of sin and slavery to the law. Faith frees a man or woman from sin, death, and the terror of facing a righteous and holy God. Faith also frees us from the impossible task of trying to earn God's favor through obedience to the law. In this freedom, the only thing that can separate us from God's love and favor is our refusal to believe and let God be God. No longer need we worry about our eternal destiny and our standing before God, for he has declared us to be righteous through the sacrificial death of his Son. We are free.

Freedom translates to servanthood. Our new freedom in faith means that now we are free to care for our neighbor in acts of the freest service and love. We love not because the law commands but in our own faith and freedom. Such love is not tainted by the possibility that we might love our neighbor because we fear the consequences if we do not. Since God has graciously forgiven us and put us in right standing before him, we no longer need to pile up loving acts like spiritual merit badges. Through the grace of God in Christ, our concern need no longer be about us and what we may or may not do. Now we are in Christ and free to love our neighbor as we would ourselves want to be loved. In this new life in Christ, there is neither paradox nor contradiction on the matter of Christian living.

First and Second Corinthians

Paul and the Corinthians

1 Corinthians 1:2–17

Paul wrote more to the church at Corinth than to any other ancient church. We know this on the basis of the two extant letters we find in the New Testament as well as other letters whose existence is theorized. Clearly, Paul's most lengthy and most vigorous correspondence was with this group of Christians with whom his relationship was also the stormiest. Some background concerning this large and prosperous city will aid our understanding.

The rapidly growing and diverse city of Corinth was situated on the isthmus, known as the Peloponnesus, that connects upper Greece with its lower peninsula. Corinth was a seaport and thus open to the entire Mediterranean world of people, goods, services, and vices. The patron goddess of Corinth was Aphrodite, the Greco-Roman goddess of love and the patron deity of sailors. The worship of Aphrodite involved temple prostitution, and during banquets held in Corinthian temples, sexual activity often was incorporated into the festivities. Apparently, the first gladiatorial contests occurred in Corinth. The city's population had a reputation for aggressiveness and a competitive spirit. In Corinth, public boasting and self-promotion were elevated to art forms.

Paul arrived in Corinth sometime during AD 49–50. Acts reports that he remained for eighteen months. We infer that the letter we call 1 Corinthians was not the first that Paul had written to this church (see 1 Cor 5:9). The best reconstruction of events leads us to conclude that Paul dictated it early in 53 or 54 from a location on the west coast of Asia Minor (modern-day Turkey). He most likely was writing from the city of Ephesus.

The letter's opening verses make it clear that Paul and the Corinthian Christians had been exchanging messages. The church had written to him, and he had already replied at least once. The picture is not pretty. The Corinthian church appears to have been populated with people who shared some of the aggressive, competitive and self-promoting characteristics of their pagan neighbors. As a result, Paul followed his customary salutation and thanksgiving by jumping directly into the first phase of a broad argument that runs nearly throughout the letter. He refers to their disunity and rivalry and appeals to the Corinthians for unity of mind and thought. Quarreling, bickering, and comparisons among themselves must stop. An important by-product of this argument was the line that Paul implicitly drew between the church and the dominant culture. Whatever the characteristics of Corinthian society, they must be left outside the church. This may have been the first occasion when Paul made such a demand in any of his letters. It surely was not the last. He expected the saints who were members of the church to live to a higher standard and forsake many of the common values of the society out of which they had been called.

Unconventional Wisdom

1 Corinthians 2:1–16

Paul wrote to many different churches for different purposes, and he employed different styles of writing. (Today scholars refer to these styles as "rhetorical.") For example, the letter to the Philippians has been compared recently to the kind of friendship letter that people wrote to one another in the ancient Mediterranean world. The letter to the Romans introduced Paul and his gospel to a church that knew him mainly by reputation. As we work our way through Paul's Corinthian letters, it will be important to keep in mind that they are extended arguments. Remember the Corinthian reputation for competitiveness and their tendency to see life issues as contests. It is as if Paul was debating members of this church. In this debate, Paul employed his considerable powers of persuasion not in pursuit of victory but to encourage faithful Christian discipleship.

In this section of 1 Corinthians, Paul's argument takes a countercultural turn. In chapter 2, he reminded the Corinthians that when he worked among them he did not use conventional rhetorical styles. His speeches did not rest on flashy turns of phrase, dramatic imagery, or intricate argument. The Corinthians and other people of the Roman world were familiar enough with those. Rather, as Paul wrote, "I resolved to know nothing while I was with you except Jesus Christ and him crucified" (2:2). Coming to Christ and the church of which he is Lord does not rest in conventional wisdom.

Richard Hays comments on the word *crucified* in 2:2: "The word *crucified*...is a perfect passive participle in the Greek;...

the perfect tense describes actions completed in the past whose effects continue in the present. Thus, when Paul summarizes the content of the gospel as 'Christ crucified,' he is identifying Jesus Christ as the one whose identity *remains* stamped by the cross. The cross has not been canceled out by the resurrection; rather, to know even the risen Jesus is to know him precisely as *the crucified one*. Any other account of his identity is not the gospel."[55]

In 1 Corinthians 3:10 and following, Paul taught that the only proper foundation for the church is Jesus Christ. It would have been difficult for nearly any person of the ancient world, but perhaps especially these proud and self-promoting Corinthians, to have accepted the lordship of a person executed as a common criminal of the lowest social class. To do so countered all logic and wisdom and cut across most tendencies of Corinthian culture. Nevertheless, Paul insisted that his readers remember Jesus as the crucified and resurrected Lord. Without the cross, no crown. The "stumbling block to Jews and foolishness to Gentiles" (1:23) is the power and wisdom of God.

Paul also elaborated on the basis by which Christians comprehend the doctrine of a crucified Lord. The active presence of the Holy Spirit is the indispensable ingredient in both the acceptance and understanding of what remains fundamentally mysterious—the gospel concerning Jesus Christ. How do we know this mystery? "We know it because we (i.e., all Christian believers, cf. 12:3b) have received God's Spirit, and God's Spirit alone discloses that the word of the cross is the truth about God.... The conclusion of all of this is summarized in 2:13: Paul and other Christians can speak now about the identity of God not because they have received advanced philosophical instruction or lessons on rhetorical declamation but because they have been taught by the Spirit of God how to speak of God through the power of the cross."[56]

Judgment on a Critical Spirit
1 Corinthians 4:1–13

Paul reserved his sharpest rebukes for the Corinthian church. First Corinthians 4 contains some of the strongest language employed by Paul in any of his letters. Up to this point, he has exhorted, encouraged, and used irony and metaphor to win the Corinthians' return to Pauline teaching. At the end of chapter 4, Paul offered the Corinthians a harsh choice: when he returns do they prefer that he bring a gentle spirit or a whip? What would prompt Paul to write in such strong terms?

We have already touched on the disunity and factionalism in the Corinthian church. This problem ran deeper than simply some people not getting along. From 4:1–5 we can infer that some of the Corinthians had presumed to judge Paul. The nature of this judgment is difficult to state, but from 4:6ff it appears to have had something to do with the presumption that Paul's authority was not very weighty and that the people of this faction were sufficiently wise to live out their own understanding of the Christian life. Paul responded to these attitudes in the bluntest of terms.

55. Hays, *First Corinthians*, 35.

56. Ibid., 45–46.

Richard Hays suggests that the Greek word translated in the New International Version as "judge" is better rendered by the words *examine* or *scrutinize.* He compares the attitude behind this word to the one taken by modern-day callers to radio talk shows. Paul summarily dismissed this kind of idle criticism, saying that it was of no consequence. To make his point, he implied a comparison between Corinthian carping and the last judgment. Paul would be examined, but not by the Corinthians or any other mortals. Praise and blame are the sole province of God—not humans.

In verses 6 and 7, Paul directly challenged the gall of the Corinthians. Who were they to be criticizing anybody anyway? As Paul asked, "What do you have that you did not receive? And if you did receive it, why do you boast as though you did not?" Every follower of Jesus lives the Christian life only through the gift of God's grace. That gift typically is mediated through the work or witness of others. It might be the ministry of teaching and preaching, which seems to be what Paul has in mind here, but the gift of God's grace can also be mediated through the witness of a Christian life or a direct testimony of evangelism. The point is that none of us, not then or now, comes to God on our own resources. Alas, the Corinthian church had forgotten this great theological truth, and the result was an ugly rift between the Corinthians and Paul.

The apostle argued further that since he was accountable to God alone, God was also the sole ground of Paul's authority. He would not permit the Corinthians to challenge it, even though this authority had made the apostles "a spectacle to the whole universe" (4:9). The Corinthians thought of themselves as wise, strong, and worthy of honor. This is the wisdom of the world that stands over against the cross. The apostles were foolish, weak, and everywhere ridiculed. In this they were aligned with the crucified Christ and the power of the gospel. In this series of comparisons and contrasts, Paul implicitly asked his readers—whether in ancient Corinth or in today's church—to be certain that the lifestyle to which they aspired did not in fact repudiate Jesus and the discipleship to which he calls every person.

Loving Church Discipline
1 Corinthians 5:1–13

The most persistent issue in the first-century church was the relationship between Jews and Gentiles and, therefore, the status of the latter in the Christian community. The problem boiled down to the question of whether Gentiles were obligated to obey all of the Mosaic Law. The Jerusalem Council resolved that question by deciding that Gentiles were not under the law except for three stipulations: Gentile Christians were to abstain from meat that had been sacrificed to idols or that had not been properly slaughtered and they were to avoid sexual immorality. Paul and Barnabas had championed the Gentile cause at the conference, so it is small wonder that Paul reacted so sharply to the sexual immorality of some members of the Corinthian church.

The problem of Corinthian sexual practices was not new to Paul. It had already been the subject of a previous and now lost correspondence. It is not difficult to imagine Paul's exasperation with people whom he had already put on notice. He had reached the limit of his patience and tolerance. A member of the church was living as husband to his father's wife. This is an odd way of stating the relationship and opens the question of whether the woman was the man's biological mother or, perhaps, his stepmother. The first possibility is a clear case of incest, which "does not occur even among pagans" (5:1), but the second relationship also violated standards governing marital partners. In either case, Paul insisted that the man be expelled from the church.

Church discipline has become increasingly rare in North American churches, but our situation scarcely matches the first-century. Today the man or woman who is expelled from a congregation for disciplinary reasons has merely to find a new church. In Paul's day, no such alternatives were open to Christians under discipline. To be expelled from a congregation meant to be cut off from the body of Christ—period. The pluralism of today's church may help to explain the infrequency of expulsion as a form of discipline. That rarity may also influence our reading of this passage.

By today's standrds, Paul's action may seem excessively harsh. It is important to understand the motive behind the expulsion of a church member and its historical precedents. Such practices as the ban and shunning were employed by some of the radical reformers of the sixteenth century—ancestors of today's Mennonite, Brethren, and German Baptist churches. In these traditions, and in the New Testament church as well, the purpose of expulsion is not simply to rid the church of a moral blemish. Rather, the ban formally separated unrepentant sinners from the church. Mennonite congregations took this step to alert such people to their dire spiritual condition. To be banned was to be warned that sin had separated that person from the church and from the church's Lord. Repentance was the only route back into fellowship.

Following the ecclesiastical ban, Mennonites took the additional social step of shunning. In this they literally applied Paul's injunction, "With such persons do not even eat." Mennonites refused to have any dealings—commercial, social, whatever—with a person who had been banned from their church, even to the extent that family members would not associate with a blood relative who was under the ban. As with the practice of banning, shunning was intended to warn the impenitent of spiritual peril. The hope was that the person would repent and seek restoration. Such forms of church discipline seem well within the likely intent of Paul's instruction here.

Marriage and Singleness
1 Corinthians 7:1–16

It is almost commonplace now in certain circles of American Protestantism to view the family as under attack. Even members of the U.S. Congress called for and enacted an end to the so-called marriage penalty built into federal tax rates. American evangelicals also earnestly support efforts to strengthen the traditional family unit and family values. Many church people who quite naturally and properly turn to the Bible for instruction and support on these issues nevertheless forget that *family* can refer to many different ways of organizing people. Those differences occur in time as well as space. The nuclear family of twenty-first-century America hardly resembles the extended family of a bygone era or the clans of the ancient Semitic world. If we are to reach solid conclusions about the implications of this text, we must take some time to look at the institution of the family as it existed in the Roman Empire of Paul's day.

Remember that the church at Corinth was a mixed assembly of Jews and Gentiles. What ideas about marriage circulated in the Greco-Roman world, surrounding and informing the earlier experience of these new Christians? For one, many marriages were arranged rather than the result of an independent decision of a young man and woman. Arranged marriages also suggest that romantic love came somewhere rather further down in the list of priorities. Marriage was often used as a way of enhancing social status, so that *concordia* (harmony) often typified the Greco-Roman idea of a good marriage.

To these ideas, we must add the observation that Paul's social world did not distinguish between public and private realms the way we do today. We are much more inclined to view the family as a haven of privacy shut off from the stresses and tensions of the public worlds of work and school. People of the Roman Empire did not erect this kind of barrier between public and private lives. Their idea of a family included many people who lived under the same roof but were not necessarily blood relatives. People also were less inclined to depend on a nuclear family for the kind of support and friendship so important in today's ideas about the family. Ancient peoples often sought such experiences in small groups and clubs. Rather quickly the church became an important place where ancient Christians found a sense of belonging and spiritual comfort. The importance of the church, in this sense, as well as the blurred line between public and private world would have given Paul a freedom even greater than he felt to address such matters.

As so often in Paul's Corinthian letters, a harmony that yields peace in the church is a dominant value, and it colors the basic objective for both married and unmarried people. Under this objective, those who are married need to know their rights and obligations. Equally, those who are unmarried must also know their status. It would be accurate to say that Paul's larger concern was with the church. Why else would he encourage, for example, people to remain single rather than marry—a truly countercultural piece of advice in Corinth? It is, therefore, fair to conclude that Paul's teaching on marriage was shaped by his view of the church. It is not that he did not value marriage but that his understanding of the church defined a view of marriage quite different from attitudes in the dominant culture. In a society where wives were regarded as inferior to their husbands, Paul's teaching that the husband's body is under the control of the wife and vice versa would have surprised some and shocked others. But then, this is hardly the first or only instance where the claims of Christ and church have set men and women at odds with the surrounding society.

Sensitive Consciences

1 Corinthians 8

In his masterful poem *The Divine Comedy*, the medieval poet Dante placed frauds and cheats lower in hell than murderers and others whom he labeled generally the "violent." He thought crimes that undercut the natural tendency of humans to live in groups were worse than crimes against individuals. Humans lose something distinctively human when we lose the basic trust in other people that is the foundation of social life. Dante therefore likely appreciated the line of thought in 1 Corinthians 8, for Paul also found it difficult, if not impossible, to think of people as individuals isolated from one another.

According to Ben Witherington, the diet of ancient peoples, regardless of their social status, did not include nearly as much meat as is the case among most North Americans today. Typically, meat was consumed only on special occasions, holidays, and—most importantly—at sacrifices. Witherington calls ancient Roman temples the "restaurants of antiquity" and states that "several temples in Corinth had dining rooms where feasts were held on many occasions, including birthdays."[57] Moreover, nearly all meat available in the marketplace had a history of being involved in temple sacrifice. All of this suggests that meat, comparatively scarce and therefore expensive, typically was associated with pagan temple worship, and that meant idols. In fact, Paul even coined a phrase for this meat—*eidolothuton*, "idol food." If poor people ever consumed meat, they would likely have done so at a feast connected with a religious celebration.

With this as background, we can reconstruct the situation that Paul addresses in 1 Corinthians 8. Within this badly divided church there were several different groups. Sorted on the basis of their loyalties to various preachers, we find some siding with Peter, others with Apollos, and still others with Paul. Sorting by social class, however, we find some who were wealthy enough to eat meat either at temples or in their homes and other poorer believers who remembered the days of meat eating connected with their pre-Christian days. The well-to-do group was also of an independent mind, likely those using phrases such as "all possess knowledge" (8:1). They seem to have wanted to convince Paul that there was nothing wrong with going to temples to eat, since the temples were places were idols could be found and every Christian knew that idols were nothing other than inert objects of wood and stone. On the other side of the issue were those Christians of "weak conscience" (8:10). This phrase, however, should be read as persons "of stronger scruples" and not as persons who "are likely to give in to temptation." Read in this light, Paul's instruction takes a middle course between those who think they are completely free and those who are entirely legalistic. With the former and against the latter, Paul concurred that meat eating is acceptable for Christians. With the latter and against the former, Paul said that temples must be forsaken; meat eating is all right, but only at home. The principle to which Paul appeals is Christian love—one ought to act first for the sake of the neighbor and not out of individualistic self-regard.

57. Witherington, *Conflict and Community*, 188.

Ethics and the Lord's Supper
1 Corinthians 11:17–34

1 Corinthians 11:17–34 contains some of the most frequently read or quoted words from the Bible. Concerning this supper, the Synoptic Gospels and Paul all agree in quoting Jesus' saying, "This is my body." They are

spoken whenever Christians gather to eat the Lord's Supper.

How ironic that the Lord's Supper, the memorial meal of suffering, sacrificial love, and unity, became an occasion for factionalism and disunity. The history of these disputes is ancient and modern. The sixteenth-century reformers Martin Luther and Ulrich Zwingli bitterly disputed the other's interpretation of the Lord's Supper at the Marburg Colloquy of 1529. And the debate still keeps Christians away from each other's tables.

Given the history of Christian disagreement over the meaning of the Lord's Supper, we should not be terribly surprised that the first-century church also had problems with the Supper's meaning and practice. In fact, problems surround the often quoted words of 1 Corinthians 12. As we approach this passage, it will be important to bear in mind an important difference between the church of the first century and today. Christians today typically gather in a church building designed for worship, while the church of Paul's day possessed no such structures. Rather, that church gathered in the homes of Christians. At Corinth, it seems that wealthier members of the congregation opened their homes but began eating and drinking prior to the arrival of others. This tangible expression of differing social status among the Corinthian Christians threatened the unity of the church.

Peter Lampe interprets this passage to contend that Paul established a clear connection between the church's ethics and its celebration of the Lord's Supper. Lampe observes that Paul often discussed the ordinances when faced with the need to correct misconduct in the church. In this case, Lampe establishes three possible Pauline connections between the supper's proclamation of Christ's death and Christian ethics: (1) Christ died for the weak; therefore, the strong Christians at Corinth should not belittle or offend in any way their weaker brothers and sisters. (2) The Lord's Supper represents Christ's self-denial on the cross for the benefit of others; in view of this example, wealthy Corinthians should not ignore the hunger of the poor. (3) In the Lord's Supper, a close relationship is established between us and Christ's suffering on the cross.

At the Lord's Table, we die with Christ, entering into the fellowship of his suffering. Such "cross-existence" includes self-denial and love for others. In the Lord's Supper, as Lampe states,

> Christ's death is proclaimed and made present by means of our giving ourselves up to others. Our love for others represents Christ's death to other human beings. Only by actively loving and caring for others does the participant in the [Lord's Supper] 'proclaim' Christ's death as something that has happened for others.[58]

Lampe helps us to see that the supper is a memorial meal with ethical consequences. In this view, Paul instructed the Corinthians concerning the Lord's Supper so they would eat and drink in remembrance of the Lord and in so doing become agents of his love and unity.

Body Life

1 Corinthians 12:4–26

In 1 Corinthians 12:4–26, we find Paul's teaching resting very clearly on the idea that human nature is social

58. Lampe, "Eucharist," 45.

and that individuals need relationships to sustain them in their individuality. This idea is quite contrary to modern Western notions about the relation of the individual and society.

Ever since John Locke and Thomas Jefferson, Americans, and other peoples as well, have organized their societies on the basis of the premise that, in the matter of the individual's relationship to society, the individual comes first. Before there are societies, there are individuals who bind themselves into societies through what is called a "social contract." As the U.S. Constitution begins, "We the people of the United States, in order to form a more perfect union...do ordain and establish this constitution." Individual people are the building blocks, and society is the product of their free choice.

People of the ancient world, Paul included, understood the relationship between the individual and the group in reverse of the social contract model. In their view, the society or group comes first and individual people are seen as its extensions. Each individual certainly owns his or her own personhood but only in relation to the group in which a person's identity is located. This view helps to explain why exile was such a terrible punishment in the ancient world. Once severed from the political body, a person became in a very real sense a nonentity and was thus condemned to a kind of living death. In today's legal system, exile hardly exists as a form of punishment. One explanation of this de-emphasis on exile is that the modern notion of the individual diminishes the severity of exile as punishment.

The ancient view of the relationship of individual and group was the foundation of Paul's instruction in 1 Corinthians 12. To make his point, he used one of his favorite and most famous metaphors for the church—the human body. Each member of the body—hands, feet, ears, eyes, and so forth—lives and has its function only insofar as it is connected to the body of which it is a part. Any member severed from the body loses the ability to carry out its function. Disconnected from an arm, a hand no longer can perform what hands do—pick up a spoon, turn a page, or, most importantly, grip a golf club. In a very real sense, a severed hand has lost its identity because it cannot function as a hand. It may still look like a hand but, functionally, it is not. Paul teaches that the relationship between each Christian and the church is just like the relationship between the hand and the body.

The Corinthian church included some Christians who believed they were superior to others. It appears that these superior-minded folk were acting independently, as if the church needed them and their gifts more than they needed the church. Paul consistently responded to such attitudes by reminding people that the church is the body of Christ and that each Christian is a member of that body. In a very real sense, Paul began with the church and its Lord and saw each individual Christian as an extension of the church. Mutual empathy and joy depended on the relationship flowing from the body to each person as did the purpose of each spiritual gift. According to Paul, the Holy Spirit distributed gifts to specific Christians not for their sake but for the strengthening of the church. After all, without a body what good are hands or feet?

The Greatest of Gifts

1 Corinthians 12:31–13:13

First Corinthians 13—the "Love Chapter"— is printed commonly in its entirety on cards, wall mottoes, and so forth, and with good reason. Paul wrote some of his most eloquent words and phrases in this description of Christian love. Our common practice of reading this chapter as a freestanding unit, however, obscures its place within an extended argument aimed at reforming a badly factionalized and divided church. Remember that Paul did not divide his original letters into chapters and verses, and neither were they so divided in the earliest manuscripts of the Greek New Testament. First Corinthians 12:31, rather than the end of one chapter, is actually a transition or introductory sentence to what Paul intended to say next. The chapter break interrupts the larger argument.

Up to chapter 13, Paul had been making an extended argument as well as an appeal for the Corinthians to let love be their guiding principle. He had just finished explaining how authentic spiritual gifts work for the common good of the church. Love, argued Paul, must be the force that binds believers together. On this, the unity of the church depends. First Corinthians 13 is, in a certain sense, not directly part of that argument. It is rather an eloquent digression but not a digression in the modern sense of straying from the main point. Ancient writers used a digression to highlight a particular point of their argument. One of the ways they did so was to change their writing style from persuasive argument to more poetic forms. If we compare Paul's language in 1 Corinthians 13 to the style he used in the surrounding sections of this letter, it seems very likely that Paul intentionally digressed from his argument in order to expand upon the kind of love that he wanted to undergird the attitudes and practices of the Corinthian church.

Many ancient writers, including both Plato and Aristotle, wrote about love as the element in human living that could overcome our divisive tendencies. In that sense, Paul stood in an already long line of commentators on love. What separated Paul's writing from the rest was the presence of the Holy Spirit. The love of which Paul wrote is impossible outside of the life of the Spirit. It is the Spirit's greatest gift and the bond of Christian unity. Paul's digression on love pointed up the specific shortcomings of the Corinthians and informed them that they had been behaving as children. On the other hand, Paul no longer thought or acted childishly. By repeating a point made in chapter 9, Paul presented himself as a good example of the way Christians are to live. In this sense, love is more than a spiritual gift. "It is meant also to be the way of life for any Christian, the norm and the guide for the exercise of all gifts."[59]

Resurrection Faith

1 Corinthians 15:20–44

Centuries before Christians began commemorating Jesus' birth, they were already celebrating Easter. In those days, new converts postponed their baptisms, often for months, in order to be baptized on Easter Sunday. There was no better day to enter into Christ's death and resurrection. Simply put, the resurrection of Jesus is the central event

59. Witherington, *Conflict and Community*, 265.

of the New Testament; therefore, early Christianity recognized it as the central event of the church's life. It is therefore somewhat surprising that in 1 Corinthians 15 Paul asked, "How can some of you say that there is no resurrection of the dead?" He seems to be quoting the opinion of some church members. Clearly that was not what Paul had taught them, but apparently this view surfaced after his departure. In this section of his letter, Paul took great pains to lay out the importance of this most basic of all New Testament doctrines.

Paul began by reminding the Corinthians of the good news, the gospel that he had taught them. In some places, Paul refers to "my gospel," but here he pointedly connects the gospel he taught the Corinthians to "what [he] received" (15:3). This is the same language he used in 1 Corinthians 11:23 where he repeated instruction concerning the Lord's Supper. The point is that Paul was no innovator on these topics; he taught the Corinthians the same good news that he himself had been taught. The core of that instruction (called by New Testament scholars the *kerygma*, the New Testament Greek word for "message") is found in 1 Corinthians 15:3–5. Paul declared that he had received this message, and thus we have a clear view of what Jesus' followers said and taught about him within approximately three years of the first Easter.

Richard Hays comments, "Paul goes back to this bedrock confession in order to make the point that 'the resurrection of the dead' is not merely some idiosyncratic speculation that can be set aside by those who claim more sophisticated knowledge; rather, it is a matter 'of first importance' (v 3). It is an integral part of the *euangelion* (good news) on which those who believe take their stand (v. 1; cf Gal 1:11). The resurrection of Jesus and his subsequent appearance to a long list of witnesses is at the heart of the gospel proclaimed in the church; without this foundational truth, there would be no church because there would be no gospel. Those who hold fast to this truth are saved by it."[60]

Later in chapter 15, Paul describes the body Christians will receive after resurrection. His Corinthian questioners seem to have asked many of the questions that are posed by people today. Left buried for a lengthy period, a body decomposes into the proverbial ashes. The bodies of those lost at sea disintegrate even more rapidly. What then is resurrected? Paul answers, "A spiritual body" (15:44).

We do not know the idea that was proposed by the Corinthians. Perhaps they were denying altogether the idea of life after death. Perhaps they were reverting to another view, one with a long history in Greek philosophy—the idea of immortality of the soul. Greeks like Socrates and Plato taught that body and soul were separable and that only the latter was immortal. Paul, of course, was raised and taught in the tradition of the Pharisees, who viewed the human as an inseparable combination of body and soul; both are necessary to make a human person. For Paul, then, life after death is about the resurrection of the body and not the merely the continuing existence of an immortal soul. Paul's teaching that we receive a spiritual body is his way of acknowledging the corruptibility of the body that now forms us while asserting that we will receive another—incorruptible—body in the resurrection. We will be the same and yet eternally different.

60. Hays, *First Corinthians*, 255.

Repairing Relationships
2 Corinthians 2:4–17

Paul's relationship with the church at Corinth was especially stormy. From evidence in the Corinthian letters, it appears that this relationship deteriorated after he wrote the letter we call 1 Corinthians. Repeated attempts were needed to patch this broken relationship, often taking the form of letters. Recall that 1 Corinthians is probably not the first letter Paul wrote to this church. Furthermore, 2 Corinthians 2:4 refers to a letter he wrote "out of great distress and anguish of heart," which many scholars agree to be a *third* letter, written between 1 and 2 Corinthians but now also lost. Second Corinthians thus may actually be the fourth letter Paul wrote to the believers in Corinth. No other congregation received such attention from him. This body of written evidence—the extant letters as well as those to which Paul refers—indicates the depth of his concern for this particular congregation and the strained relationship between them.

In 1 Corinthians, Paul addressed the problem of factionalism and the need for Christian unity. Paul was attempting to heal relationships among people *within* the church. Second Corinthians was motivated by a different purpose. Here Paul is at pains to repair the Corinthian church's relationship with *him*.

As personally important as this relationship was to Paul, spiritual consequences weighed even heavier. Ben Witherington III writes,

> Paul believed that failure to achieve this reconciliation would endanger the very Christian identity of the Corinthian *ekklesia*, since Paul was Christ's agent. To be alienated from the agent was to be alienated from the one who sent him. So not only the integrity of Paul's ministry but also the integrity of the Corinthians' faith is at stake. Paul must defend himself, his behavior, and his ministry and he must also protect his converts from the very real danger of apostasy.[61]

His trying relationship with the Corinthians gave Paul every reason to understand himself as the aggrieved partner. He was innocent of wrongdoing and even went so far as to say that the Corinthians could imitate his pattern of Christian discipleship. It was the Corinthians who were divisive, arrogant, and foolish. Their actions—not Paul's—had opened the rift between them. It is instructive for our discipleship to understand that it was the aggrieved partner, that is, Paul, who made overtures of restoration and labored so diligently to see that restoration was achieved.

When Paul listed the fruit of the Spirit in Galatians, he included the virtue of longsuffering, a character trait typically believed to reside in the weak or defenseless. Actually, longsuffering is a virtue of the strong. People who are longsuffering have a legitimate grievance and yet also possess the power to do something about it. But to make reconciliation possible they defer the exercise of that power. In the whole of Scripture, the term *longsuffering* is in point of fact applied more often to God than any other. Paul's longsuffering attitude toward the Corinthians is thus an eloquent witness of the Holy Spirit's activity in his own life.

---

61. Witherington, *Conflict and Community*, 328.

Treasure in Earthen Vessels

2 Corinthians 4:5–18

Second Corinthians 4:5–18 contains some of the most beautifully phrased verses of the New Testament, but there is more here than a well-turned phrase. In this section of 2 Corinthians, some of Paul's most memorable words reveal his own indomitable spirit as well as the depth of his confidence in God and the calling of the apostles.

Who is the "we" of whom Paul wrote in this passage? Are all Christians included under this "we," or was Paul referring to a select group within the Christian community? The first sense of "we" in 2 Corinthians 4 refers to the apostles. This word comes from the Greek *apostello*, which means "to be sent." Although sometimes we interchange this word with another New Testament word, *disciple*, the two differ significantly in meaning. Disciples are those who live under a discipline or rule. Thus a disciple must live under the authority of a master who teaches that rule; a *Christian* disciple lives under the authority of *the* Master. An apostle, on the other hand, is an ambassador, one who has been authorized to deliver a message from another. An apostle of Jesus is also a disciple, but not all disciples are necessarily apostles. Paul's word *we* in this passage needs to be read first as referring to that special group of Jesus' followers called to be his messengers. They were the "jars of clay" (4:7) in whom resided the treasure of the gospel message. The apostles were the ones who were "hard pressed...but not crushed; perplexed, but not in despair; persecuted, but not abandoned; struck down, but not destroyed" (4:9).

Did Paul here intend us to think of the whole class of Christian apostles, or did he have in mind specific individuals? By the time 2 Corinthians was written, some apostles already had been martyred. Perhaps the memory of their faces came back to Paul. He also may have been thinking of his close working associates, Barnabas, Silas, Timothy, and Titus. There is nothing in the text to force one or the other answer; we may read both meanings. Is there a sense in which all Christian disciples come under this text? Can we legitimately read it in such a way as to include all Christians or must we conclude that, if this passage refers only to apostles, today it can have meaning only for those who are called to the ministry? While it is important to respect the first reading—that "we" refers to the apostles and, by extension ordained ministers—it is also appropriate to include all Christians within its framework. What allows us to do so?

Ordination distinguishes categories of ministry but does not limit ministry to those who are called to full-time service. All Christians are called to ministry. Calling and ordination separate some Christians for full-time service, but that does not relieve the rest of us from the work and responsibility of ministry. Comparatively few are called to the ministry of preaching, but all are called to a ministry for which the Holy Spirit will individually gift us. Roman persecution widened shortly after Paul wrote these verses. In that hour, Christian disciples came to know the trials of which he wrote. Then, just like the apostles, everyday laypersons wasted away but came to view their troubles as "light and momentary" (4:17). Ordinary disciples learned to fix their eyes "not on what is seen, but on what is unseen" (4:18). They did not lose heart, and we follow in their footsteps.

Reconciling the World to Christ
2 Corinthians 5:11–21

Adam W. Miller wrote, "It is an interesting fact that these letters to the church at Corinth were preserved at all. From this correspondence we learn that disputes and disorders had arisen within the community of believers, some of the members having been guilty of immoral conduct. One might think that the Corinthians would have been ashamed of their conduct and would have hidden or destroyed the letters."[62]

Perhaps some believers at Corinth did destroy one or both of the theorized lost letters. Whether those letters were destroyed, lost, or even existed are matters of conjecture. What cannot be doubted is Paul's great concern to heal the breech between him and the Corinthians. These verses come from a section of the letter where reconciliation obviously weighs very heavily on Paul's mind and heart. Reconciliation moves back and forth from God through Christ to the world and from brothers and sisters in the church through Christ to one another. The vertical and horizontal movement of God's reconciling grace combines in the "ministry of reconciliation." God reconciled the world to God. Prior to reconciliation, humans are at war against God. They cannot win this war and yet they wage it against all possibility of success. By rights, humans should be the ones to ask God for a peace treaty. After all, they started the war in the first place. Nevertheless, God "was reconciling the world to himself in Christ" (5:19). God reconciled the world to himself through Christ, and the cross was the instrument of reconciliation. This is utterly without parallel in our experience.

Humans have a vast and intimate acquaintance with war, warriors, and kings. In war as humans have experienced it, it is the vanquished who say, "Let there be peace between us." This statement is but another form of asking for reconciliation. But kings and warriors go on to say, "Let there be peace between us and *you* pay the price of peacemaking." In conventional human reconciliation, the loser pays the price of peace, suffering the greater casualties and more extensive destruction. When the loser has had enough, peace becomes possible. One may ask whether this kind of reconciliation makes for peace or merely the absence of war.

God's way of reconciliation is quite the contrary. To a humanity making war against God, the Lord says, "Let there be peace between us, and *I* will pay the price of that peace." The name of that price is the cross.

To be reconciled to God is to no longer regard one another from "a worldly point of view" (5:16). We see the world differently because in Christ we are "a new creation; the old has gone, the new has come" (5:17). We construe the world differently because God has reconciled us to himself—through the cross.

A Collection for Needy Saints
2 Corinthians 9:1–13

Money seems to have been one of the major issues in Paul's strained relationship with the Corinthians. He had to remind them that he had not

62. Miller, *Introduction to the New Testament,* 183.

lived off their contributions during his stay in Corinth. Like everyone else, he had worked with his hands for his daily needs. Some of Paul's detractors who arrived in the city after his departure appear to have raised Corinthian suspicions about the way Paul handled money. He was forced to defend himself against false suspicions, but they likely appeared again as soon as Paul brought up his project to raise money for the destitute Christians of Judea.

Today we are curious about the origins of the poverty in Jerusalem. How did it happen that Christians there were reduced to such extremity? Famine is one likely explanation. Recall also from Acts 4:32ff that in Jerusalem believers had sold their personal goods and contributed the proceeds to a common treasury. Eventually those funds would have been exhausted and the church left with few, if any, financial options. For whatever reason, the Jerusalem Christians were hard-pressed, and Paul hoped that fellow Christians would come to the assistance of the "mother church."

Second Corinthians 9 lays heavy emphasis on giving. In the context of today's church, it is natural to explore this text for ideas and teaching on tithing. Important as tithing is to the church and Christian discipleship, it is not the kind of giving Paul had in mind. The collection for the Jerusalem church was a special project. It is not clear from the text that the actual collection of these funds would occur in the context of worship. Paul clearly told the Corinthians to lay funds aside against the day when his associates would arrive to collect them, but he says nothing about the manner of that collection. (As an aside, that it was Titus and another widely respected gospel worker who would collect the money further emphasizes Paul's determination to improve his reputation among the Corinthians. Nobody would be able to cast suspicion on him concerning the way this collection was handled.)

Important issues converge in 2 Corinthians 9. The collection for Jerusalem was extremely important to Paul, but to mention this to the Corinthian church would only raise old questions and wounds. He could legitimately imagine somebody at Corinth saying, "Oh no, there he goes talking about money again." It might have been tempting to skip the Corinthians on the collection circuit, but that church needed to be included because it was wealthier than other churches in Europe. Paul specifically pointed to the generosity of the Macedonian churches even though they were in "severe trial" and "extreme poverty." He made no reference to poverty at Corinth.

More was at stake in Paul's theological vision of the Jerusalem collection than comparisons of the financial status of the European churches. The collection was also an opportunity for some believers to acknowledge the debt they owed others. The Jerusalem church was the mother church of every congregation of Christians. Had the good news not radiated from Jerusalem to the uttermost parts of the earth, there would be no Christians in Corinth, Macedonia, Rome, or anywhere else. All of those believers were in spiritual debt to Jerusalem, and the collection was one way of reciprocating. One must also remember that the relationship between Jewish and Gentile Christians was still fragile, and the collection served the important purpose of strengthening that relationship as largely Gentile churches came to the aid of the almost exclusively Jewish church in Jerusalem. Viewed narrowly, the collection for Jerusalem is a story of aid for destitute Christians. In a larger perspective, the collection is grounded in a vision of the church as the whole people of God mutually assisting one another.

Galatians

Freedom from the Law

Galatians 1:1–2, 6–9; 2:15–21

Galatians does not take its name from a city, as in the case of Thessalonians or Philippians, but a province in Asia Minor—modern Turkey. Actually there were two districts referred to as Galatia, an older region in central Asia Minor and a newer Roman province that included such cities as Derbe and Lystra. We know that Paul evangelized the latter, and it is likely that he also preached and established churches in the former. The question of which churches he was writing to poses geographical and chronological questions rather than theological. Whichever province, it is likely that he wrote Galatians about the same years as the Corinthian letters but before he wrote Romans—between AD 53 and 56.

The letter to the Galatians has been called the "Magna Carta of Christian freedom." Paul displays here a frustration we do not find in Romans or Philippians. Clearly, he was upset with a situation in which other teachers, presumably Jewish Christians, had followed him at Galatia and modified his instruction. In Paul's view, those modifications reintroduced a subservience to the law that he believed was contrary to the gospel of grace by faith in Jesus Christ. The Christian's relation to the Law of Moses is the central theological issue in this letter. That Paul championed the cause of Christian freedom over the ritual law is no surprise; however, interpretations vary as to the implications of that Pauline cause.

Paul wasted no time in warming to his central topic. After a brief salutation he said, "I am astonished." No pleasantries, no polite exchanges—only Paul's stated amazement that the Galatians had apparently accepted serious alterations in the gospel that he had delivered to them. What were these changes? An answer to that question requires a brief excursion into the history of the first-century church.

When Paul and Barnabas first departed Antioch on the first missionary journey, the church was still largely a Jewish community. In a church where most of the members, virtually all of the leaders, and the scriptures themselves were Jewish, it was probably inevitable that these first Christians thought of themselves and the new Jesus movement as an extension of Judaism. As such, they would have seen little reason to set aside the teachings of the law. In their eyes, Jesus came not to set aside the law but to fulfill it; if new believers could not share this devotion, at least they could observe the law.

Problems arose at Antioch, however, where the gospel was preached extensively to non-Jews. The first Gentile conversions prompted the question of whether the new minority of non-Jewish Christians was obligated to live under the Law of Moses. Many answered yes, but Paul said no. A council of church leaders met in Jerusalem to settle the matter. The outcome? All agreed that Gentiles were not obligated to Torah obedience, with the proviso that they were to abstain from sexual immorality and also from eating meat that had been sacrificed to idols.

Typical of many church decisions, the legacy of the Jerusalem Council was that some wholeheartedly accepted its judgment while others subjected it to their own interpretation. Thus, there arose the "party of circumcision," a faction for whom the rite of circumcision was the symbol of participation in God's covenant with Abraham. In their view, all Christians—Jew and Gentile alike—were obligated to undergo circumcision. Representatives of this faction apparently arrived in Galatia after Paul, and they altered his gospel according to this understanding. However, in Paul's view, to require circumcision was equivalent to a reinstitution of the whole law, thereby making a dead letter of the gospel of faith in Christ. Small wonder that he wrote with such vehemence.

The Law and Christ

Galatians 3:6–9; 3:23–4:7

The letter to the Galatians has been the subject of numerous commentaries by writers of various theological and scholarly viewpoints. The great German reformer Martin Luther (1483–1546) developed two different courses of lectures on Galatians, both of which are published in the American edition of his works, and these have influenced the theology of many subsequent commentaries. The word *promise* appears prominently in these verses because it held particular importance for Luther.

Luther often described God as "the promising God" and insisted that it is God's promised salvation in Christ to which the believer clings through faith. He wrote, "For all the past promises [of God made to the Old Testament faithful] were contained in the Christ who was to come. In the same way the faith of the patriarchs was contained in Him. Therefore the faith of the patriarchs was the same as ours.... Yet the faith of the patriarchs was attached to the Christ who was to come, just as ours is attached to the One who has already come."[63]

For Luther, Christ is the fulcrum of the history of God's dealings with his people. Before the incarnation, people lived in expectation of the fulfillment of God's promises; since the incarnation, believers live in the fulfilled promises made to the patriarchs and in anticipation of the Lord's promised return. In every case, it is believers' relationship to Christ in faith that makes them heirs to God's promised salvation.

As Luther read Paul, the law substituted for faith but in an inferior manner. To rely on works of the law was to substitute human knowledge and ability for the true knowledge of God that comes only by way of faith. For Luther, human beings were bound to get into trouble whenever they relied on anything other than the salvation that God promised in Christ. This raises the question of the translation of the word *paidagogos* in Galatians 3:24. The King James Version translates this word "schoolmaster" while the New International Version takes a more roundabout route: "was put in charge." Neither translation captures the force of the word or the dynamics of the relationship Paul appears to have conveyed between the law and Christ.

63. Luther, *Works*, vol. 26, 239.

A *paidagogos* (from which we get our words *pedagogue* and *pedagogy*) was a servant, the slave who cared for the master's children when they were not in school. Included in that role was the responsibility to accompany the children, rather like a modern-day crossing guard. This was no great or demanding assignment, and therefore to translate it as "schoolmaster" leads readers away from Paul's line of thought. Without Christ, the law would have little positive function. For Paul, Christ relegates the law to a decidedly inferior status, especially regarding the issue of Gentiles and the manner in which they are made righteous before God.

Given his context and the emphasis placed on works by the late medieval church, Luther tended to read Galatians as an argument about righteousness by faith versus righteousness by works. New Testament scholar E. P. Sanders, however, helps us interpret this text in a more focused light. Sanders writes:

> The argument of Galatians 3 is... against the view that Gentiles must accept the law *as a condition* of or as a basic requirement fro membership [in the church]. Paul's argument is not in favor of faith per se, nor is it against works per se. It is much more particular: it is against requiring the Gentiles to keep the law in order to be true "sons of Abraham."
>
> We have become so sensitive to the theological issue of grace and merit that we often lose sight of the actual subject of the dispute. Many scholars who view the opposing missionaries as Jewish Christians nevertheless see Galatians 3 as Paul's rebuttal of Juda*ism*. But the quality and character of Judaism are not in view; it is only the question of how one becomes a true son of Abraham, that is, enters the people of God.[64]

Paul underscored this point by speaking historically. Since the Law was not given until centuries following Abraham's death, it could not possibly be the means by which the Gentiles can become heirs to God's promises to the patriarch of all the faithful.

Christian Freedom
Galatians 5:1–15

Freedom is one of the truly great ideas conceived by human beings. Ever since the days of Socrates in ancient Athens, philosophers have contemplated the meaning and significance of human freedom. Democracy is the political idea that places power in the hands of the people and is often therefore associated with the idea of freedom; people who govern themselves would not be likely to endorse or enact their own bondage. Since the European Enlightenment, political leaders in democracies have been charged with the responsibility of enacting policies that protect and maximize people's freedom.

The idea of freedom in North American politics bears on Galatians 5 by way of contrast. Freedom is a common idea in the Bible and Galatians in particular. But faithful Bible study must avoid the pitfall of assuming that this or any other word carries the same meaning in every time and place. Careful Bible readers and interpreters must pay attention to the social and cultural context in which words and ideas appear because context shapes meaning. Freedom in the North American political context means

64. Sanders, *Paul, the Law, and the Jewish People*, 19.

something quite different from the understanding of that idea in the world of the Bible. What is that difference?

People of the biblical era (and remember that an era spans hundreds of years) did not typically think of freedom as an end in itself. If they did, various books of the Bible stood ready to teach them otherwise. Thus, one of the first lessons learned by the children of Israel after their flight from Egyptian slavery was that the aim of the exodus was not merely to give them freedom. At Sinai, God told the Israelites that he had freed them for a purpose. Their freedom was ordered to his purpose for their existence, and that purpose was that Israel would be a people through whom all the world might come to the knowledge of God. In other words, in Exodus and throughout the Old Testament, freedom is always constrained by faithfulness. God liberates people so they might serve him in faithfulness and love.

A very similar idea underwrites Paul's understanding of freedom. As he wrote to the Galatians, "But do not use your freedom to indulge the sinful nature; rather, serve one another in love" (5:13). Freedom in Christ is not license. In the centuries since Paul, from time to time, some Christians have read his sharp criticism of the law as permission to live in complete freedom from all law. The technical term for this line of thought is *antinomianism*, literally, "opposing the law." Paul was no antinomian, for he encouraged the Galatians to serve each other lovingly because the entire law is summed up in the commandment to love our neighbors as ourselves. Christians therefore understand that freedom is not an end in itself. We are not free to do as we please. Christians are people who put their freedom to the service of others. Christians are free to love.

Flesh versus Spirit

Galatians 5:16–6:5, 7–9

In the second half of Galatians 5, Paul contrasts life in the flesh with life in the Spirit. The idea of life in the Spirit continues into chapter 6, where Paul applies it to relationships among believers.

In his discussion of the flesh versus the Spirit, Paul employed a Greek word that indicates that by "flesh" he did not mean "body." The Greek word for body is *soma*, but the word Paul used here is *sarx*. The King James Version translates this word literally as "flesh," where the New International Version employs a more theologically driven translation—"sinful nature." The early Christian exegete and preacher John Chrysostom (c. 347–407) commented on the implications of this difference of meaning:

> The body as such does not cause motion but is moved. It is not an agent but is acted upon. For desire is not of the body but of the soul...How then does Paul say that *the flesh struggles against the Spirit*? By *flesh* he means not the physical body but the evil choice...What then? Ought one to suppress the flesh? Was not the one who said this himself clothed with flesh? By *flesh* here he means earthly thoughts that are apathetic and heedless. This is not a condemnation of the body but a reproach of the apathetic soul. For the flesh [such as the body] is an instrument, and no one repudiates and hates the instrument as such, but only the one who handles the instrument badly.[65]

65. Edwards, *Galatians, Ephesians, Philippians*, 83.

Chrysostom interpreted Paul to mean that the soul of the believer chooses between opposing directions: life according to the flesh or life in the Spirit. The former leads to the vices that Paul listed in 5:19–21. It is worth noting that not all of the sins in this list are gross and external; ambition and envy lurk within the heart, unobserved by the human eye. The soul that chooses against the flesh and its works chooses freedom and a life of virtue. The famous list of these virtues in 5:22–23 is Paul's description of the moral quality of life in the Spirit. These virtues are the fruit of the Spirit. It is interesting that the Greek word that we translate as "fruit" is a singular noun. The Christian virtues of 5:22–23 are not to be understood as *fruits,* as if a believer may pick one or a combination of them; they are *fruit,* as in the "harvest" of the Spirit's activity.

The Bible commentators and preachers of the early church employed the word *virtues* to describe the characteristics of life in the Spirit. In our day, this word has come to be used almost as a synonym for *goodness,* but in the world of the early church *virtue* signified the quality of a person or object that enables it to fulfill its purpose. This often is illustrated by reference to a knife, the purpose of which is to cut things. It is the sharpness of its blade that enables the knife to fulfill this purpose, and thus the virtue of a knife is the keenness of its edge. Paul, however, was not discussing knives but people—specifically believers who have chosen life in the Spirit. The virtues of life in the Spirit are not frosting on the cake for those believers interested in living on a higher spiritual plane. Rather, the harvest of the Spirit is of the very essence of the life of discipleship.

Ephesians

A Circular Letter for Churches
Ephesians 1:1–14

Scholars of the New Testament generally agree that Ephesians was originally a circular letter because in some of the oldest and most authoritative ancient manuscripts of the Greek New Testament the phrase "in Ephesus" is not included in the salutation (1:1). Ancient circular letters commonly left a blank for the name or names of specific people at different locations to which the letter was directed. This letter also lacks the personal references characteristic of Paul's other letters. He had started the church at Ephesus and surely would have remembered gospel workers there; yet this letter gives no indication of such familiarity. The letter, then, was originally intended to circulate through a wide audience of churches—the Christians at Ephesus included.

By the end of the first century and the beginning of the second, Christians in the early church had begun copying and collecting Paul's letters. The letter that often appeared first in order was Ephesians. Broadly stated, its theme is "Christ in his church." Perhaps early Christians recognized that this letter was the best introduction to Paul's writings, a body of instruction that had risen quickly to authoritative status in the life of the church.

Some scholars ask if Paul was the author of this letter because of the letter's impersonal tone, which is so unlike Paul, for example, in his letters to the Galatians and Philippians. Its theology is Pauline, and those who think someone other than Paul wrote it believe that the letter was written by one of his closest associates. Perhaps it was written under his direction with the final authorization coming in the form of permission to send it under his name. A good bit of this is conjecture born of the desire to reconstruct events in the earliest days of Christianity. It is background important to the teacher, but we also must keep in view the letter's purpose, the strengthening of the church.

Christians are called to spiritual blessing. More than a few readers, however, will likely find themselves considering the topics of election and predestination as they are specific items of concern in this text. Of course, these theological issues have often divided Reformed or Calvinist believers from others in the church. On this theme, Ralph Martin writes, "Election here is set in a contextual framework. The author's thought begins with God whose purposes in eternity are the starting point of all Christian praise. The thought is governed by a desire to anchor the church in the divine plan....the New Testament writers proclaim God's electing mercy not as a conundrum to tease our minds but as a wonder to call forth our praise."[66]

Ephesians does not probe the mystery of God's eternal purpose as much as it celebrates the salvation that divine purpose has wrought through Christ.

The Dividing Wall of Hostility
Ephesians 2:8–22

Ephesians 2 focuses on the persistent problem of Jewish and Gentile Christian relationships. Paul faced this problem in nearly every city in which he tried to establish a church. The problem did not originate with the new Christian communities; ethnic hostility predated Christianity. Ever since the work of Ezra the scribe centuries before Christ, Jews had followed a policy of ethnic separation. Gentiles may not have had an Ezra, but they thought in largely the same terms. The Greeks, for example, believed that all non-Greeks were barbarians. This kind of us-and-them thinking was widespread throughout the ancient world.

Paul wanted no part of such divisiveness. The church transcends ethnic and tribal barriers, Paul insisted. Christians live in one fellowship without regard for the ethnic hostilities of their old life.

Paul's argument for the unity of Jewish and Gentile Christians rests on their common inheritance of faith. Readers were, and are, reminded that once they followed the ways of the world and, consequently, were dead in their sins. But God made them alive in Christ Jesus. Paul repeatedly hammered home the point that his readers did nothing to merit their salvation. "For it is by grace you have been saved, through faith—and this not from yourselves, it is the gift of God—not by works, so that no one can boast" (2:8–9). This is indicative speech. It states the way things are—matters of fact.

Paul often followed indicative statements with a "therefore" that linked the statement of fact to an ethical obligation. In Ephesians 2:11, we find the "therefore" after which Paul told his readers that they must remember certain things. On this remembrance hinges the practice of Christian unity. Paul desired both Jewish and Gentile Christians to remember their state outside of Christ. These memories would bring the realization that Christ's blood had brought them near to him and also near to one another. The

66. Martin, *Ephesians, Colossians, and Philemon*, 15–16.

memory of our former estate ought to prompt in us the Christian virtue of humility as we recall that none of us merits God's favor. We are saved and members of the church because of God's grace.

The "dividing wall of hostility" (2:14) was more than a Pauline figure of speech. In the Jerusalem temple, as Paul well knew, a wall divided the outer Court of the Gentiles from the inner precincts of the temple. Only Jews could pass beyond that barrier; Gentiles were obligated to remain outside. To be forced to remain outside was to be reminded of second-class status. The "wall of hostility" in Jerusalem was very real and so were the barriers of social customs that segregated Jews and Gentiles from each other. Christ has broken down all such barriers.

Paul viewed the church as God's only alternative to the corrupt and hopelessly divided Greco-Roman world. It was a world without God and Christ, and therefore, without hope and without peace. For Paul, Christ made the difference and in the process constituted a new social reality. In this new community, age-old animosities and rivalries were not simply overcome; they were abolished through the peace that Christ made possible through his death on the cross. The name of this new social reality is "church." It is the fellowship of the saved and it is God's alternative to a world that cannot make peace with or by itself.

Christian Unity
Ephesians 4:1–16

James Earl Massey, dean emeritus of Anderson University's School of Theology, writes that the word *unity* appears only three times in the Bible: once in Psalm 133:1 and twice in Ephesians 4. Although rarely mentioned specifically, the concept of unity, by implication and imagery, is pervasive in the Bible. This is particularly true of the people of God, the body of Christ, the church.

Unity is central in the Christology of the faith and is critical to the ongoing expansion of the church. It is questionable, Amos wrote, that two could walk together, unless they "have agreed to do so" (Amos 3:3). This need for unity was especially true of the young church. For three years, Paul had labored among believers throughout the eastern Mediterranean basin. As God's apostle to the Gentiles, he now writes from a Roman prison, fully aware of the diverse constituency receiving the letter. Many had no religious background and no common heritage to bind them together. For Paul, the barriers had already been broken down (Eph 2:14) and there was no longer "Jew nor Greek, slave nor free, male nor female" (Gal 3:28); they were now all one in Christ.

The unity of which he writes, however, is easier to believe than achieve. Theologically, unity is accomplished in Christ, the One who holds all things together. However, the practice of unity is the emphasis in Ephesians. Both Colossians and Ephesians contain a similar focus upon the all-sufficiency of Christ. In Colossians, Christ is the visible presence of the invisible God (Col 1:15), and in Ephesians, Christ is the center, uniting all things "in heaven and on earth together under one head, even Christ" (Eph 1:10).

A major concern of this circular letter, written about AD 63, is the unity of believers in Christ. Paul was attempting to assimilate the nonreligious person into the community of faith. Although he had never met these seekers, he knew that strong principles were needed if a healthy church was to emerge. Even the nonreligious knew how disharmony spoiled the beauty of music, and Paul presented Christ as the key to harmony in a discordant world.

The unity of the church does not rest on sameness. The church will not be unified because every Christian looks the same, thinks the same, or even acts entirely the same. To be sure, the one body of Christ looks to one Spirit and one hope—"one Lord, one faith, one baptism; one God and Father of all, who is over all and through all and in all" (4:5). Nevertheless, this powerful and ringing affirmation of Christianity does not yield a cookie-cutter religion where uniformity becomes a thin substitute for unity.

Paul's theology of the one church places Christ at the head. "From him the whole body, joined and held together by every supporting ligament, grows and builds itself up in love, as each part does its work" (4:16). One of Paul's favorite metaphors for the church was to call it a "body." The human body is a wonderful example of unity and diversity. Think of the enormous variation in the cells of your body. Hair cells, skin cells, nerve cells, and bone cells—some cells that serve as vision receptors; others that serve as taste receptors, brain cells, and heart muscle cells. All of them are connected by the same DNA and unified in the one body that is yours. Paul did not know the body in such detail, but his principle is nevertheless the same. Diverse as they are, Christians work together at their several tasks in one unified body called the church.

The miracle of Christian unity depends upon the connection of each single Christian to Christ. Christ is the head of the body and governs it through his distribution of roles and responsibilities necessary for the body's health and development. Verses 11 and 12 list several church offices and responsibilities and explain their primary purpose, which is ultimately the edification of the church. It is tempting to make a large distinction between the work of ordained clergy and laity at this point, but that distinction should not be pressed too far. All Christians are called to the work of ministry; all are called to works of service. Regardless of specific responsibilities, each Christian is a "supporting ligament" (4:16). The connections of the church depend on each one of us.

In the century after Paul, a man named Montanus caused a very great stir in the church through his claim that the Holy Spirit spoke through him in an extraordinary way. Some historians have concluded that Montanus claimed to be the incarnation of the Spirit. In either case, this man attracted many followers, including the very influential early theologian Tertullian. Ultimately, the church judged Montanus as a heretic and responded to his claim of direct inspiration by regularizing the procedures for ministerial ordination. The custom of the laying on hands became an important element of these procedures. A minister's calling had to be confirmed through ordination and the laying on of hands; without these procedures a call to ministry was considered invalid. So it came to be that Christ and the Spirit were understood to confer their gifts for ministry through the regular procedures of the church. While perhaps a necessary reaction to the excesses of Montanus and people like him, the regularization of ordination led to a double standard because of which only those who are ordained were thought to have a ministry. Ministry is charged with the task of preparing the people of God, but it is also true that without works of service the church is weakened and its unity threatened. Works of service reenact the works of Christ, the head of the church. Works of service embody the love that is shed on all of us by the Holy Spirit.

If Christian unity depended on uniformity, it would be no miracle. Uniformity can be enforced; all one needs is a big stick. Unity, on the other hand, is a miracle because Christ unites us even in the midst of our diversity. Thus the church is, or ought to be, the place where even Democrats and Republicans can live together in peace.

(Married) Children of Light
Ephesians 5:1–5, 21–29; 6:1–4

"Live a life worthy of the calling you have received" (4:1). Paul gave even sharper focus to this exhortation with the bold statement, "Be imitators of God" (5:1). Can he be serious? Is it possible for finite human beings to imitate the infinite Creator of the universe? The short answer is yes. This is not the only place in the Pauline letters where readers are encouraged to take God or Christ as their example. Consider Philippians 2:5: "Your attitude should be the same as that of Christ Jesus." Paul teaches that Christians can follow in the footsteps of Christ and that Christ is God. This imitation is limited to a moral sense. Of course, many are the ways that it is impossible for human beings to take God as their pattern. But through the power of the Holy Spirit it is both the privilege and duty of Christians to "live a life of love, just as Christ loved us" (5:2).

In the exhortation to imitate God and live lives of love, these verses lead to a set of ethical instructions for Christians. They depend on the same Pauline structure of indicative/imperative that we have already considered. In this case, the indicative statement can be found in 5:8: "For you were once darkness, but now you are light in the Lord." This sentence states the way things are now for believers. They are children of light. Since that is so, they are under a moral obligation to "live as children of light." Preceding and following this verse, one reads specific instructions concerning the meaning of the imperative statement to "live as children of light."

Ephesians 5:21 and the following verses contain very specific and well-known instruction for Christian wives and husbands. Much has been made of the verse, "Wives, submit to your husbands" (5:22). The interpretations of this verse by some church traditions have been the subject of recent comment and debate. Are wives to submit to their husbands? Yes, but do not stop reading there as if Paul had nothing to say to men. Husbands are to love their wives as Christ loved the church. And we already know from 5:2 that Christ's love takes the form of giving up one's own self for the sake of the beloved. A relationship in which one marriage partner submits while the other loves sacrificially can lead only to the conclusion that in Christian marriage both spouses mutually love, respect, and care for one another.

Although 5:31 is often passed over in discussions of this text, Ralph Martin takes this verse to be the central, organizing phase of this passage. "The point made by this appeal to Genesis [2:24] is the same as that in Mark 10:7–8. God created humankind as man and woman; they so yearn for each other that they are ready to leave their earthly parents... marriage sets up so fundamental a relationship between man and woman that it relativizes and even terminates the original and universal relationship of the family unit in Israel's life."[67]

The longing of one man and one woman for each other is so strong as to prompt them to leave their parents' homes and begin a life together. The power of this longing is a mystery paralleled in Paul's view by the mutual longing of Christ and the church. Once again, the norms of ethical living with regard to marriage can be found in the example of Christ. In marriage, as in the other aspects of life, Christians are taught to imitate the divine love of Christ.

Disciples' Weapons
Ephesians 6:10–24

The call to Christ is followed by his call to fellowship in the new community called the church. In the church, Christians mutually strengthen and support one another as they live out their calling to a new way of life in a world that neither understands nor appreciates it. The Ephesian letter considers all of these matters before concluding with one final, well-known exhortation.

The image of Christian warfare dominates Ephesians 6. Against whom did Christians of the first century contend? Earlier in his ministry, Paul had thought that the Roman government was a benign power that punished only evildoers (see Rom13:3–4, for example). It is also the case that Paul exploited his Roman citizenship to the advantage of gospel work. Nevertheless, by the end of his life, the nature of Paul's dealings with the imperial government had changed dramatically. Under the malignant cruelty of Emperor Nero, the government turned a hostile face toward the young Christian church. Paul was arrested, tried by a Roman official, transported to Rome in chains under the guard of Roman soldiers, and finally sentenced to die at the hands of Roman executioners.

Paul may have been one of the most famous Christian martyrs, but he was certainly not alone in suffering at the hands of the Roman Empire. Nero deflected blame for a disastrous fire in the city of Rome from himself to Christians, thus raising public opinion against them. He used the living bodies of Christians dipped in hot wax to light gardens where he hosted parties for his friends. Well before the first century had concluded, Christians knew that the Roman government had become a deadly enemy. They could not contend against the dominant culture and political arrangement with conventional force, nor were they called to do so. In this struggle, they would need to employ all of the weapons and armor of Christian discipleship.

Rome was not the only enemy of the young church. Ephesians 6 also identifies a set of spiritual foes against which Christians must contend. There are "superhuman forces arrayed against the church. The assaults of demonic powers require heavenly aid to repel, and it is the epistle's conviction, in true Pauline fashion, that God has placed at the Christians' disposal all

67. Ibid., 69.

that is needed to resist such an attack."[68] This is the well-known "full armor of God" specified in verses 13 through 18. None of this armor was worn or otherwise employed on the *backside* of a soldier's body. Christians then and now are expected to face the church's foes. The general tenor of these verses is preparedness. Christians must be prepared for conflict with the powers and principalities that pretend to rule the present age. Some of those powers are spiritual; others are temporal. In principle, all have been broken by the power of Christ and his cross.

Philippians

Friendship from Prison
Philippians 1:1–30

While New Testament scholars may debate whether Paul is the author of some of the letters that bear his name, nobody disputes the authorship of Philippians. There is nearly universal agreement that Paul is the writer. Sometimes the content of his letters modifies the actual letter format. The letter to the Romans is an introduction by way of theological statement. The Corinthian correspondence is polished argument. Philippians, on the other hand, is in both form and content genuinely a letter.

Philippians is one of a small grouping of letters called the Prison Letters. It is clear from the letter that Paul had been placed under arrest. While we can be fairly certain of his legal situation, the location of Paul's imprisonment is more difficult to determine. References to the "palace guard" (1:13) and "Caesar's household" (4:22) suggest that Paul may already have been in Rome, but other cities have been suggested as the location of this imprisonment. Caesarea and Ephesus are two of those. One thing that is clear is that Paul was in Roman rather than Jewish custody. Wherever he was and whatever the nature of Paul's incarceration, he described it in the legal terms of arrest and imprisonment. It is equally clear that Paul believed that he had been imprisoned for Christ's sake and that Christ's gospel, rather than he, would be on trial.

Because Paul had been arrested of course meant that he was not free to come and go. Travel was not possible, so he could no longer visit the churches he had founded—including the church at Philippi. His forced absence gave rise to questions about him and his work. What might be the consequences for the gospel of Paul's arrest and impending trial? His situation in jail required some interpretation, and he offered this in the first verses of Philippians.

Whether in the first or the twenty-first centuries, imprisonment is an unpleasant experience. Most of us are unacquainted with anybody who would actually enjoy imprisonment. Like us, Paul would rather be free; however, freedom is not his uppermost concern. Of greatest importance to Paul was that Christ is preached. So he can rejoice even in his own personal imprisonment because it has encouraged his "brothers in the Lord...to speak the word of God more courageously and fearlessly" (1:14). If captivity served to advance the gospel, then Paul was content to remain in prison. He could take joy that God's larger purpose, salvation for Jew and

68. Ibid., 75.

Gentile alike, was being achieved. To Paul, the most important thing was for Christ to be exalted. It is this capacity to see his own circumstances within God's larger design that enables Paul to say, "For to me, to live is Christ and to die is gain" (1:21).

Paul assured his Philippian friends that his imprisonment needed to be viewed positively. Some in the church, prone to the view that only evildoers were arrested, may have needed to hear Paul say that the gospel was being advanced through his incarceration. It is also the case that Paul often found the silver lining of evangelical advance even in the darkest clouds of suffering and obstruction. Here, however, he offered evidence of his claim. First, even his Roman captors—pagans, remember—had come to the view that Paul had been imprisoned for Jesus' sake. Second, Paul's imprisonment had the effect of encouraging and strengthening the faith of Christians in the district where Paul was a prisoner. Third, the gospel was still spreading, even though it may have been through the work of preachers who considered themselves Paul's rivals. In his view, the gospel was anything but weakened on account of his imprisonment.

Paul also wrote to reassure the Philippians about the consequences of his imprisonment personally and for them. Indiscriminate as the Romans were about executing prisoners, Paul in Roman hands meant that death lurked very near. Paul needed to consider carefully his situation. He told his readers that he was unsure: he was torn between the alternatives of release and life to continue preaching the gospel, or death and eternal salvation and deliverance in Christ. Even though death would be gain, Paul was quite content to remain at work in the church so that others might experience joy overflowing through his continued fellowship with them.

Recent studies of the letter to the Philippians describes it as a Christian version of a type known throughout the Greco-Roman world as a friendship letter. Unlike many of Paul's letters, Philippians does not attempt to settle some problem or confront some issue facing the Christians there. Unlike the Corinthian letters, the tone of Philippians is warm and cordial. Where Paul rebukes the Galatians for allowing novel interpretations of Christian discipleship to influence them away from his instruction, in Philippians Paul commends his readers and urges them to go forward in their obedience to Christ.

Throughout the ancient Roman world, all kinds of people thought relationships were a key element in the development of good character. Paul expresses this very idea in 1 Corinthians 15:33: "Bad company corrupts good character." By the same token, friendships with good people were believed to promote the development of good character. Thus, ancient people considered friendship to be a crucial moral consideration. In his letter to the Philippians, Paul takes the role of an older spiritual friend who encourages his brothers and sisters at Philippi to conduct themselves "in a manner worthy of the gospel of Christ" (1:27). Early Christian churches were communities of expectation where it was natural for a leader like Paul to exhort his readers toward Christian maturity. As their friend and older brother in the Lord, it was natural for Paul to raise such expectations of new followers of Christ. He prods, exhorts, and encourages such growth in his beloved Philippian believers—important signs of his love and friendship. Paul is a good friend and therefore writes with the expectation that the Philippians must grow as disciples of the Lord Jesus.

Paul thought especially highly of his friends at Philippi. This courageous and devoted group of men and women occupied a special place in Paul's heart. They had been willing to share in his troubles. Alone among all the congregations begun by Paul, the Philippians shared materially with him in his gospel labor (4:14–16). They had made great spiritual progress, and, because they had, he hoped for even more for them. Thus he prayed, that their love would "abound more and more in knowledge and depth of insight, so that [they would] be able to discern what is best and...be pure and blameless until the day of Christ" (1:9–10).

The Moral Example of Christ

Philippians 2:1–18

Philippians 2:1–18 should be considered under the title "Thoughts on the Cultivation of Christian Character." Two key elements in the development of Christian disciples are a moral example and a specific list of qualities that such character displays. Both are present in this text. Before considering them, it is important to consider the context of the Philippians.

In the first century, the city of Philippi was a Roman colony. The Macedonians had built a city on that site long before the arrival of the Romans, but the imperial army destroyed it when Rome first occupied that region of Europe. They could be and often did treat their enemies ruthlessly, especially those who resisted Roman occupation and rule. In such cases, imperial policy often involved the complete destruction of the city, followed by its reorganization as an official Roman colony. Increased numbers of Roman citizens often populated such colonies, and such seems to have been the case at Philippi.

American citizenship typically is a birthright, but that was not the case in the Roman Empire. To be an official citizen of Rome was a privilege restricted to a tiny minority. Roman citizens consequently were very proud of their citizenship, and when they said, "I am a Roman," they said it with a bit of arrogance thrown in. Roman achievement encouraged such attitudes. Their army and navy had turned the Mediterranean Sea into a Roman lake, creating the largest empire the ancient world had yet seen. Roman soldiers camped in tents pitched in England and on the Tigris and Euphrates rivers. Roman arms enforced the Pax Romana, the "peace of Rome," which ensured peace and safety throughout the empire. Roman achievements in law and engineering created a common imperial culture that spread with an ease unrivaled in the ancient world. Pride in Roman citizenship elevated certain personal qualities they believed ideal: swagger, pride, toughness, practicality, and courage, to name a few. Many of the Roman colonists at Philippi would naturally have thought that such characteristics make up the ideal person, the Roman citizen.

We do not know the composition of the church at Philippi, but we can say that, read in the context of a Roman colony, Paul's exhortation to the church in Philippians 2 must be seen as a sharply countercultural statement.

Paul does not want the church to be different for the sake of being different. Rather, he calls it to live counterculturally as a natural consequence of following Christ. Those who take Jesus as the pattern of their lives will live in a manner that marks them off from the dominant culture.

Possibly, some of the Philippian Christians were Roman citizens. Paul reminded them that Christian citizenship is first in heaven (3:20). As citizens of the heavenly city, they could find no moral example in Roman culture but only in the crucified and resurrected Lord. So Paul exhorts his beloved Philippian Christians, "Your attitude should be the same as that of Christ Jesus" (2:5). What follows that exhortation is a description of Christ's character that explains the qualities Paul has in mind. Although equal to God, Christ "made himself nothing, taking the very nature of a servant" (2:6–7). On Christ's example, the virtues of humility and obedience become key character traits for all who wish to be citizens of heaven (2:8). One can imagine that some of this letter's first readers found this exhortation hard to accept. The Roman world did not prize humility or obedience as personal characteristics; they were for the meek of the earth—not Roman citizens. Heavenly citizenship turned the world and its values upside down.

Later in this letter, Paul specifically directs his readers' attention to those things worthy of their consideration. He has told his readers that they are to pattern their lives on Jesus; he is their moral example as well as Savior. In chapter four, Paul lists qualities that are to be the subject matter of Christian moral reflection. In other words, he makes some specific suggestions about the qualities that are to be seriously considered by a follower of Jesus. His list includes some of the most important words in our moral vocabulary: *true, noble, right, pure, lovely, admirable, excellence, praiseworthy*. These are personal qualities that followers of Jesus are to put into practice. In this list and in the moral example of Jesus, Paul gives us crucial ideas for growth as Christian disciples.

For many years, scholars generally have agreed that Philippians 2:6–11 is an early Christian hymn. It can be broken down into three sections: (1) preexistence, (2) existence, and (3) post-existence. The terms have reference to the Logos before, during, and after the incarnation. The hymn states without reservation that the Logos, whom Paul called Christ Jesus, is "in very nature God." Later Christian theologians would argue this point until it was affirmed in the Nicene Creed, written and accepted in AD 325. The hymn goes on to say that the one who was equal to God "made himself nothing." This New International Version rendering of a form of the Greek word *kenosis* is better translated "emptied himself." We should ask ourselves, "Of what did the Logos empty himself?" One also wants to ask whether to become a human being is for the Son of God any more humiliating than to experience death. Verses 9–11 describe Jesus after the incarnation in his exaltation. Taken together, these verses constitute one of the most important early statements of Christology—the field of theology concerned with the person and work of Christ.

What a scene it will be when every knee bows and every tongue confesses the lordship of Christ! Our contemporary fascination with power and glory is not unlike the Roman colonists of Philippi, and may obscure a further insight into the manner of Christ's exaltation. If the eternal Son of God could lay aside equality with God, then perhaps humility and unselfish love lie nearer the center of the divine glory than do conventional notions of power. Perhaps it will be the beauty of holiness and the inescapable pull of suffering love that will bring all of us to our knees.

Faithful Character

Philippians 3:7–21

Faithful biblical interpretation requires that we take into account the historical situation of the New Testament church. In these first years of missionary expansion, Christianity was still very much in the process of formation. Its only scripture was the Old Testament in its Greek translation—the Septuagint. At the time that Paul wrote the Philippian letter, none of the Gospels nor most of the other New Testament books had yet been written, and Paul's letters had not yet achieved the status of scripture. Without the New Testament texts to guide them, people read the Septuagint with wide variation when it came to interpreting the implications of Jesus' life, death, and resurrection for his new followers. (As we know from church history, Christians have come to different conclusions about some of these matters even *with* the New Testament.) Some in the very early church went so far as to disregard the Old Testament entirely. At the dawn of the Christian movement, rival interpreters contested the meaning of the life and teachings of Jesus.

The letter to the Philippians illustrates three different views of the consequences of Jesus' life for his followers. One of these is the Pauline view, which eventually framed orthodox Christian teaching. On either side of Paul stood two rival interpretations that, in these early days, threatened to become normative for the church. On one side, Paul was opposed by those who saw Jesus as an extension of Judaism. We might think of them as conservatives in their determination to enforce the Old Testament law on all members of the church. Paul's attitude toward them is quite clear in Philippians 3:2. In contrast to these Judaizers, Paul taught that God's righteousness comes through faith in Christ—"the righteousness that comes from God and is by faith" (3:9).

Challenging Paul from the side opposite were those who radically interpreted his instruction on freedom in Christ. We might think of these as liberals— really, libertines—who denied the law any validity and lived utterly undisciplined lives. "Their god is their stomach and their glory is in their shame. Their mind is on earthly things" (3:19). They were people who thought that God's salvation in Christ was entirely spiritual and rendered obsolete the practices of ethical living. Against these libertines, Paul offered the example of his own life and others as testimony to faithful Christian living (3:17).

In criticizing the libertines, Paul said, "Our citizenship is in heaven" (3:20). This is more than a reminder of the Christian's ultimate destiny. Heavenly citizenship begins here and now in the confession that Christ is Savior and Lord. To become a citizen of heaven is to display in everyday life the virtues of the heavenly city. The Roman colonists of Philippi had once proudly asserted all the virtues of Roman citizenship. In arguing against the libertines' "earthly" citizenship, Paul also reminded the

Philippians that their true citizenship was no longer Roman either. Heavenly citizenship strongly implies that a new set of Christian virtues must replace the old Roman ones. Wealth, arrogance, militarism, and force had to give way to love, joy, peace, longsuffering, self-control, and the other virtues that Paul called the harvest of the Spirit's activity in the soul. In a word, heavenly citizenship meant having the same mind as Christ about the pattern of faithful character.

Love Covers a Multitude of Church Disputes

Philippians 4:4–18

As he came to the close of his letter to the Philippians, Paul touched on a range of matters. He attempted to resolve a dispute between church leaders. He urged his beloved Philippians to keep a joyful attitude toward life and also encouraged them to practice a set of virtues that he himself displayed. Finally, he expressed his deep gratitude to the Philippian church for its thoughtful generosity. Paul addressed all of these concerns in the space of twenty-three verses.

Remember, Paul wrote this letter while imprisoned. The Romans did not maintain prisons for punishment, so prison was anyplace that could serve to hold people awaiting trial: a cave, a dungeon, a jail, or perhaps a military barracks. So we do not know the precise circumstances of his incarceration. Paul's earlier references in this letter to the Praetorian Guard suggest that he was held at a barracks or guardhouse. In any case, the larger point is that Paul awaited a trial at the end of which loomed the possibility of a death sentence. The Romans applied the death penalty to a staggering variety of crimes and offenses, and Paul wrote this letter under this cloud. Fully aware of the possibility of execution, he nevertheless wrote with joy and out of concern for the Philippians' needs. Paul focused his mind and heart not on his own situation but on Christ and the church. This focus enabled him to put his own life in perspective.

From Paul's vantage point, a healthy church was of paramount concern. In sick churches, leaders allow disagreements to fester into open disputes. Apparently, two Philippian leaders, Euodia and Syntyche, had argued over some point now unknown to us. We know that they were leaders because Paul said that these women had "contended at my side in the cause of the gospel" and also referred to them as "fellow workers" (4:3). Note that these church leaders were women. Paul's written statements about the role and place of women in the church should be placed alongside his references to practice. Pauline practice was to treat men and women equally as candidates for gospel service, as this and other references repeatedly demonstrate. Whether concerning candidates for ministry or Christian unity, Paul treated matters of Christian practice with great seriousness. The unity of the church must be more than lip service, so Paul pled with Euodia and Syntyche to resolve their disagreement.

Paul also had in view the practice of Christian virtues at Philippi. To rejoice in everything and be anxious for nothing are virtues of Christian living made possible by remembering that the Lord is near. *Near* may mean that the Lord is always present or that Paul expected Christ's imminent return. In either case,

Christian awareness that the Lord is near is what underwrites joy and explains the absence of anxiety. Paul also exhorted his readers to put into practice the other virtues they had been taught, had read, or had seen embodied in Paul's own life. Clearly, Paul thought that the gospel embraced more than a set of beliefs. As crucial as faith was to the gospel, life in Christ also entails a new ethical life.

As Paul drew his letter to a conclusion, he could not fail to thank the Philippians for their abiding thoughtfulness and generosity. They had gone above and beyond the call of duty, contributing materially to Paul's support and sharing in his troubles. The fine Christians of Philippi had supported Paul from the early days of his second missionary journey down to his current imprisonment. To them, Paul expressed his deep gratitude and his assurance that the God they mutually served would never fail.

Colossians

Heresy at Colosse

Colossians 1:15–28

Nearly all of Paul's letters address a particular issue or problem. Often called the letter's "occasion," it is the primary purpose for its writing. The occasions of Paul's letters were of many different kinds. Unique among them is occasion for the letter to the Colossians, which deals with the problem of heretical teaching. One possible candidate for a heresy charge could have been the circumcision party teaching in the Galatian churches that circumcision is required of all who would be Christians. Paul does state that there can be but one gospel and that anyone who teaches another is anathema (something or someone to be shunned). But the Colossian heresy involved ideas alien to both Judaism and the emergent Jesus movement, and it must be noted that the teachings of the so-called Judaizers were at least grounded in the Judaism from which Christianity emerged.

The city of Colosse was located in Asia Minor (what is today Turkey). The city's population consisted mainly of Greeks, Phrygians, and Jews resettled there two centuries earlier by the Seleucid emperor Antiochus III. During Paul's lifetime, Colosse had become a culturally diverse city where many different philosophical and religious ideas took root. This diversity of thought created the distinct possibility that ideas from different religious and intellectual systems might merge. Apparently, some ideas alien to Pauline teaching had entered the church at Colosse, and this Colossian heresy provides the letter's occasion.

Paul did not specify the content of the heretical teaching at Colosse. A reconstruction of all its elements is therefore almost impossible, but we can say that the Colossian heresy clearly threatened the beliefs and practical living of apostolic Christianity.

> Part of the teaching was related to a theological matter and centered on the question, Where is God's true presence to be found and how may human beings gain access to that presence? The answer evidently...came back from these Colossian teachers: God's fullness is distributed throughout a series of emanations from the divine, stretching from heaven to

> earth. These "eons" or offshoots of deity must be venerated and homage paid to them as "elemental spirits" or angels or gods inhabiting the stars. They rule destiny, control human life, and hold the entrance to the divine realm in their keeping. Christ is one of them, but only one among many.[69]

The second part of our question, the means of gaining access to God's presence, evidently was answered by the Colossian heresy through rigorous abstinence, treating the body harshly, and other extreme practices (see 2:16, 21, and 23). In effect, this view insisted that believers must earn God's favor through the discipline, perhaps abuse, of the body. This teaching implicitly denied the goodness of material existence, which God had declared to be good at the creation. Such teaching constituted a comprehensive threat to the moral, spiritual, and theological health of the Colossian church.

In Colossians 1:15–28, Paul attacks false teaching at Colosse with some of the most exalted descriptions of Christ found anywhere in the New Testament. In the strongest possible terms, Paul declares that Christ is not one of a series of demigods but the "image of the invisible God" (1:15) in whom dwells all the divine fullness (1:19). The text does not open the door even the slightest crack to any misinterpretation of this apostolic teaching; it hammers the point of Christ's supremacy repeatedly in the verses from 1:15 to 1:20. In turn, they provide the theological foundation for all that follows in this letter.

69. Martin, *Ephesians, Colossians, and Philemon,* 83.

Christ and the Powers
Colossians 2:6–19

Christians are sometimes prone to see theology as an intellectual enterprise of little relevance to practical Christian living. The Colossian letter challenges that view, and Colossians 2:6–19 specifically points up theology's bearing on ethics. Not all Christians are called to be theologians, of course. But matters of Christian living are addressed in this section of Colossians by anchoring them to the letter's theological theme: "For in Christ all the fullness of the Deity dwells in bodily form" (2:9). From this theological premise follows the foundation of Christian living: "and you have been given fullness in Christ" (2:10).

"Fullness in Christ" means that participation in Christ concerns more than the redemption that Christ wrought on the cross. On that cross, Christ also "disarmed the powers and authorities" (2:15). Often this is taken as a reference to spiritual warfare, but it is also appropriate to extend the meaning of this phrase to forces of this world that pretend to rule our lives. Two people who have written very helpfully in this regard are Hendrik Berkhof, *Christ and the Powers* (Scottdale, PA.: Harold Press, 1977) and Walter Wink, *Naming the Powers* (Philadelphia: Fortress Press, 1984). Technological, political and social structures, nuclear power, and genetic engineering loom over us as only a few of the forces against which we struggle, sometimes in vain. Each of these powers and others has the potential to destabilize our lives, thereby robbing us of its fullness. But Christ has triumphed over all of them and in that triumph brings authentic fullness of life.

Paul's theological emphasis that the fullness of Christ leads to fullness of human life leads to a discussion of Christian ethics. This section of the Colossian letter—Colossians 2:6–19—takes dead aim at the rites and regulations instituted by the teachers of the Colossian heresy. Their thought and practice resembled many religious systems that placed a premium on ritual. Paul dismissed all of this as "human commands and teachings" (2:22). But it is a mistake to read Paul here as a person bent on the destruction of all religious ritual. Rather, he opposed a set of activities that crossed the boundary that separated religion from magic. He challenged those who believe that they could conjure the gods into giving them their desires or who believe that a particular set of behaviors will unlock the door to the divine presence. Verses 16–18 list the kinds of magical and quasi-religious rites that teachers of the Colossian heresy had put forward as keys to religious fulfillment. Paul described them as "idle notions" (2:18). Such activities are not harmless, since they indicate that their devotees have "lost connection with the Head"—namely Christ.

Christian discipleship is a life lived out of our theological commitments. In this sense, theology is not so much a technical discussion of beliefs and ideas as it is a set of practices. Paul's letter to the Colossians illustrates practical theology as it corrects a serious misunderstanding about religious ritual. Ethics isn't something we do once we have our theological house in order, and theology is not a discussion conducted in isolation from matters of practical living. The fullness of Christ and the fullness of life go hand in hand.

Ethics Is Not Ritual but Virtue

Colossians 3:1–17

Colossians 2 opposes the rites and rituals associated with the Colossian heresy. The root of this opposition lay in the inability of heretical ritual to bring the fullness of life. Only the fullness of God dwelling in human form can bring such fullness. Human rules and regulations are destined to perish and as such are life-denying rather than life-fulfilling. In Colossians 3, Paul moves on to consider the consequences of the Christian's participation in Christ.

Once again we find the familiar Pauline indicative and imperative. Colossians 3:1 opens with the indicative statement, "Since, then, you have been raised with Christ." Although Paul didn't state it specifically, presumably this is a reference to Christian baptism in which the believer is buried symbolically and then rises in Christ. Since that was now the case, certain ethical imperatives followed: "Set your mind on things above" (3:2) and "Put to death, therefore, whatever belongs to your earthly nature" (3:5). Paul stated these ethical obligations in the imperative mood, which is but another way of saying that they are not suggestions but obligations.

The teachers of the Colossian heresy had been enforcing a life-denying asceticism, a denial of certain goods for the sake of higher goods. Paul opposed this heretical asceticism as false. But he does not rule out all forms of asceticism, for in chapter 3 he proceeded to explain the nature and form of the true path of self-denial that Christians walk. He began this explanation with a list of vices and sins that

Christians must shun (3:5–9) followed by a catalog of Christian virtues and a general exhortation to Christlike relationships and attitudes.

The list of virtues in verses 12–14 is significant. In particular, the concept of virtue needs some further explanation. In our day the word *virtue* has become a synonym for the words *good* or *moral*. Thus we may say, "Mary is a woman of virtue" and mean "Mary is a moral person." In Paul's world, however, the word *virtue* (in Greek, *arete*) meant something quite different. In Paul's world, the word signified "excellence" and the "quality of a person or object that enabled it to fulfill its purpose or function." An illustration may be in order here. We all know that the purpose or function of a knife is to cut. It is the keen edge of the knife blade that enables it to accomplish this purpose. Thus the virtue of a knife is the sharpness of its edge, and a dull knife may be said to have lost its virtue.

Paul used the term *virtue* to refer to all the traits of Christian character he listed in Colossians 3:12–14, strongly suggesting that he thought of them as essential to Christian living. We might consider the purpose of Christian living. Paul clearly understood that purpose to lie beyond the realm of personal wishes and desires. The *Westminster Shorter Catechism* says it well: "The chief end of humanity is to serve God and enjoy God forever." The Christian virtues specified in Colossians 3 (his letter to the Galatians contains a similar list) must be understood as the qualities that enable us to fulfill our true purpose, which is to serve God here in preparation for the eternal enjoyment of divine friendship.

First and Second Thessalonians

Faith, Love, and Hope at Thessalonica

1 Thessalonians 1:2–10; 3:6–10

The books of the New Testament are not arranged in chronological sequence. Matthew was probably not the first of the Gospels nor was it the earliest New Testament book. Among Paul's correspondence, Romans is one of his later letters. They are ordered by length rather than date, but one of Paul's letters does claim the title of the oldest book of the New Testament. First Thessalonians was written in AD 49 or 50 while Paul was in Corinth on his second journey in the company of Timothy and Silas. Captivated by Paul's vision of "a man from Macedonia" (Acts 16:8–10), the little band had crossed from Asia Minor into the upper Balkans—European soil. They planted the seed of the gospel at Philippi before moving on to Thessalonica. This city sat astride the great east-west Roman highway called the Ignatian Way. Cities along this road were important commercial centers, Thessalonica among them. From there, the missionaries continued their journey, stopping at Berea, Athens, and Corinth.

Under threat of harm, Paul and his associates had been forced to leave Thessalonica hastily and perhaps prematurely. He was concerned for the fate of the new Christians community there, and for that reason he sent Timothy back to Thessalonica to look in on the church and strengthen it. Subsequently, Timothy returned to Corinth with his report. Timothy's positive news became the immediate cause for Paul's letter. He was delighted that the church was in good condition. He had been especially concerned for these new believers, as he said, "We continually remember before our God and Father your work produced by faith, your labor prompted by love, and your endurance inspired by hope in our Lord Jesus Christ." Already in the earliest of his extant letters, Paul makes reference to three central Christian virtues—faith, hope, and love. They are always intertwined in Paul's writing, but from time to time he highlights one of them. In Galatians and Romans, Paul amplifies the theme of faith. To the Corinthians, he stressed the importance of love. Faith and love were well-developed among the Thessalonians, but Paul was especially concerned that they understand and embody the virtue of hope.

Jesus was resurrected from the dead and had been seen by many still-living believers. Prior to his ascension, Jesus had promised to return, and it was widely believed that this momentous event would occur within their lifetimes. Wherever Paul brought the gospel, he taught new believers about the crucified, resurrected, and soon-to-return Lord. The ancient church lived on tiptoe in the expectation of this imminent *parousia*, the Lord's return, and this hope sustained the church through the trial and adversity.

Inevitably, the delay of that return raised questions in the minds of believers. Increased persecution lent an even greater urgency. In the face of hostility and the persecution of his church, why did the Lord tarry? The lack of a ready answer to that question threatened to undermine hope, and Paul wanted to prevent such a loss among the Thessalonians. But before turning specifically to hope, he praised them for their faith and love.

If hope is the Christian virtue oriented especially to the future and Christ's return, faith and love are the virtues to be displayed in the meantime. It will not do for Christians to hope in a manner that allows them to wait idly. There is work to be done in the meantime. Paul wrote that it is faith that yields work, and our labors are prompted by love. Love is a social virtue; it defines and supports our relationships. But Paul also regarded faith as an active virtue that implies connections with others. The Thessalonians had questions concerning the Christian hope, but faith and love were alive and well and the source of much well-doing.

Problems in a New Church

1 Thessalonians 4:1–8; 5:12–24

The Thessalonian manuscript is one of our earliest sources, possibly dated about AD 50 or 51, as early as twenty years following the resurrection of Christ. As a cradle of Christian faith, this church's history can be compacted into three small words: potential, problems, and prayer—words that can be applied to every church in every age.

Paul believed that he had been divinely directed to Thessalonica because of the city's potential. As a financial center, it was the hub of commerce for land and sea. As a free city, it was essentially Greek and therefore intellectually alive. In such an atmosphere of exploration and expansion, faithful converts responded to the gospel of Christ. Although a good response brought about the establishment of a strong church, it was not without its problems. Rapid growth, then as now, confronts the church with change, and after Paul's departure, he was informed that some problems did in fact need attention. Paul addressed each of these in this first letter:

- Theological confusion about the resurrection (1 Thess 4:11–18).
- Rejection of authority, with some believers questioning Paul's leadership (1 Thess 5:12–14).
- Constant temptation for converts to return to former pagan practices of immorality (1 Thess 4:3–8).
- Lack of discipline in accepting responsibility for the life of the local church (1 Thess 4:9; 5:13).

Solutions to such problems were not to be found in the financial or intellectual resources of the Thessalonians. Instead, Paul insisted, the answers were theological, relational, and spiritual. Repeatedly, he supports a practical theology of holiness with the words "mentioning you in our *prayers*" (1:2), "we *pray* most earnestly" (3:10), "*pray* continually" (5:17), and "*pray* for us" (5:25).

These verses sound a call to holiness. A call to personal, ethical holiness as indicated in 4:1–8 is followed by a challenge to relational holiness in the context of the community of faith (5:12–24). Personal holiness enables people to conduct their lives in ways acceptable to God. It makes possible the practice of abstinence and fidelity in moral matters of individual conduct, and integrity in all other aspects of life. In 5:12–24, the emphasis is placed upon holiness as it affects our relationship within the church. Specifically, Paul reminds us to love, accept, cherish, and encourage one another. And, should it appear to be more than we are capable of doing, he reminds us that God is the one who enables us to be holy.

Hopeful Grief

1 Thessalonians 4:13–18; 5:2–11

In writing to the new church at Thessalonica, Paul emphasized the Christian virtue of hope. He stated quite frankly that there was no need to lecture them about brotherly love; in that, they had been apt students of God himself. They need do nothing differently—only more of the same (4:9–12). (May that be said of Christians in our time and place!) Paul turned from love to the subject of hope because it was there that the Thessalonians were in need of clearer understanding and for a simple reason that is the universal fact of human existence—death.

During the period when Paul, Silas, and Timothy stayed in Thessalonica, they worked as evangelists. Part of the work of evangelism included an explanation of the gospel. Part of this would have included the expectation that the end of the age was near and that the Lord would soon return. After the missionaries' departure, the Thessalonian church continued in this expectation. It appears to be the case, however, that either some believers or their loved ones died during this period. Because such deaths had occurred prior to Christ's return, the question of the status of those who had died in the meantime naturally arose. What happens to those who die before Christ's return? Does a believer need to be alive when Christ returns in order to live eternally with him? Such questions led to further questions concerning the nature of Christ's return. As much to instruct concerning the return of Christ as to deal with the issue of the status of the dead in Christ, Paul wrote this first letter to the Thessalonians.

As for all flesh, so also even for those who believe in salvation and eternal life through Christ Jesus—sooner or later death will come. When its shadow falls across our lives, touching a friend or a loved one, what is an appropriate Christian response? Paul did not gloss over grief. He did not write in a way that suggests that Christian funerals may not permit sadness. The faith of a disciple may soften the pain of loss, but it is not a narcotic that masks or dulls sorrow. Paul took grief seriously: We grieve, but not as those "who have no hope." Christians may grieve and appropriately so; hope circumscribes this grief, surrounding it and closing it off through the promise of a loving Father. It was to this promise that Paul turned. Those who have died in the Lord are with God, who "will bring with Jesus those who have fallen asleep in him" (4:14). For all of the pain we may still feel at the loss of a loved one, this promise makes Christian grief qualitatively different.

Paul tells us that God will bring the dead in Christ with Jesus at the return of the Lord. Paul is not teaching concerning the kingdom of God; instead, this is instruction concerning the end of time. If it is teaching on the kingdom that one seeks, better to read the Gospels than the letters of the New Testament. In Thessalonians, we are instructed regarding the end of time. It is not at all self-evident that the kingdom and the end of the age concern the same issues. Jesus teaching on the kingdom concerns the present reign and ruling activity of God. Jesus' statement that the kingdom is "among you" is phrased in the present tense—the kingdom is here, and it is also in a certain sense "not yet." But in 1 Thessalonians, Paul was speaking of the return of Christ at the end of the age. In the wake of this return, Christians will be caught up to meet him in the air. Christian hope is sustained by the vision of eternal friendship with God.

One final question remains. What do we do in the meantime? How shall we occupy the time while we wait for the Lord's return? Are we to wait like airline passengers idly whiling away the time as they wait for the boarding call? From Paul's point of view, idleness is bad Christian practice. There is work to be done, prompted by our faith. And there is love, God's love, of which the world cannot get enough and of which it is our privilege to offer in imitation of the Christ who one day will return. So we live and work in hope.

Growing Hostility and the End of Time

2 Thessalonians 1:3–4, 11–12; 2:13–3:4

The church's situation at Thessalonica appears to have changed markedly for the worse in the interval between 1 and 2 Thessalonians. Friendly relationships characterize the first letter, which is full of warmth and affection for a church that Paul clearly loved and respected. He celebrates their faith, love, and activity on behalf of the gospel. The warm familial words characteristic of 1 Thessalonians do not appear as frequently in the second letter. Moreover, several of the first letter's concerns are muted or receive no comment in the second. One explanation for these differences is that the church had heeded Paul's instruction, and there was no longer any need to address those matters. However, the issue of eschatology (teaching concerning the "last things," the end of the age) dominates the second letter far beyond the level of discussion in 1 Thessalonians. One explanation for this intensified emphasis is that persecution had become a fact of life at Thessalonica.

As the first century wore on, the shadow of persecution lengthened, and the early church found persecution increasingly difficult to avoid. This is not to say that Christians were persecuted constantly and everywhere in the Roman Empire. Even after the imperial government became aware of Christians and regarded them as enemies of the state, persecutions came in waves and were conducted regionally. The church in one area of the empire might lead a tranquil life while in another region believers might experience terrible trial. Periods of intense persecution were often followed by long years of peace when pagan Romans left Christians to themselves. It is also the case that official policy was not popular among all pagans; there were those who thought persecution was ineffective and misguided. Before Christians came to the attention of the imperial Roman government, however, they experienced some degree of persecution at the hands of the Jews.

Acts documents persecution of the first followers of Jesus. Paul himself was, of course, among the early Jews most determined to identify and punish Christians. The period of Jewish persecution was most intense until AD 70 when the Romans destroyed Jerusalem and the temple and effectively ended Jewish leadership in the city. In such imperial cities as Thessalonica or any of the other locations of Pauline churches, the minority status of Jews meant that they could not act officially against Christians. Instead, Jewish policy often appears to have been to incite opposition to Christians by portraying them as troublemakers and disturbers of the peace. It's worth remembering that criminal and civil legal procedures in the ancient world differed markedly from ours. It was comparatively easy to harass an enemy, or worse, by denouncing that person before a magistrate, especially if one could produce corroborating witnesses. This seems to have been the way Jews prompted imperial officials into action against Christians.

Second Thessalonians addresses the increasingly hostile world in which Christians found themselves. The letter describes their situation with apocalyptic clarity: the forces of darkness were arrayed against God, and Christians prayed fervently to God to inaugurate the end of the world through Christ's return. In such circumstances, the virtue of perseverance naturally received heightened apostolic attention. Jesus' followers needed encouragement to stand fast until the very end. A striking feature of this exhortation is the letter's encouragement of the practice of reciprocal prayer (2 Thess 2:16–3:3). Pauline churches apparently thought of themselves as bound together, each connected to the other through the Christian practice of mutual intercessory prayer. In this way, no group of believers was left to fend for itself—a state of isolation that would be unacceptable for people whom Paul described as the body of Christ.

First and Second Timothy, Titus

Neither, or Both, Jew and Greek
1 Timothy 1:1–3

Timothy, perhaps more than any other person in the New Testament church, combined the ancient division that separated Jew from Gentile. Timothy was Paul's beloved son in the gospel, a faithful gospel minister, and child of a marriage between a Jewish woman and a Gentile man. Timothy symbolizes the possibility and the need of the church to overcome old misunderstandings and suspicions.

Even in the twenty-first century, people are still divided by race or religion. This knowledge can help us understand the ancient world's ethnic and caste divisions. Jews separated themselves from the *goyim*, the Gentiles, through a system of rules and regulations called *kashrut* (kosher). Gentiles, that is to say all those who were not Jews, were declared unclean. They ate foods that Torah prohibited—pork, lobster, and shrimp—and sometimes prepared kosher foods by methods that were not kosher. From our perspective, such sanctions appear to govern elements of everyday life that have nothing to do with religious faith. But first-century Judaism believed that God's law covered every aspect of life—from religious ceremonies in the temple to the manner in which dishes were cooked, cleaned, and stored. The religion of the covenant people of the Lord God was not restricted to the spiritual realm. Rather, religion, according to the Torah, concerned all aspects of life, physical and material as well as spiritual. Circumcision was the most important symbol of this bond, the covenant between Yahweh and Israel.

Jews, especially of the Diaspora and therefore living in a Gentile culture, were still not of that world. Some Jews became followers of Jesus, but conversion did not mean that they stopped being Jewish or abandoned all the customs of *kashrut*. The large-scale conversion of Gentiles raised some very large questions in the early and largely Jewish church. Since Jewish Christians viewed Jesus as the promised Messiah, they quite naturally understood him to be the fulfillment of the Torah predicted by the prophets. For these Christians, Torah remained very much in force. From their perspective, any Gentile who became a Christian was expected to keep the commandments. Through their conversion to Christianity, they became children of Yahweh's covenant with Abraham. These Gentiles needed to carry the sign of that covenant—circumcision. At least, that is what the Jewish Christians contended.

Paul appears to have met Timothy for the first time on his second missionary journey. The young man's spiritual legacy was impressive, as were the signs of his own faith. Paul saw great potential in him and determined to take him along as companion and fellow minister. Timothy appeared to have gifts that would prove of great benefit to the church, and this was always Paul's litmus test: Will this person, will this action, add to the life of the church? Will it strengthen the body of Christ?

Prior to leaving Lystra, however, a technicality had to be remedied. Timothy's father was a Gentile, and because fathers controlled the lives of their children in the ancient world, Timothy had never been circumcised. The Jerusalem Council had declared that Gentiles need not submit to this procedure; nevertheless, Paul, who had argued that very point in Jerusalem, now required Timothy to be circumcised before joining him and Silas. Paul the rabbi even performed the procedure himself. That Timothy agreed to undergo circumcision is perhaps an indication that the decision at Jerusalem had not yet persuaded Jewish Christians. It is surely a sign of submission and an expression of the young man's willingness to be of service to Christ and the church. Timothy was willing to place his life in service—not on his terms, but on those of others.

Bishops and Elders

1 Timothy 3:1–13; 5:17–19

The two letters addressed to Timothy and the letter to Titus are known as the Pastoral Letters. This name comes from the fact that much of their content is taken up with discussions and instruction concerning the ministry and oversight of the church.

For more than a century, scholars have debated the authorship of these letters. Since the letters address advanced organizational developments in the early church—for example, the church offices of bishop, elder, and deacon—some speculate that they were written too late to have come from the hand of Paul. Others maintain that he wrote sections of each letter, but that a close associate later incorporated these into larger, more complete versions. Still others maintain Pauline authorship of each letter in the whole. Regardless of the theory of authorship, as canonical books of the New Testament, the Pastoral Letters offer us guidance on important matters of pastoral and parish life.

Three different classes of church workers and their qualifications are the subject of these two passages. The words that refer to these church offices need special attention. The NIV translates the Greek word *episkopos*, from which comes the English word *episcopal*, as "overseer." The KJV uses the more traditional "bishop." The term appears in the New Testament only five times, and one of those is in reference to Christ as the head of the church (1 Peter 2:25). The other four instances occur in Acts and the Pastoral Letters. The words *overseer* and *bishop* are equally legitimate translations; bishops oversaw church thought and practice, but it was not until the second century that bishops came to be recognized as possessing authority over parish priests.

The English word *elder* translates the Greek word *presbuteros*, from which derives the word *presbyter*, as in *Presbyterian*. The term seems to derive from Christianity's Jewish roots, as in its Hebrew form the word referred to the rulers of synagogues. Early Christian churches took over many aspects of synagogue governance. A *presbuteros* was a spiritual leader, and apostles and elders are described as those responsible for overseeing the whole Christian church. On the basis of these verses. it seems quite likely that *elder* referred not only to church office but also to the age of the officeholder, as maturity and wisdom are two of its principle criteria. Many scholars believe that at the time the pastoral letters were written no clear distinction existed between bishops and elders and that the titles and responsibilities were interchangeable.

The word *deacon* also appears in this text. The word translates the Greek *diakonos*, meaning "one who serves." First-century deacons were likely assistants to the pastor or overseer, although they also could hold some pastoral responsibilities. The chief focus of their work was oversight of the material aspects of church life—the administration of the church treasury and charity extended especially to widows and orphans.

Taken together, these somewhat technical terms indicate that by the time the pastoral letters were written, some degree of separation was developing between clergy and laity. We also know this to be the case from extra-biblical documents from approximately the same time. Passages in 1 Timothy 3 and 5 spell out the qualifications that presumably separated laypersons from overseers and deacons. In some respects, these qualifications were moral in that they refer to character traits necessary to the proper discharge of the responsibilities of the offices. In other cases, the qualifications are more intellectual, as in the case of the wisdom that the text implies is required of elders and deacons. In terms of both moral and intellectual qualifications, the New Testament clearly teaches that church offices make high expectations of those who are called to ministerial service.

Advice to a Younger Colleague in Ministry

1 Timothy 4:7–16; 5:1–8

These two passages in 1 Timothy might be appropriately summarized as an older and more seasoned minister's advice to a younger colleague. This advice can be divided into the following subject categories: theology, relationships, public leadership, and care for the elderly. While we work our way through these categories, it will be good to hold certain questions before us: What is the difference between the ministry of the laity and ordained ministry? What aspects of this advice apply more to one than the other? What aspects apply equally to both?

Ministers are expected to be theological leaders in the church. Timothy had not come to his present position without instruction. In his discipleship, he had been "brought up in the truths of the faith and of…good teaching" (4:6). Furthermore, he was exhorted to have nothing to do with "godless myths and old wives' tales" (4:7). Such a warning illustrates ancient Christianity's perennial problem with teachers of false doctrine. Many individuals on the fringe of the Christian movement believed that they held a clearer vision of the meaning of Jesus' life and ministry.

One especially persistent and pernicious group was the Gnostics, who spun out extremely fanciful interpretations of Jesus. They constituted a serious threat to early Christianity, and Timothy was cautioned to have nothing to do with them. In theological matters, godliness carries far greater weight. "Godliness strengthens and enlightens the mind, subjugates the passions, quiets the conscience, brings internal peace, and disarms death of its terrors. In our social relationships it makes happy adjustments, fosters harmony and good will. It grows out of love. It makes life a safe pattern for others."[70]

There is more to ministry than theological leadership. Relationships also hold crucial importance. A young

70. Linn, *Studies in the New Testament*, vol. 2, 165.

minister faces particular challenges associated with age. Is this baby-faced youngster really qualified for ministry? It is not age, however, but calling that authorizes ministry. A better indicator of ministerial readiness than age is the presence of the fruits of godliness. The question of readiness is not answered as much by age as it is by the kind of example set by ministers. What kind of speech do they employ? What kind of lives do they lead? Do they exemplify virtuous Christian living?

Ministry also has a formal, public dimension. Ministers are leaders in public worship, and at the center of worship we find preaching and teaching. Today we tend to think of these as separate functions, but the early church did not make that hard-and-fast distinction. Christian preaching centered in what was called the *kerygma*, the "message." The gospel to which Paul referred specifically had a definite content: "Christ died for our sins according to the Scriptures, that he was buried, that he was raised on the third day according to the Scriptures, and that he appeared to Peter, and then to the Twelve" (1 Cor 15:3–5). The importance of delivering this message "according to the Scriptures" is manifestly evident, hence the importance of careful biblical study.

In the Jewish culture from which Christianity emerged, the elderly were to be treated respectfully. We see this concern carried over in the advice to Timothy that he must not rebuke elderly men. Widows rather quickly came to have a special status in the church. In the man's world of ancient civilization, elderly women without families were special objects of the church's charitable support. "Widow" appears to have become a minor church office as well as an indication of marital status. They were expected to be involved in the life of the church by performing works of charity on behalf of members of the congregation. First-century ministry involved responsibility for the physical care as well as the spiritual direction of elderly saints.

A Last Will and Testament
2 Timothy 2:1–15

Commentator Otto Linn observes that 2 Timothy was the last letter written by Paul before his martyrdom. Tradition varies slightly in identifying the date of his death. Some authorities put the date at AD 67, others at 68, but all agree that Paul was beheaded, the form of execution typically employed in the case of a Roman citizen, along the Ostian Way outside of Rome. "His busy career came to rest in the loneliness of a Roman dungeon with the issuing of his last testament, the Second Epistle to Timothy. Inactivity is the bane of a feverish and surging disposition like Paul's, and when you add to it the chill of loneliness and the sting of want you have an alliance sufficiently strong to break the spirit of anyone but a genius. But Paul's spirit was not broken; his life was not embittered by suffering, but sweetened and lifted with an anticipation born of a faith that could not die even though he regarded his fate as sealed."[71]

As a spiritual last will and testament, 2 Timothy bears the gravity of final thoughts. In the last days of one's earthly life, what ideas and encouragement, what final thoughts would you want to entrust to someone you referred to as your "son in the faith"? Second

71. Ibid., 167–68

Timothy has the tone of a person who has answered that question and is now ready to set those thoughts on paper. The general mood is one of encouragement: Remain strong in the grace of Christ. Keep your focus. Expect to encounter difficulty and hardship. The cultural sea on which a first-century evangelist labored was likely to be rough, so Timothy should not expect smooth sailing. Pay attention to the calling and supervision of the next generation of gospel workers. Stay centered on the apostolic gospel: "Jesus Christ [crucified], raised from the dead, descended from David [and thus the Messiah, the Christ]" (v. 8).

Much of this final exhortation centers on the word of God. Paul may have been a prisoner, but the Word remained unchained. At the close of this text, Timothy is encouraged to live before God as a gospel laborer who "correctly handles the word of truth." The "word" is at the center of 2 Timothy, and we need to give special attention to its rich range of meaning. The New Testament speaks with a Greek tongue, but it possesses a Hebrew heart, so we must draw on the Jewish understanding of "word."

The word of truth and the word of the gospel ultimately derive from the word of God. When used with reference to God, the Hebrew *dabar*, which translates into *logos* in New Testament Greek, rests on the prior act of God's speech. This is already a strong claim for biblical religion. It is a characteristic of God that to speak is to effect an action: God speaks and things happen. The divine word is effective; it accomplishes its purpose. When God speaks his word into the world, not only does that word act, but it also carries something of God. When God speaks a word, it does not stop being God's word, and that word is to be understood as an extension of God.

The Swiss-German theologian Karl Barth made three distinctions of the Word of God. First there is Jesus Christ, the living and incarnate Word. Second, the Bible is the Word of God that witnesses to Jesus Christ through human words. Third, said Barth, following a point made by Martin Luther, the church's proclamation of Christ is also a form of the Word of God. Primarily through preaching, but also in other forms of witness, the church makes the Word alive. It is in each of these aspects that Timothy—and all other Christians—must rightly handle the Word of truth, whether the Christ, the Scripture, or our witness to Christ in the world.

Inspired Scripture

2 Timothy 3:1–5; 3:12–4:5

Two related themes seize the attention of 2 Timothy 3:1–5 and 3:12–4:5. Paul warned Timothy of a coming decline in the church's spiritual and moral character. There is an antidote to this disease, however, and its name is sound teaching that rests on Scripture. It sounds simple enough: "Preach the Word," but an imperative runs the risk of becoming an unfortunate and simplistic slogan. There is more to sound doctrinal instruction than biblical preaching. Since we believe the Scriptures to be inspired and desire to interpret the Bible faithfully, it remains for us to understand the significance of that imperative in Paul's day and how our faith may rest upon Scripture.

The text opens with a warning of spiritual and moral decay. It is a catalog of sins and vices sure to lead to problems in the church. Let there be no mistake here; the passage refers to Christians who have lost their first love. Paul is not describing the pagan world. Pagans would not be interested in presenting a "form of godliness" (3:5). The substitution of money and pleasure for God as the object of Christian love, indulgence in slanderous gossip, a lost love of the good, and unforgiving lives out of control name only the worst characteristics of "men of depraved minds" (3:8).

Augustine's definition of depravity gets to the origins of such wickedness. He described depravity as being "turned in on the self." It is the root problem of the human condition without God's grace. Depravity means that human beings act with reference only to themselves. It is the very opposite of God's love. The only remedy for depravity is God's grace, manifested in Jesus and available through the ministry of the Holy Spirit. Humanity's gracious salvation in Christ is the core of what Paul sometimes called "my gospel."

It is this gospel that had been entrusted to Timothy, who is exhorted to "continue in what you have learned" (3:14). What he had learned, however, encompassed more than a set of rationally stated propositions. Doctrine is more than a body of teaching; a crucial aspect of doctrine has to do with Christian practice. Prayer, worship, forgiveness, and Christian charity are a few of many practices whereby beliefs sink deep into our lives, transforming the way we live in the world. In one way or another, each of these ultimately rests on Scripture, which the text tells us is inspired. The Greek word translated as "inspired" is *theopneustos*, literally, "God-breathed." Theologians differ in their interpretation of this word. Some argue that inspiration extends to every word of the Bible and that the text is inerrant. Others contend that the Bible's words express ideas that were inspired by God. An early Church of God writer said that it was the people who wrote the Bible who were inspired.[72]

In this connection, it is worth asking how to interpret 2 Timothy's use of the term *Scriptures*. What Bible did first-century Christians read? The fact that some of the canonical gospels and letters had not been written by the time of Paul's death means that, in this context, *Scriptures* must refer first of all to the Old Testament. But before Paul's day, the Old Testament already circulated in Greek translation as well as Hebrew, and the differences between them extend further than a simple matter of language. The Greek translation, known today as the Septuagint, contained more books than the Hebrew Old Testament. Because almost no Gentiles could read Hebrew, it was the Septuagint that Paul used and which became the Bible of the early church.

By the close of the first-century, Paul's letters had been collected, were circulating through the church, and had acquired authoritative, if not canonical, status. In the second and third centuries, the church determined which of the many writings that interpreted Jesus' life and teachings were inspired like the Old Testament and therefore were entitled to be read as authoritative for Christian teaching and life. Through this lengthy historical process, the twenty-seven books of the New Testament came to have the same status as the Old Testament—the Scriptures of the church.

---

72. Wickersham, *Holiness Bible Subjects*, 18–19.

Regardless of one's theory of inspiration, Scripture is the standard of the church. It is "useful for teaching, rebuking, correcting and training in righteousness" (3:16). Those four participial verbs identify four critical functions of the church. The church teaches, rebukes (disciplines), corrects, and trains. The church does not engage in these tasks on the basis of Scripture. The church performs these tasks in order that her people might grow and be "thoroughly equipped for every good work."

Send the Parchments
2 Timothy 4:13

Psalm 119 sings of biblical tradition as a lamp for our feet and the light by which we can walk through life as God's people. Our life path may take us through green pastures and beside still waters; it may take us through the valley of the shadow of death. In 2 Timothy 4:13, we hear Paul's appeal for "my scrolls, especially the parchments" to be brought to him, imprisoned in Rome. From the previous verses, we can fairly conclude that he is under sentence of death and, further, that the execution of his sentence is imminent: "the time has come for my departure" (4:6). Samuel Johnson is reported to have said that when a man has been sentenced to hang in two weeks, it concentrates his mind something wondrous. What is of such importance that Paul would ask Timothy to bring it to him as soon as possible?

Paul asks only for a cloak for warmth against the damp cold of a Roman dungeon and his scrolls and parchments. We do not know their contents for certain. The text does not provide enough information to warrant strong inferences. Might these scrolls have contained notes and sketches of theological ideas that Paul wanted to work out in further detail? Perhaps. If time was short, however, and only a month or two remained in Paul's life, it is not unrealistic to think that he would want scrolls containing scriptures to read for comfort and light.

Remember that any scriptures read by Paul would have been what Christians call the Old Testament. None of the Gospels existed yet, his own letters being the earliest written elements of the New Testament. That Paul would have read from the Old Testament means he would have been reading from the same books that delighted the psalmist. Perhaps he was reading the Torah, a collection of psalms, or a scroll of one of the prophets—any and all of which carry the word that he celebrated as a "lamp to [his] feet and a light for [his] path."

Practicing Our Convictions
Titus 2:7–8, 11–14; 3:1–10

Little is known of the man named Titus. From Galatians 2:3, it appears that he was Greek and therefore a Gentile convert to Christianity. Although Paul did not regard him with the same deep affection he held for Timothy, he certainly respected Titus. They had worked together at Antioch, and Titus was a member of the Pauline party at the Jerusalem Council (see Acts 15). The precise occasion that prompted the letter to Titus is unclear. The perennial problem of false teachers is part of the letter's background. Sharper focus is given to issues dealing with Christian ethics, and a general disregard for Christian standards of living may have been more in the forefront of Paul's mind.

A crucial concern of Christian ethical teaching is the need for good examples. Ethics is more a matter of practice than convictions or moral reasoning. High ethical standards can be achieved easily if all that is entailed is agreeing to statements written on a chalkboard. But convictions must be practiced as well as affirmed, and one of the important aspects of moral learning involves seeing what ethical convictions look like when lived out in human experience. Without examples, we will have difficulty learning how to put ethics into practice. An example from the world of manners makes the point.

Like young people everywhere in American society these days, many of the male students at the institution where I teach wear caps. The insignia may be of endless variety, but caps themselves seem to be standard issue for many college-age males (and more than a few females as well). Men over the age of fifty-five or veterans of military service may recall learning that males were formerly expected to remove their head covering upon entering a building; this was considered good manners. Generations of young men learned this practice through precept and example, watching their fathers and other men remove hats or caps when they came indoors. This practice is largely lost among men today; heads remain covered by caps or hats in restaurants, theaters, and sometimes even in churches. This breach of etiquette sometimes prompts older men to wonder about the manners of the younger generation. Thus come the questions: What's the matter with them? Don't they know any better? In many cases the answer is, No, they don't. But without good examples, how is a younger generation to acquire manners? They are not something we instinctively know.

The issue at stake in this text is much more important than the manners governing the use of hats and caps, but the illustration still serves to make a point. Ethics, like manners, is not instinctive. In both cases, we learn in part by watching good examples. Without them, we may find a way to ethical living, but it will be a longer and more difficult road. The letter to Titus views ethics as a public practice rather than a set of private convictions. Its first concern is for moral growth in the next generation of Christian believers. If they are to develop into faithful disciples, older generations will need to demonstrate ethical Christian practice. Ethical practice is important for a second reason. It is through such moral living that a line is drawn between church and world. This line is crucial if the world is to know that it is the world. Such recognition—the awareness that one is a sinner and far from God—is the first step in conversion. In this view, Christian ethics is intimately connected to evangelism.

Philemon

Obligations of Being in Christ
Philemon vv. 4–21

Regardless of its brevity, the letter to Philemon stands out among the books of the New Testament. It is the shortest of Paul's letters, containing only 335 words. Unlike all other Pauline letters, Philemon is a personal note. Furthermore, from verse 19 it appears that Paul wrote the original himself, another departure from his usual practice. In the ancient world, when all letters were handwritten, it was customary to employ an amanuensis, a professional copyist whose fine penmanship ensured the final copy's legibility. Paul followed this practice, often adding personal greetings in his own handwriting at the letter's conclusion. In the case of his letter to Philemon, Paul seems to have employed no amanuensis.

Commenting on this letter's inclusion into the canon of the New Testament, Ralph Martin says, "It is surprising that the church would want to retain this simple appeal and incorporate it into its library of what later became sacred Scripture. The truth is that Paul's advocacy of the slave's case was genuinely revolutionary and marks the opening of a new chapter in social relationships. The letter speaks about how the members of Christ's church are to relate to one another and treat one another."[73]

The background and circumstances of this letter help us grasp the importance of Paul's personal appeal to his friend. Some time before the actual composition of this note, Paul had befriended Philemon, who became indebted to the apostle. Although not stated explicitly, verse 19 allows us to infer that Philemon's debt to Paul was spiritual; probably, it was through Paul's witness that Philemon had become a Christian.

Subsequent to these events, Philemon's slave Onesimus fled his master and apparently took refuge with Paul. Greek law permitted a runaway slave to seek asylum in the home of a friend. It is often assumed that Onesimus had done his master some wrong, perhaps stolen some property, but the text does not support that assumption. Paul took responsibility for any indebtedness that Onesimus had with Philemon, but that act may have been based in a Roman law that required those who harbored runaway slaves to pay the owner a day's wage in compensation for every day the runaway was absent from duty. These relationships were altered when Onesimus converted to Christianity. When that happened, Paul decided the runaway slave ought to return to his master and fellow Christian.

Onesimus stood on shaky legal ground. Roman law granted wide latitude to owners of runaway slaves. Masters could take steps to pursue runaways and have them arrested. Runaway slaves could be imprisoned and whipped. Masters were even permitted to have the slave crucified. In the face of this legal tradition, Paul makes bold to ask Philemon to forgive Onesimus. Against the backdrop of Roman law and custom, Paul's request must be seen for the revolutionary policy that it was. Paul did not base his request on Philemon's *rights* over Onesimus but in their new *relationship* in Christ. The theme of indebtedness runs throughout this moving personal note. Philemon was in Paul's debt. Onesimus was in Philemon's debt. Paul was willing to give Philemon an IOU for damages he may have suffered through Onesimus's escape and absence. In this situation, Paul could ask his friend and brother Philemon to receive as a brother in Christ the runaway slave who was now a brother in the Lord to both Paul and Philemon. Where all are debtors in Christ, common fellowship in Christ becomes a new possibility.

73. Martin, *Ephesians, Colossians, and Philemon*, 133.

Hebrews

An Anonymous Sermon on Christ

Hebrews 1:1–9; 2:1–4

Questions abound concerning the authorship and structure of Hebrews. It is not a letter, following neither the epistle form found in Paul's writings nor the General Epistles. There is neither signature nor salutation. Many scholars suggest that we would do better to read this book as a sermon. In this connection, it is worth observing that nearly all ancient books, secular as well as sacred, were written to be read aloud. About the book of Hebrews, commentator Thomas Long says, it has "an especially strong oral, sermonic quality…[that employs] language in ways that would have aural impact when spoken aloud to a group gathered for worship."[74] Long believes that Hebrews may originally have been a sermon manuscript written for wider distribution in the church.

Since this sermon contains no signature, questions of authorship and date are bound to arise. For many centuries, Paul was believed to be the author, but contemporary scholars generally dismiss that supposition. The topics, themes, and style of Hebrews are quite unlike any of Paul's letters. Several other New Testament personalities—Apollos, Barnabas, Priscilla, and Silas, to name but a few—have also been suggested as possible authors. None of these suggestions rests on a very strong case, leaving us to agree with the opinion of the great Bible scholar of the ancient church, Origen, who said, "But who wrote the epistle, in truth God knows."[75]

Because we cannot confidently name the author of Hebrews, it is also difficult to assign it a date. About the best estimate we can make is that this treatise was written sometime between AD 60 and 100. Equally mysterious is its original destination. The title simply states, "To the Hebrews," but the word does not necessarily refer to Jewish Christians and most likely not to Jews. By the second half of the first century, it was commonplace for Christians to refer to themselves as "Jews" in respect of the idea that they were the spiritual Israel and heirs to God's promise to Abraham. This usage ultimately came to mean a generalized reference to the church as the New Israel of God.

Thomas Long identifies the occasion for delivering Hebrews as one in which the author is attempting to minister to a church burdened by serious problems. "His congregation is exhausted…The threat here is that, worn down and worn out, they will drop their end of the rope and drift away. Tired of walking the walk, many of them are considering taking a walk, leaving the community and falling away from the faith."[76] In this view, Hebrews is an extended exhortation intended to inspire and mobilize a congregation of Christians to faithful obedience and action. This exhortation is built around the meaning of Jesus Christ.

74. Long, *Hebrews*, 5.

75. Ibid., 1.

76. Ibid., 3.

From the very opening verses, Hebrews focuses attention on Christ's nature and purpose. In olden days, God spoke through prophets, but more recently he has spoken though his Son. To say that Jesus is the Son of God is already to make a strong claim about who Jesus is. "The Son is the radiance of God's glory and the exact representation of his being, sustaining all things by his powerful word" (1:3). This is not simply praise language aimed at exciting a band of weary disciples. The opening verses of Hebrews announce the central theme of the sermon in the highest Christological terms. Unlike the prophets of old who *carried* the word, the Son *is* the Word. The writer reminds his readers of the nature and purpose of the Christ they served—a reminder that would prompt his readers to more faithful discipleship.

In his published lectures on Christ, the German martyr-theologian Dietrich Bonhoeffer asks of the Christ, "The only real question which now remains is: 'Who are you? Speak for yourself!'...It is also the question of faith: 'Who are you? Are you God himself?'"[77] The early church struggled profoundly with these questions about the person and work of Christ. When considered against the background of basic religious and theological assumptions, texts like Hebrews 1:3 raised crucial questions about the nature of Christ and his ministry. Some early Christians were devoted to the idea that God is one and therefore read Hebrews 1:3 to mean that *radiance* signifies "similar to" but not "the same as" and *representation* means one who stands in the place of another. At the same time, other Christians insisted that the Logos and the Father were "of the same essence." In AD 381 at the Council of Constantinople, Christians formalized an elaborated version of the Nicene Creed, which declares that God is "one essence in three persons." Centuries later, such theologians as Bonhoeffer wondered whether the council had asked an inappropriate question. It appeared to him that the question uppermost on their minds was, *What are you?* The question that mattered most to Bonhoeffer in addressing Christ was not *What?* but *Who?*

The *Who* question cuts to the heart of the matter. When we ask, "What are you?" Jesus becomes an object for analysis; he becomes a "thing" to be examined and analyzed. Such questions ought to be bracketed out. Instead, we must come to terms with Jesus as the subject, the person who initiates. The question *Who are you?* forces us to consider Jesus in relation to us. Carried to its logical conclusion, the question forces each person to consider Jesus in relation to himself or herself.

Why God Became a Human
Hebrews 2:5–18

Very late in the eleventh century, an Italian monk became archbishop of Canterbury in England and wrote his most important theological work, *Why God Became a Human*. Anselm of Canterbury's masterpiece offered a theory of the atonement. The word literally means "at-one-ment," and in Christian thought is understood to be the explanation of humanity's reconciliation to God. Hebrews takes Christ's nature and work to be crucial to the life of the church and the aspect of that work called atonement is the heart of Hebrews 2:5–18.

77. Bonhoeffer, *Christ the Center*, 30.

Judaism is a continuous reference point in Hebrews. It provided the background for Christian teaching in at least two ways, demonstrated in this text. In the first place, Hebrews quotes from the Old Testament. It is important to remember that the books of the New Testament were only in the process of being written during the first century. There was no "Old" Testament; Christian and Jew alike read from the same scriptures. Hebrews 2 quotes the Psalms and Isaiah. That the Jewish scriptures were also the Bible of early Christians lent a Jewish cast to their understanding of Jesus. Second, Jewish religious traditions also shaped the teaching of Hebrews, and no clearer example of this shaping influence can be found than this book's understanding of Jesus as the sacrifice that makes possible reconciliation between God and human beings.

Once a year, the Jewish calendar marked Yom Kippur, the Day of Atonement. Prescribed in Leviticus 23:27, it was the holiest day of the entire year. People were to fast, pray, and reflect for the entire day. The Day of Atonement was dedicated to repentance for sins committed against God, and sins against one's neighbor were to be forgiven by making amends and asking the personal forgiveness of the aggrieved person. According to Leviticus, sins against God were to be atoned through a burnt sacrifice. This sacrifice, offered on the Day of Atonement, carried the sins of the people and thus expiated their sins before God. This day and its attending ritual provide the backdrop for Hebrews' discussion of Jesus as the One making atonement for human sin.

Not just anybody or anything can take the part of the atoning sacrifice. Thus, Hebrews must explain the nature of the One who was sacrificed. Here Hebrews cites Psalm 8:4–6. Read in context, Psalm 8 is a meditation on human beings; it is they who are "made a little lower than the angels" (2:7), yet Hebrews 2:9 applies that description to Jesus. The text goes on to say that Christ is "now crowned with glory and honor." Hebrews takes the view that it is through suffering and death that Jesus was "made perfect" and crowned with glory and honor. Jesus' sacrificial death is, for Hebrews, both the means of his exaltation and our reconciliation. Jesus' atoning death also explains, to use Anselm's phrase, why God became a human being. "For surely it is not angels he helps, but Abraham's descendants" (2:16), which we should take to mean all human beings. Abraham is the patriarch of peoples other than Israel. In order "to help" human beings, Christ "had to be made like his brothers in every way" (2:17). Suffering and temptation were aspects of humanity that Jesus also needed to experience if he was to be the means of atonement.

Anselm took a different tack to arrive at the same theological port. He argued that sin offended God, who demanded satisfaction for this slur on his honor. The offended party in this case, however, is the infinite God, and no human being can adequately pay the price of satisfaction. Only an infinite sacrifice can satisfy the breach of God's honor. It is at this point that Christ enters the picture and becomes incarnate—the God-Man, if you will—who as human could offer the infinite sacrifice of himself and make at-one-ment possible.

Faithful Obedience

Hebrews 3:12–4:2; 4:9–13

Had Martin Luther been responsible for determining the canonical books of the New Testament, it is possible that fewer than our twenty-seven books would have been included. The great reformer placed Hebrews, along with James, at the very end of his German translation of the Bible. Luther labeled James a "letter of straw," and given the emphasis of this text, it is not difficult to understand why he also relegated Hebrews to an inferior position. Luther championed the theological view that faith and faith alone appropriates God's saving work in Christ for our salvation. In Luther's judgment, good works are of no value; in fact, they may tempt us to trust them to secure our righteousness before God. From this perspective, any positive estimate of works or human obedience to God's will was questionable in Luther's mind. So, when James says, "Faith without works is dead," or where Hebrews hinges salvation on obedience (4:6), Luther was quick to find fault in such apparent devaluation of the word of the gospel of faith.

Hebrews teaches that hearing the gospel must be combined with faith. None of us is to have an "unbelieving heart" (3:12), which is the opposite of faith. How, then, are we to understand the meaning of *faith* here? Three points in the text will help us define this critically important word. First, Hebrews insists, don't be like the children of Israel. Unbelief is closely associated with rebellion, as in the case of the Israelites, who were led out of Egypt only to turn their backs on God in the wilderness. Such attitudes and actions come under the general category of disobedience. In the view of Hebrews, to only *hear* the gospel of Christ is insufficient; one must also follow Christ's instruction. To hear *and* follow is Christian obedience.

A second point considers the concept of rest: "The promise of entering his rest still stands" (4:1). This promise is yet to be fulfilled; therefore, believers must live and act in a consistent manner that will enable us to enter that rest when it finally is made manifest. The concept of rest draws its meaning from the Sabbath day of rest at the end of the creation. Only after the work of creation, the expression of God's will, was completed, did the Lord God institute the Sabbath as the day of rest. But, writes commentator Thomas Long, rest does not only point back to the first Sabbath, "it points forward to the completed work of redemption."[78] However, continues Long, "rest is not just a concept applying to the beginning and the end; it is also a quality of Christian life in the middle of time, a calm assurance of participating in the will of God (4:3)."[79]

A third point in these verses is that the church must live in memory of Israel's disobedient folly; it could happen again. The time for obedient living is now—"Today..." (4:7).

Taken together, the points made in this passage help us understand faith as faithful obedience. This is very much along the same lines as the text in James that reminds us that "faith without deeds is dead" (2:26). Faith that only hears or merely confesses with the lips is inadequate as faith. Faith, understood as trusting in the Lord with all one's heart, mind, and strength is not an isolated act. At its core it is a relationship

78. Long, *Hebrews*, 58.

79. Ibid., 59.

between the believer and God. *Fidelity*—faithfulness—is a term that more adequately expresses this relationship. When we consider what it means to live in relationship with God, faithfulness is the key to its health. Luther was right to take "The just shall live by faith" as the watchword of the Protestant Reformation. We might also agree with Luther that salvation is by faith alone, if he would allow us to enlarge the meaning of faith to include faithfulness—living in obedient relationship to God.

Jesus the Royal High Priest
Hebrews 4:14–5:10

Hebrews never strays far from the Old Testament for its images and interpretive ideas, and the passage in Hebrews 4:14–5:10 illustrates the point. Jesus is identified here as the Great High Priest. The writer of Hebrews turned to the Jewish priesthood and the mysterious figure of the priest-king Melchizedek for definitions of Jesus' high priestly role. Since we learn here that Jesus stands in the tradition of the Hebrew scriptures and, more importantly, fulfills them, our understanding and application of the text will be well served by background study into these two ideas.

The English word *priest* translates the Hebrew *kohen*, which comes from a root that means "to stand." A priest is one who stands before God as representative of the people. Priests also are mediators or bridges between God and humanity. Before Moses, no Old Testament reference identifies an Israelite priesthood. That silence does not mean, however, that no priestly functions were performed. In the period of the Patriarchs, the head of the clan—Abraham, Isaac, Jacob, Joseph, etc.—took the role of priest in their family groups. These patriarchs built altars and offered sacrifices on behalf of their families and servants.

Moses was of the tribe of Levi, and with this tribe the office of the Levitical priesthood began. Aaron, his brother, was consecrated priest, and from him descended the official line of tabernacle priests. When David became king over all of Israel and Judah, the priesthood came under the patronage of the monarchy. After the construction of the temple under Solomon, the worship of Yahweh in the new religious center of Jerusalem gradually assumed growing importance. Priests serving in the temple came to have higher status, and the Babylonian exile only served to intensify this tendency.

By Jesus' day, the significance of the high priest at Jerusalem had been solidified. The high priest was the principal administrator of the temple sanctuary, including its worship and treasury, and presided over the Jewish ruling council, the Sanhedrin. His most important priestly act occurred annually on the Day of Atonement. On that one day each year, and only once, the high priest entered the innermost chamber of the temple, the Holy of Holies, and sprinkled the blood of a sacrificial animal on the mercy seat in expiation of the people's sins.

Some ancient societies combined the offices of priest and king. This was natural enough in cultures where kings were often considered to have a special relationship with the gods, and it is out of such a shadowy past that the figure of Melchizedek emerges. This name first appears in Genesis 14 where he is identified as the priest-king of Salem, who, like Abraham, worshiped the one true

God. In Melchizedek, a relationship is established concerning royalty, priesthood, and Jerusalem, which, like the City of David, also brings the Davidic monarchy into the picture. Psalm 110 takes up Melchizedek as the priest-king who is the model of a line that will last forever.

The author of Hebrews was steeped in Old Testament imagery and traditions and adapted the person of Melchizedek to Jesus in a form of interpretation called typology. Hebrews combines the name's meaning (king of peace, king of justice) with Melchizedek's appearance without genealogy or stated ancestry. To this, Hebrews adds that Melchizedek blessed Abraham and, in this act, established the later idea of a priesthood higher and nobler than the Levitical order in Jerusalem. It is to this higher order that Jesus belongs. This is one argument by which Hebrews establishes the idea that the Great High Priest Jesus is not only superior to all others but is of a qualitatively different order of priesthood. More than this, even though Jesus was the Son of God, he "learned obedience from what he suffered" (5:8) and thus his priesthood is of a completely different character from that in the Jerusalem temple. For it is through his own suffering that he became the means of our salvation.

Maturity
Hebrews 5:11–6:12

We have noted the possibility that Hebrews was originally a sermon. A feature of this book that lends strength to this idea is a recurring rhetorical pattern that moves from theological considerations to ethical application. Hebrews appears to have been composed according to a plan that gives maximum emphasis to an ethical teaching by grounding it on a theological foundation, repeating the same pattern to make a new ethical point. It is a highly effective sermonic technique that not only instructs but also provides the theological grounds on which that teaching rests.

Hebrews 5:11 to 6:12 contains a body of ethical instruction founded on a theological argument made in 4:14–5:10. The 4:14–5:10 section considers Jesus as the Great High Priest, one of the three christological titles—Prophet, Priest, and King—that define his ministry. Once this point has been established, Hebrews moves on to consider ethical implications for followers of Jesus the Great High Priest as well as the fate of those who fall away.

Here the writer of Hebrews takes a very pointed line of argument. The original audience was "slow to learn" (5:11). The use of the word *ought* also tells us that their slow rate of growth in the gospel was not because of incapacity; these people had not matured because of a failure of will rather than ability. They had not been diligent. Even after a considerable period of time in the faith, they had not advanced beyond the most elementary levels of understanding and practice. Difficult lessons lay ahead. Would this congregation be up to the challenge? If Christian discipleship is growth in service to the Master, one aspect of that discipleship will be to follow his example. But as we learn in 5:8, Jesus was made perfect through his obedient suffering. Does this mean that the maturation of disciples hinges on obedient suffering, and when the text exhorts Jesus' followers to "go on to maturity," what does that entail?

The United Methodist *Book of Discipline* asks all candidates for ordination, "Are you going on to perfection?" The question finds its origin in the exhortation in Hebrews 6:1 in the King James Version. The Greek word here derives from *teleios*, which can be translated as either "perfection" or "maturity." These two English words connote something of the same image; to be mature is to be complete or whole, and completion is a kind of perfection. If the church to which Hebrews was addressed was to achieve spiritual maturity, believers had to become diligent students. Christian discipleship cannot, however, be reduced to memorizing a creed. The mastery of doctrine describes not the essence of discipleship but only a minimal faith that the Puritans called historical. Even Satan possessed historical faith. Although necessary, the mastery of theological truths is an insufficient standard of Christian maturity. In addition to the faith that is believed, there is also the faith that believes—the practice of faith. Teaching must take root in the lives of disciples and be encouraged to grow; the name for such growth is the "practice of the Christian faith." Beyond a catechism there must be the lived experience of believers.

The writer of Hebrews threatened readers with dire warnings. Christian maturity is an imperative; without it, apostasy looms. Few believers would willingly participate in the re-crucifixion of Jesus, and yet, those guilty of apostasy commit precisely that sin. It is impossible for such to be restored to the life of salvation. The mere idea of an unpardonable sin sends shivers down the spine of any sensitive Christian. To those, the text offers a consoling word: God is just. The Guardian of Israel does not slumber; he has seen the good works of his faithful people and will not turn his face from those who love him.

Jesus and Jeremiah's New Covenant

Hebrews 8:6–12

Hebrews 8:6–12 is taken up nearly in its entirety with a quotation from the Old Testament, Jeremiah 31:31–34, one of the high watermarks of Old Testament faith. From a terrible moment in Israel's life, this prophetic oracle looks forward to a future filled with God's forgiveness and grace. Jeremiah surveyed the religious and moral climate of Jerusalem in the late seventh- and sixth-century BC and found little that was encouraging. God's people had wandered into the far country of idolatry, callously disregarding the first four commandments of the Decalogue. Their religious life had become unrighteous living. Where little righteousness is to be found, justice will also be wanting. So it was in Jeremiah's Jerusalem. Legal, political, and religious leaders not only failed to do justice but also perverted social structures to serve their own ends. So it was that Jeremiah pronounced the Lord God's judgment against a people who took comfort in the false belief that their city and society would always stand. When that judgment came calling in the form of Babylonian invasion and exile, the people of Jerusalem wondered whether God had abandoned them forever. To these anxious and sorrowful souls, Jeremiah spoke a new word of hope and comfort in the midst of ruin and despair. That new word is quoted in Hebrews 8.

More than mere quotation is at work here, however. The text announces that the new covenant prophesied by Jeremiah has been established in accordance with the Word of the Lord. Jesus is the new high priest who fulfills this prophetic promise. The quotation from Jeremiah 31 occurs in the midst of a lengthy argument intended to demonstrate that Jesus is the Great High Priest, who by his sacrificial death puts an end to the old covenant and its sacrificial system. Hebrews takes Jeremiah's promise of a new covenant as self-evident proof of God's dissatisfaction with the old arrangement. If there had been nothing wrong with the first covenant, why would the Lord promise a new one, and why would the new covenant be of such a radically different nature? It is not written on tables of stone or even stony human hearts; it is written on hearts softened by the grace and forgiveness available through the life and sacrificial death of Jesus.

Hebrews argues that both the new covenant and the Great High Priest who represented humanity on the cross before God are vastly superior to the old covenant and priesthood. Hebrews is far too indebted to the Old Testament to say that under the new covenant the law has disappeared. No, the law remains, but thanks to the work of Jesus the High Priest, that law is no longer something external to our lives. Under the new covenant God writes the law upon human hearts and minds. In this new situation, there is no longer need of human mediators—all will know of the Lord.

Strength for Trying Times
Hebrews 10:19–39

The New Testament does not gloss over the sometimes harsh realities of life as a Christian. So we read in Hebrews words like "suffering," "insult," "persecution," and "confiscation." The people to whom this sermon was originally preached endured all of this and more. They stood in dire need of encouragement and instruction about the way to be disciples under the threat of persecution.

In Hebrews 10:19–39, the author encourages the congregations in some very practical matters. But even practical matters must be grounded in theological concepts so that we do not substitute other, alien footings. Christians, states the text, find themselves in a unique covenant with God that offers them privileges that they are to claim. Central to the covenant's uniqueness is Jesus as the Great High Priest of the church. The one-of-a-kind High Priest makes the one-of-a-kind covenant a reality. Hebrews reads the new covenant as the outgrowth of God's covenant with Israel, and thus we find here numerous references to features of Jewish religious life. The application of these Jewish symbols to a Christian context illustrates the potential of symbols to carry more than one meaning. Indeed, this multiplicity of meanings is one important source of the friction between first-century Jews and Christians. Each group believed that it alone correctly interpreted the story and symbols of Yahweh's covenant with Abraham.

Medieval Christians commonly placed the three theological virtues of faith, hope, and love alongside the cardinal virtues of justice, courage, temperance, and practical wisdom. Not surprisingly, Hebrews 10:19–39 refers to all three. We are here reminded of our privileges under the new covenant in Christ and exhorted to live out their consequences. God's love for us in Christ the High

Priest is also resident in the Christian community. These, coupled with faith and hope, also privileges of the new covenant, strengthen us for a life even under trial as the people who walk with the promising God.

Faith and Faithfulness

Hebrews 11:1–13

Having made the point that Christ's death on the cross is the once-and-for-all and therefore superior sacrifice (10:1–18), Hebrews turns to ethical considerations that follow from this theological claim. These considerations have to do with perseverance (10:19–39) and the closely related virtue of faith. Christians are not to be found among "those who shrink back and are destroyed, but of those who believe and are saved" (10:39). Faith is that quality of character that makes possible courageous Christian living, so Hebrews offers us the famous "faith chapter" to light our way. Before proceeding to the examples of faithful living that fill this chapter, a working definition of faith is in order.

Systematic theologians will sometimes complain that the definition of *faith* found in Hebrews is incomplete. *Faith* is an enormously rich and complex term that encompasses a great range of meaning. Hebrews 11:1–2 describes aspects of faith that are necessary to our understanding. When Hebrews "names faith as the 'assurance of things hoped for,' [it] is describing what faith *has*: it already possesses in the present what God has promised for the future. This possession is partly an inward reality and partly an outward force."[80]

80. Ibid., 113.

Hebrews, however, is not content to offer a textbook definition of faith. This virtue can also be defined by example, and the balance of the chapter turns to a long series of examples. Abel, Enoch, Noah, and Abraham are lifted up as examples of the faith-filled life. They are followed in turn by Isaac, Jacob, Joseph, Moses, and many other Old Testament giants. To become faithful, we must do more than master a definition; acquiring the virtues necessarily involves their embodiment. In order to understand faith fully, we must see faith practiced in the lives of others. Their example of faithful living encourages us to believe that we too can live in a similar manner as they.

We have previously considered the way Hebrews alternates between theology and the ethical obligation. Perhaps trained in the classical rhetoric of the ancient world, the author writes in a rhythm that swings from church doctrine to church practice and back again. Indeed, it is not too much to say that in Hebrews, theology has a very practical bent; church doctrine here is not so much a set of propositions as a set of convictions that require practice.

Chapter 11 illustrates Hebrews' practical understanding of church doctrine. It would be difficult to claim that Hebrews uses the word *faith* as though it was simply a collection of propositions to which a believer must give assent. Here *faith* is more verb than noun; the church is to practice faith. It is action and a way of being. The giants of faith cited in Hebrews 11 exemplify faith as action—a practical virtue.

If we follow the example of Hebrews 11, one of the key elements in the practice of faith is the act of remembering.

The chapter is an act of remembering that links the church, the new people of God, to Israel, the people of the first covenant. But we do not remember only to establish connections between the distant past and ourselves. Memory played a crucial role in the ethical and spiritual formation of ancient Israel. The great festival of Passover served to remind Israel that once it had been a slave people, nobodies whom God had rescued from Pharaoh's oppression. In the ritual of the Passover meal, not to mention other great annual festivals like the Feast of Tabernacles, Israel remembered and by this act was reconstituted as the people of Yahweh called to live in faithful covenant with him.

Faithful Christian living entails certain features. People of faith "must believe that [God] exists and that he rewards those who earnestly seek him" (11:6). Second, the outward faith of believers condemns the world (see v. 7). Third, faith results in a new and revolutionary relationship with God that also makes believers "aliens and strangers on earth" (11:13). Faith has a specific reference point; for Christians there can be no generalized faith in faith. Faith is oriented toward God as the Christian's ultimate concern. Moreover, the relationship is personal; God is not an abstract, philosophical principle but a personal being whom we can address and who not only addresses but also blesses those who live by faith.

Faith that is practiced identifies the believer and also the world for what it is, namely, the world and not God. It is not necessary that Christians verbally condemn the world. Faith-filled Christian living exposes the world, in the process illuminating its judgment under God. This kind of faithful witness also results in a kind of alienation from the world. Christians become, in Stanley Hauerwas' and William Willimon's phrase, "resident aliens."[81] Empowered by faith Christians look hopefully toward a future filled with the love of God.

Running Before an Expert Crowd
Hebrews 12:1–11

Hebrews 12:1–11 begins with a famous verse, one that many of us may have memorized as children. If the themes of Hebrews 11 are faith and memory, the themes of chapter 12 are perseverance and encouragers.

The first verses of chapter 12 announce the theme: cast off everything that slows us down spiritually and run the race with perseverance. The images are clear—an arena where athletic contests are conducted. Runners strip off their warm-ups and prepare for the start of the race. They strain against each other as the finish line comes into view. The crowd rises to its feet and shouts as if with a single voice. The scene could be ancient or modern, the Atlanta Olympics or the games in Rome or at Olympus.

Remember that in the earliest Greek manuscripts the books of the New Testament are not divided into chapters and verses. They were a later editorial addition to simplify reference and study. The artificiality of these divisions appears at places like Hebrews 12:1–2, which easily can be read as the summary of chapter 11. "Therefore" at the beginning of 12:1 is a clue; the

81. See Hauerwas and Willimon, *Resident Aliens.*

writer of this letter is summing up the work of the previous verses. He is not simply concluding, however, for there is more to be said about the consequences of living with the kind of faith described in chapter 11. As we have seen again and again, the opening verses of chapter 12 serve as a transition or bridge from the theological statement through memory of chapter 11 to the practical exhortations of the first part of chapter 12.

Hebrews 12 makes much of the idea of struggle. This struggle takes several different forms: the struggle against sin, the struggle against hardship, and the struggle that is part of the Lord's disciplining of his beloved. The metaphors that illustrate this last form of struggle come straight from the world of parent-child relationships. Reading Hebrews 12:7–11, one can almost hear someone saying, "This will hurt me much more than it will hurt you." That oft-stated parental comfort takes on the heavy weight of eternity when we reflect on Calvary. It did hurt him far more than us, and yet he does not leave us to struggle alone. We are surrounded by experts who are intimately acquainted with the race we now run.

The day of the women's marathon race at the 1984 Los Angeles Olympic Games dawned warmer and more humid than ideal for a long-distance race. The conditions did not deter American Joan Benoit from winning the gold medal, but they proved too severe for a woman who entered the Coliseum long after Benoit and the other contestants had finished. Dazed by heat and hours of extreme exertion, unable to keep the pace of a weekend jogger, the woman scarcely responded to the race official who pointed her in the correct direction on the track. Spectators immediately recognized the symptoms of heat exhaustion in her sagging posture and halting step. Only four hundred meters from the finish line, it appeared that she would not complete the race. It was then that the great crowd rose to its feet and began cheering. Louder and louder their single voice rolled down to the stadium floor, enveloping the staggering figure on the track with encouragement to finish. Step after painful step the contestant went on, enabled by a rising crescendo of cheers that reached its peak only as she crossed the finish line.

Sometimes athletics imitates life—or even the Bible. This true-life illustration resembles the opening verses of Hebrews 12. The writer seems to have in mind a situation much like the 1984 women's marathon, minus only the degree of drama. The imagery of this chapter is drawn from sport, namely running the races contested during the great athletic festivals that were part of the ancient world. Runners competed for the victor's prize, a wreath of laurel leaves in the Pan-Athenaic games of ancient Greece. In other words, they ran with a goal in view—the finish line and victory. No athlete worth his or her salt can compete successfully without training, and there is no training without discipline. As the sign in the weight room reads: "No pain, no gain." Hebrews applies this aspect of an athlete's life to Christian discipleship.

The prize and the perfect exemplar for the Christian "athlete" is Jesus. He is the goal of Christian existence. Eternal fellowship with him is the prize to be won, but he is also our example, the One who endured to the very end. He ran his race to perfection, for the sake of the "joy set before him"—the prize waiting to be won. We may grow weary as we run our own race; in such moments, exhorts Hebrews, consider the example of Jesus. His race was ever so much more difficult and demanding, yet he proved the victor. So, says Hebrews, can we. Jesus is both example and goal.

To reach this goal, however, the Christian "athlete" will need to be disciplined. The text tells us to "endure hardship as discipline" (12:7), and we are exhorted to take a particular perspective on the hardships that come our way. They are not merely afflictions or misery. Drawing on Proverbs 3:11–12, Hebrews reminds believers that hardship may be divine discipline by a God who disciplines only those he loves. Even as parental discipline was meted out for our good, so does God discipline us so we also may win the race.

The race is everything. Can we finish? Will we finish? The finish line is the beautiful face of our Savior, who at the same time is our example of faithfulness. We have been or will be in training, subject to the Lord's loving discipline. But even these incomparable aids do not exhaust the spiritual resources at our disposal as we set out on the racecourse. There is also the crowd. These are no mere armchair spectators; they have taken their seat in the stadium only after completing the race themselves. They have participated in the great race; they know what it is to run and stay the course. When we become dazed and weary from effort, we will find this crowd surrounding us. They will rise to their feet and cheer us on.

James

A Universal Call to Active Faith
James 1:1–18

Sometimes the secular world has a benign attitude concerning people of faith; at other times, it has been very hostile. This changeable society—sometimes referred to as the world or the dominant culture—always presents influences with which Christian men and women must deal. The letter of James is one of the most practical and down-to-earth of all the letters of the New Testament. It is focused on Christian practice and has served believers as a guide for many of the practical considerations of Christian living, especially matters concerning the church's life within the dominant culture.

Along with Jude, 1 and 2 Peter, and 1, 2, and 3 John, James is called one of the Catholic or General Letters. They were written to the church at large rather than to a specific congregation, such as Rome or Corinth. They are known by the name of the persons said to be their authors rather than by an intended destination, unlike Paul's letters written to a specific congregation. Some Reformers considered James and Jude, along with Hebrews and the Revelation, to be of lesser usefulness. Until 1539, four years after William Tyndale was martyred, his English translation segregated these four books from the rest of the New Testament. Even today some Christians rarely find their way to the section of the Bible where the General Letters are to be found. Such neglect ignores the fact that they are part of the canon of Scripture. We may hope that the church will share the attitude of the early Christian historian Eusebius, who said that James and Jude "have been regularly used in very many churches."[82] Church tradition says that this letter was written by James, the brother of Jesus. Scholars are divided as to whether that is actually the case. The strongest evidence against the tradition is that the Greek of the letter is of a fine quality believed to be beyond the ability of a Galilean peasant such as James. In this case, some scholars say, James the brother of Jesus authored an earlier version of the letter that was then edited and polished by a Christian more accomplished in Greek. This theory has the advantage of connecting the letter with a man who was one of the first martyrs of the early church; life under trial is one of the themes of the letter of James.

The opening salutation of this letter contains an important guide to the contemporary Christian appropriation of its message. James wrote to "the twelve tribes scattered among the nations." Other New Testament writers also used this way of speaking to indicate that the young church was the new people of God, the new community expected in the age of the Messiah. Scattered like Israel, the church in James is directly descended from the old people of God. Remember that the first followers of Jesus were all Jewish. Later the church grew among non-Jewish peoples to the extent that it became almost exclusively a Gentile community. But we Gentiles must never think that the church is given to us independently of Israel, the old people of God. Through the work of Christ, we have been grafted into the vine of Abraham.

82. Quoted in Perkins, *First and Second Peter*, 1.

James was also Jewish Christian because he thinks of discipleship under Jesus as action oriented. This letter exhorts Christians to *do* rather than simply to *be*. Christian maturity is connected to Christian action, but James does not teach the idea that maturity (in some translations "perfection") comes by careful and close observance of the law and custom; rather, maturity or perfection is God's gift to those who wait patiently, putting their faith into action. Indeed, it is not too much to say that in James *faith* is very much an action word. Under the trial experienced increasingly by the young Christian community, life provides many opportunities to exercise faith. When put into action, faith strengthens believers' relationships with God. In this strengthened relationship, maturity grows. To be mature, of course, is to be whole or complete. That is one of the definitions of the Greek word the English Bible translates as "salvation." In the letter of James, to be saved is to practice faith actively, in the process not earning but receiving from God a wholeness or completion that is Christian maturity.

Practical Faith, Close to Home

James 1:22–27; 2:8–9, 14–17; 5:13–16

Faith, hope, and love are called the theological virtues because they have their origin in God. God is the gracious giver of these virtues. We do not earn faith, hope, and love; they are gifts. Because they are gifts, however, does not mean that they are not to be used or that they cannot be refined through practice. As James says, the man or woman who merely listens but never acts lacks the Christian's foremost reference point for life. James teaches us that it is insufficient for Christian disciples to think that faith is fulfilled when they say, "I believe." Rather, faith is a matter of applying the gifts of grace we have received. These texts touch on a matter of everyday life and its connection to faith. To reflect on them is to explore faith, the first of the theological virtues, as the active principle of practical daily living.

We are accustomed to thinking of faith in grand terms, but James forces us to apply faith to the homeliest of situations. We want to scale mountains; James insists that we first think about the words we thoughtlessly utter. Who of us has not spoken rashly or hurtfully only to wish immediately that we could reclaim those words? We must consider the power of words not only to harm but also to build up and to heal. True, we need to watch our tongues that they speak no evil or hurt. On the other hand, the church cannot thrive in silence. The body of Christ lives through our mutual encouragement of one another. Beyond encouragement, there is also instruction, and this depends in some measure upon words.

The church grows and matures as faith is passed from one person, from one generation, to another. Tongues that witness to the faith and tongues that teach are crucial to growth. James' warning about the power of speech has two sides. One cautions us to wait before saying something that might harm. The other encourages all of us to teach, that is, to speak when our words can build up or, in the language of the church of an earlier day, edify.

Relentlessly, these verses press believers to action. A kind thought or a generous impulse only starts one down the road to Christian discipleship. So, for example, to see a person in need and only think of helping without actually offering assistance earns James' rhetorical question in rebuke: "What good is it?" Neither is it sufficient for disciples to bless the needy with mere words. People in hunger or without proper clothing need more than a word of blessing. This instruction is reminiscent of Jesus' saying about fathers who would give a stone to a child who asked for bread. When considered in the light of such practical circumstances as hunger or nakedness, faith requires action for its completion—no action, no faith.

That James refers to the needy as "brother" or "sister" raises another aspect of these texts, which may cause some readers to infer that such terms mean the church's first obligation is the assistance of believers. Perhaps, but one ought not, therefore, conclude that the need of the saints is the church's only obligation. The church that aids only other believers risks the criticism of being exclusively concerned with its own. On the other hand, the church that fails to assist needy believers risks the criticism that Christians neglect one another. In either case, verbal blessings without action indicate incomplete faith.

Martin Luther famously declared James to be a "letter of straw," yet the great reformer also provided an important key to reading James 2:8–9. Luther took it to be a principle of Christian living that faith was active in love. In his view, the awareness that we are justified by faith frees believers to love authentically. Justified by grace through faith, they need not attempt to earn God's favor by performing good deeds. Freed of this worry that leads to unholy self-preoccupation, believers can turn their attention completely and unselfishly toward their neighbor. James similarly connects faith and love, adding for good measure that love shows no favoritism. Christian disciples may not extend their love preferentially only to those they like. Jesus taught us to love our neighbor and in one of the best known of all his parables made the point that our neighbor is anybody we chance to meet along the way.

The Power of the Tongue

James 3

James 3 is an extended meditation on responsible Christian discourse. From this letter's view, those who teach bear an acute responsibility for their speech. It is one thing to live by one's own convictions and accept the consequences they may bring. One of the marks of maturity is the ability to own one's actions, to be able to say, "Yes, I did that," and accept the consequences of that declaration. Comedian Flip Wilson, who often performed as "Geraldine Jones," earned lots of laughs with the line, "The devil made me do it." In a comedy sketch, the line is funny, but it will not hold up in court. Neither is it the mark of maturity. Accepting the consequences of our own actions is a responsibility born especially by teachers who profess their convictions with students. Those who take their teachers seriously may very well adopt some of the teacher's convictions and choose to live by them. To watch students live by convictions learned from their teachers can be no clearer an illustration of the awesome responsibility that rests on the shoulders of those who teach.

In case the point escaped his readers, James draws a wonderful analogy from the world of mechanics and technology to underscore the Christian practice of holding one's tongue. Think of a mammoth aircraft carrier or the supertankers that carry oil across the seas. These huge ships displace tens of thousands of tons of water, yet measured against such massive weight their rudders are of an insignificant size. Nevertheless, it is this comparatively little part that steers the mighty vessel. Such is the power of the tongue.

James is not finished. Next he finds a negative example in the natural world. Creation holds all manner of animals and birds that have been domesticated, which is to say they have been brought under human control. Able to tame some of the animals, we seem almost incapable of taming our own tongues. James stops just short of an entirely pessimistic view of the human ability to speak graciously. We might turn his comparisons around. The tongue that curses its neighbor is also the tongue that offers praise to God. James declares that this should not be, but at least it demonstrates that we are not hopelessly lost; our tongues do not only gossip, nor do we employ them only to curse. But since speaking out both sides of our mouths is not worthy of a follower of Jesus, we must ask, "What are we to do?"

The tongue, of course, does not speak of its own accord. It is *supposed* to be connected to a brain. It is the self who is expected to exercise some control; but if the tongue is less capable of being tamed than a wild beast, what can be done? In the last verses of chapter 3, James returns to a subject that appears earlier in the letter—wisdom. Schooled in wisdom, followers of Jesus do actually stand a chance of harnessing their tongues. Clearly, to do so will require some effort on the part of Christians, and James explicitly challenges casual attitudes toward our speech. However, the efforts that we make to curb our tongues finally cannot be determined on our own. There is a wisdom that comes from God that can help us achieve mastery over our tongues.

This wisdom is most definitely not a human achievement. Quite the contrary, it is a gift from God. James tells us that only through such wisdom will we stand a chance against the power of the tongue. This wisdom is described in 3:17 by means of a list of familiar Christian virtues. We have seen similar words in other New Testament passages, and here they are again—peace-loving, considerate, submissive, merciful, impartial, and sincere. The wisdom that comes from God is not the wisdom of this world. That kind of wisdom leads to strife. But divine wisdom leads to wholeness and the possibility that we might be able to govern the unruly tongue.

Need Versus Desire

James 4:1–10, 13–17

To learn the difference between need and desire is to overcome one of life's great challenges. James uses the Greek word *hedonai* here more in the sense of "desires" than its customary translation, "pleasures." The subject of 4:1–6 is the improper desire that flows from disordered passions. The ancient Greeks thought extensively about the way to live a serene and unified life. Many, particularly Plato, regarded the passions or feelings as especially disruptive. He developed his philosophy in a way that considered the ability to control one's feelings as critical to the achievement of a good life, for the passions are the sources of our desires. Control passions and we control the futile search for things that offer only fleeting satisfaction. (Eastern religions also identify desire as an important obstacle to harmonious existence. In Buddhism, to eliminate all desire is to achieve a state of blessedness.)

In James, passions and desires also are seen as problems, but in a way that fundamentally differs from Plato or Buddhism. The letter of James sees disordered passions as interrupting our relationship with God. We cannot pray faithfully because disordered passions prompt wrong desires; we ask God for what we should not want, and God will not honor such prayer. Sometimes we know that we want what we do not need or what we should not desire, and so we do not even ask God to grant this request. Ashamed of our petty self-centeredness, we may even stop praying, and once again our relationship with God suffers. In the manner of an Old Testament prophet, James labeled such people adulterers. The charge here does not necessarily mean sexual sin. OT prophets used the term as a metaphor for faithlessness. In the context of James 4, it makes sense to think of adultery as the charge that Christians had their eyes on the world more than on Jesus. They desired the world rather than Christ. Their passions were disordered, which is to say, misdirected.

Verses 7–10 offer the cure for passions and desires that are out of control. James teaches that the solution to the problem of disordered passions lies in their redirection rather than elimination.

The Christian ordering of our feelings and desires begins in humility. This distinctly Christian virtue enables us to see God and the world in proper relationship. To humble oneself before God is to remember the first commandment: only God is God, and there is no other. For those who have forgotten that commandment, repentance is in order. With repentance comes restoration, and James promises that God will draw near to those who genuinely seek his face. Repentance, of course, means an about-face. To love God is to see the world in its proper light. As the song says, "Turn your eyes upon Jesus." The world grows dim, but it does not disappear. To love God is to live in proper relationship to the world. To love God is now to live with ordered passions, desiring what we need rather than what we want. It is in that spirit that Augustine offered this ethical advice, "Love God and do what you will."

Verses 13–17 put a theological exclamation point on these reflections. Human beings control the details of their lives only conditionally. The plans we make are subject to a future that is not ours to control. In the early Church of God, it was customary to announce one's plans for the future and then add the initials "d. v." They were an abbreviation for the Latin *Deus vult,* a phrase that means "God willing." In ordinary language, the saints exemplified the truth that James here teaches. It is appropriate to plan ahead, but only in accordance with a faith that confesses that we live and move and have our being by the mercy of God Almighty, Maker of heaven and earth. An old saying puts the matter in these simple words: Man proposes; God disposes.

First and Second Peter

Resident Aliens
1 Peter 1

First Peter is another of the General or Catholic Letters of the New Testament. Scholars are divided as to whether this letter was actually written by Peter, but by the time of the early church historian Eusebius, Christians accepted the letter as authored by him (even though the letter itself tells us that Silas, also called Silvanus, served as the copyist or amanuensis). The letter is addressed to believers who are "strangers in the world, scattered throughout" provinces in Asia Minor, modern Turkey.

We must understand the status of these exiles. New Testament writers often made use of the term *Diaspora* (or such other similar words as *exile, resident aliens*) to describe the Christian's situation in the social world of the Roman Empire. Each of these terms suggests the second-class status that was the lot of noncitizens. Aliens could be forced out of cities and were subject to forms of taxation from which Roman citizens were exempt. To be an exile or a resident alien was to live without the ties to a political community that the ancient world regarded as essential to selfhood.

Hostility toward the Christian community was familiar to many Christians by the end of the first century, and persecution thus serves as a backdrop for both 1 and 2 Peter. Already in the salutation, certain words or phrases appear that would have sent clear signals to first-century readers that trial and difficulty could be expected at the hands of the world. First, Peter 1:1 refers to "strangers in the world, scattered..." This is a reference to the dispersion of Jews throughout the Roman world. However distant they were to become, a memory of a connection still remained between Jews and the young Christian movement. This relationship made life difficult for Christians since they were often lumped together with Jews and made to suffer the same social stigma.

Jews were subject to a number of social restrictions. They could not become citizens of the cities where they resided, making them automatically aliens. They were prohibited from using such public facilities as gymnasiums and athletic arenas. Christians came under some of the same restrictions, and the result was a fair degree of social tension.

This background of hostile environment led to the writing of 1 Peter. There was a real danger that ongoing persecution might weaken faith. This letter was intended to encourage Christians in the face of trials. Thus, we read in verses 6–7: "... though now for a little while you may have had to suffer grief in all kinds of trials. These have come so that your faith...may be proved genuine and may result in praise, glory and honor."

We should not overlook the fact that many of the people to whom 1 Peter was written were converts from paganism. They had taken a step that severed many of the connections important to their social life: conversion to Christianity alienated new believers from their families, friends, civil authorities, and former religious practices. Worship of the Greco-Roman gods was considered a civic obligation. Romans did not object to people choosing other religious beliefs as long as they were added to the imperial civil religion. Christians refused to make that compromise. The new faith could not be constructed on a pagan foundation. To convert to the way of Christ required the rejection of the religious beliefs of the dominant culture. Imperial authorities considered Christian converts to be atheists and traitors to Rome; therefore, they were outside the boundaries of conventional society. They may still have been living in the same houses they had always occupied, but in a real sense these converts were exiles in their own hometowns.

In the ancient world, a person's connection to a community established identity. A person was not an individual. One's individuality was established as an extension of the body politic. For this reason, 1 Peter emphasizes the point that conversion has made these pagan converts members of the new and true community—the church. Conversion may have severed their former relationships, but more importantly it joined them to the body of Christ. This was not just any association, but a "royal priesthood, a holy nation, a people belonging to God" (1:9). Just as former relationships had once legitimized their social being, the new connection to the church meant they were no longer exiles. Membership in the body of Christ conferred benefits far superior to anything the old order could offer. There was no mercy, no forgiveness, and no hope to be found in those old political associations, but fellowship with Jesus and the new people of God conferred light where formerly there was darkness. Aliens in a world that was passing away, these converts had been grafted by the experience of salvation into a new community founded on God's mercy and hope.

Before they became Christians, God (1:2) had destined converts. Before conversion they desired only ignorance (1:14), but they were sanctified by the Spirit (1:2, 22) and redeemed by Christ's blood (1:2, 18–19). Redemption and sanctification had cast believers into a Christian present where they were to live obediently (1:2, 14, 22), with a living hope (1:3, 13, 21), guarded by God's power (1:5), even while they rejoiced in their trials (1:6–7). The power of hope that resided in a future squarely under God's control sustained them through the present and gave them confidence for the future. In that future, salvation is to be revealed (1:5, 9, 13) and with it glory and honor for those who have lived in faith and obedience to the Lord (1:7). In this line of thought, 1 Peter addresses all phases of Christian living, from the past to the present and into God's glorious future. Sustained by such a comprehensive vision of their lives within God's plan, first-century readers of this letter could rest easier and with more confidence despite their hostile environment.

A Spiritual Temple
1 Peter 2:1–10

This text has a strong ethical quality to it as it lists a number of sins and vices of which Christians are to rid themselves. In sharp contrast to Hebrews, whose immature readers are encouraged to leave behind the milk of elementary Christian teaching, 1 Peter exhorts its readers to compare themselves with "newborn babies [and] crave pure spiritual milk" (2:2). It may be that Peter's first readers were babes in Christ who only recently had tasted that the Lord was good and needed the nourishment of elementary instruction. This would make especially good sense if these new converts immediately found themselves facing hostility.

These verses help readers to see themselves and the early Christian movement within the larger framework of God's life with Israel, the original people of God. The passage repeatedly refers to builders, building materials, and the finished building. The letter was likely written after the destruction of the Jerusalem temple, and we may infer that these references to construction were prompted by that disaster. But 1 Peter does not linger in mourning over the lost temple. Instead, the letter helps Christians to see that the church is a new, spiritual temple. Christ, the stone rejected by the original people of God, is the cornerstone of the new construction project. Each individual Christian is a living stone in God's new temple—a spiritual people of God. The metaphor is changed in 2:5; Christians are now encouraged to think of themselves as a new and holy priesthood. Unlike the old temple priesthood, however, the sacrifices offered by Christians are not physical but spiritual and mediated by Jesus Christ himself.

Verses 6–8 quote several passages from the Old Testament to support Peter's interpretation of the church. These all refer to stones and a "cornerstone chosen and precious" (2:6 NRSV). It is Christ, the cornerstone of the spiritual temple, who is cast aside as unfit by the original people of God. He has become the great stumbling block. For first-century Jewish Christians, their fellow Jews' persistent rejection of Jesus proved to be an enduring and mysterious problem. For men like Paul and Peter, Jewish resistance was a continuing source of hurt. Despite this, they insisted that Jesus was indeed the cornerstone of a new spiritual Israel.

The passage concludes by reinforcing the theme of Christians as members of the spiritual Israel. As God once called a ragtag collection of slaves out of Egypt, forging them into a people, so in Christ, God again has made a church out of an assortment of people who came from a wide variety of social and ethnic backgrounds. The foundation of this new people called the church is the mercy and grace of God revealed in Jesus.

Called to Exemplary Living

1 Peter 2:11–12; 3:13–17; 4:7–11; 5:8–10

First Peter 2:11 takes for granted the alien status of Christians. It is the premise upon which good Christian conduct can be based. Moreover, it is important that Christians live upright, morally praiseworthy lives before the pagan world that surrounds them. One aspect of this importance has to do with some of the moral assumptions of the ancient world.

Classical Greek and Roman moralists taught the idea of self-control in at least two different respects. The ancient Greeks in particular were concerned about what they termed the nonrational parts of the soul—appetites, desires, and passions—and their potential to throw a harmonious life out of balance. For example, Plato and the tragic poet Sophocles both thought that romantic love was a kind of madness. Men and women sometimes behave very strangely when they are in love, and this odd behavior struck many pagan thinkers as irrational. They stressed the importance of reason or intellect remaining in control of the passions for the person who wanted to achieve happiness. Similarly, the philosopher Aristotle considered the moral plight of the person who knew the good but failed to do it. The term he used to describe this problem was *akrasia*, "to be weak-willed." In his view, the morally self-sufficient person needed to control his or her desires through the exercise of the intellect. Self-control of this kind, thought Aristotle, contributed to a life of happiness.

A second strategy by which ancient pagan moralists taught the idea of self-control had to do with their attitude toward external circumstances. Sooner or later we are likely to find ourselves confronted by a situation or circumstances over which we have little control but that nevertheless may seriously affect us for good or ill. It might be a chronic illness, the consequences of an accident, or the actions toward us of another person. While people often cannot control the circumstances of their lives, Stoic philosophers believed that it is possible to control one's attitude. In this manner, the Stoics believed, we remain self-controlled. Whether as taught by Plato or the Stoics, self-control was an important ethical concept in ancient pagan moral thought.

First-century Christian writers were aware of these ideas. This awareness shows up in this text's emphasis on the importance of self-control and a morally praiseworthy life in a pagan culture. Early Christian writers knew that the church's critics were watching. They exhorted believers to live holy and blamelessly so as to bring no reproach on the church or the Savior whose name they had taken as their own. Morally upright lives served to ground Christians' claims that their religion, rather than the pagans', was true.

It would be wonderful if people were never harassed on account of their good deeds. But in the increasingly hostile climate of the late first century, it was no longer possible to assure Christians that a Christlike life would never result in harm or violence. The shadow of persecution falls across the third chapter of 1 Peter with a reminder that suffering for good is far better than being punished for evil. That believers suffer because of their beliefs is a consequence of doing good. It is also a sign of the world's depravity. It might also nurture the hope that even those who are depraved might be ashamed of their actions by the gracious and winsome character of the saints.

Do Not Fear Suffering

1 Peter 3:13–21; 4:12–16

Once again the shadows of hostility and the beginnings of persecution are felt in the events behind this letter. First Peter 3:13–21 and 4:12–16 offer comfort to those who experience such trials, even as they also suffer hardship and hostility in a larger theological context.

Most North American Christians experience little hostility or trial for the sake of Jesus. So how does this passage address us and our situation? One might be tempted to enlarge the theme to suffering in general, but that would be an interpretive mistake. First Peter really is addressed to those who endure hardship for the sake of Jesus rather than those who encounter illness, calamity, or heartache. It is not that illness, calamity, or heartache are unimportant or do not need attention, but 1 Peter simply deals with the matter of hostility directed toward the faithful. This hostility was the immediate problem facing the young Christians to whom the letter was written.

What of us, then, who do not share the first-century church's hostile situation? One way to approach this question would be to ask, "Is it possible that we might someday face opposition and trial for the sake of Christ? How would this letter help us if we ever found ourselves in such circumstances?" Another approach would be to consider the fact that there always have been Christians somewhere in the world, down to the very present day, who have faced hostility because of their profession of faith. How does this letter benefit them? These are two approaches to this passage that retain an awareness of its basic theme of hostility. Chapter 3, verses 8–12, offers instruction that will build strong congregations. Internal strength will serve young churches well as they face the pressure of external attack. In time of trial, the healthy relationships Christians enjoy with one another are crucial to the stability of the church.

Verse 13 asks a question that we might read as ironic, "Who is going to harm you if you are eager to do good?" The early church knew that the answer to this question was, "Rome." The original readers of this letter knew that the empire's law enforcement agencies, authorized to protect the innocent and punish the guilty, stood ready to arrest them. The text gives meaning to trials by referring to Christ as the example of suffering. Our trials pale in comparison to what Christ underwent for us;

nevertheless, those who suffer for the sake of the gospel join in Christ's suffering. When Christ is revealed in all his glory, this fellowship of suffering will be transformed into overflowing joy.

Go About Your Lives

1 Peter 5:1–11

The instruction offered by 1 Peter in the letter's final chapter barely mentions this hostility. The letter expects its readers to continue with their daily lives, calmly going about their affairs as leaders and members of the church.

Special instructions were given to the elders of the congregations. *Elder* is a term drawn from the church's Jewish background. In the very earliest days of the Christian movement, pastors were referred to as elders and, in the Pastoral Letters, sometimes as bishops. First Peter 5 instructs leaders to be calm and generous examples to their congregations.

As Christianity spread, pagan critics often accused Christians of atheism and social radicalism. The Christian refusal to sacrifice to Roman gods was seen as atheism. People who refused to make these sacrifices were believed to disturb the system of gods that brought stability and order to the empire. Pagan critics charged that such folk were capable of the worst sorts of social upheaval and radicalism; they threatened to "turn the world upside down." In a word, Christians made their pagan Roman neighbors nervous.

In the face of this suspicion, how then were Christians to live publicly? One wise course of action called upon Christians to live conservatively and follow established social convention wherever possible. We find an example of this kind of advice in 5:5–6. Young men were to mind their place, respecting the age and wisdom of their elders. Everyone, young and old, was to be respectful and act humbly toward others even as they are to live alert to the possibility of temptation and under self-control. This not only followed the words of Proverbs 3:34, cited in verse 5, but it also had become standard Christian teaching. Living this way would result in a lower-profile public life than one lived in haughty arrogance. A life characterized by haughty arrogance was much more likely to attract the attention of Roman authorities. This conservative approach to Christian living was eminently practical advice for those living under the watchful imperial eye.

First Peter expects young Christians to keep on with their lives in the face of hostility. They were to live calmly as they continued their everyday affairs. They were to keep a low profile even as they were to live confidently in the hope of Christ's glorious return. If suffering should be their lot, believers could take consolation and find hope in the faith that "the God of all grace, who called you to his eternal glory in Christ, after you have suffered a little while, will...make you strong, firm and steadfast" (5:10). Suffering and death are not the worst things that can happen to a Christian, especially when God awaits with a crown of glory.

A Catalog of Virtues

2 Peter 1:3–15

Second Peter is a spiritual "last will and testament." The letter's tone suggests the awareness that the author's days were numbered. He was under sentence of death, and in the Roman justice system, executions were not delayed by years of legal appeals. Soon he would lay aside the "tent of this body" (1:13). People who speak or write from this extreme situation offer their most important words and advice. Time is too short for small talk; we must say only what is critically important. That is the setting and mood of 2 Peter.

The writer was a member of the older generation that was passing from the scene. He had important things to transmit to the next generation and wanted to give all the wisdom and insight into the nature of the Christian life that he possibly could. He had spent his entire adult life in the service of the Master. He wished to share with his readers—then and now—the accumulated wisdom of those years.

Several different New Testament passages list the qualities of Christian character. The most famous of these is Galatians 5:22–23, the often-cited fruit of the Spirit. Another can be found in Colossians 3:12–14. In 2 Peter, we find a third list. Colossians refers to such characteristics as virtues, and it will be important that we consider these qualities against the backdrop of the ancient world's understanding of that term.

The English word *virtue* translates the Greek term *arete,* a word that also can be translated "excellence." Ancient pagan moral philosophers used this word to describe human excellence in the sense of a person who lived a complete, well-ordered, and fulfilled life. The Greek word for such a life was *eudaimonia,* "happiness," meaning a flourishing, well-lived life in all aspects. In our ordinary language today, we use the word *virtuous* more or less as a synonym for *good* or *morally upright.* Modern usage strays from the ancient world's definition.

In the first-century Roman world, *virtue* meant the quality that enables a person or object to fulfill its purpose. In that world, the purpose or function of a thing or person was crucial to understanding what or who it was. Moreover, to achieve that purpose was to be employed to the fullest intention of its creator. The list of Christian virtues in 2 Peter 1:5–7 refers to people and not things, so we must ask about the purpose of human beings. Do human beings have a purpose or function? Many in the dominant culture would answer, "No, human beings have no intrinsic purpose other than those they choose for themselves." To such views, the Christian tradition has typically reacted sharply and negatively. The vast majority of Christians have affirmed that humans do have a purpose and that we do not determine it for ourselves. That purpose was determined at the moment of creation by the One who created us. As the Westminster Confession states, "The chief end [purpose] of [humanity] is to serve God and enjoy God forever."

We begin now to see the importance of the Christian virtues to human flourishing or, to use a more biblical word, blessedness. In the Christian context, the virtues are those qualities that enable believers to fulfill their purpose, which is to serve God and enjoy God forever. This means that the qualities listed in 2 Peter 1—or Galatians 5 or Colossians 3—are not characteristics only of the super-spiritual. Quite the contrary, the Christian virtues are essential for all of us if we are to fulfill our divinely intended purpose. The Christian virtues are not frosting on a cake; they are the meat and potatoes of Christian living. The virtues listed in

2 Peter 1:5–7 are qualities that enable us to fulfill our purpose as creatures of the living God. As the letter itself says, "If you possess these qualities in increasing measure, they will keep you from being ineffective and unproductive in your knowledge of our Lord Jesus Christ. But if anyone does not have them, he is nearsighted and blind" (1:8–9). An older Christian, steeped in the wisdom and experience of a life of service to Christ, would want to tell us such things before departing this life for the eternal presence of God.

Heterodox Teaching
2 Peter 2:1–10, 17–19

The interpretation of 2 Peter 2:1–10, 17–19, requires some additional information about the earliest decades of Christianity. The Christian movement spread into the Mediterranean world by word of mouth. Decades before the appearance of the first New Testament documents, believers were telling the story of Jesus and testifying to the experience of the risen Lord. Paul's first letters were not written until AD 50, and they were the earliest documents of what Christians call the New Testament. Mark, the earliest of the Gospels, was not written until at least one and perhaps two decades later. The latest of the New Testament books was written about the turn of the century, but decisions about which books should be included in the canon of Scripture still lay far in the future.

In addition to the twenty-seven books eventually canonized as the New Testament, many other interpretations of Jesus' life and ministry also circulated during this same period. Some of these have been discovered and translated for use by scholars who want to understand the religious background of the New Testament. Much of this literature presents Jesus and his teaching in dramatically different terms from the familiar presentations we know from the New Testament. Most Christians today would recognize the teaching in these other sources as divergent from normative Christianity. The first-century church, however, did not have the long historical perspective we enjoy. They found themselves in the position of determining authentic Christian teaching and setting aside the rest. It seems clear that this was the situation confronting 2 Peter.

Chapter 2 takes up the problem of false teachers who were offering different interpretations of Jesus' life and ministry. "The word 'ruin' or 'destruction' echoes through this section. On the one hand, false teaching provides the occasion for bad morals and destroys true piety. On the other, destruction awaits false teachers and their followers. Whatever they may think about the future, divine judgment has already been passed against them."[83] Second Peter attributes the worst possible motives to these false teachers. He accuses them of teaching out of greed (2:3) and the desire to indulge perverse sexual appetites (2:13–14).

Debate aside, Bible scholar Pheme Perkins notes that 2 Peter 2 raises an important question for modern Christians. "Are we too unconcerned about the truth of religious claims? Many people have [adapted to] the [religious] pluralism of our culture...by holding religious beliefs to be private and

83. Perkins, *First and Second Peter*, 180.

individual, not public."[84]People whose children or friends no longer practice an identifiable form of Christianity will often say, "Well, they're really good people, so I guess it's okay." Perkins continues, "In other words, a general moral or behavioral test substitutes for belief, convictions, and in some cases for a morally coherent way of life."[85]In the face of this attitude's undermining effects on Christian belief, we ought to pause and ask ourselves which is the more damaging corrupter of the church—a permissive attitude or the presence of false teachers within the church?

The Delay of Christ's Return
2 Peter 3:1–18

Writing late in the second century, Tertullian, the early Christian theologian, affirmed that believers longed for the end of the world, but he also declared that they prayed that God would delay it. Tertullian explained that although the end of the world posed no threat to Christians, they hoped for its delay in order to provide additional time for the salvation of their pagan friends and loved ones. The possibility that the world would soon end was still very much in the minds of Christians in Tertullian's day. Nevertheless, the farther in time the church drew away from the days of Jesus' life and ministry, the more difficult it became to sustain the hope of his return. That difficulty lies at the heart of this text.

The issue of authorship is even more in play for 2 Peter than the first letter bearing this name. In addition to changes in vocabulary, 2 Peter appears to have been written at a time significantly later than 1 Peter. Second Peter 3:15–16 refers to Paul's letters in a way that indicates they were circulating in the church with the same authority as the Old Testament. Some time would have had to elapse before Paul's letters achieved the status of Scripture. It is not unreasonable to suggest, therefore, that 2 Peter dates from the second generation of church leaders.

What about the letter's signature? Its salutation begins, "Simon Peter." Doesn't this signature count for something and signify the writer's identity? Certainly that would be the case today, but in the ancient world it was quite common for people to sign another person's name to a document so that the "forger's" ideas would be considered seriously. So, for example, a monk living in Syria many centuries after the close of the New Testament wrote a series of works under the name of Dionysius—a convert under Paul's preaching in Athens. Unless his lifespan exceeded five hundred years, there is no way that Dionysius the Areopagite could be the man converted on Mars Hill and the one who wrote mystical theological essays in Syria, one and the same person. Readers may then ask whether the possibility of forgery raises questions about the legitimacy of this letter as Scripture, but the answer to that question is "only in part." Forgery was no more acceptable in the ancient world than it is today, but the signature did not finally determine a book's status as canonical. Were that not so, several other books carrying Peter's name would have to be included in Scripture. The signature may have gotten the letter an initial reading, but the contents stood the test of time.

84. Ibid., 182

85. Ibid.

The letter, not its signature, sustained the church through time of trial and nurtured its life; this spiritual sustenance is the primary reason this letter is found in the canon of Scripture.

The reason for this letter is in the delay of Christ's return. The first generation of church leadership was dying; still the Lord had not returned. With no sign of the second coming, the faith of the second generation slackened or, perhaps, was even undermined. It was one thing to die prematurely at the hands of Roman persecutors, it was quite another to reach old age wondering why the Lord tarried. Why had he not returned for his followers as he had promised? The further away Christians lived from the days of Jesus and the apostles, the more intense this question became. From the contents of the letter, it is clear that there were people who doubted whether Christ would ever return. These critics may have been church members or pagan outsiders. In either case, disbelief was a source of deep concern, and it may very well have weakened the church's moral life. Some Christians may have lost their commitment to the virtuous lifestyle of a follower of Jesus as they despaired of his imminent return. Second Peter was written to counter this criticism and the problem of a diminished moral life by bolstering trust that Christ would keep his promise and return to claim his own.

Of special concern in 2 Peter 3 is the problem of scoffers. Apparently there were some who raised doubt among believers by pointing to the undeniable fact that Jesus had not returned. Every passing year made it easier to undermine Christians' belief in the promised return of Christ. Doubt about Christ's return was just the opening argument. If that promise failed, what others might also not be true? Second Peter is directed at allaying the fears of believers against the malicious slander of these scoffers. The letter attacks their charges and insinuations by connecting the Christian hope in Christ's return to the end of the world. The world suffered destruction at the hand of God's justice once before. Back in the time of Noah, the great flood covered the earth with water. God's judgment was a fact. Even as it was a fact in the distant past, it will once again be a fact. The future destruction will be by fire, not water, because God promised Noah that never again would such a flood occur. Why fire? Along with water, it was one of the four elements that ancient peoples believed went together to compose the earth, and it seemed right that one of those elements would be the agent of the earth's undoing. The chapter's point, however, is not to explain the cause of the earth's destruction but to strengthen Christian hope in Christ's promised return by linking that return and the earth's end. After the end of the present age, Christians would dwell in a new heaven and a new earth, the "home of righteousness."

With what attitude should Christians anticipate the return of Christ? Over the centuries, not a few believers have mistakenly thought they could calculate the day of his appearing. Thus, followers of William Miller, dressed in white robes, climbed hills in upstate New York on an autumn day in 1844, expecting to see Jesus descend that very day. Some must have been embarrassed when their neighbors saw them returning to their homes that evening. Those who had quit their jobs or sold their businesses felt much worse. Even if we stop short of such extremes as the Millerites, what is the appropriate attitude to take toward the hope of Jesus' appearing? Certainly his promise is not to be forgotten or held in abeyance. Second Peter taught believers then and teaches believers today to trust in this promise and live as men and women whose present-day activities and relationships are sustained by this hope.

Tertullian had pagan friends and critics who were troubled by the Christian belief that Christ would soon return and that the world would be destroyed. What kind of people could these Christians be to hope for a day that would bring unimaginable terror? Tertullian reassured his friends by telling them that Christians indeed prayed for the delay of Christ's return. They were seeking more time for the sake of the world's conversion.

First, Second, and Third John

Real Revelation with Real Consequences

1 John 1:5–10; 2:3–11

We commonly refer to this book as the first letter of John, but a quick look at the opening line of 1 John shows that it does not carry the personal signature we find in the letters of Paul and Peter. The absence of a signature suggests that this may have been a tract or intended for the instruction and encouragement of the early church. Clearly, it is written in the same style and with much of the same vocabulary and theology as the gospel according to John as well as 2 and 3 John.

It seems clear that the writer of 1 John was aware of substandard behavior among some Christians and criticized it sharply. Some of this behavior, especially the failure to love, was simply unacceptable among Christians; this tract insists that such behavior must change.

First John emphasizes the real-life, not theoretical, experience of God's revelation in Jesus. The opening verses refer to what has been heard, seen, and touched. None of this is imaginary or illusory. God's revelation is as real as any flesh-and-blood person, but in the man Jesus is the word of life. This real-life, tactile revelation of God in Christ makes possible human fellowship. We now enjoy fellowship with God and with one another because of the Word of life.

God is light. This statement means "that God is freedom from darkness or death. To say that the gospel—good news—of God's salvation is the proclamation of God as light evokes the statement in the Gospel [of John's] prologue (1:5) that 'the light shines in the darkness, and the darkness has not overcome it.' It is also a clear allusion to the coming of Jesus as the light and life of humankind...Otherwise, to say that the message is that God is light and without any darkness sounds strangely abstract, but it is a proposition to which many people in the ancient world, pagan or Jewish, could easily have agreed. John's point is that in Jesus the light has shone in such a way as really to illumine human life."[86]

86. Smith, *First, Second, and Third John*, 42.

Repeatedly through 1 John 1:8–10, we find the phrase "If we say" or "If we claim." Clearly, *saying* is in tension with *doing*. This tension is something like the expectation that people who talk the talk had better walk the walk. The most important of these "if" phrases, however, is "If we confess." Now the burden of performance is thrown onto God's shoulders. In this case, our speech—confession of sin—initiates God's forgiving and redeeming action because God is faithful and just. John could say this because he had seen the gospel of Jesus with his own eyes, heard it with his own ears, and touched it with his hand.

Christ or Culture?

1 John 1:5–2:6; 2:15–17; 2:29–3:1

Although rather brief in comparison with many other New Testament letters, the Johannine letters contain some of the most memorable passages in all of the New Testament. They describe God in a forthright language that sharply contrasts God and the world. These letters confront the readers with a stark choice: will you follow Christ or culture?

Most New Testament letters were written to address specific problems or situations. The occasion behind 3 John is quite clear while the occasion for 2 John is a little more difficult to identify; it is even more difficult for 1 John. It may very well have been that 1 John's great affirmations of the faith were occasioned by the ongoing presence of ideas that differed from what was increasingly the normative teaching of the church. The theological health of the young church made it important to write words about the Word. First John testifies that this Word—the *Logos*—dwelled with God from all time and became incarnate in Jesus of Nazareth. The writer affirms that he has seen and heard this Word and lives in the joy of fellowship with the Word. This letter is written that others might know this joy and life born in fellowship with the Word, the *Logos* of God.

Prominent in this letter is the contrast it makes between God and the world. God is light, and the world is darkness. Believers therefore must choose: they can love either God or the world—they cannot love both. Two outstanding American theologians, the brothers H. Richard and Reinhold Niebuhr, noted this contrast and its consequent choice. H. Richard Niebuhr described the attitude of the Johannine letters as "Christ against culture." By culture he meant something similar to what John calls "the world," signifying the products of human activity over against the natural world of creation. The arts, education, government, economics, and work are all aspects of culture or "the world." In John's vision, this world is anything but eternal; it is indeed "passing away" and therefore merits little or no attention from believers. Many Christians across the ages have understood their spirituality within the paradigm of "Christ against culture." They see the world as dangerous and seductive. The Puritan writer John Bunyan, for example, portrayed the world as Vanity Fair in *The Pilgrim's Progress*, a place to be avoided by honest and sincere Christians.

In their determination to love God, some believers have attempted to sever most relationships with the world. Amish Christians are famous for a distinctive way of life that refuses physical connections to the outside world. This leads to an important question—where exactly is the world that John exhorts believers to flee? Is it "out there," a place that can be avoided simply by walking in the opposite direction? Or is "the world" much nearer than we realize? First John gives us a clue in the phrase "the cravings of the sinful man, the lust of his eyes and the boasting of what he has and does" (2:16). This is translated more famously as "the desire of the flesh, the lust of the eye, and the pride of life." The early Christian theologian Augustine saw in these the occasions of human sin. In his view, these characteristics are not "out there," but are found in the human character bent down by sinfulness. The world may indeed be a dangerous and seductive place, but we have a hand in making it so. It turns out that the line separating the church from the world runs through each and every human heart.

Troublemaking Love
1 John 3:1–5, 9–18

A deep suspicion of the world runs through the gospel of John and the three letters that bear his name. To John, the world is a dangerous place, and there was a strict line of separation that divided it from the community of those who believed in Jesus. The Johannine literature asserts that the world is hostile toward Christians, even as it insists that belief in Christ is accompanied by an abandonment of the world. John set the two against each other in mutually exclusive terms: Christ *or* the world. People should not think of this as a "both/and" possibility; it is either one or the other.

Since this tract presents the issue to its readers in uncompromising terms, we should not be surprised to read this sentence: "Do not be surprised...if the world hates you" (3:13). We might wonder, however, why the world would hate Christians. John's tract instructs Christians in the way of love. They are to follow the example of their Lord and Master and love one another. How could anybody incur the hatred of the world for being a loving person? Why would the world hate people who are kind and loving?

These questions are important to remember whenever anyone suggests that Jesus came to teach love. It is hard to imagine that the Roman Empire would think it worth its time to crucify somebody who went around encouraging people to love one another. There was more to Jesus' teaching than that, and there is more to discipleship than simply being nice. The truth of the matter is that loving in Jesus' radical way can get people in trouble with the powers that be. Love, as 1 John tells us in 3:16, involves the possibility of self-sacrifice.

This tract takes love to the point of being willing to share personal property: "If anyone has material possessions and sees his brother in need but has no pity on him, how can the love of God be in him?" (3:17). Such radical love upsets the "principalities and powers" that have a vested interest in the status quo of the world. Such powers benefit from people's selfishness; they even make a profit from it. The radical love proposed by 1 John will upset the world's way of operating; the powers and principalities will find their comfortable arrangements disturbed and ultimately threatened. In the face of such disturbance and threat, they eventually will seek to compromise or eliminate its source. This explains why Rome had to eliminate Jesus, and that is why the world hates his followers.

The writer presses his point to its logical conclusion. We have mentioned how he insisted on actions being consistent with our profession of love. As he draws his radical teaching on love to a close, once again John exhorts readers to put love in action rather than to live it only in hollow sounds upon their lips.

God Is Love

1 John 3:11, 14–16; 4:7–16

Augustine identified only two motives behind human behavior: we act either with reference to self or with reference to God. The first motive considers the self before anyone or anything: "What's in it for me?" The Latin word for this kind of self-regard is *cupiditas*, from which we get the word *cupidity* (yes, also *cupid*). Associated with self-regard is self-gratification. Augustine thought that this motive tainted all human action. Because human beings are turned in on themselves—in a word, depraved—cupidity is always with us. Endlessly preoccupied with ourselves, our actions always have at least a hint of self-regard hanging about them. This motive describes the human predicament of sinfulness. In Augustine's mind, it is not that we commit sins and become sinners; it is rather that we are sinful and therefore sin. The essence of sinfulness is cupidity. No human being escapes self-regard. Augustine thought that he observed it even in infants who jealously eyed another child nursing at their mother's breast.

Action with reference to self, of course, is a motive completely foreign to the motive of God's action. First John tells us that God is love. This is *agape* love. The second of Augustine's two motives—action with reference to God—connects us to the love that is God. Action in this case is motivated by the love that God has demonstrated for humanity since creation but most clearly and in the most costly manner in Jesus' cross. To act out of this godly *agape* love is to place the needs and concerns of the other ahead of our own. In other words, it is the very opposite of cupidity.

Godly love is unnatural to human beings in their depravity, but God's grace empowers us to love as God. This is not a higher road for the especially devoted follower of Jesus. The New Testament commands all of his disciples to love. Nowhere is that commandment stated any more specifically than here in 1 John, which also explains why we are to love. Just as this letter leaves us with a choice between God and the world, so also it presents us with only two bases for our actions. We can either love or not love, but since those who love are of God, those who do not love have no part in him.

Psychology students sooner or later learn Abraham Maslow's hierarchy of needs. At the very bottom are the basic needs for survival—food, shelter, and so forth. Higher are social needs—for example, companionship. Modern society has become accustomed to think that a good human life necessarily entails the satisfaction of needs. So it is that we may say that human beings *need* love. We *need* some other person to love us, to consider our needs and desires. That may be so, but 1 John puts our need *to* love ahead of a need *for* love. The love to which he invites us *gives* rather than *receives*. It is the love that God has for all of us. In Augustine's terms, this love is action with reference to God.

One more word must be said about this love. The text tells us that God *is* love—not that God *has* love or that God *shows* love: God *is* love. To love is to enter into a relationship, and to live in relationship is to be vulnerable to another—the one who is loved. Here 1 John tells us something very important about God and the nature of God's power under the category of love. God has great power—a word for this power is *omnipotence*—but nowhere in the Bible does it say that God *is* power. It says only that God is love.

God's Love for the World
1 John 4:7–17

In 1 John, we have the church's mature theological reflection on Jesus and the event of his birth and life—what some scholars refer to as the "Christ event." The gospel according to Matthew tells us that Jesus came to be God with us and that Jesus came to save us. First John lengthens this theological reflection to explain how and why God sent Jesus.

By the time of 1 John's writing, people had had years to consider the meaning and significance of the Christ event. Many sermons had already been preached, many testimonies given, and 1 John 4 is an eloquently crafted statement that sums up some of this reflection. God sent Jesus into the world so that humans might have life through him. This possibility was purchased through Christ's atoning sacrifice. In chapter three, we saw how John linked sacrificial living to divine fellowship. That idea is repeated here; Christians ought to love in the manner of the self-sacrificing love God has for the world.

When 1 John uses the word *ought,* we shift from theology to ethics. Jesus' birth, life, sacrificial death, and resurrection compose the elements of our way to life, to be sure. But the way to life has moral consequences for our life in the world. Since we are children of light, people in whom new life is now found, we are to live like it. Since the God in whom we now live is love, we are to love: "Whoever lives in love lives in God, and God in him" (4:16). Only to speak or merely to claim it is inadequate; a godly life must flow from the profession of the disciple's lips.

Why does 1 John make these clear and forthright statements about the nature and purpose of the coming of Jesus? From the opening verses of chapter 4, it seems clear that the writer was aware of the presence of people who were teaching contrary views of Jesus' incarnation and its theological meaning. These people had been claiming the authority of the Spirit for a body of teaching that contradicted John's. He had to counter these heretical teachers. "Whether in Spirit-inspired utterance or otherwise, they…have not espoused the necessary and proper confession that Jesus has come in the flesh (cf. 2 John 7). Thus, they do not confess Jesus."[87] John meant to correct this false confession by setting the theological record straight.

Faith Is the Victory
1 John 5:1–12

Earlier in this tract, John taught his readers that their love for God is demonstrated through loving God's children. In chapter 5, the tables are turned: "Proof of loving the children of

87. Ibid., 99.

God is loving God and obeying God's commandments."[88] It is clear that these commandments are directed toward the people of God. To them, God's commandments are not a burden (5:3), and one immediately thinks of Jesus' saying that his yoke is easy and his burden is light.

God's commandments may not be burdensome, but obedience to them enlists believers in the struggle between the children of light and the children of darkness. In this struggle, however, victory is assured. Those who love God are born of God. Those who are born of God keep his commandments and overcome the world. We have already seen how John sets up a strong contrast between believers and the world. The struggle is between these two opposing value systems; however, the struggle has in principle already been decided; "for everyone born of God overcomes the world. This is the victory that has overcome the world, even our faith" (5:4).

We should ask whether the struggle in which believers are victorious is external or internal. Is the struggle a cosmic battle between the forces of God and good versus the Devil and evil? Or might this struggle be interpreted as internal? Is the struggle between the temptations of the world and faith? Some of the Johannine literature takes the first point of view; the struggle is between the forces of evil and God. In 1 John 5:1–12, the sense is more of the internal struggle waged in the heart of everyone who seeks to follow Jesus. "Those who have conquered the world have risen above it so that it no longer taints or influences, much less determines, them. They have successfully fulfilled the injunction of 1 John 2:15: 'Do not love the world or the things in the world.'"[89]

The last section of the passage collects some difficult verses. Interpreted individually, they seem clear enough, but taken together they present more difficulty. Some commentators think that this section of 1 John 5 is a series of affirmations that lead to a ringing affirmation in verses 11 and 12. Interpreters have differed, for instance, over the meaning of the phrase "born of water and blood" (5:6, 8). Traditionally, this has been interpreted to mean that "water" refers to Jesus' natural birth and "blood" to the crucifixion. On the other hand, John Calvin took this phrase to mean the crucifixion, where both water and blood flowed from Jesus' side. Several such verses present themselves in this section, and it is best to proceed on a verse-by-verse reading, rather than try to tie together whole paragraphs.

One final word about the Johannine literature. We often find the repeating phrase "believe in Christ" or "believe in the Son." In both the gospel and letters of John, this phrase is better translated "believe into the Son." In John, believers are taken into the very life of God in Christ; in faith they now dwell in Christ. This is the victory that overcomes the world.

The Johannine Comma
1 John 5:1–15

Those who compare the NIV and KJV translations will note the difference in the renderings of 1 John 5:7–8. This is known as the "Johannine Comma." The KJV reads, "For there are three that bear

88. Ibid., 117

89. Ibid., 119

record in heaven, the Father, the Word, and the Holy Ghost: and these three are one." This sentence is not included in the NIV. How do we account for this serious difference?

The answer is to be found in the history of the text of Scripture. The English Bible is, of course, a translation from the original languages—Greek for the New Testament and Hebrew for the Old. But even the Hebrew and Greek testaments are themselves composite products of careful study and comparison of many ancient manuscripts. At some points, these manuscripts vary. Because they also differ in reliability, it is up to a scholar or committee of scholars to select which manuscript gives the best reading of a particular text. It was a great step forward when the Dutch scholar Erasmus prepared a critical edition of the Greek New Testament in 1516, providing what he called a "new instrument" for Christian discipleship. His work enabled such people as William Tyndale to prepare fresh translations of the New Testament into English based on the best Greek manuscripts available. Along with other translations, the Tyndale New Testament contributed to the Authorized Version of 1611, known for centuries since as the King James Bible.

The work of translation and critical comparison of manuscripts is ongoing. In some cases, more recent discoveries of ancient manuscripts mandate this work. For example, in 1844 a man named Tischendorf discovered a nearly complete Greek manuscript of the New Testament at St. Catherine's monastery on the Sinai Peninsula. Named *Codex Sinaiticus*, this fourth-century manuscript gave scholars another textual authority with which to compare manuscripts already available. Since the KJV had been translated without awareness of *Sinaiticus*, a new translation of the English Bible was almost obligatory. What has this to do with the difference between the KJV and NIV readings in 1 John 5? Simply put, no *ancient* Greek manuscript contains the sentence called the Johannine Comma. It is found in some ancient Latin manuscripts and apparently was inserted into the text of 1 John from them. Erasmus had serious reservations about including the sentence; Luther and Calvin both had their doubts. On the other hand, John Wesley argued vigorously in favor of it.[90] At first blush, this excursion into the field of textual criticism and history may seem irrelevant. After all, isn't the primary reason of Bible study to learn how we can live more faithfully as followers of Jesus? Instead of Greek or Latin manuscripts and what they do or don't say, shouldn't we be considering 1 John's insistence that believers' love for God and his children enables them to overcome the world and is indeed obedience to the commandments? Perhaps so, for indeed the first task of the body of Christ is not critical scholarship but the performance of Scripture. The Bible is not given to us merely for textual analysis or even simply to be believed. Belief in the Bible is crucial, of course, but finally it is the book to be lived. It is the script for faithful Christian discipleship.

If we are to live faithfully according to its teachings, however, we must understand what the Bible says. Therefore, the church's performance of the Scripture depends to some degree on the work of scholars who do the very important work of textual criticism. Their work provides the foundation on which

90. Ibid., 121–22.

translators build. Ultimately, we, the church, rely on the diligent work of many scholars to provide us with the Bible in which God calls us to daily performance of our discipleship. Some of them gave their lives that we might have the book of books. We ought to know a little of these men and women and their work—and thank God for them.

False Teachers and Freeloaders
2 & 3 John

As we read through the New Testament letters, we become aware of the variety of problems facing the early church. Not everybody who listened to Paul's teaching immediately got it straight. For example, he found it necessary to write to the Thessalonians to correct mistaken ideas about the end of time and the return of Christ. Corinth was unwilling to accept Paul's apostolic authority. There was also the problem common to many New Testament churches—the relationship between Jewish and Gentile Christians. Increasingly, the church took on the character of the non-Jews who rapidly became the numerical majority. Theologically and in many instances morally, however, Gentile Christians started from scratch; they knew little or nothing of the God of Israel and Jesus; they did not understand life in relationship with this God. It is understandable that there would be mistakes in comprehension and ethical behavior.

One problem that persisted throughout the early church was false teaching. Paul as well as the other apostles and gospel workers were not the only missionary teachers. There were those who differed with Paul, for example, but believed they possessed a clearer understanding of the nature and purpose of Jesus' life and death. The early church judged these teachers to be false prophets because they were maliciously motivated. No doubt great evil was done in the church, but the presence of these teachers also indicates the different paths that early Christianity might have taken. By the same token, the presence of variant teachers helps us appreciate the extraordinary labors and achievement of those who gave us the letters and books of the canonical New Testament. The problem of false teaching reared its head in the churches to which the Johannine letters were written.

Verse 7 of 2 John refers to the deceivers who taught a message that did not acknowledge the incarnation, that is, that Christ came "in the flesh." They believed in Jesus but thought that they possessed a better grasp of his nature and life on earth. Without more details, we cannot be completely certain, but it appears that these false teachers were Gnostics. Many different forms of gnostic teaching vexed ancient Christianity during the New Testament era and for more than a century afterward.

One form took the name of Docetism, from the Greek word *dokeo*, meaning "to appear" or "to seem." Like other Gnostics, Docetists were dualists; they believed that spirit was good and matter evil—despite God's pronouncement in Genesis that all creation is good. This dualism prompted Docetists to believe that Christ could not actually dwell in material human flesh without contamination. Consequently, they taught the idea that the incarnation (as 2 John states, that Jesus came "in the flesh") was apparent but not real. John strongly cautioned against any view that refuses to take seriously Jesus' full humanity. There is also Jesus' complete divinity, of course, but 2 John will not allow anything less than the confession that Jesus was fully human. Jesus' life on earth was not a phantasm, not some sort of appearance, but the incarnation of the Logos of God.

Third John addresses another problem that troubled the early church. This one surrounds the hospitality that Christians were to practice, particularly toward traveling evangelists and gospel workers. Apparently a man named Diotrephes had wearied of extending hospitality to "the brothers," but not only "brothers" circulated among the churches. Sometimes false teachers and freeloaders also requested food and housing. Christians had to learn to discriminate between authentic gospel workers and false teachers as well as those merely looking for a free ride. Diotrephes may simply have made a blanket judgment—no more hospitality to anybody, whether they were fakes or authentic preachers. Third John offers a standard by which to judge true ministers and believers from false: "Anyone who does what is good is from God" (verse 11). And what is good is consistent with the love that is God and that has been revealed to us in the person of Jesus.

Jude

Questions of Authorship

Along with the letters of Peter, James, and John, Jude is one of the Catholic or General Letters of the New Testament. The salutation addresses Christians living at no specific location but to "those who have been called, who are loved by God the Father and kept by Jesus Christ" (v. 1). Any sincere Christian is the intended reader of this letter.

Strong parallels exist between Jude and 2 Peter. Some scholars believe that the writer of 2 Peter borrowed from Jude's letter to write his. If that is so, it would not be the first or only case of one New Testament writer borrowing from another. For many years, scholars who studied the three Synoptic Gospels—Matthew, Mark, and Luke—have demonstrated that Matthew and Luke borrowed from Mark. Luke himself wrote us that he investigated other accounts of Jesus' life and ministry as he worked on his gospel (Luke 1:1–3). This kind of scholarly work helps us get a picture of the earliest days of the Christian community, how it expanded, and how its beliefs spread.

Who was the writer? The salutation identifies him as the brother of James. This James is probably the brother of the Lord. Leader of the Jerusalem church, he possessed great stature in the early days of Christianity. But this very means of identification raises questions about the writer. If this Jude was the brother of James, he also would have been the brother of Jesus. Why not claim that relationship as well?

Commentator Pheme Perkins identifies several characteristics internal to the letter that suggest that its author was a second-generation Christian. This letter is written in polished Greek, indicating that its author had studied Greek rather than simply picked it up.. Second, unlike Paul, for example, the writer never claimed apostolic status and authority. Another interesting feature of this letter is the authorities that it cites. The argument relies heavily on

Jewish apocryphal sources rather than the Hebrew Bible exclusively. The letter refers to stories and ideas found in such apocryphal books as *1 Enoch* and the *Testament of Moses*, books written during the period between the close of the Old Testament era and the beginning of the New.

New Leadership Confronts Challenges

Jude vv. 3–4, 8, 10, 12–13, 16–23

Christianity is an undeniable presence around the world. In the United States and Canada, in every town, village, and in many hamlets, we will likely see church buildings and other signs of Christian presence. There are sites in Europe where Christians have worshiped since antiquity. Many of our practices are rooted in a nearly two-thousand-year-old tradition. From this secure vantage point, we look back on the earliest days of the Christian movement and can scarcely believe there was a time when it was tiny and Christians were uncertain and even confused about what they believed and practiced. Nevertheless, that was the situation in many locations as Christianity entered the second century, and it is the situation that Jude addressed.

The dominant theme of this letter is false doctrine. The letter demonstrates a pronounced concern for orthodoxy; there were many differences of opinion about the nature of Christianity troubling the New Testament church. These differences were not found only among lay people. Teachers of false doctrine had found their way into positions of leadership and offered a view of Jesus that differed from the consensus teaching of the church. Jude says that they denied "Jesus Christ our only Sovereign and Lord" (v. 4). These teachers did, however, attend worship; they even participated in the church's meals and the service of the Lord's Supper. It seems likely they were not simply atheists, otherwise they would not bother participating in the life of the church. Instead, they probably offered a different interpretation of Christ, perhaps the same false doctrine opposed in the letter to the Colossians.

The letter of Jude does not contain an elaborate theology; rather, it consists of sharp warnings and rebukes to the false teachers who threaten the young Christian community. Jude reminded his readers of their salvation in Christ. "Since Jude consistently castigates the false teachers for immorality, slavery to passion, self-interested flattery and the like, [these] Christians must have been taught that life in the Spirit required a serious moral transformation. Those who fall away from that holiness of life will be condemned at the judgment."[91] During the first two centuries of its life, the ancient church continued to battle against individuals who taught a surprisingly wide variety of ideas about the person and nature of Jesus. For example, sometime about the year AD 185, Irenaeus, bishop of Lyons, published *Against Heresies*. In this book, he catalogued and criticized many different speculations about Christ. During the first centuries of Christianity, an orthodox theological consensus about the person and work of Christ was in the process of development, but did not yet exist. In AD 100, the New Testament was not yet canonized—nor would it be for more than two hundred years.

91. Perkins, *First and Second Peter*, 144.

Christians read the Old Testament as Scripture as well as other ancient literature and took some of that literature to be authoritative.

All of this means that one of the fundamental tasks confronting the early church was the establishment of orthodox Christian doctrine. The letter of Jude was an important part of that process. It called attention to the problem of false teaching and earnestly exhorted its readers to cling to the specific line of apostolic instruction—the faith once delivered to the saints. "As we read Jude, we have the opportunity to watch a small part of the [second-generation] church take charge of preserving the faith it has inherited."[92]

Revelation

Secret Code
Revelation 5:1–10

The book of Revelation (there is no *s*) is the only book of its kind in the New Testament. It is written in the apocalyptic style that emerged late in the Old Testament era and during the intertestamental period. *Apocalyptic* comes from a Greek word meaning "revealed," and the book's title, translated literally, is the Apocalypse of John. Apocalyptic literature means more, however, than "revealed." This literature emphasizes the imminent end of the world and God's ultimate victory over the forces of darkness and evil. As such, the apocalyptic message was addressed first of all to the people of God who were undergoing trial.

The apocalyptic style of writing was first employed by Jewish writers in time of trial. In roughly 200 BC, under the Seleucid emperors Antiochus III and IV, the Jewish people experienced persecution through occupation; pagans who had seized control of Jerusalem dominated them. In an act of ultimate desecration, a swine was sacrificed on the altar of the temple. It was during this approximate period that apocalyptic writing developed as a highly symbolic code language.

As the Roman persecution of Christians intensified near the conclusion of the first century, Jewish-Christian writers adapted apocalyptic themes to their own specifically Christian context. Persecution is the common factor connecting Jewish and Christian apocalyptic literature. Under Roman attack, the church looked for relief through God's sudden and redemptive action. The apocalyptic message encouraged both groups in that hope.

Perhaps it was this association with Jewish apocalyptic literature—not to mention the difficult contents of the book itself—that made the ancient church cautious in its reception of the Revelation into the Christian canon. Second- and third-century Christian interpreters and theologians used the book, but it was not included in some lists of canonical books. The great Bible translator and interpreter Jerome (340–420) and his contemporary Augustine (354–430) lent their prestige to the book. As a result, it was more widely received as scripture in the Western Empire.

The book of Revelation has proved to be an endless source of Christian reflection across the centuries. Perhaps with no other book of the Bible is

92. Ibid., 145.

the starting point more crucial to the interpreter's task. Different interpretive assumptions and methods lead to vastly different conclusions. So-called historical interpretations take the book to be a symbolic map of the future, whether of the church or the entire sweep of world history. According to this method, when the meaning of the symbols is unlocked one can discern future events down to the end of time. Preterist interpretations, in contrast, restrict the apocalyptic message to the first-century church under trial. The method that guides these reflections understands Revelation as "a pastoral letter to Christians in Asia in the late first century who were confronted with a critical [social and political] situation," and which "has an urgently needed message for the contemporary church."[93]

Ancient writers intended their works to be read aloud. Revelation was not only intended to be read aloud but all the way through in one sitting. When we attempt to exegete or interpret each individual verse, we risk a serious mistake. Better interpretive practice is to see this letter's big picture. So, for example, in Revelation 5:1–10 we find the book's first use of the symbol of the lamb. This important symbol is John's favorite metaphorical device to refer to Christ, the "Lamb slain from the foundation of the world" (13:8 KJV). In Revelation, it is this slain lamb that takes the place reserved for the lion—Judah and the old Davidic monarchy. What once belonged to the lion now belongs to the Lamb, not just any lamb but the Lamb of God. Victory and glory belong to him. Now there is a message for a weary church discouraged by persecution's trials.

93. Boring, *Revelation*, 1.

Hope in Time of Trial
Revelation 7:1–3, 9–10, 14–17

Sometimes the symbolism and interpretive challenges of the book of Revelation obscure the fact that this book is actually a letter. Revelation 1:4 uses an ancient letter's standard form of salutation: "John, to the seven churches in... Asia." Although the vocabulary differs markedly, let us say, from the language of Paul's letters, like those letters, Revelation was written for an occasion or with a specific purpose in mind.

By the end of the first century, Christian confession had become dangerous. The worship of the divine Roman Emperor had been accepted as a fact of life.

> This was the same as a declaration of war against the church, for to recognize another lord than Christ would be fatal to Christianity. The defiant message from the prophet of Patmos gives the church's reply to the challenge. Coming as it did out of cruelly hard times with still darker forebodings regarding the immediate future, its primary purpose was to strengthen and brace believers for the inevitable shock of the dreadful "things which must shortly come to pass" (1:1). There could be no compromise. It was a matter of life and death to the church.
>
> By its symbolism of fantastic imagery...it sought to convey its God-inspired message of exhortation, warning, and inspiration to the understanding few.[94]

A further word on interpretation of Revelation will clarify Revelation 7:1–3, 9–10, 14–17. Historical interpreters

94. Linn, *Studies in the New Testament*, vol. 3, 83–84.

read the book in linear fashion, assuming that each chapter unfolds a new epoch or aspect of the future of the world or church. The interpretation followed here, on the other hand, is that the message of Revelation is a recurrent series of cycles through new and different sets of symbols. Thus, for example, the chapters on either side of Revelation 7:1–3, 9–10, and 14–17 warn of impending trials. The woes change, but in both cases a crescendo of catastrophe escalates until we finally arrive at the great triumph that is the theme.

Numbers are particularly important in the scheme of apocalyptic symbolism. Seven is the number that connotes perfection, since the Lord God created the world in seven days. Twelve is another number to express completion, following the notion that Israel was composed of the twelve tribes. In this sense 144,000 (7:4) is not to be taken as the literal number of the redeemed. Rather, as the product of twelve times 12,000, it is symbolic of the whole body of the saved in Christ—the complete number of the redeemed. When Revelation refers to this number, it is symbolic of all who have been sealed and therefore protected in the harrowing time to come.

As persecutor of the saints, Rome falls under the severest judgment of God. In announcing this destruction, John was following the practice of Jesus and the prophets of Israel who had connected national disasters with God's judgment at the last day, and pagan Romans believed that if the empire fell, the end of the world would be at hand. It would have been quite natural, therefore, for Christians to ask, "What will happen to us when God pours out his wrath against our persecutor, the Roman Empire?" The message of Revelation 7 assures Christians that the true Israel of God, the church, will be preserved from the horrors that await. Under the shelter of God's tent and drinking from the waters of life, every tear will be wiped from their eyes. The hurt and pain of mortal life will be forever past.

"Babylon Is Fallen"
Revelation 14:6–13

It is useful to remind ourselves that biblical notation (divisions into chapters and verses) is not found in the ancient manuscripts from which the English Bible is translated. Stephen Langton divided the Vulgate Bible into chapters in 1205, which Robert Stephanus later subdivided into verses. The Reformed theologian Theodore Beza adopted Stephanus' system for the received edition of the Greek New Testament in 1565. These divisions can convey a mistaken impression that there is a break in the flow or ideas of the text and thus make more difficult our understanding of larger connections. Such seems to be the case with Revelation 14. Commentator Eugene Boring identifies this chapter as belonging to a unit that includes the previous two chapters as well. In his view, this is "a cosmic operatic drama in which all the characters and actions are exaggerated, larger than life. Chapters 12–13 pull away the curtain that hides the transcendent world from ordinary sight and offers a behind-the-scenes view of the powers of evil at work in the present, while chapter 14...presents a behind-the-scenes view of the victory of God in salvation and judgment."[95]

95. Boring, *Revelation*, 150.

Boring's comment will prove helpful as we interpret key symbols and ideas in Revelation 14. Here John reports a vision of three angels whose messages provide the substance of this text. The first angel calls the faithful to the worship of the true God, the Creator of the heavens, the earth, and all that they contain. This is more than a call to worship, for it means to contrast faithful worship of the true God with worship of false gods. But John had in mind a particular false god whose symbolic name is Babylon. The worship of this false god is futile, for "fallen is Babylon the Great, which made all the nations drink the maddening wine of her adulteries" (14:8). Who is this Babylon and what does the text mean when it says that Babylon *is* fallen?

Recall that we identified the growing worship of the emperor as a great challenge to early Christianity. Emperor worship was not optional in the Roman Empire. As part of their oath of allegiance, Roman soldiers were required to sacrifice a pinch of incense to the divinity of the emperor. One need not make the worship of Caesar a regular part of religious life, but a bow toward Rome was expected of everyone. But even a small nod was objectionable to Christians, who regarded imperial enforcement of this practice as drunkenness. In this view, Babylon the Great is a symbolic reference to the Roman Empire that enforced the practice of emperor worship repugnant to Christians.

To solidify this interpretation we can consider the comment of Otto F. Linn:

> The Hebrew numerical value for Nero-Caesar is 666. John identifies this person with the beast whose death stroke was healed (13:3, 18). This again seems to refer to Nero, for it was at his death that this beast which stood as a symbol of the emperor was threatened with death.... Since the number six falls below seven, which is the emblem of completeness, its symbolic value becomes significant. It was a number that was dreaded by the Jews, and even the sixth day of the week is considered unlucky by many to this day. This seeker after divine honors was aptly symbolized by endless imperfection, 666.[96]

The antichrist and Babylon are thus symbols referring to the emperor who would require his image to be worshiped throughout the empire and whose power was employed to enforce this usurpation of God's rightful place as the only One worthy of human worship.

The third angel of John's vision issues a stern warning to any who might be tempted to follow the ways of the Roman world. Here we find a bold line drawn between Christ and culture. One cannot serve God and mammon. God in Christ will have no other gods before him. Those who follow the way of the world will drink from the cup of the Lord's wrath. In the face of very real threats of persecution and the seductions of the surrounding culture, John exhorted Christians to hold fast against this abomination. Patience and endurance are the virtues that sustain Christians against the day when the Lord's ultimate victory, already assured, will be manifest to all the nations.

96. Linn, *Studies in the New Testament*, vol. 3, 127–28.

The Heavenly City

Revelation 21:1–7, 22–27

A little more than four centuries after John wrote to the seven churches of Asia, Augustine, the Christian theologian and bishop of Hippo Regius, a city in the North African province of Numidia, wrote a lengthy and detailed defense of Christianity. By the date of this writing, the empire that so disgusted John had become in some measure Christian. In AD 313 the new convert Emperor Constantine had issued the Edict of Milan granting official legal status to Christianity, and little more than a half-century later another Christian emperor, Theodosius I, decreed Christianity the official religion of the Roman Empire.

As barbarian invaders threatened the security of the empire to the west, the few remaining pagan critics charged that Christians were the ones responsible for the impending collapse. Against this criticism, Augustine wrote one of his greatest works, *The City of God*. Ancient pagans customarily referred to Rome as "the City," but Augustine argued that there were in fact two cities; Rome was but one and decidedly inferior to the other infinitely greater city—the City of God. It was the latter that determined the course of history and human destiny. John's vision of the new Jerusalem anticipated Augustine's great defense, even as it articulated some of the same themes. The course of human history is not the work of human hands but determined by the God who is both Alpha and Omega, beginning and end. The new Jerusalem is the end—the goal—of history, and as such it also represents a return to the beginning, the peaceful kingdom that was in place when the earth was new.

In a sense, we have come full circle. We are brought back to the beginning, and know this hauntingly familiar place for the first time. As John took pen in hand, there were still terrors to be endured; the Roman Empire remained and wielded great power to achieve its corrupt ends. However, that power had been broken in principle by the blood of the Lamb slain on the cross. God's final victory was therefore assured; in effect, it had already happened. There remained the death struggle of the "city of man," "Babylon the Great," but the outcome had already been determined in the resurrection. John's vision looked beyond this struggle to a day of unclouded light where only goodness and love exist in a shining creation, new as Eden's first morning.

> The earthly lot of the suffering church, cruel as it was, could be borne for it was not final. Hope has a way of lingering on through the desolation wrought by conflicting passions and energies of wicked men, of nursing into a healthy, undying life the submerged qualities of the eternal self until even in their present temporal insecurity men have had the vision of the protecting walls of the "new Jerusalem" and feel the infinite calm of the eternal Presence. There is a realm even here which is undesecrated by evil forces, "a mighty fortress" where the securities of the coming life are inviolably held. The new Jerusalem is an experience that begins here and continues on forever…
>
> To the ancients a city was a place of security. Its walls were built to afford protection against the most determined enemies. Heaven with its

jasper walls assures the saint of a future of unmolested quietness and peace.... Heaven is itself one vast temple filled with the glory of God. Its twelve gates welcome the new Israel, those whose names "are written in the Lamb's book of life" (21:27). It is a city of the redeemed upon whom shines the light of God's eternal presence.[97]

97. Ibid., 149–50.

Bibliography

Achtemeier, Elizabeth. *Nahum–Malachi*. Interpretation: A Bible Commentary for Teaching and Preaching. Atlanta: John Knox Press, 1986.

Achtemeier, Paul. *Romans*. Interpretation: A Bible Commentary for Teaching and Preaching. Atlanta: John Knox Press, 1985.

Barna, George. *What Americans Believe*. Ventura, CA: Regal Books, 1991.

Bellah, Robert N., et al. *Habits of the Heart: Individualism and Commitment in American Life*. Berkeley: University of California Press, 1985.

Blenkinsopp, Joseph. *A History of Prophecy in Israel*. Philadelphia: Westminster Press, 1983.

Bonhoeffer, Dietrich. *Letters and Papers from Prison*. Rev. ed. Edited by Eberhard Bethge. Translated by Reginald Fuller. New York: Macmillan, 1967.

———. *Christ the Center*. Translated by Edwin H. Robertson. San Francisco: Harper and Row, 1978.

———. *The Cost of Discipleship*. New York: Macmillan, 1949; Touchstone, 1995.

Borg, Marcus, J. *Jesus—A New Vision: Spirit, Culture, and the Life of Discipleship*. San Francisco: Harper and Row, 1987

Boring, M. Eugene. *Revelation*. Interpretation: A Bible Commentary for Teaching and Preaching. Louisville: John Knox Press, 1989.

Bray, Gerald, ed. *Romans*. Ancient Christian Commentary on Scripture. Downers Grove, IL: InterVarsity Press, 2005.

Bright, John. *A History of Israel*. Philadelphia: Westminster Press, 1959.

———. *A History of Israel*. 3rd ed. Philadelphia: Westminster Press, 1981.

Brown, Raymond E. *The Birth of the Messiah*. New York: Doubleday and Company, 1977.

Brown, William P. *Ecclesiastes*. Interpretation: A Bible Commentary for Teaching and Preaching. Louisville: John Knox Press, 2000.

Brueggemann, Walter. *A Commentary on Jeremiah: Exile and Homecoming.* Grand Rapids: William B. Eerdmanns, 1998.

———. *Genesis*. Interpretation: A Bible Commentary for Teaching and Preaching. Atlanta: John Knox Press, 1982.

———. *Theology of the Old Testament*. Minneapolis: Fortress Press, 1997.

Craddock, Fred B. *Luke*. Interpretation: A Bible Commentary for Teaching and Preaching. Louisville: John Knox Press, 1990.

Dodd, C. H. *The Parables of the Kingdom.* London: Nisbet & Co. Ltd.,1935.

Edwards, Mark J., ed. *Galatians, Ephesian, Philippians*. Ancient Christian Commentary. Downer's Grove, IL: InterVarsity Press, 1999.

Gentz, William H., ed. *The Dictionary of Bible and Religion.* Nashville: Abingdon Press, 1986.

Gundry, Robert H. *Mark: A Commentary on His Apology for the Cross.* Grand Rapids: William B. Eerdmans, 1993.

Hanson, Paul D. *Isaiah 40–66*. Interpretation: A Bible Commentary for Teaching and Preaching. Louisville: John Knox Press, 1995.

Hauerwas, Stanley, and William H. Willimon. *Resident Aliens: Life in the Christian Colony*. Nashville: Abingdon Press, 1989.

Hays, Richard B. *First Corinthians*. Interpretation: A Bible Commentary for Teaching and Preaching. Louisville: John Knox Press, 1997.

Jeremias, Joachim. *The Parables of Jesus*. 2nd ed. rev. Translated by S. H. Hooke. New York: Charles Scribner's Sons, 1972.

Lampe, Peter. "The Eucharist: Identifying with Christ on the Cross," *Interpretation* 48, no. 1 (January 1994) 36–49.

Lash, Nicholas. *Theology on the Way to Emmaus*. London: SCM Press, 1986.

Levenson, Jon D. *Esther*. Interpretation: A Bible Commentary for Teaching and Preaching. Louisville: Westminster John Knox Press, 1997.

Limburg, James. *Hosea–Micah*. Interpretation: A Bible Commentary for Teaching and Preaching. Atlanta: John Knox Press, 1988.

Linn, Otto F. *Studies in the New Testament*. 3 vols. Anderson, IN: Warner Press, 1942.

Long, Thomas G. *Hebrews*. Interpretation: A Bible Commentary for Teaching and Preaching. Louisville: John Knox Press, 1997.

Luther, Martin. *Works*. 55 vols. Edited by Jaroslav Pelikan. St. Louis: Concordia Publishing House, 1963.

Martin, Ralph P. *Ephesians, Colossians, and Philemon*. Interpretation: A Bible Commentary for Teaching and Preaching. Atlanta: John Knox Press, 1991.

McKane, William. *Proverbs: A New Approach*. Philadelphia: Westminster Press, 1970.

Miller, Adam W. *An Introduction to the New Testament*. Anderson, IN: Gospel Trumpet Company, 1943.

Milton, John. *Paradise Lost*. New York: Penguin Books, 1961, 1981.

Moessner, David P. *Lord of the Banquet*. Minneapolis: Fortress Press, 1989.

Niebuhr, H. Richard. *Christ and Culture*. New York: Harper and Row, 1951.

Oden, Thomas C. and Christopher A. Hall, eds. *Mark*. Ancient Christian Commentary on Scripture. Downers Grove, IL: InterVarsity Press, 1998.

Perkins, Pheme. *First and Second Peter, James and Jude*. Interpretation, A Bible Commentary for Teaching and Preaching. Louisville: John Knox Press, 1995.

Petersen, David L. *Haggai and Zechariah 1–8: A Commentary*. Philadelphia: Westminster Press, 1984.

Sanders, E. P. *The Historical Figure of Jesus*. New York: Penguin Books, 1993.

———. *Paul, the Law, and the Jewish People*. Philadelphia: Fortress Press, 1983.

Simonetti, Manlio, ed. *Matthew 14–28*. Ancient Christian Commentary on Scripture. Downer's Grove, IL: InterVarsity Press, 2002.

Sloyan, Gerard. *John*. Interpretation: A Bible Commentary for Teaching and Preaching. Atlanta: John Knox Press, 1988.

Smith, D. Moody. *First, Second, and Third John*. Interpretation: A Bible Commentary for Teaching and Preaching. Louisville, John Knox Press, 1991.

Strege, Merle D. "Ecclesiology and the Lord's Supper: The Memorial Meal of a Peaceable Community." In *The Lord's Supper: Believers' Church Perspectives,* edited by Dale R. Stoffer. Scottdale, PA: Herald Press, 1997.

———. *Tell Me the Tale: Historical Reflections on the Church of God.* Anderson, IN: Warner Press, 1991.

Strege, Merle D., and Richard L. Willowby. *God's Redeeming Story: A Theological Primer.* Anderson, IN.: Warner Press, 1996.

Teasley, D. O. *The Bible and How to Interpret It.* Anderson, IN: Gospel Trumpet Company, 1918.

Towner, W. Sibley. *Daniel.* Interpretation: A Bible Commentary for Teaching and Preaching. Atlanta: John Knox Press, 1984.

Von Rad, Gerhard. *Old Testament Theology,* vol. 2. Translated by D. M. G. Stalker. New York: Harper and Row, 1965.

Weiser, Artur. *The Psalms.* Philadelphia: Westminster Press, 1962.

Wickersham, H. C. *Holiness Bible Subjects.* 2nd ed. Grand Junction, MI: Gospel Trumpet Publishing Company, 1894.

Williamson, Lamar, Jr. *Mark.* Interpretation: A Bible Commentary for Teaching and Preaching. Atlanta: John Knox Press, 1983.

Willimon, William H. *Acts.* Interpretation: A Bible Commentary for Teaching and Preaching. Atlanta: John Knox Press, 1988.

Witherington, Ben, III. *Conflict and Community in Corinth.* Grand Rapids: William B. Eerdmans, 1995.

Yoder, John Howard. *The Politics of Jesus.* 2nd ed. rev. Grand Rapids: William B. Eerdmanns, 1994.

Scripture Index

John

Acts

Romans

1 Corinthians

2 Corinthians

Galatians

Ephesians

Names Index

Please note that this index of proper names excludes the following due to their frequency within the text: Jews, Christians, Greeks, Romans, Hebrews, Gentiles, *and* Israel *(people, nation).*